Edward G. E. L. B-L Lytton

**Lord Lytton's novels**

Edward G. E. L. B-L Lytton

**Lord Lytton's novels**

ISBN/EAN: 9783741140938

Manufactured in Europe, USA, Canada, Australia, Japa

Cover: Foto ©Andreas Hilbeck / pixelio.de

Manufactured and distributed by brebook publishing software (www.brebook.com)

Edward G. E. L. B-L Lytton

**Lord Lytton's novels**

*Frontispiece*

# "My Novel"

### By Pisistratus Caxton

OR

## VARIETIES IN ENGLISH LIFE

> " Neque enim notare singulos mens est mihi,
> Verum ipsam vitam et mores hominum ostendere."
> — PHÆDRUS.

IN TWO VOLUMES

VOL. II.

LONDON
GEORGE ROUTLEDGE AND SONS
BROADWAY, LUDGATE HILL
NEW YORK: 9 LAFAYETTE PLACE

# LORD LYTTON'S NOVELS.

## KNEBWORTH EDITION.

EUGENE ARAM.
NIGHT AND MORNING.
PELHAM.
ERNEST MALTRAVERS.
ALICE.
THE LAST DAYS OF POMPEII.
THE CAXTONS.
DEVEREUX.
THE DISOWNED.
GODOLPHIN.
HAROLD.
PAUL CLIFFORD.
A STRANGE STORY.
THE LAST OF THE BARONS.
LEILA, AND THE PILGRIMS ON THE RHINE.

LUCRETIA.
MY NOVEL. VOL. 1.
MY NOVEL. VOL. 2.
RIENZI.
WHAT WILL HE DO WITH IT? VOL. 1.
WHAT WILL HE DO WITH IT? VOL. 2.
ZANONI.
THE COMING RACE.
KENELM CHILLINGLY.
THE PARISIANS. VOL. 1.
THE PARISIANS. VOL. 2.
FALKLAND AND ZICCI.
PAUSANIAS THE SPARTAN.

*Price 3s. 6d. each volume;
Or, the Complete Set, in 28 vols., Crown 8vo, cloth, £4 18s. 0d.*

# MY NOVEL.

## BOOK VIII.

### INITIAL CHAPTER.

#### THE ABUSE OF INTELLECT.

THERE is at present so vehement a flourish of trumpets, and so prodigious a roll of the drum, whenever we are called upon to throw up our hats, and cry "Huzza" to the "March of Enlightenment,"- that, out of that very spirit of contradiction natural to all rational animals, one is tempted to stop one's ears, and say, "Gently, gently; LIGHT is noiseless; how comes 'Enlightenment' to make such a clatter? Meanwhile if it be not impertinent, pray, where is Enlightenment marching to?" Ask that question of any six of the loudest bawlers in the procession, and I'll wager tenpence to California that you get six very unsatisfactory answers. One respectable gentleman, who, to our great astonishment, insists upon calling himself "a slave," but has a remarkably free way of expressing his opinions, will reply—"Enlightenment is marching towards the seven points of the Charter." Another, with his hair *à la jeune France*, who has taken a fancy to his friend's wife, and is rather embarrassed with his own, asserts that Enlightenment is proceeding towards the Rights of Women, the reign of Social Love, and the annihilation of Tyrannical Prejudice. A third, who has the air of a man well to do in the middle class, more modest in his hopes, because he neither wishes to have his head broken by his errand-boy, nor his wife carried off to an Agapemoné by his apprentice, does not take Enlightenment a step farther than a siege on Debrett, and a cannonade on the Budget. Illiberal man! the march that he swells will soon trample *him* under foot. No one fares so ill in a crowd as the man who is wedged in the middle. A fourth, looking wild and dreamy, as if he had come out of the cave of Trophonius, and who is a mesmeriser and a mystic, thinks Enlightenment is in full career towards the good old days of alchemists and necromancers. A fifth, whom one might take for a Quaker, asserts that the march of Enlightenment is a crusade for universal philanthropy, vegetable diet, and the perpetuation of peace by means of speeches, which certainly do produce a very contrary effect from the Philippics of Demosthenes! The sixth—(good fellow without a rag on his back)—does not care a straw where the march goes. He can't be worse off than he is; and it is quite immaterial to him whether he goes to the dog-star above, or the bottomless pit below. I say nothing, however, against the march, while we take it altogether. Whatever happens, one is in good company; and though I am somewhat indolent by nature, and would rather stay at home with Locke and Burke, (dull dogs though they were,) than have my thoughts set off helter-skelter with those cursed trumpets and drums, blown and dub-a-dubbed by fellows whom I vow to heaven I would not trust with a five-pound note—still, if I must march, I must; and so deuce take the hindmost. But when it comes to individual marchers upon their own account—privateers and condottieri of Enlightenment—who have filled their pockets with lucifer-matches, and have a sublime contempt for their neighbours' barns and hay-ricks, I don't see why I should throw myself into the seventh heaven of admiration and ecstacy.

If those who are eternally rhapsodising on the celestial blessings that are to follow Enlightenment, Universal Knowledge, and so forth, would just take their eyes out of their pockets, and look about them, I would respectfully inquire if they have never met any very knowing and enlightened gentleman, whose acquaintance is by no means desirable. If not, they are monstrous lucky. Every man must judge by his own experience; and the worst rogues I have ever encountered were amazingly well-informed clever fellows! From dunderheads and dunces we can protect ourselves, but from your sharp-witted gentleman, all enlightenment and no prejudice, we have but to cry, "Heaven defend us!" It is true, that the rogue (let him be ever so enlightened) usually comes to no good himself, (though not before he has done harm enough to his neighbours). But that only shows that the world wants something else in those it rewards, besides intelligence *per se* and in the abstract; and is much too old a world to allow any Jack Horner to pick out its plums for his own personal gratification. Hence a man of very moderate intelligence, who believes in God, suffers his heart to beat with human sympathies, and keeps his eyes off your strong-box, will perhaps gain a vast deal more power than knowledge ever gives to a rogue.

Wherefore, though I anticipate an outcry against me on the part of the blockheads, who, strange to say, are the most credulous idolaters of enlightenment, and, if knowledge were power, would rot on a dunghill; yet, nevertheless, I think all really enlightened men will agree with me, that when one falls in with detached sharpshooters from the general March of Enlightenment, it is no reason that we should make ourselves a target, because Enlightenment has furnished them with a gun. It has, doubtless, been already remarked by the judicious reader, that of the numerous characters introduced into this work, the larger portion belong to that species which we call the INTELLECTUAL—that through them are analysed and developed human intellect, in various forms and directions. So that this History, rightly considered, is a kind of humble familiar Epic, or, if you prefer it, a long Serio-Comedy, upon the Varieties of English Life in this our Century, set in movement by the intelligences most prevalent. And where more ordinary and less refined types of the species round and complete the survey of our passing generation, they will often suggest, by contrast, the deficiencies which mere intellectual culture leaves in the human being. Certainly, I have no spite against intellect and enlightenment. Heaven forbid I should be such a Goth! I am only the advocate for common sense and fair play. I don't think an able man necessarily an angel; but I think if his heart match his head, and both proceed in the Great March under the divine Oriflamme, he goes as near to the angel as humanity will permit: if not, if he has but a penn'orth of heart to a pound of brains, I say, "*Bon jour, mon ange!* I see not the starry upward wings, but the grovelling cloven-hoof." I'd rather be offuscated by the Squire of Hazeldean, than enlightened by Randal Leslie. Every man to his taste. But intellect itself (not in the philosophical but the ordinary sense of the term) is rarely, if ever, one completed harmonious agency: it is not one faculty, but a compound of many, some of which are often at war with each other, and mar the concord of the whole. Few of us but have some predominant faculty, in itself a strength; but which, usurping unseasonably dominion over the rest, shares the lot of all tyranny, however brilliant, and leaves the empire weak against disaffection within, and invasion from without. Hence, intellect may be perverted in a man of evil disposition, and sometimes merely wasted in a man of excellent impulses, for want of the necessary discipline, or of a strong ruling motive. I doubt if there be one person in the world, who has obtained a high reputation for talent, who has not met somebody much cleverer than himself, which said somebody has never obtained any reputation at all! Men like Audley Egerton are constantly seen in the great positions of life; while men like Harley L'Estrange, who could have beaten them hollow in anything equally striven for by both, float away down the stream, and, unless some sudden stimulant arouse their dreamy energies, vanish out of sight into silent graves. If Hamlet and Polonius were living now, Polonius would have a much better chance of being a Cabinet Minister, though Hamlet would unquestionably be a much more intellectual character. What would become of Hamlet? Heaven knows! Dr. Arnold said, from his experience of a school, that the difference between one man and another was not mere ability—it was energy. There is a great deal of truth in that saying.

Submitting these hints to the judgment and penetration of the sagacious, I enter on the fresh division of this work, and see already Randal Leslie gnawing his lips on the back-ground. The German poet observes, that the Cow of Isis is to some the divine symbol of knowledge, to others but the milch cow, only regarded for the pounds of butter she will yield. O tendency of our age, to look on Isis as the milch cow! O prostitution of the grandest desires to the basest uses! Gaze on the goddess, Randal Leslie, and get ready thy churn and thy scales. Let us see what the butter will fetch in the market.

## CHAPTER II.

A NEW Reign has commenced. There has been a general election; the unpopularity of the Administration has been apparent at the hustings. Audley Egerton, hitherto returned by vast majorities, has barely escaped defeat—thanks to a majority of five. The expenses of his election are said to have been prodigious. "But who can stand against such wealth as Egerton's—no doubt backed, too, by the Treasury purse?" said the defeated candidate. It is towards the close of October; London is already full; Parliament will meet in less than a fortnight.

In one of the principal apartments of that hotel in which foreigners may discover what is meant by English comfort, and the price which foreigners must pay for it, there sat two persons side by side, engaged in close conversation. The one was a female, in whose pale clear complexion and raven hair —in whose eyes, vivid with a power of expression rarely bestowed on the beauties of the north, we recognise Beatrice, Marchesa di Negra. Undeniably handsome as was the Italian lady, her companion, though a man, and far advanced into middle age, was yet more remarkable for personal advantages. There was a strong family likeness between the two; but there was also a striking contrast in air, manner, and all that stamps on the physiognomy the idiosyncrasies of character. There was something of gravity, of earnestness and passion, in Beatrice's countenance when carefully examined: her smile at times might be false, but it was rarely ironical, never cynical. Her gestures, though graceful, were unrestrained and frequent. You could see she was a daughter of the south. Her companion, on the contrary, preserved on the fair, smooth face, to which years had given scarcely a line or wrinkle, something that might have passed, at first glance, for the levity and thoughtlessness of a gay and youthful nature; but the smile, though exquisitely polished, took at times the derision of a sneer. In his manners he was as composed and as free from gesture as an Englishman. His hair was of that red brown with which the Italian painters produce such marvellous effects of colour; and if here and there a silver thread gleamed through the locks, it was lost at once amidst their luxuriance. His eyes were light, and his complexion, though without much colour, was singularly transparent. His beauty, indeed, would have been rather womanly than masculine, but for the height and sinewy spareness of a frame in which muscular strength was rather adorned than concealed by an admirable elegance of proportion. You would never have guessed this man to be an Italian; more likely you would have supposed him a Parisian. He conversed in French, his dress was of French fashion, his mode of thought seemed French. Not that he was like the Frenchman of the present day—an animal, either rude or reserved; but your ideal of the *Marquis* of the old *régime*—the *roué* of the Regency.

Italian, however, he was, and of a race renowned in Italian history. But, as if ashamed of his country and his birth, he affected to be a citizen of the world. Heaven help the world if it hold only such citizens !

"But, Giulio," said Beatrice di Negra, speaking in Italian, "even granting that you discover this girl, can you suppose that her father will ever consent to your alliance? Surely you know too well the nature of your kinsman?"

"*Tu te trompes, ma sœur*," replied Giulio Franzini, Count di Peschiera, in French, as usual—"*tu te trompes;* I knew it before he had gone through exile and penury. How can I know it now? But comfort yourself, my too anxious Beatrice, I shall not care for his consent, till I've made sure of his daughter's."

"But how win that in despite of the father?"

"*Eh, mordieu!*" interrupted the Count, with true French gaiety; "what would become of all the comedies ever written, if marriages were not made in despite of the father? Look you," he resumed, with a very slight compression of his lip, and a still slighter movement in his chair—"look you, this is no question of ifs and buts! it is a question of must and shall —a question of existence to you and to me. When Danton was condemned to the guillotine, he said, flinging a pellet of bread at the nose of his respectable judge—'*Mon individu sera bientôt dans le néant*'—My patrimony is there already! I am loaded with debts. I see before me, on the one side, ruin or suicide; on the other side, wedlock and wealth."

"But from those vast possessions which you have been permitted to enjoy so long, have you really saved nothing against the time when they might be reclaimed at your hands?"

"My sister," replied the Count, "do I look like a man who saved? Besides, when the Austrian Emperor, unwilling to raze from his Lombard domains a name and a house so illustrious as our kinsman's, and desirous, while punishing that kinsman's rebellion, to reward my adherence, forbore the peremptory confiscation of those vast possessions at which my mouth waters while we speak, but, annexing them to the crown during pleasure, allowed me, as the next of male kin, to retain the revenues of one-half for the same very indefinite period—had I not every reason to suppose, that, before long, I could so influence his Imperial Majesty or his minister, as to obtain a decree that might transfer the whole, unconditionally and absolutely, to myself? And methinks I should have done so, but for this accursed, intermeddling English Milord, who has never ceased to besiege the court or the minister with alleged extenuations of our cousin's rebellion, and proofless assertions that I shared it in order to entangle my kinsman, and betrayed it in order to profit by his spoils. So that, at last, in return for all my services, and in answer to all my claims, I received from the minister himself this cold reply—'Count of Peschiera, your aid was important, and your reward has been large. That reward it would not be for your honour to extend, and justify the ill opinion of your Italian countrymen by formally appropriating to yourself all that was forfeited by the treason you denounced. A name so noble as yours should be dearer to you than fortune itself.'"

"Ah, Giulio," cried Beatrice, her face lighting up, changed in its whole character—" those were words that might make the demon that tempts to avarice fly from your breast in shame."

The Count opened his eyes in great amaze; then he glanced round the room and said, quietly—

"Nobody else hears you, my dear Beatrice; talk common sense. Heroics sound well in mixed society; but there is nothing less suited to the tone of a family conversation."

Madame di Negra bent down her head abashed, and that sudden change in the expression of her countenance which had seemed to betray susceptibility to generous emotion, faded as suddenly away.

"But still," she said, coldly, "you enjoy one-half of those ample revenues—why talk, then, of suicide and ruin?"

"I enjoy them at the pleasure of the crown; and what if it be the pleasure of the crown to recall our cousin, and reinstate him in his possessions?"

"There is a *probability*, then, of that pardon? When you first employed me in your researches, you only thought there was a *possibility*."

"There is a great probability of it, and therefore I am here. I learned some little time since that the question of such recall had been suggested by the Emperor, and discussed in Council. The danger to the State which might arise from our cousin's wealth, his alleged abilities—(abilities! bah!)—and his popular name, deferred any decision on the point; and, indeed, the difficulty of dealing with myself must have embarrassed the minister. But it is a mere question of time. He cannot long remain excluded from the general amnesty already extended to the other refugees. The person who gave me this information is high in power, and friendly to myself; and he added a piece of advice on which I acted. 'It was intimated,' said he, 'by one of the partisans of your kinsman, that the exile could give a hostage for his loyalty in the person of his daughter and heiress; that she had arrived at marriageable age; that if she were to wed, with the Emperor's consent, some one whose attachment to the Austrian crown was unquestionable, there would be a guarantee both for the faith of the father, and for the transmission of so important a heritage to safe and loyal hands. Why not' (continued my friend) 'apply to the Emperor for his consent to that alliance for yourself?—you, on whom he can depend;—you who, if the daughter should die, would be the legal heir to those lands?' On that hint I spoke."

"You saw the Emperor?"

"And after combating the unjust prepossessions against me, I stated, that so far from my cousin having any fair cause of resentment against me, when all was duly explained to him, I did not doubt that he would willingly give me the hand of his child."

"You did!" cried the Marchesa, amazed.

"And," continued the Count imperturbably, as he smoothed, with careless hand, the snowy plaits of his shirt front—"and that I should thus have the happiness of becoming myself the guarantee of my kinsman's loyalty—the agent for the restoration of his honours, while, in the eyes of the envious and malignant, I should clear up my own name from all suspicion that I had wronged him."

"And the Emperor consented?"

"*Pardieu*, my dear sister, what else could his majesty do? My proposition smoothed every obstacle, and reconciled policy with mercy. It remains, therefore, only to find out what has hitherto baffled all our researches, the retreat of our dear kinsfolk, and to make myself a welcome lover to the demoiselle. There is some disparity of years, I own; but—unless your sex and my glass flatter me overmuch—I am still a match for many a gallant of five-and-twenty."

The Count said this with so charming a smile, and looked so pre-eminently handsome, that he carried off the coxcombry of the words as gracefully as if they had been spoken by some dazzling hero of the grand old comedy of Parisian life.

Then interlacing his fingers, and lightly leaning his hands, thus clasped, upon his sister's shoulder, he looked into her face, and said slowly—"And now, my sister, for some gentle but deserved reproach. Have you not sadly failed me in the task I imposed on your regard for my interests? Is it not some years since you first came to England on the mission of discovering these worthy relations of ours? Did I not entreat you to seduce into your toils the man whom I knew to be my enemy, and who was indubitably acquainted with our cousin's retreat—a secret he has hitherto locked within his bosom?

D.d you not tell me, that though he was then in England, you could find no occasion even to meet him, but that you had obtained the friendship of the statesman to whom I directed your attention, as his most intimate associate? And yet you, whose charms are usually so irresistible, learn nothing from the statesman, as you see nothing of *Milord*. Nay, baffled and misled, you actually suppose that the quarry has taken refuge in France. You go thither—you pretend to search the capital —the provinces, Switzerland, *que sais-je?*—all in vain,— though—*foi de gentilhomme*—your police cost me dearly—you return to England—the same chace, and the same result *Palsambleu ma sœur*, I do too much credit to your talents not to question your zeal. In a word, have you been in earnest— or have you not had some womanly pleasure in amusing yourself and abusing my trust?"

"Giulio," answered Beatrice, sadly, "you know the influence you have exercised over my character and my fate. Your reproaches are not just. I made such inquiries as were in my power, and I have now cause to believe that I know one who is possessed of this secret, and can guide us to it."

"Ah, you do!" exclaimed the Count. Beatrice did not heed the exclamation, and hurried on.

"But grant that my heart shrunk from the task you imposed on me, would it not have been natural? When I first came to England, you informed me that your object in discovering the exiles was one which I could honestly aid. You naturally wished first to know if the daughter lived; if not, you were the heir. If she did, you assured me you desired to effect, through my mediation, some liberal compromise with Alphonso, by which you would have sought to obtain his restoration, provided he would leave you for life in possession of the grant you hold from the crown. While these were your objects, I did my best, ineffectual as it was, to obtain the information required."

"And what made me lose so important, though so ineffectual an ally?" asked the Count, still smiling; but a gleam that belied the smile shot from his eye.

"What! when you bade me receive and co-operate with the miserable spies—the false Italians—whom you sent over, and seek to entangle this poor exile, when found, in some rash correspondence to be revealed to the court;—when you sought to seduce the daughter of the Count of Peschiera, the descendant of those who had ruled in Italy, into the informer, the corruptor, and the traitress; No, Giulio—then I recoiled;

and then, fearful of your own sway over me, I retreated into France. I have answered you frankly."

The Count removed his hands from the shoulder on which they had reclined so cordially.

"And this," said he, "is your wisdom, and this your gratitude. You, whose fortunes are bound up in mine—you, who subsist on my bounty—you, who——"

"Hold," cried the Marchesa, rising, and with a burst of emotion, as if stung to the utmost, and breaking into revolt from the tyranny of years—"hold—gratitude! bounty! Brother, brother—what, indeed, do I owe to you? The shame and the misery of a life. While yet a child, you condemned me to marry against my will—against my heart—against my prayers—and laughed at my tears when I knelt to you for mercy. I was pure then, Giulio—pure and innocent as the flowers in my virgin crown. And now—now—"

Beatrice stopped abruptly, and clasped her hands before her face.

"Now you upbraid me," said the Count, unruffled by her sudden passion, "because I gave you in marriage to a man young and noble?"

"Old in vices, and mean of soul! The marriage I forgave you. You had the right, according to the customs of our country, to dispose of my hand. But I forgave you not the consolations that you whispered in the ear of a wretched and insulted wife."

"Pardon me the remark," replied the Count, with a courtly bend of his head, "but those consolations were also conformable to the customs of our country, and I was not aware till now that you had wholly disdained them. And," continued the Count, "you were not so long a wife that the gall of the chain should smart still. You were soon left a widow—free, childless, young, beautiful."

"And penniless."

"True, Di Negra was a gambler, and very unlucky; no fault of mine. I could neither keep the cards from his hands, nor advise him how to play them."

"And my own portion? Oh Giulio, I knew but at his death why you had condemned me to that renegade Genoese. He owed you money, and, against honour, and I believe against law, you had accepted my fortune in discharge of the debt."

"He had no other way to discharge it—a debt of honour must be paid—old stories these. What matters? Since then my purse has been open to you."

"Yes, not as your sister, but your instrument—your spy! Yes, your purse has been open—with a niggard hand."

"*Un peu de conscience, ma chère,* you are so extravagant. But come, be plain. What would you?"

"I would be free from you."

"That is, you would form some second marriage with one of these rich island lords. *Ma foi,* I respect your ambition."

"It is not so high. I aim but to escape from slavery—to be placed beyond dishonourable temptation. I desire," cried Beatrice, with increased emotion—"I desire to re-enter the life of woman."

"Eno'!" said the Count, with a visible impatience; is there anything in the attainment of your object that should render you indifferent to mine? You desire to marry, if I comprehend you right. And to marry, as becomes you, you should bring to your husband not debts, but a dowry. Be it so. I will restore the portion that I saved from the spendthrift clutch of the Genoese—the moment that it is mine to bestow —the moment that I am husband to my kinsman's heiress. And now, Beatrice, you imply that my former notions revolted your conscience; my present plan should content it; for by this marriage shall our kinsman regain his country, and repossess, at least, half his lands. And if I am not an excellent husband to the demoiselle, it will be her own fault. I have sown my wild oats. *Je suis bon prince,* when I have things a little my own way. It is my hope and my intention, and certainly it will be my interest, to become *digne époux et irréprochable père de famille.* I speak lightly—'tis my way. I mean seriously. The little girl will be very happy with me, and I shall succeed in soothing all resentment her father may retain. Will you aid me then—yes or no? Aid me, and you shall indeed be free. The magician will release the fair spirit he has bound to his will. Aid me not, *ma chère,* and mark, I do not threaten— I do but warn—aid me not; grant that I become a beggar, and ask yourself what is to become of you—still young, still beautiful, and still penniless? Nay, worse than penniless; you have done me the honour, (and here the Count, looking on the table, drew a letter from a portfolio emblazoned with his arms and coronet,) you have done me the honour to consult me as to your debts."

"You will restore my fortune?" said the Marchesa, irresolutely—and averting her head from an odious schedule of figures.

"When my own, with your aid, is secured."

"But do you not overrate the value of my aid?"

"Possibly," said the Count, with a caressing suavity—and he kissed his sister's forehead. "Possibly; but, by my honour, I wish to repair to you any wrong, real or supposed, I may have done you in past times. I wish to find again my own dear sister. I may over-value your aid, but not the affection from which it comes. Let us be friends, *cara Beatrice mia*," added the Count, for the first time employing Italian words.

The Marchesa laid her head on his shoulder and her tears flowed softly. Evidently this man had great influence over her—and evidently, whatever her cause for complaint, her affection for him was still sisterly and strong. A nature with fine flashes of generosity, spirit, honour, and passion, was hers —but uncultured, unguided—spoilt by the worst social examples—easily led into wrong—not always aware where the wrong was—letting affections good or bad whisper away her conscience or blind her reason. Such women are often far more dangerous when induced to wrong, than those who are thoroughly abandoned—such women are the accomplices men like the Count of Peschiera most desire to obtain.

"Ah, Giulio," said Beatrice, after a pause, and looking up at him through her tears, "when you speak to me thus, you know you can do with me what you will. Fatherless and motherless, whom had my childhood to love and obey but you?"

"Dear Beatrice," murmured the Count tenderly—and he again kissed her forehead. "So," he continued, more carelessly—"so the reconciliation is effected, and our interests and our hearts re-allied. Now, alas! to descend to business. You say that you know some one whom you believe to be acquainted with the lurking-place of my father-in-law—that is to be!"

"I think so. You remind me that I have an appointment with him this day: it is near the hour—I must leave you."

"To learn the secret?—Quick—quick. I have no fear of your success, if it is by his heart that you lead him!"

"You mistake; on his heart I have no hold. But he has a friend who loves me, and honourably, and whose cause he pleads. I think here that I have some means to control or persuade him. If not—ah, he is of a character that perplexes me in all but his worldly ambition; and how can we foreigners influence him through *that?*"

"Is he poor, or is he extravagant?"

"Not extravagant, and not positively poor, but dependent."

"Then we have him," said the Count, composedly. "If his assistance be worth buying, we can bid high for it. *Sur mon âme*, I never yet knew money fail with any man who was both worldly and dependent. I put him and myself in your hands."

Thus saying, the Count opened the door, and conducted his sister with formal politeness to her carriage. He then returned, reseated himself, and mused in silence. As he did so, the muscles of his countenance relaxed. The levity of the Frenchman fled from his visage, and in his eye, as it gazed abstractedly into space, there was that steady depth so remarkable in the old portraits of Florentine diplomatist or Venetian Oligarch. Thus seen, there was in that face, despite all its beauty, something that would have awed back even the fond gaze of love; something hard, collected, inscrutable, remorseless. But this change of countenance did not last long. Evidently thought, though intense for the moment, was not habitual to the man. Evidently he had lived the life which takes all things lightly—so he rose with a look of fatigue, shook and stretched himself, as if to cast off, or grow out of, an unwelcome and irksome mood. An hour afterwards, the Count of Peschiera was charming all eyes, and pleasing all ears, in the saloon of a high-born beauty, whose acquaintance he had made at Vienna, and whose charms, according to that old and never-truth-speaking oracle, Polite Scandal, were now said to have attracted to London the brilliant foreigner.

## CHAPTER III.

THE Marchesa regained her house, which was in Curzon Street, and withdrew to her own room, to readjust her dress, and remove from her countenance all trace of the tears she had shed.

Half an hour afterwards she was seated in her drawing-room, composed and calm; nor, seeing her then, could you have guessed that she was capable of so much emotion and so much weakness. In that stately exterior, in that quiet attitude, in that elaborate and finished elegance which comes alike from the arts of the toilet and the conventional repose of rank, you could see but the woman of the world and the great lady.

A knock at the door was heard, and in a few moments there entered a visitor, with the easy familiarity of intimate acquaintance—a young man, but with none of the bloom of youth. His hair, fine as a woman's, was thin and scanty, but it fell low over the forehead, and concealed that noblest of our human features. "A gentleman," says Apuleius, "ought to wear his whole mind on his forehead."* The young visitor would never have committed so frank an imprudence. His cheek was pale, and in his step and his movements there was a languor that spoke of fatigued nerves or delicate health. But the light of the eye and the tone of the voice were those of a mental temperament controlling the bodily—vigorous and energetic. For the rest, his general appearance was distinguished by a refinement alike intellectual and social. Once seen, you would not easily forget him. And the reader, no doubt, already recognises Randal Leslie. His salutation, as I before said, was that of intimate familiarity; yet it was given and replied to with that unreserved openness which denotes the absence of a more tender sentiment.

Seating himself by the Marchesa's side, Randal began first to converse on the fashionable topics and gossip of the day; but it was observable that while he extracted from her the current anecdote and scandal of the great world, neither anecdote nor scandal did he communicate in return. Randal Leslie had already learned the art not to commit himself, nor to have quoted against him one ill-natured remark upon the eminent. Nothing more injures the man who would rise beyond the fame of the *salons*, than to be considered backbiter and gossip; "yet it is always useful," thought Randal Leslie, "to know the foibles—the small social and private springs by which the great are moved. Critical occasions may arise in which such knowledge may be power." And hence, perhaps, (besides a more private motive, soon to be perceived,) Randal did not consider his time thrown away in cultivating Madame di Negra's friendship. For, despite much that was whispered against her, she had succeeded in dispelling the coldness with which she had at first been received in the London circles. Her beauty, her grace, and her high birth, had raised her into fashion, and the homage of men of the first station, while it perhaps injured her reputation as woman, added to her celebrity as fine lady. So much do we cold English, prudes though we be, forgive to the foreigner what we avenge on the native.

Sliding at last from these general topics into very well-bred

* "Hominem liberum et magnificum debere, si queat, in primori fronte, animum gestare."

and elegant personal compliment, and reciting various eulogies, which Lord this and the Duke of that had passed on the Marchesa's charms, Randal laid his hand on hers, with the license of admitted friendship, and said—

"But since you have deigned to confide in me, since when (happily for me, and with a generosity of which no *coquette* could have been capable) you, in good time, repressed into friendship feelings that might else have ripened into those you are formed to inspire and disdain to return, you told me with your charming smile, 'Let no one speak to me of love who does not offer me his hand, and with it the means to supply tastes that I fear are terribly extravagant;'—since thus you allowed me to divine your natural objects, and upon that understanding our intimacy has been founded, you will pardon me for saying that the admiration you excite amongst these *grands seigneurs* I have named, only serves to defeat your own purpose, and scare away admirers less brilliant, but more in earnest. Most of these gentlemen are unfortunately married; and they who are not belong to those members of our aristocracy who, in marriage, seek more than beauty and wit— namely, connexions to strengthen their political station, or wealth to redeem a mortgage and sustain a title."

"My dear Mr. Leslie," replied the Marchesa—and a certain sadness might be detected in the tone of the voice and the droop of the eye—"I have lived long enough in the real world to appreciate the baseness and the falsehood of most of those sentiments which take the noblest names. I see through the hearts of the admirers you parade before me, and know that not one of them would shelter with his ermine the woman to whom he talks of his heart. Ah," continued Beatrice, with a softness of which she was unconscious, but which might have been extremely dangerous to youth less steeled and self-guarded than was Randal Leslie's—"Ah, I am less ambitious than you suppose. I have dreamed of a friend, a companion, a protector, with feelings still fresh, undebased by the low round of vulgar dissipation and mean pleasures—of a heart so new, that it might restore my own to what it was in its happy spring. I have seen in your country some marriages, the mere contemplation of which has filled my eyes with delicious tears. I have learned in England to know the value of home. And with such a heart as I describe, and such a home, I could forget that I ever knew a less pure ambition."

"This language does not surprise me," said Randal; "yet it does not harmonise with your former answer to me."

"To you," repeated Beatrice, smiling, and regaining her lighter manner: "to you—true. But I never had the vanity to think that your affection for me could bear the sacrifices it would cost you in marriage; that you, with your ambition, could bound your dreams of happiness to home. And then, too," said she, raising her head, and with a certain grave pride in her air—"and *then*, I could not have consented to share my fate with one whom my poverty would cripple. I could not listen to my heart, if it had beat for a lover without fortune, for to him I could then have brought but a burden, and betrayed him into a union with poverty and debt. *Now*, it may be different. Now I may have the dowry that befits my birth. And now I may be free to choose according to my heart as woman, not according to my necessities, as one poor, harassed, and despairing."

"Ah," said Randal, interested, and drawing still closer towards his fair companion—"ah, I congratulate you sincerely; you have cause, then, to think that you shall be—rich?"

The Marchesa paused before she answered, and during that pause Randal relaxed the web of the scheme which he had been secretly weaving, and rapidly considered whether, if Beatrice di Negra would indeed be rich, she might answer to himself as a wife; and in what way, if so, he had best change his tone from that of friendship into that of love. While thus reflecting, Beatrice answered—

"Not rich for an Englishwoman; for an Italian, yes. My fortune should be half a million—"

"Half a million!" cried Randal, and with difficulty he restrained himself from falling at her feet in adoration.

"Of francs!" continued the Marchesa.

"Francs! Ah," said Randal, with a long-drawn breath, and recovering from his sudden enthusiasm, "about twenty thousand pounds?—eight hundred a-year at four per cent. A very handsome portion, certainly (Genteel poverty! he murmured to himself. What an escape I have had! but I see—I see. This will smooth all difficulties in the way of my better and earlier project. I see)—a very handsome portion," he repeated aloud—"not for a *grand seigneur*, indeed, but still for a gentleman of birth and expectations worthy of your choice, if ambition be not your first object. Ah, while you spoke with such endearing eloquence of feelings that were fresh, of a heart that was new, of the happy English home, you might guess that my thoughts ran to my friend who loves you so devotedly, and who so realises your idol. Proverbially, with us, happy marriages and happy homes are found not in the gay circles of London fashion, but at the hearths of our rural nobility—our untitled country gentlemen. And who, amongst all your adorers, can offer you a lot so really enviable as the one whom, I see by your blush, you already guess that I refer to?"

"Did I blush?" said the Marchesa, with a silvery laugh. "Nay, I think that your zeal for your friend misled you. But I will own frankly, I have been touched by his honest ingenuous love—so evident, yet rather looked than spoken. I have contrasted the love that honours me with the suitors that seek to degrade; more I cannot say. For though I grant that your friend is handsome, high-spirited, and generous, still he is not what—"

"You mistake, believe me," interrupted Randal. "You shall not finish your sentence. He *is* all that you do not yet suppose him; for his shyness, and his very love, his very respect for your superiority, do not allow his mind and his nature to appear to advantage. You, it is true, have a taste for letters and poetry rare among your countrywomen. He has not at present—few men have. But what Cimon would not be refined by so fair an Iphigenia? Such frivolities as he now shows belong but to youth and inexperience of life. Happy the brother who could see his sister the wife of Frank Hazeldean."

The Marchesa leant her cheek on her hand in silence. To her, marriage was more than it usually seems to dreaming maiden or to disconsolate widow. So had the strong desire to escape from the control of her unprincipled and remorseless brother grown a part of her very soul—so had whatever was best and highest in her very mixed and complex character been galled and outraged by her friendless and exposed position, the equivocal worship rendered to her beauty, the various debasements to which pecuniary embarrassments had subjected her—(not without design on the part of the Count, who though grasping, was not miserly, and who by precarious and seemingly capricious gifts at one time, and refusals of all aid at another, had involved her in debt in order to retain his hold on her)—so utterly painful and humiliating to a woman of her pride and her birth was the station that she held in the world—that in marriage she saw liberty, life, honour, self-redemption; and these thoughts, while they compelled her to co-operate with the schemes, by which the Count, on securing to himself a bride, was to bestow on herself a dower, also disposed her now to receive with favour Randal Leslie's pleadings on behalf of his friend.

The advocate saw that he had made an impression, and with the marvellous skill which his knowledge of those natures that engaged his study bestowed on his intelligence, he continued to improve his cause by such representations as were likely to be most effective. With what admirable tact he avoided panegyric of Frank as the mere individual, and drew him rather as the type, the ideal of what a woman in Beatrice's position might desire, in the safety, peace, and honour of a home, in the trust, and constancy, and honest confiding love of its partner! He did not paint an elysium; he described a haven; he did not glowingly delineate a hero of romance— he soberly portrayed that Representative of the Respectable and the Real which a woman turns to when romance begins to seem to her but delusion. Verily, if you could have looked into the heart of the person he addressed, and heard him speak, you would have cried admiringly, "Knowledge *is* power; and this man, if as able on a larger field of action, should play no mean part in the history of his time."

Slowly Beatrice roused herself from the reveries which crept over her as he spoke—slowly, and with a deep sigh, and said—

"Well, well, grant all you say; at least before I can listen to so honourable a love, I must be relieved from the base and sordid pressure that weighs on me. I cannot say to the man who woos me, 'Will you pay the debts of the daughter of Franzini, and the widow of di Negra?'"

"Nay, your debts, surely, make so slight a portion of your dowry."

"But the dowry has to be secured;" and here, turning the tables upon her companion, as the apt proverb expresses it, Madame di Negra extended her hand to Randal, and said in the most winning accents, "You are, then, truly and sincerely my friend?"

"Can you doubt it?"

"I prove that I do not, for I ask your assistance."

"Mine? How?"

"Listen; my brother has arrived in London—"

"I see that arrival announced in the papers."

"And he comes, empowered by the consent of the Emperor, to ask the hand of a relation and countrywoman of his; an alliance that will heal long family dissensions, and add to his own fortunes those of an heiress. My brother, like myself, has been extravagant. The dowry which by law he still owes me it would distress him to pay till this marriage be assured."

"I understand," said Randal. "But how can I aid this marriage?"

"By assisting us to discover the bride. She, with her father, sought refuge and concealment in England."

"The father had, then, taken part in some political disaffections, and was proscribed?"

"Exactly; and so well has he concealed himself, that he has baffled all our efforts to discover his retreat. My brother can obtain him his pardon in cementing this alliance—"

"Proceed."

"Ah, Randal, Randal, is this the frankness of friendship? You know that I have before sought to obtain the secret of our relation's retreat—sought in vain to obtain it from Mr. Egerton, who assuredly knows it—"

"But who communicates no secrets to living man," said Randal, almost bitterly; "who, close and compact as iron, is as little malleable to me as to you."

"Pardon me. I know you so well that I believe you could attain to any secret you sought earnestly to acquire. Nay, more, I believe that you know already that secret which I ask you to share with me."

"What on earth makes you think so?"

"When, some weeks ago, you asked me to describe the personal appearance and manners of the exile, which I did partly from the recollections of my childhood, partly from the description given to me by others, I could not but notice your countenance, and remark its change; in spite," said the Marchesa, smiling, and watching Randal while she spoke—"in spite of your habitual self-command. And when I pressed you to own that you had actually seen some one who tallied with that description, your denial did not deceive me. Still more, when returning recently, of your own accord, to the subject, you questioned me so shrewdly as to my motives in seeking the clue to our refugees, and I did not then answer you satisfactorily, I could detect—"

"Ha, ha," interrupted Randal with the low soft laugh by which occasionally he infringed upon Lord Chesterfield's recommendations to shun a merriment so natural as to be illbred—"Ha, ha, you have the fault of all observers too minute and refined. But even granting that I may have seen some Italian exiles, (which is likely enough,) what could be more natural than my seeking to compare your description with their appearance; and granting that I might suspect some one amongst them to be the man you search for, what more natural also, than that I should desire to know if you meant him harm or good in discovering his 'whereabout?'  For ill," added Randal, with an air of prudery—"ill would it become me to betray, even to friendship, the retreat of one who would hide from persecution; and even if I did so—for honour itself is a weak safeguard against your fascinations—such indiscretion might be fatal to my future career."

"How?"

"Do you not say that Egerton knows the secret, yet will not communicate?—and is he a man who would ever forgive in me an imprudence that committed himself? My dear friend, I will tell you more. When Audley Egerton first noticed my growing intimacy with you, he said, with his usual dryness of counsel, 'Randal, I do not ask you to discontinue acquaintance with Madame di Negra—for an acquaintance with women like her forms the manners, and refines the intellect; but charming women are dangerous, and Madame di Negra is—a charming woman.'"

The Marchesa's face flushed. Randal resumed: "'Your fair acquaintance' (I am still quoting Egerton) 'seeks to discover the home of a countryman of hers. She suspects that I know it. She may try to learn it through you. Accident may possibly give you the information she requires. Beware how you betray it. By one such weakness I should judge of your general character. He from whom a woman can extract a secret will never be fit for public life.' Therefore, my dear Marchesa, even supposing I possess this secret, you would be no true friend of mine to ask me to reveal what would imperil all my prospects. For as yet," added Randal, with a gloomy shade on his brow—"as yet, I do not stand alone and erect—I *lean;*—I am dependent."

"There may be a way," replied Madame di Negra, persisting, "to communicate this intelligence, without the possibility of Mr. Egerton's tracing our discovery to yourself; and, though I will not press you farther, I add this—You urge me to accept your friend's hand; you seem interested in the success of his suit, and you plead it with a warmth that shows how much you regard what you suppose is his happiness; I will never accept his hand till I can do so without blush for my penury—till my dowry is secured, and that can only be by my brother's union with the exile's daughter. For your friend's sake, therefore, think well how you can aid me in the first step to that alliance. The young lady once discovered, and my brother has no fear for the success of his suit."

"And you would marry Frank if the dower was secured?"

"Your arguments in his favour seem irresistible," replied Beatrice, looking down.

A flash went from Randal's eyes, and he mused a few moments.

Then slowly rising and drawing on his gloves, he said—

"Well, at least you so far reconcile my honour towards aiding your research, that you now inform me you mean no ill to the exile."

"Ill!—the restoration to fortune, honours, his native land."

"And you so far enlist my heart on your side, that you inspire me with the hope to contribute to the happiness of two friends whom I dearly love. I will, therefore, diligently try to ascertain if, among the refugees I have met with, lurk those whom you seek; and if so, I will thoughtfully consider how to give you the clue. Meanwhile, not one incautious word to Egerton."

"Trust me—I am a woman of the world."

Randal now had gained the door. He paused, and renewed carelessly—

"This young lady must be heiress to great wealth, to induce a man of your brother's rank to take so much pains to discover her."

"Her wealth *will* be vast," replied the Marchesa; "and if anything from wealth or influence in a foreign state could be permitted to prove my brother's gratitude—"

"Ah, fie!" interrupted Randal; and, approaching Madame di Negra, he lifted her hand to his lips, and said gallantly—

"This is reward enough to your *preux chevalier*."

With those words he took his leave.

## CHAPTER IV.

WITH his hands behind him, and his head drooping on his breast—slow, stealthy, noiseless, Randal Leslie glided along the streets on leaving the Italian's house. Across the scheme he had before revolved, there glanced another yet more glittering, for its gain might be more sure and immediate. If the exile's daughter were heiress to such wealth, might he himself hope ——. He stopped short even in his own soliloquy, and his breath came quick. Now, in his last visit to Hazeldean, he had come in contact with Riccabocca, and been struck by the beauty of Violante. A vague suspicion had crossed him that these might be the persons of whom the Marchesa was in search, and the suspicion had been confirmed by Beatrice's description of the refugee she desired to discover. But as he had not then learned the reason for her inquiries, nor conceived the possibility that he could have any personal interest in ascertaining the truth, he had only classed the secret in question among those the farther research into which might be left to time and occasion. Certainly the reader will not do the unscrupulous intellect of Randal Leslie the injustice to suppose that he was deterred from confiding to his fair friend all that he knew of Riccabocca, by the refinement of honour to which he had so chivalrously alluded. He had correctly stated Audley Egerton's warning against any indiscreet confidence, though he had forborne to mention a more recent and direct renewal of the same caution. His first vist to Hazeldean had been paid without consulting Egerton. He had been passing some days at his father's house, and had gone over thence to the Squire's. On his return to London, he had, however, mentioned this visit to Audley, who had seemed annoyed and even displeased at it, though Randal knew sufficient of Egerton's character to guess that such feelings could scarce be occasioned merely by his estrangement from his half-brother. This dissatisfaction had, therefore, puzzled the young man. But, as it was necessary to his views to establish intimacy with the Squire, he did not yield the point with his customary deference to his patron's whims. Accordingly he observed, that he should be very sorry to do anything displeasing to his benefactor, but that his father had been naturally anxious that he should not appear positively to slight the friendly overtures of Mr. Hazeldean.

"Why naturally?" asked Egerton.

"Because you know that Mr. Hazeldean is a relation of mine—that my grandmother was a Hazeldean."

"Ah!" said Egerton, who, as it has been before said, knew little and cared less, about the Hazeldean pedigree, "I was either not aware of that circumstance, or had forgotten it. And your father thinks that the Squire may leave you a legacy?"

"Oh, sir, my father is not so mercenary—such an idea never

entered his head. But the Squire himself has indeed said—
' Why, if anything happened to Frank, you would be next heir to my lands, and therefore we ought to know each other.' But—"

"Enough," interrupted Egerton. "I am the last man to pretend to the right of standing between you and a single chance of fortune, or of aid to it. And whom did you meet at Hazeldean?"

"There was no one there, sir; not even Frank."

"Hum. Is the Squire not on good terms with his parson? Any quarrel about tithes?"

"Oh, no quarrel. I forgot Mr. Dale; I saw him pretty often. He admires and praises you very much, sir."

"Me—and why? What did he say of me?"

"That your heart was as sound as your head; that he had once seen you about some old parishioners of his, and that he had been much impressed with the depth of feeling he could not have anticipated in a man of the world, and a statesman."

"Oh, that was all; some affair when I was member for Lansmere?"

"I suppose so."

Here the conversation had broken off; but the next time Randal was led to visit the Squire he had formally asked Egerton's consent, who, after a moment's hesitation, had as formally replied, "I have no objection."

On returning from this visit, Randal mentioned that he had seen Riccabocca: and Egerton, a little startled at first, said, composedly, "Doubtless one of the political refugees; take care not to set Madame di Negra on his track. Remember, she is suspected of being a spy of the Austrian government."

"Rely on me, sir," said Randal; "but I should think this poor Doctor can scarcely be the person she seeks to discover."

"That is no affair of ours," answered Egerton: "we are English gentlemen, and make not a step towards the secrets of another."

Now, when Randal revolved this rather ambiguous answer, and recalled the uneasiness with which Egerton had first heard of his visit to Hazeldean, he thought that he was indeed near the secret which Egerton desired to conceal from him and from all—viz., the incognito of the Italian whom Lord L'Estrange had taken under his protection.

"My cards," said Randal to himself, as with a deep-drawn sigh he resumed his soliloquy, "are become difficult to play.

On the one hand, to entangle Frank into marriage with this foreigner, the Squire could never forgive him. On the other hand, if she will not marry him without the dowry—and that depends on her brother's wedding this countrywoman—and that countrywoman be, as I surmise, Violante—and Violante be this heiress, and to be won by me! Tush, tush. Such delicate scruples in a woman so placed and so constituted as Beatrice di Negra must be easily talked away. Nay the loss itself of this alliance to her brother, the loss of her own dowry —the very pressure of poverty and debt—would compel her into the sole escape left to her option. I will then follow up the old plan; I will go down to Hazeldean, and see if there be any substance in the new one;—and then to reconcile both. Aha—the House of Leslie shall rise yet from its ruin—and—"

Here he was startled from his reverie by a friendly slap on the shoulder, and an exclamation—"Why, Randal, you are more absent than when you used to steal away from the cricket-ground, muttering Greek verses, at Eton."

"My dear Frank," said Randal, "you—you are so *brusque*, and I was just thinking of you."

"Were you? And kindly, then, I am sure," said Frank Hazeldean, his honest, handsome face lighted up with the unsuspecting genial trust of friendship; "and heaven knows," he added, with a sadder voice, and a graver expression on his eye and lip,—"Heaven knows I want all the kindness you can give me!"

"I thought," said Randal, "that your father's last supply, of which I was fortunate enough to be the bearer, would clear off your more pressing debts. I don't pretend to preach, but really I must say, once more, you should not be so extravagant."

FRANK (seriously).—"I have done my best to reform. I have sold off my horses, and I have not touched dice nor card these six months; I would not even put into the raffle for the last Derby." This last was said with the air of a man who doubted the possibility of obtaining belief to some assertion of preternatural abstinence and virtue.

RANDAL.—"Is it possible? But, with such self-conquest, how is it that you cannot contrive to live within the bounds of a very liberal allowance?"

FRANK (despondingly).—"Why, when a man once gets his head under water, it is so hard to float back again on the surface. You see, I attribute all my embarrassments to that first concealment of my debts from my father, when they could have been so easily met, and when he came up to town so kindly."

"I am sorry, then, that I gave you that advice."

"Oh, you meant it so kindly, I don't reproach you; it was all my own fault."

"Why, indeed, I did urge you to pay off that moiety of your debts left unpaid, with your allowance. Had you done so, all had been well."

"Yes; but poor Borrowell got into such a scrape at Goodwood—I could not resist him; a debt of honour—*that* must be paid; so when I signed another bill for him, he could not pay it, poor fellow! Really he would have shot himself, if I had not renewed it. And now it is swelled to such an amount with that cursed interest, that *he* never can pay it; and one bill, of course, begets another—and to be renewed every three months; 'tis the devil and all! So little as I ever got for all I have borrowed," added Frank, with a kind of rueful amaze. "Not £1500 ready money; and the interest would cost me almost as much yearly—if I had it."

"Only £1500!"

"Well—besides seven large chests of the worst cigars you ever smoked, three pipes of wine that no one would drink; and a great bear that had been imported from Greenland for the sake of its grease."

"That should, at least, have saved you a bill with your hair-dresser."

"I paid his bill with it," said Frank, "and very good-natured he was to take the monster off my hands—it had already hugged two soldiers and one groom into the shape of a flounder. I tell you what," resumed Frank, after a short pause, "I have a great mind even now to tell my father honestly all my embarrassments."

RANDAL (solemnly).—"Hum!"

FRANK.—"What? don't you think it would be the best way? I never can save enough—never can pay off what I owe? and it rolls like a snowball."

RANDAL.—"Judging by the Squire's talk, I think that with the first sight of your affairs you would forfeit his favour for ever; and your mother would be so shocked, especially after supposing that the sum I brought you so lately sufficed to pay off every claim on you. If you had not assured her of that it might be different; but she who so hates an untruth, and who said to the Squire, 'Frank says this will clear him; and with all his faults, Frank never yet told a lie!'"

"Oh, my dear mother!—I fancy I hear her!" cried Frank, with deep emotion. "But I did not tell a lie, Randal; I did not say that that sum would clear me."

"You empowered and begged me to say so," replied Randal, with grave coldness; "and don't blame me if I believed you."

"No, no! I only said it would clear me for the moment."

"I misunderstood you, then, sadly; and such mistakes involve my own honour. Pardon me, Frank; don't ask my aid in future. You see with the best intentions, I only compromise myself.'

"If you forsake me, I may as well go and throw myself into the river," said Frank, in a tone of despair; "and sooner or later, my father must know my necessities. The Jews threaten to go to him already; and the longer the delay, the more terrible the explanation."

"I don't see why your father should ever learn the state of your affairs; and it seems to me that you could pay off these usurers, and get rid of these bills, by raising money on comparatively easy terms—"

"How?" cried Frank, eagerly.

"Why, the Casino property is entailed on you, and you might obtain a sum upon that, not to be paid till the property becomes yours."

"At my poor father's death? Oh, no—no! I cannot bear the idea of this cold-blooded calculation on a father's death. I know it is not uncommon; I know other fellows who have done it, but they never had parents so kind as mine; and even in them it shocked and revolted me. The contemplating a father's death, and profiting by the contemplation,—it seems a kind of parricide: it is not natural, Randal. Besides, don't you remember what the Governor said—he actually wept while he said it—'Never calculate on my death; I could not bear that.' Oh, Randal, don't speak of it!"

"I respect your sentiments; but still, all the post-obits you could raise could not shorten Mr. Hazeldean's life by a day. However, dismiss that idea; we must think of some other device. Ha, Frank! you are a handsome fellow, and your expectations are great—why don't you marry some woman with money?"

"Pooh!" exclaimed Frank, colouring. "You know, Randal, that there is but one woman in the world I can ever think of; and I love her so devotedly, that, though I was as gay as most men before, I really feel as if the rest of her sex had lost every charm. I was passing through the street now—merely to look up at her windows."

"You speak of Madame di Negra? I have just left her. Certainly she is two or three years older than you; but if you can get over that misfortune, why not marry her?"

"Marry her!" cried Frank, in amaze, and all his colour fled from his cheeks. "Marry her! Are you serious?"

"Why not?"

"But even if she, who is so accomplished, so admired—even if she would accept me, she is, you know, poorer than myself. She has told me so frankly. That woman has such a noble heart! and—and—my father would never consent, nor my mother either. I know they would not."

"Because she is a foreigner?"

"Yes—partly."

"Yet the Squire suffered his cousin to marry a foreigner."

"That was different. He had no control over Jemima; and a daughter-in-law is so different; and my father is so English in his notions; and Madame di Negra, you see, is altogether so foreign. Her very graces would be against her in his eyes."

"I think you do both your parents injustice. A foreigner of low birth—an actress or singer, for instance—of course would be highly objectionable; but a woman, like Madame di Negra, of such high birth and connexions—"

Frank shook his head. "I don't think the Governor would care a straw about her connexions, if she were a king's daughter. He considers all foreigners pretty much alike. And then, you know" (Frank's voice sank into a whisper)— "you know that one of the very reasons why she is so dear to me, would be an insuperable objection to the old-fashioned folks at home."

"I don't understand you, Frank."

"I love her the more," said young Hazeldean, raising his front with a noble pride, that seemed to speak of his descent from a race of cavaliers and gentlemen—"I love her the more because the world has slandered her name—because I believe her to be pure and wronged. But would they at the Hall— they who do not see with a lover's eyes—they who have all the stubborn English notions about the indecorum and license of Continental manners, and will so readily credit the worst? —Oh, no—I love, I cannot help it—but I have no hope."

"It is very possible that you may be right," exclaimed Randal, as if struck and half convinced by his companion's argument—" very possible; and certainly I think that th homely folks at the Hall would fret and fume at first, if they heard you were married to Madame di Negra. Yet still, when your father learned that you had done so, not from passion alone, but to save him from all pecuniary sacrifice—to clear yourself of debt—to—"

"What do you mean?" exclaimed Frank, impatiently.

"I have reason to know that Madame di Negra will have as large a portion as your father could reasonably expect you to receive with any English wife. And when this is properly stated to the Squire, and the high position and rank of your wife fully established and brought home to him—for I must think that these would tell, despite your exaggerated notions of his prejudices—and then, when he really sees Madame di Negra, and can judge of her beauty and rare gifts, upon my word, I think, Frank, that there would be no cause for fear. After all, too, you are his only son. He will have no option but to forgive you; and I know how anxiously both your parents wish to see you settled in life."

Frank's whole countenance became illuminated. "There is no one who understands the Squire like you, certainly," said he, with lively joy. "He has the highest opinion of your judgment. And you really believe you could smooth matters?"

"I believe so; but I should be sorry to induce you to run any risk; and if, on cool consideration, you think that risk is incurred, I strongly advise you to avoid all occasion of seeing the poor Marchesa. Ah, you wince; but I say it for her sake as well as your own. First you must be aware, that, unless you have serious thoughts of marriage, your attentions can but add to the very rumours that, equally groundless, you so feelingly resent; and, secondly, because I don't think any man has a right to win the affections of a woman—especially a woman who seems to me likely to love with her whole heart and soul—merely to gratify his own vanity."

"Vanity! Good heavens! can you think so poorly of me? But as to the Marchesa's affections" continued Frank, with a faltering voice, "do you really and honestly believe that they are to be won by me?"

"I fear lest they may be half won already," said Randal, with a smile and a shake of the head; but she is too proud to let you see any effect you may produce on her, especially when, as I take it for granted, you have never hinted at the hope of obtaining her hand."

"I never till now conceived such a hope. My dear Randal,

all my cares have vanished—I tread upon air—I have a great mind to call on her at once."

"Stay, stay," said Randal. "Let me give you a caution. I have just informed you that Madame di Negra will have, what you suspected not before, a fortune suitable to her birth. Any abrupt change in your manner at present might induce her to believe that you were influenced by that intelligence."

"Ah!" exclaimed Frank, stopping short, as if wounded to the quick. "And I feel guilty—feel as if I *was* influenced by that intelligence. So I am, too, when I reflect," he continued, with a *naïveté* that was half pathetic; "but I hope she will not be *very* rich—if so, I'll not call."

"Make your mind easy, it is but a portion of some twenty or thirty thousand pounds, that would just suffice to discharge all your debts, clear away all obstacle to your union, and in return for which you could secure a more than adequate jointure and settlement on the Casino property. Now I am on that head, I will be yet more communicative. Madame di Negra has a noble heart, as you say, and told me herself, that, until her brother on his arrival had assured her of this dowry, she would never have consented to marry you—never crippled with her own embarrassments the man she loves. Ah! with what delight she will hail the thought of assisting you to win back your father's heart! But be guarded meanwhile. And now, Frank, what say you—would it not be well if I ran down to Hazeldean to sound your parents? It is rather inconvenient to me, to be sure, to leave town just at present; but I will do more than that to render you a smaller service. Yes, I'll go to Rood Hall to-morrow, and thence to Hazeldean. I am sure your father will press me to stay, and I shall have ample opportunities to judge of the manner in which he would be likely to regard your marriage with Madame di Negra—supposing always it were properly put to him. We can then act accordingly."

"My dear, dear Randal, how can I thank you? If ever a poor fellow like me can serve you in return—but that's impossible."

"Why certainly, I will never ask you to be security to a bill of mine," said Randal, laughing. "I practise the economy I preach."

"Ah!" said Frank, with a groan, "that is because your mind is cultivated—you have so many resources; and all my faults have come from idleness. If I had had anything to do on a rainy day, I should never have got into these scrapes."

"Oh! you will have enough to do some day managing your property. We who have no property must find one in knowledge. Adieu, my dear Frank—I must go home now. By the way, you have never, by chance, spoken of the Riccaboccas to Madame di Negra?"

"The Riccaboccas? No. That's well thought of. It may interest her to know that a relation of mine has married her countryman. Very odd that I never did mention it; but, to say truth, I really do talk so little to her: she is so superior, and I feel positively shy with her."

"Do me the favour, Frank," said Randal, waiting patiently till this reply ended—for he was devising all the time what reason to give for his request—"never to allude to the Riccaboccas either to her or to her brother, to whom you are sure to be presented."

"Why not allude to them?"

Randal hesitated a moment. His invention was still at fault, and, for a wonder, he thought it the best policy to go pretty near the truth.

"Why, I will tell you. The Marchesa conceals nothing from her brother, and he is one of the few Italians who are in high favour with the Austrian court."

"Well!"

"And I suspect that poor Dr. Riccabocca fled his country from some mad experiment at revolution, and is still hiding from the Austrian police."

"But they can't hurt him here," said Frank, with an Englishman's dogged inborn conviction of the sanctity of his native island. "I should like to see an Austrian pretend to dictate to us whom to receive and whom to reject."

"Hum—that's true and constitutional, no doubt; but Riccabocca may have excellent reasons—and, to speak plainly, I know he has (perhaps as affecting the safety of friends in Italy)—for preserving his incognito, and we are bound to respect those reasons without inquiring further."

"Still I cannot think so meanly of Madame di Negra," persisted Frank (shrewd here, though credulous elsewhere, and both from his sense of honour), "as to suppose that she would decend to be a spy, and injure a poor countryman of her own, who trusts to the same hospitality she receives herself at our English hands. Oh! if I thought that, I could not love her!" added Frank, with energy.

"Certainly you are right. But see in what a false position you would place both her brother and herself. If they knew

Riccabocca's secret, and proclaimed it to the Austrian Government, as you say, it would be cruel and mean; but if they knew it and concealed it, it might involve them both in the most serious consequences. You know the Austrian policy is proverbially so jealous and tyrannical?"

" Well, the newspapers say so, certainly."

" And, in short, your discretion can do no harm, and your indiscretion may. Therefore, give me your word, Frank. I can't stay to argue now."

" I'll not allude to the Riccaboccas, upon my honour," answered Frank; " still, I am sure that they would be as safe with the Marchesa as with——"

" I rely on your honour," interrupted Randal, hastily, and hurried off.

## CHAPTER V.

Towards the evening of the following day, Randal Leslie walked slowly from a village in the main road (about two miles from Rood Hall,) at which he had got out of the coach. He passed through meads and cornfields, and by the skirts of woods which had formerly belonged to his ancestors, but had been long since alienated. He was alone amidst the haunts of his boyhood, the scenes in which he had first invoked the grand Spirit of Knowledge, to bid the Celestial Still One minister to the commands of an earthly and turbulent ambition. He paused often in his path, especially when the undulations of the ground gave a glimpse of the grey church tower, or the gloomy firs that rose above the desolate wastes of Rood.

" Here," thought Randal, with a softening eye—" here, how often, comparing the fertility of the lands passed away from the inheritance of my fathers, with the forlorn wilds that are left to their mouldering hall—here, how often have I said to myself—' I will rebuild the fortunes of my house.' And straightway Toil lost its aspect of drudge, and grew kingly, and books became as living armies to serve my thought. Again—again—O thou haughty Past, brace and strengthen me in the battle with the Future." His pale lips writhed as he soliloquised, for his conscience spoke to him while he thus addressed his will, and its voice was heard more audibly in the quiet of the rural landscape, than amidst the turmoil and din of that armed and sleepless camp which we call a city.

Doubtless, though Ambition have objects more vast and beneficent than the restoration of a name,—*that* in itself is high and chivalrous, and appeals to a strong interest in the human heart. But all emotions, and all ends, of a nobler character, had seemed to filter themselves free from every golden grain in passing through the mechanism of Randal's intellect, and came forth at last into egotism clear and unalloyed. Nevertheless, it is a strange truth that, to a man of cultivated mind, however perverted and vicious, there are vouchsafed gleams of brighter sentiments, irregular perceptions of moral beauty, denied to the brutal unreasoning wickedness of uneducated villany—which perhaps ultimately serve as his punishment—according to the old thought of the satirist, that there is no greater curse than to perceive virtue yet adopt vice. And as the solitary schemer walked slowly on, and his childhood—innocent at least in deed—came distinct before him through the halo of bygone dreams— dreams far purer than those from which he now rose each morning to the active world of Man—a profound, melancholy crept over him, and suddenly he exclaimed aloud, "*Then* I aspired to be renowned and great—*now*, how is it that, so advanced in my career, all that seemed lofty in the end has vanished from me, and the only means that I contemplate are those which my childhood would have called poor and vile? Ah! is it that I then read but books, and now my knowledge has passed onward, and men contaminate more than books? But," he continued, in a lower voice, as if arguing with himself,—" if power is only so to be won—and of what use is knowledge if it be not power—does not success in life justify all things? And who prizes the wise man if he fails?" He continued his way, but still the soft tranquillity around rebuked him, and still his reason was dissatisfied, as well as his conscience. There are times when Nature, like a bath of youth, seems to restore to the jaded soul its freshness—times from which some men have emerged, as if re-born. The crises of life are very silent. Suddenly the scene opened on Randal Leslie's eyes. The bare desert common—the dilapidated church—the old house, partially seen in the dank dreary hollow, into which it seemed to Randal to have sunken deeper and lowlier than when he saw it last. And on the common were some young men playing at hockey. That old-fashioned game, now very uncommon in England, except at schools, was still preserved in the primitive vicinity of Rood by the young yoemen and farmers. Randal stood by the stile and looked on, for among the players he recognized his brother Oliver. Presently the ball was struck towards Oliver, and the group instantly gathered round that young gentleman and snatched him from Randal's eye; but the elder brother heard a displeasing din, a derisive laughter. Oliver had shrunk from the danger of the thick clubbed sticks that plied around him, and received some stroke across the legs, for his voice rose whining, and was drowned by shouts of, "Go to your mammy. That's Noll Leslie—all over. Butter shins."

Randal's sallow face became scarlet. "The jest of boors—a Leslie!" he muttered, and ground his teeth. He sprang over the stile and walked erect and haughtily across the ground. The players cried out indignantly. Randal raised his hat, and they recognised him, and stopped the game. For him at least a certain respect was felt. Oliver turned round quickly, and ran up to him. Randal caught his arm firmly, and without saying a word to the rest, drew him away towards the house. Oliver cast a regretful, lingering look behind him, rubbed his shins, and then stole a timid glance towards Randal's severe and moody countenance.

"You are not angry that I was playing at hocky with our neighbours," said he deprecatingly, observing that Randal would not break the silence.

"No," replied the elder brother; "but, in associating with his inferiors, a gentleman still knows how to maintain his dignity. There is no harm in playing with inferiors, but it is necessary to a gentleman to play so that he is not the laughing-stock of clowns."

Oliver hung his head, and made no answer. They came into the slovenly precincts of the court, and the pigs stared at them from the palings, as their progenitors had stared, years before, at Frank Hazeldean.

Mr. Leslie senior, in a shabby straw-hat, was engaged in feeding the chickens before the threshold, and he performed even that occupation with a maundering lack-a-daisical slothfulness, dropping down the grains almost one by one from his inert dreamy fingers.

Randal's sister, her hair still and for ever hanging about her ears, was seated on a rush-bottom chair, reading a tattered novel; and from the parlour window was heard the querulous voice of Mrs. Leslie, in high fidget and complaint.

Somehow or other, as the young heir to all this helpless

poverty stood in the courtyard, with his sharp, refined, intelligent features, and his strange elegance of dress and aspect, one better comprehended how, left solely to the egotism of his knowledge and his ambition, in such a family, and without any of the sweet nameless lessons of Home, he had grown up into such close and secret solitude of soul—how the mind had taken so little nutriment from the heart, and how that affection and respect which the warm circle of the hearth usually calls forth had passed with him to the graves of dead fathers, growing, as it were, bloodless and ghoul-like amidst the charnels on which they fed.

"Ha, Randal, boy," said Mr. Leslie, looking up, lazily, "how d'ye do? Who could have expected you? My dear—my dear," he cried, in a broken voice, and as if in helpless dismay, "here's Randal, and he'll be wanting dinner, or supper, or something." But, in the meanwhile, Randal's sister Juliet had sprung up and thrown her arms round her brother's neck, and he had drawn her aside caressingly, for Randal's strongest human affection was for this sister.

"You are growing very pretty, Juliet," said he, smoothing back her hair; "why do yourself such injustice—why not pay more attention to your appearance, as I have so often begged you to do?"

"I did not expect you, dear Randal; you always come so suddenly, and catch us *en dish-a-bill.*"

"Dish-abill!" echoed Randal, with a groan. "*Dishabille!*—you ought never to be so caught!"

"No one else does so catch us—nobody else ever comes—Heigho!" and the young lady sighed very heartily.

"Patience, patience; my day is coming, and then yours, my sister," replied Randal, with genuine pity, as he gazed upon what a little care could have trained into so fair a flower, and what now looked so like a weed.

Here Mrs. Leslie, in a state of intense excitement—having rushed through the parlour—leaving a fragment of her gown between the yawning brass of the never-mended Brummagem work-table—tore across the hall—whirled out of the door, scattering the chickens to the right and left, and clutched hold of Randal in her motherly embrace. "La, how you do shake my nerves," she cried, after giving him a most hasty and uncomfortable kiss. "And you are hungry too, and nothing in the house but cold mutton! Jenny, Jenny—I say, Jenny! Juliet, have you seen Jenny? Where's Jenny? Out with the odd man, I'll be bound."

"I am not hungry, mother," said Randal; "I wish for nothing but tea." Juliet, scrambling up her hair, darted into the house to prepare the tea, and also to "tidy herself." She dearly loved her fine brother, but she was greatly in awe of him.

Randal seated himself on the broken pales. "Take care they don't come down," said Mr. Leslie, with some anxiety.

"Oh, sir, I am very light; nothing comes down with me."

The pigs stared up, and grunted in amaze at the stranger.

"Mother," said the young man, detaining Mrs. Leslie, who wanted to set off in chase of Jenny—"Mother, you should not let Oliver associate with those village boors. It is time to think of a profession for him."

"Oh, he eats us out of house and home—such an appetite! But as to a profession—what is he fit for! He will never be a scholar."

Randal nodded a moody assent; for, indeed Oliver had been sent to Cambridge, and supported there out of Randal's income from his official pay; and Oliver had been plucked for his Little Go.

"There is the army," said the elder brother—a gentleman's calling. How handsome Juliet ought to be—but—I left money for masters—and she pronounces French like a chambermaid."

"Yet she is fond of her book too. She's always reading, and good for nothing else."

"Reading!—those trashy novels!"

"So like you—you always come to scold, and make things unpleasant," said Mrs. Leslie, peevishly. "You are grown too fine for us, and I am sure we suffer affronts enough from others, not to want a little respect from our own children."

"I did not mean to affront you," said Randal, sadly. "Pardon me. But who else has done so?"

Then Mrs. Leslie went into a minute and most irritating catalogue of all the mortifications and insults she had received; the grievances of a petty provincial family, with much pretension and small power; of all people, indeed, without the disposition to please—without the ability to serve—who exaggerate every offence, and are thankful for no kindness. Farmer Jones had insolently refused to send his waggon twenty miles for coals. Mr. Giles, the butcher, requesting the payment of his bill, had stated that the custom at Rood was too small for him to allow credit. Squire Thornhill, who was the present owner of the fairest slice of the old Leslie

domains, had taken the liberty to ask permission to shoot
over Mr. Leslie's land, since Mr. Leslie did not preserve.
Lady Spratt (new people from the city, who hired a neighbouring country-seat) had taken a discharged servant of
Mrs. Leslie's without applying for the character. The Lord-
Lieutenant had given a ball, and had not invited the Leslies.
Mr. Leslie's tenants had voted against their landlord's wish at
the recent election. More than all, Squire Hazeldean and his
Harry had called at Rood, and though Mrs. Leslie had
screamed out to Jenny, "Not at home," she had been seen at
the window, and the Squire had actually forced his way in,
and caught the whole family "in a state not fit to be seen."
That was a trifle, but the Squire had presumed to instruct
Mr. Leslie how to manage his property, and Mrs. Hazeldean
had actually told Juliet to hold up her head, and tie up her
hair, "as if we were her cottagers!" said Mrs. Leslie, with
the pride of a Montfydget.

All these, and various other annoyances, though Randal
was too sensible not to perceive their insignificance, still galled
and mortified the listening heir of Rood. They showed, at
least, even to the well-meant officiousness of the Hazeldeans,
the small account in which the fallen family was held. As
he sat still on the moss-grown pales, gloomy and taciturn,
his mother standing beside him, with her cap awry, Mr. Leslie
shamblingly sauntered up, and said in a pensive, dolorous
whine—

"I wish we had a good sum of money, Randal, boy!"

To do Mr. Leslie justice, he seldom gave vent to any wish
that savoured of avarice. His mind must be singularly
aroused, to wander out of its normal limits of sluggish, dull
content.

So Randal looked at him in surprise, and said, "Do you,
sir?—why?"

"The manors of Rood and Dulmansberry, and all the lands
therein, which my great-grandfather sold away, are to be sold
again when Squire Thornhill's eldest son comes of age, to cut
off the entail. Sir John Spratt talks of buying them. I
should like to have them back again! 'Tis a shame to see
the Leslie estates hawked about, and bought by Spratts and
people. I wish I had a great—great sum of ready money."

The poor gentleman extended his helpless fingers as he
spoke, and fell into a dejected reverie.

Randal sprang from the paling, a movement which
frightened the contemplative pigs, and set them off squalling

and scampering, "When does young Thornhill come of age?"

"He was nineteen last August. I know it, because the day he was born, I picked up my fossil of the sea-horse, just by Dulmansberry church, when the joy-bells were ringing. My fossil sea-horse! It will be an heirloom, Randal——"

"Two years—nearly two years—yet—ah, ah!" said Randal; and his sister now appearing, to announce that tea was ready, he threw his arm round her neck and kissed her. Juliet had arranged her hair and trimmed up her dress. She looked very pretty, and she had now the air of a gentlewoman—something of Randal's own refinement in her slender proportions and well-shaped head.

"Be patient, patient still, my dear sister," whispered Randal, "and keep your heart whole for two years longer."

The young man was gay and good-humoured over his simple meal, while his family grouped round him. When it was over, Mr. Leslie lighted his pipe, and called for his brandy-and-water. Mrs. Leslie began to question about London and Court, and the new King and the new Queen, and Mr. Audley Egerton, and hoped Mr. Egerton would leave Randal all his money, and that Randal would marry a rich woman, and that the King would make him a prime-minister one of these days; and then she should like to see if Farmer Jones would refuse to send his wagon for coals! And, every now and then, as the word "riches" or "money" caught Mr. Leslie's ears, he shook his head, drew his pipe from his mouth, "A Spratt should not have what belonged to my great-great-grandfather. If I had a good sum of ready money!—the old family estates!" Oliver and Juliet sat silent, and on their good behaviour; and Randal, indulging his own reveries, dreamily heard the words "money," "Spratt," "great-great-grandfather," "rich wife," "family estates;" and they sounded to him vague and afar off, like whispers from the world of romance and legend—weird prophecies of things to be.

Such was the hearth which warmed the viper that nestled and gnawed at the heart of Randal, poisoning all the aspirations that youth should have rendered pure, ambition lofty, and knowledge beneficent and divine.

## CHAPTER VI.

When the rest of the household were in deep sleep, Randal stood long at his open window, looking over the dreary, comfortless scene—the moon gleaming from skies half-autumnal, half-wintry, upon squalid decay, through the ragged fissures of the firs; and when he lay down to rest, his sleep was feverish, and troubled by turbulent dreams.

However, he was up early, and with an unwonted colour in his cheeks, which his sister ascribed to the country air. After breakfast, he took his way towards Hazeldean, mounted upon a tolerable horse, which he borrowed of a neighbouring farmer who occasionally hunted. Before noon, the garden and terrace of the Casino came in sight. He reined in his horse, and by the little fountain at which Leonard had been wont to eat his radishes and con his book, he saw Riccabocca seated under the shade of the red umbrella. And by the Italian's side stood a form that a Greek of old might have deemed the Naïad of the Fount; for in its youthful beauty there was something so full of poetry—something at once so sweet and so stately—that it spoke to the imagination while it charmed the sense.

Randal dismounted, tied his horse to the gate, and, walking down a trellised alley, came suddenly to the spot. His dark shadow fell over the clear mirror of the fountain just as Riccabocca had said, "All here is so secure from evil!—the waves of the fountain are never troubled like those of the river!" and Violante had answered in her soft native tongue, and lifting her dark, spiritual eyes—"But the fountain would be but a lifeless pool, oh, my father, if the spray did not mount towards the skies!"

## CHAPTER VII.

Randal advanced—"I fear, Signor Riccabocca, that I am guilty of some want of ceremony."

"To dispense with ceremony is the most delicate mode of conferring a compliment," replied the urbane Italian, as he recovered from his first surprise at Randal's sudden address, and extended his hand.

Violante bowed her graceful head to the young man's respectful salutation. "I am on my way to Hazeldean," resumed Randal, "and, seeing you in the garden, could not resist this intrusion."

RICCABOCCA.—"You come from London? Stirring times for you English, but I do not ask you the news? No news can affect us."

RANDAL (softly).—"Perhaps yes."

RICCABOCCA (startled).—"How?"

VIOLANTE.—"Surely he speaks of Italy, and news from that country affects you still, my father."

RICCABOCCA.—"Nay, nay, nothing affects me like this country; its east winds might affect a pyramid! Draw your mantle round you, child, and go in; the air has suddenly grown chill."

Violante smiled on her father, glanced uneasily towards Randal's grave brow, and went slowly towards the house.

Riccabocca, after waiting some moments in silence, as if expecting Randal to speak, said, with affected carelessness, "So you think that you have news that might affect me? *Corpo di Bacco!* I am curious to learn what!"

"I may be mistaken—that depends on your answer to one question. Do you know the Count of Peschiera?"

Riccabocca winced, and turned pale. He could not baffle the watchful eye of the questioner.

"Enough," said Randal; "I see that I am right. Believe in my sincerity. I speak but to warn and to serve you. The Count seeks to discover the retreat of a countryman and kinsman of his own."

"And for what end?" cried Riccabocca, thrown off his guard, and his breast dilated, his crest rose, and his eye flashed; valour and defiance broke from habitual caution and self-control. "But—pooh!" he added, striving to regain his ordinary and half-ironical calm, "it matters not to me. I grant, sir, that I know the Count di Peschiera; but what has Dr. Riccabocca to do with the kinsman of so grand a personage?"

"Dr. Riccabocca—nothing. But—" here Randal put his lip close to the Italian's ear, and whispered a brief sentence. Then retreating a step, but laying his hand on the exile's shoulder, he added—"Need I say that your secret is safe with me?"

Riccabocca made no answer. His eyes rested on the ground musingly.

Randal continued—"And I shall esteem it the highest honour you can bestow on me, to be permitted to assist you in forestalling danger."

RICCABOCCA (slowly).—"Sir, I thank you; you have my secret, and I feel assured it is safe, for I speak to an English gentleman. There may be family reasons why I should avoid the Count di Peschiera; and, indeed, he is safest from shoals who steers clearest of his—relations."

The poor Italian regained his caustic smile as he uttered that wise villanous Italian maxim.

RANDAL.—"I know little of the Count of Peschiera save from the current talk of the world. He is said to hold the estates of a kinsman who took part in a conspiracy against the Austrian power."

RICCABOCCA.—"It is true. Let that content him; what more does he desire? You spoke of forestalling danger; what danger? I am on the soil of England, and protected by its laws."

RANDAL.—"Allow me to inquire if, had the kinsman no child, the Count di Peschiera would be legitimate and natural heir to the estates he holds?"

RICCABOCCA.—"He would—What then?"

RANDAL.—"Does that thought suggest no danger to the child of the kinsman?"

Riccabocca recoiled, and gasped forth, "The child! You do not mean to imply that this man, infamous though he be, can contemplate the crime of an assassin?"

Randal paused perplexed. His ground was delicate. He knew not what causes of resentment the exile entertained against the Count. He knew not whether Riccabocca would not assent to an alliance that might restore him to his country —and he resolved to feel his way with precaution.

"I did not," said he, smiling gravely, "mean to insinuate so horrible a charge against a man whom I have never seen. He seeks you—that is all I know. I imagine, from his general character, that in this search he consults his interest. Perhaps all matters might be conciliated by an interview!"

"An interview!" exclaimed Riccabocca; "there is but one way we should meet—foot to foot, and hand to hand."

"Is it so? Then you would not listen to the Count if he proposed some amicable compromise—if, for instance, he was a candidate for the hand of your daughter?"

The poor Italian, so wise and so subtle in his talk, was as

rash and blind when it came to action, as if he had been born in Ireland, and nourished on potatoes and Repeal. He bared his whole soul to the merciless eye of Randal.

"My daughter!" he exclaimed. "Sir, your very question is an insult."

Randal's way became clear at once. "Forgive me," he said, mildly; "I will tell you frankly all that I know. I am acquainted with the Count's sister. I have some little influence over her. It was she who informed me that the Count had come here, bent upon discovering your refuge, and resolved to wed your daughter. This is the danger of which I spoke. And when I asked your permission to aid in forestalling it, I only intended to suggest that it might be wise to find some securer home, and that I, if permitted to know that home, and to visit you, could apprise you from time to time of the Count's plans and movements."

"Sir, I thank you sincerely," said Riccabocca, with emotion; "but am I not safe here?"

"I doubt it. Many people have visited the Squire in the shooting season, who will have heard of you—perhaps seen you, and who are likely to meet the Count in London. And Frank Hazeldean, too, who knows the Count's sister——"

"True, true," interrupted Riccabocca. "I see, I see. I will consider. I will reflect. Meanwhile you are going to Hazeldean. Do not say a word to the Squire. He knows not the secret you have discovered."

With those words Riccabocca turned slightly away, and Randal took the hint to depart.

"At all times command and rely on me," said the young traitor, and he regained the pale to which he had fastened his horse.

As he remounted, he cast his eyes towards the place where he had left Riccabocca. The Italian was still standing there. Presently the form of Jackeymo was seen emerging from the shrubs. Riccabocca turned hastily round, recognized his servant, uttered an exclamation loud enough to reach Randal's ear, and then, catching Jackeymo by the arm, disappeared with him amidst the deep recesses of the garden.

"It will be indeed in my favour," thought Randal, as he rode on, "if I can get them into the neighbourhood of London —all occasion there to woo, and if expedient, to win—the heiress."

## CHAPTER VIII.

"By the Lord Harry!" cried the Squire, as he stood with his wife in the park, on a visit of inspection to some first-rate South-Downs just added to his stock—"By the Lord, if that is not Randal Leslie trying to get into the park at the back gate! Hollo, Randal! you must come round by the lodge, my boy," said he. "You see this gate is locked, to keep out trespassers."

"A pity," said Randal. "I like short cuts, and you have shut up a very short one."

"So the trespassers said," quoth the Squire; "but Stirn insisted on it;—valuable man, Stirn. But ride round to the lodge. Put up your horse, and you'll join us before we can get to the house."

Randal nodded and smiled, and rode briskly on.

The squire rejoined his Harry.

"Ah, William," said she, anxiously, "though certainly Randal Leslie means well, I always dread his visits."

"So do I, in one sense," quoth the Squire, "for he always carries away a bank-note for Frank."

"I hope he is really Frank's friend," said Mrs. Hazeldean.

"Who's else can he be? Not his own, poor fellow, for he will never accept a shilling from me, though his grandmother was as good a Hazeldean as I am. But, zounds, I like his pride, and his economy too. As for Frank—"

"Hush, William!" cried Mrs. Hazeldean, and put her fair hand before the Squire's mouth. The Squire was softened, and kissed the fair hand gallantly—perhaps he kissed the lips too: at all events, the worthy pair were walking lovingly arm-in-arm when Randal joined them.

He did not affect to perceive a certain coldness in the manner of Mrs. Hazeldean, but began immediately to talk to her about Frank; praise that young gentleman's appearance; expatiate on his health, his popularity, and his good gifts, personal and mental—and this with so much warmth, that any dim and undeveloped suspicions Mrs. Hazeldean might have formed, soon melted away.

Randal continued to make himself thus agreeable, until the Squire, persuaded that his young kinsman was a first-rate agriculturalist, insisted upon carrying him off to the home farm; and Harry turned towards the house, to order Randal's room to be got ready: "For," said Randal, "knowing that you will excuse my morning dress, I venture to invite myself to dine and sleep at the Hall."

On approaching the farm-buildings, Randal was seized with the terror of an impostor; for, despite all the theoretical learning on Bucolics and Georgics with which he had dazzled the Squire, poor Frank, so despised, would have beat him hollow when it came to the judging of the points of an ox, or the show of a crop.

"Ha, ha!" cried the Squire, chuckling, "I long to see how you'll astonish Stirn. Why, you'll guess in a moment where we put the top-dressing; and when you come to handle my short-horns, I dare swear you'll know to a pound how much oil-cake has gone into their sides."

"Oh, you do me too much honour—indeed you do. I only know the general principles of agriculture; the details are eminently interesting, but I have not had the opportunity to acquire them."

"Stuff!" cried the Squire. "How can a man know general principles unless he has first studied the details? You are too modest, my boy. Ho! there's Stirn looking out for us!"

Randal saw the grim visage of Stirn peering out of a cattle-shed, and felt undone. He made a desperate rush towards changing the Squire's humour.

"Well, sir, perhaps Frank may soon gratify your wish, and turn farmer himself."

"Eh!" quoth the Squire, stopping short—"what now?"

"Suppose he were to marry?"

"I'd give him the two best farms on the property rent free. Ha, ha! Has he seen the girl yet? I'd leave him free to choose; sir, I chose for myself—every man should. Not but what Miss Sticktorights is an heiress, and, I hear, a very decent girl, and that would join the two properties, and put an end to that lawsuit about the right of way, which began in the reign of King Charles the Second, and is likely otherwise to last till the day of judgment. But never mind her; let Frank choose to please himself."

"I'll not fail to tell him so, sir. I did fear you might have some prejudices. But here we are at the farmyard."

"Burn the farmyard! How can I think of farmyards when you talk of Frank's marriage? Come on—this way. What were you saying about prejudices?"

"Why you might wish him to marry an Englishwoman, for instance."

"English! Good heavens, sir, does he mean to marry a Hindoo?"

"Nay, I don't know that he means to marry at all: I am only surmising; but if he did fall in love with a foreigner—"

"A foreigner! Ah, then Harry was—" The Squire stopped short.

"Who might, perhaps," observed Randal—not truly, if he referred to Madame di Negra—"who might, perhaps, speak very little English?"

"Lord ha' mercy?"

"And a Roman Catholic—"

"Worshipping idols, and roasting people who don't worship them."

"Signor Riccabocca is not so bad as that."

"Rickeybockey! Well, if it was his daughter! But not speak English! and not go to the parish church! By George, if Frank thought of such a thing, I'd cut him off with a shilling. Don't talk to me, sir; I would. I'm a mild man, and an easy man; but when I say a thing, I say it, Mr. Leslie. Oh, but it is a jest—you are laughing at me. There's no such painted good-for-nothing creature in Frank's eye—eh?"

"Indeed, sir, if ever I find there is, I will give you notice in time. At present, I was only trying to ascertain what you wished for a daughter-in-law. You said you had no prejudice."

"No more I have—not a bit of it."

"You don't like a foreigner and a Catholic?"

"Who the devil would?"

"But if she had rank and title?"

"Rank and title! Bubble and squeak! No, not half so good as bubble and squeak. English beef and good cabbage. But foreign rank and title!—foreign cabbage and beef!—foreign bubble and foreign squeak!" And the Squire made a wry face, and spat forth his disgust and indignation.

"You must have an Englishwoman?"

"Of course."

"Money?"

"Don't care, provided she is a tidy, sensible, active lass, with a good character for her dower."

"Character—ah, that is indispensable?"

"I should think so, indeed. A Mrs. Hazeldean of Hazeldean—You frighten me. He's not going to run off with a divorced woman, or a—"

The Squire stopped, and looked so red in the face that

Randal feared he might be seized with apoplexy before Frank's crimes had made him alter his will.

Therefore he hastened to relieve Mr. Hazeldean's mind, and assured him that he had been only talking at random; that Frank was in the habit, indeed, of seeing foreign ladies occasionally, as all persons in the London world were; but that he was sure Frank would never marry without the full consent and approval of his parents. He ended by repeating his assurance, that he would warn the Squire if ever it became necessary. Still, however, he left Mr. Hazeldean so disturbed and uneasy that that gentleman forgot all about the farm, and went moodily on in the opposite direction, re-entering the park at its farther extremity. As soon as they approached the house, the Squire hastened to shut himself with his wife in full parental consultation; and Randal, seated upon a bench on the terrace, revolved the mischief he had done, and its chances of success.

While thus seated, and thus thinking, a footstep approached cautiously, and a low voice said, in broken English, "Sare, sare, let me speak vid you."

Randal turned in surprise, and beheld a swarthy saturnine face, with grizzled hair and marked features. He recognised the figure that had joined Riccabocca in the Italian's garden.

"Speak-a you Italian?" resumed Jackeymo.

Randal, who had made himself an excellent linguist, nodded assent; and Jackeymo, rejoiced, begged him to withdraw into a more private part of the grounds.

Randal obeyed, and the two gained the shade of a stately chestnut avenue.

"Sir," then said Jackeymo, speaking in his native tongue, and expressing himself with a certain simple pathos, "I am but a poor man; my name is Giacomo. You have heard of me; servant to the Signore whom you saw to-day—only a servant; but he honours me with his confidence. We have known danger together; and of all his friends and followers, I alone came with him to the stranger's land."

"Good, faithful fellow," said Randal, examining the man's face, "say on. Your master confides in you? He has confided that which I told him this day?"

"He did. Ah, sir; the Padrone was too proud to ask you to explain more—too proud to show fear of another. But he does fear—he ought to fear—he shall fear," (continued Jackeymo, working himself up to passion)—"for the Padrone has a daughter, and his enemy is a villain. Oh, sir, tell me all that you did not tell to the Padrone. You hinted that this man might wish to marry the Signora. Marry her!—I could cut his throat at the altar!"

"Indeed," said Randal;—"I believe that such is his object."

"But why? He is rich—she is penniless;—no, not quite that, for we have saved—but penniless, compared to him."

"My good friend, I know not yet his motives: but I can easily learn them. If, however, this Count be your master's enemy, it is surely well to guard against him, whatever his designs; and, to do so, you should move into London or its neighbourhood. I fear that, while we speak, the Count may get upon his track."

"He had better not come here!" cried the servant, menacingly, and putting his hand where the knife was *not*.

"Beware of your own anger, Giacomo. One act of violence, and you would be transported from England, and your master would lose a friend."

Jackeymo seemed struck by this caution.

"And if the Padrone were to meet him, do you think the Padrone would meekly say, '*Come stà sa Signoria?*' The Padrone would strike him dead!"

"Hush—hush! You speak of what in England is called murder, and is punished by the gallows. If you really love your master, for Heaven's sake get him from this place—get him from all chance of such passion and peril. I go to town to-morrow; I will find him a house that shall be safe from all spies—all discovery. And there, too, my friend, I can do—what I cannot at this distance—watch over him, and keep watch also on his enemy."

Jackeymo seized Randal's hand, and lifted it towards his lip; then, as if struck by a sudden suspicion, dropped the hand, and said bluntly, "Signore, I think you have seen the Padrone twice. Why do you take this interest in him?"

"Is it so uncommon to take interest even in a stranger who is menaced by some peril?"

Jackeymo, who believed little in general philanthropy, shook his head sceptically.

"Besides," continued Randal, suddenly bethinking himself of a more plausible reason—"besides, I am a friend and connection of Mr. Egerton; and Mr. Egerton's most intimate friend is Lord L'Estrange; and I have heard that Lord L'Estrange—"

"The good Lord! Oh, now I understand." interrupted

Jackeymo, and his brow cleared. "Ah, if *he* were in England! But you will let us know when he comes?"

"Certainly. Now, tell me, Giacomo, is this Count really unprincipled and dangerous? Remember I know him not personally."

"He has neither heart nor conscience."

"That defect makes him dangerous to men; perhaps not less so to women. Could it be possible, if he obtained any interview with the Signora, that he could win her affections?"

Jackeymo crossed himself rapidly and made no answer.

"I have heard that he is still very handsome."

Jackeymo groaned.

Randal resumed—"Enough; persuade the Padrone to come to town."

"But if the Count is in town?"

"That makes no difference; the safest place is always the largest city. Everywhere else, a foreigner is in himself an object of attention and curiosity."

"True."

"Let your master, then, come to London, or rather, into its neighbourhood. He can reside in one of the suburbs most remote from the Count's haunts. In two days I will have found him a lodging and write to him. You trust to me now?"

"I do indeed—I do, Excellency. Ah, if the Signorina were married, we would not care!"

"Married! But she looks so high!"

"Alas! not now—not here!"

Randal sighed heavily. Jackeymo's eyes sparkled. He thought he had detected a new motive for Randal's interest—a motive to an Italian the most natural, the most laudable of all.

"Find the house, Signore—write to the Padrone. He shall come. I'll talk to him. I can manage him. Holy San Giacomo, bestir thyself now—'tis long since I troubled thee!"

Jackeymo strode off through the fading trees, smiling and muttering as he went.

The first dinner-bell rang, and on entering the drawing-room, Randal found Parson Dale and his wife, who had been invited in haste to meet the unexpected visitor.

The preliminary greetings over, Mr. Dale took the opportunity afforded by the Squire's absence to inquire after the health of Mr. Egerton.

"He is always well," said Randal. "I believe he is made of iron."

"His heart is of gold," said the Parson.

"Ah," said Randal, inquisitively, "you told me you had come in contact with him once, respecting, I think, some of your old parishioners at Lansmere?"

The parson nodded, and there was a moment's silence.

"Do you remember your battle by the stocks, Mr. Leslie?" said Mr. Dale, with a good-humoured laugh.

"Indeed, yes. By the way, now you speak of it, I met my old opponent in London the first year I went up to it."

"You did!—where?"

"At a literary scamp's—a cleverish man called Burley."

"Burley! I have seen some burlesque verses in Greek by a Mr. Burley."

"No doubt, the same person. He has disappeared—gone to the dogs, I dare say. Burlesque Greek is not a knowledge very much in power at present."

"Well, but Leonard Fairfield?—you have seen him since?"

"No."

"Nor heard of him?"

"No!—have you?"

"Strange to say, not for a long time. But I have reason to believe that he must be doing well."

"You surprise me! Why?"

"Because two years ago he sent for his mother. She went to him."

"Is that all?"

"It is enough; for he would not have sent for her if he could not maintain her."

Here the Hazeldeans entered, arm-in-arm, and the fat butler announced dinner.

The squire was unusually taciturn—Mrs. Hazeldean thoughtful—Mrs. Dale languid and headachy. The Parson, who seldom enjoyed the luxury of converse with a scholar, save when he quarrelled with Dr. Riccabocca, was animated by Randal's repute for ability, into a great desire for argument.

"A glass of wine, Mr. Leslie. You were saying, before dinner, that burlesque Greek is not a knowledge very much in power at present. Pray, sir, what knowledge is in power?"

RANDAL, (laconically.)—"Practical knowledge."

PARSON.—"What of?"

RANDAL.—"Men."

PARSON, (candidly.)—"Well, I suppose that is the most available sort of knowledge, in a wordly point of view. How does one learn it? Do books help?"

RANDAL.—"According as they are read, they help or injure."

PARSON.—"How should they be read in order to help?"

RANDAL.—"Read specially to apply to purposes that lead to power."

PARSON, (very much struck with Randal's pithy and Spartan logic.)—"Upon my word, sir, you express yourself very well. I must own that I began these questions in the hope of differing from you; for I like an argument."

"That he does," growled the Squire; the most contradictory creature!"

PARSON.—"Argument is the salt of talk. But now I am afraid I must agree with you, which I was not at all prepared for."

Randal bowed and answered—"No two men of our education can dispute upon the application of knowledge."

PARSON, (pricking up his ears.)—"Eh?—what to?"

RANDAL.—"Power, of course."

PARSON, (overjoyed.)—"Power!—the vulgarest application of it, or the loftiest? But you mean the loftiest?"

RANDAL, (in his turn interested and interrogative.)—"What do you call the loftiest, and what the vulgarist?"

PARSON.—"The vulgarest, self-interest; the loftiest, beneficence."

Randal suppressed the half-disdainful smile that rose to his lip.

"You speak, sir, as a clergyman should do. I admire your sentiment, and adopt it; but I fear that the knowledge which aims only at beneficence very rarely in this world gets any power at all."

SQUIRE, (seriously.)—"That's true; I never get my own way when I want to do a kindness, and Stirn always gets his when he insists on something diabolically brutal and harsh."

PARSON.—"Pray, Mr. Leslie, what does intellectual power refined to the utmost, but entirely stripped of beneficence, most resemble?"

RANDAL.—Resemble?—I can hardly say. Some very great man—almost any very great man—who has baffled all his foes, and attained all his ends."

PARSON.—"I doubt if any man has ever become very great who has not meant to be beneficent, though he might err in the means. Cæsar was naturally beneficent, and so was Alexander. But intellectual power refined to the utmost, and wholly void of beneficence, resembles only one being, and that, sir, is the Principle of Evil."

RANDAL, (startled.)—"Do you mean the Devil?"

PARSON.—"Yes, sir—the Devil; and even he, sir, did not succeed! Even he, sir, is what your great men would call a most decided failure."

MRS. DALE.—"My dear—my dear!"

PARSON.—"Our religion proves it, my love; he was an angel, and he fell."

There was a solemn pause. Randal was more impressed than he liked to own to himself. By this time the dinner was over, and the servants had retired. Harry glanced at Carry. Carry smoothed her gown and rose.

The gentlemen remained over their wine; and the Parson, satisfied with what he deemed a clencher upon his favourite subject of discussion, changed the subject to lighter topics, till, happening to fall upon tithes, the Squire struck in, and by dint of loudness of voice, and truculence of brow, fairly overwhelmed both his guests, and proved to his own satisfaction that tithes were an unjust and unchristianlike usurpation on the part of the Church generally, and a most especial and iniquitous infliction upon the Hazeldean estates in particular.

## CHAPTER IX.

ON entering the drawing-room, Randal found the two ladies seated close together, in a position much more appropriate to the familiarity of their school-days, than to the politeness of the friendship now existing between them. Mrs. Hazeldean's hand hung affectionately over Carry's shoulder, and both those fair English faces were bent over the same book It was pretty to see these sober matrons, so different from each other in character and aspect, thus unconsciously restored to the intimacy of happy maiden youth by the golden link of some Magician from the still land of Truth or Fancy—brought together in heart, as each eye rested on the same thought;—closer and closer, as sympathy, lost in the actual world, grew out of that world which unites in one bond of feeling the readers of some gentle book.

"And what work interests you so much?" asked Randal, pausing by the table.

"One you have read, of course," replied Mrs. Dale, putting a book-mark embroidered by herself into the page, and handing the volume to Randal. "It has made a great sensation, I believe."

Randal glanced at the title of the work. "True," said he, "I have heard much of it in London, but I have not yet had time to read it."

MRS. DALE.—"I can lend it to you, if you like to look over it to-night, and you can leave it for me with Mrs. Hazeldean."

PARSON, (approaching.)—"Oh! that book!—yes, you must read it. I do not know a work more instructive."

RANDAL.—"Instructive! Certainly I will read it then. But I thought it was a mere work of amusement—of fancy. It seems so as I look over it."

PARSON.—"So is the *Vicar of Wakefield;* yet what book more instructive?"

RANDAL.—"I should not have said *that* of the *Vicar of Wakefield.* A pretty book enough, though the story is most improbable. But how is it instructive?"

PARSON.—"By its results: it leaves us happier and better. What can any instruction do more? Some works instruct through the head, some through the heart. The last reach the widest circle, and often produce the most genial influence on the character. This book belongs to the last. You will grant my proposition when you have read it."

Randal smiled and took the volume.

MRS. DALE.—"Is the author known yet?"

RANDAL.—"I have heard it ascribed to many writers, but I believe no one has claimed it."

PARSON.—"I think it must have been written by my old college friend, Professor Moss; the naturalist—its descriptions of scenery are so accurate."

MRS. DALE.—"La, Charles, dear! that snuffy, tiresome, prosy professor? How can you talk such nonsense? I am sure the author must be young—there is so much freshness of feeling."

MRS. HAZELDEAN, (positively.)—"Yes, certainly, young."

PARSON, (no less positively.)—"I should say just the contrary. Its tone is too serene, and its style too simple, for a young man. Besides I don't know any young man who would send me his book, and this book has been sent me—very handsomely bound, too, you see. Depend upon it Moss is the man—quite his turn of mind."

Mrs. Dale.—"You are too provoking, Charles, dear! Mr. Moss is so remarkably plain, too."

Randal.—"Must an author be handsome?"

Parson.—"Ha! ha! Answer that if you can, Carry."

Carry remained mute and disdainful.

Squire, (with great *naïveté*.)—"Well, I don't think there's much in the book, whoever wrote it; for I've read it myself, and understand every word of it."

Mrs. Dale.—"I don't see why you should suppose it was written by a man at all. For my part, I think it must be a woman."

Mrs. Hazeldean.—"Yes, there's a passage about maternal affection, which only a woman could have written."

Parson.—"Pooh! pooh! I should like to see a woman who could have written that description of an August evening before a thunderstorm; every wildflower in the hedgerow exactly the flowers of August—every sign in the air exactly those of the month. Bless you! a woman would have filled the hedge with violets and cowslips. Nobody else but my friend Moss could have written that description."

Squire.—"I don't know; there's a simile about the waste of corn-seed in hand-sowing, which makes me think he must be a farmer!"

Mrs. Dale, (scornfully.)—"A farmer! In hobnailed shoes, I suppose! I say it is a woman."

Mrs. Hazeldean.—"A woman, and a mother!"

Parson.—"A middle-aged man, and a naturalist."

Squire.—"No, no, Parson—certainly a young man; for that love-scene puts me in mind of my own young days, when I would have given my ears to tell Harry how handsome I thought her; and all I could say was, 'Fine weather for the crops, Miss.' Yes, a young man and a farmer. I should not wonder if he had held the plough himself."

Randal, (who had been turning over the pages.)—"This sketch of Night in London comes from a man who has lived the life of cities and looked at wealth with the eyes of poverty. Not bad! I will read the book."

"Strange," said the parson, smiling, "that this little work should so have entered into our minds, suggested to all of us different ideas, yet equally charmed all—given a new and fresh current to our dull country life—animated us as with the sight of a world in our breasts we had never seen before save in dreams: a little work like this by a man we don't know and never may! Well, *that* knowledge *is* power, and a noble one!"

"A sort of power, certainly, sir," said Randal, candidly; and that night, when Randal retired to his own room, he suspended his schemes and projects, and read, as he rarely did, without an object to gain by the reading.

The work surprised him by the pleasure it gave. Its charm lay in the writer's calm enjoyment of the beautiful. It seemed like some happy soul sunning itself in the light of its own thoughts. Its power was so tranquil and even, that it was only a critic who could perceive how much force and vigour were necessary to sustain the wing that floated aloft with so imperceptible an effort. There was no one faculty predominating tyrannically over the others; all seemed proportioned in the felicitous symmetry of a nature rounded, integral, and complete. And when the work was closed, it left behind it a tender warmth that played round the heart of the reader and vivified feelings which seemed unknown before. Randal laid down the book softly; and for five minutes the ignoble and base purposes to which his own knowledge was applied, stood before him, naked and unmasked.

"Tut!" said he, wrenching himself violently away from the benign influence, "it was not to sympathise with Hector, but to conquer with Achilles, that Alexander of Macedon kept Homer under his pillow. Such should be the true use of books to him who has the practical world to subdue; let parsons and women construe it otherwise, as they may!"

And the Principle of Evil descended again upon the intellect, from which the guide of Beneficence was gone.

## CHAPTER X.

RANDAL rose at the sound of the first breakfast bell, and on the staircase met Mrs. Hazeldean. He gave her back the book; and as he was about to speak, she beckoned to him to follow her into a little morning-room appropriated to herself. No boudoir of white and gold, with pictures by Watteau, but lined with large walnut-tree presses, that held the old heirloom linen, strewed with lavender—stores for the housekeeper, and medicines for the poor.

Seating herself on a large chair in this sanctum, Mrs. Hazeldean looked formidably at home.

"Pray," said the lady, coming at once to the point, with her usual straightforward candour, "what is all this you have been saying to my husband as to the possibility of Frank's marrying a foreigner?"

RANDAL.—"Would you be as averse to such a notion as Mr. Hazeldean is?"

MRS. HAZELDEAN.—"You ask me a question, instead of answering mine."

Randal was greatly put out in his fence by these rude thrusts. For indeed he had a double purpose to serve—first, thoroughly to know if Frank's marriage with a woman like Madame di Negra would irritate the Squire sufficiently to endanger the son's inheritance; and, secondly, to prevent Mr. and Mrs. Hazeldean believing seriously that such a marriage was to be apprehended, lest they should prematurely address Frank on the subject, and frustrate the marriage itself. Yet, withal, he must so express himself, that he could not be afterwards accused by the parents of disguising matters. In his talk to the Squire the preceding day, he had gone a little too far—farther than he would have done but for his desire of escaping the cattle-shed and short-horns. While he mused, Mrs. Hazeldean observed him with her honest sensible eyes, and finally exclaimed—

"Out with it, Mr. Leslie!"

"Out with what, my dear madam? The Squire has sadly exaggerated the importance of what was said mainly in jest. But I will own to you plainly, that Frank has appeared to me a little smitten with a certain fair Italian."

"Italian!" cried Mrs. Hazeldean. "Well, I said so from the first. Italian!—that's all, is it?" and she smiled.

Randal was more and more perplexed. The pupil of his eye contracted, as it does when we retreat into ourselves, and think, watch, and keep guard.

"And perhaps," resumed Mrs. Hazeldean, with a very sunny expression of countenance, "you have noticed this in Frank since he was here?"

"It is true," murmured Randal; "but I think his heart or his fancy was touched even before."

"Very natural," said Mrs. Hazeldean; "how could he help it?—such a beautiful creature! Well, I must not ask you to tell Frank's secrets; but I guess the object of attraction; and though she will have no fortune to speak of—and it is not such a match as he might form—still she is so amiable, and has been so well brought up, and is so little like one's general notions of a Roman Catholic, that I think I could persuade Hazeldean into giving his consent."

"Ah," said Randal, drawing a long breath, and beginning with his practised acuteness to detect Mrs. Hazeldean's error; "I am very much relieved and rejoiced to hear this; and I may venture to give Frank some hope, if I find him disheartened and desponding, poor fellow!"

"I think you may," replied Mrs. Hazeldean, laughing pleasantly. "But you should not have frightened poor William so, hinting that the lady knew very little English. She has an accent, to be sure; but she speaks our tongue very prettily. I always forget that she's not English born! Ha, ha, poor William!"

RANDAL.—"Ha, ha!"

MRS. HAZELDEAN.—"We had once thought of another match for Frank—a girl of good English family."

RANDAL.—"Miss Sticktorights?"

MRS. HAZELDEAN.—"No; that's an old whim of Hazeldean's. But I doubt if the Sticktorights would ever merge their property in ours. Bless you, it would be all off the moment they came to settlements, and had to give up the right of way. We thought of a very different match; but there's no dictating to young hearts, Mr. Leslie."

RANDAL.—"Indeed no, Mrs. Hazeldean. But since we now understand each other so well, excuse me if I suggest that you had better leave things to themselves, and not write to Frank on the subject. Young hearts, you know, are often stimulated by apparent difficulties, and grow cool when the obstacle vanishes."

MRS. HAZELDEAN.—"Very possibly; it was not so with Hazeldean and me. But I shall not write to Frank on the subject for a different reason—though I would consent to the match, and so would William; yet we both would rather, after all, that Frank married an Englishwoman, and a Protestant. We will not, therefore, do anything to encourage the idea. But if Frank's happiness becomes really at stake, *then* we will step in. In short, we would neither encourage nor oppose. You understand?"

"Perfectly."

"And in the meanwhile, it is quite right that Frank should see the world, and try to distract his mind, or at least to know it. And I dare say it has been some thought of that kind which has prevented his coming here."

Randal, dreading a farther and plainer *éclaircissement*, now rose, and saying, "Pardon me, but I must hurry over breakfast, and be back in time to catch the coach"—offered his arm to his hostess, and led her into the breakfast-parlour. Devouring his meal, as if in great haste, he then mounted his horse, and, taking cordial leave of his entertainers, trotted briskly away.

All things favoured his project—even chance had befriended him in Mrs. Hazeldean's mistake. She had, not unnaturally, supposed Violante to have captivated Frank on his last visit to the Hall. Thus, while Randal had certified his own mind that nothing could more exasperate the Squire than an alliance with Madame di Negra, he could yet assure Frank that Mrs. Hazeldean was all on his side. And when the error was discovered, Mrs. Hazeldean would only have to blame herself for it. Still more successful had his diplomacy proved with the Riccaboccas : he had ascertained the secret he had come to discover ; he should induce the Italian to remove to the neighbourhood of London ; and if Violante were the great heiress he suspected her to prove, whom else of her own age would she see but him ? And the old Leslie domains, to be sold in two years—a portion of the dowry might purchase them ! Flushed by the triumph of his craft, all former vacillations of conscience ceased. In high and fervent spirits he passed the Casino, the garden of which was solitary and deserted, reached his home, and, telling Oliver to be studious, and Juliet to be patient, walked thence to meet the coach and regain the capital.

## CHAPTER XI.

VIOLANTE was seated in her own little room, and looking from the window on the terrace that stretched below. The day was warm for the time of year. The orange-trees had been removed under shelter for the approach of winter; but where they had stood sate Mrs. Riccabocca at work. In the Belvidere, Riccabocca himself was conversing with his favourite servant. But the casements and the door of the Belvidere were open; and where they sate, both wife and daughter could see the Padrone leaning against the wall, with his arms folded, and his eyes fixed on the floor; while Jackeymo, with one finger on his master's arm, was talking to him with visible earnestness. And the daughter from the window, and the wife from her work, directed tender, anxious eyes towards the still thoughtful form so dear to both. For the last day or two, Riccabocca had been peculiarly abstracted, even to gloom. Each felt there was something stirring at his heart—neither, as yet, knew what.

Violante's room silently revealed the nature of the education by which her character had been formed. Save a sketchbook, which lay open on a desk at hand, and which showed talent exquisitely taught (for in this Riccabocca had been her teacher), there was nothing that spoke of the ordinary female accomplishments. No piano stood open, no harp occupied yon nook, which seemed made for one; no broidery-frame, nor implements of work, betrayed the usual and graceful resources of a girl; but ranged on shelves against the wall were the best writers in English, Italian, and French; and these betokened an extent of reading, that he who wishes for a companion to his mind in the sweet commune of woman, which softens and refines all it gives and takes in interchange, will never condemn as masculine. You had but to look into Violante's face to see how noble was the intelligence that brought soul to those lovely features. Nothing hard, nothing dry and stern was there. Even as you detected knowledge, it was lost in the gentleness of grace. In fact, whatever she gained in the graver kinds of information, became transmuted, through her heart and her fancy, into spiritual golden stores. Give her some tedious and arid history, her imagination seized upon beauties other readers had passed by, and, like the eye of the artist, detected everywhere the Picturesque. Something in her mind seemed to reject all that was mean and commonplace, and to bring out all that was rare and elevated in whatever it received. Living so apart from all companions of her age, she scarcely belonged to the Present time. She dwelt in the Past, as Sabrina in her crystal well. Images of chivalry—of the Beautiful and the Heroic—such as, in reading the silvery line of Tasso, rise before us, softening force and valour into love and song—haunted the reveries of the fair Italian maid.

Tell us not that the Past, examined by cold Philosophy, was no better and no loftier than the Present: it is not thus seen by pure and generous eyes. Let the Past perish, when it ceases to reflect on its magic mirror the beautiful Romance which is its noblest reality, though perchance but the shadow of Delusion.

Yet Violante was not merely the dreamer. In her, life was so puissant and rich, that action seemed necessary to its glorious development—action, but still in the woman's sphere —action to bless and to refine and to exalt all around her, and to pour whatever else of ambition was left unsatisfied into sympathy with the aspirations of man. Despite her father's fears of the bleak air of England, in that air she had strengthened the delicate health of her childhood. Her elastic step—her eyes full of sweetness and light—her bloom, at once soft and luxuriant—all spoke of the vital powers fit to sustain a mind of such exquisite mould, and the emotions of a heart that, once aroused, could ennoble the passions of the South with the purity and devotion of the North.

Solitude makes some natures more timid, some more bold. Violante was fearless. When she spoke, her eyes frankly met your own; and she was so ignorant of evil, that as yet she seemed nearly unacquainted with shame. From this courage, combined with affluence of idea, came a delightful flow of happy converse. Though possessing so imperfectly the accomplishments ordinarily taught to young women, and which may be cultured to the utmost, and yet leave the thoughts so barren, and the talk so vapid—she had that accomplishment which most pleases the taste, and commands the love, of the man of talent; especially if his talent be not so actively employed as to make him desire only relaxation where he seeks companionship—the accomplishment of facility in intellectual interchange—the charm that clothes in musical words beautiful womanly ideas.

"I hear him sigh at this distance," said Violante, softly, as she still watched her father; "and methinks this is a new grief; and not for his country. He spoke twice yesterday of that dear English friend, and wished that he were here."

As she said this, unconsciously the virgin blushed, her hands drooped on her knee, and she fell herself into thought as profound as her father's, but less gloomy. From her arrival in England, Violante had been taught a grateful interest in the name of Harley L'Estrange. Her father, preserving a silence, that seemed disdain, of all his old Italian intimates, had been pleased to converse with open heart of the Englishman who had saved where countrymen had betrayed. He spoke of the soldier, then in the full bloom of

youth, who, unconsoled by fame, had nursed the memory of
some hidden sorrow amidst the pine-trees that cast their
shadow over the sunny Italian lake; how Riccabocca, then
honoured and happy, had courted from his seclusion the
English Signore, then the mourner and the voluntary exile;
how they had grown friends amidst the landscapes in which
her eyes had opened to the day; how Harley had vainly
warned him from the rash schemes in which he had sought to
reconstruct in an hour the ruins of weary ages; how, when
abandoned, deserted, proscribed, pursued, he had fled for life
—the infant Violante clasped to his bosom—the English
soldier had given him refuge, baffled the pursuers, armed his
servants, accompanied the fugitive at night towards the defile
in the Apennines, and, when the emissaries of a perfidious
enemy, hot in the chase, came near, had said, "You have your
child to save! Fly on! Another league, and you are beyond
the borders. We will delay the foes with parley; they will
not harm us." And not till escape was gained did the father
know that the English friend had delayed the foe, not by
parley, but by the sword, holding the pass against numbers,
with a breast as dauntless as Bayard's on the glorious bridge.

And since then, the same Englishman had never ceased
to vindicate his name, to urge his cause; and if hope yet
remained of restoration to land and honours, it was in that
untiring zeal.

Hence, naturally and insensibly, this secluded and musing
girl had associated all that she read in tales of romance and
chivalry with the image of the brave and loyal stranger. He
it was who animated her dreams of the Past, and seemed
born to be, in the destined hour, the deliverer of the Future.
Around this image grouped all the charms that the fancy of
virgin woman can raise from the enchanted lore of old Heroic
Fable. Once in her early girlhood, her father (to satisfy her
curiosity, eager for general description) had drawn from
memory a sketch of the features of the Englishman—drawn
Harley, as he was in that first youth, flattered and idealised,
no doubt, by art, and by partial gratitude—but still resembling him as he was then, while the deep mournfulness of
recent sorrow yet shadowed and concentrated all the varying
expressions of his countenance; and to look on him was to
say—"So sad, yet so young!" Never did Violante pause to
remember that the same years which ripened herself from
infancy into woman, were passing less gently over that smooth
cheek and dreamy brow—that the world might be altering

the nature as time the aspect. To her the hero of the Ideal remained immortal in bloom and youth. Bright illusion, common to us all, where Poetry once hallows the human form! Whoever thinks of Petrarch as the old time-worn man? Who does not see him as when he first gazed on Laura?—

"Ogni altra cosa ogni pensier va fore;
E sol ivi con voi rimansi Amore!"

## CHAPTER XII.

AND Violante, thus absorbed in reverie, forgot to keep watch on the Belvidere. And the Belvidere was now deserted. The wife, who had no other ideal to distract *her* thoughts, saw Riccabocca pass into the house.

The exile entered his daughter's room, and she started to feel his hand upon her locks and his kiss upon her brow.

"My child!" cried Riccabocca, seating himself, "I have resolved to leave for a time this retreat, and to seek the neighbourhood of London."

"Ah, dear father, *that*, then, was your thought? But what can be your reason? Do not turn away; you know how carefully I have obeyed your command and kept your secret. Ah, you will confide in me."

"I do, indeed," returned Riccabocca, with emotion. "I leave this place, in the fear lest my enemies discover me. I shall say to others that you are of an age to require teachers, not to be obtained here. But I should like none to know where we go."

The Italian said these last words through his teeth, and hanging his head. He said them in shame.

"My mother—(so Violante always called Jemima)—my mother—you have spoken to her?"

"Not yet. *There* is the difficulty."

"No difficulty, for she loves you so well," replied Violante, with soft reproach. "Ah, why not also confide in her? Who so true? so good?"

"Good—I grant it?" exclaimed Riccabocca. "What then? *Da cattiva Donna guardati, ed alla buona non fidar niente,*' (from the bad woman, guard thyself; to the good woman trust nothing). And if you must trust," added the abominable man, "trust her with anything but a secret!"

"Fie," said Violante, with arch reproach, for she knew her father's humours too well to interpret his horrible sentiments literally—"fie on your consistency, *Padre carissimo*. Do you not trust your secret to me?"

"You! A kitten is not a cat, and a girl is not a woman. Besides, the secret was already known to you, and I had no choice. Peace, Jemima will stay here for the present. See to what you wish to take with you; we shall leave to-night."

Not waiting for an answer, Riccabocca hurried away, and with a firm step strode the terrace, and approached his wife.

"*Anima mia*," said the pupil of Machiavelli, disguising in the tenderest words the cruellest intentions—for one of his most cherished Italian proverbs was to the effect, that there is no getting on with a mule or a woman unless you coax them,—"*Anima mia*, soul of my being, you have already seen that Violante mopes herself to death here."

"She, poor child! Oh no!"

"She does, core of my heart—she does—and is as ignorant of music as I am of tent-stitch."

"She sings beautifully."

"Just as birds do, against all the rules, and in defiance of gamut. Therefore, to come to the point, O treasure of my soul! I am going to take her with me for a short time, perhaps to Cheltenham or Brighton. We shall see."

"All places with you are the same to me, Alphonso. When shall we go?"

"*We* shall go to-night; but terrible as it is to part from you—you—"

"Ah!" interrupted the wife, and covered her face with her hands.

Riccabocca, the wiliest and most relentless of men in his maxims, melted into absolute uxorial imbecility at the sight of that mute distress. He put his arm round his wife's waist, with genuine affection, and without a single proverb at his heart—"*Carissima*, do not grieve so; we shall be back soon, and travelling is expensive; rolling stones gather no moss, and there is so much to see to at home."

Mrs. Riccabocca gently escaped from her husband's arm. She withdrew her hands from her face and brushed away the tears that stood in her eyes.

"Alphonso," she said, touchingly, "hear me! What you think good, that shall ever be good to me. But do not think that I grieve solely because of our parting. No; I grieve to think that, despite all these years in which I have been the partner of your hearth, and slept on your breast—all these years in which I have had no thought but, however humbly, to do my duty to you and yours, and could have wished that you had read my heart, and seen there but yourself and your child—I grieve to think that you still deem me as unworthy your trust as when you stood by my side at the altar."

"Trust!" repeated Riccabocca, startled and conscience-stricken: "why do you say 'trust?' In what have I distrusted you? I am sure," he continued, with the artful volubility of guilt, "that I never doubted your fidelity—hook-nosed, long-visaged foreigner though I be; never pryed into your letters; never inquired into your solitary walks; never heeded your flirtations with that good-looking Parson Dale; never kept the money; and never looked into the account books!" Mrs. Riccabocca refused even a smile of contempt at these revolting evasions; nay, she seemed scarcely to hear them.

"Can you think," she resumed, pressing her hand on her heart to still its struggles for relief in sobs—"can you think that I could have watched, and thought, and taxed my poor mind so constantly, to conjecture what might best soothe or please you, and not seen, long since, that you have secrets known to your daughter—your servant—not to me? Fear not—the secrets cannot be evil, or you would not tell them to your innocent child. Besides, do I not know your nature? and do I not love you because I know it?—it is for something connected with those secrets that you leave your home. You think that I should be incautious—imprudent. You will not take me with you. Be it so. I go to prepare for your departure. Forgive me if I have displeased you, husband."

Mrs. Riccabocca turned away; but a soft hand touched the Italian's arm. "O father, can you resist this? Trust her! trust her!—I am a woman like her! I answer for her woman's faith. Be yourself—ever nobler than all others, my own father."

"*Diavolo!* Never one door shuts but another opens," groaned Riccabocca. "Are you a fool, child? Don't you see that it was for your sake only I feared—and would be cautious?"

"For mine! O then do not make me deem myself mean, and the cause of meanness. For mine! Am I not your daughter—the descendant of men who never feared?"

Violante looked sublime while she spoke; and as she ended

she led her father gently on towards the door, which his wife had now gained.

"Jemima—wife mine!—pardon, pardon," cried the Italian, whose heart had been yearning to repay such tenderness and devotion,—" come back to my breast—it has been long closed —it shall be open to you now and for ever."

In another moment the wife was in her right place—on her husband's bosom ; and Violante, beautiful peacemaker, stood smiling awhile at both, and then lifted her eyes gratefully to Heaven, and stole away.

## CHAPTER XIII.

ON Randal's return to town, he heard mixed and contradictory rumours in the streets, and at the clubs, of the probable downfall of the Government at the approaching session of Parliament. These rumours had sprung up suddenly, as if in an hour. True that, for some time, the sagacious had shaken their heads and said, "Ministers could not last." True, that certain changes in policy, a year or two before, had divided the party on which the Government depended, and strengthened that which opposed it. But still the more important members of that Government had been so long identified with official station, and there seemed so little power in the Opposition to form a cabinet of names familiar to official ears, that the general public had anticipated, at most, a few partial changes. Rumour now went far beyond this. Randal, whose whole prospects at present were but reflections from the greatness of his patron, was alarmed. He sought Egerton, but the minister was impenetrable, and seemed calm, confident, and imperturbed. Somewhat relieved, Randal then set himself to work to find a safe home for Riccabocca ; for the greater need to succeed in obtaining fortune there, if he failed in getting it through Egerton. He found a quiet house, detached and secluded, in the neighbourhood of Norwood. No vicinity more secure from espionage and remark. He wrote to Riccabocca, and communicated the address, adding fresh assurances of his own power to be of use. The next morning he was seated in his office, thinking very little of the details, that he mastered, however, with mechanical precision, when the minister who presided over that department of the public service, sent for him into his private room, and begged him to take a letter to Egerton, with whom he wished to consult relative to a very important point to be decided in the Cabinet that day. "I want you to take it," said the minister smiling, (the minister was a frank homely man,) "because you are in Mr. Egerton's confidence, and he may give you some verbal message besides a written reply. Egerton is often *over* cautious and brief in the *litera scripta.*"

Randal went first to Egerton's neighbouring office—Egerton had not been there that day. He then took a cabriolet and drove to Grosvenor Square. A quiet-looking chariot was at the door. Mr. Egerton was at home; but the servant said, "Dr. F. is with him, sir; and perhaps he may not like to be disturbed."

"What—is your master ill?"

"Not that I know of, sir. He never says he is ill. But he has looked poorly the last day or two."

Randal hesitated a moment; but his commission might be important, and Egerton was a man who so held the maxim, that health and all else must give way to business, that he resolved to enter; and, unannounced and unceremoniously, as was his wont, he opened the door of the library. He started as he did so. Audley Egerton was leaning back on the sofa, and the doctor, on his knees before him, was applying the stethoscope to his breast. Egerton's eyes were partially closed as the door opened. But at the noise he sprang up, nearly oversetting the doctor. "Who's that?—How dare you?" he exclaimed, in a voice of great anger. Then recognising Randal, he changed colour, bit his lip, and muttered drily, "I beg pardon for my abruptness; what do you want, Mr. Leslie?"

"This letter from Lord ——; I was told to deliver it immediately into your own hands. I beg pardon—"

"There is no cause," said Egerton, coldly. "I have had a slight attack of bronchitis; and as Parliament meets so soon, I must take advice from my doctor, if I would be heard by the reporters. Lay the letter on the table, and be kind enough to wait for my reply."

Randal withdrew. He had never seen a physician in that house before, and it seemed surprising that Egerton should even take a medical opinion upon a slight attack. While waiting in the ante-room there was a knock at the street door, and presently a gentleman, exceedingly well dressed, was shown in, and honoured Randal with an easy and half-familiar bow. Randal remembered to have met this personage at dinner, and at the house of a young nobleman of high fashion, but had not been introduced to him, and did not even know him by name. The visitor was better informed.

"Our friend Egerton is busy, I hear, Mr. Leslie," said he, arranging the camelia in his button-hole.

"Our friend Egerton!" It must be a very great man to say, "Our friend Egerton."

"He will not be engaged long, I dare say," returned Randal, glancing his shrewd inquiring eye over the stranger's person.

"I trust not; my time is almost as precious as his own. I was not so fortunate as to be presented to you when we met at Lord Spendquick's. Good fellow, Spendquick; and decidedly clever."

Lord Spendquick was usually esteemed a gentleman without three ideas.

Randal smiled.

In the meanwhile the visitor had taken out a card from an embossed morocco case, and now presented it to Randal, who read thereon, "Baron Levy, No. —, Bruton St."

The name was not unknown to Randal. It was a name too often on the lips of men of fashion not to have reached the ears of an *habitué* of good society.

Mr. Levy had been a solicitor by profession. He had of late years relinquished his ostensible calling: and not long since, in consequence of some services towards the negotiation of a loan, had been created a baron by one of the German kings. The wealth of Mr. Levy was said to be only equalled by his good nature to all who were in want of a temporary loan, and with sound expectations of repaying it some day or other.

You seldom saw a finer-looking man than Baron Levy—about the same age as Egerton, but looking younger: so well preserved—such magnificent black whiskers—such superb teeth! Despite his name and his dark complexion, he did not, however, resemble a Jew—at least externally; and, in fact, he was not a Jew on the father's side, but the natural son of a rich English *grand seigneur*, by a Hebrew lady of distinction—in the opera. After his birth, this lady had married a German trader of her own persuasion, and her husband had been prevailed upon, for the convenience of all parties, to adopt his wife's son, and accord to him his own Hebrew name. Mr. Levy, senior, was soon left a widower, and then the real father, though never actually owning the boy, had shown him great attention—had him frequently at his house—initiated him betimes into his own high-born society, for which the boy showed great taste. But when my Lord died, and left but a moderate legacy to the younger Levy, who was then about eighteen, that ambiguous person was articled to an attorney by his putative sire, who shortly afterwards returned to his native land, and was buried at Prague, where his tombstone may yet be seen. Young Levy, however, contrived to do very well without him. His real birth was generally known, and rather advantageous to him in a social point of view. His legacy enabled him to become a partner where he had been a clerk, and his practice became great amongst the fashionable classes of society. Indeed he was so useful, so pleasant, so much a man of the world, that he grew intimate with his clients—chiefly young men of rank; was on good terms with both Jew and Christian; and being neither one nor the other, resembled (to use Sheridan's incomparable simile) the blank page between the Old and the New Testament.

Vulgar, some might call Mr. Levy, from his assurance, but it was not the vulgarity of a man accustomed to low and coarse society—rather the *mauvais ton* of a person not sure of his own position, but who has resolved to swagger into the best one he can get. When it is remembered that he had made his way in the world, and gleaned together an immense fortune, it is needless to add that he was as sharp as a needle, and as hard as a flint. No man had had more friends, and no man had stuck by them more firmly—so long as there was a pound in their pockets!

Something of this character had Randal heard of the Baron, and he now gazed, first at his card, and then at him with—admiration.

"I met a friend of yours at Borrowell's the other day," resumed the Baron—"Young Hazeldean. Careful fellow—quite a man of the world."

As this was the last praise poor Frank deserved, Randal again smiled.

The Baron went on—"I hear, Mr. Leslie, that you have much influence over this same Hazeldean. His affairs are in a sad state. I should be very happy to be of use to him, as a relation of my friend Egerton's; but he understands business so well that he despises my advice."

"I am sure you do him injustice."

"Injustice! I honour his caution. I say to every man, 'Don't come to me—I can get you money on much easier terms than any one else; and what's the result! You come so often that you ruin yourself; whereas a regular usurer without conscience frightens you. "Cent. per cent.," you say; "oh, I must pull in."' If you have influence over your friend, tell him to stick to his bill-brokers, and have nothing to do with Baron Levy."

Here the minister's bell rung, and Randal, looking through the window, saw Dr. F. walking to his carriage, which had made way for Baron Levy's splendid cabriolet—a cabriolet in the most perfect taste—Baron's coronet on the dark-brown panels—horse black, with such action!—harness just relieved with plating. The servant now entered, and requested Randal to step in; and addressing the Baron, assured him that he would not be detained a minute.

"Leslie," said the minister, sealing a note, "take this back to Lord ——, and say that I shall be with him in an hour."

"No other message—he seemed to expect one."

"I dare say he did. Well, my letter is official, my message is not: beg him to see Mr. —— before we meet—he will understand—all rests upon that interview."

Egerton then, extending the letter, resumed gravely—"Of course, you will not mention to any one that Dr. F. was with me: the health of public men is not to be suspected. Hum— were you in your own room or the ante-room?"

"The ante-room, sir."

Egerton's brow contracted slightly. "And Mr. Levy was there, eh?"

"Yes—the Baron."

"Baron! true. Come to plague me about the Mexican loan, I suppose. I will keep you no longer."

Randal, much meditating, left the house, and re-entered his hack cab. The Baron was admitted to the statesman's presence.

## CHAPTER XIV.

EGERTON had thrown himself at full length on the sofa, a position exceedingly rare with him; and about his whole air and manner, as Levy entered, there was something singularly different from that stateliness of port common to the austere legislator. The very tone of his voice was different. It was as if the statesman—the man of business—had vanished; it was rather the man of fashion and the idler, who, nodding languidly to his visitor, said, "Levy, what money can I have for a year?"

"The estate will bear very little more. My dear fellow, that last election was the very devil. You cannot go on thus much longer."

"My dear fellow!" Baron Levy hailed Audley Egerton as "my dear fellow." And Audley Egerton, perhaps, saw nothing strange in the words, though his lip curled.

"I shall not want to go on thus much longer," answered Egerton, as the curl on his lip changed to a gloomy smile "The estate must, meanwhile, bear £5000 more."

"A hard pull on it. You had really better sell."

"I cannot afford to sell at present. I cannot afford men to say, 'Audley Egerton is done up—his property is for sale.'"

"It is very sad when one thinks what a rich man you have been—and may be yet!"

"Be yet! How?"

Baron Levy glanced towards the thick mahogany doors—thick and impervious as should be the doors of statesmen. "Why, you know that, with three words from you, I could produce an effect upon the stocks of three nations, that might give us each a hundred thousand pounds. We would go shares."

"Levy," said Egerton, coldly, though a deep blush overspread his face, "you are a scoundrel; that is your look-out. I interfere with no man's tastes and conscience. I don't intend to be a scoundrel myself. I have told you that long ago."

The usurer's brows darkened, but he dispelled the cloud with an easy laugh.

"Well, said he, "you are neither wise nor complimentary, but you shall have the money. But yet, would it not be better," added Levy, with emphasis, "to borrow it without interest, of your friend L'Estrange?"

Egerton started as if stung.

"You mean to taunt me, sir!" he exclaimed, passionately. "I accept pecuniary favours from Lord L'Estrange!—I!"

"Tut, my dear Egerton, I dare say my Lord would not think so ill now of that act in your life which—"

"Hold!" exclaimed Egerton, writhing. "Hold!"

He stopped, and paced the room, muttering, in broken

sentences, "To blush before this man! Chastisement, chastisement!"

Levy gazed on him with hard and sinister eyes. The minister turned abruptly.

"Look you, Levy," said he, with forced composure—"you hate me—why, I know not."

"Hate you! How have I shown hatred? Would you ever have lived in this palace, and ruled this country as one of the most influential of its ministers, but for my management—my whispers to the wealthy Miss Leslie? Come, but for me what would you have been—perhaps a beggar?"

"What shall I be now, if I live? And this fortune which my marriage brought to me—it has passed for the main part into your hands. Be patient, you will have it all ere long. But there is one man in the world who has loved me from a boy, and woe to you if ever he learn that he has the right to despise me!"

"Egerton, my good fellow," said Levy, with great composure, "you need not threaten me, for what interest can I possibly have in tale-telling to Lord L'Estrange? Again, dismiss from your mind the absurd thought that I hate you. True, you snub me in private, you cut me in public, you refuse to come to my dinners, you'll not ask me to your own; still, there is no man I like better, nor would more willingly serve. When do you want the £5000?"

"Perhaps in one month, perhaps not for three or four. Let it be ready when required."

"Enough; depend on it. Have you any other commands?"

"None."

"I will take my leave, then. By-the-by, what do you suppose the Hazeldean rental is worth—net?"

"I don't know, nor care. You have no designs upon *that* too?"

"Well, I like keeping up family connections. Mr. Frank seems a liberal young gentleman."

Before Egerton could answer, the Baron had glided to the door, and, nodding pleasantly, vanished with that nod.

Egerton remained, standing on his solitary hearth. A drear, single man's room it was, from wall to wall, despite its fretted ceilings and official pomp of Bramah escritoires and red boxes. Drear and cheerless—no trace of woman's habitation—no vestige of intruding, happy children. There stood the austere man alone. And then with a deep sigh he muttered, "Thank heaven, not for long—it will not last long."

Repeating those words, he mechanically locked up his papers, and pressed his hand to his heart for an instant, as if a spasm had shot through it.

"So—I must shun all emotion!" said he, shaking his head gently.

In five minutes more, Audley Egerton was in the streets, his mien erect, and his step firm as ever.

"That man is made of Bronze," said a leader of the Opposition to a friend as they rode past the minister. "What would I not give for his nerves!"

# BOOK NINTH.

## INITIAL CHAPTER.

#### ON PUBLIC LIFE.

Now that I am fairly in the heart of my story, these preliminary chapters must shrink into comparatively small dimensions, and not encroach upon the space required by the various personages whose acquaintance I have picked up here and there, and who are now all crowding upon me like poor relations to whom one has unadvisedly given a general invitation, and who descend upon one simultaneously about Christmas time. Where they are to be stowed, and what is to become of them all, Heaven knows; in the meanwhile, the reader will have already observed that the Caxton Family themselves are turned out of their own rooms, sent a-packing, in order to make way for the new comers.

But to proceed.—Note the heading to the present Chapter "ON PUBLIC LIFE,"—a thesis pertinent to this portion of my narrative, and if somewhat trite in itself, the greater is the stimulus to suggest thereon some original hints for reflection.

Were you ever in public life, my dear reader? I don't mean, by that question, to ask whether you were ever Lord Chancellor, Prime Minister, Leader of the Opposition, or even a member of the House of Commons. An author hopes to find readers far beyond that very egregious but very limited segment of the Great Circle. Were you ever a busy man in your vestry, active in a municipal corporation, one of a committee for furthering the interests of an enlightened candidate for your native burgh, town, or shire?—in a word, did you ever resign your private comforts as men in order to share the public troubles of mankind? If ever you have so far departed from the Lucretian philosophy, just look back—was it life at all that you lived?—were you an individual distinct existence—a passenger in the railway?—or were you merely an indistinct portion of that common flame which heated the boiler and generated the steam that set off the monster train? —very hot, very active, very useful, no doubt; but all your identity fused in flame, and all your forces vanishing in gas.

And do you think the people in the railway carriages care for you?—do you think that the gentleman in the worsted wrapper is saying to his neighbour with the striped rug on his comfortable knees, "How grateful we ought to be for that fiery particle which is crackling and hissing under the boiler! It helps us on a fraction of an inch from Vauxhall to Putney!" Not a bit of it. Ten to one but he is saying —"Not sixteen miles an hour! What the deuce is the matter with the stoker?"

Look at our friend Audley Egerton. You have just had a glimpse of the real being that struggles under the huge copper;—you have heard the hollow sound of the rich man's coffers under the tap of Baron Levy's friendly knuckle— heard the strong man's heart give out its dull warning sound to the scientific ear of Dr. F——. And away once more vanishes the separate existence, lost again in the flame that heats the boiler, and the smoke that curls into air from the grimy furnace.

Look to it, O Public Man, whoever thou art, and whatsoever thy degree—see if thou canst not compound matters, so as to keep a little nook apart for thy private life; that is, for *thyself!* Let the Great Popkins Question not absorb wholly the individual soul of thee, as Smith or Johnson. Don't so entirely consume thyself under that insatiable boiler, that when thy poor little monad rushes out from the sooty furnace, and arrives at the stars, thou mayest find no vocation for thee there, and feel as if thou hadst nothing to do amidst the still splendours of the Infinite. I don't deny to thee the uses of "Public Life;" I grant that it is much to have helped to carry that great Popkins Question; but Private Life, my friend, is the life of thy private soul; and there may be matters concerned with that which, on consideration, thou mayest allow, cannot be wholly mixed up with the Great Popkins Question—and were not finally settled when thou didst exclaim—"I have not lived in vain—the Popkins Question is carried at last!" Oh, immortal soul, for one quarter of an hour *per diem*—de-Popkinise thine immortality!

## CHAPTER II.

It had not been without much persuasion on the part of Jackeymo, that Riccabocca had consented to settle himself in the house which Randal had recommended to him. Not that the exile conceived any suspicion of the young man beyond that which he might have shared with Jackeymo, viz., that Randal's interest in the father was increased by a very natural and excusable admiration of the daughter. But the Italian had the pride common to misfortune,—he did not like to be indebted to others, and he shrank from the pity of those to whom it was known that he had held a higher station in his own land. These scruples gave way to the strength of his affection for his daughter and his dread of his foe. Good men, however able and brave, who have suffered from the wicked, are apt to form exaggerated notions of the power that has prevailed against them. Jackeymo had conceived a superstitious terror of Peschiera; and Riccabocca, though by no means addicted to superstition, still had a certain creep of the flesh whenever he thought of his foe.

But Riccabocca—than whom no man was more physically brave, and no man in some respects, more morally timid— feared the Count less as a foe than as a gallant. He remembered his kinsman's surpassing beauty—the power he had obtained over women. He knew him versed in every art that corrupts, and wholly void of the conscience that deters. And Riccabocca had unhappily nursed himself into so poor an estimate of the female character, that even the pure and lofty nature of Violante did not seem to him a sufficient safeguard against the craft and determination of a practised and remorseless intriguer. But of all the precautions he could take, none appeared more likely to conduce to safety, than his establishing a friendly communication with one who professed to be able to get at all the Count's plans and movements, and who could apprise Riccabocca at once should his retreat be discovered. "Forewarned is forearmed," said he to himself, in one of the proverbs common to all nations. However, as with his usual sagacity he came to reflect upon the alarming intelligence conveyed to him by Randal, viz., that the Count sought his daughter's hand, he divined that there was some strong personal interest under such ambition; and what could be that interest save the probability of Riccabocca's ultimate admission to the Imperial grace, and the

Count's desire to assure himself of the heritage to an estate that he might be permitted to retain no more? Riccabocca was not indeed aware of the condition (not according to usual customs in Austria) on which the Count held the forfeited domains. He knew not that they had been granted merely on pleasure; but he was too well aware of Peschiera's nature to suppose that he would woo a bride without a dower, or be moved by remorse in any overture of reconciliation. He felt assured too—and this increased all his fears—that Peschiera would never venture to seek an interview with himself; all the Count's designs on Violante would be dark, secret, and clandestine. He was perplexed and tormented by the doubt, whether or not to express openly to Violante his apprehensions of the nature of the danger to be apprehended. He had told her vaguely that it was for her sake that he desired secrecy and concealment. But that might mean anything: what danger to himself would not menace her? Yet to say more was so contrary to a man of his Italian notions and Machiavellian maxims! To say to a young girl, "There is a man come over to England on purpose to woo and win you. For Heaven's sake take care of him; he is diabolically handsome; he never fails where he sets his heart."—"*Cospetto!*" cried the Doctor, aloud, as these admonitions shaped themselves to speech in the camera-obscura of his brain; "such a warning would have undone a Cornelia while she was yet an innocent spinster." No, he resolved to say nothing to Violante of the Count's intention, only to keep guard, and make himself and Jackeymo all eyes and all ears.

The house Randal had selected pleased Riccabocca at first glance. It stood alone, upon a little eminence; its upper windows commanded the high road. It had been a school, and was surrounded by high walls, which contained a garden and lawn sufficiently large for exercise. The garden doors were thick, fortified by strong bolts, and had a little wicket lattice, shut and opened at pleasure, from which Jackeymo could inspect all visitors before he permitted them to enter.

An old female servant from the neighbourhood was cautiously hired; Riccabocca renounced his Italian name, and abjured his origin. He spoke English sufficiently well to think he could pass as an Englishman. He called himself Mr. Richmouth (a liberal translation of Riccabocca). He bought a blunderbuss, two pair of pistols, and a huge house-dog. Thus provided for, he allowed Jackeymo to write a line to Randal and communicate his arrival.

Randal lost no time in calling. With his usual adaptability, and his powers of dissimulation, he contrived easily to please Mrs. Riccabocca, and to increase the good opinion the exile was disposed to form of him. He engaged Violante in conversation on Italy and its poets. He promised to bring her books. He began, though more distantly than he could have desired—for her sweet stateliness awed him—the preliminaries of courtship. He established himself at once as a familiar guest, riding down daily in the dusk of evening, after the toils of office, and retiring at night. In four or five days he thought he had made great progress with all. Riccabocca watched him narrowly, and grew absorbed in thought after every visit. At length one night, when he and Mrs. Riccabocca were alone in the drawing-room, Violante having retired to rest, he thus spoke as he filled his pipe :—

"Happy is the man who has no children! Thrice happy he who has no girls!"

"My dear Alphonso!" said the wife, looking up from the wristband to which she was attaching a neat mother-o'-pearl button. She said no more; it was the sharpest rebuke she was in the custom of administering to her husband's cynical and odious observations. Riccabocca lighted his pipe with a thread paper, gave three great puffs, and resumed.

"One blunderbuss, four pistols, and a house-dog called Pompey, who would have made mincemeat of Julius Cæsar!"

"He certainly eats a great deal, does Pompey!" said Mrs. Riccabocca, simply. "But if he relieves your mind!"

"He does not relieve it in the least, ma'am," groaned Riccabocca; "and that is the point I was coming to. This is a most harassing life, and a most undignified life. And I who have only asked from Heaven dignity and repose! But, if Violante were once married, I should want neither blunderbuss, pistol, nor Pompey. And it is that which would relieve my mind, *cara mia*,—Pompey only relieves my larder!"

Now Riccabocca had been more communicative to Jemima than he had been to Violante. Having once trusted her with one secret, he had every motive to trust her with another; and he had accordingly spoken out his fears of the Count di Peschiera. Therefore she answered, laying down the work, and taking her husband's hand tenderly—

"Indeed, my love, since you dread so much (though I own

that I must think unreasonably) this wicked, dangerous man it would be the happiest thing in the world to see dear Violante well married; because, you see, if she is married to one person she cannot be married to another; and all fear of this Count, as you say, would be at an end."

"You cannot express yourself better. It is a great comfort to unbosom one's-self to a wife, after all;" quoth Riccabocca

"But," said the wife, after a grateful kiss—"but, where and how can we find a husband suitable to the rank of your daughter?"

"There—there—there," cried Riccabocca, pushing back his chair to the farther end of the room—"that comes of unbosoming one's-self! Out flies one's secret; it is opening the lid of Pandora's box; one is betrayed, ruined, undone!"

"Why, there's not a soul that can hear us!" said Mrs. Riccabocca, soothingly.

"That's chance, ma'am! If you once contract the habit of blabbing out a secret when nobody's by, how on earth can you resist it when you have the pleasurable excitement of telling it to all the world? Vanity, vanity—woman's vanity! Woman never could withstand rank—never!" The Doctor went on railing for a quarter of an hour, and was very reluctantly appeased by Mrs. Riccabocca's repeated and tearful assurances that she would never even whisper to herself that her husband had ever held any other rank than that of Doctor. Riccabocca, with a dubious shake of the head, renewed—

"I have done with all pomp and pretension. Besides, the young man is a born gentleman: he seems in good circumstances; he has energy and latent ambition; he is akin to L'Estrange's intimate friend: he seems attached to Violante. I don't think it probable that we could do better. Nay, if Peschiera fears that I shall be restored to my country, and I learn the wherefore, and the ground to take, through this young man—why, gratitude is the first virtue of the noble!"

"You speak, then, of Mr. Leslie?"

"To be sure—of whom else?"

Mrs. Riccabocca leaned her cheek on her hand thoughtfully. "Now you have told me *that*, I will observe him with different eyes."

"*Anima mia*, I don't see how the difference of your eyes will alter the object they look upon!" grumbled Riccabocca, shaking the ashes out of his pipe.

"The object alters when we see it in a different point of

view!" replied Jemima, modestly. "This thread does very well when I look at it in order to sew on a button, but I should say it would never do to tie up Pompey in his kennel."

"Reasoning by illustration, upon my soul!" ejaculated Riccabocca, amazed.

"And," continued Jemima, "when I am to regard one who is to constitute the happiness of that dear child, and for life, can I regard him as I would the pleasant guest of an evening? Ah, trust me, Alphonso; I don't pretend to be wise like you; but, when a woman considers what a man is likely to prove to woman—his sincerity—his honour—his heart—oh, trust me, she is wiser than the wisest man!"

Riccabocca continued to gaze on Jemima with unaffected admiration and surprise. And, certainly, to use his phrase, since he had unbosomed himself to his better half—since he had confided in her, consulted with her, her sense had seemed to quicken—her whole mind to expand.

"My dear," said the sage, "I vow and declare that Machiavelli was a fool to you. And I have been as dull as the chair I sit upon, to deny myself so many years the comfort and counsel of such a —— but, *corpo di Bacco!* forget all about rank; and so now to bed.—One must not holloa till one's out of the wood," muttered the ungrateful, suspicious villain, as he lighted the chamber candle.


## CHAPTER III.

RICCABOCCA could not confine himself to the precincts within the walls to which he condemned Violante. Resuming his spectacles, and wrapped in his cloak, he occasionally sallied forth upon a kind of outwatch or reconnoitring expedition—restricting himself, however, to the immediate neighbourhood, and never going quite out of sight of his house. His favourite walk was to the summit of a hillock overgrown with stunted bush-wood. Here he would sit himself musingly, often till the hoofs of Randal's horse rang on the winding road, as the sun set, over fading herbage, red and vaporous, in autumnal skies. Just below the hillock, and not two hundred yards from his own house, was the only other habitation in view—a charming, thoroughly English cottage, though somewhat imitated from the Swiss—with gable ends, thatched roof, and pretty, projecting casements, opening through creepers and climbing roses. From his height he commanded the gardens of this cottage, and his eye of artist was pleased, from the first sight, with the beauty which some exquisite taste had given to the ground. Even in that cheerless season of the year, the garden wore a summer smile; the evergreens were so bright and various, and the few flowers, still left, so hardy and so healthful. Facing the south, a colonnade, or covered gallery, of rustic woodwork had been formed, and creeping plants, lately set, were already beginning to clothe its columns. Opposite to this colonnade there was a fountain which reminded Riccabocca of his own at the deserted Casino. It was indeed singularly like it; the same circular shape, the same girdle of flowers around it. But the jet from it varied every day—fantastic and multiform, like the sports of a Naïad—sometimes shooting up like a tree, sometimes shaped as a convolvulus, sometimes tossing from its silver spray a flower of vermillion, or a fruit of gold—as if at play with its toy like a happy child. And near the fountain was a large aviary, large enough to enclose a tree. The Italian could just catch a gleam of rich colour from the wings of the birds, as they glanced to and fro within the network, and could hear their songs, contrasting the silence of the freer populace of air, whom the coming winter had already stilled.

Riccabocca's eye, so alive to all aspects of beauty, luxuriated in the view of this garden. Its pleasantness had a charm that stole him from his anxious fear and melancholy memories.

He never saw but two forms within the demesnes, and he could not distinguish their features. One was a woman, who seemed to him of staid manner and homely appearance: she was seen but rarely. The other a man, often pacing to and fro the colonnade, with frequent pauses before the playful fountain, or the birds that sang louder as he approached. This latter form would then disappear within a room, the glass door of which was at the extreme end of the colonnade; and if the door were left open, Riccabocca could catch a glimpse of the figure bending over a table covered with books.

Always, however, before the sun set, the man would step forth more briskly, and occupy himself with the garden, often working at it with good heart, as if at a task of delight; and then, too, the woman would come out, and stand by as if talking to her companion. Riccabocca's curiosity grew aroused. He bade Jemima inquire of the old maid-servant who lived at the cottage, and heard that its owner was a Mr. Oran—a quiet gentleman, and fond of his book.

While Riccabocca thus amused himself, Randal had not been prevented, either by his official cares or his schemes on Violante's heart and fortune, from furthering the project that was to unite Frank Hazeldean and Beatrice di Negra. Indeed, as to the first, a ray of hope was sufficient to fire the ardent and unsuspecting lover. And Randal's artful misrepresentation of his conference with Mrs. Hazeldean, removed all fear of parental displeasure from a mind always too disposed to give itself up to the temptation of the moment. Beatrice, though her feelings for Frank were not those of love, became more and more influenced by Randal's arguments and representations, the more especially as her brother grew morose, and even menacing, as days slipt on, and she could give no clue to the retreat of those whom he sought for. Her debts, too, were really urgent. As Randal's profound knowledge of human infirmity had shrewdly conjectured, the scruples of honour and pride, that had made her declare she would not bring to a husband her own encumbrances, began to yield to the pressure of necessity. She listened already, with but faint objections, when Randal urged her not to wait for the uncertain discovery that was to secure her dowry, but by a private marriage with Frank escape at once into freedom and security. While, though he had first held out to young Hazeldean the inducement of Beatrice's dowry as a reason of self-justification in the eyes of the Squire, it was still easier to drop that inducement, which had always rather damped than fired the high spirit and generous heart of the poor Guardsman. And Randal could conscientiously say, that when he had asked the Squire if he expected fortune with Frank's bride, the Squire had replied—"I don't care." Thus encouraged by his friend and his own heart, and the softening manner of a woman who might have charmed many a colder, and fooled many a wiser man, Frank rapidly yielded to the snares held out for his perdition. And though as yet he honestly shrank from proposing to Beatrice or himself a marriage without the consent, and even the knowledge, of his parents, yet Randal was quite content to leave a nature, however good, so thoroughly impulsive and undisciplined, to the influences of the first strong passion it had ever known. Meanwhile, it was so easy to dissuade Frank from even giving a hint to the folks at home. "For," said the wily and able traitor, "though we may be sure of Mrs. Hazeldean's consent, and her power over your father, when the step is once taken, yet we cannot count for certain on the Squire—he is so choleric and hasty. He might hurry to town—see Madame di Negra, blurt out some passionate, rude expressions, which would wake her resentment, and cause her instant rejection. And it might be too late if he repented afterwards—as he would be sure to do."

Meanwhile Randal Leslie gave a dinner at the Clarendon Hotel, (an extravagance most contrary to his habits,) and invited Frank, Mr. Borrowell, and Baron Levy.

But this house-spider, which glided with so much ease after its flies, through webs so numerous and mazy, had yet to amuse Madame di Negra with assurances that the fugitives sought for would sooner or later be discovered. Though Randal baffled and eluded her suspicion that he was already acquainted with the exiles, ("the persons he had thought of were," he said, "quite different from her description;" and he even presented to her an old singing-master, and a sallow-faced daughter, as the Italians who had caused this mistake,) it was necessary for Beatrice to prove the sincerity of the aid she had promised to her brother, and to introduce Randal to the Count. It was no less desirable to Randal to know, and even win the confidence of this man—his rival.

The two met at Madame di Negra's house. There is something very strange, and almost mesmerical, in the *rapport* between two evil natures. Bring two honest men together, and it is ten to one if they recognise each other as honest; differences in temper, manner, even politics, may make each misjudge the other. But bring together two men, unprincipled and perverted—men who, if born in a cellar, would have been food for the hulks or gallows—and they understand each other by instant sympathy. The eyes of Franzini, Count of Peschiera, and Randal Leslie no sooner met, than a gleam of intelligence shot from both. They talked on indifferent subjects—weather, gossip, politics—what not. They bowed and they smiled; but, all the while, each was watching, plumbing the other's heart, each measuring his strength with his companion; each inly saying, "This is a very remarkable rascal; am I a match for him?" It was at dinner they met; and following the English fashion, Madame di Negra left them alone with their wine.

Then, for the first time, Count di Peschiera cautiously and adroitly made a covered push towards the object of the meeting.

"You have never been abroad, my dear sir? You must contrive to visit me at Vienna. I grant the splendour of your London world; but, honestly speaking, it wants the freedom of ours—a freedom which unites gaiety with polish. For as your society is mixed, there are pretension and effort with those who have no right to be in it, and artificial condescension and chilling arrogance with those who have to keep their inferiors at a certain distance. With us, all being of fixed rank and acknowledged birth, familiarity is at once established. Hence," added the Count, with his French lively smile—"hence there is no place like Vienna for a young man —no place like Vienna for *bonnes fortunes*."

"Those make the paradise of the idle," replied Randal, "but the purgatory of the busy. I confess frankly to you, my dear Count, that I have as little of the leisure which becomes the aspirer to *bonnes fortunes* as I have the personal graces which obtain them without an effort;" and he inclined his head as in compliment.

"So," thought the Count, "woman is not his weak side. What is?"

"*Morbleu!* my dear Mr. Leslie—had I thought as you do some years since, I had saved myself from many a trouble. After all, Ambition is the best mistress to woo; for with her there is always the hope, and never the possession."

"Ambition, Count," replied Randal, still guarding himself in dry sententiousness, "is the luxury of the rich, and the necessity of the poor."

"Aha," thought the Count, "it comes, as I anticipated from the first—comes to the bribe." He passed the wine to Randal, filling his own glass, and draining it carelessly: "*Sur mon âme mon chér*," said the Count, "luxury is ever pleasanter than necessity; and I am resolved at least to give Ambition a trial—*je vais me réfugier dans le sein du bonheur domestique*—a married life and a settled home. *Peste!* If it were not for ambition, one would die of ennui. Apropos, my dear sir, I have to thank you for promising my sister your aid in finding a near and dear kinsman of mine, who has taken refuge in your country, and hides himself even from me."

"I should be most happy to assist in your search. As yet, however, I have only to regret that all my good wishes are fruitless. I should have thought, however, that a man of such rank had been easily found, even through the medium of your own ambassador."

"Our own ambassador is no very warm friend of mine;

and the rank would be no clue, for it is clear that my kinsman has never assumed it since he quitted his country."

"He quitted it, I understand, not exactly from choice," said Randal, smiling. "Pardon my freedom and curiosity, but will you explain to me a little more than I learn from English rumour, (which never accurately reports upon foreign matters still more notorious,) how a person who had so much to lose, and so little to win, by revolution, could put himself into the same crazy boat with a crew of hair-brained adventurers and visionary professors."

"Professors!" repeated the Count; "I think you have hit on the very answer to your question; not but what men of high birth were as mad as the *canaille*. I am the more willing to gratify your curiosity, since it will perhaps serve to guide your kind search in my favour. You must know, then, that my kinsman was not born the heir to the rank he obtained. He was but a distant relation to the head of the house which he afterwards represented. Brought up in an Italian university, he was distinguished for his learning and his eccentricities. There too, I suppose, brooding over old wives' tales about freedom, and so forth, he contracted his *carbonaro*, chimerical notions for the independence of Italy. Suddenly, by three deaths, he was elevated, while yet young, to a station and honours which might have satisfied any man in his senses. *Que diable!* what could the independence of Italy do for *him!* He and I were cousins; we had played together as boys; but our lives had been separated till his succession to rank brought us necessarily together. We became exceedingly intimate. And you may judge how I loved him," said the Count, averting his eyes slightly from Randal's quiet, watchful gaze, "when I add, that I forgave him for enjoying a heritage that, but for him, had been mine."

"Ah, you were next heir?"

"And it is a hard trial to be very near a great fortune, and yet just to miss it."

"True," cried Randal, almost impetuously. The Count now raised his eyes, and again the two men looked into each other's souls.

"Harder still, perhaps," resumed the Count, after a short pause—"harder still might it have been to some men to forgive the rival as well as the heir."

"Rival! how?"

"A lady, who had been destined by her parents to myself,

though we had never, I own, been formally betrothed, became the wife of my kinsman."

"Did he know of your pretensions?"

"I do him the justice to say he did not. He saw and fell in love with the young lady I speak of. Her parents were dazzled. Her father sent for me. He apologised—he explained; he set before me, mildly enough, certain youthful imprudences or errors of my own, as an excuse for his change of mind; and he asked me not only to resign all hope of his daughter, but to conceal from her new suitor that I had ever ventured to hope."

"And you consented?"

"I consented."

"That was generous. You must indeed have been much attached to your kinsman. As a lover, I cannot comprehend it; perhaps, my dear Count, you may enable me to understand it better—as a man of the world."

"Well," said the Count, with his most *roué* air, "I suppose we *are* both men of the world?"

"*Both!* certainly," replied Randal, just in the tone which Peachum might have used in courting the confidence of Lockit.

"As a man of the world, then, I own," said the Count, playing with the rings on his fingers, "that if I could not marry the lady myself, (and that seemed to me clear,) it was very natural that I should wish to see her married to my wealthy kinsman."

"Very natural; it might bring your wealthy kinsman and yourself still closer together."

"This is really a very clever fellow!" thought the Count, but he made no direct reply.

"*Enfin*, to cut short a long story, my cousin afterwards got entangled in attempts, the failure of which is historically known. His projects were detected—himself denounced. He fled, and the Emperor, in sequestrating his estates, was pleased, with rare and singular clemency, to permit me, as his nearest kinsman, to enjoy the revenues of half those estates during the royal pleasure; nor was the other half formally confiscated. It was no doubt his Majesty's desire not to extinguish a great Italian name; and if my cousin and his child died in exile, why, of that name, I, a loyal subject of Austria—I, Franzini, Count di Peschiera, would become the representative. Such, in a similar case, has been sometimes the Russian policy towards Polish insurgents."

"I comprehend perfectly; and I can also conceive that you, in profiting so largely, though so justly, by the fall of your kinsman, may have been exposed to much unpopularity—even to painful suspicion."

'*Entre nous, mon cher*, I care not a stiver for popularity; and as to suspicion, who is he that can escape from the calumny of the envious? But, unquestionably, it would be most desirable to unite the divided members of our house; and this union I can now effect, by the consent of the Emperor to my marriage with my kinsman's daughter. You see, therefore, why I have so great an interest in this research?"

"By the marriage articles you could no doubt secure the retention of the half you hold; and if you survive your kinsman, you would enjoy the whole. A most desirable marriage; and, if made, I suppose that would suffice to obtain your cousin's amnesty and grace?"

"You say it."

"But even without such marriage, since the Emperor's clemency has been extended to so many of the proscribed, it is perhaps probable that your cousin might be restored?"

"It once seemed to me possible," said the Count, reluctantly; "but since I have been in England, I think not. The recent revolution in France, the democratic spirit rising in Europe, tend to throw back the cause of a proscribed rebel. England swarms with revolutionists; my cousin's residence in this country is in itself suspicious. The suspicion is increased by his strange seclusion. There are many Italians here who would aver that they had met with him, and that he was still engaged in revolutionary projects."

"Aver—untruly?"

"*Ma foi*—it comes to the same thing; *les absens ont toujours tort*. I speak to a man of the world. No; without some such guarantee for his faith, as his daughter's marriage with myself would give, his recall is improbable. By the heaven above us, it shall be *impossible!*" The Count rose as he said this—rose as if the mask of simulation had fairly fallen from the visage of crime—rose tall and towering, a very image of masculine power and strength, beside the slight, bended form and sickly face of the intellectual schemer. And had you seen them thus confronted and contrasted, you would have felt that if ever the time should come when the interest of the one would compel him openly to denounce or boldly to expose the other, the odds were that the brilliant and audacious reprobate would master the weaker nerve but superior wit of the furtive traitor. Randal was startled; but rising also, he said, carelessly—

"What if this guarantee can no longer be given?—what if, in despair of return, and in resignation to his altered fortunes, your cousin has already married his daughter to some English suitor?"

"Ah, that would indeed be, next to my own marriage with her, the most fortunate thing that could happen to myself."

"How? I don't understand!"

"Why, if my cousin has so abjured his birthright, and forsworn his rank—if this heritage, which is so dangerous from its grandeur, pass, in case of his pardon, to some obscure Englishman—a foreigner—a native of a country that has no ties with ours—a country that is the very refuge of levellers and Carbonari—*mort de ma vie*—do you think that such would not annihilate all chance of my cousin's restoration, and be an excuse even in the eyes of Italy for formally conferring the sequestrated estates on an Italian? No; unless, indeed, the girl were to marry an Englishman of such name and birth and connection as would in themselves be a guarantee (and how in poverty is this likely?) I should go back to Vienna with a light heart, if I could say, 'My kinswoman is an Englishman's wife—shall her children be the heirs to a house so renowned for its lineage, and so formidable for its wealth?' *Parbleu!* if my cousin were but an adventurer, or merely a professor, he had been pardoned long ago. The great enjoy the honour not to be pardoned easily."

Randal fell into deep but brief thought. The Count observed him, not face to face, but by the reflection of an opposite mirror. "This man knows something; this man is deliberating; this man can help me," thought the Count.

But Randal said nothing to confirm these hypotheses. Recovering from his abstraction, he expressed courteously his satisfaction at the Count's prospects, either way. "And since, after all," he added, "you mean so well to your cousin, it occurs to me that you might discover him by a very simple English process."

"How?"

"Advertise that, if he will come to some place appointed, he will hear of something to his advantage."

The Count shook his head. "He would suspect me, and not come."

"But he was intimate with you. He joined an insurrection;—you were more prudent. You did not injure him, though you may have benefited yourself. Why should he shun you?"

"The conspirators forgive none who do not conspire; besides, to speak frankly, he thought I injured him."

"Could you not conciliate him through his wife—whom you resigned to him?"

"She is dead—died before he left the country."

"Oh, that is unlucky! Still I think an advertisement might do good. Allow me to reflect on that subject. Shall we now join *Madame la Marquise?*"

On re-entering the drawing-room, the gentlemen found Beatrice in full dress, seated by the fire, and reading so intently that she did not remark them enter.

"What so interests you, *ma sœur?*—the last novel by Balzac, no doubt?"

Beatrice started, and, looking up, showed eyes that were full of tears. "Oh, no! no picture of miserable, vicious, Parisian life. This is beautiful; there is *soul* here."

Randal took up the book which the Marchesa laid down; it was the same which had charmed the circle at Hazeldean— charmed the innocent and fresh-hearted—charmed now the wearied and tempted votaress of the world.

"Hum," murmured Randal; "the parson was right. This is power—a sort of a power."

"How I should like to know the author! Who can he be —can you guess?"

"Not I. Some old pedant in spectacles."

"I think not—I am sure not.—Here beats a heart I have ever sighed to find, and never found."

"Oh, *la naïve enfant!*" cried the Count; "*comme son imagination s'égare en rêves enchantés.* And to think that, while you talk like an Arcadian, you are dressed like a princess."

"Ah, I forgot—the Austrian ambassador's. I shall not go to-night. This book unfits me for the artificial world."

"Just as you will, my sister. I shall go. I dislike the man, and he me; but ceremonies before men!"

"You are going to the Austrian Embassy?" said Randal. "I, too, shall be there. We shall meet." And he took his leave.

"I like your young friend prodigiously," said the Count, yawning. "I am sure that he knows of the lost birds, and will stand to them like a pointer, if I can but make it his interest to do so. We shall see."

## CHAPTER IV.

RANDAL arrived at the ambassador's before the Count, and contrived to mix with the young noblemen attached to the embassy, and to whom he was known. Standing among these was a young Austrian, on his travels, of very high birth, and with an air of noble grace that suited the ideal of the old German chivalry. Randal was presented to him, and, after some talk on general topics, observed, "By the way, Prince, there is now in London a countryman of yours, with whom you are, doubtless, familiarly acquainted—the Count di Peschiera."

"He is no countryman of mine. He is an Italian. I know him but by sight and by name," said the Prince, stiffly.

"He is of very ancient birth, I believe."

"Unquestionably. His ancestors were gentlemen."

"And very rich."

"Indeed! I have understood the contrary. He enjoys, it is true, a large revenue."

A young *attaché*, less discreet than the Prince, here observed, "Oh, Peschiera!—Poor fellow, he is too fond of play to be rich."

"And there is some chance that the kinsman whose revenue he holds may obtain his pardon, and re-enter into possession of his fortunes—so I hear, at least," said Randal, artfully.

"I shall be glad if it be true," said the Prince with decision; "and I speak the common sentiment at Vienna. That kinsman had a noble spirit, and was, I believe, equally duped and betrayed. Pardon me, sir; but we Austrians are not so bad as we are painted. Have you ever met in England the kinsman you speak of?"

"Never, though he is supposed to reside here; and the Count tells me that he has a daughter."

"The Count—ha! I heard something of a scheme—a wager of that—that Count's;—a daughter! Poor girl! I hope she will escape his pursuit; for, no doubt, he pursues her."

"Possibly she may already have married an Englishman."

"I trust not, said the Prince, seriously; "that might at present be a serious obstacle to her father's return."

"You think so?"

"There can be no doubt of it," interposed the *attaché*, with a grand and positive air; "unless, indeed, the Englishman were of a rank equal to her own."

Here there was a slight, well-bred murmur and buzz at the door; for the Count di Peschiera himself was announced; and as he entered, his presence was so striking, and his beauty so dazzling, that whatever there might be to the prejudice of his character, it seemed instantly effaced or forgotten in that irresistible admiration which it is the prerogative of personal attributes alone to create.

The Prince, with a slight curve of his lip at the groups that collected round the Count, turned to Randal, and said, "Can you tell me if a distinguished countryman of yours is in England—Lord L'Estrange?"

"No, Prince—he is not. You know him?"

"Well."

"He is acquainted with the Count's kinsman; and perhaps from him you have learned to think so highly of that kinsman?"

The Prince bowed, and answered as he moved away, "When one man of high honour vouches for another, he commands the belief of all."

"Certainly," soliloquised Randal, "I must not be precipitate. I was very near falling into a terrible trap. If I were to marry the girl, and only, by so doing, settle away her inheritance on Peschiera!—How hard it is to be sufficiently cautious in this world!"

While thus meditating, a member of Parliament tapped him on the shoulder.

"Melancholy, Leslie! I lay a wager I guess your thoughts."

"Guess," answered Randal.

"You were thinking of the place you are so soon to lose."

"Soon to lose!"

"Why, if ministers go out, you could hardly keep it, I suppose."

This ominous and horrid member of Parliament, Squire Hazeldean's favourite county member, Sir John, was one of those legislators especially odious to officials—an independent "large-acred" member, who would no more take office himself than he would cut down the oaks in his park, and who had no bowels of human feeling for those who had opposite tastes and less magnificent means.

"Hem!" said Randal, rather surlily. "In the first place, Sir John, ministers are not going out."

"Oh yes, they will go. You know I vote with them generally, and would willingly keep them in; but they are men of honour and spirit; and if they can't carry their measures, they must resign; otherwise, by Jove, I would turn round and vote them out myself!"

"I have no doubt you would, Sir John; you are quite capable of it; that rests with you and your constituents. But even if ministers did go out, I am but a poor subaltern in a public office. I am no minister—why should I go out too?"

"Why? Hang it, Leslie, you are laughing at me. A young fellow like you could never be mean enough to stay in, under the very men who drove out your friend Egerton?"

"It is not usual for those in the public offices to retire with every change of Government."

"Certainly not; but always those who are the relations of a retiring minister—always those who have been regarded as politicians, and who mean to enter Parliament, as of course you will do at the next election. But you know that as well as I do—you who are so decided a politician—the writer of that admirable pamphlet! I should not like to tell my friend Hazeldean, who has a sincere interest in you, that you ever doubted on a question of honour as plain as your A, B, C."

"Indeed, Sir John," said Randal, recovering his suavity, while he inly breathed a dire anathema on his county member, "I am so new to these things, that what you say never struck me before. No doubt you must be right; at all events I cannot have a better guide and adviser than Mr. Egerton himself."

SIR JOHN.—"No, certainly—perfect gentleman, Egerton! I wish we could make it up with him and Hazeldean."

RANDAL, (sighing.)—"Ah, I wish we could!"

SIR JOHN.—"And some chance of it now; for the time is coming when all true men of the old school must stick together."

RANDAL.—"Wisely, admirably said, my dear Sir John. But, pardon me, I must pay my respects to the ambassador."

Randal escaped, and passing on, saw the ambassador himself in the next room, conferring in a corner with Audley

Egerton. The ambassador seemed very grave—Egerton calm and impenetrable, as usual. Presently the Count passed by, and the ambassador bowed to him very stiffly.

As Randal, some time later, was searching for his cloak below, Audley Egerton unexpectedly joined him.

"Ah, Leslie," said the minister, with more kindness than usual, "if you don't think the night air too cold for you, let us walk home together. I have sent away the carriage."

This condescension in his patron was so singular, that it quite startled Randal, and gave him a presentiment of some evil. When they were in the street, Egerton, after a pause, began—

"My dear Mr. Leslie, it was my hope and belief that I had provided for you at least a competence; and that I might open to you, later, a career yet more brilliant. Hush! I don't doubt your gratitude; let me proceed. There is a possible chance, after certain decisions that the Government have come to, that we may be beaten in the House of Commons, and of course resign. I tell you this beforehand, for I wish you to have time to consider what, in that case, would be your best course. My power of serving you may then probably be over. It would, no doubt, (seeing our close connection, and my views with regard to your future being so well known,)—no doubt, be expected that you should give up the place you hold, and follow my fortunes for good or ill. But as I have no personal enemies with the opposite party—and as I have sufficient position in the world to uphold and sanction your choice, whatever it may be, if you think it more prudent to retain your place, tell me so openly, and I think I can contrive that you may do it without loss of character and credit. In that case, confine your ambition merely to rising gradually in your office, without mixing in politics. If, on the other hand, you should prefer to take your chance of my return to office, and so resign your present place; and, furthermore, should commit yourself to a policy that may then be not only in opposition, but unpopular, I will do my best to introduce you into parliamentary life. I cannot say that I advise the latter."

Randal felt as a man feels after a severe fall—he was literally stunned. At length he faltered out—

"Can you think, sir, that I should ever desert your fortunes—your party—your cause?"

"My dear Leslie," replied the minister, "you are too young to have committed yourself to any men or to any party, except, indeed, in that unlucky pamphlet. This must not be an affair of sentiment, but of sense and reflection. Let us say no more on the point now ; but by considering the *pros* and the *cons*, you can better judge what to do, should the time for option suddenly arrive."

"But I hope that time may not come."

"I hope so too, and most sincerely," said the minister, with deliberate and genuine emphasis.

"What could be so bad for the country?" ejaculated Randal. "It does not seem to me possible, in the nature of things, that you and your party should ever go out!"

"And when we are once out, there will be plenty of wiseacres to say it is out of the nature of things that we should ever come in again. Here we are at the door."

## CHAPTER V.

RANDAL passed a sleepless night; but, indeed, he was one of those persons who neither need, nor are accustomed to, much sleep. However, towards morning, when dreams are said to be prophetic, he fell into a most delightful slumber— a slumber peopled by visions fitted to lure on, through labyrinths of law, predestined chancellors, or wreck upon the rocks of glory the inebriate souls of youthful ensigns—dreams from which Rood Hall emerged crowned with the towers of Belvoir or Raby, and looking over subject lands and manors wrested from the nefarious usurpation of Thornhills and Hazeldeans—dreams in which Audley Egerton's gold and power—rooms in Downing Street, and saloons in Grosvenor Square—had passed away to the smiling dreamer, as the empire of Chaldæa passed to Darius the Median. Why visions so belying the gloomy and anxious thoughts that preceded them should visit the pillow of Randal Leslie, surpasses my philosophy to conjecture. He yielded, however, passively to their spell, and was startled to hear the clock strike eleven as he descended the stairs to breakfast. He was vexed at the lateness of the hour, for he had meant to have taken advantage of the unwonted softness of Egerton, and drawn therefrom some promises or proffers to cheer the prospects which the minister had so chillingly expanded before him the preceding night. And it was only at breakfast that he usually found the opportunity of private conference with his busy patron. But Audley Egerton would be sure to have sallied forth—and so he had—only Randal was surprised to hear that he had gone out in his carriage, instead of on foot, as was his habit. Randal soon despatched his solitary meal, and with a new and sudden affection for his office, thitherwards bent his way. As he passed through Piccadilly, he heard behind a voice that had lately become familiar to him, and turning round, saw Baron Levy walking side by side, though not arm-in-arm, with a gentleman almost as smart as himself, but with a jauntier step and a brisker air—a step that, like Diomed's, as described by Shakespeare—

"Rises on the toe;—that spirit of his
In aspiration lifts him from the earth."

Indeed, one may judge of the spirits and disposition of a man by his ordinary gait and mien in walking. He who habitually pursues abstract thought, looks down on the ground. He who is accustomed to sudden impulses, or is trying to seize upon some necessary recollection, looks up with a kind of jerk. He who is a steady, cautious, merely practical man, walks on deliberately, his eyes straight before him; and, even in his most musing moods, observes things around sufficiently to avoid a porter's knot or a butcher's tray. But the man with strong ganglions—of pushing, lively temperament, who, though practical, is yet speculative—the man who is emulous and active, and ever trying to rise in life—sanguine, alert, bold—walks with a spring—looks rather above the heads of his fellow-passengers—but with a quick, easy turn of his own, which is lightly set on his shoulders; his mouth is a little open—his eye is bright, rather restless, but penetrative—his port has something of defiance—his form is erect, but without stiffness. Such was the appearance of the Baron's companion. And as Randal turned round at Levy's voice, the Baron said to his companion, "A young man in the first circles—you should book him for your fair lady's parties. How d'ye do, Mr. Leslie? Let me introduce you to Mr. Richard Avenel." Then, as he hooked his arm into Randal's, he whispered, "Man of first-rate talent—monstrous rich—has two or three parliamentary seats in his pocket—wife gives parties—her foible."

"Proud to make your acquaintance, sir," said Mr. Avenel, lifting his hat. "Fine day."

"Rather cold too," said Leslie, who, like all thin persons,

with weak digestions, was chilly by temperament; besides, he had enough on his mind to chill his body.

"So much the healthier—braces the nerves," said Mr. Avenel; "but you young fellows relax the system by hot rooms and late hours. Fond of dancing of course, sir?" Then, without waiting for Randal's negative, Mr. Richard continued rapidly, "Mrs. Avenel has a *soirée dansante* on Thursday—shall be very happy to see you in Eaton Square. Stop, I have a card;" and he drew out a dozen large invitation cards, from which he selected one, and presented it to Randal. The Baron pressed that young gentleman's arm, and Randal replied courteously that it would give him great pleasure to be introduced to Mrs. Avenel. Then, as he was not desirous to be seen under the wing of Baron Levy, like a pigeon under that of a hawk, he gently extricated himself, and pleading great haste, walked quickly on towards his office.

"That young man will make a figure some day," said the Baron. "I don't know any one of his age with so few prejudices. He is a connection by marriage to Audley Egerton, who—"

"Audley Egerton!" exclaimed Mr. Avenel; "a d—d haughty, aristocratic, disagreeable, ungrateful fellow!"

"Why, what do you know of him?"

"He owed his first seat in Parliament to the votes of two near relations of mine, and when I called upon him some time ago, in his office, he absolutely ordered me out of the room. Hang his impertinence; if ever I can pay him off, I guess I shan't fail for want of good will!"

"Ordered you out of the room? That's not like Egerton, who is civil, if formal—at least to most men. You must have offended him in his weak point."

"A man whom the public pays so handsomely should have no weak point. What is Egerton's?"

"Oh, he values himself on being a thorough gentleman—a man of the nicest honour," said Levy, with a sneer. "You must have ruffled his plumes there. How was it?"

"I forget," answered Mr. Avenel, who was far too well versed in the London scale of human dignities since his marriage, not to look back with a blush at his desire of knighthood. "No use bothering our heads now about the plumes of an arrogant popinjay. To return to the subject we were discussing. You must be sure to let me have this money next week."

"Rely on it."

"And you'll not let my bills get into the market; keep them under lock and key."

"So we agreed."

"It is but a temporary difficulty—royal mourning, such nonsense—panic in trade, lest these precious ministers go out. I shall soon float over the troubled waters."

"By the help of a paper boat," said the Baron, laughing; and the two gentlemen shook hands and parted.

## CHAPTER VI.

MEANWHILE Audley Egerton's carriage had deposited him at the door of Lord Lansmere's house, at Knightsbridge. He asked for the Countess, and was shown into the drawing-room, which was deserted. Egerton was paler than usual; and as the door opened, he wiped the unwonted moisture from his forehead, and there was a quiver on his firm lip. The Countess too, on entering, showed an emotion almost equally unusual to her self-control. She pressed Audley's hand in silence, and seating herself by his side, seemed to collect her thoughts. At length she said—

"It is rarely indeed that we meet, Mr. Egerton, in spite of your intimacy with Lansmere and Harley. I go so little into your world, and you will not voluntarily come to me."

"Madam," replied Egerton, "I might evade your kind reproach by stating that my hours are not at my disposal; but I answer you with plain truth,—it must be painful to both of us to meet."

The Countess coloured and sighed, but did not dispute the assertion.

Audley resumed. "And therefore, I presume that, in sending for me, you have something of moment to communicate?"

"It relates to Harley," said the Countess, as if in apology; "and I would take your advice."

"To Harley! Speak on, I beseech you."

"My son has probably told you that he has educated and reared a young girl, with the intention to make her Lady L'Estrange, and hereafter Countess of Lansmere."

"Harley has no secrets from me," said Egerton mournfully.

"This young lady has arrived in England—is here—in this house."

"And Harley too?"

"No, she came over with Lady N—— and her daughters. Harley was to follow shortly, and I expect him daily. Here is his letter. Observe, he has never yet communicated his intentions to this young person, now intrusted to my care— never spoken to her as the lover."

Egerton took the letter and read it rapidly, though with attention.

"True," said he, as he returned the letter: "and before he does so he wishes you to see Miss Digby and to judge of her yourself—wishes to know if you will approve and sanction his choice."

"It is on this that I would consult you—a girl without rank;—the father, it is true, a gentleman, though almost equivocally one,—but the mother, I know not what. And Harley, for whom I hoped an alliance with the first houses in England!" The Countess pressed her hands convulsively together.

EGERTON.—"He is no more a boy. His talents have been wasted—his life a wanderer's. He presents to you a chance of resettling his mind, of re-arousing his native powers, of a home beside your own. Lady Lansmere, you cannot hesitate!"

LADY LANSMERE.—"I do, I do! After all that I have hoped, after all that I did to prevent—"

EGERTON, (interrupting her.) — "You owe him now an atonement; that is in your power—it is not in mine."

The Countess again pressed Audley's hand, and the tears gushed from her eyes.

"It shall be so. I consent—I consent. I will silence, I will crush back this proud heart. Alas! it well-nigh broke his own! I am glad you speak thus. I like to think he owes my consent to you. In that there is atonement for both."

"You are too generous, madam," said Egerton, evidently moved, though still, as ever, striving to repress emotion. "And now may I see the young lady? This conference pains me; you see even my strong nerves quiver; and at this time I have much to go through—need of all my strength and firmness."

"I hear, indeed, that the Government will probably retire. But it is with honour: it will be soon called back by the voice of the nation."

"Let me see the future wife of Harley L'Estrange," said Egerton, without heed of this consolatory exclamation.

The Countess rose and left the room. In a few minutes she returned with Helen Digby.

Helen was wondrously improved from the pale, delicate child, with the soft smile and intelligent eyes, who had sate by the side of Leonard in his garret. She was about the middle height, still slight, but beautifully formed; that exquisite roundness of proportion which conveys so well the idea of woman, in its undulating pliant grace—formed to embellish life, and soften away its rude angles—formed to embellish, not to protect. Her face might not have satisfied the critical eye of an artist—it was not without defects in regularity; but its expression was eminently gentle and prepossessing; and there were few who would not have exclaimed, "What a lovely countenance!" The mildness of her brow was touched with melancholy—her childhood had left its traces on her youth. Her step was slow, and her manner shy, subdued, and timid.

Audley gazed on her with earnestness as she approached him; and then coming forward, took her hand and kissed it.

"I am your guardian's constant friend," said he, and he drew her gently to a seat beside him, in the recess of a window. With a quick glance of his eye towards the Countess, he seemed to imply the wish to converse with Helen somewhat apart. So the Countess interpreted the glance; and though she remained in the room, she seated herself at a distance, and bent over a book.

It was touching to see how the austere man of business lent himself to draw forth the mind of this quiet, shrinking girl; and if you had listened, you would have comprehended how he came to possess such social influence, and how well, some time or other in the course of his life, he had learned to adapt himself to women.

He spoke first of Harley L'Estrange—spoke with tact and delicacy. Helen at first answered by monosyllables, and then, by degrees, with grateful and open affection. Audley's brow grew shaded. He then spoke of Italy, and though no man had less of the poet in his nature, yet with the dexterity of one long versed in the world, and who had been accustomed to extract evidences from characters most opposed to his own, he suggested such topics as might serve to arouse poetry in others. Helen's replies betrayed a cultivated taste, and a charming womanly mind; but they betrayed, also, one accustomed to take its colourings from another's—to appreciate, admire, revere the Lofty and the Beautiful, but humbly and meekly. There was no vivid enthusiasm, no remark of striking originality, no flash of the self-kindling, creative faculty. Lastly, Egerton turned to England—to the critical nature of the times—to the claims which the country possessed upon all who had the ability to serve and guide its troubled destinies. He enlarged warmly on Harley's natural talents, and rejoiced that he had returned to England, perhaps to commence some great career. Helen looked surprised, but her face caught no correspondent glow from Audley's eloquence. He rose, and an expression of disappointment passed over his grave, handsome features, and as quickly vanished.

"Adieu! my dear Miss Digby; I fear I have wearied you, especially with my politics. Adieu, Lady Lansmere; no doubt I shall see Harley as soon as he returns."

Then he hastened from the room, gained his carriage, and ordered the coachman to drive to Downing Street. He drew down the blinds, and leant back. A certain languor became visible in his face, and once or twice he mechanically put his hand to his heart.

"She is good, amiable, docile—will make an excellent wife, no doubt," said he, murmuringly. "But does she love Harley as he has dreamed of love? No! Has she the power and energy to arouse his faculties, and restore to the world the Harley of old? No! Meant by Heaven to be the shadow of another's sun—not herself the sun—this child is not the one who can atone for the Past and illume the Future."

## CHAPTER VII.

THAT evening Harley L'Estrange arrived at his father's house. The few years that had passed since we saw him last had made no perceptible change in his appearance. He still preserved his elastic youthfulness of form, and singular variety and play of countenance. He seemed unaffectedly rejoiced to greet his parents, and had something of the gaiety and tenderness of a boy returned from school. His manner to Helen bespoke the chivalry that pervaded all the complexities and curves of his character. It was affectionate, but respectful. Hers to him, subdued—but innocently sweet and gently cordial. Harley was the chief talker. The aspect of the times was so critical that he could not avoid questions on politics; and, indeed, he showed an interest in them which he had never evinced before. Lord Lansmere was delighted.

"Why, Harley, you love your country after all?"

"The moment she seems in danger—yes!" replied the Patrician; and the Sybarite seemed to rise into the Athenian.

Then he asked with eagerness about his old friend Audley; and, his curiosity satisfied there, he inquired the last literary news. He had heard much of a book lately published. He named the one ascribed by Parson Dale to Professor Moss; none of his listeners had read it.

Harley pished at this, and accused them all of indolence and stupidity, in his own quaint, metaphorical style. Then he said—"And town gossip?"

"We never hear it," said Lady Lansmere.

"There is a new plough much talked of at Boodles," said Lord Lansmere.

"God speed it. But is not there a new man much talked of at White's?"

"I don't belong to White's."

"Nevertheless, you may have heard of him—a foreigner, a Count di Peschiera."

"Yes," said Lord Lansmere; "he was pointed out to me in the park—a handsome man for a foreigner; wears his hair properly cut; looks gentlemanlike and English."

"Ah, ah! He is here then!" and Harley rubbed his hands.

"Which road did you take? Did you pass the Simplon?"

"No; I came straight from Vienna."

Then, relating with lively vein his adventures by the way, he continued to delight Lord Lansmere by his gaiety till the time came to retire to rest. As soon as Harley was in his own room, his mother joined him.

"Well," said he, "I need not ask if you like Miss Digby? Who would not?"

"Harley, my own son," said the mother, bursting into tears, "be happy your own way; only be happy, that is all I ask."

Harley, much affected, replied gratefully and soothingly to this fond injunction. And then gradually leading his mother on to converse of Helen, asked abruptly—" And of the chance of our happiness—her happiness as well as mine—what is your opinion ? Speak frankly."

"Of *her* happiness there can be no doubt," replied the mother proudly. "Of yours, how can you ask me? Have you not decided on that yourself?"

"But still it cheers and encourages one in any experiment, however well considered, to hear the approval of another. Helen has certainly a most gentle temper."

"I should conjecture so. But her mind—"

"Is very well stored."

"She speaks so little—"

"Yes. I wonder why? She's surely a woman."

"Pshaw," said the Countess, smiling, in spite of herself. "But tell me more of the process of your experiment. You took her as a child, and resolved to train her according to your own ideal. Was that easy?"

"It seemed so. I desired to instil habits of truth: she was already by nature truthful as the day; a taste for nature and all things natural—that seemed inborn; perceptions of Art as the interpreter of Nature—those were more difficult to teach. I think they may come. You have heard her play and sing?"

"No."

"She will surprise you. She has less talent for drawing; still, all that teaching could do has been done—in a word, she is accomplished. Temper, heart, mind—these all are excellent." Harley stopped and suppressed a sigh. "Certainly I ought to be very happy," said he; and he began to wind up his watch.

"Of course she must love you," said the Countess, after a pause. "How could she fail?"

"Love me! My dear mother, that is the very question I shall have to ask."

"Ask! Love is discovered by a glance; it has no need of asking."

"I have never discovered it, then, I assure you. The fact is, that before her childhood was passed, I removed her, as you may suppose, from my roof. She resided with an Italian family, near my usual abode. I visited her often, directed her studies, watched her improvement—"

"And fell in love with her?"

"Fall is such a very violent word. No; I don't remember to have had a fall. It was all a smooth inclined plane from the first step, until at last I said to myself, 'Harley L'Estrange, thy time has come. The bud has blossomed into flower. Take it to thy breast.' And myself replied to myself, meekly, 'So be it.' Then I found that Lady N—— with her daughters, was coming to England. I asked her ladyship to take my ward to your house. I wrote to you, and prayed your assent; and, that granted, I knew you would obtain my father's. I am here—you give me the approval I sought for. I will speak to Helen to-morrow. Perhaps, after all, she may reject me."

"Strange, strange—you speak thus coldly, thus lightly; you so capable of ardent love!"

"Mother," said Harley, earnestly, "be satisfied! *I* am! Love, as of old, I feel, alas! too well, can visit me never more. But gentle companionship, tender friendship, the relief and the sunlight of woman's smile—hereafter the voices of children—music that, striking on the hearts of both parents, wakens the most lasting and the purest of all sympathies: these are my hope. Is the hope so mean, my fond mother?"

Again the Countess wept, and her tears were not dried when she left the room.

## CHAPTER VIII.

OH! Helen, fair Helen—type of the quiet, serene, unnoticed, deepfelt excellence of woman! Woman, less as the ideal that a poet conjures from the air, than as the companion of a poet on the earth! Woman, who, with her clear sunny vision of things actual, and the exquisite fibre of her delicate sense, supplies the deficiencies of him whose foot stumbles on the soil, because his eye is too intent upon the stars! Woman, the provident, the comforting—angel whose pinions are folded round the heart, guarding there a divine spring unmarred by the winter of the world! Helen, soft Helen, is it indeed in thee that the wild and brilliant "lord of wantonness and ease" is to find the regeneration of his life—the rebaptism of his soul? Of what avail thy meek prudent household virtues to one whom Fortune screens from rough trial?—whose sorrows lie remote from thy ken?—whose spirit, erratic and perturbed, now rising, now falling, needs a vision more subtle than thine to pursue, and a strength that can sustain the reason, when it droops, on the wings of enthusiasm and passion?

And thou, thyself, O nature, shrinking and humble, that needest to be courted forth from the shelter, and developed under the calm and genial atmosphere of holy, happy love—can such affection as Harley L'Estrange may proffer suffice to thee? Will not the blossoms, yet folded in the petal, wither away beneath the shade that may protect them from the storm, and yet shut them from the sun? Thou who, where thou givest love, seekest, though meekly, for love in return;—to be the soul's sweet necessity, the life's household partner to him who receives all thy faith and devotion—canst thou influence the sources of joy and of sorrow in the heart that does not heave at thy name? Hast thou the charm and the force of the moon, that the tides of that wayward sea shall ebb and flow at thy will? Yet who shall say—who conjecture how near two hearts can become, when no guilt lies between them, and time brings the ties all its own? Rarest of all things on earth is the union in which both, by their contrasts, make harmonious their blending; each supplying the defects of the helpmate, and completing, by fusion, one strong human soul! Happiness enough, where even Peace does but seldom preside, when each can bring to the altar, if not the flame, still the incense. Where man's thoughts are all noble and generous, woman's feelings all gentle and pure, love may follow, if it does not precede;—and if not—, if the roses be missed from the garland, one may sigh for the rose, but one is safe from the thorn.

The morning was mild, yet somewhat overcast by the mist which announces coming winter in London, and Helen walked musingly beneath the trees that surrounded the garden of Lord Lansmere's house. Many leaves were yet left on the boughs; but they were sere and withered. And the birds chirped at times; but their note was mournful and complaining. All within this house, until Harley's arrival, had been strange and saddening to Helen's timid and subdued spirits. Lady Lansmere had received her kindly, but with a certain restraint; and the loftiness of manner, common to the Countess with all but Harley, had awed and chilled the diffident orphan. Lady Lansmere's very interest in Harley's choice—her attempts to draw Helen out of her reserve—her watchful eyes whenever Helen shyly spoke, or shyly moved, frightened the poor child, and made her unjust to herself.

The very servants, though staid, grave, and respectful, as suited a dignified, old-fashioned household, painfully contrasted the bright welcoming smiles and free talk of Italian domestics. Her recollections of the happy warm Continental manner, which so sets the bashful at their ease, made the stately and cold precision of all around her doubly awful and dispiriting. Lord Lansmere himself, who did not as yet know the views of Harley, and little dreamed that he was to anticipate a daughter-in-law in the ward, whom he understood Harley, in a freak of generous romance, had adopted, was familiar and courteous, as became a host. But he looked upon Helen as a mere child, and naturally left her to the Countess. The dim sense of her equivocal position—of her comparative humbleness of birth and fortunes, oppressed and pained her; and even her gratitude to Harley was made burthensome by a sentiment of helplessness. The grateful long to requite. And what could she ever do for him?

Thus musing, she wandered alone through the curving walks; and this sort of mock country landscape—London loud, and even visible, beyond the high gloomy walls, and no escape from the windows of the square formal house—seemed a type of the prison bounds of Rank to one whose soul yearns for simple loving Nature.

Helen's reverie was interrupted by Nero's joyous bark. He had caught sight of her, and came bounding up, and thrust his large head into her hand. As she stooped to caress the dog, happy at his honest greeting, and tears that had been long gathering to the lids fell silently on his face (for I know nothing that more moves us to tears than the hearty kindness of a dog, when something in human beings has pained or chilled us), she heard behind the musical voice of Harley. Hastily she dried or repressed her tears, as her guardian come up, and drew her arm within his own.

"I had so little of your conversation last evening, my dear ward, that I may well monopolise you now, even to the privation of Nero. And so you are once more in your native land?"

Helen sighed softly.

"May I not hope that you return under fairer auspices than those which your childhood knew?"

Helen turned her eyes with ingenuous thankfulness to her guardian, and the memory of all she owed to him rushed upon her heart.

Harley renewed, and with earnest, though melancholy

sweetness—" Helen, your eyes thank me; but hear me before your words do. I deserve no thanks. I am about to make to you a strange confession of egotism and selfishness."

"You!—oh, impossible!"

"Judge yourself, and then decide which of us shall have cause to be grateful. Helen, when I was scarcely your age—a boy in years, but more, methinks, a man at heart, with man's strong energies and sublime aspirings, than I have ever since been—I loved, and deeply—"

He paused a moment, in evident struggle. Helen listened in mute surprise, but his emotion awakened her own; her tender woman's heart yearned to console. Unconsciously her arm rested on his less lightly.

"Deeply, and for sorrow. It is a long tale, that may be told hereafter. The worldly would call my love a madness. I did not reason on it then—I cannot reason on it now. Enough: death smote suddenly, terribly, and to me mysteriously, her whom I loved. The love lived on. Fortunately, perhaps, for me, I had quick distraction, not to grief, but to its inert indulgence. I was a soldier; I joined our armies. Men called me brave. Flattery! I was a coward before the thought of life. I sought death: like sleep, it does not come at our call. Peace ensued. As when the winds fall the sails droop—so when excitement ceased, all seemed to me flat and objectless. Heavy, heavy was my heart. Perhaps grief had been less obstinate, but that I feared I had causes for self-reproach. Since then I have been a wanderer—a self-made exile. My boyhood had been ambitious—all ambition ceased. Flames, when they reach the core of the heart, spread, and leave all in ashes. Let me be brief: I did not mean thus weakly to complain—I to whom Heaven has given so many blessings! I felt, as it were, separated from the common objects and joys of men. I grew startled to see how, year by year, wayward humours possessed me. I resolved again to attach myself to some living heart—it was my sole chance to rekindle my own. But the one I had loved remained as my type of woman, and she was different from all I saw. Therefore I said to myself, 'I will rear from childhood some young fresh life, to grow up into my ideal.' As this thought began to haunt me, I chanced to discover you. Struck with the romance of your early life, touched by your courage, charmed by your affectionate nature, I said to myself, 'Here is what I seek.' Helen, in assuming the guardianship of your life, in all the culture which I have sought to bestow on your docile childhood, I repeat, that I have been but the egotist. And now, when you have reached that age, when it becomes me to speak, and you to listen—now, when you are under the sacred roof of my own mother—now I ask you, can you accept this heart, such as wasted years, and griefs too fondly nursed, have left it? Can you be, at least, my comforter? Can you aid me to regard life as a duty, and recover those aspirations which once soared from the paltry and miserable confines of our frivolous daily being? Helen, here I ask you, can you be all this, and under the name of—Wife?"

It would be in vain to describe the rapid, varying, indefinable emotions that passed through the inexperienced heart of the youthful listener as Harley thus spoke. He so moved all the springs of amaze, compassion, tender respect, sympathy, childlike gratitude, that when he paused and gently took her hand, she remained bewildered, speechless, overpowered. Harley smiled as he gazed upon her blushing, downcast, expressive face. He conjectured at once that the idea of such proposals had never crossed her mind; that she had never contemplated him in the character of wooer; never even sounded her heart as to the nature of such feelings as his image had aroused.

"My Helen," he resumed, with a calm pathos of voice, "there is some disparity of years between us, and perhaps I may not hope henceforth for that love which youth gives to the young. Permit me simply to ask, what you will frankly answer—'Can you have seen in our quiet life abroad, or under the roof of your Italian friends, any one you prefer to me?'"

"No, indeed, no!" murmured Helen. "How could I?—who is like you?" Then, with a sudden effort—for her innate truthfulness took alarm, and her very affection for Harley, childlike and reverent, made her tremble lest she should deceive him—she drew a little aside, and spoke thus:—

"Oh my dear guardian, noblest of all human beings, at least in my eyes, forgive, forgive me, if I seem ungrateful, hesitating; but I cannot, cannot think of myself as worthy of you. I never so lifted my eyes. Your rank, your position—"

"Why should they be eternally my curse? Forget them, and go on."

"It is not only they," said Helen, almost sobbing, "though they are much; but I your type, your ideal!—I?—impos sible! Oh, how can I ever be anything even of use, of aid, of comfort to one like you!"

"You can, Helen—you can," cried Harley, charmed by such ingenuous modesty. "May I not keep this hand?"

And Helen left her hand in Harley's, and turned away her face, fairly weeping. A stately step passed under the wintry trees.

"My mother," said Harley L'Estrange, looking up, "I present to you my future wife."

## CHAPTER IX.

WITH a slow step and an abstracted air, Harley L'Estrange bent his way towards Egerton's house, after his eventful interview with Helen. He had just entered one of the streets leading into Grosvenor Square, when a young man, walking quickly from the opposite direction, came full against him, and drawing back with a brief apology, recognised him, and exclaimed, "What! you in England, Lord L'Estrange! Accept my congratulations on your return. But you seem scarcely to remember me."

"I beg your pardon, Mr. Leslie. I remember you now by your smile; but you are of an age in which it is permitted me to say that you look older than when I saw you last."

"And yet, Lord L'Estrange, it seems to me that you look younger."

Indeed, this reply was so far true that there appeared less difference of years than before between Leslie and L'Estrange; for the wrinkles in the schemer's mind were visible in his visage, while Harley's dreamy worship of Truth and Beauty, seemed to have preserved to the votary the enduring youth of the divinities.

Harley received the compliment with a supreme indifference, which might have been suitable to a Stoic, but which seemed scarcely natural to a gentleman who had just proposed to a lady many years younger than himself.

Leslie renewed—"Perhaps you are on your way to Mr. Egerton's. If so, you will not find him at home; he is at his office."

"Thank you. Then to his office I must re-direct my steps."

"I am going to him myself," said Randal, hesitatingly.

L'Estrange had no prepossessions in favour of Leslie, from the little he had seen of that young gentleman; but Randal's remark was an appeal to his habitual urbanity, and he replied, with well-bred readiness, "Let us be companions so far."

Randal accepted the arm proffered to him; and Lord L'Estrange, as is usual with one long absent from his native land, bore part as a questioner in the dialogue that ensued.

"Egerton is always the same man, I suppose—too busy for illness, and too firm for sorrow?"

"If he ever feel either, he will never stoop to complain. But, indeed, my dear lord, I should like much to know what you think of his health."

"How! You alarm me!"

"Nay, I did not mean to do that; and pray do not let him know that I went so far. But I have fancied that he looks a little worn and suffering."

"Poor Audley!" said L'Estrange, in a tone of deep affection. "I will sound him, and, be assured, without naming you; for I know well how little he likes to be supposed capable of human infirmity. I am obliged to you for your hint—obliged to you for your interest in one so dear to me."

And Harley's voice was more cordial to Randal than it had ever been before. He then began to inquire what Randal thought of the rumours that had reached himself as to the probable defeat of the Government, and how far Audley's spirits were affected by such risks. But Randal here, seeing that Harley could communicate nothing, was reserved and guarded.

"Loss of office could not, I think, affect a man like Audley," observed Lord L'Estrange. "He would be as great in opposition—perhaps greater; and as to emoluments—"

"The emoluments are good," interposed Randal, with a half sigh.

"Good enough, I suppose, to pay him back about a tenth of what his place costs our magnificent friend—No, I will say one thing for English statesmen, no man amongst them ever yet was the richer for place."

"And Mr. Egerton's private fortune must be large, I take for granted," said Randal, carelessly.

"It ought to be, if he has time to look to it."

Here they passed by the hotel in which lodged the Count di Peschiera.

"Randal stopped. "Will you excuse me for an instant? As we are passing this hotel, I will just leave my card here." So saying he gave his card to a waiter lounging by the door. "For the Count di Peschiera," said he aloud.

L'Estrange started; and as Randal again took his arm, said—"So that Italian lodges here? and you know him?"

"I know him but slightly, as one knows any foreigner who makes a sensation."

"He makes a sensation?"

"Naturally: for he is handsome, witty, and said to be very rich—that is, as long as he receives the revenues of his exiled kinsman."

"I see you are well informed, Mr. Leslie. And what is supposed to bring hither the Count di Peschiera?"

"I did hear something, which I did not quite understand, about a bet of his that he would marry his kinsman's daughter; and so, I conclude, secure to himself all the inheritance; and that he is therefore here to discover the kinsman and win the heiress. But probably you know the rights of the story, and can tell me what credit to give to such gossip."

"I know this at least, that if he did lay such a wager, I would advise you to take any odds against him that his backers may give," said L'Estrange drily; and while his lip quivered with anger, his eye gleamed with arch ironical humour.

"You think, then, that this poor kinsman will not need such an alliance in order to regain his estates?"

"Yes; for I never yet knew a rogue whom I would not bet against, when he backed his own luck as a rogue against Justice and Providence."

Randal winced, and felt as if an arrow had grazed his heart; but he soon recovered.

"And indeed there is another vague rumour that the young lady in question is married already—to some Englishman."

This time it was Harley who winced. "Good Heavens! that cannot be true—that would undo all! An Englishman just at this moment! But some Englishman of correspondent rank I trust, or at least one known for opinions opposed to what an Austrian would call Revolutionary doctrines?"

"I know nothing. But it was supposed, merely a private

gentleman of good family. Would not that suffice? Can the Austrian Court dictate a marriage to the daughter as a condition for grace to the father?"

"No—not that!" said Harley, greatly disturbed. "But put yourself in the position of any minister to one of the great European monarchies. Suppose a political insurgent, formidable for station and wealth, had been proscribed, much interest made on his behalf, a powerful party striving against it, and just when the minister is disposed to relent, he hears that the heiress to this wealth and this station is married to the native of a country in which sentiments friendly to the very opinions for which the insurgent was proscribed are popularly entertained, and thus that the fortune to be restored may be so employed as to disturb the national security—the existing order of things;—this, too, at the very time when a popular revolution has just occurred in France,* and its effects are felt most in the very land of the exile;—suppose all this, and then say if anything could be more untoward for the hopes of the banished man, or furnish his adversaries with stronger arguments against the restoration of his fortune? But pshaw—this must be a chimera! If true, I should have known of it."

"I quite agree with your lordship—there can be no truth in such a rumour. Some Englishman, hearing, perhaps, of the probable pardon of the exile, may have counted on an heiress, and spread the report in order to keep off other candidates. By your account, if successful in his suit, he might fail to find an heiress in the bride."

"No doubt of that. Whatever might be arranged, I can't conceive that he would be allowed to get at the fortune, though it might be held in suspense for his children. But indeed it so rarely happens that an Italian girl of high name marries a foreigner, that we must dismiss this notion with a smile at the long face of the hypothetical fortune-hunter. Heaven help him, if he exist!"

"Amen!" echoed Randal, devoutly.

"I hear that Peschiera's sister is returned to England. Do you know her too?"

"A little."

"My dear Mr. Leslie, pardon me if I take a liberty not

---

* As there have been so many Revolutions in France, it may be convenient to suggest that, according to the dates of this story, Harley no doubt alludes to that revolution which exiled Charles X. and placed Louis Philippe on the throne.

warranted by our acquaintance. Against the lady I say nothing. Indeed, I have heard some things which appear to entitle her to compassion and respect. But as to Peschiera, all who prize honour suspect him to be a knave—I know him to be one. Now, I think that the longer we preserve that abhorrence for knavery which is the generous instinct of youth, why, the fairer will be our manhood, and the more reverend our age. You agree with me?" And Harley suddenly turning, his eyes fell like a flood of light upon Randal's pale and secret countenance.

"To be sure," murmured the schemer.

Harley, surveying him, mechanically recoiled, and withdrew his arm.

Fortunately for Randal, who somehow or other felt himself slipped into a false position, he scarce knew how or why, he was here seized by the arm; and a clear, open, manly voice cried, "My dear fellow, how are you? I see you are engaged now; but look into my rooms when you can, in the course of the day."

And with a bow of excuse for his interruption, to Lord L'Estrange, the speaker was then turning away, when Harley said—

"No, don't let me take you from your friend, Mr. Leslie. And you need not be in a hurry to see Egerton; for I shall claim the privilege of older friendship for the first interview."

"It is Mr. Egerton's nephew, Frank Hazeldean."

"Pray, call him back, and present me to him. He has a face that would have gone far to reconcile Timon to Athens."

Randal obeyed, and after a few kindly words to Frank, Harley insisted on leaving the two young men together, and walked on to Downing Street with a brisker step.

---

## CHAPTER X.

"THAT Lord L'Estrange seems a very good fellow."

"So-so;—an effeminate humorist—says the most absurd things, and fancies them wise. Never mind him. You wanted to speak to me, Frank?"

"Yes; I am so obliged to you for introducing me to Levy. I must tell you how handsomely he has behaved."

"Stop; allow me to remind you that I did not introduce you to Levy; you had met him before at Borrowell's, if I recollect right, and he dined with us at the Clarendon—that is all I had to do with bringing you together. Indeed I rather cautioned you against him than not. Pray don't think I introduced you to a man who, however pleasant and perhaps honest, is still a money-lender. Your father would be justly angry with me if I had done so."

"Oh, pooh! you are prejudiced against poor Levy. But just hear: I was sitting very ruefully, thinking over those cursed bills, and how the deuce I should renew them, when Levy walked into my rooms; and, after telling me of his long friendship for my uncle Egerton and his admiration for yourself, and (give me your hand, Randal) saying how touched he felt by your kind sympathy in my troubles, he opened his pocket-book, and showed me the bills safe and sound in his own possession."

"How?"

"He had bought them up. 'It must be so disagreeable to me,' he said, 'to have them flying about the London money-market, and those Jews would be sure sooner or later to apply to my father. And now,' added Levy, 'I am in no immediate hurry for the money, and we must put the interest upon fairer terms.' In short, nothing could be more liberal than his tone. And he says, 'he is thinking of a way to relieve me altogether, and will call about it in a few days, when his plan is matured.' After all, I must owe this to you, Randal. I dare swear you put it into his head."

"O no, indeed! On the contrary, I still say, 'Be cautious in all your dealings with Levy.' I don't know, I'm sure, what he means to propose. Have you heard from the Hall lately?"

"Yes—to-day. Only think—the Riccaboccas have disappeared. My mother writes me word of it—a very odd letter. She seems to suspect that I know where they are, and reproaches me for 'mystery'—quite enigmatical. But there is one sentence in her letter—see, here it is in the postscript—which seems to refer to Beatrice: 'I don't ask you to tell me your secrets, Frank, but Randal will no doubt have assured you that my first consideration will be for your own happiness, in any matter in which your heart is really engaged.'"

"Yes," said Randal, slowly; "no doubt this refers to Beatrice; but, as I told you, your mother will not interfere one way or the other—such interference would weaken her influence with the Squire. Besides, as she said, she can't *wish* you to marry a foreigner; though once married, she would—— But how do you stand now with the Marchesa? Has she consented to accept you?"

"Not quite; indeed I have not actually proposed. Her manner, though much softened, has not so far emboldened me; and, besides, before a positive declaration, I certainly must go down to the Hall and speak at least to my mother."

"You must judge for yourself, but don't do anything rash: talk first to me. Here we are at my office. Good-bye; and —and pray believe that, in whatever you do with Levy, I have no hand in it."

## CHAPTER XI.

Towards the evening, Randal was riding fast on the road to Norwood. The arrival of Harley, and the conversation that had passed between that nobleman and Randal, made the latter anxious to ascertain how far Riccabocca was likely to learn L'Estrange's return to England, and to meet with him. For he felt that, should the latter come to know that Riccabocca, in his movements, had gone by Randal's advice, Harley would find that Randal had spoken to him disingenuously; and, on the other hand, Riccabocca, placed under the friendly protection of Lord L'Estrange, would no longer need Randal Leslie to defend him from the machinations of Peschiera. To a reader happily unaccustomed to dive into the deep and mazy recesses of a schemer's mind, it might seem that Randal's interest in retaining a hold over the exile's confidence would terminate with the assurances that had reached him, from more than one quarter, that Violante might cease to be an heiress if she married himself. "But perhaps," suggests some candid and youthful conjecturer—" perhaps Randal Leslie is in love with this fair creature?" Randal in love!—no! He was too absorbed by harder passions for that blissful folly. Nor, if he could have fallen in love, was Violante the one to attract that sullen, secret heart; her instinctive nobleness, the very stateliness of her beauty, womanlike though it was, awed him. Men of that kind may love some soft slave—they cannot lift their eyes to a queen. They may look down—they cannot look up. But, on the one hand, Randal could not resign altogether the *chance* securing a fortune that would realise his most dazzling dreams, upon the mere assurance, however probable, which had so dismayed him; and, on the other hand, should he be compelled to relinquish all idea of such alliance, though he did not contemplate the base perfidy of actually assisting Peschiera's avowed designs, still, if Frank's marriage with Beatrice should absolutely depend upon her brother's obtaining the knowledge of Violante's retreat, and that marriage should be as conducive to his interests as he thought he could make it, why,—he did not then push his deductions farther, even to himself—they seemed too black; but he sighed heavily, and that sigh foreboded how weak would be honour and virtue against avarice and ambition. Therefore, on all accounts, Riccabocca was one of those cards in a sequence, which so calculating a player would not throw out of his hand: it *might* serve for repique—at the worst it might score well in the game. Intimacy with the Italian was still part and parcel in that knowledge which was the synonym of power.

While the young man was thus meditating, on his road to Norwood, Riccabocca and his Jemima were close conferring in their drawing-room. And if you could have there seen them, reader, you would have been seized with equal surprise and curiosity: for some extraordinary communication had certainly passed between them. Riccabocca was evidently much agitated, and with emotions not familiar to him. The tears stood in his eyes at the same time that a smile the reverse of cynical or sardonic, curved his lips; while his wife was leaning her head on his shoulder, her hand clasped in his, and, by the expression of her face, you might guess that he had paid her some very gratifying compliment, of a nature more genuine and sincere than those which characterised his habitual hollow and dissimulating gallantry. But just at this moment Giacomo entered, and Jemima, with her native English modesty, withdrew in haste from Riccabocca's sheltering side.

"Padrone," said Giacomo, who, whatever his astonishment at the connubial position he had disturbed, was much too discreet to betray it—"Padrone, I see the young Englishman riding towards the house, and I hope when he arrives, you will not forget the alarming information I gave to you this morning."

"Ah—ah!" said Riccabocca, his face falling.

"If the Signorina were but married!"

"My very thought—my constant thought!" exclaimed Riccabocca. "And you really believe the young Englishman loves her?"

"Why else should he come, Excellency?" asked Giacomo, with great *naïveté*.

"Very true; why, indeed?" said Riccabocca. "Jemima, I cannot endure the terrors I suffer on that poor child's account. I will open myself frankly to Randal Leslie. And now, too, that which might have been a serious consideration, in case I return to Italy, will no longer stand in our way, Jemima."

Jemima smiled faintly, and whispered something to Riccabocca, to which he replied—

"Nonsense, *anima mia*. I know it *will* be—have not a doubt of it. I tell you it is as nine to four, according to the nicest calculations. I will speak at once to Randal. He is too young—too timid to speak himself."

"Certainly," interposed Giacomo; "how could he dare to speak, let him love ever so well?"

Jemima shook her head.

"Oh, never fear," said Riccabocca, observing this gesture; "I will give him the trial. If he entertain but mercenary views, I shall soon detect them. I know human nature pretty well, I think, my love; and, Giacomo,—just get me my Machiavelli;—that's right. Now leave me, my dear; I must reflect and prepare myself."

When Randal entered the house, Giacomo, with a smile of peculiar suavity, ushered him into the drawing-room. He found Riccabocca alone, and seated before the fire-place, leaning his face on his hand, with the great folio of Machiavelli lying open on the table.

The Italian received him as courteously as usual; but there was in his manner a certain serious and thoughtful dignity, which was perhaps the more imposing, because but rarely assumed. After a few preliminary observations, Randal remarked that Frank Hazeldean had informed him of the curiosity which the disappearance of the Riccaboccas had excited at the Hall, and inquired carelessly if the Doctor had left instructions as to the forwarding of any letters that might be directed to him at the Casino.

"Letters," said Riccabocca, simply, "I never receive any; or, at least, so rarely, that it was not worth while to take an event so little to be expected into consideration. No; if any letters do reach the Casino, there they will wait."

"Then I can see no possibility of indiscretion; no chance of a clue to your address."

"Nor I either."

Satisfied so far, and knowing that it was not in Riccabocca's habits to read the newspapers, by which he might otherwise have learnt of L'Estrange's arrival in London, Randal then proceeded to inquire, with much seeming interest, into the health of Violante—hoped it did not suffer by confinement, &c. Riccabocca eyed him gravely while he spoke, and then suddenly rising, that air of dignity to which I have before referred, became yet more striking.

"My young friend," said he, "hear me attentively, and answer me frankly. I know human nature—" Here a slight smile of proud complacency passed the sage's lips, and his eye glanced toward his Machiavelli.

"I know human nature—at least I have studied it," he renewed more earnestly, and with less evident self-conceit; "and I believe that when a perfect stranger to me exhibits an interest in my affairs, which occasions him no small trouble —an interest (continued the wise man, laying his hand on Randal's shoulder) which scarcely a son could exceed, he must be under the influence of some strong personal motive."

"Oh, sir!" cried Randal, turning a shade more pale, and with a faltering tone. Riccabocca surveyed him with the tenderness of a superior being, and pursued his deductive theories.

"In your case, what is that motive? Not political; for I conclude you share the opinions of your government, and those opinions have not favoured mine. Not that of pecuniary or ambitious calculations; for how can such calculations enlist you on behalf of a ruined exile? What remains? Why, the motive which at your age is ever the most natural and the strongest. I don't blame you. Machiavelli himself allows that such a motive has swayed the wisest minds, and overturned the most solid states. In a word, young man, you are in love, and with my daughter Violante."

Randal was so startled by this direct and unexpected charge upon his own masked batteries, that he did not even attempt his defence. His head drooped on his breast, and he remained speechless.

"I do not doubt," resumed the penetrating judge of human nature, "that you would have been withheld by the laudable and generous scruples which characterise your happy age, from voluntarily disclosing to me the state of your heart.

You might suppose that, proud of the position I once held, or sanguine in the hope of regaining my inheritance, I might be over-ambitious in my matrimonial views for Violante; or that you, anticipating my restoration to honours and fortune, might seem actuated by the last motives which influence love and youth; and, therefore, my dear young friend, I have departed from the ordinary custom in England, and adopted a very common one in my own country. With us, a suitor seldom presents himself till he is assured of the consent of a father. I have only to say this—if I am right, and you love my daughter, my first object in life is to see her safe and secure; and, in a word—you understand me."

Now, mightily may it comfort and console us ordinary mortals, who advance no pretence to superior wisdom and ability, to see the huge mistakes made by both these very sagacious personages—Dr. Riccabocca, valuing himself on his profound acquaintance with character, and Randal Leslie, accustomed to grope into every hole and corner of thought and action, wherefrom to extract that knowledge which is power! For whereas the sage, judging not only by his own heart in youth, but by the general influence of the master passion on the young, had ascribed to Randal sentiments wholly foreign to that able diplomatist's nature; so no sooner had Riccabocca brought his speech to a close, than Randal, judging also by his own heart, and by the general laws which influence men of the mature age and boasted worldly wisdom of the pupil of Machiavelli, instantly decided that Riccabocca presumed upon his youth and inexperience, and meant most nefariously to take him in.

"The poor youth!" thought Riccabocca, "how unprepared he is for the happiness I give him!"

"The cunning old Jesuit!" thought Randal; "he has certainly learned, since we met last, that he has no chance of regaining his patrimony, and so he wants to impose on me the hand of a girl without a shilling. What other motive can he possibly have! Had his daughter the remotest probability of becoming the greatest heiress in Italy, would he dream of bestowing her on me in this off-hand way? The thing stands to reason."

Actuated by his resentment at the trap thus laid for him, Randal was about to disclaim altogether the disinterested and absurd affection laid to his charge, when it occurred to him that, by so doing, he might mortally offend the Italian—since the cunning never forgive those who refuse to be duped by them—and it might still be conducive to his interest to preserve intimate and familiar terms with Riccabocca; therefore, subduing his first impulse, he exclaimed,

"O too generous man! pardon me if I have so long been unable to express my amaze, my gratitude; but I cannot—no, I cannot, while your prospects remain thus uncertain, avail myself of your—of your inconsiderate magnanimity. Your rare conduct can only redouble my own scruples, if you, as I firmly hope and believe, are restored to your great possessions —you would naturally look so much higher than me. Should these hopes fail, then, indeed, it may be different; yet even then, what position, what fortune, have I to offer to your daughter worthy of her?"

"You are well born! all gentlemen are equals," said Riccabocca, with a sort of easy nobleness. "You have youth, information, talent—sources of certain wealth in this happy country — powerful connections; and, in fine, if you are satisfied with marrying for love, I shall be contented;—if not, speak openly. As to the restoration to my possessions, I can scarcely think that probable while my enemy lives. And even in that case, since I saw you last, something has occurred (added Riccabocca, with a strange smile, which seemed to Randal singularly sinister and malignant) that may remove all difficulties. Meanwhile, do not think me so extravagantly magnanimous—do not underrate the satisfaction I must feel at knowing Violante safe from the designs of Peschiera— safe, and for ever, under a husband's roof. I will tell you an Italian proverb—it contains a truth full of wisdom and terror:—

"'Hai cinquanta Amici?—non basta.—Hai un Nemico?—è troppo.'"*

"Something has occurred!" echoed Randal, not heeding the conclusion of this speech, and scarcely hearing the proverb which the sage delivered in his most emphatic and tragic tone. "Something has occurred! My dear friend, be plainer. What has occurred?" Riccabocca remained silent. "Something that induces you to bestow your daughter on me?"

Riccabocca nodded, and emitted a low chuckle.

"The very laugh of a fiend," muttered Randal. "Something that makes her not worth bestowing. He betrays himself. Cunning people always do."

---

* Have you fifty friends?—it is not enough.—Have you one enemy?—it is too much.

"Pardon me," said the Italian at last, "if I don't answer your question; you will know later; but, at present, this is a family secret. And now I must turn to another and more alarming cause for my frankness to you." Here Riccabocca's face changed, and assumed an expression of mingled rage and fear. "You must know," he added, sinking his voice, "that Giacomo has seen a strange person loitering about the house, and looking up at the windows; and he has no doubt—nor have I—that this is some spy or emissary of Peschiera's."

"Impossible; how could he discover you?"

"I know not; but no one else has any interest in doing so. The man kept at a distance, and Giacomo could not see his face."

"It may be but a mere idler. Is this all?"

"No; the old woman who serves us said that she was asked at a shop 'if we were not Italians?'"

"And she answered?"

"'No;' but owned that 'we had a foreign servant, Giacomo.'"

"I will see to this. Rely on it that if Peschiera has discovered you, I will learn it. Nay, I will hasten from you in order to commence inquiry."

"I cannot detain you. May I think that we have now an interest in common?"

"O, indeed yes; but—but—your daughter! how can I dream that one so beautiful, so peerless, will confirm the hope you have extended to me?"

"The daughter of an Italian is brought up to consider that it is a father's right to dispose of her hand."

"But the heart?"

"*Cospetto!*" said the Italian, true to his infamous notions as to the sex, "the heart of a girl is like a convent—the holier the cloister, the more charitable the door."

## CHAPTER XII.

RANDAL had scarcely left the house before Mrs. Riccabocca, who was affectionately anxious in all that concerned Violante, rejoined her husband.

"I like the young man very well," said the sage—"very well indeed. I find him just what I expected, from my general knowledge of human nature; for as love ordinarily goes with youth, so modesty usually accompanies talent. He is young, *ergo* he is in love; he has talent, *ergo* he is modest—modest and ingenuous."

"And you think not in any way swayed by interest in his affections?"

"Quite the contrary; and to prove him the more, I have not said a word as to the worldly advantages which, in any case, would accrue to him from an alliance with my daughter. In any case; for if I regain my country, her fortune is assured; and if not, I trust (said the poor exile, lifting his brow with stately and becoming pride) that I am too well aware of my child's dignity, as well as my own, to ask any one to marry her to his own worldly injury."

"Eh! I don't quite understand you, Alphonso. To be sure, your dear life is insured for her marriage portion; but—"

"*Pazzie*—stuff!" said Riccabocca, petulantly; "her marriage portion would be as nothing to a young man of Randal's birth and prospects. I think not of that. But listen: I have never consented to profit by Harley L'Estrange's friendship for me; my scruples would not extend to my son-in-law. This noble friend has not only high rank, but considerable influence —influence with the government—influence with Randal's patron—who, between ourselves, does not seem to push the young man as he might do; I judge by what Randal says. I should write, therefore, before anything was settled, to L'Estrange, and I should say to him simply, 'I never asked you to save me from penury, but I do ask you to save a daughter of my house from humiliation. I can give to her no dowry; can her husband owe to my friend that advance in an honourable career—that opening to energy and talent—which is more than a dowry to generous ambition?"

"Oh, it is in vain you would disguise your rank," cried Jemima, with enthusiasm, "it speaks in all you utter, when your passions are moved."

The Italian did not seem flattered by that eulogy. "Pish," said he, "there you are! rank again!"

But Jemima was right. There was something about her husband that was grandiose and princely, whenever he escaped from his accursed Machiavelli, and gave fair play to his heart.

And he spent the next hour or so in thinking over all that he could do for Randal, and devising for his intended son-in-law the agreeable surprises, which Randal was at that very time racking his yet cleverer brains to disappoint.

These plans conned sufficiently, Riccabocca shut up his Machiavelli, and hunted out of his scanty collection of books Buffon on Man, and various other psychological volumes, in which he soon became deeply absorbed. Why were these works the object of the sage's study? Perhaps he will let us know soon, for it is clearly a secret known to his wife; and though she has hitherto kept one secret, that is precisely the reason why Riccabocca would not wish long to overburthen her discretion with another.

## CHAPTER XIII.

RANDAL reached home in time to dress for a late dinner at Baron Levy's.

The Baron's style of living was of that character especially affected both by the most acknowledged exquisites of that day, and, it must be owned, also, by the most egregious *parvenus*. For it is noticeable that it is your *parvenu* who always comes nearest in fashion (so far as externals are concerned) to your genuine exquisite. It is your *parvenu* who is most particular as to the cut of his coat, and the precision of his equipage, and the minutiæ of his *ménage*. Those between the *parvenu* and the exquisite who know their own consequence, and have something solid to rest upon, are slow in following all the caprices of fashion, and obtuse in observation as to those niceties which neither give them another ancestor, nor add another thousand to the account at their banker's;—as to the last, rather indeed the contrary! There was a decided elegance about the Baron's house and his dinner. If he had been one of the lawful kings of the dandies, you would have cried, "What perfect taste!"—but such is human nature, that the dandies who dined with him said to each other, "He pretend to imitate D——! vulgar dog!" There was little affectation of your more showy opulence. The furniture in the rooms was apparently simple, but, in truth, costly, from its luxurious comfort—the ornaments and china scattered about the commodes were of curious rarity and great value; and the pictures on the walls were gems. At dinner, no plate was admitted on the table. The Russian fashion, then uncommon, now more prevalent, was adopted—fruit and flowers in old

*Sèvres* dishes of priceless *vertu*, and in sparkling glass of Bohemian fabric. No livery servant was permitted to wait; behind each guest stood a gentleman dressed so like the guest himself, in fine linen and simple black, that guest and lacquey seemed stereotypes from one plate.

The viands were exquisite; the wine came from the cellars of deceased archbishops and ambassadors. The company was select; the party did not exceed eight. Four were the eldest sons of peers, (from a baron to a duke;) one was a professed wit, never to be got without a month's notice, and, where a *parvenu* was host, a certainty of green peas and peaches—out of season; the sixth, to Randal's astonishment, was Mr. Richard Avenel; himself and the Baron made up the complement.

The eldest sons recognized each other with a meaning smile; the most juvenile of them, indeed, (it was his first year in London,) had the grace to blush and look sheepish. The others were more hardened; but they all united in regarding with surprise both Randal and Dick Avenel. The former was known to most of them personally, and to all, by repute, as a grave, clever, promising young man, rather prudent than lavish, and never suspected to have got into a scrape. What the deuce did he do there? Mr. Avenel puzzled them yet more. A middle-aged man, said to be in business, whom they had observed "about town" (for he had a noticeable face and figure)—that is, seen riding in the park, or lounging in the pit at the opera, but never set eyes on at a recognized club, or in the coteries of their "set;" a man whose wife gave horrid third-rate parties, that took up half a column in the *Morning Post* with a list of "The Company Present," in which a sprinkling of dowagers fading out of fashion, and a foreign title or two, made the darkness of the obscurer names doubly dark. Why this man should be asked to meet *them*, by Baron Levy, too—a decided tuft-hunt and would-be exclusive— called all their faculties into exercise. The wit, who, being the son of a small tradesman, but in the very best society, gave himself far greater airs than the young lords, impertinently solved the mystery.—"Depend on it," whispered he to Spendquick—"depend on it the man is the X.Y. of the *Times* who offers to lend any sum of money from £10 to half-a-million. He's the man who has all your bills; Levy is only his jackal."

"'Pon my soul," said Spendquick, rather alarmed, "if that's the case, one may as well be civil to him."

"*You*, certainly," said the wit. "But I never have found an X.Y. who would advance me the L. s.; and therefore, I shall not be more respectful to X.Y. than to any other unknown quantity."

By degrees, as the wine circulated, the party grew gay and sociable. Levy was really an entertaining fellow; had all the gossip of the town at his fingers' ends; and possessed, moreover, that pleasant art of saying ill-natured things of the absent, which those present always enjoy. By degrees, too, Mr. Richard Avenel came out; and, as the whisper had circulated round the table that he was X.Y., he was listened to with a profound respect, which greatly elevated his spirits. Nay, when the wit tried once to show him up or mystify him, Dick answered with a bluff spirit, that, though very coarse, was found so humorous by Lord Spendquick and other gentlemen similarly situated in the money-market, that they turned the laugh against the wit, and silenced him for the rest of the night—a circumstance which made the party go off much more pleasantly. After dinner, the conversation, quite that of single men, easy and *débonnaire*, glanced from the turf, and the ballet, and the last scandal, towards politics; for the times were such that politics were discussed everywhere, and three of the young lords were county members.

Randal said little, but, as was his wont, listened attentively; and he was aghast to find how general was the belief that the Government was doomed. Out of regard to him, and with that delicacy of breeding which belongs to a certain society, nothing personal to Egerton was said, except by Avenel, who, however, on blurting out some rude expressions respecting that minister, was instantly checked by the Baron.

"Spare my friend, and Mr. Leslie's near connection," said he, with a polite but grave smile.

"Oh," said Avenel, "public men, whom we pay, are public property—aren't they, my lord?" appealing to Spendquick.

"Certainly," said Spendquick, with great spirit—"public property, or why should we pay them? There must be a very strong motive to induce us to do that! I hate paying people. In fact," he subjoined in an aside, "I never do."

"However," resumed Mr. Avenel, graciously, "I don't want to hurt your feelings, Mr. Leslie. As to the feelings of our host, the Baron, I calculate that they have got tolerably tough by the exercise they have gone through."

"Nevertheless," said the Baron, joining in the laugh which any lively saying by the supposed X.Y. was sure to excite—

"nevertheless, 'love me, love my dog,' love me, love my Egerton."

Randal started, for his quick ear and subtle intelligence caught something sinister and hostile in the tone with which Levy uttered this equivocal comparison, and his eye darted towards the Baron. But the Baron had bent down his face, and was regaling himself upon an olive.

By-and-by the party rose from table. The four young noblemen had their engagements elsewhere, and proposed to separate without re-entering the drawing-room. As, in Goethe's theory, monads which have affinities with each other are irresistibly drawn together, so these gay children of pleasure had, by a common impulse, on rising from table, moved each to each, and formed a group round the fireplace. Randal stood a little apart, musing; the wit examined the pictures through his eye-glass; and Mr. Avenel drew the Baron towards the sideboard, and there held him in whispered conference. This colloquy did not escape the young gentlemen round the fireplace; they glanced towards each other.

"Settling the percentage on renewal," said one, *sotto voce*.

"X.Y. does not seem such a very bad fellow," said another.

"He looks rich, and talks rich," said a third.

"A decided independent way of expressing his sentiments; those moneyed men generally have."

"Good heavens!" ejaculated Spendquick, who had been keeping his eye anxiously fixed on the pair, "do look; X.Y. is actually taking out his pocket-book; he is coming this way. Depend on it he has got our bills—mine is due to-morrow!"

"And mine too," said another, edging off. "Why, it is a perfect *guet-apens*."

Meanwhile, breaking away from the Baron, who appeared anxious to detain him, and failing in that attempt, turned aside, as if not to see Dick's movements—a circumstance which did not escape the notice of the group, and confirmed all their suspicions, Mr. Avenel, with a serious, thoughtful face, and a slow step, approached the group. Nor did the great Roman general more nervously "flutter the dove-cots in Corioli," than did the advance of the supposed X.Y. agitate the bosoms of Lord Spendquick and his sympathising friends. Pocket-book in hand, and apparently feeling for something formidable within its mystic recesses, step by step came Dick Avenel towards the fireplace. The group stood still, fascinated by horror.

"Hum," said Mr. Avenel, clearing his throat.

## VARIETIES IN ENGLISH LIFE. 127

"I don't like that hum at all," muttered Spendquick.

"Proud to have made your acquaintance, gentlemen," said Dick, bowing.

The gentlemen, thus addressed, bowed low in return.

"My friend the Baron thought this not exactly the time to—" Dick stopped a moment; you might have knocked down those four young gentlemen, though four finer specimens of humanity no aristocracy in Europe could produce— you might have knocked them down with a feather! "But," renewed Avenel, not finishing his sentence, "I have made it a rule in life never to lose securing a good opportunity; in short, to make the most of the present moment. And," added he, with a smile which froze the blood in Lord Spendquick's veins, "the rule has made me a very warm man! Therefore, gentlemen, allow me to present you each with one of these "—every hand retreated behind the back of its wellborn owner—when, to the inexpressible relief of all, Dick concluded with—" a little *soirée dansante*," and extended four cards of invitation.

"Most happy!" exclaimed Spendquick. "I don't dance in general; but to oblige X—— I mean to have a better acquaintance, sir, with *you*—I would dance on the tightrope."

There was a good-humoured, pleasant laugh at Spendquick's enthusiasm, and a general shaking of hands and pocketing of the invitation cards.

"You don't look like a dancing man," said Avenel, turning to the wit, who was plump and somewhat gouty—as wits who dine out five days in the week generally are; "but we shall have supper at one o'clock."

Infinitely offended and disgusted, the wit replied, drily, "that every hour of his time was engaged for the rest of the season," and, with a stiff salutation to the Baron, took his departure. The rest, in good spirits, hurried away to their respective cabriolets; and Leslie was following them into the hall, when the Baron, catching hold of him, said, "Stay, I want to talk to you."

## CHAPTER XIV.

THE Baron turned into his drawing-room, and Leslie followed.

"Pleasant young men, those," said Levy, with a slight sneer, as he threw himself into an easy chair and stirred the fire. "And not at all proud; but, to be sure, they are—under great obligations to me. Yes; they owe me a great deal. *Apropos,* I have had a long talk with Frank Hazeldean—fine young man—remarkable capacities for business. I can arrange his affairs for him. I find, on reference to the Will Office, that you were quite right; the Casino property is entailed on Frank. He will have the fee simple. He can dispose of the reversion entirely. So that there will be no difficulty in our arrangements."

"But I told you also that Frank had scruples about borrowing on the event of his father's death."

"Ay—you did so. Filial affection! I never take that into account in matters of business. Such little scruples, though they are highly honourable to human nature, soon vanish before the prospect of the King's Bench. And, too, as you so judiciously remarked, our clever young friend is in love with Madame di Negra."

"Did he tell you that?"

"No; but Madame di Negra did!"

"You know her?"

"I know most people in good society, who now and then require a friend in the management of their affairs. And having made sure of the fact you stated, as to Hazeldean's contingent property (excuse my prudence), I have accommodated Madame di Negra, and bought up her debts."

"You have—you surprise me!"

"The surprise will vanish on reflection. But you are very new to the world yet, my dear Leslie. By the way, I have had an interview with Peschiera—"

"About his sister's debts?"

"Partly. A man of the nicest honour is Peschiera."

Aware of Levy's habit of praising people for the qualities in which, according to the judgment of less penetrating mortals, they were most deficient, Randal only smiled at this eulogy, and waited for Levy to resume. But the Baron sate silent and thoughtful for a minute or two, and then wholly changed the subject.

"I think your father has some property in ——shire, and you probably can give me a little information as to certain estates of a Mr. Thornhill, estates which, on examination of the title-deeds, I find once, indeed, belonged to your family." The Baron glanced at a very elegant memorandum-book.— "The manors of Rood and Dulmansberry, with sundry farms thereon. Mr. Thornhill wants to sell them—an old client of mine, Thornhill. He has applied to me on the matter. Do you think it an improvable property?"

Randal listened with a livid cheek and a throbbing heart. We have seen that, if there was one ambitious scheme in his calculation which, though not absolutely generous and heroic, still might win its way to a certain sympathy in the undebased human mind, it was the hope to restore the fallen fortunes of his ancient house, and repossess himself of the long alienated lands that surrounded the dismal wastes of the mouldering hall. And now to hear that those lands were getting into the inexorable gripe of Levy—tears of bitterness stood in his eyes.

"Thornhill," continued Levy, who watched the young man's countenance—"Thornhill tells me that that part of his property—the old Leslie lands—produces £2000 a-year, and that the rental could be raised. He would take £50,000 for it—£20,000 down, and suffer the remaining £30,000 to lie on mortgage at four per cent. It seems a very good purchase. What do you say?"

"Don't ask me," said Randal, stung into rare honesty; "for I had hoped I might live to repossess myself of that property."

"Ah! indeed. It would be a very great addition to your consequence in the world—not from the mere size of the estate, but from its hereditary associations. And if you have any idea of the purchase—believe me, I'll not stand in your way."

"How can I have any idea of it?"

"But I thought you said you had."

"I understood that these lands could not be sold till Mr. Thornhill's son came of age, and joined in getting rid of the entail."

"Yes, so Thornhill himself supposed, till, on examining the title-deeds, I found he was under a mistake. These lands are not comprised in the settlement made by old Jasper Thornhill, which ties up the rest of the property. The title will be perfect. Thornhill wants to settle the matter at once—losses on the turf, you understand; an immediate purchaser would get still better terms. A Sir John Spratt would give the money;—but the addition of these lands would make the Spratt property of more consequence in the county than the Thornhill. So my client would rather take a few thousands less from a man who don't set up to be his rival. Balance of power in counties as well as nations."

Randal was silent.

"Well," said Levy, with great kindness of manner, "I see I pain you; and though I am what my very pleasant guests would call a *parvenu*, I comprehend your natural feelings as a gentleman of ancient birth. *Parvenu!* Ah! is it not strange, Leslie, that no wealth, no fashion, no fame can wipe out that blot. They call me a *parvenu*, and borrow my money. They call our friend the wit, a *parvenu*, and submit to all his insolence—if they condescend to regard his birth at all— provided they can but get him to dinner. They call the best debater in the Parliament of England a *parvenu*, and will entreat him, some day or other, to be prime minister, and ask him for stars and garters. A droll world, and no wonder the *parvenus* want to upset it.

Randal had hitherto supposed that this notorious tuft- hunter—this dandy capitalist—this money-lender, whose whole fortune had been wrung from the wants and follies of an aristocracy, was naturally a firm supporter of things as they are—how could things be better for men like Baron Levy? But the usurer's burst of democratic spleen did not surprise his precocious and acute faculty of observation. He had before remarked, that it is the persons who fawn most upon an aristocracy, and profit the most by the fawning, who are ever at heart its bitterest disparagers. Why is this? Because one full half of democratic opinion is made up of envy; and we can only envy what is brought before our eyes, and what, while very near to us, is still unattainable. No man envies an archangel.

"But," said Levy, throwing himself back in his chair, "a new order of things is commencing; we shall see. Leslie, it is lucky for you that you did not enter parliament under the government; it would be your political ruin for life."

"You think, then, that the ministry really cannot last?"

"Of course I do; and what is more, I think that a ministry of the same principles cannot be restored. You are a young man of talent and spirit; your birth is nothing compared to the rank of the reigning party; it would tell, to a certain degree, in a democratic one. I say, you should be more civil to Avenel; he could return you to parliament at the next election."

"The next election! In six years! We have just had a general election."

"There will be another before this year, or half of it, or perhaps a quarter of it, is out."

"What makes you think so?"

"Leslie, let there be confidence between us; we can help each other. Shall we be friends?"

"With all my heart. But though you may help me, how can I help you?"

"You have helped me already to Frank Hazeldean and the Casino estate. All clever men can help me. Come, then, we are friends; and what I say is secret. You ask me why I think there will be a general election so soon? I will answer you frankly. Of all the public men I ever met with, there is no one who had so clear a vision of things immediately before him as Audley Egerton."

"He has that character. Not *far*-seeing, but *clear*-sighted to a certain limit."

"Exactly so. No one better, therefore, knows public opinion, and its immediate ebb and flow."

"Granted."

"Egerton, then, counts on a general election within three months; and I have lent him the money for it."

"Lent him the money! Egerton borrow money of you— the rich Audley Egerton!"

"Rich!" repeated Levy in a tone impossible to describe, and accompanying the word with that movement of the middle finger and thumb, commonly called a "snap," which indicates profound contempt.

He said no more. Randal sate stupified. At length the latter muttered, "But if Egerton is really not rich—if he lose office, and without the hope of return to it——"

"If so, he is ruined!" said Levy, coldly; "and therefore, from regard to you, and feeling interest in your future fate, I say—Rest no hopes of fortune or career upon Audley Egerton. Keep your place for the present, but be prepared at the next election to stand upon popular principles. Avenel shall return you to parliament; and the rest is with luck and energy. And now, I'll not detain you longer," said Levy, rising and ringing the bell. The servant entered.

"Is my carriage here?"

"Yes, Baron."

"Can I set you down anywhere?"

"No, thank you, I prefer walking."

"Adieu, then. And mind you remember the *soirée dansant*. at Mrs. Avenel's." Randal mechanically shook the hand extended to him, and went down the stairs.

The fresh frosty air roused his intellectual faculties, which Levy's ominous words had almost paralysed.

And the first thing the clever schemer said to himself was this—

"But what can be the man's motive in what he said to me?"

The next was—

"Egerton ruined! What am I, then?"

And the third was—

"And that fair remnant of the old Leslie property! £20,000 down—how to get the sum? Why should Levy have spoken to me of this?"

And lastly, the soliloquy rounded back—"The man's motives! His motives?"

Meanwhile, the Baron threw himself into his chariot—the most comfortable easy chariot you can possibly conceive—single man's chariot—perfect taste—no married man ever had such a chariot; and in a few minutes he was at ——'s hotel, and in the presence of Giulio Franzini, Count di Peschiera.

"*Mon cher*," said the Baron, in very good French, and in a tone of the most familiar equality with the descendant of the princes and heroes of grand mediæval Italy—"*Mon cher*, give me one of your excellent cigars. I think I have put all matters in train."

"You have found out—"

"No; not so fast yet," said the Baron, lighting the cigar extended to him. "But you said that you should be perfectly contented if it only cost you £20,000 to marry off your sister, (to whom that sum is legally due,) and to marry yourself to the heiress."

"I did, indeed."

"Then I have no doubt I shall manage both objects for that sum, if Randal Leslie really knows where the young lady is, and can assist you. Most promising able man is Randal Leslie—but innocent as a babe just born."

"Ha, ha! Innocent? *Que diable!*"

"Innocent as this cigar, *mon cher*—strong certainly, but smoked very easily. *Soyez tranquille!*"

## CHAPTER XV.

WHO has not seen, who not admired, that noble picture by Daniel Maclise, which refreshes the immortal name of my ancestor Caxton! For myself, while with national pride I heard the admiring murmurs of the foreigners who grouped around it (nothing, indeed, of which our nation may be more proud had they seen in the Crystal Palace)—heard, with no less a pride in the generous nature of fellow-artists, the warm applause of living and deathless masters, sanctioning the enthusiasm of the popular crowd;—what struck me more than the precision of drawing, for which the artist has been always renowned, and the just, though gorgeous affluence of colour which he has more recently acquired, was the profound depth of conception, out of which this great work had so elaborately arisen. That monk, with his scowl towards the printer and his back on the Bible over which *his form casts a shadow*—the whole transition between the mediæval Christianity of cell and cloister, and the modern Christianity that rejoices in the daylight, is depicted there, in the shadow that obscures the Book—in the scowl that is fixed upon the Book-diffuser;—that sombre, musing face of Richard, Duke of Gloucester, with the beauty of Napoleon, darkened to the expression of a Fiend, looking far and anxiously into futurity as if foreseeing there what antagonism was about to be created to the schemes of secret crime and unrelenting force;—the chivalrous head of the accomplished Rivers, seen but in profile, under his helmet, as if the age when Chivalry must defend its noble attributes, in steel, was already half passed away: and, not least grand of all, the rude thews and sinews of the artisan forced into service on the type, and the ray of intellect, fierce, and menacing revolutions yet to be, struggling through his rugged features, and across his low knitted brow;—all this, which showed how deeply the idea of the discovery in its good and its evil, its saving light and its perilous storms, had sunk into the artist's soul, charmed me as effecting the exact union between sentiment and execution, which is the true and rare consummation of the Ideal in Art. But observe, while in these personages of the group are depicted the deeper and graver agencies implicated in the bright but terrible invention—observe how little the light epicures of the hour heed the scowl of the monk, or the restless gesture of Richard, or the troubled gleam in the eyes of the artisan—King Edward, handsome *Poco curante*, delighted in the surprise of a child, with a new toy; and Clarence, with his curious, yet careless, glance—all the while Caxton himself, calm, serene, untroubled, intent solely upon the manifestation of his discovery, and no doubt supremely indifferent whether the first proofs of it shall be dedicated to a Rivers or an Edward, a Richard or a Henry, Plantagenet or Tudor—'tis all the same to that comely, gentle-looking man. So is it ever with your Abstract Science!—not a jot cares its passionless logic for the woe or weal of a generation or two. The stream, once emerged from its source, passes on into the great Intellectual Sea, smiling over the wretch that it drowns, or under the keel of the ship which it serves as a slave.

Now, when about to commence the present chapter on the Varieties of Life, this masterpiece of thoughtful art forced itself on my recollection, and illustrated what I designed to convey. In the surface of every age, it is often that which but amuses, for the moment, the ordinary children of pleasant existence, the Edwards and the Clarences (be they kings and dukes, or simplest of simple subjects), which afterwards towers out as the great serious epoch of the time. When we look back upon human records, how the eye settles upon WRITERS as the main land-marks of the past! We talk of the age of Augustus, of Elizabeth, of Louis XIV., of Anne, as the notable eras of the world. Why? Because it is their writers who have made them so. Intervals between one age of authors and another lie unnoticed, as the flats and common lands of uncultured history. And yet, strange to say, when these authors are living amongst us, they occupy a very small portion of our thoughts, and fill up but desultory interstices in the bitumen and tufo wherefrom we build up the Babylon of our lives! So it is, and perhaps so it should be, whether it pleases the conceit of penmen or not. Life is meant to be active; and books, though they give the action to future generations, administer but to the holiday of the present.

And so, with this long preface, I turn suddenly from the Randals and the Egertons, and the Levys, Avenels, and Peschieras—from the plots and passions of practical life, and drop the reader suddenly into one of those obscure retreats wherein Thought weaves, from unnoticed moments, a new link to the chain that unites the ages.

Within a small room, the single window of which opened on a fanciful and fairy-like garden, that has been before described, sate a young man alone. He had been writing; the ink was not dry on his manuscript, but his thoughts had been suddenly interrupted from his work, and his eyes, now lifted from the letter which had occasioned that interruption, sparkled with delight. "He will come," exclaimed the young man; " come here—to the home which I owe to him. I have not been unworthy of his friendship. And she"—his breast heaved, but the joy faded from his face. " Oh, strange, strange, that I feel sad at the thought to see her again. See *her*—Ah no! my own comforting Helen—my own Child-angel! *Her* I can never see again! The grown woman—that is not my Helen. And yet—and yet (he resumed after a pause), if ever she read the pages in which thought flowed and trembled under her distant starry light—if ever she see how her image has rested with me, and feel that, while others believe that I invent, I have but remembered—will she not, for a moment, be my own Helen again! Again, in heart and in fancy, stand by my side on the desolate bridge—hand in hand—orphans both, as we stood in the days so sorrowful, yet, as I recall them, so sweet.—Helen in England, it is a dream!"

He rose, half-consciously, and went to the window. The fountain played merrily before his eyes, and the birds in the aviary carolled loud to his ear. "And in this house," he murmured, " I saw her last! And there, where the fountain now throws its spray on high—there her benefactor and mine told me that I was to lose *her*, that I might win—fame. Alas!"

At this time a woman, whose dress was somewhat above her mien and air, which, though not without a certain respectability, were very homely, entered the room; and, seeing the young man standing thus thoughtful by the window, paused. She was used to his habits; and since his success in life, had learned to respect them. So she did not disturb his reverie, but began softly to arrange the room—dusting, with the corner of her apron, the various articles of furniture, putting a stray chair or two in its right place, but not touching a single paper. Virtuous woman, and rare as virtuous!

The young man turned at last, with a deep, **yet not** altogether painful sigh—

"My dear mother, good day to you. Ah, you do well to make the room look its best. Happy news! I expect a visitor!"

"Dear me, Leonard, will he want lunch—or what?"

"Nay, I think not, mother. It is he to whom we owe all—'*Hæc otia fecit.*' Pardon my Latin; it is Lord L'Estrange."

The face of Mrs. Fairfield (the reader has long since divined the name) changed instantly, and betrayed a nervous twitch of all the muscles, which gave her a family likeness to old Mrs. Avenel.

"Do not be alarmed, mother. He is the kindest—"

"Don't talk so; I can't bear it!" cried Mrs. Fairfield.

"No wonder you are affected by the recollection of all his benefits. But when once you have seen him, you will find yourself ever after at your ease. And so, pray smile and look as good as you are; for I am proud of your open honest look when you are pleased, mother. And he must see your heart in your face, as I do."

With this, Leonard put his arm round the widow's neck and kissed her. She clung to him fondly for a moment, and he felt her tremble from head to foot. Then she broke from his embrace, and hurried out of the room. Leonard thought perhaps she had gone to improve her dress, or to carry her housewife energies to the decoration of the other rooms; for "the house" was Mrs. Fairfield's hobby and passion; and now that she worked no more, save for her amusement, it was her main occupation. The hours she contrived to spend daily in bustling about those little rooms, and leaving everything therein to all appearance precisely the same, were among the marvels in life which the genius of Leonard had never comprehended. But she was always so delighted when Mr. Norreys or some rare visitor came; and said, (Mr. Norreys never failed to do so,) "How neatly all is kept here. What could Leonard do without you, Mrs. Fairfield?"

And, to Norreys' infinite amusement, Mrs. Fairfield always returned the same answer. "'Deed, sir, and thank you kindly, but 'tis my belief that the drawin'-room would be awful dusty."

Once more left alone, Leonard's mind returned to the state of reverie, and his face assumed the expression that had now become to it habitual. Thus seen, he was changed much since we last beheld him. His cheek was more pale and thin, his lips more firmly compressed, his eye more fixed and abstract. You could detect, if I may borrow a touching French expression, that "sorrow had passed by there." But the melancholy on his countenance was ineffably sweet and serene, and on his ample forehead there was that power, so rarely seen in early youth—the power that has conquered, and betrays its conquests but in calm. The period of doubt, of struggle, of defiance, was gone perhaps for ever; genius and soul were reconciled to human life. It was a face most loveable; so gentle and peaceful in its character. No want of fire: on the contrary, the fire was so clear and so steadfast, that it conveyed but the impression of light. The candour of boyhood; the simplicity of the villager were still there—refined by intelligence, but intelligence that seemed to have traversed through knowledge—not with the footstep, but the wing—unsullied by the mire—tending towards the star—seeking through the various grades of Being but the lovelier forms of truth and goodness; at home as should be the Art that consummates the Beautiful—

"In den heitern Regionen
Wo die reinen Formen wohnen."*

From this reverie Leonard did not seek to rouse himself, till the bell at the garden gate rang loud and shrill; and then starting up and hurrying into the hall, his hand was grasped in Harley's.

## CHAPTER XVI.

A FULL and happy hour passed away in Harley's questions and Leonard's answers; the dialogue that naturally ensued between the two, on the first interview after an absence of years so eventful to the younger man.

The history of Leonard during this interval was almost solely internal, the struggle of intellect with its own difficulties, the wanderings of imagination through its own adventurous worlds.

The first aim of Norreys, in preparing the mind of his pupil for its vocation, had been to establish the equilibrium of its powers, to calm into harmony the elements rudely shaken by the trials and passions of the old hard outer life.

* At home—"In the serene regions
Where dwell the pure forms."

The theory of Norreys was briefly this. The education of a superior human being is but the development of ideas in one for the benefit of others. To this end, attention should be directed—1st, To the value of the ideas collected; 2ndly, To their discipline; 3rdly, To their expression. For the first, acquirement is necessary; for the second, discipline; for the third, art. The first comprehends knowledge, purely intellectual, whether derived from observation, memory, reflection, books or men, Aristotle or Fleet Street. The second demands *training*, not only intellectual, but moral; the purifying and exaltation of motives; the formation of habits; in which method is but a part of a divine and harmonious symmetry—an union of intellect and conscience. Ideas of value, stored by the first process; marshalled into force, and placed under guidance, by the second; it is the result of the third, to place them before the world in the most attractive or commanding form. This may be done by actions no less than words; but the adaptation of means to end, the passage of ideas from the brain of one man into the lives and souls of all, no less in action than in books, requires study. Action has its art as well as literature. Here Norreys had but to deal with the calling of the scholar, the formation of the writer, and so to guide the perceptions towards those varieties in the sublime and beautiful, the just combination of which is at once CREATION. Man himself is but a combination of elements. He who combines in nature, creates in art.

Such, very succinctly and inadequately expressed, was the system upon which Norreys proceeded to regulate and perfect the great native powers of his pupil; and though the reader may perhaps say that no system laid down by another can either form genius or dictate to its results, yet probably nine-tenths at least of those in whom we recognise the luminaries of our race, have passed, unconsciously to themselves (for self-education is rarely conscious of its phases), through each of these processes. And no one who pauses to reflect will deny, that, according to this theory, illustrated by a man of vast experience, profound knowledge, and exquisite taste, the struggles of genius would be infinitely lessened; its vision cleared and strengthened, and the distance between effort and success notably abridged.

Norreys, however, was far too deep a reasoner to fall into the error of modern teachers, who suppose that education can dispense with labour. No mind becomes muscular without rude and early exercise. Labour should be strenuous, but in right directions. All that we can do for it is to save the waste of time in blundering into needless toils.

The master had thus first employed his neophyte in arranging and compiling materials for a great critical work in which Norreys himself was engaged. In this stage of scholastic preparation, Leonard was necessarily led to the acquisition of languages, for which he had great aptitude—the foundations of a large and comprehensive erudition were solidly constructed. He traced by the ploughshare the walls of the destined city. Habits of accuracy and of generalisation became formed insensibly; and that precious faculty which seizes, amidst accumulated materials, those that serve the object for which they are explored,—(that faculty which quadruples all force, by concentrating it on one point)—once roused into action, gave purpose to every toil and quickness to each perception. But Norreys did not confine his pupil solely to the mute world of a library; he introduced him to some of the first minds in arts, science, and letters—and active life. "These," said he, "are the living ideas of the present, out of which books for the future will be written: study them; and here, as in the volumes of the past, diligently amass and deliberately compile."

By degrees Norreys led on that young, ardent mind from the selection of ideas to their æsthetic analysis—from compilation to criticism; but criticism severe, close, and logical—a reason for each word of praise or of blame. Led in this stage of his career to examine into the laws of beauty, a new light broke upon his mind; from amidst the masses of marble he had piled around him, rose the vision of the statue.

And so, suddenly one day Norreys said to him, "I need a compiler no longer—maintain yourself by your own creations." And Leonard wrote, and a work flowered up from the seed deep buried, and the soil well cleared to the rays of the sun and the healthful influence of expanded air.

That first work did not penetrate to a very wide circle of readers, not from any perceptible fault of its own—there is luck in these things; the first anonymous work of an original genius is rarely at once eminently successful. But the more experienced recognised the promise of the book. Publishers, who have an instinct in the discovery of available talent, which often forestalls the appreciation of the public, volunteered liberal offers. "Be fully successful this time," said Norreys; "think not of models nor of style. Strike at once at the common human heart—throw away the corks—swim out boldly. One word more—never write a page till you have walked from your room to Temple Bar, and, mingling with men, and reading the human face, learn why great poets have mostly passed their lives in cities."

Thus Leonard wrote again, and woke one morning to find himself famous. So far as the chances of all professions dependent on health will permit, present independence, and, with foresight and economy, the prospects of future competence were secured.

"And, indeed," said Leonard, concluding a longer but a simpler narrative than is here told—"indeed, there is some chance that I may obtain at once a sum that will leave me free for the rest of my life to select my own subjects and write without care for remuneration. This is what I call the true (and, perhaps, alas! the rare) independence of him who devotes himself to letters. Norreys, having seen my boyish plan for the improvement of certain machinery in the steam-engine, insisted on my giving much time to mechanics. The study that once pleased me so greatly, now seemed dull; but I went into it with good heart; and the result is, that I have improved so far on my original idea, that my scheme has met the approbation of one of our most scientific engineers: and I am assured that the patent for it will be purchased of me upon terms which I am ashamed to name to you, so disproportioned do they seem to the value of so simple a discovery. Meanwhile, I am already rich enough to have realised the two dreams of my heart—to make a home in the cottage where I had last seen you and Helen—I mean Miss Digby; and to invite to that home her who had sheltered my infancy."

"Your mother, where is she? Let me see her."

Leonard ran out to call the widow, but to his surprise and vexation, learned that she had quitted the house before L'Estrange arrived.

He came back perplexed how to explain what seemed ungracious and ungrateful, and spoke with hesitating lip and flushed cheek of the widow's natural timidity and sense of her own homely station. "And so overpowered is she," added Leonard, "by the recollection of all that we owe to you, that she never hears your name without agitation or tears, and trembled like a leaf at the thought of seeing you."

"Ha!" said Harley, with visible emotion. "Is it so?" And he bent down, shading his face with his hand. "And," he renewed, after a pause, but not looking up—"and you ascribe this fear of seeing me, this agitation at my name, solely to an exaggerated sense of—of the circumstances attending my acquaintance with yourself?"

"And, perhaps to a sort of shame that the mother of one you have made her proud of is but a peasant."

"That is all," said Harley, earnestly, now looking up and fixing eyes in which stood tears, upon Leonard's ingenuous brow.

"Oh, my dear lord, what else can it be? Do not judge her harshly."

L'Estrange arose abruptly, pressed Leonard's hand, muttered something not audible, and then drawing his young friend's arm in his, led him into the garden, and turned the conversation back to its former topics.

Leonard's heart yearned to ask after Helen, and yet something withheld him from doing so, till, seeing Harley did not volunteer to speak of her, he could not resist his impulse. "And Helen—Miss Digby—is she much changed?"

"Changed, no—yes; very much."

"Very much!" Leonard sighed.

"I shall see her again?"

"Certainly," said Harley, in a tone of surprise. "How can you doubt it? And I reserve to you the pleasure of saying that you are renowned. You blush; well, I will say that for you. But you shall give her your books."

"She has not yet read them, then?—not the last? The first was not worthy of her attention," said Leonard, disappointed.

"She has only just arrived in England; and, though your books reached me in Germany, she was not then with me. When I have settled some business that will take me from town, I shall present you to her and my mother." There was a certain embarrassment in Harley's voice as he spoke; and, turning round abruptly, he exclaimed, "But you have shown poetry even here. I could not have conceived that so much beauty could be drawn from what appeared to me the most common-place of all suburban gardens. Why, surely, where that charming fountain now plays stood the rude bench in which I read your verses."

"It is true; I wished to unite all together my happiest associations. I think I told you, my lord, in one of my letters, that I had owed a very happy, yet very struggling time in my boyhood to the singular kindness and generous instructions of a foreigner whom I served. This fountain is copied from one that I made in his garden, and by the margin of which many a summer day I have sat and dreamt of fame and knowledge."

"True, you told me of that; and your foreigner will be pleased to hear of your success, and no less so of your grateful recollections. By the way, you did not mention his name."

"Riccabocca."

"Riccabocca! My own dear and noble friend!—is it possible? One of my reasons for returning to England is connected with him. You shall go down with me and see him. I meant to start this evening."

"My dear Lord," said Leonard, "I think that you may spare yourself so long a journey. I have reason to suspect that Signor Riccabocca is my nearest neighbour. Two days ago I was in the garden, when suddenly lifting my eyes to yon hillock I perceived the form of a man seated amongst the brushwood; and, though I could not see his features, there was something in the very outline of his figure and his peculiar posture, that irresistibly reminded me of Riccabocca. I hastened out of the garden and ascended the hill, but he was gone. My supicions were so strong that I caused inquiry to be made at the different shops scattered about, and learned that a family consisting of a gentleman, his wife, and daughter, had lately come to live in a house that you must have passed in your way hither, standing a little back from the road, surrounded by high walls; and though they were said to be English, yet from the description given to me of the gentleman's person by one who had noticed it, by the fact of a foreign servant in their employ, and by the very name 'Richmouth,' assigned to the new comers, I can scarcely doubt that it is the family you seek."

"And you have not called to ascertain?"

"Pardon me, but the family so evidently shunning observation, (no one but the master himself ever seen without the walls,) the adoption of another name too—led me to infer that Signor Riccabocca has some strong motive for concealment; and now, with my improved knowledge of life, and recalling all the past, I cannot but suppose that Riccabocca was not what he appeared. Hence, I have hesitated on formally obtruding myself upon his secrets, whatever they be, and have rather watched for some chance occasion to meet him in his walks."

"You did right, my dear Leonard; but my reasons for seeing my old friend forbid all scruples of delicacy, and I will go at once to his house."

"You will tell me, my Lord, if I am right."

"I hope to be allowed to do so. Pray, stay at home till I return. And now, ere I go, one question more: You indulge conjectures as to Riccabocca, because he has changed his name—why have you dropped your own?"

"I wished to have no name," said Leonard, colouring deeply, "but that which I could make myself."

"Proud poet, this I can comprehend. But from what reason did you assume the strange and fantastic name of Oran?"

The flush on Leonard's face became deeper. "My lord, said he, in a low voice, "it is a childish fancy of mine; it is an anagram."

"Ah!"

"At a time when my cravings after knowledge were likely much to mislead, and perhaps undo me, I chanced on some poems that suddenly affected my whole mind, and led me up into purer air; and I was told that these poems were written in youth, by one who had beauty and genius—one who was in her grave—a relation of my own, and her familiar name was Nora—"

"Ah!" again ejaculated Lord L'Estrange, and his arm pressed heavily upon Leonard's.

"So, somehow or other," continued the young author, falteringly, "I wished that if ever I won to a poet's fame, it might be to my own heart, at least, associated with this name of Nora—with her whom death had robbed of the fame that she might otherwise have won—with her who—"

"He paused, greatly agitated.

Harley was no less so. But, as if by a sudden impulse, the soldier bent down his manly head and kissed the poet's brow; then he hastened to the gate, flung himself on his horse, and rode away.

## CHAPTER XVII.

LORD L'ESTRANGE did not proceed at once to Riccabocca's house. He was under the influence of a remembrance too deep and too strong to yield easily to the lukewarm claim of friendship. He rode fast and far; and impossible it would be to define the feelings that passed through a mind so acutely sensitive, and so rootedly tenacious of all affections. When recalling his duty to the Italian, he once more struck into the road to Norwood, the slow pace of his horse was significant of his own exhausted spirits; a deep dejection had succeeded to feverish excitement. "Vain task," he murmured, "to wean myself from the dead! Yet I am now betrothed to another; and she, with all her virtues, is not the one to—" He stopped short in generous self-rebuke. "Too late to think of that! Now, all that should remain to me is to insure the happiness of the life to which I have pledged my own. But—" He sighed as he so murmured. On reaching the vicinity of Riccabocca's house, he put up his horse at a little inn, and proceeded on foot across the heathland towards the dull square building, which Leonard's description had sufficed to indicate as the exile's new home. It was long before any one answered his summons at the gate. Not till he had thrice rung did he hear a heavy step on the gravel walk within; then the wicket within the gate was partially drawn aside, a dark eye gleamed out, and a voice in imperfect English asked who was there.

"Lord L'Estrange; and if I am right as to the person I seek, that name will at once admit me."

The door flew open as did that of the mystic cavern at the sound of "Open, Sesame;" and Giacomo, almost weeping with joyous emotion, exclaimed, in Italian, "The good Lord! Holy San Giacomo! thou hast heard me at last! We are safe now." And dropping the blunderbuss with which he had taken the precaution to arm himself, he lifted Harley's hand to his lips, in the affectionate greeting familiar to his countrymen.

"And the Padrone?" asked Harley, as he entered the jealous precincts.

"Oh, he is just gone out; but he will not be long. You will wait for him?"

"Certainly. What lady is that I see at the far end of the garden?"

"Bless her, it is our Signorina. I will run and tell her you are come."

"That I am come; but she cannot know me even by name."

"Ah, Excellency, can you think so? Many and many a time has she talked to me of you, and I have heard her pray to the holy Madonna to bless you, and in a voice so sweet—"

"Stay, I will present myself to her. Go, into the house, and we will wait without for the Padrone. Nay, I need the air, my friend." Harley, as he said this, broke from Giacomo, and approached Violante.

The poor child, in her solitary walk in the obscurer parts of the dull garden, had escaped the eye of Giacomo when he had gone forth to answer the bell; and she, unconscious of the fears of which she was the object, had felt something of youthful curiosity at the summons at the gate, and the sight of a stranger in close and friendly conference with the unsocial Giacomo.

As Harley now neared her with that singular grace of movement which belonged to him, a thrill shot through her heart—she knew not why. She did not recognise his likeness to the sketch taken by her father from his recollections of Harley's early youth. She did not guess who he was; and yet she felt herself colour, and, naturally fearless though she was, turned away with a vague alarm.

"Pardon my want of ceremony, Signorina," said Harley, in Italian; "but I am so old a friend of your father's that I cannot feel as a stranger to yourself."

Then Violante lifted to him her dark eyes so intelligent and so innocent—eyes full of surprise, but not displeased surprise. And Harley himself stood amazed, and almost abashed, by the rich and marvellous beauty that beamed upon him. "My father's friend," she said, hesitatingly, "and I never to have seen you!"

"Ah, Signorina," said Harley, (and something of its native humour, half arch, half sad, played round his lip,) "you are mistaken there; you have seen me before, and you received me much more kindly then—"

"Signor!" said Violante, more and more surprised, and with a yet richer colour on her cheeks.

Harley, who had now recovered from the first effect of her beauty, and who regarded her as men of his years and character are apt to regard ladies in their teens, as more child than woman, suffered himself to be amused by her perplexity; for it was in his nature, that the graver and more mournful he felt at heart, the more he sought to give play and whim to his spirits.

"Indeed, Signorina," said he, demurely, "you insisted then on placing one of those fair hands in mine; the other (forgive me the fidelity of my recollections) was affectionately thrown around my neck."

"Signor!" again exclaimed Violante; but this time there was anger in her voice as well as surprise, and nothing could be more charming than her look of pride and resentment.

Harley smiled again, but with so much kindly sweetness, that the anger vanished at once, or rather Violante felt angry with herself that she was no longer angry with him. But she had looked so beautiful in her anger, that Harley wished, perhaps, to see her angry again. So, composing his lips from their propitiatory smile, he resumed, gravely—

"Your flatterers will tell you, Signorina, that you are much improved since then, but I liked you better as you were; not but what I hope to return some day what you then so generously pressed upon me."

"Pressed upon you!—I? Signor, you are under some strange mistake."

"Alas! no; but the female heart is so capricious and fickle! You pressed it upon me, I assure you. I own that I was not loath to accept it."

"Pressed it! Pressed what?"

"Your kiss, my child," said Harley; and then added, with a serious tenderness, "And I again say that I hope to return it some day—when I see you, by the side of father and of husband, in your native land—the fairest bride on whom the skies of Italy ever smiled! And now, pardon a hermit and a soldier for his rude jests, and give your hand, in token of that pardon,—to Harley L'Estrange."

Violante, who at the first words of his address had recoiled, with a vague belief that the stranger was out of his mind, sprang forward as it closed, and, in all the vivid enthusiasm of her nature, pressed the hand held out to her, with both her own. "Harley L'Estrange—the preserver of my father's life!" she cried; and her eyes were fixed on his with such evident gratitude and reverence, that Harley felt at once confused and delighted. She did not think at that instant of the hero of her dreams—she thought but of him who had saved her father. But, as his eyes sank before her own, and his head uncovered, bowed over the hand he held, she recognised the likeness to the features on which she had so often gazed. The first bloom of youth was gone, but enough of youth still remained to soften the lapse of years, and to leave to manhood the attractions which charm the eye. Instinctively she withdrew her hands from his clasp, and, in her turn, looked down.

In this pause of embarrassment to both, Riccabocca let himself into the garden by his own latch-key, and, startled to see a man by the side of Violante, sprang forward with an abrupt and angry cry. Harley heard, and turned.

As if restored to courage and self-possession by the sense of her father's presence, Violante again took the hand of the visitor. "Father," she said, simply, "it is he—*he* is come at last." And then, retiring a few steps, she contemplated them both; and her face was radiant with happiness—as if something, long silently missed and looked for, was as silently found, and life had no more a want, nor the heart a void.

# BOOK TENTH.

### INITIAL CHAPTER.

UPON THIS FACT—THAT THE WORLD IS STILL MUCH THE SAME AS IT ALWAYS HAS BEEN.

It is observed by a very pleasant writer—read now-a-days only by the brave pertinacious few who still struggle hard to rescue from the House of Pluto the souls of departed authors, jostled and chased as those souls are by the noisy footsteps of the living—it is observed by the admirable Charron, that "judgment and wisdom is not only the best, but the happiest portion God Almighty hath distributed amongst men; for though this distribution be made with a very uneven hand, yet nobody thinks himself stinted or ill-dealt with, but he that hath never so little is contented in *this* respect." \*

And, certainly, the present narrative may serve in notable illustration of the remark so drily made by the witty and wise preacher. For whether our friend Riccabocca deduce theories for daily life from the great folio of Machiavelli; or that promising young gentleman, Mr. Randal Leslie, interpret the power of knowledge into the art of being too knowing for dull honest folks to cope with him; or acute Dick Avenel push his way up the social ascent with a blow for those before, and a kick for those behind him, after the approved fashion of your strong New Man; or Baron Levy—that cynical impersonation of Gold—compare himself to the Magnetic Rock in the Arabian tale, to which the nails in every ship that approaches the influence of the loadstone fly from the planks, and a shipwreck per day adds its waifs to the Rock; questionless, at least,. it is, that each of those personages believes that Providence has bestowed on him an elder son's inheritance of wisdom. Nor, were we to glance towards the obscurer paths of life, should we find good Parson Dale deem

---

\* Translation of *Charron on Wisdom.* By G. STANHOPE, D.D., late Dean of Canterbury (1729.) A translation remarkable for ease, vigour, and (despite that contempt for the strict rules of grammar, which was common enough amongst writers at the commencement of the last century) for the idiomatic raciness of its English.

himself worse off than the rest of the world in this precious commodity—as, indeed, he has signally evinced of late in that shrewd guess of his touching Professor Moss;—even plain Squire Hazeldean takes it for granted that he could teach Audley Egerton a thing or two worth knowing in politics; Mr. Stirn thinks that there is no branch of useful lore on which he could not instruct the Squire; while Sprott, the tinker, with his bag full of tracts and lucifer matches, regards the whole framework of modern society, from a rick to a constitution, with the profound disdain of a revolutionary philosopher. Considering that every individual thus brings into the stock of the world so vast a share of intelligence, it cannot but excite our wonder to find that Oxenstiern is popularly held to be right when he said, " See, my son, how little wisdom it requires to govern States;"—that is, Men! That so many millions of persons, each with a profound assurance that he is possessed of an exalted sagacity, should concur in the ascendancy of a few inferior intellects, according to a few stupid, prosy, matter-of-fact rules as old as the hills, is a phenomenon very discreditable to the spirit and energy of the aggregate human species! It creates no surprise that one sensible watch-dog should control the movements of a flock of silly grass-eating sheep; but that two or three silly grass-eating sheep should give the law to whole flocks of such mighty sensible watch-dogs—*Diavolo!* Dr. Riccabocca, explain *that*, if you can! And wonderfully strange it is, that notwithstanding all the march of enlightenment, notwithstanding our progressive discoveries in the laws of nature—our railways, steam-engines, animal magnetism, and electro-biology—we have never made any improvement that is generally acknowledged, since men ceased to be troglodytes and nomads, in the old-fashioned gamut of flats and sharps, which attunes into irregular social jog-trot all the generations that pass from the cradle to the grave; still, " *the desire for something we have not* " impels all the energies that keep us in movement, for good or for ill, according to the checks or the directions of each favourite desire.

A friend of mine once said to a *millionaire*, whom he saw for ever engaged in making money which he never seemed to have any pleasure in spending, " Pray, Mr. ——, will you answer me one question: You are said to have two millions, and you spend £600 a-year. In order to rest and enjoy, what will content you ? "

" A little more," answered the *millionaire*. That " little

more" is the mainspring of civilisation. Nobody ever gets it!

"Philus," saith a Latin writer, "was not so rich as Lælius; Lælius was not so rich as Scipio; Scipio was not so rich as Crassus; and Crassus was not so rich—as he wished to be!" If John Bull were once contented, Manchester might shut up its mills. It is the "little more" that makes a mere trifle of the National Debt!—Long life to it!

Still, mend our law-books as we will, one is forced to confess that knaves are often seen in fine linen, and honest men in the most shabby old rags; and still, notwithstanding the exceptions, knavery is a very hazardous game; and honesty, on the whole, by far the best policy. Still, most of the Ten Commandments remain at the core of all the Pandects and Institutes that keep our hands off our neighbours' throats, wives, and pockets; still, every year shows that the Parson's maxim—*non quieta movere*—is as prudent for the health of communities as when Apollo recommended his votaries not to rake up a fever by stirring the Lake Camarina; still people, thank Heaven, decline to reside in parallelograms, and the surest token that we live under a free government is, when we are governed by persons whom we have a full right to imply, by our censure and ridicule, are blockheads compared to ourselves! Stop that delightful privilege, and, by Jove! sir, there is neither pleasure nor honour in being governed at all! You might as well be—a Frenchman!

## CHAPTER II.

THE Italian and his friend are closeted together.

"And why have you left your home in ———shire? and why this new change of name?"

"Peschiera is in England."

"I know it."

"And bent on discovering me; and, it is said, of stealing from me my child."

"He has had the assurance to lay wagers that he will win the hand of your heiress. I know that too; and therefore I have come to England—first to baffle his design—for I do not think your fears altogether exaggerated—and next to learn from you how to follow up a clue which, unless I am too sanguine, may lead to his ruin, and your unconditional restoration. Listen to me. You are aware that, after the skirmish with Peschiera's armed hirelings sent in search of you, I received a polite message from the Austrian government, requesting me to leave its Italian domains. Now, as I hold it the obvious duty of any foreigner, admitted to the hospitality of a state, to refrain from all participation in its civil disturbances, so I thought my honour assailed at this intimation, and went at once to Vienna to explain to the Minister there (to whom I was personally known), that though I had, as became man to man, aided to protect a refugee, who had taken shelter under my roof, from the infuriated soldiers at the command of his private foe, I had not only not shared in any attempt at revolt, but dissuaded, as far as I could, my Italian friends from their enterprise; and that, because, without discussing its merits, I believed, as a military man and a cool spectator, the enterprise could only terminate in fruitless bloodshed. I was enabled to establish my explanation by satisfactory proof; and my acquaintance with the Minister assumed something of the character of friendship. I was then in a position to advocate your cause, and to state your original reluctance to enter into the plots of the insurgents. I admitted freely that you had such natural desire for the independence of your native land, that, had the standard of Italy been boldly hoisted by its legitimate chiefs, or at the common uprising of its whole people, you would have been found in the van, amidst the ranks of your countrymen; but I maintained that you would never have shared in a conspiracy frantic in itself, and defiled by the lawless schemes and sordid ambition of its main projectors, had you not been betrayed and decoyed into it by the misrepresentations and domestic treachery of your kinsman—the very man who denounced you. Unfortunately, of this statement I had no proof but your own word. I made, however, so far an impression in your favour, and, it may be, against the traitor, that your property was not confiscated to the State, nor handed over, upon the plea of your civil death, to your kinsman."

"How!—I do not understand. Peschiera has the property?"

"He holds the revenues but of one half upon pleasure, and they would be withdrawn, could I succeed in establishing the case that exists against him. I was forbidden before to mention this to you; the Minister, not inexcusably, submitted you to the probation of unconditional exile. Your grace might

depend upon your own forbearance from further conspiracies
—forgive the word. I need not say I was permitted to return
to Lombardy. I found, on my arrival, that—that your unhappy wife had been to my house, and exhibited great despair
at hearing of my departure."

Riccabocca knit his dark brows, and breathed hard.

"I did not judge it necessary to acquaint you with this
circumstance, nor did it much affect me. I believed in her
guilt—and what could now avail her remorse, if remorse she
felt? Shortly afterwards, I heard that she was no more."

"Yes," muttered Riccabocca, "she died in the same year
that I left Italy. It must be a strong reason that can excuse
a friend for reminding me even that she once lived!"

"I come at once to that reason," said L'Estrange, gently.
"This autumn I was roaming through Switzerland, and, in
one of my pedestrian excursions amidst the mountains, I met
with an accident, which confined me for some days to a sofa
at a little inn in an obscure village. My hostess was an
Italian; and, as I had left my servant at a town at some
distance, I required her attention till I could write to him to
come to me. I was thankful for her cares, and amused by
her Italian babble. We became very good friends. She told
me she had been servant to a lady of great rank, who had
died in Switzerland; and that, being enriched by the generosity
of her mistress, she had married a Swiss innkeeper, and his
people had become hers. My servant arrived, and my hostess
learned my name, which she did not know before. She came
into my room greatly agitated. In brief, this woman had
been servant to your wife. She had accompanied her to my
villa, and known of her anxiety to see me, as your friend.
The government had assigned to your wife your palace at
Milan, with a competent income. She had refused to accept
of either. Failing to see me, she had set off towards England,
resolved upon seeing yourself; for the journals had stated
that to England you had escaped."

"She dared!—shameless! And see, but a moment before,
I had forgotten all but her grave in a foreign soil—and these
tears had forgiven her," murmured the Italian.

"Let them forgive her still," said Harley, with all his
exquisite sweetness of look and tone. "I resume. On entering Switzerland your wife's health, which you know was
always delicate, gave way. To fatigue and anxiety succeeded
fever, and delirium ensued. She had taken with her but this
one female attendant—the sole one she could trust—on

leaving home. She suspected Peschiera to have bribed her household. In the presence of this woman she raved of her innocence—in accents of terror and aversion, denounced your kinsman—and called on you to vindicate her name and your own."

"Ravings indeed! Poor Paulina!" groaned Riccabocca, covering his face with both hands.

"But in her delirium there were lucid intervals. In one of these she rose, in spite of all her servant could do to restrain her, took from her desk several letters, and reading them over, exclaimed piteously, 'But how to get them to him?—whom to trust? And his friend is gone!' Then an idea seemed suddenly to flash upon her, for she uttered a joyous exclamation, sate down, and wrote long and rapidly, enclosed what she wrote with all the letters, in one packet, which she sealed carefully, and bade her servant carry to the post, with many injunctions to take it with her own hand, and pay the charge on it. 'For oh!' said she (I repeat the words as my informant told them to me)—'for, oh! this is my sole chance to prove to my husband that, though I have erred, I am not the guilty thing he believes me; the sole chance, too, to redeem my error, and restore, perhaps, to my husband his country, to my child her heritage.' The servant took the letter to the post; and when she returned, her lady was asleep, with a smile upon her face. But from that sleep, she woke again delirious, and before the next morning her soul had fled." Here Riccabocca lifted one hand from his face and grasped Harley's arm, as if mutely beseeching him to pause. The heart of the man struggled hard with his pride and his philosophy; and it was long before Harley could lead him to regard the worldly prospects which this last communication from his wife might open to his ruined fortunes. Not, indeed, till Riccabocca had persuaded himself, and half persuaded Harley (for strong indeed, was all presumption of guilt against the dead), that his wife's protestations of innocence from all but error had been but ravings.

"Be this as it may," said Harley, "there seems every reason to suppose that the letters enclosed were Peschiera's correspondence, and that, if so, these would establish the proof of his influence over your wife, and of his perfidious machinations against yourself. I resolved, before coming hither, to go round by Vienna. There I heard, with dismay, that Peschiera had not only obtained the imperial sanction to demand your daughter's hand, but had boasted to his profligate circle that he should succeed; and he was actually on his road to England. I saw at once that could this design, by any fraud or artifice, be successful with Violante, (for of your consent, I need not say, I did not dream,) the discovery of the packet, whatever its contents, would be useless: Peschiera's end would be secured. I saw also that his success would suffice for ever to clear his name; for his success must imply your consent (it would be to disgrace your daughter, to assert that she had married without it), and your consent would be his acquittal. I saw, too, with alarm, that to all means for the accomplishment of his project he would be urged by despair; for his debts are great, and his character nothing but new wealth can support. I knew that he was able, bold, determined, and that he had taken with him a large supply of money borrowed upon usury;—in a word, I trembled for you both. I have now seen your daughter, and I tremble no more. Accomplished seducer as Peschiera boasts himself, the first look upon her face so sweet, yet so noble, convinced me that she is proof against a legion of Peschieras. Now, then, return we to this all-important subject—to this packet. It never reached you. Long years have passed since then. Does it exist still? Into whose hands would it have fallen? Try to summon up all your recollections. The servant could not remember the name of the person to whom it was addressed; she only insisted that the name began with a B, that it was directed to England, and that to England she accordingly paid the postage. Whom then, with a name that begins with B, or (in case the servant's memory here mislead her) whom did you or your wife know, during your visit to England, with sufficient intimacy to make it probable that she would select such a person for her confidant?"

"I cannot conceive," said Riccabocca, shaking his head. "We came to England shortly after our marriage. Paulina was affected by the climate. She spoke not a word of English, and indeed not even French, as might have been expected from her birth, for her father was poor, and thoroughly Italian. She refused all society. I went, it is true, somewhat into the London world—enough to induce me to shrink from the contrast that my second visit as a beggared refugee would have made to the reception I met with on my first—but I formed no intimate friendships. I recall no one whom she could have written to as intimate with me."

"But," persisted Harley, "think again. Was there no lady well acquainted with Italian, and with whom, perhaps, for that very reason, your wife became familiar?"

"Ah, it is true. There was one old lady of retired habits, but who had been much in Italy. Lady—Lady—I remember —Lady Jane Horton."

"Horton—Lady Jane!" exclaimed Harley; "again! thrice in one day—is this wound never to scar over?" Then, noting Riccabocca's look of surprise, he said, "Excuse me, my friend; I listen to you with renewed interest. Lady Jane was a distant relation of my own; she judged me, perhaps, harshly—and I have some painful associations with her name; but she was a woman of many virtues. Your wife knew her?"

"Not, however, intimately—still, better than any one else in London. But Paulina would not have written to her; she knew that Lady Jane had died shortly after her own departure from England. I myself was summoned back to Italy on pressing business; she was too unwell to journey with me as rapidly as I was obliged to travel; indeed, illness detained her several weeks in England. In this interval she might have made acquaintances. Ah, now I see; I guess. You say the name began with B. Paulina, in my absence, engaged a companion—a Mrs. Bertram. This lady accompanied her abroad. Paulina became excessively attached to her, she knew Italian so well. Mrs. Bertram left her on the road, and returned to England, for some private affairs of her own. I forget why or wherefore; if, indeed, I ever asked or learned. Paulina missed her sadly, often talked of her, wondered why she never heard from her. No doubt it was to this Mrs. Bertram that she wrote!"

"And you don't know the lady's friends, or address?"

"No."

"Nor who recommended her to your wife?"

"No."

"Probably Lady Jane Horton?"

"It may be so. Very likely."

"I will follow up this track, slight as it is."

"But if Mrs. Bertram received the communication, how comes it that it never reached myself—O, fool that I am, how should it! I, who guarded so carefully my incognito!"

"True. This your wife could not foresee; she would naturally imagine that your residence in England would be easily discovered. But many years must have passed since your wife lost sight of this Mrs. Bertram, if their acquaintance was made so soon after your marriage; and now it is a long time to retrace—before even your Violante was born."

"Alas! yes. I lost two fair sons in the interval. Violante was born to me as the child of sorrow."

"And to make sorrow lovely! how beautiful she is!"

The father smiled proudly.

"Where, in the loftiest houses of Europe, find a husband worthy of such a prize?"

"You forget that I am still an exile—she still dowerless. You forget that I am pursued by Peschiera; that I would rather see her a beggar's wife—than—Pah, the very thought maddens me, it is so foul. *Corpo di Bacco!* I have been glad to find her a husband already."

"Already! Then that young man spoke truly?"

"What young man?"

"Randal Leslie. How! You know him?" Here a brief explanation followed. Harley heard with attentive ear, and marked vexation, the particulars of Riccabocca's connection and implied engagement with Leslie.

"There is something very suspicious to me in all this," said he. "Why should this young man have so sounded me as to Violante's chance of losing fortune if she married an Englishman?"

"Did he? O, pooh! Excuse him. It was but his natural wish to seem ignorant of all about me. He did not know enough of my intimacy with you to betray my secret."

"But he knew enough of it—must have known enough to have made it right that he should tell you I was in England. He does not seem to have done so."

"No—*that* is strange—yet scarcely strange; for, when we last met, his head was full of other things—love and marriage. *Basta!* youth will be youth."

"He has no youth left in him!" exclaimed Harley, passionately. "I doubt if he ever had any. He is one of those men who come into the world with the pulse of a centenarian. You and I never shall be as old—as he was in long clothes. Ah, you may laugh; but I am never wrong in my instincts. I disliked him at the first—his eye, his smile, his voice, his very footstep. It is madness in you to countenance such a marriage; it may destroy all chance of your restoration."

"Better that than infringe my word once passed."

"No, no," exclaimed Harley; "your word is not passed— it shall not be passed. Nay, never look so piteously at me. At all events, pause till we know more of this young man. If he be worthy of her without a dower, why, then, let him lose you your heritage. I should have no more to say."

"But why lose me my heritage? There is no law in Austria which can dictate to a father what husband to choose for his daughter."

"Certainly not. But you are out of the pale of law itself just at present; and it would surely be a reason for state policy to withhold your pardon, and it would be to the loss of that favour with your own countrymen, which would now make that pardon so popular, if it were known that the representative of your name were debased by your daughter's alliance with an English adventurer—a clerk in a public office! O, sage in theory, why are you such a simpleton in action?"

Nothing moved by this taunt, Riccabocca rubbed his hands, and then stretched them comfortably over the fire.

"My friend," said he, "the representation of my name would pass to my son."

"But you have no son?"

"Hush! I am going to have one; my Jemima informed me of it yesterday morning; and it was upon that information that I resolved to speak to Leslie. Am I a simpleton now?"

"Going to have a son," repeated Harley, looking very bewildered; "how do you know it is to be a son?"

"Physiologists are agreed," said the sage, positively, "that where the husband is much older than the wife, and there has been a long interval without children before she condescends to increase the population of the world—she (that is, it is at least as nine to four)—she brings into the world a male. I consider that point, therefore, as settled, according to the calculations of statisticians and the researches of naturalists."

Harley could not help laughing, though he was still angry and disturbed.

"The same man as ever; always the fool of philosophy."

"*Cospetto!*" said Riccabocca. "I am rather the philosopher of fools. And talking of that, shall I present you to my Jemima?"

"Yes; but in turn I must present you to one who remembers with gratitude your kindness, and whom your philosophy, for a wonder, has not ruined. Some time or other you must explain that to me. Excuse me for a moment; I will go for him."

"For him;—for whom? In my position I must be cautious; and—"

"I will answer for his faith and discretion. Meanwhile order dinner, and let me and my friend stay to share it."

"Dinner? *Corpo di Bacco!*—not that Bacchus can help us here. What will Jemima say?"

"Henpecked man, settle that with your connubial tyrant. But dinner it must be."

I leave the reader to imagine the delight of Leonard at seeing once more Riccabocca unchanged and Violante so improved; and the kind Jemima too. And their wonder at him and his history, his books and his fame. He narrated his struggles and adventures with a simplicity that removed from a story so personal the character of egotism. But when he came to speak of Helen, he was brief and reserved.

Violante would have questioned more closely; but, to Leonard's relief, Harley interposed.

"You shall see her whom he speaks of before long, and question her yourself."

With these words, Harley turned the young man's narrative into new directions; and Leonard's words again flowed freely. Thus the evening passed away happily to all save Riccabocca. For the thought of his dead wife rose ever and anon before the exile; but when it did, and became too painful, he crept nearer to Jemima, and looked in her simple face, and pressed her cordial hand. And yet the monster had implied to Harley that his comforter was a fool—so she was, to love so contemptible a slanderer of herself, and her sex.

Violante was in a state of blissful excitement; she could not analyse her own joy. But her conversation was chiefly with Leonard; and the most silent of all was Harley. He sate listening to Leonard's warm, yet unpretending eloquence —that eloquence which flows so naturally from genius, when thoroughly at its ease, and not chilled back on itself by hard, unsympathising hearers—listened, yet more charmed, to the sentiments less profound, yet no less earnest—sentiments so feminine, yet so noble, with which Violante's fresh virgin heart responded to the poet's kindling soul. Those sentiments of hers were so unlike all he heard in the common world—so akin to himself in his gone youth! Occasionally—at some high thought of her own, or some lofty line from Italian song, that she cited with lighted eyes, and in melodious accents— occasionally he reared his knightly head, and his lip quivered, as if he had heard the sound of a trumpet. The inertness of long years was shaken. The Heroic, that lay deep beneath all the humours of his temperament, was reached, appealed to; and stirred within him, rousing up all the bright associations connected with it, and long dormant. When he arose to take leave, surprised at the lateness of the hour, Harley said, in a tone that bespoke the sincerity of the compliment, "I thank you for the happiest hours I have known for years." His eye dwelt on Violante as he spoke. But timidity returned to her with his words—at his look; and it was no longer the inspired muse, but the bashful girl that stood before him.

"And when shall I see you again?" asked Riccabocca, disconsolately, following his guest to the door.

"When? Why, of course, to-morrow. Adieu! my friend. No wonder you have borne your exile so patiently,—with such a child!"

He took Leonard's arm, and walked with him to the inn where he had left his horse. Leonard spoke of Violante with enthusiasm. Harley was silent.

## CHAPTER III.

THE next day a somewhat old-fashioned, but exceedingly patrician, equipage stopped at Riccabocca's garden-gate. Giacomo, who, from a bedroom window, had caught sight of its winding towards the house, was seized with undefinable terror when he beheld it pause before their walls, and heard the shrill summons at the portal. He rushed into his master's presence, and implored him not to stir—not to allow any one to give ingress to the enemies the machine might disgorge. "I have heard," said he, "how a town in Italy—I think it was Bologna—was once taken and given to the sword, by incautiously admitting a wooden horse, full of the troops of Barbarossa, and all manner of bombs and Congreve rockets."

"The story is differently told in Virgil," quoth Riccabocca, peeping out of the window. "Nevertheless, the machine looks very large and suspicious; unloose Pompey."

"Father," said Violante, colouring, "it is your friend, Lord L'Estrange; I hear his voice."

"Are you sure?"

"Quite. How can I be mistaken?"

"Go, then, Giacomo; but take Pompey with thee—and give the alarm, if we are deceived."

But Violante was right, and in a few moments Lord L'Estrange was seen walking up the garden, and giving the arm to two ladies.

"Ah," said Riccabocca, composing his dressing-robe round him, "go, my child, and summon Jemima. Man to man; but, for Heaven's sake, woman to woman."

Harley had brought his mother and Helen, in compliment to the ladies of his friend's household.

The proud Countess knew that she was in the presence of Adversity, and her salute to Riccabocca was only less respectful than that with which she would have rendered homage to her sovereign. But Riccabocca, always gallant to the sex that he pretended to despise, was not to be outdone in ceremony; and the bow which replied to the curtsey would have edified the rising generation, and delighted such surviving relics of the old Court breeding as may linger yet amidst the gloomy pomp of the Faubourg St. Germain. These dues paid to etiquette, the Countess briefly introduced Helen, as Miss Digby, and seated herself near the exile. In a few moments the two elder personages became quite at home with each other; and, really, perhaps Riccabocca had never, since we have known him, showed to such advantage as by the side of his polished, but somewhat formal visitor. Both had lived so little with our modern, ill-bred age! They took out their manners of a former race, with a sort of pride in airing once more such fine lace and superb brocade. Riccabocca gave truce to the shrewd but homely wisdom of his proverbs— perhaps he remembered that Lord Chesterfield denounces proverbs as vulgar;—and gaunt though his figure, and far from elegant though his dressing-robe, there was that about him which spoke undeniably of the *grand seigneur*—of one to whom a Marquis de Dangeau would have offered a *fauteuil* by the side of the Rohans and Montmorencies.

Meanwhile Helen and Harley seated themselves a little apart, and were both silent—the first, from timidity; the second, from abstraction. At length the door opened, and Harley suddenly sprang to his feet—Violante and Jemima entered. Lady Lansmere's eyes first rested on the daughter, and she could scarcely refrain from an exclamation of admiring surprise; but then, when she caught sight of Mrs. Riccabocca's somewhat humble, yet not obsequious mien— looking a little shy, a little homely, yet still thoroughly a gentlewoman (though of your plain, rural kind of that genus) —she turned from the daughter, and with the *savoir vivre* the fine old school, paid her first respects to the wife; respects literally, for her manner implied respect,—but it was more kind, simple, and cordial than the respect she had shown to Riccabocca;—as the sage himself had said, here "it was Woman to Woman." And then she took Violante's hand in both hers, and gazed on her as if she could not resist the pleasure of contemplating so much beauty. "My son," she said, softly, and with a half sigh—"my son in vain told me not to be surprised. This is the first time I have ever known reality exceed description!"

Violante's blush here made her still more beautiful; and as the Countess returned to Riccabocca, she stole gently to Helen's side.

"Miss Digby, my ward," said Harley, pointedly, observing that his mother had neglected her duty of presenting Helen to the ladies. He then reseated himself, and conversed with Mrs. Riccabocca; but his bright, quick eye glanced over at the two girls. They were about the same age—and youth was all that, to the superficial eye, they seemed to have in common. A greater contrast could not well be conceived; and, what is strange, both gained by it. Violante's brilliant loveliness seemed yet more dazzling, and Helen's fair, gentle face yet more winning. Neither had mixed much with girls of her own age; each took to the other at first sight. Violante, as the less shy, began the conversation.

"You are his ward—Lord L'Estrange's?"

"Yes."

"Perhaps you came with him from Italy?"

"No, not exactly. But I have been in Italy for some years."

"Ah! you regret—nay, I am foolish—you return to your native land. But the skies in Italy are so blue—here it seems as if nature wanted colours."

"Lord L'Estrange says that you were very young when you left Italy; you remember it well. He, too, prefers Italy to England."

"He! Impossible!"

"Why impossible, fair sceptic?" cried Harley, interrupting himself in the midst of a speech to Jemima.

Violante had not dreamed that she could be overheard—she was speaking low; but, though visibly embarrassed, she answered, distinctly—

"Because in England there is the noblest career for noble minds."

Harley was startled, and replied, with a slight sigh, "At your age I should have said as you do. But this England of ours is so crowded with noble minds, that they only jostle each other, and the career is one cloud of dust."

"So, I have read, seems a battle to a common soldier, but not to the chief."

"You have read good descriptions of battles, I see."

Mrs. Riccabocca, who thought this remark a taunt upon her step-daughter's studies, hastened to Violante's relief.

"Her papa made her read the history of Italy, and I believe that is full of battles."

HARLEY.—"All history is, and all women are fond of war and of warriors. I wonder why?"

VIOLANTE, (turning to Helen, and in a very low voice, resolved that Harley should not hear this time.)—"We can guess why—can we not?"

HARLEY, (hearing every word, as if it had been spoken in St. Paul's Whispering Gallery.)—"If you can guess, Helen, pray tell me."

HELEN, (shaking her pretty head, and answering, with a livelier smile than usual.)—"But I am not fond of war and warriors."

HARLEY to Violante.—"Then I must appeal at once to you, self-convicted Bellona that you are. Is it from the cruelty natural to the female disposition?"

VIOLANTE, (with a sweet musical laugh.)—"From two propensities still more natural to it."

HARLEY.—"You puzzle me: what can they be?"

VIOLANTE.—"Pity and admiration; we pity the weak and admire the brave."

Harley inclined his head, and was silent.

Lady Lansmere had suspended her conversation with Riccabocca to listen to this dialogue. "Charming!" she cried. "You have explained what has often perplexed me. Ah, Harley, I am glad to see that your satire is foiled: you have no reply to that."

"No; I willingly own myself defeated, too glad to claim the Signorina's pity, since my cavalry sword hangs on the wall, and I can have no longer a professional pretence to her admiration."

He then rose, and glanced towards the window. "But I see a more formidable disputant for my conqueror to encounter is coming into the field—one whose profession it is to substitute some other romance for that of camp and siege."

"Our friend Leonard," said Riccabocca, turning his eye also towards the window. "True; as Quevedo says, wittily, 'Ever since there has been so great a demand for type, there has been much less lead to spare for cannon-balls.'"

Here Leonard entered. Harley had sent Lady Lansmere's footman to him with a note, that prepared him to meet Helen. As he came into the room, Harley took him by the hand and led him to Lady Lansmere.

"The friend of whom I spoke. Welcome him now for my sake, ever after for his own;" and then, scarcely allowing time for the Countess's elegant and gracious response, he drew Leonard towards Helen. "Children," said he, with a touching voice, that thrilled through the hearts of both, "go and seat yourselves yonder, and talk together of the past. Signorina, I invite you to renewed discussion upon the abstruse metaphysical subject you have started; let us see if we cannot find gentler sources for pity and admiration than war and warriors." He took Violante aside to the window. "You remember that Leonard, in telling you his history last night, spoke, you thought, rather too briefly of the little girl who had been his companion in the rudest time of his trials. When you would have questioned more, I interrupted you, and said, 'You should see her shortly, and question her yourself.' And now what think you of Helen Digby? Hush, speak low. But her ears are not so sharp as mine."

VIOLANTE.—"Ah! that is the fair creature whom Leonard called his child-angel? What a lovely innocent face!—the angel is there still."

HARLEY, (pleased both at the praise and with her who gave it.)—"You think so; and you are right. Helen is not communicative. But fine natures are like fine poems—a glance at the first two lines suffices for a guess into the beauty that waits you if you read on."

Violante gazed on Leonard and Helen as they sat apart. Leonard was the speaker, Helen the listener; and though the former had, in his narrative the night before, been indeed brief as to the episode in his life connected with the orphan, enough had been said to interest Violante in the pathos of their former position towards each other, and in the happiness they must feel in their meeting again—separated for years on the wide sea of life, now both saved from the storm and shipwreck. The tears came into her eyes. "True," she said, very softly, "there is more here to move pity and admiration than in—" She paused.

HARLEY.—" Complete the sentence. Are you ashamed to retract? Fie on your pride and obstinacy."

VIOLANTE.—" No; but even here there have been war and heroism—the war of genius with adversity, and heroism in the comforter who shared it and consoled. Ah! wherever pity and admiration are both felt, something nobler than mere sorrow must have gone before: the heroic must exist."

"Helen does not know what the word heroic means," said Harley, rather sadly; "you must teach her."

"Is it possible," thought he as he spoke, "that a Randal Leslie could have charmed this grand creature? No 'Heroic' surely, in that sleek young placeman." "Your father," he said aloud, and fixing his eyes on her face, "sees much, he tells me, of a young man about Leonard's age, as to date; but I never estimate the age of men by the parish register; and I should speak of that so-called young man as a contemporary of my great-grandfather;—I mean Mr. Randal Leslie. Do you like him?"

"Like him?" said Violante, slowly, and as if sounding her own mind.—" Like him—yes."

"Why?" asked Harley, with dry and curt indignation.

"His visits seem to please my dear father. Certainly I like him."

"Hum. He professes to like you, I suppose?"

Violante laughed unsuspiciously. She had half a mind to reply, "Is that so strange?" But her respect for Harley stopped her. The words would have seemed to her pert.

"I am told he is clever," resumed Harley.

"O, certainly."

"And he is rather handsome. But I like Leonard's face better."

"Better—that is not the word. Leonard's face is as that of one who has gazed so often upon Heaven; and Mr. Leslie's—there is neither sunlight nor starlight reflected there."

"My dear Violante!" exclaimed Harley, overjoyed; and he pressed her hand.

The blood rushed over the girl's cheek and brow; her hand trembled in his. But Harley's familiar exclamation might have come from a father's lips.

At this moment Helen softly approached them, and looking timidly into her guardian's face, said, "Leonard's mother is with him: he asks me to call and see her. May I?"

"May you! A pretty notion the Signorina must form of

your enslaved state of pupilage, when she hears you ask that question. Of course you may."

"Will you come with us?"

Harley looked embarrassed. He thought of the widow's agitation at his name; of that desire to shun him, which Leonard had confessed, and of which he thought he divined the cause. And so divining, he too shrank from such a meeting.

"Another time, then," said he, after a pause.

Helen looked disappointed, but said no more.

Violante was surprised at this ungracious answer. She would have blamed it as unfeeling in another. But all that Harley did was right in her eyes.

"Cannot I go with Miss Digby?" said she, "and my mother will go too. We both know Mrs. Fairfield. We shall be so pleased to see her again."

"So be it," said Harley; "I will wait here with your father till you come back. O, as to my mother, she will excuse the—excuse Madame Riccabocca, and you too. See how charmed she is with *your* father. I must stay to watch over the conjugal interests of *mine*."

But Mrs. Riccabocca had too much good old country breeding to leave the Countess; and Harley was forced himself to appeal to Lady Lansmere. When he had explained the case in point, the Countess rose and said—

"But I will call myself, with Miss Digby."

"No," said Harley, gravely, but in a whisper. "No—I would rather not. I will explain later."

"Then," said the Countess aloud, after a glance of surprise at her son, " I must insist on your performing this visit, my dear madam, and you Signorina. In truth, I have something to say confidentially to—"

"To me," interrupted Riccabocca. "Ah, Madame la Comtesse, you restore me to five-and-twenty. Go, quick—O jealous and injured wife; go, both of you, quick; and you, too, Harley."

"Nay," said Lady Lansmere, in the same tone, "Harley must stay, for my design is not at present upon destroying your matrimonial happiness, whatever it may be later. It is a design so innocent that my son will be a partner in it."

Here the Countess put her lips to Harley's ear, and whispered. He received her communication in attentive silence; but when she had done, pressed her hand, and bowed his head, as if in assent to a proposal.

In a few minutes the three ladies and Leonard were on their road to the neighbouring cottage.

Violante, with her usual delicate intuition, thought that Leonard and Helen must have much to say to each other; and (ignorant, as Leonard himself was, of Helen's engagement to Harley) began already, in the romance natural to her age, to predict for them happy and united days in the future. So she took her stepmother's arm, and left Helen and Leonard to follow.

"I wonder," she said, musingly, "how Miss Digby became Lord L'Estrange's ward. I hope she is not very rich, nor very high-born."

"La, my love," said the good Jemima, "that is not like you; you are not envious of her, poor girl?"

"Envious! Dear mamma, what a word! But don't you think Leonard and Miss Digby seem born for each other? And then the recollections of their childhood—the thoughts of childhood are so deep, and its memories so strangely soft!" The long lashes drooped over Violante's musing eyes as she spoke. "And therefore," she said, after a pause—"therefore I hoped that Miss Digby might not be very rich nor very high-born."

"I understand you now, Violante," exclaimed Jemima, her own early passion for match-making instantly returning to her; "for as Leonard, however clever and distinguished, is still the son of Mark Fairfield, the carpenter, it would spoil all if Miss Digby was, as you say, rich and high-born. I agree with you—a very pretty match—a very pretty match, indeed I wish dear Mrs. Dale were here now—she is so clever in settling such matters."

Meanwhile Leonard and Helen walked side by side a few paces in the rear. He had not offered her his arm. They had been silent hitherto since they left Riccabocca's house.

Helen now spoke first. In similar cases it is generally the woman, be she ever so timid, who does speak first. And here Helen was the bolder; for Leonard did not disguise from himself the nature of his feelings, and Helen was engaged to another; and her pure heart was fortified by the trust reposed in it.

"And have you ever heard more of the good Dr. Morgan, who had powders against sorrow, and who meant to be so kind to us—though," she added, colouring, "we did not think so then?"

"He took my child-angel from me," said Leonard, with

visible emotion; "and if she had not returned, where and what should I be now? But I have forgiven him. No, I have never met him since."

"And that terrible Mr. Burley?"

"Poor, poor Burley! He, too, is vanished out of my present life. I have made many inquiries after him; all I can hear is that he went abroad, supposed as a correspondent to some journal. I should like so much to see him again, now that perhaps I could help him as he helped me."

"*Helped* you—ah!"

Leonard smiled with a beating heart, as he saw again the dear prudent, warning look, and involuntarily drew closer to Helen. She seemed more restored to him and to her former self.

"Helped me much by his instructions; more, perhaps, by his very faults. You cannot guess, Helen,—I beg pardon, Miss Digby—but I forgot that we are no longer children: you cannot guess how much we men and more than all, perhaps, we writers whose task it is to unravel the web of human actions, owe even to our own past errors; and if we learned nothing by the errors of others, we should be dull indeed. We must know where the roads divide, and have marked where they lead to, before we can erect our sign-post; and books are the sign-posts in human life."

"Books! and I have not yet read yours. And Lord L'Estrange tells me you are famous now. Yet you remember me still—the poor orphan-child, whom you first saw weeping at her father's grave, and with whom you burdened your own young life, over-burdened already. No, still call me Helen—you must always be to me—a brother! Lord L'Estrange feels *that;* he said so to me when he told me that we were to meet again. He is so generous, so noble. Brother!" cried Helen, suddenly, and extending her hand, with a sweet but sublime look in her gentle face—"brother, we will never forfeit his esteem; we will both do our best to repay him! Will we not?—say so!"

Leonard felt overpowered by contending and unanalysed emotions. Touched almost to tears by the affectionate address—thrilled by the hand that pressed his own—and yet with a vague fear, a consciousness that something more than the words themselves was implied—something that checked all hope. And this word "brother," once so precious and so dear, why did he shrink from it now?—why could he not too say the sweet word "sister?"

"She is above me now and evermore!" he thought, mournfully; and the tones of his voice, when he spoke again, were changed. The appeal to renewed intimacy but made him more distant; and to that appeal itself he made no direct answer; for Mrs. Riccabocca, now turning round, and pointing to the cottage which came in view, with its picturesque gable-ends, cried out—

"But is that your house, Leonard? I never saw anything so pretty."

"You do not remember it then," said Leonard to Helen, in accents of melancholy reproach—"there where I saw you last! I doubted whether to keep it exactly as it was, and I said, 'No! the association is not changed because we try to surround it with whatever beauty we can create; the dearer the association, the more the Beautiful becomes to it natural.' Perhaps you don't understand this—perhaps it is only we poor poets who do."

"I understand it," said Helen, gently. She looked wistfully at the cottage.

"So changed—I have so often pictured it to myself—never, never like this; yet I loved it, commonplace as it was to my recollection; and the garret, and the tree in the carpenter's yard."

She did not give these thoughts utterance. And they now entered the garden.

## CHAPTER IV.

Mrs. FAIRFIELD was a proud woman when she received Mrs. Riccabocca and Violante in her grand house; for a grand house to her was that cottage to which her boy Lenny had brought her home. Proud, indeed, ever was Widow Fairfield; but she thought then in her secret heart, that if ever she could receive in the drawing-room of that grand house the great Mrs. Hazeldean, who had so lectured her for refusing to live any longer in the humble tenement rented of the Squire, the cup of human bliss would be filled, and she could contentedly die of the pride of it. She did not much notice Helen—her attention was too absorbed by the ladies who renewed their old acquaintance with her, and she carried them all over the house, yea, into the very kitchen; and so, somehow or other, there was a short time when Helen and Leonard found themselves alone. It was in the study. Helen had unconsciously seated herself in Leonard's own chair, and she was gazing with anxious and wistful interest on the scattered papers, looking so disorderly (though, in truth, in that disorder there was method, but method only known to the owner), and at the venerable well-worn books, in all languages, lying on the floor, on the chairs—anywhere. I must confess that Helen's first tidy womanlike idea was a great desire to arrange the litter. "Poor Leonard," she thought to herself—" the rest of the house so neat, but no one to take care of his own room and of him!"

As if he divined her thought, Leonard smiled and said, "It would be a cruel kindness to the spider, if the gentlest hand in the world tried to set its cobweb to rights."

HELEN.—"You were not quite so bad in the old days."

LEONARD.—"Yet even then, you were obliged to take care of the money. I have more books now, and more money. My present housekeeper lets me take care of the books, but she is less indulgent as to the money."

HELEN, (archly.)—"Are you as absent as ever?"

LEONARD.—"Much more so, I fear. The habit is incorrigible. Miss Digby—"

HELEN.—"Not Miss Digby—sister, if you like."

LEONARD, (evading the word that implied so forbidden an affinity.)—"Helen, will you grant me a favour? Your eyes and your smile say, 'yes.' Will you lay aside, for one minute, your shawl and bonnet? What! can you be surprised that I ask it? Can you not understand that I wish for one minute to think that you are at home again under this roof?"

Helen cast down her eyes, and seemed troubled; then she raised them, with a soft angelic candour in their dovelike blue, and, as if in shelter from all thoughts of more warm affection, again murmured "*brother*," and did as he asked her.

So there she sate, amongst the dull books, by his table, near the open window—her fair hair parted on her forehead —looking so good, so calm, so happy! Leonard wondered at his own self-command. His heart yearned to her with such inexpressible love—his lips so longed to murmur—"Ah, as now so could it be for ever! Is the home too mean?" But that word "brother" was as a talisman between her and him.

Yet she looked so at home—perhaps so at home she felt!—

more certainly than she had yet learned to do in that stiff stately house in which she was soon to have a daughter's rights. Was she suddenly made aware of this—that she so suddenly arose—and with a look of alarm and distress on her face—

"But—we are keeping Lady Lansmere too long," she said, falteringly. "We must go now," and she hastily took up her shawl and bonnet.

Just then Mrs. Fairfield entered with the visitors, and began making excuses for inattention to Miss Digby, whose identity with Leonard's child-angel she had not yet learned.

Helen received these apologies with her usual sweetness. "Nay," she said, "your son and I are such old friends, how could you stand on ceremony with me?"

"Old friends!" Mrs. Fairfield stared amazed, and then surveyed the fair speaker more curiously than she had yet done. "Pretty nice spoken thing," thought the widow; "as nice spoken as Miss Violante, and humbler-looking like,— though, as to dress, I never see anything so elegant out of a picter."

Helen now appropriated Mrs. Riccabocca's arm; and, after a kind leave-taking with the widow, the ladies returned towards Riccabocca's house.

Mrs. Fairfield, however, ran after them with Leonard's hat and gloves, which he had forgotten.

"'Deed, boy," she said, kindly, yet scoldingly, "but there'd be no more fine books, if the Lord had not fixed your head on your shoulders. You would not think it, marm," she added to Mrs. Riccabocca, "but sin' he has left you, he's not the 'cute lad he was; very helpless at times, marm!"

Helen could not resist turning round, and looking at Leonard, with a sly smile.

The widow saw the smile, and catching Leonard by the arm, whispered, "But, where before have you seen that pretty young lady? Old friends!"

"Ah, mother," said Leonard sadly, "it is a long tale; you have heard the beginning—who can guess the end?"— and he escaped. But Helen still leant on the arm of Mrs. Riccabocca, and, in the walk back, it seemed to Leonard as if the winter had re-settled in the sky.

Yet he was by the side of Violante, and she spoke to him with such praise of Helen! Alas! it is not always so sweet as folks say, to hear the praises of one we love. Sometimes those praises seem to ask ironically, "And what right hast thou to hope because thou lovest? *All* love *her.*"

## CHAPTER V.

No sooner had Lady Lansmere found herself alone with Riccabocca and Harley, than she laid her hand on the exile's arm, and, addressing him by a title she had not before given him, and from which he appeared to shrink nervously, said— "Harley, in bringing me to visit you, was forced to reveal to me your incognito, for I should have discovered it. You may not remember me, in spite of your gallantry. But I mixed more in the world than I do now, during your first visit to England, and once sate next to you at dinner at Carlton House. Nay, no compliments, but listen to me. Harley tells me you have cause for some alarm respecting the designs of an audacious and unprincipled adventurer, I may call him; for adventurers are of all ranks. Suffer your daughter to come to me, on a visit, as long as you please. With me, at least, she will be safe; and if you too, and the—"

"Stop, my dear madam," interrupted Riccabocca, with great vivacity, "your kindness overpowers me. I thank you most gratefully for your invitation to my child; but—"

"Nay," in his turn interrupted Harley, "no buts. I was not aware of my mother's intention when she entered this room. But since she whispered it to me, I have reflected on it, and am convinced that it is but a prudent precaution. Your retreat is known to Mr. Leslie—he is known to Peschiera. Grant that no indiscretion of Mr. Leslie's betray the secret; still I have reason to believe that the Count guesses Randal's acquaintance with you. Audley Egerton this morning told me he had gathered that, not from the young man himself, but from questions put to himself by Madame di Negra; and Peschiera might, and would set spies to track Leslie to every house that he visits—might and would, still more naturally, set spies to track myself. Were this man an Englishman, I should laugh at his machinations; but he is an Italian, and has been a conspirator. What he could do I know not; but an assassin can penetrate into a camp, and a traitor can creep through closed walls to one's hearth. With my mother, Violante must be safe; that you cannot oppose. And why not come yourself?"

Riccabocca had no reply to these arguments, so far as they affected Violante; indeed, they awakened the almost superstitious terror with which he regarded his enemy, and he consented at once that Violante should accept the invitation proffered. But he refused it for himself and Jemima.

"To say truth," said he, simply, "I made a secret vow, on re-entering England, that I would associate with none who knew the rank I had formerly held in my own land. I felt that all my philosophy was needed, to reconcile and habituate myself to my altered circumstances. In order to find in my present existence, however humble, those blessings which make all life noble—dignity and peace—it was necessary for poor, weak human nature, wholly to dismiss the past. It would unsettle me sadly, could I come to your house, renew awhile, in your kindness and respect—nay, in the very atmosphere of your society—the sense of what I have been; and then (should the more than doubtful chance of recall from my exile fail me) to awake, and find myself for the rest of life what I am. And though, were I alone, I might trust myself perhaps to the danger—yet my wife: she is happy and contented now; would she be so, if you had once spoiled her for the simple position of Dr. Riccabocca's wife? Should I not have to listen to regrets, and hopes, and fears that would prick sharp through my thin cloak of philosophy? Even as it is, since in a moment of weakness I confided my secret to her, I have had 'my rank' thrown at me—with a careless hand, it is true—but it hits hard nevertheless. No stone hurts like one taken from the ruins of one's own home; and the grander the home, why, the heavier the stone! Protect, dear madam—protect my daughter, since her father doubts his own power to do so. But—ask no more."

Riccabocca was immovable here. And the matter was settled as he decided, it being agreed that Violante should be still styled but the daughter of Dr. Riccabocca.

"And now, one word more," said Harley. "Do not confide to Mr. Leslie these arrangements; do not let him know where Violante is placed—at least, until I authorise such confidence in him. It is sufficient excuse, that it is no use to know unless he called to see her, and his movements, as I said before, may be watched. You can give the same reason to suspend his visits to yourself. Suffer me, meanwhile, to mature my judgment on this young man. In the meanwhile, also, I think that I shall have means of ascertaining the real nature of Peschiera's schemes. His sister has sought to know me; I will give her the occasion. I have heard some things of her in my last residence abroad, which make me believe that she cannot be wholly the Count's tool in any schemes nakedly villanous; that she has some finer qualities in her than I once supposed; and that she can be won from his influence. It is a state of war; we will carry it into the enemy's camp. You will promise me, then, to refrain from all further confidence in Mr. Leslie."

"For the present, yes," said Riccabocca, reluctantly.

"Do not even say that you have seen me, unless he first tell you that I am in England, and wish to learn your residence. I will give him full occasion to do so. Pish! don't hesitate; you know your own proverb—

> 'Boccha chiusa, ed occhio aperto
> Non fece mai nissun deserto.'

'The closed mouth and the open eye,' &c."

"That's very true," said the Doctor, much struck. "Very true. '*In boccha chiusa non c'entrano mosche.*' One can't swallow flies if one keeps one's mouth shut. *Corpo di Bacco!* that's very true indeed."

## CHAPTER VI.

VIOLANTE and Jemima were both greatly surprised, as the reader may suppose, when they heard, on their return, the arrangements already made for the former. The Countess insisted on taking her at once, and Riccabocca briefly said, "Certainly, the sooner the better." Violante was stunned and bewildered. Jemima hastened to make up a little bundle of things necessary, with many a woman's sigh that the poor wardrobe contained so few things befitting. But among the clothes she slipped a purse, containing the savings of months, perhaps of years, and with it a few affectionate lines, begging Violante to ask the Countess to buy her all that was proper for her father's child. There is always something hurried and uncomfortable in the abrupt and unexpected withdrawal of any member from a quiet household. The small party broke into still smaller knots. Violante hung on her father, and listened vaguely to his not very lucid explanations. The Countess approached Leonard, and, according to the usual mode with persons of quality addressing young authors, complimented him highly on the books she had not read, but which her son assured her were so remarkable. She was a little anxious to know where Harley had first met with Mr. Oran, whom he called his friend; but she was too high-bred to inquire, or to express any wonder that rank should be friends with genius. She took it for granted that they had formed their acquaintance abroad.

Harley conversed with Helen.—"You are not sorry that Violante is coming to us? She will be just such a companion for you as I could desire; of your own years too."

HELEN, (ingenuously.)—"It is hard to think I am not younger than she is."

HARLEY.—"Why, my dear Helen?"

HELEN.—"She is so brilliant. She talks so beautifully. And I—"

HARLEY.—"And you want but the habit of talking, to do justice to your own beautiful thoughts."

Helen looked at him gratefully, but shook her head. It was a common trick of hers, and always when she was praised.

At last the preparations were made—the farewell was said. Violante was in the carriage by Lady Lansmere's side. Slowly moved on the stately equipage with its four horses and trim postilions, heraldic badges on their shoulders, in the style rarely seen in the neighbourhood of the metropolis, and now fast vanishing even amidst distant counties.

Riccabocca, Jemima, and Jackeymo continued to gaze after it from the gate.

"She is gone," said Jackeymo, brushing his eyes with his coat-sleeve. "But it is a load off one's mind."

"And another load on one's heart," murmured Riccabocca. "Don't cry, Jemima; it may be bad for you, and bad for *him* that is to come. It is astonishing how the humours of the mother may affect the unborn. I should not like to have a son who has a more than usual propensity to tears."

The poor philosopher tried to smile; but it was a bad attempt. He went slowly in, and shut himself with his books. But he could not read. His whole mind was unsettled. And though, like all parents, he had been anxious to rid himself of a beloved daughter for life, now that she was gone but for a while, a string seemed broken in the Music of Home.

## CHAPTER VII.

THE evening of the same day, as Egerton, who was to entertain a large party at dinner, was changing his dress, Harley walked into his room.

Egerton dismissed his valet by a sign, and continued his toilet.

"Excuse me, my dear Harley, I have only ten minutes to give you. I expect one of the royal dukes, and punctuality is the stern virtue of men of business, and the graceful courtesy of princes."

Harley had usually a jest for his friend's aphorisms; but he had none now. He laid his hand kindly on Egerton's shoulder—"Before I speak of my business, tell me how you are—better?"

"Better—nay, I am always well. Pooh! I may look a little tired—years of toil will tell on the countenance. But that matters little: the period of life has passed with me when one cares how one looks in the glass."

As he spoke, Egerton completed his dress, and came to the hearth, standing there, erect and dignified as usual, still far handsomer than many a younger man, and with a form that seemed to have ample vigour to support for many a year the sad and glorious burthen of power.

"So now to your business, Harley."

"In the first place, I want you to present me, at the earliest opportunity, to Madame di Negra. You say she wished to know me."

"Are you serious?"

"Yes."

"Well, then, she receives this evening. I did not mean to go; but when my party breaks up—"

"You can call for me at 'The Travellers.' Do!"

"Next—you knew Lady Jane Horton better even than I did, at least in the last year of her life." Harley sighed, and Egerton turned and stirred the fire.

"Pray, did you ever see at her house, or hear her speak of, a Mrs. Bertram?"

"Of whom?" said Egerton, in a hollow voice, his face still turned towards the fire.

"A. Mrs. Bertram; but Heavens! my dear fellow, what is the matter? Are you ill?"

"A spasm at the heart, that is all—don't ring—I shall be better presently—go on talking. Mrs. —— why do you ask?"

"Why? I have hardly time to explain; but I am, as I told you, resolved on righting my old Italian friend, if Heaven will help me, as it ever does help the just when they bestir themselves; and this Mrs. Bertram is mixed up in my friend's affairs."

"His! How is that possible?"

Harley rapidly and succinctly explained. Audley listened attentively, with his eyes fixed on the floor, and still seeming to labour under great difficulty of breathing.

At last he answered, "I remember something of this Mrs.—Mrs.—Bertram. But your inquiries after her would be useless. I think I have heard that she is long since dead; nay, I am sure of it."

"Dead!—that is most unfortunate. But do you know any of her relations or friends? Can you suggest any mode of tracing this packet, if it came to her hands?"

"No."

"And Lady Jane had scarcely any friend that I remember, except my mother, and she knows nothing of this Mrs. Bertram. How unlucky! I think I shall advertise. Yet, no. I could only distinguish this Mrs. Bertram from any other of the same name, by stating with whom she had gone abroad, and that would catch the attention of Peschiera, and set him to counterwork us."

"And what avails it?" said Egerton. "She whom you seek is no more—no more!" He paused, and went on rapidly—"The packet did not arrive in England till years after her death—was no doubt returned to the post-office—is destroyed long ago."

Harley looked very much disappointed. Egerton went on in a sort of set mechanical voice, as if not thinking of what he said, but speaking from the dry practical mode of reasoning which was habitual to him, and by which the man of the world destroys the hopes of an enthusiast. Then starting up at the sound of the first thundering knock at the street door, he said, "Hark! you must excuse me."

"I leave you, my dear Audley. But I must again ask—Are you better now?"

"Much, much—quite well. I will call for you—probably between eleven and twelve."

## CHAPTER VIII.

If any one could be more surprised **at seeing** Lord L'Estrange at the house of Madame di Negra that evening than the fair hostess herself, it was Randal Leslie. Something instinctively told him that this visit threatened interference with whatever might be his ultimate projects in regard to Riccabocca and Violante. But Randal Leslie was not one of those who shrink from an intellectual combat. On the contrary, he was too confident of his powers of intrigue, not to take a delight in their exercise. He could not conceive that the indolent Harley could be a match for his own restless activity and dogged perseverance. But in a very few moments fear crept on him. No man of his day could produce a more brilliant effect than Lord L'Estrange, when he deigned to desire it. Without much pretence to that personal beauty which strikes at first sight, he still retained all the charm of countenance, and all the grace of manner, which had made him in boyhood the spoiled darling of society. Madame di Negra had collected but a small circle round her, still it was of the *élite* of the great world; not, indeed, those more precise and reserved *dames de chateau*, whom the lighter and easier of the fair dispensers of fashion ridicule as prudes; but nevertheless, ladies were there, as unblemished in reputation, as high in rank; flirts and coquettes, perhaps—nothing more; in short, "charming women"—the gay butterflies that hover over the stiff parterre. And there were ambassadors and ministers, and wits and brilliant debaters, and first-rate dandies (dandies, when first-rate, are generally very agreeable men). Amongst all these various persons, Harley, so long a stranger to the London world, seemed to make himself at home with the ease of an Alcibiades. Many of the less juvenile ladies remembered him, and rushed to claim his acquaintance, with nods and becks, and wreathed smiles. He had ready compliment for each. And few indeed were there, men or women, for whom Harley L'Estrange had not appropriate attraction. Distinguished reputation as soldier and scholar for the grave; whim and pleasantry for the gay; novelty for the sated; and for the more vulgar natures was he not Lord L'Estrange, unmarried, possessed already of a large independence, and heir to an ancient earldom, and some fifty thousands a-year?

Not till he had succeeded in the general effect—which, it must be owned, he did his best to create—did Harley seriously and especially devote himself to his hostess. And then he seated himself by her side; and, as if in compliment to both, less pressing admirers insensibly slipped away and edged off.

Frank Hazeldean was the last to quit his ground behind Madame di Negra's chair; but when he found that the two began to talk in Italian, and he could not understand a word they said, he too—fancying, poor fellow, that he looked foolish, and cursing his Eton education that had neglected, for languages spoken by the dead, of which he had learned little, those still in use among the living, of which he had learned nought—retreated towards Randal, and asked wistfully, "Pray, what age should you say L'Estrange was? He must be devilish old, in spite of his looks. Why, he was at Waterloo!"

"He is young enough to be a terrible rival," answered Randal, with artful truth.

Frank turned pale, and began to meditate dreadful bloodthirsty thoughts, of which hair-triggers and Lord's Cricket-ground formed the staple.

Certainly there was apparent ground for a lover's jealousy. For Harley and Beatrice now conversed in a low tone, and Beatrice seemed agitated, and Harley earnest. Randal himself grew more and more perplexed. Was Lord L'Estrange really enamoured of the Marchesa? If so, farewell to all hopes of Frank's marriage with her! Or was he merely playing a part in Riccabocca's interest; pretending to be the lover, in order to obtain an influence over her mind, rule her through her ambition, and secure an ally against her brother? Was this *finesse* compatible with Randal's notions of Harley's character? Was it consistent with that chivalric and soldierly spirit of honour which the frank nobleman affected, to make love to a woman in mere *ruse de guerre?* Could mere friendship for Riccabocca be a sufficient inducement to a man, who, whatever his weaknesses or his errors, seemed to wear on his very forehead a soul above deceit, to stoop to paltry means, even for a worthy end? At this question, a new thought flashed upon Randal—might not Lord L'Estrange have speculated himself upon winning Violante?—would not that account for all the exertions he had made on behalf of her inheritance at the court of Vienna—exertions of which Peschiera and Beatrice had both complained? Those objections which the Austrian government might take to Violante's marriage with some obscure Englishman would probably not exist against a man like Harley L'Estrange, whose family not only belonged to the highest aristocracy of England, but had always supported opinions in vogue amongst the leading governments of Europe. Harley himself, it is true, had never taken part in politics, but his notions were, no doubt, those of a high-born soldier, who had fought, in alliance with Austria, for the restoration of the Bourbons. And this immense wealth—which Violante might lose, if she married one like Randal himself—her marriage with the heir of the Lansmeres might actually tend only to secure. Could Harley, with all his own expectations, be indifferent to such a prize? —and no doubt he had learned Violante's rare beauty in his correspondence with Riccabocca.

Thus considered, it seemed natural to Randal's estimate of human nature, that Harley's more prudish scruples of honour, as regards what is due to women, could not resist a temptation so strong. Mere friendship was not a motive powerful enough to shake them, but ambition was.

While Randal was thus cogitating, Frank thus suffering, and many a whisper, in comment on the evident flirtation between the beautiful hostess and the accomplished guest, reached the ears both of the brooding schemer and the jealous lover, the conversation between the two objects of remark and gossip had taken a new turn. Indeed, Beatrice had made an effort to change it.

"It is long, my lord," said she, still speaking Italian, "since I have heard sentiments like those you address to me; and if I do not feel myself wholly unworthy of them, it is from the pleasure I have felt in reading sentiments equally foreign to the language of the world in which I live." She took a book from the table as she spoke: "Have you seen this work?"

Harley glanced at the title-page. "To be sure I have, and I know the author."

"I envy you that honour. I should so like also to know one who has discovered to me deeps in my own heart which I had never explored."

"Charming Marchesa, if the book has done this, believe me that I have paid you no false compliment—formed no overflattering estimate of your nature; for the charm of the work is but in its simple appeal to good and generous emotions, and it can charm none in whom those emotions exist not!"

"Nay, that cannot be true, or why is it so popular?"

"Because good and generous emotions are more common to the human heart than we are aware of till the appeal comes."

"Don't ask me to think that! I have found the world so base."

"Pardon me a rude question; but what do you know of the world?"

Beatrice looked first in surprise at Harley, then glanced round the room with significant irony.

"As I thought; you call this little room 'the world.' Be it so. I will venture to say, that if the people in this room were suddenly converted into an audience before a stage, and you were as consummate in the actor's art as you are in all others that please and command—"

"Well?"

"And were to deliver a speech full of sordid and base sentiments, you would be hissed. But let any other woman, with half your powers, arise and utter sentiments sweet and womanly, or honest and lofty—and applause would flow from every lip, and tears rush to many a worldly eye. The true proof of the inherent nobleness of our common nature is in the sympathy it betrays with what is noble wherever crowds are collected. Never believe the world is base;—if it were so, no society could hold together for a day. But you would know the author of this book? I will bring him to you."

"Do."

"And now," said Harley, rising, and with his candid, winning smile, "do you think we shall ever be friends?"

"You have startled me so, that I can scarcely answer. But why would you be friends with me?"

"Because you need a friend. You have none?"

"Strange flatterer!" said Beatrice, smiling, though very sadly; and looking up, her eye caught Randal's.

"Pooh!" said Harley, "you are too penetrating to believe that you inspire friendship *there*. Ah, do you suppose that, all the while I have been conversing with you, I have not noticed the watchful gaze of Mr. Randal Leslie? What tie can possibly connect you together I know not yet; but I soon shall."

"Indeed! you talk like one of the old Council of Venice. You try hard to make me fear you," said Beatrice, seeking to escape from the graver kind of impression Harley had made on her, by the affectation, partly of coquetry, partly of levity

"And I," said L'Estrange, calmly, "tell you already, that I fear you no more." He bowed, and passed through the crowd to rejoin Audley, who was seated in a corner whispering with some of his political colleagues. Before Harley reached the minister, he found himself close to Randal and young Hazeldean.

He bowed to the first, and extended his hand to the last. Randal felt the distinction, and his sullen, bitter pride was deeply galled—a feeling of hate towards Harley passed into his mind. He was pleased to see the cold hesitation with which Frank just touched the hand offered to him. But Randal had not been the only person whose watch upon Beatrice the keen-eyed Harley had noticed. Harley had seen the angry looks of Frank Hazeldean, and divined the cause. So he smiled forgivingly at the slight he had received.

"You are like me, Mr. Hazeldean," said he. "You think something of the heart should go with all courtesy that bespeaks friendship—

'The hand of Douglas is his own.'"

Here Harley drew aside Randal. "Mr. Leslie, a word with you. If I wished to know the retreat of Dr. Riccabocca, in order to render him a great service, would you confide to me that secret?"

"That woman has let out her suspicions that I know the exile's retreat," thought Randal; and with quick presence of mind, he replied at once—

"My Lord, yonder stands a connection of Dr. Riccabocca's. Mr. Hazeldean is surely the person to whom you should address this inquiry."

"Not so, Mr. Leslie; for I suspect that he cannot answer it, and that you can. Well, I will ask something that it seems to me you may grant without hesitation. Should you see Dr. Riccabocca, tell him that I am in England, and so leave it to him to communicate with me or not; but perhaps you have already done so?"

"Lord L'Estrange," said Randal, bowing low, with pointed formality, "excuse me if I decline either to disclaim or acquiesce in the knowledge you impute to me. If I am acquainted with any secret intrusted to me by Dr. Riccabocca, it is for me to use my own discretion how best to guard it. And for the rest, after the Scotch earl, whose words your lordship has quoted, refused to touch the hand of Marmion,

Douglas could scarcely have called Marmion back in order to give him—a message!"

Harley was not prepared for this tone in Mr. Egerton's *protégé*, and his own gallant nature was rather pleased than irritated by a haughtiness that at least seemed to bespeak independence of spirit. Nevertheless, L'Estrange's suspicions of Randal were too strong to be easily set aside, and therefore he replied, civilly, but with covert taunt—

"I submit to your rebuke, Mr. Leslie, though I meant not the offence you would ascribe to me. I regret my unlucky quotation yet the more, since the wit of your retort has obliged you to identify yourself with Marmion, who, though a clever and brave fellow, was an uncommonly—tricky one." And so Harley, certainly having the best of it, moved on, and joining Egerton, in a few minutes more both left the room.

"What was L'Estrange saying to you?" asked Frank, "Something about Beatrice I am sure."

"No; only quoting poetry."

"Then what made you look so angry, my dear fellow? I know it was your kind feeling for me. As you say, he is a formidable rival. But that can't be his own hair. Do you think he wears a *toupet?* I am sure he was praising Beatrice. He is evidently very much smitten with her. But I don't think she is a woman to be caught by *mere* rank and fortune! Do you? Why can't you speak?"

"If you do not get her consent soon, I think she is lost to you," said Randal, slowly; and before Frank could recover his dismay, glided from the house.

## CHAPTER IX.

VIOLANTE'S first evening at the Lansmeres had passed more happily to her than the first evening under the same roof had done to Helen. True that she missed her father much— Jemima somewhat; but she so identified her father's cause with Harley, that she had a sort of vague feeling that it was to promote that cause that she was on this visit to Harley's parents. And the Countess, it must be owned, was more emphatically cordial to her than she had ever yet been to Captain Digby's orphan. But perhaps the real difference in the heart of either girl was this, that Helen felt awe of Lady Lansmere, and Violante felt only love for Lord L'Estrange's mother. Violante, too, was one of those persons whom a reserved and formal person, like the Countess, "can get on with," as the phrase goes. Not so poor little Helen—so shy herself, and so hard to coax into more than gentle monosyllables. And Lady Lansmere's favourite talk was always of Harley. Helen had listened to such talk with respect and interest. Violante listened to it with inquisitive eagerness—with blushing delight. The mother's heart noticed the distinction between the two, and no wonder that that heart moved more to Violante than to Helen. Lord Lansmere, too, like most gentlemen of his age, clumped all young ladies together, as a harmless, amiable, but singularly stupid class of the genus-Petticoat, meant to look pretty, play the piano, and talk to each other about frocks and sweethearts. Therefore this animated dazzling creature, with her infinite variety of look and play of mind, took him by surprise, charmed him into attention, and warmed him into gallantry. Helen sate in her quiet corner, at her work, sometimes listening with almost mournful, though certainly unenvious, admiration at Violante's vivid, yet ever unconscious, eloquence of word and thought—sometimes plunged deep into her own secret meditations. And all the while the work went on the same, under the small, noiseless fingers. This was one of Helen's habits that irritated the nerves of Lady Lansmere. She despised young ladies who were fond of work. She did not comprehend how often it is the resource of the sweet womanly mind, not from want of thought, but from the silence and the depth of it. Violante was surprised, and perhaps disappointed, that Harley had left the house before dinner, and did not return all the evening. But Lady Lansmere, in making excuse for his absence, on the plea of engagements, found so good an opportunity to talk of his ways in general—of his rare promise in boyhood—of her regret at the inaction of his maturity—of her hope to see him yet do justice to his natural powers, that Violante almost ceased to miss him.

And when Lady Lansmere conducted her to her room, and, kissing her cheek tenderly, said, "But you are just the person Harley admires—just the person to rouse him from melancholy dreams, of which his wild humours are now but the vain disguise "—Violante crossed her arms on her bosom, and her bright eyes, deepened into tenderness, seemed to ask, "He melancholy—and why?"

On leaving Violante's room, Lady Lansmere paused before the door of Helen's; and, after musing a little while, entered softly.

Helen had dismissed her maid; and, at the moment Lady Lansmere entered, she was kneeling at the foot of the bed, her hands clasped before her face.

Her form, thus seen, looked so youthful and child-like—the attitude itself was so holy and so touching, that the proud and cold expression on Lady Lansmere's face changed. She shaded the light involuntarily, and seated herself in silence that she might not disturb the act of prayer.

When Helen rose, she was startled to see the Countess seated by the fire; and hastily drew her hand across her eyes. She had been weeping.

Lady Lansmere did not, however, turn to observe those traces of tears, which Helen feared were too visible. The Countess was too absorbed in her own thoughts; and as Helen timidly approached, she said—still with her eyes on the clear low fire—"I beg your pardon, Miss Digby, for my intrusion; but my son has left it to me to prepare Lord Lansmere to learn the offer you have done Harley the honour to accept. I have not yet spoken to my lord; it may be days before I find a fitting occasion to do so; meanwhile I feel assured that your sense of propriety will make you agree with me that it is due to Lord L'Estrange's father, that strangers should not learn arrangements of such moment in his family, before his own consent be obtained."

Here the Countess came to a full pause; and poor Helen, finding herself called upon for some reply to this chilling speech, stammered out, scarce audibly—

"Certainly, madam, I never dreamed of—"

"That is right, my dear," interrupted Lady Lansmere rising suddenly, and as if greatly relieved. "I could not doubt your superiority to ordinary girls of your age, with whom these matters are never secret for a moment. Therefore, of course, you will not mention, at present, what has passed between you and Harley, to any of the friends with whom you may correspond."

"I have no correspondents—no friends, Lady Lansmere," said Helen, deprecatingly, and trying hard not to cry.

"I am very glad to hear it, my dear; young ladies never should have. Friends, especially friends who correspond, are the worst enemies they can have. Good night, Miss Digby. I need not add, by the way, that though we are bound to show all kindness to this young Italian lady, still she is wholly unconnected with our family; and you will be as prudent with her as you would have been with your correspondents—had you had the misfortune to have any."

Lady Lansmere said the last words with a smile, and left an ungenial kiss (the stepmother's kiss) on Helen's bended brow. She then left the room, and Helen sate on the seat vacated by the stately unloving form, and again covered her face with her hands, and again wept. But when she rose at last, and the light fell upon her face, that soft face was sad indeed, but serene—serene, as if with some inward sense of duty—sad, as with the resignation which accepts patience instead of hope.

## CHAPTER X.

The next morning Harley appeared at breakfast. He was in gay spirits, and conversed more freely with Violante than he had yet done. He seemed to amuse himself by attacking all she said, and provoking her to argument. Violante was naturally a very earnest person; whether grave or gay, she spoke with her heart on her lips, and her soul in her eyes. She did not yet comprehend the light vein of Harley's irony, so she grew piqued and chafed; and she was so lovely in anger; it so brightened her beauty and animated her words, that no wonder Harley thus maliciously teased her. But what perhaps, she liked still less than the teasing—though she could not tell why—was the kind of familiarity that Harley assumed with her—a familiarity as if he had known her all her life—that of a good-humoured elder brother, or a bachelor uncle. To Helen, on the contrary, when he did not address her apart, his manner was more respectful. He did not call *her* by her Christian name, as he did Violante, but "Miss Digby," and softened his tone and inclined his head when he spoke to her. Nor did he presume to jest at the very few and brief sentences he drew from Helen, but rather listened to them with deference, and invariably honoured them with approval. After breakfast he asked Violante to play or sing; and when she frankly owned how little she had cultivated those accomplishments, he persuaded Helen to sit down to the piano, and stood by her side while she did so, turning over the leaves of her music-book with the ready devotion of an admiring amateur. Helen always played well, but less well than usual that day, for her generous nature felt abashed. It was as if she were showing off to mortify Violante. But Violante, on the other hand, was so passionately fond of music that she had no feeling left for the sense of her own inferiority. Yet she sighed when Helen rose, and Harley thanked Miss Digby for the delight she had given him.

The day was fine. Lady Lansmere proposed to walk in the garden. While the ladies went up-stairs for their shawls and bonnets, Harley lighted his cigar, and stept from the window upon the lawn. Lady Lansmere joined him before the girls came out.

"Harley," said she, taking his arm, "what a charming companion you have introduced to us! I never met with any that both pleased and delighted me like this dear Violante. Most girls who possess some power of conversation, and who have dared to think for themselves, are so pedantic, or so masculine; but *she* is always so simple, and always still the girl. Ah, Harley!"

"Why that sigh, my dear mother?"

"I was thinking how exactly she would have suited you—how proud I should have been of such a daughter-in-law—and how happy you would have been with such a wife."

Harley started. "Tut," said he, peevishly, "she is a mere child; you forget my years."

"Why," said Lady Lansmere, surprised, "Helen is quite as young as Violante."

"In dates—yes. But Helen's character is so staid;—what it is now it will be ever; and Helen, from gratitude, respect, or pity, condescends to accept the ruins of my heart;—while this bright Italian has the soul of a Juliet, and would expect in a husband all the passion of a Romeo. Nay, mother, hush. Do you forget that I am engaged—and of my own free will and choice? Poor dear Helen! Apropos, have you spoken to my father, as you undertook to do?"

"Not yet. I must seize the right moment. You know that my lord requires management."

"My dear mother, that female notion of managing us, men, costs you, ladies, a great waste of time, and occasions us a great deal of sorrow. Men are easily managed by plain truth. *We* are brought up to respect it, strange as it may seem to you!"

Lady Lansmere smiled with the air of superior wisdom, and

the experience of an accomplished wife. "Leave it to me, Harley, and rely on my lord's consent."

Harley knew that Lady Lansmere always succeeded in obtaining her way with his father; and he felt that the Earl might naturally be disappointed in such an alliance, and, without due propitiation, evince that disappointment in his manner to Helen. Harley was bound to save her from all chance of such humiliation. He did not wish her to think that she was not welcomed into his family; therefore he said, "I resign myself to your promise and your diplomacy. Meanwhile, as you love me, be kind to my betrothed."

"Am I not so?"

"Hem. Are you as kind as if she were the great heiress you believe Violante to be?"

"Is it," answered Lady Lansmere, evading the question—"is it because one is an heiress and the other is not that you make so marked a difference in your own manner to the two; treating Violante as a spoilt child, and Miss Digby as—"

"The destined wife of Lord L'Estrange, and the daughter-in-law of Lady Lansmere—yes."

The Countess suppressed an impatient exclamation that rose to her lips, for Harley's brow wore that serious aspect which it rarely assumed save when he was in those moods in which men must be soothed, not resisted. And after a pause he went on—"I am going to leave you to-day. I have engaged apartments at the Clarendon. I intend to gratify your wish, so often expressed, that I should enjoy what are called the pleasures of my rank, and the privileges of single-blessedness—celebrate my adieu to celibacy, and blaze once more, with the splendour of a setting sun, upon Hyde Park and May Fair."

"You are a positive enigma. Leave our house, just when you are betrothed to its inmate! Is that the natural conduct of a lover?"

"How can your woman eyes be so dull, and your woman heart so obtuse?" answered Harley, half-laughing, half-scolding. "Can you not guess that I wish that Helen and myself should both lose the association of mere ward and guardian; that the very familiarity of our intercourse under the same roof almost forbids us to be lovers; that we lose the joy to meet, and the pang to part. Don't you remember the story of the Frenchman, who for twenty years loved a lady, and never missed passing his evenings at her house. She became a widow. 'I wish you joy,' cried his friend; 'you may now marry the woman you have so long adored.' 'Alas,' said the poor Frenchman, profoundly dejected; 'and if so, where shall I spend my evenings?'"

Here Violante and Helen were seen in the garden, walking affectionately arm in arm.

"I don't perceive the point of your witty, heartless anecdote," said Lady Lansmere, obstinately. "Settle that, however, with Miss Digby. But, to leave the very day after your friend's daughter comes as a guest!—what will *she* think of it?"

Lord L'Estrange looked steadfastly at his mother. "Does it matter much what she thinks of me?—of a man engaged to another; and old enough to be—"

"I wish to heaven you would not talk of your age, Harley; it is a reflection upon mine; and I never saw you look so well nor so handsome." With that she drew him on towards the young ladies; and, taking Helen's arm, asked her, aside, "If she knew that Lord L'Estrange had engaged rooms at the Clarendon; and if she understood why?" As, while she said this she moved on, Harley was left by Violante's side.

"You will be very dull here, I fear, my poor child," said he.

"Dull! But why *will* you call me child? Am I so very —very child-like?"

"Certainly, you are to me—a mere infant. Have I not seen you one; have I not held you in my arms?"

VIOLANTE.—"But that was a long time ago!"

HARLEY.—"True. But if years have not stood still for you, they have not been stationary for me. There is the same difference between us now that there was then. And, therefore, permit me still to call you child, and as child to treat you!"

VIOLANTE.—"I will do no such thing. Do you know that I always thought I was good-tempered till this morning."

HARLEY.—"And what undeceived you? Did you break your doll?"

VIOLANTE, (with an indignant flash from her dark eyes.)— "There!—again!—you delight in provoking me!"

HARLEY.—"It *was* the doll, then. Don't cry; I will get you another."

Violante plucked her arm from him, and walked away towards the Countess in speechless scorn. Harley's brow contracted, in thought and in gloom. He stood still for a moment or so, and then joined the ladies.

"I am trespassing sadly on your morning; but I wait for a visitor whom I sent to before you were up. He is to be here at twelve. With your permission, I will dine with you to-morrow, and you will invite him to meet me."

"Certainly. And who is your friend. I guess—the young author?"

"Leonard Fairfield," cried Violante, who had conquered, or felt ashamed, of her short-lived anger.

"Fairfield!" repeated Lady Lansmere. "I thought, Harley, you said the name was Oran."

"He has assumed the latter name. He is the son of Mark Fairfield, who married an Avenel. Did you recognise no family likeness?—none in those eyes—mother?" said Harley, sinking his voice into a whisper.

"No," answered the Countess, falteringly.

Harley, observing that Violante was now speaking to Helen about Leonard, and that neither was listening to him, resumed in the same low tone, "And his mother—Nora's sister,—shrank from seeing me! That is the reason why I wished you not to call. She has not told the young man *why* she shrank from seeing me; nor have I explained it to him as yet. Perhaps I never shall."

"Indeed, dearest Harley," said the Countess, with great gentleness, "I wish you too much to forget the folly—well, I will not say that word—the sorrows of your boyhood, not to hope that you will rather strive against such painful memories than renew them by unnecessary confidence to any one; least of all to the relation of—"

"Enough!—don't name her; the very name pains me. And as to confidence, there are but two persons in the world to whom I ever bare the old wounds—yourself and Egerton. Let this pass. Ha!—a ring at the bell—that is he!"

---

## CHAPTER XI.

LEONARD entered on the scene, and joined the party in the garden. The Countess, perhaps to please her son, was more than civil—she was markedly kind to him. She noticed him more attentively than she had hitherto done; and, with all her prejudices of birth, was struck to find the son of Mark Fairfield the carpenter so thoroughly the gentleman. He might not have the exact tone and phrase by which Convention stereotypes those born and schooled in a certain world; but the aristocrats of Nature can dispense with such trite minutiæ. And Leonard had lived, of late at least, in the best society that exists, for the polish of language and the refinement of manners,—the society in which the most graceful ideas are clothed in the most graceful forms—the society which really, though indirectly, gives the law to courts—the society of the most classic authors, in the various ages in which literature has flowered forth from civilization. And if there was something in the exquisite sweetness of Leonard's voice, look, and manner, which the Countess acknowledged to attain that perfection in high breeding, which, under the name of "suavity," steals its way into the heart, so her interest in him was aroused by a certain subdued melancholy which is rarely without distinction, and never without charm. He and Helen exchanged but few words. There was but one occasion in which they could have spoken apart, and Helen herself contrived to elude it. His face brightened at Lady Lansmere's cordial invitation, and he glanced at Helen as he accepted it; but her eye did not meet his own.

"And now," said Harley, whistling to Nero, whom his ward was silently caressing, "I must take Leonard away. Adieu! all of you, till to-morrow at dinner. Miss Violante, is the doll to have blue eyes or black?"

Violante turned her own black eyes in mute appeal to Lady Lansmere, and nestled to that lady's side as if in refuge from unworthy insult.

## CHAPTER XII.

"LET the carriage go to the Clarendon," said Harley to his servant; "I and Mr. Oran will walk to town. Leonard, I think you would rejoice at an occasion to serve your old friends, Dr. Riccabocca and his daughter?"

"Serve them! O yes." And there instantly returned to Leonard the recollection of Violante's words when, on leaving his quiet village, he had sighed to part from all those he loved; and the little dark-eyed girl had said, proudly, yet consolingly, "But to SERVE those you love!" He turned to L'Estrange, with beaming, inquisitive eyes.

"I said to our friend," resumed Harley, "that I would vouch for your honour as my own. I am about to prove my words, and to confide the secrets which your penetration has indeed divined;—our friend is not what he seems." Harley then briefly related to Leonard the particulars of the exile's history, the rank he had held in his native land, the manner in which, partly through the misrepresentations of a kinsman he had trusted, partly through the influence of a wife he had loved, he had been drawn into schemes which he believed bounded to the emancipation of Italy from a foreign yoke by the united exertions of her best and bravest sons.

"A noble ambition," interrupted Leonard, manfully. "And pardon me, my lord, I should not have thought that you would speak of it in a tone that implies blame."

"The ambition in itself was noble," answered Harley. "But the cause to which it was devoted became defiled in its dark channel through Secret Societies. It is the misfortune of all miscellaneous political combinations, that with the purest motives of their more generous members are ever mixed the most sordid interests, and the fiercest passions of mean confederates. When those combinations act openly, and in day-light, under the eye of Public Opinion, the healthier elements usually prevail; where they are shrouded in mystery —where they are subjected to no censor in the discussion of the impartial and dispassionate—where chiefs working in the dark exact blind obedience, and every man who is at war with law is at once admitted as a friend of freedom—the history of the world tells us that patriotism soon passes away. Where all is in public, public virtue, by the natural sympathies of the common mind, and by the wholesome control of shame, is likely to obtain ascendancy; where all is in private, and shame is but for him who refuses the abnegation of his conscience, each man seeks the indulgence of his private vice. And hence, in Secret Societies (from which may yet proceed great danger to all Europe), we find but foul and hateful Eleusinia, affording pretexts to the ambition of the great, to the licence of the penniless, to the passions of the revengeful, to the anarchy of the ignorant. In a word, the societies of these Italian Carbonari did but engender schemes in which the abler chiefs disguised new forms of despotism, and in which the revolutionary many looked forward to the overthrow of all the institutions that stand between Law and

Chaos. Naturally, therefore" (added L'Estrange, drily), "when their schemes were detected, and the conspiracy foiled, it was for the silly, honest men entrapped into the league to suffer—the leaders turned king's evidence, and the common mercenaries became—banditti." Harley then proceeded to state that it was just when the *soi-disant* Riccabocca had discovered the true nature and ulterior views of the conspirators he had joined, and actually withdrawn from their councils, that he was denounced by the kinsman who had duped him into the enterprise, and who now profited by his treason. Harley next spoke of the packet despatched by Riccabocca's dying wife, as it was supposed, to Mrs. Bertram, and of the hopes he founded on the contents of that packet, if discovered. He then referred to the design which had brought Peschiera to England—a design which that personage had avowed with such effrontery to his companions at Vienna, that he had publicly laid wagers on his success.

"But these men can know nothing of England—of the safety of English laws," said Leonard, naturally. "We take it for granted that Riccabocca, if I am still so to call him, refuses his consent to the marriage between his daughter and his foe. Where, then, the danger? This Count, even if Violante were not under your mother's roof, could not get an opportunity to see her. He could not attack the house and carry her off like a feudal baron in the middle ages."

"All this is very true," answered Harley. "Yet I have found through life that we cannot estimate danger by external circumstances, but by the character of those from whom it is threatened. This Count is a man of singular audacity, of no mean natural talents—talents practised in every art of duplicity and intrigue; one of those men whose boast it is that they succeed in whatever they undertake; and he is, here, urged on the one hand by all that can whet the avarice, and on the other, by all that can give invention to despair. Therefore, though I cannot guess what plan he may possibly adopt, I never doubt that some plan, formed with cunning and pursued with daring, will be embraced the moment he discovers Violante's retreat, unless, indeed, we can forestall all peril by the restoration of her father, and the detection of the fraud and falsehood to which Peschiera owes the fortune he appropriates. Thus, while we must prosecute to the utmost our inquiries for the missing documents, so it should be our care to possess ourselves, if possible, of such knowledge of the Count's machinations as may enable us to defeat them. Now, it was with satisfaction that I learned in Germany that Peschiera's sister was in London. I knew enough both of his disposition and of the intimacy between himself and this lady, to make me think it probable he will seek to make her his instrument and accomplice, should he require one. Peschiera (as you may suppose by his audacious wager) is not one of those secret villains who would cut off their right hand if it could betray the knowledge of what was done by the left—rather one of those self-confident vaunting knaves of high animal spirits, and conscience so obtuse that it clouds their intellect—who must have some one to whom they can boast of their abilities and confide their projects. And Peschiera has done all he can to render this poor woman so wholly dependent on him, as to be his slave and his tool. But I have learned certain traits in her character that show it to be impressionable to good, and with tendencies to honour. Peschiera had taken advantage of the admiration she excited, some years ago, in a rich young Englishman, to entice this admirer into gambling, and sought to make his sister both a decoy and an instrument in his designs of plunder. She did not encourage the addresses of our countryman, but she warned him of the snare laid for him, and entreated him to leave the place lest her brother should discover and punish her honesty. The Englishman told me this himself. In fine, my hope of detaching this lady from Peschiera's interests, and inducing her to forewarn us of his purpose, consists but in the innocent, and, I hope, laudable artifice, of redeeming herself—of appealing to, and calling into disused exercise, the better springs of her nature."

Leonard listened with admiration and some surprise to the singularly subtle and sagacious insight into character which Harley evinced in the brief clear strokes by which he had thus depicted Peschiera and Beatrice, and was struck by the boldness with which Harley rested a whole system of action upon a few deductions drawn from his reasonings on human motive and characteristic bias. Leonard had not expected to find so much practical acuteness in a man who, however accomplished, usually seemed indifferent, dreamy, and abstracted to the ordinary things of life. But Harley L'Estrange was one of those whose powers lie dormant till circumstance supplies to them all they need for activity—the stimulant of a motive.

Harley resumed—"After a conversation I had with the lady last night, it occurred to me that in this part of our diplomacy you could render us essential service. Madame di

Negra—such is the sister's name—has conceived an admiration for your genius, and a strong desire to know you personally. I have promised to present you to her; and I shall do so after a preliminary caution. The lady is very handsome, and very fascinating. It is possible that your heart and your senses may not be proof against her attractions."

"O, do not fear that!" exclaimed Leonard, with a tone of conviction so earnest that Harley smiled.

"Forewarned is not always forearmed against the might of beauty, my dear Leonard; so I cannot at once accept your assurance. But listen to me! Watch yourself narrowly, and if you find that you are likely to be captivated, promise, on your honour, to retreat at once from the field. I have no right, for the sake of another, to expose you to danger; and Madame di Negra, whatever may be her good qualities, is the last person I should wish to see you in love with."

"In love with her! Impossible!"

"Impossible is a strong word," returned Harley; "still, I own fairly (and this belief alone warrants me in trusting you to her fascinations) that I do think, as far as one man can judge of another, that she is not the woman to attract you; and, if filled by one pure and generous object in your intercourse with her, you will see her with purged eyes. Still I claim your promise as one of honour."

"I give it," said Leonard, positively. "But how can I serve Riccabocca? How aid in—"

"Thus," interrupted Harley.—"The spell of your writings is, that, unconsciously to ourselves, they make us better and nobler. And your writings are but the impressions struck off from your mind. Your conversation, when you are roused, has the same effect. And as you grow more familiar with Madame di Negra, I wish you to speak of your boyhood, your youth. Describe the exile as you have seen him—so touching amidst his foibles, so grand amidst the petty privations of his fallen fortunes, so benevolent while poring over his hateful Machiavelli, so stingless in his wisdom of the serpent, so playfully astute in his innocence of the dove—I leave the picture to your knowledge of humour and pathos. Describe Violante brooding over her Italian Poets, and filled with dreams of her fatherland; describe her with all the flashes of her princely nature, shining forth through humble circumstance and obscure position; waken in your listener compassion, respect, admiration for her kindred exiles;—and I think our work is done. She will recognise evidently those whom her brother seeks. She will question you closely where you met with them—where they now are. Protect that secret; say at once that it is not your own. Against your descriptions and the feelings they excite, she will not be guarded as against mine. And there are other reasons why your influence over this woman of mixed nature may be more direct and effectual than my own."

"Nay, I cannot conceive that."

"Believe it, without asking me to explain," answered Harley.

For he did not judge it necessary to say to Leonard, "I am high-born and wealthy—you a peasant's son, and living by your exertions. This woman is ambitious and distressed. She might have projects on me that would counteract mine on her. You she would but listen to, and receive, through the sentiments of good or of poetical that are in her—you she would have no interest to subjugate, no motive to ensnare."

"And now," said Harley, turning the subject, "I have another object in view. This foolish sage friend of ours, in his bewilderment and fears, has sought to save Violante from one rogue by promising her hand to a man who, unless my instincts deceive me, I suspect much disposed to be another. Sacrifice such exuberance of life and spirit to that bloodless heart, to that cold and earthward intellect! By Heaven, it shall not be!"

"But whom can the exile possibly have seen of birth and fortunes to render him a fitting spouse for his daughter? Whom, my lord, except yourself?"

"Me!" exclaimed Harley, angrily, and changing colour. "I worthy of such a creature? I—with my habits! I—silken egotist that I am! And you, a poet, to form such an estimate of one who might be the queen of a poet's dream!"

"My lord, when we sate the other night round Riccabocca's hearth—when I heard her speak, and observed you listen, I said to myself, from such knowledge of human nature as comes, we know not how, to us poets—I said, 'Harley L'Estrange has looked long and wistfully on the heavens, and he now hears the murmur of the wings that can waft him towards them.' And then I sighed, for I thought how the world rules us all in spite of ourselves, and I said, 'What pity for both, that the exile's daughter is not the worldly equal of the peer's son!' And you too sighed, as I thus thought; and I fancied that, while you listened to the music of the wing, you felt the iron of the chain. But the exile's daughter *is* your equal in birth, and you are her equal in heart and in soul."

"My poor Leonard, you rave," answered Harley, calmly. "And if Violante is not to be some young prince's bride, she should be some young poet's."

"Poet's! O, no!" said Leonard, with a gentle laugh. "Poets need repose where *they* love!"

Harley was struck by the answer, and mused over it in silence. "I comprehend," thought he; "it is a new light that dawns on me. What is needed by the man whose whole life is one strain after glory—whose soul sinks, in fatigue, to the companionship of earth—is not the love of a nature like his own. He is right—it is repose! While I!—it is true—boy that he is, his intuitions are wiser than all my experience! It *is* excitement—energy—elevation, that Love should bestow on me. But I have chosen; and, at least, with Helen, my life will be calm, and my hearth sacred. Let the rest sleep in the same grave as my youth."

"But," said Leonard, wishing kindly to arouse his noble friend from a reverie which he felt was mournful, though he did not divine its true cause—"but you have not yet told me the name of the Signora's suitor. May I know?"

"Probably one you never heard of. Randal Leslie—a placeman. You refused a place;—you were right."

"Randal Leslie? Heaven forbid!" cried Leonard, revealing his surprise at the name.

"Amen! But what do you know of him?"

Leonard related the story of Burley's pamphlet.

Harley seemed delighted to hear his suspicions of Randal confirmed. "The paltry pretender!—and yet I fancied that he might be formidable! However, we must dismiss him for the present;—we are approaching Madame di Negra's house. Prepare yourself, and remember your promise."

## CHAPTER XIII.

Some days have passed by. Leonard and Beatrice di Negra have already made friends. Harley is satisfied with his young friend's report. He himself has been actively occupied. He has sought, but hitherto in vain, all trace of Mrs. Bertram; he has put that investigation into the hands of his lawyer, and his lawyer has not been more fortunate than himself. Moreover, Harley has blazed forth again in the London world, and promises again *de faire fureur;* but he has always found time to spend some hours in the twenty-four at his father's house. He has continued much the same tone with Violante, and she begins to accustom herself to it, and reply saucily. His calm courtship to Helen flows on in silence. Leonard, too, has been a frequent guest at the Lansmeres: all welcome and like him there. Peschiera has not evinced any sign of the deadly machinations ascribed to him. He goes less into the drawing-room world; for in that world he meets Lord L'Estrange; and brilliant and handsome though Peschiera be, Lord L'Estrange, like Rob Roy Macgregor, is "on his native heath," and has the decided advantage over the foreigner. Peschiera, however, shines in the clubs, and plays high. Still scarcely an evening passes in which he and Baron Levy do not meet.

Audley Egerton has been intensely occupied with affairs. Only seen once by Harley. Harley then was about to deliver himself of his sentiments respecting Randal Leslie, and to communicate the story of Burley and the pamphlet. Egerton stopped him short.

"My dear Harley, don't try to set me against this young man. I wish to hear nothing in his disfavour. In the first place, it would not alter the line of conduct I mean to adopt with regard to him. He is my wife's kinsman; I charged myself with his career, as a wish of hers, and therefore as a duty to myself. In attaching him so young to my own fate, I drew him necessarily away from the professions in which his industry and talents (for he has both in no common degree) would have secured his fortunes; therefore, be he bad, be he good, I shall try to provide for him as I best can; and, moreover, cold as I am to him, and worldly though perhaps he be, I have somehow or other conceived an interest in him—a liking to him. He has been under my roof, he is dependent on me; he has been docile and prudent, and I am a lone childless man; therefore, spare him, since in so doing you spare me; and ah, Harley, I have so many cares on me *now,* that—"

"O, say no more, my dear, dear Audley," cried the generous friend; "how little people know you!"

Audley's hand trembled. Certainly his nerves began to show wear and tear.

Meanwhile, the object of this dialogue—the type of

perverted intellect—of mind without heart—of knowledge which had no aim but power—was in a state of anxious perturbed gloom. He did not know whether wholly to believe Levy's assurance of his patron's ruin. He could not believe it when he saw that great house in Grosvenor Square, its hall crowded with lacqueys, its sideboard blazing with plate; when no dun was ever seen in the antechamber; when not a tradesman was ever known to call twice for a bill. He hinted to Levy the doubts all these phenomena suggested to him; but the Baron only smiled ominously, and said,—

"True, the tradesmen are always paid; but the *how* is the question! Randal, *mon cher*, you are too innocent. I have but two pieces of advice to suggest, in the shape of two proverbs—'Wise rats run from a falling house,' and, 'Make hay while the sun shines.' Apropos, Mr. Avenel likes you greatly, and has been talking of the borough of Lansmere for you. He has contrived to get together a great interest there. Make much of him."

Randal had indeed been to Mrs. Avenel's *soirée dansante*, and called twice and found her at home, and been very bland and civil, and admired the children. She had two, a boy and a girl, very like their father, with open faces as bold as brass. And as all this had won Mrs. Avenel's good graces, so it had propitiated her husband's. Avenel was shrewd enough to see how clever Randal was. He called him "smart," and said "he would have got on in America," which was the highest praise Dick Avenel ever accorded to any man. But Dick himself looked a little careworn; and this was the first year in which he had murmured at the bills of his wife's dress-maker, and said with an oath, that "there was such a thing as going *too* much ahead."

Randal had visited Dr. Riccabocca, and found Violante flown. True to his promise to Harley, the Italian refused to say where, and suggested, as was agreed, that for the present it would be more prudent if Randal suspended his visits to himself. Leslie, not liking this proposition, attempted to make himself still necessary, by working on Riccabocca's fears as to that espionage on his retreat, which had been among the reasons that had hurried the sage into offering Randal Violante's hand. But Riccabocca had already learned that the fancied spy was but his neighbour Leonard; and, without so saying, he cleverly contrived to make the supposition of such espionage an additional reason for the cessation of Leslie's visits. Randal then, in his own artful, quiet, roundabout way, had sought to find out if any communication had passed between L'Estrange and Riccabocca. Brooding over Harley's words to him, he suspected there had been such communication, with his usual penetrating astuteness. Riccabocca, here, was less on his guard, and rather parried the sidelong questions than denied their inferences.

Randal began already to surmise the truth. Where was it likely Violante should go but to the Lansmeres? This confirmed his idea of Harley's pretensions to her hand. With such a rival what chance had he? Randal never doubted for a moment that the pupil of Machiavelli would "throw him over," if such an alliance to his daughter really presented itself. The schemer at once discarded from his projects all further aim on Violante; either she would be poor, and he would not have her; or she would be rich, and her father would give her to another. As his heart had never been touched by the fair Italian, so the moment her inheritance became more doubtful, it gave him no pang to lose her; but he did feel very sore and resentful at the thought of being supplanted by Lord L'Estrange,—the man who had insulted him.

Neither, as yet, had Randal made any way in his designs on Frank. For several days Madame di Negra had not been at home either to himself or young Hazeldean; and Frank, though very unhappy, was piqued and angry; and Randal suspected, and suspected, and suspected, he knew not exactly what, but that the devil was not so kind to him there as that father of lies ought to have been to a son so dutiful. Yet, with all these discouragements, there was in Randal Leslie so dogged and determined a conviction of his own success—there was so great a tenacity of purpose under obstacles, and so vigilant an eye upon all chances that could be turned to his favour, that he never once abandoned hope, nor did more than change the details in his main schemes. Out of calculations apparently the most far-fetched and improbable, he had constructed a patient policy, to which he obstinately clung. How far his reasonings and patience served to his ends, remains yet to be seen. But could our contempt for the baseness of Randal himself be separated from the faculties which he elaborately degraded to the service of that baseness, one might allow that there was something one could scarcely despise in this still self-reliance, this inflexible resolve. Had such qualities, aided as they were by abilities of no ordinary acuteness, been applied to objects commonly honest, one would have backed Randal Leslie against any fifty picked prize-men from the colleges. But there are judges of weight and metal who do that now, especially Baron Levy, who says to himself as he eyes that pale face all intellect, and that spare form all nerve, "This is a man who must make way in life; he is worth helping."

By the words "worth helping," Baron Levy meant "worth getting into my power, that he may help me."

## CHAPTER XIV.

BUT Parliament had met. Events that belong to history had contributed yet more to weaken the administration. Randal Leslie's interest became absorbed in politics; for the stake to him was his whole political career. Should Audley lose office, and for good, Audley could aid him no more; but to abandon his patron, as Levy recommended, and pin himself, in the hope of a seat in Parliament, to a stranger—an obscure stranger, like Dick Avenel—that was a policy not to be adopted at a breath. Meanwhile, almost every night, when the House met, that pale face and spare form, which Levy so identified with shrewdness and energy, might be seen amongst the benches appropriated to those more select strangers who obtain the Speaker's order of admission. There, Randal heard the great men of that day, and with the half-contemptuous surprise at their fame, which is common enough amongst clever, well-educated young men, who know not what it is to speak in the House of Commons. He heard much slovenly English, much trite reasoning, some eloquent thoughts, and close argument, often delivered in a jerking tone of voice (popularly called the Parliamentary *twang*), and often accompanied by gesticulations that would have shocked the manager of a provincial theatre. He thought how much better than these great dons (with but one or two exceptions) he himself could speak—with what more refined logic—with what more polished periods—how much more like Cicero and Burke! Very probably he might have so spoken, and for that very reason have made that deadest of all dead failures—a pretentious imitation of Burke and Cicero. One thing, however, he was obliged to own, viz., that in a popular representative assembly it is not precisely knowledge which is power, or if knowledge, it is but the knowledge of that particular assembly, and what will best take with it;—passion, invective, sarcasm, bold declamation, shrewd common sense, the readiness so rarely found in a very profound mind—he owned that all these were the qualities that told; when a man who exhibited nothing but "knowledge," in the ordinary sense of the word, stood an imminent chance of being coughed down.

There at his left—last but one in the row of the ministerial chiefs—Randal watched Audley Egerton, his arms folded on his breast, his hat drawn over his brows, his eyes fixed with steady courage on whatever speaker in the Opposition held possession of the floor. And twice Randal heard Egerton speak, and marvelled much at the effect that minister produced. For of those qualities enumerated above, and which Randal had observed to be most sure of success, Audley Egerton only exhibited to a marked degree—the common sense and the readiness. And yet, though but little applauded by noisy cheers, no speaker seemed more to satisfy friends, and command respect from foes. The true secret was this, which Randal might well not divine, since that young person, despite his ancient birth, his Eton rearing, and his refined air, was not one of Nature's gentlemen;—the true secret was, that Audley Egerton moved, looked, and spoke like a thorough gentleman of England. A gentleman of more than average talents and of long experience, speaking his sincere opinions —not a rhetorician aiming at effect. Moreover, Egerton was a consummate man of the world. He said, with nervous simplicity, what his party desired to be said, and put what his opponents felt to be the strong points of the case. Calm and decorous, yet spirited and energetic, with little variety of tone, and action subdued and rare, but yet signalised by earnest vigour, Audley Egerton impressed the understanding of the dullest, and pleased the taste of the most fastidious.

But once, when allusions were made to a certain popular question, on which the premier had announced his resolution to refuse all concession, and on the expediency of which it was announced that the cabinet was nevertheless divided—and when such allusions were coupled with direct appeals to Mr. Egerton, as "the enlightened member of a great commercial constituency," and with a flattering doubt that "that Right Honourable gentleman, member for that great city, identified with the cause of the Burgher class, could be so far behind the spirit of the age as his official chief,"—Randal observed that Egerton drew his hat still more closely over his brows, and turned to whisper with one of his colleagues. He could not be *got up* to speak.

That evening Randal walked home with Egerton, and intimated his surprise that the minister had declined what seemed to him a good occasion for one of those brief, weighty replies by which Audley was chiefly distinguished—an occasion to which he had been loudly invited by the "hears" of the House.

"Leslie," answered the statesman, briefly, "I owe all my success in Parliament to this rule—I have never spoken against my convictions. I intend to abide by it to the last."

"But if the question at issue comes before the House, you will vote against it?"

"Certainly, I vote as a member of the cabinet. But since I am not leader and mouthpiece of the party, I retain as an individual the privilege to speak or keep silence."

"Ah, my dear Mr. Egerton," exclaimed Randal, "forgive me. But this question, right or wrong, has got such hold of the public mind. So little, if conceded in time, would give content; and it is so clear (if I may judge by the talk I hear everywhere I go) that by refusing all concessions, the Government must fall, that I wish—"

"So do I wish," interrupted Egerton, with a gloomy, impatient sigh—"so do I wish! But what avails it? If my advice had been taken but three weeks ago—now it is too late—we could have doubled the rock; we refused, we must split upon it."

This speech was so unlike the discreet and reserved minister, that Randal gathered courage to proceed with an idea that had occurred to his own sagacity. And before I state it, I must add that Egerton had of late shown much more personal kindness to his *protégé;* whether his spirits were broken, or that at last, close and compact as his nature of bronze was, he felt the imperious want to groan aloud in some loving ear, the stern Audley seemed tamed and softened. So Randal went on.

"May I say what I have heard expressed with regard to you and your position—in the streets—in the clubs?"

"Yes, it is in the streets and the clubs that statesmen should go to school. Say on."

"Well, then, I have heard it made a matter of wonder why you, and one or two others I will not name, do not at once retire from the ministry, and on the avowed ground that you side with the public feeling on this irresistible question."

"Eh!"

"It is clear that in so doing you would become the most popular man in the country—clear that you would be summoned back to power on the shoulders of the people. No new cabinet could be formed without you, and your station in it would perhaps be higher, for life, than that which you may now retain but for a few weeks longer. Has not this ever occurred to you?"

"Never," said Audley, with dry composure.

Amazed at such obtuseness, Randal exclaimed, "Is it possible! And, yet, forgive me if I say I think you are ambitious, and love power."

"No man more ambitious; and if by power you mean office, it has grown the habit of my life, and I shall not know what to do without it."

"And how, then, has what seems to me so obvious never occurred to you?"

"Because you are young, and therefore I forgive you; but not the gossips who could wonder why Audley Egerton refused to betray the friends of his whole career, and to profit by the treason."

"But one should love one's country before a party."

"No doubt of that; and the first interest of a country is the honour of its public men."

"But men may leave their party without dishonour!"

"Who doubts that? Do you suppose that if I were an ordinary independent member of Parliament, loaded with no obligations, charged with no trust, I could hesitate for a moment what course to pursue? Oh, that I were but the member for * * *! Oh, that I had the full right to be a free agent! But if a member of a cabinet, a chief in whom thousands confide, because he is outvoted in a council of his colleagues, suddenly retires, and by so doing breaks up the whole party whose confidence he has enjoyed, whose rewards he has reaped, to whom he owes the very position which he employs to their ruin—own that though his choice may be honest, it is one which requires all the consolations of conscience."

"But you will have those consolations. And," added Randal, energetically, "the gain to your career will be so immense!"

"That is precisely what it cannot be," answered Egerton, gloomily. "I grant that I may, if I choose, resign office with the present Government, and so at once destroy that Government; for my resignation on such ground would suffice to do it. I grant this; but for that very reason I could not the next day take office with another administration. I could not accept wages for desertion. No gentleman could! and therefore—" Audley stopped short, and buttoned his coat over his broad breast. The action was significant; it said that the man's mind was made up.

In fact, whether Audley Egerton was right or wrong in his theory depends upon much subtler, and perhaps loftier views in the casuistry of political duties, than it was in his character to take. And I guard myself from saying anything in praise or disfavour of his notions, or implying that he is a fit or unfit example in a parallel case. I am but describing the man as he was, and as a man like him would inevitably be, under the influences in which he lived, and in that peculiar world of which he was so emphatically a member. "*Ce n'est pas moi qui parle, c'est Marc Aurèle.*"

He speaks, not I.

Randal had no time for further discussion. They now reached Egerton's house, and the minister, taking the chamber candlestick from his servant's hand, nodded a silent good-night to Leslie, and with a jaded look retired to his room.

## CHAPTER XV.

BUT not on the threatened question was that eventful campaign of Party decided. The Government fell less in battle than skirmish. It was one fatal Monday—a dull question of finance and figures. Prosy and few were the speakers. All the Government silent, save the Chancellor of the Exchequer, and another business-like personage connected with the Board of Trade, whom the House would hardly condescend to hear. The House was in no mood to think of facts and figures. Early in the evening, between nine and ten, the Speaker's sonorous voice sounded, "Strangers must withdraw!" And Randal, anxious and foreboding, descended from his seat and went out of the fatal doors. He turned to take a last glance at Audley Egerton. The whipper-in was whispering to Audley; and the minister pushed back his hat from his brows, and glanced round the House, and up into the galleries, as if to calculate rapidly the relative numbers of the two armies in the field; then he smiled bitterly, and threw himself back into his seat. That smile long haunted Leslie.

Amongst the strangers thus banished with Randal, while the division was being taken, were many young men, like himself, connected with the administration—some by blood, some by place. Hearts beat loud in the swarming lobbies. Ominous mournful whispers were exchanged. "They say the Government will have a majority of ten." "No; I hear they will certainly be beaten." "H—— says by fifty." "I don't believe it," said a Lord of the Bedchamber; "it is impossible. I left five Government members dining at the 'Travellers.'" "No one thought the division would be so early." "A trick of the Whigs—shameful." "Wonder some one was not set up to talk for time; very odd P—— did not speak; however, he is so cursedly rich, he does not care whether he is out or in." "Yes; and Audley Egerton too, just such another: glad, no doubt, to be set free to look after his property; very different tactics if we had men to whom office was as necessary as it is— to me!" said a candid young placeman. Suddenly the silent Leslie felt a friendly grasp on his arm. He turned and saw Levy.

"Did I not tell you?" said the Baron, with an exulting smile.

"You are sure, then, that the Government will be outvoted?"

"I spent the morning in going over the list of members with a parliamentary client of mine, who knows them all as a shepherd does his sheep. Majority for the Opposition at least twenty-five."

"And in that case must the Government resign, sir?" asked the candid young placeman, who had been listening to the smart well-dressed Baron, "his soul planted in his ears."

"Of course, sir," replied the Baron, blandly, and offering his snuff-box, (true Louis Quinze, with a miniature of Madame de Pompadour, set in pearls.) "You are a friend to the present ministers? You could not wish them to be mean enough to stay in?" Randal drew aside the Baron.

"If Audley's affairs are as you state, what can he do?"

"I shall ask him that question to-morrow," answered the Baron, with a look of visible hate. "And I have come here just to see how he bears the prospect before him."

"You will not discover that in his face. And those absurd scruples of his! If he had but gone out in time—to come in again with the New Men!"

"Oh, of course, our Right Honourable is too punctilious for that!" answered the Baron, sneering.

Suddenly the doors opened—in rushed the breathless expectants. "What are the numbers? What is the division?"

"Majority against ministers," said a member of Opposition, peeling an orange, "twenty-nine."

The Baron, too, had a Speaker's order; and he came into the House with Randal, and sate by his side. But, to their disgust, some member was talking about the other motions before the House.

"What! has nothing been said as to the division?" asked the Baron of a young county member, who was talking to some non-parliamentary friend in the bench before Levy. The county member was one of the Baron's pet eldest sons —had dined often with Levy—was under "obligations" to him. The young legislator looked very much ashamed of Levy's friendly pat on his shoulder, and answered, hurriedly, "O yes; H—— asked, 'if, after such an expression of the House, it was the intention of ministers to retain their places, and carry on the business of the Government?'"

"Just like H——! Very inquisitive mind! And what was the answer he got?"

"None," said the county member; and returned in haste to his proper seat in the body of the House.

"There comes Egerton," said the Baron. And, indeed, as most of the members were now leaving the House, to talk over affairs at clubs or in saloons, and spread through town the great tidings, Audley Egerton's tall head was seen towering above the rest. And Levy turned away disappointed. For not only was the minister's handsome face, though pale, serene and cheerful, but there was an obvious courtesy, a marked respect, in the mode in which that assembly—heated though it was—made way for the fallen minister as he passed through the jostling crowd. And the frank urbane nobleman, who afterwards, from the force, not of talent but of character, became the leader in that House, pressed the hand of his old opponent, as they met in the throng near the doors, and said aloud, "I shall not be a proud man if ever I live to have office; but I shall be proud if ever I leave it with as little to be said against me as your bitterest opponents can say against you, Egerton."

"I wonder," exclaimed the Baron aloud, and leaning over the partition that divided him from the throng below, so that his voice reached Egerton—and there was a cry from formal, indignant members, "Order in the strangers' gallery!" "I wonder what Lord L'Estrange will say!"

Audley lifted his dark brows, surveyed the Baron for an instant with flashing eyes, then walked down the narrow defile between the last benches, and vanished from the scene in which, alas! so few of the most admired **performers leave** more than an actor's short-lived name!

## CHAPTER XVI.

BARON LEVY did not execute his threat of calling on Egerton the next morning. Perhaps he shrank from again meeting the flash of those indignant eyes. And indeed Egerton was too busied all the forenoon to see any one not upon public affairs, except Harley, who hastened to console or cheer him. When the House met, it was announced that the ministers had resigned, only holding their offices till their successors were appointed. But already there was some reaction in their favour; and when it became generally known that the new administration was to be formed of men, few indeed of whom had ever before held office, the common superstition in the public mind that government is like a trade, in which a regular apprenticeship must be served, began to prevail; and the talk at the clubs was, that the new men could not stand; that the former ministry, with some modification, would be back in a month. Perhaps that too might be a reason why Baron Levy thought it prudent not prematurely to offer vindictive condolences to Mr. Egerton. Randal spent part of his morning in inquiries, as to what gentlemen in his situation meant to do with regard to their places; he heard with great satisfaction that very few intended to volunteer retirement from their desks. As Randal himself had observed to Egerton, "their country before their party!"

Randal's place was of great moment to him; its duties were easy, its salary amply sufficient for his wants, and defrayed such expenses as were bestowed on the education of Oliver and his sister. For I am bound to do justice to this young man—indifferent as he was towards his species in general, the ties of family were strong with him; and he stinted himself in many temptations most alluring to his age, in the endeavour to raise the dull honest Oliver and the loose-haired pretty Juliet somewhat more to his own level of culture and refinement. Men essentially griping and unscrupulous, often do make the care for their family an apology for their sins against the world. Even Richard III., if the chroniclers are to be trusted, excused the murder of his nephews by his passionate affection for his son. With the loss of that place, Randal lost all means of support, save what Audley could give him; and if Audley were in truth ruined? Moreover, Randal had already established at the office a reputation for ability and industry. It was a career in which, if he abstained from party politics, he might rise to a fair station and to a considerable income. Therefore, much contented with what he learned as to the general determination of his fellow officials, a determination warranted by ordinary precedent in such cases, Randal dined at a club with good relish, and much Christian resignation for the reverse of his patron, and then walked to Grosvenor Square, on the chance of finding Audley within. Learning that he was so, from the porter who opened the door, Randal entered the library. Three gentlemen were seated there with Egerton: one of the three was Lord L'Estrange; the other two were members of the really defunct, though nominally still existing, Government. He was about to withdraw from intruding on this conclave, when Egerton said to him gently, " Come in, Leslie; I was just speaking about yourself."

"About me, sir?"

"Yes; about you and the place you hold. I had asked Sir —— (pointing to a fellow minister) whether I might not, with propriety, request your chief to leave some note of his opinion of your talents, which I know is high, and which might serve you with his successor."

"Oh, sir, at such a time to think of me!" exclaimed Randal, and he was genuinely touched.

"But," resumed Audley, with his usual dryness, "Sir ——, to my surprise, thinks that it would better become you that you should resign. Unless his reasons, which he has not yet stated, are very strong, such would not be my advice."

"My reasons," said Sir ——, with official formality, "are simply these: I have a nephew in a similar situation; he will resign, as a matter of course. Every one in the public offices whose relations and near connections hold high appointments in the Government, will do so. I do not think Mr. Leslie will like to feel himself a solitary exception."

"Mr. Leslie is no relation of mine—not even a near connection," answered Egerton.

"But his name is so associated with your own—he has resided so long in your house—is so well known in society, (and don't think I compliment when I add, that we hope so well of him,) that I can't think it worth his while to keep this paltry place, which incapacitates him too from a seat in Parliament."

Sir —— was one of those terribly rich men, to whom all considerations of mere bread and cheese are paltry. But I must add that he supposed Egerton to be still wealthier than himself, and sure to provide handsomely for Randal, whom Sir —— rather liked than not; and for Randal's own sake, Sir —— thought it would lower him in the estimation of Egerton himself, despite that gentleman's advocacy, if he did not follow the example of his avowed and notorious patron.

"You see, Leslie," said Egerton, checking Randal's meditated reply, "that nothing can be said against your honour if you stay where you are; it is a mere question of expediency; I will judge that for you; keep your place."

Unhappily the other member of the Government, who had hitherto been silent, was a literary man. Unhappily, while this talk had proceeded, he had placed his hand upon Randal Leslie's celebrated pamphlet, which lay on the library table; and, turning over the leaves, the whole spirit and matter of that masterly composition in defence of the administration (a composition steeped in all the essence of party) recurred to his too faithful recollection. He, too, liked Randal; he did more—he admired the author of that striking and effective pamphlet. And therefore, rousing himself from the sublime indifference he had before felt for the fate of a subaltern, he said, with a bland and complimentary smile, "No; the writer of this most able publication is no ordinary placeman. His opinions here are too vigorously stated; this fine irony on the very person who in all probability will be the chief in his office, has excited too lively an attention, to allow him the *sedet eternumque sedebit* on an official stool. Ha, ha! this is so good! Read it, L'Estrange. What say you?"

Harley glanced over the page pointed out to him. The original was in one of Burley's broad, coarse, but telling burlesques, strained fine through Randal's more polished satire. It was capital. Harley smiled, and lifted his eyes to

Randal. The unlucky plagiarist's face was flushed—the beads stood on his brow. Harley was a good hater; he loved too warmly not to err on the opposite side; but he was one of those men who forget hate when its object is distressed and humbled. He put down the pamphlet and said, "I am no politician; but Egerton is so well known to be fastidious and over-scrupulous in all points of official etiquette, that Mr. Leslie cannot follow a safer counsellor."

"Read that yourself, Egerton," said Sir ———; and he pushed the pamphlet to Audley.

Now Egerton had a dim recollection that that pamphlet was unlucky; but he had skimmed over its contents hastily, and at that moment had forgotten all about it. He took up the too famous work with a reluctant hand, but he read attentively the passages pointed out to him, and then said gravely and sadly—

"Mr. Leslie, I retract my advice. I believe Sir ——— is right; that the nobleman here so keenly satirised will be the chief in your office. I doubt whether he will not compel your dismissal; at all events, he could scarcely be expected to promote your advancement. Under the circumstances, I fear you have no option as a ———" Egerton paused a moment, and, with a sigh that seemed to settle the question, concluded with—"as a gentleman."

Never did Jack Cade, never did Wat Tyler, feel a more deadly hate to that word "gentleman," than the well-born Leslie felt then; but he bowed his head, and answered with his usual presence of mind—

"You utter my own sentiment."

"You think we are right, Harley?" asked Egerton, with an irresolution that surprised all present.

"I think," answered Harley, with a compassion for Randal that was almost over generous, and yet with an *équivoque* on the words, despite the compassion—"I think whoever has served Audley Egerton, never yet has been a loser by it; and if Mr. Leslie wrote this pamphlet, he must have well served Audley Egerton. If he undergoes the penalty, we may safely trust to Egerton for the compensation."

"My compensation has long since been made," answered Randal, with grace; "and that Mr. Egerton could thus have cared for my fortunes, at an hour so occupied, is a thought of pride which—"

"Enough Leslie! enough!" interrupted Egerton, rising and pressing his *protégé's* hand. "See me before you go to bed."

Then the two other ministers rose also and shook hands with Leslie, and told him he had done the right thing, and that they hoped soon to see him in Parliament; and hinted, smilingly, that the next administration did not promise to be very long-lived; and one asked him to dinner, and the other to spend a week at his country seat. And amidst these congratulations at the stroke that left him penniless, the distinguished pamphleteer left the room. How he cursed big John Burley!

## CHAPTER XVII.

It was past midnight when Audley Egerton summoned Randal. The statesman was then alone, seated before his great desk, with its manifold compartments, and engaged on the task of transferring various papers and letters, some to the waste-basket, some to the flames, some to two great iron chests with patent locks, that stood, open-mouthed, at his feet. Strong, stern, and grim, looked those iron chests, silently receiving the relics of power departed; strong, stern, and grim as the grave. Audley lifted his eyes at Randal's entrance, signed to him to take a chair, continued his task for a few moments, and then turning round, as if by an effort, he plucked himself from his master-passion—Public Life,—he said, with deliberate tones—

"I know not, Randal Leslie, whether you thought me needlessly cautious, or wantonly unkind, when I told you never to expect from me more than such advance to your career as my then position could effect—never to expect from my liberality in life, nor from my testament in death—an addition to your private fortunes. I see by your gesture what would be your reply, and I thank you for it. I now tell you, as yet in confidence, though before long it can be no secret to the world, that my pecuniary affairs have been so neglected by me in my devotion to those of the state, that I am somewhat like the man who portioned out his capital at so much a day, calculating to live just long enough to make it last. Unfortunately he lived too long." Audley smiled— but the smile was cold as a sunbeam upon ice—and went on with the same firm, unfaltering accents! "The prospects that face me I am prepared for; they do not take me by surprise. I knew long since how this would end, if I survived the loss of office. I knew it before you came to me, and therefore I spoke to you as I did, judging it manful and right to guard you against hopes which you might otherwise have naturally entertained. On this head, I need say no more. It may excite your surprise, possibly your blame, that I, esteemed methodical and practical enough in the affairs of the state, should be so imprudent as to my own."

"Oh, sir! you owe no account to me."

"To you, at least, as much as to any one. I am a solitary man; my few relations need nothing from me. I had a right to spend what I possessed as I pleased; and if I have spent it recklessly as regards myself, I have not spent it ill in its effect on others. It has been my object for many years to have no *Private Life*—to dispense with its sorrows, joys, affections; and as to its duties, they did not exist for me.— I have said." Mechanically, as he ended, the minister's hand closed the lid of one of the iron boxes, and on the closed lid he rested his firm foot. "But now," he resumed, "I have failed to advance your career. True, I warned you that you drew into a lottery; but you had more chance of a prize than a blank. A blank, however, it has turned out, and the question becomes grave—What are you to do?"

Here, seeing that Egerton came to a full pause, Randal answered readily—

"Still, sir, to go by your advice."

"My advice," said Audley, with a softened look, "would perhaps be rude and unpalatable. I would rather place before you an option. On the one hand, recommence life again. I told you that I would keep your name on your college books. You can return—you can take your degree—after that, you can go to the bar—you have just the talents calculated to succeed in that profession. Success will be slow, it is true; but, with perseverance it will be sure. And, believe me Leslie, Ambition is only sweet while it is but the loftier name for Hope. Who would care for a fox's brush if it had not been rendered a prize by the excitement of the chase?"

"Oxford—again! It is a long step back in life," said Randal, drearily, and little heeding Egerton's unusual indulgence of illustration. "A long step back—and to what? To a profession in which one never begins to rise till one's hair is grey? Besides, how live in the meanwhile?"

"Do not let that thought disturb you. The modest income that suffices for a student at the bar, I trust, at least, to insure you from the wrecks of my fortune."

"Ah, sir, I would not burthen you farther. What right have I to such kindness, save my name of Leslie?" And in spite of himself, as Randal concluded, a tone of bitterness, that betrayed reproach, broke forth. Egerton was too much the man of the world not to comprehend the reproach, and not to pardon it.

"Certainly," he answered, calmly, "as a Leslie you are entitled to my consideration, and would have been entitled perhaps to more, had I not so explicitly warned you to the contrary. But the bar does not seem to please you?"

"What is the alternative, sir? Let me decide when I hear it," answered Randal, sullenly. He began to lose respect for the man who owned he could do so little for him, and who evidently recommended him to shift for himself.

If one could have pierced into Egerton's gloomy heart as he noted the young man's change of tone, it may be a doubt whether one would have seen there, pain or pleasure—pain, for merely from the force of habit he had begun to like Randal—or pleasure, at the thought that he might have reason to withdraw that liking. So lone and stoical had grown the man, who had made it his object to have no private life! Revealing, however, neither pleasure nor pain, but with the composed calmness of a judge upon the bench, Egerton replied—

"The alternative is, to continue in the course you have begun, and still to rely on me."

"Sir, my dear Mr. Egerton," exclaimed Randal, regaining all his usual tenderness of look and voice, "rely on you! But that is all I ask! Only—"

"Only, you would say, I am going out of power, and you don't see the chance of my return?"

"I did not mean that."

"Permit me to suppose that you did: very true; but the party I belong to is as sure of return as the pendulum of that clock is sure to obey the mechanism that moves it from left to right. Our successors profess to come in upon a popular question. All administrations who do that are necessarily short-lived. Either they do not go far enough to please present supporters, or they go so far as to arm new enemies in the rivals who outbid them with the people. 'Tis the history of all revolutions, and of all reforms. Our own administration in reality is destroyed for having passed what was called a popular measure a year ago, which lost us half our friends, and refusing to propose another popular measure this year, in the which we are outstripped by the men who halloo'd us on to the last. Therefore, whatever our successors do, we shall, by the law of reaction, have another experiment of power afforded to ourselves. It is but a question of time; you can wait for it; whether I can is uncertain. But if I die before that day arrives, I have influence enough still left with those who will come in, to obtain a promise of a better provision for you than that which you have lost. The promises of public men are proverbially uncertain. But I shall entrust your cause to a man who never failed a friend, and whose rank will enable him to see that justice is done to you—I speak of Lord L'Estrange."

"Oh, not him; he is unjust to me; he dislikes me; he—"

"May dislike you (he has his whims), but he loves me; and though for no other human being but you would I ask Harley L'Estrange a favour, yet for *you* I will," said Egerton, betraying, for the first time in that dialogue, a visible emotion —"for you, a Leslie, a kinsman, however remote, to the wife from whom I received my fortune! And despite all my cautions, it is possible that in wasting that fortune I may have wronged you. Enough: You have now before you the two options, much as you had at first; but you have at present more experience to aid you in your choice. You are a man, and with more brains than most men; think over it well, and decide for yourself. Now to bed, and postpone thought till the morrow. Poor Randal, you look pale!"

Audley, as he said the last words, put his hand on Randal's shoulder, almost with a father's gentleness; and then suddenly drawing himself up, as the hard inflexible expression, stamped on that face by years, returned, he moved away and resettled to Public Life and the iron box.

## CHAPTER XVIII.

EARLY the next day Randal Leslie was in the luxurious business-room of Baron Levy. How unlike the cold Doric simplicity of the statesman's library! Axminster carpets, three inches thick, *portières à la Française* before the doors; Parisian bronzes on the chimney-piece; and all the receptacles that lined the room, and contained title-deeds, and post-obits, and

bills, and promises to pay, and lawyer-like japan boxes, with
many a noble name written thereon in large white capitals—
"making ruin pompous"—all these sepulchres of departed
patrimonies veneered in rosewood that gleamed with French
polish, and blazed with ormolu. There was a coquetry, an
air of *petit maître*, so diffused over the whole room, that you
could not for the life of you, recollect you were with an
usurer! Plutus wore the aspect of his enemy Cupid; and
how realise your idea of Harpagon in that Baron, with his easy
French "*Mon cher*," and his white, warm hands that pressed
yours so genially, and his dress so exquisite, even at the
earliest morn? No man ever yet saw that Baron in a dressing-
gown and slippers! As one fancies some feudal baron of old
(not half so terrible) everlastingly clad in mail, so all one's
notions of this grand marauder of civilisation were inseparably
associated with varnished boots and a camelia in the button-
hole.

"And this is all that he does for you!" cried the Baron,
pressing together the points of his ten taper fingers. Had he
but let you conclude your career at Oxford, I have heard
enough of your scholarship to know that you would have
taken high honours—been secure of a fellowship—have
betaken yourself with content to a slow and laborious profession, and prepared yourself to die on the woolsack."

"He proposes to me now to return to Oxford," said Randal.
"It is not too late!"

"Yes it is," said the Baron. "Neither individuals nor
nations ever go back of their own accord. There must be an
earthquake before a river recedes to its source."

"You speak well," answered Randal, "and I cannot gain-
say you. But now!"

"Ah, the *now* is the grand question in life—the *then* is
obsolete, gone by—out of fashion; and *now, mon cher*, you
come to ask my advice?"

"No, Baron, I come to ask your explanation."

"Of what?"

"I want to know why you spoke to me of Mr. Egerton's
ruin; why you spoke to me of the lands to be sold by Mr.
Thornhill; and why you spoke to me of Count Peschiera.
You touched on each of those points within ten minutes—you
omitted to indicate what link can connect them?"

"By Jove," said the Baron, rising, and with more admiration in his face than you could have conceived that face, so
smiling and so cynical, could exhibit—"by Jove, Randal

Leslie, but your shrewdness is wonderful. You really are the first young man of your day; and I will 'help you,' as I helped Audley Egerton. Perhaps you will be more grateful."

Randal thought of Egerton's ruin. The parallel implied by the Baron did not suggest to him the rare enthusiasm of gratitude. However, he merely said, "Pray, proceed—I listen to you with interest."

"As for politics, then," said the Baron, "we will discuss that topic later. I am waiting myself to see how these new men get on. The first consideration is for your private fortunes. You should buy this ancient Leslie property—Rood and Dulmansberry—only £20,000 down; the rest may remain on mortgage for ever—or at least till I find you a rich wife—as in fact I did for Egerton. Thornhill wants the £20,000 now—wants them very much."

"And where," said Randal, with an iron smile, "are the £20,000 you ascribe to me to come from?"

"Ten thousand shall come to you the day Count Peschiera marries the daughter of his kinsman with your help and aid —the remaining ten thousand I will lend you. No scruple— I shall hazard nothing—the estates will bear that additional burden. What say you—shall it be so?"

"Ten thousand pounds from Count Peschiera!" said Randal, breathing hard. "You cannot be serious? Such a sum—for what?—for a mere piece of information? How otherwise can I aid him? There must be trick and deception intended here."

"My dear fellow," answered Levy, "I will give you a hint. There is such a thing in life as being over-suspicious. If you have a fault, it is that. The information you allude to is, of course, the first assistance you are to give. Perhaps more may be needed—perhaps not. Of that you will judge yourself, since the £10,000 are contingent on the marriage aforesaid."

"Over-suspicious or not," answered Randal, "the amount of the sum is too improbable, and the security too bad, for me to listen to this proposition, even if I could descend to—"

"Stop, *mon cher*. Business first, scruples afterwards. The security too bad—what security?"

"The word of Count di Peschiera."

"He has nothing to do with it—he need know nothing about it. 'Tis my word you doubt. I am your security."

Randal thought of that dry witticism in Gibbon, "Abu Rafe says he will be witness for this fact, but who will be witness for Abu Rafe?" but he remained silent, only fixing on Levy those dark observant eyes, with their contracted, wary pupils.

"The fact is simply this," resumed Levy: "Count di Peschiera has promised to pay his sister a dowry of £20,000, in case he has the money to spare. He can only have it to spare by the marriage we are discussing. On my part, as I manage his affairs in England for him, I have promised that, for the said sum of £20,000, I will guarantee the expenses in the way of that marriage, and settle with Madame di Negra. Now, though Peschiera is a very liberal, warm-hearted fellow, I don't say that he would have named so large a sum for his sister's dowry, if in strict truth he did not owe it to her. It is the amount of her own fortune, which, by some arrangements with her late husband, not exactly legal, he possessed himself of. If Madame di Negra went to law with him for it, she could get it back. I have explained this to him; and, in short, you now understand why the sum is thus assessed. But I have bought up Madame di Negra's debts. I have bought up young Hazeldean's (for we must make a match between these two a part of our arrangements). I shall present to Peschiera, and to these excellent young persons, an account that will absorb the whole £20,000. That sum will come into my hands. If I settle the claims against them for half the money, which, making myself the sole creditor, I have the right to do, the moiety will remain. And if I choose to give it to you in return for the services which provide Peschiera with a princely fortune—discharge the debts of his sister—and secure her a husband in my promising young client, Mr. Hazeldean, that is my look-out—all parties are satisfied, and no one need ever be the wiser. The sum is large, no doubt; it answers to me to give it to you; does it answer to you to receive it?"

Randal was greatly agitated; but, vile as he was, and systematically as in thought he had brought himself to regard others merely as they could be made subservient to his own interest, still, with all who have not hardened themselves in actual crime, there is a wide distinction between the thought and the act; and though, in the exercise of ingenuity and cunning, he would have had few scruples in that moral swindling which is mildly called "outwitting another," yet thus nakedly and openly to accept a bribe for a deed of treachery towards the poor Italian who had so generously trusted him—he recoiled. He was nerving himself to refuse, when Levy, opening his pocket-book, glanced over the memoranda therein, and said, as to himself, "Rood Manor—Dulmansberry, sold to the Thornhills by Sir Gilbert Leslie, knight of the shire; estimated present net rental £2250 7s. 0d. It is the greatest bargain I ever knew. And with this estate in hand, and your talents, Leslie, I don't see why you should not rise higher than Audley Egerton. He was poorer than you once!"

The old Leslie lands—a positive stake in the country—the restoration of the fallen family; and on the other hand, either long drudgery at the bar,—a scanty allowance on Egerton's bounty—his sister wasting her youth at slovenly, dismal Rood—Oliver debased into a boor!—or a mendicant's dependence on the contemptuous pity of Harley L'Estrange—Harley who had refused his hand to him—Harley, who perhaps would become the husband of Violante! Rage seized him as these contrasting pictures rose before his view. He walked to and fro in disorder, striving to recollect his thoughts, and reduce himself from the passions of the human heart into the mere mechanism of calculating intellect. "I cannot conceive," said he, abruptly, "why you should tempt me thus—what interest it is to you!"

Baron Levy smiled, and put up his pocket-book. He saw from that moment that the victory was gained.

"My dear boy," said he, with the most agreeable *bonhommie*, "it is very natural that you should think a man would have a personal interest in whatever he does for another. I believe that view of human nature is called utilitarian philosophy, and is much in fashion at present. Let me try and explain to you. In this affair I shan't injure myself. True, you will say, if I settle claims, which amount to £20,000, for £10,000, I might put the surplus into my own pocket instead of yours. Agreed. But I shall not get the £20,000, nor repay myself Madame di Negra's debts, (whatever I may do as to Hazeldean's,) unless the Count gets this heiress. You can help in this. I want you; and I don't think I could get you by a less offer than I make. I shall soon pay myself back the £10,000 if the Count get hold of the lady and her fortune. Brief—I see my way here to my own interests. Do you want more reasons—you shall have them. I am now a very rich man. How have I become so? Through attaching myself from the first to persons of expectations, whether from fortune or talent. I have made connections in society, and society has enriched me. I have still a passion for making money. *Que voulez vous?* It is my profession, my hobby. It will be useful to me in a thousand ways, to secure as a friend a young man who will have influence with other young men, heirs to something better than Rood Hall. You may succeed in public life. A man in public life may attain to the knowledge of state secrets that are very profitable to one who dabbles a little in the Funds. We can perhaps hereafter do business together that may put yourself in a way of clearing off all mortgages on these estates—on the encumbered possession of which I shall soon congratulate you. You see I am frank; 'tis the only way of coming to the point with so clever a fellow as you. And now, since the less we rake up the mud in a pond from which we have resolved to drink, the better, let us dismiss all other thoughts but that of securing our end. Will you tell Peschiera where the young lady is, or shall I? Better do it yourself; reason enough for it, that he has confided to you his hope, and asked you to help him; why should not you? Not a word to him about our little arrangement; he need never know it. You need never be troubled." Levy rang the bell: "Order my carriage round."

Randal made no objection. He was deathlike pale, but there was a sinister expression of firmness on his thin, bloodless lips.

"The next point," Levy resumed, "is to hasten the match between Frank and the fair widow. How does that stand?"

"She will not see me, nor receive him."

"Oh, learn why! And if you find on either side there is a hitch, just let me know; I will soon remove it."

"Has Hazeldean consented to the post-obit?"

"Not yet; I have not pressed it; I wait the right moment, if necessary."

"It will be necessary."

"Ah, you wish it. It shall be so."

Randal Leslie again paced the room, and after a silent self-commune came up close to the Baron, and said—

"Look you, sir, I am poor and ambitious; you have tempted me at the right moment, and with the right inducement. I succumb. But what guarantee have I that this money will be paid—these estates made mine upon the conditions stipulated?"

"Before anything is settled," replied the Baron, "go and ask my character of any of our young friends, Borrowell,

Spendquick—whom you please; you will hear me abused, of course; but they will all say this of me, that when I pass my word, I keep it. If I say, '*Mon cher*, you shall have the money,' a man has it; if I say, 'I renew your bill for six months,' it is renewed. 'Tis my way of doing business. In all cases my word is my bond. In this case, where no writing can pass between us, my only bond must be my word. Go, then, make your mind clear as to your security, and come here and dine at eight. We will call on Peschiera afterwards."

"Yes," said Randal, "I will at all events take the day to consider. Meanwhile, I say this, I do not disguise from myself the nature of the proposed transaction, but what I have once resolved I go through with. My sole vindication to myself is, that if I play here with a false die, it will be for a stake so grand, as once won, the magnitude of the prize will cancel the ignominy of the play. It is not this sum of money for which I sell myself—it is for what that sum will aid me to achieve. And in the marriage of young Hazeldean with the Italian woman, I have another, and it may be a larger interest. I have slept on it lately—I wake to it now. Insure that marriage, obtain the post-obit from Hazeldean, and whatever the issue of the more direct scheme for which you seek my services, rely on my gratitude, and believe that you will have put me in the way to render gratitude of avail. At eight I will be with you."

Randal left the room.

The Baron sate thoughtful. "It is true," said he to himself, "this young man is the next of kin to the Hazeldean estate, if Frank displease his father sufficiently to lose his inheritance; that must be the clever boy's design. Well, in the long-run, I should make as much, or more, out of him than out of the spendthrift Frank. Frank's faults are those of youth. He will reform and retrench. But *this* man! No, I shall have *him* for life. And should he fail in this project, and have but this encumbered property—a landed proprietor mortgaged up to his ears—why, he is my slave, and I can foreclose when I wish, or if he prove useless;—no, I risk nothing. And if I did—if I lost ten thousand pounds—what then? I can afford it for revenge!—afford it for the luxury of leaving Audley Egerton alone with penury and ruin, deserted, in his hour of need, by the pensioner of his bounty—as he will be by the last friend of his youth—when it so pleases me—me whom he has called 'scoundrel!' and whom he—"

Levy's soliloquy halted there, for the servant entered to

announce the carriage. And the Baron hurried his hand over his features, as if to sweep away all trace of the passions that distorted their smiling effrontery. And so, as he took up his cane and gloves, and glanced at the glass, the face of the fashionable usurer was once more as varnished as his boots.

## CHAPTER XIX.

WHEN a clever man resolves on a villanous action, he hastens, by the exercise of his cleverness, to get rid of the sense of his villany. With more than his usual alertness, Randal employed the next hour or two in ascertaining how far Baron Levy merited the character he boasted, and how far his word might be his bond. He repaired to young men whom he esteemed better judges on these points than Spendquick and Borrowwell—young men who resembled the Merry Monarch, inasmuch as

> "They never said a foolish thing,
> And never did a wise one."

There are many such young men about town—sharp and able in all affairs except their own. No one knows the world better, nor judges of character more truly than your half-beggared *roué*. From all these Baron Levy obtained much the same testimonials: he was ridiculed as a would-be dandy, but respected as a very responsible man of business, and rather liked as a friendly accommodating species of the Sir Epicure Mammon, who very often did what were thought handsome, liberal things; and, "in short," said one of these experienced referees, "he is the best fellow going—for a money-lender! You may always rely on what he promises, and he is generally very forbearing and indulgent to *us* of good society; perhaps for the same reason that our tailors are;—to send one of us to prison would hurt his custom. His foible is to be thought a gentleman. I believe, much as I suppose he loves money, he would give up half his fortune rather than do anything for which we could cut him. He allows a pension of three-hundred a-year to Lord S——. True; he was his man of business for twenty years, and before then S—— was rather a prudent fellow, and had fifteen thousand a-year. He has helped on, too, many a clever young man;—the best boroughmonger you ever knew. He likes having friends in Parliament. In fact of course, he is a rogue; but if one wants a rogue, one can't find a pleasanter. I should like to see him on the French stage—a prosperous *Macaire;* Le Maître could hit him off to the life."

From information in these more fashionable quarters, gleaned with his usual tact, Randal turned to a source less elevated, but to which he attached more importance. Dick Avenel associated with the Baron—Dick Avenel must be in his clutches. Now Randal did justice to that gentleman's practical shrewdness. Moreover, Avenel was by profession a man of business. He must know more of Levy that these men of pleasure could; and, as he was a plain-spoken person, and evidently honest, in the ordinary acceptation of the word, Randal did not doubt that out of Dick Avenel he should get the truth.

On arriving in Eaton Square, and asking for Mr. Avenel, Randal was at once ushered into the drawing-room. The apartment was not in such good, solid, mercantile taste as had characterised Avenel's more humble bachelor's residence at Screwstown. The taste now was the Honourable Mrs. Avenel's; and, truth to say, no taste could be worse. Furniture of all epochs heterogeneously clumped together here a sofa *à la renaissance* in *Gobelin* — there a rosewood Console from Gillow—a tall mock-Elizabethan chair in black oak, by the side of a modern Florentine table of mosaic marbles. All kinds of colours in the room, and all at war with each other. Very bad copies of the best-known pictures in the world, in the most gaudy frames, and impudently labelled by the names of their murdered originals—"Raffaele," "Corregio," "Titian," "Sebastian del Piombo." Nevertheless, there had been plenty of money spent, and there was plenty to show for it. Mrs. Avenel was seated on her sofa *à la renaissance*, with one of her children at her feet, who was employed in reading a new Annual in crimson silk binding. Mrs. Avenel was in an attitude as if sitting for her portrait.

Polite society is most capricious in its adoptions or rejections. You see many a very vulgar person firmly established in the *beau monde;* others, with very good pretensions as to birth, fortune, &c., either rigorously excluded, or only permitted a peep over the pales. The Honourable Mrs. Avenel belonged to families unquestionably noble, both by her own descent and by her first marriage; and if poverty had kept her down in her earlier career, she now, at least, did not want wealth to back her pretensions. Nevertheless, all the dispensers of fashion concurred in refusing their support to the Honourable Mrs. Avenel. One might suppose it was solely on account of her plebeian husband; but indeed it was not so. Many a woman of high family can marry a low-born man not so presentable as Avenel, and, by the help of his money, get the fine world at her feet. But Mrs. Avenel had not that art. She was still a very handsome, showy woman; and as for dress, no duchess could be more extravagant. Yet these very circumstances had perhaps gone against her ambition; for your quiet little plain woman, provoking no envy, slips into the *coteries*, when a handsome, flaunting lady —whom, once seen in your drawing-room, can be no more overlooked than a scarlet poppy amidst a violet bed—is pretty sure to be weeded out as ruthlessly as a poppy would be in a similar position.

Mr. Avenel was sitting by the fire, rather moodily, his hands in his pockets, and whistling to himself. To say truth, that active mind of his was very much bored in London, at least during the fore part of the day. He hailed Randal's entrance with a smile of relief, and rising and posting himself before the fire—a coat tail under each arm—he scarcely allowed Randal to shake hands with Mrs. Avenel, and pat the child on the head, murmuring, "Beautiful creature." (Randal was ever civil to children—that sort of wolf in sheep's clothing always is—don't be taken in, O you foolish young mothers!) Dick, I say, scarcely allowed his visitor these preliminary courtesies, before he plunged far beyond depth of wife and child, into the political ocean. "Things now were coming right—a vile oligarchy was to be destroyed. British respectability and British talent were to have fair play." To have heard him you would have thought the day fixed for the millennium! "And what is more," said Avenel, bringing down the fist of his right hand upon the palm of his left, "if there is to be a new parliament, we must have new men—not worn-out old brooms that never sweep clean, but men who understand how to govern the country, sir. I INTEND TO COME IN MYSELF!"

"Yes," said Mrs. Avenel, hooking in a word at last, "I am sure, Mr. Leslie, you will think I did right. I persuaded Mr. Avenel that, with his talents and property, he ought, for the sake of his country, to make a sacrifice; and then you know his opinions now are all the fashion, Mr. Leslie; formerly they would have been called shocking and vulgar!"

Thus saying, she looked with fond pride at Dick's comely face, which at that moment, however, was all scowl and frown. I must do justice to Mrs. Avenel; she was a weak, silly woman in some things, and a cunning one in others, but she was a good wife, as wives go. Scotch women generally are.

"Bother!" said Dick, "What do women know about politics. I wish you'd mind the child—it is crumpling up, and playing almighty smash with that flim-flam book, which cost me one pound one."

Mrs. Avenel submissively bowed her head, and removed the Annual from the hands of the young destructive; the destructive set up a squall, as destructives usually do when they don't have their own way. Dick clapped his hand to his ears. "Whe-e-ew, I can't stand this; come and take a walk, Leslie: I want stretching!" He stretched himself as he spoke, first half-way up to the ceiling, and then fairly out of the room.

Randal, with his May Fair manner, turned towards Mrs. Avenel as if to apologise for her husband and himself.

"Poor Richard!" said she, "he is in one of his humours—all men have them. Come and see me again soon. When does Almacks open?"

"Nay, I ought to ask you that question, you who know everything that goes on in our set," said the young serpent. Any tree planted in "our set," if it had been but a crab-tree, would have tempted Mr. Avenel's Eve to jump at its boughs.

"*Are* you coming, there?" cried Dick from the foot of the stairs.

## CHAPTER XX.

"I HAVE just been at our friend Levy's," said Randal, when he and Dick were outside the street door. "He, like you, is full of politics—pleasant man—for the business he is said to do."

"Well," said Dick, slowly, "I suppose he *is* pleasant, but make the best of it—and still—"

"Still what, my dear Avenel?" (Randal here for the first time discarded the formal Mister.)

MR. AVENEL.—"Still the thing itself is not pleasant."

RANDAL, (with his soft hollow laugh.)—"You mean borrowing money upon more than five per cent."

"Oh, curse the per centage. I agree with Bentham on the Usury Laws—no shackles in trade for me, whether in money or anything else. That's not it. But when one owes a fellow money even at two per cent., and 'tis not convenient to pay him, why, somehow or other, it makes one feel small; it takes the British Liberty out of a man!"

"I should have thought you more likely to lend money than to borrow it."

"Well, I guess you are right there, as a general rule. But I tell you what it is, sir; there is too great a mania for competition getting up in this rotten old country of ours. I am as liberal as most men. I like competition to a certain extent, but there is too much of it, sir—too much of it."

Randal looked sad and convinced. But if Leonard had heard Dick Avenel, what would have been his amaze? Dick Avenel rail against competition! Think there could be too much of it! Of course, "heaven and earth are coming together," said the spider, when the housemaid's broom invaded its cobweb. Dick was all for sweeping away other cobwebs; but he certainly thought heaven and earth coming together when he saw a great Turk's-head besom poked up at his own.

Mr. Avenel, in his genius for speculation and improvement, had established a factory at Screwstown, the first which had ever eclipsed the church spire with its Titanic chimney. It succeeded well at first. Mr. Avenel transferred to this speculation nearly all his capital. "Nothing," quoth he, "paid such an interest. Manchester was getting worn out—time to show what Screwstown could do. Nothing like competition." But by-and-by a still greater capitalist than Dick Avenel, finding out that Screwstown was at the mouth of a coal mine, and that Dick's profits were great, erected a still uglier edifice, with a still taller chimney. And having been brought up to the business, and making his residence in the town, while Dick employed a foreman and flourished in London, this infamous competitor so managed, first to share, and then gradually to sequester, the profits which Dick had hitherto monopolised, that no wonder Mr. Avenel thought competition should have its limits. "The tongue touches where the tooth aches," as Dr. Riccabocca would tell us. By little and little our Juvenile Talleyrand (I beg the elder great man's pardon) wormed out from Dick this grievance, and in the grievance discovered the origin of Dick's connection with the money-lender.

"But Levy," said Avenel, candidly, "is a decentish chap in his way—friendly too. Mrs. A. finds him useful; brings some of your young highflyers to her *soirées*. To be sure, they don't dance—stand all in a row at the door, like mutes at a funeral. Not but what they have been uncommon civil to me lately—Spendquick particularly. By-the-by, I dine with him to-morrow. The aristocracy are behindhand—not smart, sir—not up to the march; but when a man knows how to take 'em, they beat the New Yorkers in good manners. I'll say that for them. I have no prejudice."

"I never saw a man with less; no prejudice even against Levy."

"No, not a bit of it! Every one says he's a Jew; he says he's not. I don't care a button what he is. His money is English—that's enough for any man of a liberal turn of mind. His charges, too, are moderate. To be sure, he knows I shall pay them; only what I don't like in him is a sort of way he has of *mon-cher*-ing and my-good-fellow-ing one, to do things quite out of the natural way of that sort of business. He knows I have got Parliamentary influence. I could return a couple of members for Screwstown, and one, or perhaps two, for Lansmere, where I have of late been cooking up an interest; and he dictates to—no, not *dictates*—but tries to *humbug* me into putting in his own men. However, in one respect, we are likely to agree. He says you want to come into Parliament. You seem a smart young fellow; but you must throw over that stiff red-tapist of yours, and go with Public Opinion, and—Myself."

"You are very kind, Avenel; perhaps when we come to compare opinions we may find that we agree entirely. Still, in Egerton's present position, delicacy to him—however, we'll not discuss that now. But you really think I might come in for Lansmere—against the L'Estrange interest, too, which must be strong there?"

"It *was* very strong, but I've smashed it, I calculate."

"Would a contest there cost very much?"

"Well, I guess you must come down with the ready. But, as you say, time enough to discuss that when you have squared your account with 'delicacy;' come to me then, and we'll go into it."

Randal, having now squeezed his orange dry, had no desire to waste his time in brushing up the rind with his coat-sleeve, so he unhooked his arm from Avenel's, and, looking at his watch, discovered he should be just in time for an appointment of the most urgent business—hailed a cab, and drove off.

Dick looked hipped and disconsolate at being left alone; he yawned very loud, to the astonishment of three prim old maiden Belgravians who were passing that way; and then his mind began to turn towards his factory at Screwstown, which had led to his connection with the Baron; and he thought over a letter he had received from his foreman that morning, informing him that it was rumoured at Screwstown that Mr. Dyce, his rival, was about to have new machinery on an improved principle; and that Mr. Dyce had already gone up to town, it was supposed, with the intention of concluding a purchase for a patent discovery to be applied to the new machinery, and which that gentleman had publicly declared in the corn-market "would shut up Mr. Avenel's factory before the year was out." As this menacing epistle recurred to him, Dick felt his desire to yawn incontinently checked. His brow grew very dark; and he walked, with restless strides, on and on, till he found himself in the Strand. He then got into an omnibus, and proceeded to the city, wherein he spent the rest of the day, looking over machines and foundries, and trying in vain to find out what diabolical invention the over-competition of Mr. Dyce had got hold of. "If," said Dick Avenel to himself, as he returned fretfully homeward—" if a man like me, who has done so much for British industry and go-a-head principles, is to be catawampously champed up by a mercenary selfish cormorant of a capitalist like that interloping blockhead in drab breeches, Tom Dyce, all I can say is, that the sooner this cursed old country goes to the dogs, the better pleased I shall be. I wash my hands of it."

## CHAPTER XXI.

RANDAL's mind was made up. All he had learned in regard to Levy had confirmed his resolves or dissipated his scruples. He had started from the improbability that Peschiera would offer, and the still greater improbability that Peshiera would pay him, ten thousand pounds for such information or aid as he could bestow in furthering the Count's object. But when

Levy took such proposals entirely on himself, the main question to Randal became this—could it be Levy's interest to make so considerable a sacrifice? Had the Baron implied only friendly sentiments as his motives, Randal would have felt sure he was to be taken in; but the usurer's frank assurance that it would answer to him in the long-run to concede to Randal terms so advantageous, altered the case, and led our young philosopher to look at the affair with calm contemplative eyes. Was it sufficiently obvious that Levy counted on an adequate return? Might he calculate on reaping help by the bushel if he sowed it by the handful? The result of Randal's cogitations was, that the Baron might fairly deem himself no wasteful sower. In the first place, it was clear that Levy, not without reasonable ground, believed that he could soon replace, with exceeding good interest, any sum he might advance to Randal, out of the wealth which Randal's prompt information might bestow on Levy's client, the Count; and, secondly, Randal's self-esteem was immense, and could he but succeed in securing a pecuniary independence on the instant, to free him from the slow drudgery of the bar, or from a precarious reliance on Audley Egerton, as a politician out of power—his convictions of rapid triumph in public life were as strong as if whispered by an angel or promised by a fiend. On such triumphs, with all the social position they would secure, Levy might well calculate for repayment by a thousand indirect channels. Randal's sagacity detected that, through all the good-natured or liberal actions ascribed to the usurer, Levy had steadily pursued his own interests—he saw that Levy meant to get him into his power, and use his abilities as instruments for digging new mines, in which Baron Levy would claim the right of large royalties. But at that thought Randal's pale lip curled disdainfully; he confided too much in his own powers not to think that he could elude the grasp of the usurer, whenever it suited him to do so. Thus, on a survey, all conscience hushed itself—his mind rushed buoyantly on to anticipations of the future. He saw the hereditary estates regained—no matter how mortgaged—for the moment still his own—legally his own—yielding for the present what would suffice for competence to one of few wants, and freeing his name from that title of Adventurer, which is so prodigally given in rich old countries to those who have no estates but their brains. He thought of Violante but as the civilised trader thinks of a trifling coin, of a glass bead, which he exchanges with some barbarian for gold dust;—he thought of Frank Hazeldean married to the foreign woman of beggared means, and repute that had known the breath of scandal—married, and living on post-obit instalments of the Casino property;—he thought of the poor Squire's resentment;—his avarice swept from the lands annexed to Rood on to the broad fields of Hazeldean;— he thought of Avenel, of Lansmere, of Parliament;—with one hand he grasped fortune, with the next power. "And yet I entered on life with no patrimony—(save a ruined hall and a barren waste)—no patrimony but knowledge. I have but turned knowledge from books to men; for books may give fame after death, but men give us power in life." And all the while he thus ruminated, his act was speeding his purpose. Though it was but in a miserable hack cab that he erected airy scaffoldings round airy castles, still the miserable hack cab was flying fast, to secure the first foot of solid ground whereon to transfer the mental plan of the architect to foundations of positive slime and clay. The cab stopped at the door of Lord Lansmere's house. Randal had suspected Violante to be there: he resolved to ascertain. Randal descended from his vehicle and rang the bell. The lodge-keeper opened the great wooden gates.

"I have called to see the young lady staying here—the foreign young lady."

Lady Lansmere had been too confident of the security of her roof to condescend to give any orders to her servants with regard to her guest, and the lodge-keeper answered directly—

"At home, I believe, sir. I rather think she is in the garden with my lady."

"I see," said Randal. And he did see the form of Violante at a distance. "But, since she is walking, I will not disturb her at present. I will call another day."

The lodge-keeper bowed respectfully, Randal jumped into his cab—"To Curzon Street—quick!"

## CHAPTER XXII.

HARLEY had made one notable oversight in that appeal to Beatrice's better and gentler nature, which he entrusted to the advocacy of Leonard—a scheme in itself very character-istic of Harley's romantic temper, and either wise or foolish, according as his indulgent theory of human idiosyncrasies in general, and of those peculiar to Beatrice di Negra in especial, was the dream of an enthusiast, or the inductive conclusion of a sound philosopher.

Harley had warned Leonard not to fall in love with the Italian—he had forgotten to warn the Italian not to fall in love with Leonard; nor had he ever anticipated the probability of that event. This is not to be very much wondered at; for if there be anything on which the most sensible men are dull-eyed, where those eyes are not lighted by jealousy, it is as to the probabilities of another male creature being beloved. All, the least vain of the whiskered gender, think it prudent to guard themselves against being too irresistible to the fair sex; and each says of his friend, "Good fellow enough, but the last man for *that* woman to fall in love with!"

But certainly there appeared on the surface more than ordinary cause for Harley's blindness in the special instance of Leonard.

Whatever Beatrice's better qualities, she was generally esteemed worldly and ambitious. She was pinched in circumstances—she was luxuriant and extravagant; how was it likely that she could distinguish any aspirant of the humble birth and fortunes of the young peasant author? As a coquette, she might try to win his admiration and attract his fancy; but her own heart would surely be guarded in the triple mail of pride, poverty, and the conventional opinions of the world in which she lived. Had Harley thought it possible that Madame di Negra could stoop below her station, and love, not wisely, but too well, he would rather have thought that the object would be some brilliant adventurer of fashion —some one who could turn against herself all the arts of deliberate fascination, and all the experience bestowed by frequent conquest. One so simple as Leonard—so young and so new! Harley L'Estrange would have smiled at himself, if the idea of that image subjugating the ambitious woman to the disinterested love of a village maid, had once crossed his mind. Nevertheless, so it was, and precisely from those causes which would have seemed to Harley to forbid the weakness.

It *was* that fresh, pure heart—it was that simple, earnest sweetness—it was that contrast in look, in tone, in sentiment, and in reasonings, to all that had jaded and disgusted her in the circle of her admirers—it was all this that captivated

Beatrice at the first interview with Leonard. Here was what she had confessed to the sceptical Randal she had dreamed and sighed for. Her earliest youth had passed into abhorrent marriage, without the soft, innocent crisis of human life— virgin love. Many a wooer might have touched her vanity, pleased her fancy, excited her ambition—her heart had never been awakened; it woke now. The world, and the years that the world had wasted, seemed to fleet away as a cloud. She was as if restored to the blush and the sigh of youth— the youth of the Italian maid. As in the restoration of our golden age is the spell of poetry with us all, so such was the spell of the poet himself on her.

Oh, how exquisite was that brief episode in the life of the woman palled with the "hack sights and sounds" of worldly life! How strangely happy were those hours, when, lured on by her silent sympathy, the young scholar spoke of his early struggles between circumstance and impulse, musing amidst the flowers, and hearkening to the fountain; or of his wanderings in the desolate, lamp-lit streets, while the vision of Chatterton's glittering eyes shone dread through the friendless shadows. And as he spoke, whether of his hopes or his fears, her looks dwelt fondly on the young face, that varied between pride and sadness—pride ever so gentle, and sadness ever so nobly touching. She was never weary of gazing on that brow, with its quiet power; but her lids dropped before those eyes, with their serene, unfathomable passion. She felt, as they haunted her, what a deep and holy thing love in such souls must be. Leonard never spoke to her of Helen—that reserve every reader can comprehend. To natures like his, first love is a mystery; to confide it is to profane. But he fulfilled his commission of interesting her in the exile and his daughter. And his description of them brought tears to her eyes. She inly resolved not to aid Peschiera in his designs on Violante. She forgot for the moment that her own fortune was to depend on the success of those designs.—Levy had arranged so that she was not reminded of her poverty by creditors—she knew not how. She knew nothing of business. She gave herself up to the delight of the present hour, and to vague prospects of a future, associated with that young image—with that face of a guardian angel that she saw before her, fairest in the moments of absence; for in those moments came the life of fairy-land, when we shut our eyes on the world, and see through the haze of golden reverie. Dangerous, indeed, to Leonard would have been the soft society of Beatrice di Negra, had not his heart been wholly devoted to one object, and had not his ideal of woman been from that object one sole and indivisible reflection. But Beatrice guessed not this barrier between herself and him. Amidst the shadows that he conjured up from his past life, she beheld no rival form. She saw him lonely in the world as she was herself. And in his lowly birth, his youth, in the freedom from presumption which characterised him in all things (save that confidence in his intellectual destinies, which is the essential attribute of genius), she but grew the bolder by the belief that, even if he loved her, he would not dare to hazard the avowal.

And thus, one day, yielding, as she had ever been wont to yield, to the impulse of her quick Italian heart—how she never remembered—in what words she could never recall—she spoke—she owned her love—she pleaded, with tears and blushes, for love in return. All that passed was to her as a dream—a dream from which she woke with a fierce sense of agony, of humiliation—woke as the woman "scorned." No matter how gratefully, how tenderly Leonard had replied—the reply was refusal. For the first time she learned she had a rival; that all he could give of love was long since, from his boyhood, given to another. For the first time in her life, that ardent nature knew jealousy, its torturing stings, its thirst for vengeance, its tempest of loving hate. But, to outward appearance, silent and cold she stood as marble. Words that sought to soothe fell on her ear unheeded: they were drowned by the storm within. Pride was the first feeling which dominated the warring elements that raged in her soul. She tore her hand from that which clasped hers with so loyal a respect. She could have spurned the form that knelt at her feet, not for love, but for pardon. She pointed to the door with the gesture of an insulted queen. She knew no more till she was alone. Then came that rapid flash of conjecture peculiar to the storms of jealousy; that which seems to single from all nature the one object to dread and to destroy; the conjecture so often false; yet received at once by our convictions as the revelation of instinctive truth. He to whom she had humbled herself loved another; whom but Violante?—whom else, young and beautiful, had he named in the record of his life?—None! And he had sought to interest her, Beatrice di Negra, in the object of his love;—hinted at dangers which Beatrice knew too well;—implied trust in Beatrice's will to protect. Blind fool that she had been! This, then, was the reason why he had come, day after day, to

Beatrice's house; this was the charm that had drawn him thither; this—she pressed her hands to her burning temples, as if to stop the torture of thought. Suddenly a voice was heard below, the door opened, and Randal Leslie entered.

## CHAPTER XXIII.

PUNCTUALLY at eight o'clock that evening, Baron Levy welcomed the new ally he had secured. The pair dined *en tête à tête*, discussing general matters till the servants left them to their wine. Then said the Baron, rising and stirring the fire —then said the Baron, briefly and significantly—

"Well!"

"As regards the property you spoke of," answered Randal, "I am willing to purchase it on the terms you name. The only point that perplexes me is how to account to Audley Egerton, to my parents, to the world, for the power of purchasing it."

"True," said the Baron, without even a smile at the ingenious and truly Greek manner in which Randal had contrived to denote his meaning, and conceal the ugliness of it—" true, we must think of that. If we could manage to conceal the real name of the purchaser for a year or so—it might be easy —you may be supposed to have speculated in the Funds; or Egerton may die, and people may believe that he had secured to you something handsome from the ruins of his fortune."

"Little chance of Egerton's dying."

"Humph!" said the Baron. "However, this is a mere detail, reserved for consideration. You can now tell us where the young lady is?"

"Certainly. I could not this morning—I can now. I will go with you to the Count. Meanwhile, I have seen Madame di Negra; she will accept Frank Hazeldean if he will but offer himself at once."

"Will he not?"

"No! I have been to him. He is overjoyed at my representations, but considers it his duty to ask the consent of his parents. Of course they will not give it; and if there be delay, she will retract. She is under the influence of passions, on the duration of which there is no reliance."

"What passions? Love?"

"Love; but not for Hazeldean. The passions that bring

her to accept his hand are pique and jealousy. She believes, in a word, that one, who seems to have gained the mastery over her affections with a strange suddenness, is but blind to her charms, because dazzled by Violante's. She is prepared to aid in all that can give her rival to Peschiera; and yet, such is the inconsistency of woman, (added the young philosopher, with a shrug of the shoulders,) that she is also prepared to lose all chance of securing him she loves, by bestowing herself on another!"

"Woman, indeed, all over!" said the Baron, tapping his snuff-box (Louis Quinze), and regaling his nostrils with a scornful pinch. "But who is the man whom the fair Beatrice has thus honoured? Superb creature! I had some idea of her myself when I bought up her debts; but it might have embarrassed me, in more general plans, as regards the Count. All for the best. Who's the man? Not Lord L'Estrange?"

"I do not think it is he; but I have not yet ascertained. I have told you all I know. I found her in a state so excited, so unlike herself, that I had no little difficulty in soothing her into confidence so far. I could not venture more."

"And she will accept Frank?"

"Had he offered to-day she would have accepted him!"

"It may be a great help to your fortunes, *mon cher*, if Frank Hazeldean married this lady without his father's consent. Perhaps he may be disinherited. You are next of kin."

"How do you know that?" asked Randal, sullenly.

"It is my business to know all about the chances and connections of any one with whom I do money matters. I do money matters with young Mr. Hazeldean; so I know that the Hazeldean property is not entailed; and, as the Squire's half-brother has no Hazeldean blood in him, you have excellent expectations."

"Did Frank tell you I was next of kin?"

"I rather think so; but I am sure *you* did."

"I—when?"

"When you told me how important it was to you that Frank should marry Madame di Negra. *Peste! mon cher*, do you think I am a blockhead?"

"Well, Baron, Frank is of age, and can marry to please himself. You implied to me that you could help him in this."

"I will try. See that he call at Madame di Negra's to-morrow, at two precisely."

## VARIETIES IN ENGLISH LIFE. 235

"I would rather keep clear of all apparent interference in this matter. Will you not arrange that he call on her? And do not forget to entangle him in a *post-obit*."

"Leave it to me. Any more wine? No;—then let us go to the Count's."

## CHAPTER XXIV.

THE next morning Frank Hazeldean was sitting over his solitary breakfast-table. It was long past noon. The young man had risen early, it is true, to attend his military duties, but he had contracted the habit of breakfasting late. One's appetite does not come early when one lives in London, and never goes to bed before daybreak.

There was nothing very luxurious or effeminate about Frank's rooms, though they were in a very dear street, and he paid a monstrous high price for them. Still, to a practised eye, they betrayed an inmate who can get through his money, and make very little show for it. The walls were covered with coloured prints of racers and steeple-chases, interspersed with the portraits of opera-dancers—all smirk and caper. Then there was a semi-circular recess covered with red cloth, and fitted up for smoking, as you might perceive by sundry stands full of Turkish pipes in cherry-stick and jessamine, with amber mouthpieces; while a great serpent hookah, from which Frank could no more have smoked than he could have smoked out of the head of a boa constrictor, coiled itself up on the floor; over the chimney-piece was a collection of Moorish arms. What use on earth, ataghan and scimitar, and damasquined pistols, that would not carry straight three yards, could be to an officer in his Majesty's Guards is more than I can conjecture, or even Frank satisfactorily explain. I have strong suspicions that this valuable arsenal passed to Frank in part payment of a bill to be discounted. At all events, if so, it was an improvement on the bear that he had sold to the hair-dresser. No books were to be seen anywhere, except a Court Guide, a Racing Calendar, an Army List, the Sporting Magazine complete, (whole bound in scarlet morocco, at about a guinea per volume,) and a small book, as small as an Elzevir, on the chimney-piece, by the side of a cigar-case. That small book had cost Frank more than all the rest put together; it was his Own Book, his book *par excellence;* book made up by himself—his BETTING BOOK!

On a centre table were deposited Frank's well-brushed hat —a satinwood box, containing kid-gloves, of various delicate tints, from primrose to lilac—a tray full of cards and three-cornered notes—an opera-glass, and an ivory subscription ticket to his opera stall.

In one corner was an ingenious receptacle for canes, sticks, and whips—I should not like, in these bad times, to have paid the bill for them; and mounting guard by that receptacle, stood a pair of boots as bright as Baron Levy's— "the force of brightness could no further go." Frank was in his dressing-gown—very good taste—quite Oriental— guaranteed to be true India cachmere, and charged as such. Nothing could be more neat, though perfectly simple, than the appurtenances of his breakfast-table:—silver tea-pot, ewer and basin—all fitting into his dressing-box—(for the which may Storr and Mortimer be now praised, and some day paid!) Frank looked very handsome—rather tired, and exceedingly bored. He had been trying to read the *Morning Post,* but the effort had proved too much for him.

Poor dear Frank Hazeldean!—true type of many a poor dear fellow who has long since gone to the dogs. And if, in this road to ruin, there had been the least thing to do the traveller any credit by the way! One feels a respect for the ruin of a man like Audley Egerton. He is ruined *en roi!* From the wrecks of his fortune he can look down and see stately monuments built from the stones of that dismantled edifice. In every institution which attests the humanity of England, was a record of the princely bounty of the public man. In those objects of party, for which the proverbial sinews of war are necessary—in those rewards for service, which private liberality can confer—the hand of Egerton had been opened as with the heart of a king. Many a rising member of Parliament, in those days when talent was brought forward through the aid of wealth and rank, owed his career to the seat which Audley Egerton's large subscription had secured to him; many an obscure supporter in letters and the press looked back to the day when he had been freed from the gaol by the gratitude of the patron. The city he represented was embellished at his cost; through the shire that held his mortgaged lands, which he had rarely ever visited, his gold had flowed as a Pactolus;

all that could animate its public spirit, or increase its civilization, claimed kindred with his munificence, and never had a claim disallowed. Even in his grand, careless household, with its large retinue and superb hospitality, there was something worthy of a representative of that time-honoured portion of our true nobility—the untitled gentlemen of the land. The Great Commoner had, indeed, "something to show" for the money he had disdained and squandered. But for Frank Hazeldean's mode of getting rid of the dross, when gone, what would be left to tell the tale? Paltry prints in a bachelor's lodging; a collection of canes and cherry-sticks; half-a-dozen letters in ill-spelt French from a *figurante;* some long-legged horses, fit for nothing but to lose a race; that damnable Betting-Book; and—*sic transit gloria*—down sweeps some hawk of a Levy, on the wings of an I O U, and not a feather is left of the pigeon!

Yet Frank Hazeldean has stuff in him—a good heart, and strict honour. Fool though he seem, there is sound sterling sense in some odd corner of his brains, if one could but get at it. All he wants to save him from perdition is, to do what he has never yet done—viz., pause and think. But, to be sure, that same operation of thinking is not so easy for folks unaccustomed to it, as people who think—think!

"I can't bear this," said Frank, suddenly, and springing to his feet. "This woman, I cannot get her out of my head. I ought to go down to the governor's; but then if he gets into a passion, and refuses his consent, where am I? And he will, too, I fear. I wish I could make out what Randal advises. He seems to recommend that I should marry Beatrice at once, and trust to my mother's influence to make all right afterwards. But when I ask, '*Is* that your advice?' he backs out of it. Well, I suppose he is right there. I can understand that he is unwilling, good fellow, to recommend anything that my father would disapprove. But still—"

Here Frank stopped in his soliloquy, and did make his first desperate effort to—think!

Now, O dear reader, I assume, of course, that thou art one of the class to which thought is familiar; and, perhaps, thou hast smiled in disdain or incredulity at that remark on the difficulty of thinking which preceded Frank Hazeldean's discourse to himself. But art thou quite sure that when thou hast tried to *think* thou hast always succeeded? Hast thou not often been duped by that pale visionary simulatrum of thought which goes by the name of *reverie?* Honest old Montaigne confessed that he did not understand that process of sitting down to think, on which some folks express themselves so glibly. He could not think unless he had a pen in his hand, and a sheet of paper before him; and so, by a manual operation, seized and connected the links of ratiocination. Very often has it happened to myself, when I have said to Thought peremptorily, "Bestir thyself—a serious matter is before thee—ponder it well—think of it," that that same thought has behaved in the most refractory, rebellious manner conceivable—and, instead of concentrating its rays into a single stream of light, has broken into all the desultory tints of the rainbow, colouring senseless clouds, and running off into the seventh heaven—so that after sitting a good hour by the clock, with brows as knit as if I was intent on squaring the circle, I have suddenly discovered that I might as well have gone comfortably to sleep—I have been doing nothing but dream—and the most nonsensical dreams! So when Frank Hazeldean, as he stopped at that meditative "But still"—and leaning his arm on the chimney-piece, and resting his face on his hand, felt himself at the grave crisis of life, and fancied he was going "to think on it," there only rose before him a succession of shadowy pictures. Randal Leslie, with an unsatisfactory countenance, from which he could extract nothing;—the Squire, looking as black as thunder in his study at Hazeldean;—his mother trying to plead for him, and getting herself properly scolded for her pains;—and then off went that Will-o'-the-wisp which pretended to call itself Thought, and began playing round the pale charming face of Beatrice di Negra, in the drawing-room at Curzon Street, and repeating, with small elfin voice, Randal Leslie's assurance of the preceding day, "as to her affection for you, Frank, there is no doubt of *that;* she only begins to think you are trifling with her." And then there was a rapturous vision of a young gentleman on his knee, and the fair pale face bathed in blushes, and a clergyman standing by the altar, and a carriage-and-four with white favours at the church-door; and of a honeymoon, which would have astonished as to honey all the bees of Hymettus. And in the midst of these phantasmagoria, which composed what Frank fondly styled "making up his mind," there came a single man's elegant rat-tat-tat at the street door.

"One never *has* a moment for *thinking*," cried Frank, and he called out to his valet, "Not at home."

But it was too late. Lord Spendquick was in the hall, and presently within the room. How d'ye do's were exchanged and hands shaken.

LORD SPENDQUICK.—" I have a note for you, Hazeldean."

FRANK, (lazily.)—" From whom ? "

LORD SPENDQUICK.—" Levy. Just come from him—never saw him in such a fidget. He was going into the city—I suppose to see X. Y. Dashed off this note for you—and would have sent it by a servant, but I said I would bring it."

FRANK, (looking fearfully at the note.)—" I hope he does not want his money yet. 'Private and confidential'—that looks bad."

SPENDQUICK.—" Devilish bad, indeed."

Frank opens the note and reads, half aloud, " Dear Hazeldean."

SPENDQUICK, (interrupting.)—" Good sign ! He always 'Spendquicks' me when he lends me money; and 'tis 'My dear Lord' when he wants it back. Capital sign !"

Frank reads on, but to himself, and with a changing countenance—

"DEAR HAZELDEAN,—I am very sorry to tell you that, in consequence of the sudden failure of a house at Paris with which I had large dealings, I am pressed on a sudden for all the ready money I can get. I don't want to inconvenience you, but do try and see if you can take up those bills of yours which I hold, and which, as you know, have been due some little time. I had hit on a way of arranging your affairs; but when I hinted at it, you seemed to dislike the idea; and Leslie has since told me that you have strong objections to giving any security on your prospective property. So no more of that, my dear fellow. I am called out in haste to try what I can do for a very charming client of mine, who is in great pecuniary distress, though she has for a brother a foreign Count, as rich as a Crœsus. There is an execution in her house. I am going down to the tradesman who put it in, but have no hope of softening him; and I fear there will be others before the day is out. Another reason for wanting money, if you can help me, *mon cher!*—An execution in the house of one of the most brilliant women in London—an execution in Curzon Street, May Fair ! It will be all over the town, if I can't stop it.—Yours in haste, LEVY.

"*P.S.*—Don't let what I have said vex you too much. I should not trouble you if Spendquick and Borrowell would pay me something. Perhaps you can get them to do so."

Struck by Frank's silence and paleness, Lord Spendquick here, in the kindest way possible, laid his hand on the young Guardsman's shoulder, and looked over the note with that freedom which gentlemen in difficulties take with each other's private and confidential correspondence. His eye fell on the postscript. "Oh, damn it," cried Spendquick, "but that's too bad—employing you to get me to pay him! Such horrid treachery. Make yourself easy, my dear Frank; I could never suspect you of anything so unhandsome. I could as soon suspect myself of—paying him—"

"Curzon Street! Count!" muttered Frank, as if waking from a dream. "It must be so." To thrust on his boots—change his dressing-robe for a frock-coat—snatch at his hat, gloves, and cane—break from Spendquick—descend the stairs—a flight at a leap—gain the street—throw himself into a cabriolet; all this was done before his astounded visitor could even recover breath enough to ask "What's the matter?"

Left thus alone, Lord Spendquick shook his head—shook it twice, as if fully to convince himself that there was nothing in it; and then re-arranging his hat before the looking-glass, and drawing on his gloves deliberately, he walked down stairs, and strolled into White's, but with a bewildered and absent air. Standing at the celebrated bow-window for some moments in musing silence, Lord Spendquick at last thus addressed an exceedingly cynical, sceptical, old *roué*—

"Pray, do you think there is any truth in the stories about people in former times selling themselves to the devil?"

"Ugh," answered the *roué*, much too wise ever to be surprised. "Have you any personal interest in the question?"

"I!—no; but a friend of mine has just received a letter from Levy, and he flew out of the room in the most ex-tra-or-di-na-ry manner—just as people did in those days when their time was up! And Levy, you know, is—"

"Not quite as great a fool as the other dark gentleman to whom you would compare him: for Levy never made such bad bargains for himself. Time up! No doubt it is. I should not like to be in your friend's shoes."

"Shoes!" said Spendquick, with a sort of shudder; "you never saw a neater fellow, nor one, to do him justice, who takes more time in dressing than he does in general. And talking of shoes—he rushed out with the right boot on the left foot, and the left boot on the right. Very mysterious." And a third time Lord Spendquick shook his head—and a third time that head seemed to him wondrous empty.

## CHAPTER XXV.

But Frank had arrived in Curzon Street—leapt from the cabriolet—knocked at the door, which was opened by a strange-looking man in a buff waistcoat and corduroy smalls. Frank gave a glance at this personage—pushed him aside—and rushed up stairs. He burst into the drawing-room—no Beatrice was there. A thin elderly man, with a manuscript book in his hands, appeared engaged in examining the furniture and making an inventory, with the aid of Madame di Negra's upper servant. The thin man stared at Frank, and touched the hat which was on his head. The servant, who was a foreigner, approached Frank, and said, in broken English, that his lady did not receive—that she was unwell, and kept her room. Frank thrust a sovereign into the servant's hand, and begged him to tell Madame di Negra that Mr. Hazeldean entreated the honour of an interview. As soon as the servant vanished on this errand, Frank seized the thin man by the arm—" What is this?—an execution?"

"Yes, sir."

"For what sum?"

"Fifteen hundred and forty-seven pounds. We are the first in possession."

" There are others, then?"

" Or else, sir, we should never have taken this step. Most painful to our feelings, sir; but these foreigners are here to-day, and gone to-morrow. And—"

The servant re-entered. Madame di Negra would see Mr. Hazeldean. Would he walk up stairs? Frank hastened to obey this summons.

Madame di Negra was in a small room which was fitted up as a boudoir. Her eyes showed the traces of recent tears, but her face was composed, and even rigid, in its haughty, though mournful expression. Frank, however, did not pause to notice her countenance—to hear her dignified salutation. All his timidity was gone. He saw but the woman whom he loved, in distress and humiliation. As the door closed on him, he flung himself at her feet. He caught at her hand—the skirt of her robe.

"Oh! Madame di Negra!—Beatrice!" he exclaimed, tears in his eyes, and his voice half-broken by generous emotion; "forgive me—forgive me; don't see in me a mere acquaintance. By accident I learned, or, rather, guessed—this—this strange insult to which you are so unworthily exposed. I am here. Think of me—but as a friend—the truest friend. Oh! Beatrice,"—and he bent his head over the hand he held—"I never dared say so before—it seems presuming to say it now—but I cannot help it. I love you—I love you with my whole heart and soul;—to serve you—if only but to serve you!—I ask nothing else." And a sob went from his warm, young, foolish heart.

The Italian was deeply moved. Nor was her nature that of the mere sordid adventuress. So much love and so much confidence! She was not prepared to betray the one, and entrap the other.

"Rise—rise," she said, softly; "I thank you gratefully. But do not suppose that I—"

"Hush—hush!—you must not refuse me. Hush! don't let your pride speak."

"No—it is not my pride. You exaggerate what is occurring here. You forget that I have a brother. I have sent for him. He is the only one I can apply to. Ah! that is his knock! But I shall never, never forget that I have found one generous noble heart in this hollow world."

Frank would have replied, but he heard the Count's voice on the stairs, and had only time to rise and withdraw to the window, trying hard to repress his agitation and compose his countenance. Count di Peschiera entered—entered as a very personation of the beauty and magnificence of careless, luxurious, pampered, egotistical wealth. His surtout, trimmed with the costliest sables, flung back from his splendid chest. Amidst the folds of the glossy satin that enveloped his throat, gleamed a turquoise, of such value as a jeweller might have kept for fifty years before he could find a customer rich and frivolous enough to buy it. The very head of his cane was a masterpiece of art, and the man himself, so elegant despite his strength, and so fresh despite his years!—It is astonishing how well men wear when they think of no one but themselves!

"Pr-rr!" said the Count, not observing Frank behind the draperies of the window; "Pr-rr—. It seems to me that you must have passed a very unpleasant quarter of an hour And now—*Dieu me damne—quoi faire!*"

Beatrice pointed to the window, and felt as if she could have sunk into the earth for shame. But as the Count spoke in French, and Frank did not very readily comprehend that language, the words escaped him; though his ear was shocked by a certain satirical levity of tone.

Frank came forward. The Count held out his hand, and with a rapid change of voice and manner, said, "One whom my sister admits at such a moment must be a friend to me."

"Mr. Hazeldean," said Beatrice, with meaning, "would indeed have nobly pressed on me the offer of an aid which I need no more, since you, my brother, are here."

"Certainly," said the Count, with his superb air of *grand seigneur*; "I will go down and clear your house of this impertinent *canaille*. But I thought your affairs were with Baron Levy. He should be here."

"I expect him every moment. Adieu! Mr. Hazeldean." Beatrice extended her hand to her young lover with a frankness which was not without a certain pathetic and cordial dignity. Restrained from farther words by the Count's presence, Frank bowed over the fair hand in silence, and retired. He was on the stairs when he was joined by Peschiera.

"Mr. Hazeldean," said the latter, in a low tone, "will you come into the drawing-room?"

Frank obeyed. The man employed in his examination of the furniture was still at his task: but at a short whisper from the Count he withdrew.

"My dear sir," said Peschiera, "I am so unacquainted with your English laws, and your mode of settling embarrassments of this degrading nature, and you have evidently showed so kind a sympathy in my sister's distress, that I venture to ask you to stay here, and aid me in consulting with Baron Levy."

Frank was just expressing his unfeigned pleasure to be of the slightest use, when Levy's knock resounded at the street-door, and in another moment the Baron entered.

"Ouf!" said Levy, wiping his brows, and sinking into a chair as if he had been engaged in toils the most exhausting— "Ouf! this is a very sad business—very; and nothing, my dear Count, nothing but ready money can save us here."

"You know my affairs, Levy," replied Peschiera, mournfully shaking his head, "and that though in a few months, or it may be weeks, I could discharge with ease my sister's debts, whatever their amount, yet at this moment, and in a strange land, I have not the power to do so. The money I brought with me is nearly exhausted. Can you not advance the requisite sum?"

"Impossible!—Mr. Hazeldean is aware of the distress under which I labour myself."

"In that case," said the Count, "all we can do to-day is to remove my sister, and let the execution proceed. Meanwhile I will go among my friends, and see what I can borrow from them."

"Alas!" said Levy, rising and looking out of the window— "alas! we cannot remove the Marchesa—the worst is to come. Look!—you see those three men; they have a writ against her person: the moment she sets her foot out of these doors she will be arrested."\*

"Arrested!" exclaimed Peschiera and Frank in a breath.

"I have done my best to prevent this disgrace, but in vain," said the Baron, looking very wretched. "You see these English tradespeople fancy they have no hold upon foreigners. But we can get bail; she must not go to prison—"

"Prison!" echoed Frank. He hastened to Levy and drew him aside. The Count seemed paralyzed by shame and grief. Throwing himself back on the sofa, he covered his face with his hands.

"My sister!" groaned the Count—"daughter to a Peschiera, widow to a di Negra!" There was something affecting in the proud woe of this grand patrician.

"What is the sum?" whispered Frank, anxious that the poor Count should not overhear him; and indeed the Count seemed too stunned and overwhelmed to hear anything less loud than a clap of thunder!

"We may settle all liabilities for £5000. Nothing to Peschiera, who is enormously rich. *Entre nous*, I doubt his assurance that he is without ready money. It may be so, but—"

"Five thousand pounds! How can I raise such a sum?"

"You, my dear Hazeldean? What are you talking about? To be sure you could raise twice as much with a stroke of your pen, and throw your own debts into the bargain. But— to be so generous to an acquaintance!"

"Acquaintance!—Madame di Negra! the height of my ambition is to claim her as my wife!"

"And these debts don't startle you?"

"If a man loves," answered Frank, simply, "he feels it most when the woman he loves is in affliction. And," he added, after a pause, "though these debts are faults, kindness

---

\* At that date the law of *mesne process* existed still.

at this moment may give me the power to cure for ever both her faults and my own. I can raise this money by a stroke of the pen! How?"

"On the Casino property."

Frank drew back.

"No other way?"

"Of course not. But I know your scruples; let us see if they can be conciliated. You would marry Madame di Negra; she will have £20,000 on her wedding-day. Why not arrange that, out of this sum, your anticipative charge on the Casino property be paid at once? Thus, in truth, it will be but for a few weeks that the charge will exist. The bond will remain locked in my desk—it can never come to your father's knowledge, nor wound his feelings. And when you marry (if you will but be prudent in the meanwhile), you will not owe a debt in the world."

Here the Count suddenly started up.

"Mr. Hazeldean, I asked you to stay and aid us by your counsel; I see now that counsel is unavailing. This blow on our house must fall! I thank you, sir—I thank you. Farewell. Levy, come with me to my poor sister, and prepare her for the worst."

"Count," said Frank, "hear me. My acquaintance with you is but slight, but I have long known and—and esteemed your sister. Baron Levy has suggested a mode in which I can have the honour and the happiness of removing this temporary but painful embarrassment. I can advance the money."

"No—no!" exclaimed Peschiera. "How can you suppose that I will hear of such a proposition? Your youth and benevolence mislead and blind you. Impossible, sir—impossible! Why, even if I had no pride, no delicacy of my own, my sister's fair fame—"

"Would suffer indeed," interrupted Levy, "if she were under such obligation to any one but her affianced husband. Nor, whatever my regard for you, Count, could I suffer my client, Mr. Hazeldean, to make this advance upon any less valid security than that of the fortune to which Madame di Negra is entitled."

"Ha!—is this indeed so? You are a suitor for my sister's hand, Mr. Hazeldean?"

"But not at this moment—not to owe her hand to the compulsion of gratitude," answered gentleman Frank.

"Gratitude! And you do not know her heart, then? Do

not know—" the Count interrupted himself, and went on after a pause. "Mr. Hazeldean, I need not say, that we rank among the first houses in Europe. My pride led me formerly into the error of disposing of my sister's hand to one whom she did not love—merely because in rank he was her equal. I will not again commit such an error, nor would Beatrice again obey me if I sought to constrain her. Where she marries, there she will love. If, indeed, she accepts you, as I believe she will, it will be from affection solely. If she does, I cannot scruple to accept this loan—a loan from a brother-in-law—loan to me, and not charged against her fortune! *That*, sir, (turning to Levy, with his grand air,) you will take care to arrange. If she do not accept you, Mr. Hazeldean, the loan, I repeat, is not to be thought of. Pardon me, if I leave you. This, one way or other, must be decided at once." The Count inclined his head with much stateliness, and then quitted the room. His step was heard ascending the stairs.

"If," said Levy, in the tone of a mere man of business—"if the Count pay the debts, and the lady's fortune be only charged with your own—after all it will not be a bad marriage in the world's eye, nor ought it to be in a father's. Trust me, we shall get Mr. Hazeldean's consent, and cheerfully too."

Frank did not listen; he could only listen to his love, to his heart beating loud with hope and with fear.

Levy sate down before the table, and drew up a long list of figures in a very neat hand—a list of figures on *two* accounts, which the *post-obit* on the Casino was destined to efface.

After a lapse of time, which to Frank seemed interminable, the Count re-appeared. He took Frank aside, with a gesture to Levy, who rose, and retired into the drawing-room.

"My dear young friend," said Peschiera, "as I suspected, my sister's heart is wholly yours. Stop; hear me out. But, unluckily I informed her of your generous proposal; it was most unguarded, most ill-judged in me, and that has well-nigh spoiled all; she has so much pride and spirit; so great a fear that you may think yourself betrayed into an imprudence which you may hereafter regret, that I am sure she will tell you that she does not love you, she cannot accept you, and so forth. Lovers like you are not easily deceived. Don't go by her words; but you shall see her yourself and judge. Come."

Followed mechanically by Frank, the Count ascended the stairs and threw open the door of Beatrice's room. The

Marchesa's back was turned; but Frank could see that she was weeping.

"I have brought my friend to plead for himself," said the Count, in French; "and take my advice, sister, and do not throw away all prospect of real and solid happiness for a vain scruple. *Heed me!*" He retired and left Frank alone with Beatrice.

Then the Marchesa, as if by a violent effort, so sudden was her movement, and so wild her look, turned her face to her wooer, and came up to him, where he stood.

"Oh!" she said, clasping her hands, "is this true? You would save me from disgrace, from a prison—and what can I give you in return? My love! No, no. I will not deceive you. Young, fair, noble, as you are, I do not love you, as you should be loved. Go; leave this house; you do not know my brother. Go, go—while I have still strength, still virtue enough to reject whatever may protect me from him! whatever—may—Oh—go, go."

"You do not love me," said Frank. "Well, I don't wonder at it; you are so brilliant, so superior to me. I will abandon hope—I will leave you as you command me. But at least I will not part with my privilege to serve you. As for the rest—shame on me if I could be mean enough to boast of love, and enforce a suit, at such a moment."

Frank turned his face and stole away softly. He did not arrest his steps at the drawing-room; he went into the parlour, wrote a brief line to Levy charging him quietly to dismiss the execution, and to come to Frank's rooms with the necessary deeds; and, above all, to say nothing to the Count. Then he went out of the house and walked back to his lodgings.

That evening Levy came to him, and accounts were gone into, and papers signed; and the next morning Madame di Negra was free from debt; and there was a great claim on the reversion of the Casino estates; and at the noon of that next day Randal was closeted with Beatrice; and before the night, came a note from Madame di Negra, hurried, blurred with tears, summoning Frank to Curzon Street. And when he entered the Marchesa's drawing-room, Peschiera was seated beside his sister; and rising at Frank's entrance, said, "My dear brother-in-law!" and placed Frank's hand in Beatrice's.

"You accept—you accept me—and of your own free will and choice?"

And Beatrice answered, "Bear with me a little, and I will

try to repay you with all my—all my—" She stopped short, and sobbed aloud.

"I never thought her capable of such acute feelings, such strong attachment," whispered the Count.

Frank heard, and his face was radiant. By degrees Madame di Negra recovered composure, and she listened with what her young lover deemed a tender interest, but what in fact, was mournful and humbled resignation, to his joyous talk of the future. To him the hours passed by, brief and bright, like a flash of sunlight. And his dreams when he retired to rest, were so golden! But, when he awoke the next morning, he said to himself, "What—what will they say at the Hall?"

At that same hour Beatrice, burying her face on her pillow, turned from the loathsome day, and could have prayed for death. At that same hour, Giulio Franzini, Count di Peschiera, dismissing some gaunt haggard Italians, with whom he had been in close conference, sallied forth to reconnoitre the house that contained Violante. At that same hour, Baron Levy was seated before his desk casting up a deadly array of figures, headed, Account with the Right Hon. Audley Egerton, M.P., *Dr.* and *Cr.*"—title-deeds strewed around him, and Frank Hazeldean's post-obit peeping out fresh from the elder parchments. At that same hour, Audley Egerton had just concluded a letter from the chairman of his committee in the city he represented, which letter informed him that he had not a chance of being re-elected. And the lines of his face were as composed as usual, and his foot rested as firm on the grim iron box; but his hand was pressed to his heart, and his eye was on the clock; and his voice muttered—"Dr. F—— should be here!" And that hour Harley L'Estrange, who the previous night had charmed courtly crowds with his gay humour, was pacing to and fro the room in his hotel with restless strides and many a heavy sigh;—and Leonard was standing by the fountain in his garden, and watching the wintry sunbeams that sparkled athwart the spray;—and Violante was leaning on Helen's shoulder, and trying archly, yet innocently, to lead Helen to talk of Leonard;—and Helen was gazing stedfastly on the floor, and answering but by monosyllables;—and Randal Leslie was walking down to his office for the last time, and reading, as he passed across the Green Park, a letter from *home*, from his sister; and then, suddenly crumpling the letter in his thin pale hand, he looked up, beheld in the distance the spires of the great national Abbey; and recalling the words of our hero Nelson, he muttered — "Victory *and* Westminster, but *not* the Abbey!" And Randal Leslie felt that, within the last few days, he had made a vast stride in his ambition;—his grasp on the old Leslie lands—Frank Hazeldean betrothed, and possibly disinherited; and Dick Avenel, in the back ground, opening against the hated Lansmere interest, that same seat in Parliament which had first welcomed into public life Randal's ruined patron.

" But some must laugh, and some must weep·
   Thus runs the world away!"

# BOOK ELEVENTH.

## INITIAL CHAPTER.

ON THE IMPORTANCE OF HATE AS AN AGENT IN CIVILISED LIFE.

It is not an uncommon crotchet amongst benevolent men to maintain that wickedness is necessarily a sort of insanity, and that nobody would make a violent start out of the straight path unless stung to such disorder by a bee in his bonnet. Certainly, when some very clever, well-educated person like our friend, Randal Leslie, acts upon the fallacious principle that "roguery is the best policy," it is curious to see how many points he has in common with the insane: what overcunning —what irritable restlessness—what suspicious belief that the rest of the world are in a conspiracy against him, which it requires all his wit to baffle and turn to his own proper aggrandisement and profit. Perhaps some of my readers may have thought that I have represented Randal as unnaturally far-fetched in his schemes, too wiredrawn and subtle in his speculations; yet that is commonly the case with very refining intellects, when they choose to play the knave; it helps to disguise from themselves the ugliness of their ambition, just as a philosopher delights in the ingenuity of some metaphysical process, which ends in what plain men call "atheism," who would be infinitely shocked and offended if he were called an atheist.

Having premised thus much on behalf of the "Natural" in Randal Leslie's character, I must here fly off to say a word or two on the agency in human life exercised by a passion rarely seen without a mask in our debonair and civilised age —I mean Hate.

In the good old days of our forefathers, when plain speaking and hard blows were in fashion—when a man had his heart at the tip of his tongue, and four feet of sharp iron dangling at his side, Hate playing an honest, open part in the theatre of the world. In fact, when we read History, Hate seems to have "starred it" on the stage. But now, where is Hate? —who ever sees its face? Is it that smiling, good-tempered creature, that presses you by the hand so cordially? or that dignified figure of state that calls you its "Right Honourable friend?" Is it that bowing, grateful dependent?—is it that soft-eyed Amaryllis? Ask not, guess not: you will only know it to be hate when the poison is in your cup, or the poinard in your breast. In the Gothic age, grim Humour painted "the Dance of Death;" in our polished-century, some sardonic wit should give us "the Masquerade of Hate."

Certainly, the counter-passion betrays itself with ease to our gaze. Love is rarely a hypocrite. But Hate—how detect, and how guard against it? It lurks where you least suspect it; it is created by causes that you can the least foresee; and Civilisation multiplies its varieties, whilst it favours its disguise: for Civilisation increases the number of contending interests, and Refinement renders more susceptible to the least irritation the cuticle of Self-Love. But Hate comes covertly forth from some self-interest we have crossed, or some self-love we have wounded; and, dullards that we are, how seldom we are aware of our offence! You may be hated by a man you have never seen in your life: you may be hated as often by one you have loaded with benefits;—you may so walk as not to tread on a worm; but you must sit fast on your easy chair till you are carried out to your bier, if you would be sure not to tread on some snake of a foe. But, then, what harm does the hate do us? Very often the harm is as unseen by the world as the hate is unrecognised by us. It may come on us, unawares, in some solitary byway of our life; strike us in our unsuspecting privacy; thwart us in some blessed hope we have never told to another; for the moment the world sees that it is Hate that strikes us, its worst power of mischief is gone.

We have a great many names for the same passion—Envy, Jealousy, Spite, Prejudice, Rivalry; but they are so many synonyms for the one old heathen demon. When the death-giving shaft of Apollo sent the plague to some unhappy Achæan, it did not much matter to the victim whether the god were called Helios or Smintheus.

No man you ever met in the world seemed more raised above the malice of Hate than Audley Egerton: even in the hot war of politics he had scarcely a personal foe; and in private life he kept himself so aloof and apart from others that he was little known, save by the benefits the waste of his wealth conferred. That the hate of any one could reach the austere statesman on his high pinnacle of esteem,—you would have smiled at the idea! But Hate is now, as it ever has been, an actual Power amidst "the Varieties of Life;" and, in spite of bars to the door, and policemen in the street, no one can be said to sleep in safety while there wakes the eye of a single foe.

## CHAPTER II.

THE glory of Bond Street is no more. The title of Bond Street Lounger has faded from our lips. In vain the crowd of equipages and the blaze of shops: the renown of Bond Street was in its pavement—its pedestrians. Art thou old enough, O reader! to remember the Bond Street Lounger and his incomparable generation? For my part, I can just recall the decline of the grand era. It was on its wane when, in the ambition of boyhood, I first began to muse upon high neckcloths and Wellington boots. But the ancient *habitués*— the *magni nominis umbræ*—contemporaries of Brummell in his zenith—boon companions of George IV. in his regency—still haunted the spot. From four to six in the hot month of June, they sauntered stately to and fro, looking somewhat mournful even then—foreboding the extinction of their race. The Bond Street Lounger was rarely seen alone: he was a social animal, and walked arm in arm with his fellow-man. He did not seem born for the cares of these ruder times; not made was he for an age in which Finsbury returns members to Parliament. He loved his small talk; and never since then has talk been so pleasingly small. Your true Bond Street Lounger had a very dissipated look. His youth had been spent with heroes who loved their bottle. He himself had perhaps supped with Sheridan. He was by nature a spendthrift: you saw it in the roll of his walk. Men who make money rarely saunter; men who save money rarely swagger. But saunter and swagger both united to stamp PRODIGAL on the Bond Street Lounger. And so familiar as he was with his own set, and so amusingly supercilious with the vulgar residue of mortals whose faces were strange to Bond Street. But he is gone. The world, though sadder for his loss, still strives to do its best without him; and our young men, now-a-days, attend to model cottages, and incline to Tractarianism. Still the place, to an unreflecting eye, has its brilliancy and bustle. But it is a thoroughfare, not a lounge. And adown the thoroughfare, somewhat before the hour when the throng is thickest, passed two gentlemen of an appearance exceedingly out of keeping with the place. Yet both had the air of men pretending to aristocracy—an old-world air of respectability and stake in the country, and Church-and-Stateism. The burlier of the two was even rather a beau in his way. He had first learned to dress, indeed, when Bond Street was at its acmé, and Brummell in his pride. He still retained in his garb the fashion of his youth; only what then had spoken of the town, now betrayed the life of the country. His neckcloth ample and high, and of snowy whiteness, set off to comely advantage a face smooth-shaven, and of clear florid hues; his coat of royal blue, with buttons in which you might have seen yourself *veluti in speculum*, was, rather jauntily, buttoned across a waist that spoke of lusty middle age, free from the ambition, the avarice, and the anxieties that fret Londoners into threadpapers; his small-clothes, of greyish drab, loose at the thigh and tight at the knee, were made by Brummell's own breeches-maker, and the gaiters to match (thrust half-way down the calf), had a manly dandyism that would have done honour to the beau-ideal of a county member. The profession of this gentleman's companion was unmistakable—the shovel-hat, the clerical cut of the coat, the neckcloth without collar, that seemed made for its accessory —the band, and something very decorous, yet very mild, in the whole mien of this personage, all spoke of one who was every inch the gentleman and the parson.

"No," said the portlier of these two persons—"no, I can't say I like Frank's looks at all. There's certainly something on his mind. However, I suppose it will be all out this evening."

"He dines with you at your hotel, Squire? Well, you must be kind to him. We can't put old heads upon young shoulders."

"I don't object to his head being young," returned the Squire; "but I wish he had a little of Randal Leslie's good sense in it. I see how it will end; I must take him back to the country; and if he wants occupation, why he shall keep the hounds, and I'll put him into Brooksby farm."

"As for the hounds," replied the Parson, "hounds necessitate horses; and I think more mischief comes to a young man of spirit, from the stables, than from any other place in the world. They ought to be exposed from the pulpit, those stables!" added Mr. Dale, thoughtfully; "see what they entailed upon Nimrod! But Agriculture is a healthful and noble pursuit, honoured by sacred nations, and cherished by the greatest men in classical times. For instance, the Athenians were—"

"Bother the Athenians!" cried the Squire, irreverently; "you need not go so far back for an example. It is enough for a Hazeldean that his father, and his grandfather, and his great grandfather all farmed before him; and a devilish deal better, I take it, than any of those musty old Athenians—no offence to them. But I'll tell you one thing, Parson—a man, to farm well, and live in the country, should have a wife; it is half the battle."

"As to a battle, a man who is married is pretty sure of half, though not always the better half, of it," answered the Parson, who seemed peculiarly facetious that day. "Ah, Squire, I wish I could think Mrs. Hazeldean right in her conjecture!—you would have the prettiest daughter-in-law in the three kingdoms. And I do believe that, if I could have a good talk with the young lady apart from her father, we could remove the only objection I know to the marriage. Those Popish errors—"

"Ah, very true!" cried the Squire; "that Pope sticks hard in my gizzard. I could excuse her being a foreigner, and not having, I suppose, a shilling in her pocket—bless her handsome face!—but to be worshipping images in her room instead of going to the parish church, that will never do. But you think you could talk her out of the Pope, and into the family pew?"

"Why, I could have talked her father out of the Pope, only, when he had not a word to say for himself, he bolted out of the window. Youth is more ingenuous in confessing its errors."

"I own," said the Squire, "that both Harry and I had a favourite notion of ours till this Italian girl got into our heads. Do you know we both took a great fancy to Randal's little sister—pretty, blushing, English-faced girl as ever you saw. And it went to Harry's good heart to see her so neglected by that silly, fidgetty mother of hers, her hair hanging about her ears; and I thought it would be a fine way to bring Randal and Frank more together, and enable me to do something for Randal himself—a good boy with Hazeldean blood in his veins. But Violante is so handsome, that I don't wonder at the boy's choice; and then it is our fault—we let them see so much of each other as children. However, I should be very angry if Rickeybockey had been playing sly, and running away from the Casino in order to give Frank an opportunity to carry on a clandestine intercourse with his daughter."

"I don't think that would be like Riccabocca; more like him to run away in order to deprive Frank of the best of all occasions to court Violante, if he so desired; for where could he see more of her than at the Casino?"

SQUIRE.—"That's well put. Considering he was only a foreign doctor, and, for aught we know, once went about in a caravan, he is a gentleman-like fellow, that Rickeybockey. I speak of people as I find them. But what is your notion about Frank? I see you don't think he is in love with Violante, after all. Out with it, man; speak plain."

PARSON.—"Since you so urge me, I own I do not think him in love with her; neither does my Carry, who is uncommonly shrewd in such matters."

SQUIRE.—"Your Carry, indeed!—as if she were half as shrewd as my Harry. Carry—nonsense!"

PARSON, (reddening.)—"I don't want to make invidious remarks; but, Mr. Hazeldean, when you sneer at my Carry, I should not be a man if I did not say that—"

SQUIRE, (interrupting.)—"She is a good little woman enough; but to compare her to my Harry!"

PARSON.—"I don't compare her to your Harry; I don't compare her to any woman in England, sir. But you are losing your temper, Mr. Hazeldean!"

SQUIRE.—"I!"

PARSON.—"And people are staring at you, Mr. Hazeldean. For decency's sake, compose yourself, and change the subject. We are just at the Albany. I hope that we shall not find poor Captain Higginbotham as ill as he represents himself in his letter. Ah, is it possible? No, it cannot be. Look—look!"

SQUIRE.—"Where—what—where? Don't pinch so hard. Bless me, do you see a ghost?"

PARSON.—"There—the gentleman in black!"

SQUIRE.—"Gentleman in black! What!—in broad daylight! Nonsense!"

Here the Parson made a spring forward, and, catching the arm of the person in question, who himself had stopped, and was gazing intently on the pair, exclaimed—

"Sir, pardon me; but is not your name Fairfield? Ah, it is Leonard—it is—my dear, dear boy! What joy! So altered, so improved, but still the same honest face. Squire, come here—your old friend, Leonard Fairfield."

"And he wanted to persuade me," said the Squire, shaking Leonard heartily by the hand, "That you were the Gentleman in Black; but, indeed, he has been in strange humours and tantrums all the morning. Well, Master Lenny; why, you are grown quite a gentleman! The world thrives with you —eh! I suppose you are head-gardener to some grandee."

"Not that, sir," said Leonard, smiling. "But the world has thriven with me at last, though not without some rough usage at starting. Ah, Mr. Dale, you can little guess how often I have thought of you and your discourse on Knowledge; and, what is more, how I have lived to feel the truth of your words, and to bless the lesson."

PARSON, (much touched and flattered.)—"I expected nothing less from you, Leonard; you were always a lad of great sense, and sound judgment. So you have thought of my little discourse on Knowledge, have you?"

SQUIRE.—"Hang knowledge! I have reason to hate the word. It burned down three ricks of mine; the finest ricks you ever set eyes on, Mr. Fairfield."

PARSON.—"That was not knowledge, Squire; that was ignorance."

SQUIRE.—"Ignorance! The deuce it was. I'll just appeal to you, Mr. Fairfield. We have been having sad riots in the shire, and the ringleader was just such another lad as you were!"

LEONARD.—"I am very much obliged to you, Mr. Hazeldean. In what respect?"

SQUIRE.—"Why he was a village genius, and always reading some cursed little tract or other; and got mighty discontented with King, Lords, and Commons, I suppose, and went about talking of the wrongs of the poor, and the crimes of the rich, till, by Jove, sir, the whole mob rose one day with pitchforks and sickles, and smash went Farmer Smart's thrashing-machines; and on the same night my ricks were on fire. We caught the rogues, and they were all tried; but the poor deluded labourers were let off with a short imprisonment. The village genius, thank heaven, is sent packing to Botany Bay."

LEONARD.—"But, did his books teach him to burn ricks and smash machines?"

PARSON.—"No; he said quite the contrary, and declared that he had no hand in those misdoings."

Squire.—"But he was proved to have excited, with his wild talk, the boobies who had! 'Gad, sir, there was a hypocritical Quaker once, who said to his enemy, 'I can't shed thy blood, friend, but I will hold thy head under water till thou art drowned.' And so there is a set of demagogical fellows, who keep calling out, 'Farmer, this is an oppressor, and Squire that is a vampire! But no violence! Don't smash their machines, don't burn their ricks! Moral force, and a curse on all tyrants!' Well, and if poor Hodge thinks moral force is all my eye, and that the recommendation is to be read backwards, in the devil's way of reading the Lord's prayer, I should like to know which of the two ought to go to Botany Bay—Hodge, who comes out like a man, if he thinks he is wronged, or 'tother sneaking chap, who makes use of his knowledge to keep himself out of the scrape?"

Parson.—"It may be very true; but when I saw that poor fellow at the bar, with his intelligent face, and heard his bold clear defence, and thought of all his hard struggles for knowledge, and how they had ended, because he forgot that knowledge is like fire, and must not be thrown amongst flax—why, I could have given my right hand to save him. And, oh, Squire, do you remember his poor mother's shriek of despair when he was sentenced to transportation for life—I hear it now! And what Leonard—what do you think had misled him? At the bottom of all the mischief was a Tinker's bag. You cannot forget Sprott?"

Leonard.—"Tinker's bag!—Sprott!"

Squire.—"That rascal, sir, was the hardest fellow to nab you could possibly conceive; as full of quips and quirks as an Old Bailey lawyer. But we managed to bring it home to him. Lord! his bag was choke-full of tracts against every man who had a good coat on his back; and as if that was not enough, cheek by jowl with the tracts were lucifers, contrived on a new principle, for teaching my ricks the theory of spontaneous combustion. The labourers bought the lucifers—"

Parson.—"And the poor village genius bought the tracts."

Squire.—"All headed with a motto—'To teach the working classes that knowledge is power.' So that I was right in saying that knowledge had burnt my ricks; knowledge inflamed the village genius, the village genius inflamed fellows more ignorant than himself, and they inflamed my stack-yard. However, lucifers, tracts, village genius, and Sprott, are all off to Botany Bay; and the shire has gone on much the better for it. So no more of your knowledge for me, begging your pardon, Mr. Fairfield. Such uncommonly fine ricks as mine were too! I declare, parson, you are looking as if you felt pity for Sprott; and I saw you, indeed, whispering to him as he was taken out of court."

PARSON (looking sheepish).—"Indeed, Squire, I was only asking him what had become of his donkey, an unoffending creature."

SQUIRE.—"Unoffending! Upset me amidst a thistle bed in my own village green. I remember it. Well, what did he say *had* become of the donkey?"

PARSON.—"He said but one word; but that showed all the vindictiveness of his disposition. He said it with a horrid wink, that made my blood run cold. 'What's become of your poor donkey?' said I, and he answered—"

SQUIRE.—"Go on. He answered—"

PARSON.—"'Sausages.'"

SQUIRE.—"Sausages! Like enough; and sold to the poor; and that's what the poor will come to if they listen to such revolutionising villains. Sausages! Donkey sausages!— (spitting)—'Tis as b— as eating one another; perfect cannibalism."

Leonard, who had been thrown into grave thought by the history of Sprott and the village genius, now pressing the Parson's hand, asked permission to wait on him before Mr. Dale quitted London; and was about to withdraw, when the Parson, gently detaining him, said—"No; don't leave me yet, Leonard—I have so much to ask you, and to talk about. I shall be at leisure shortly. We are just now going to call on a relation of the Squire's, whom you must recollect, I am sure—Captain Higginbotham—Barnabas Higginbotham. He is very poorly."

"And I am sure he would take it kind in you to call too," said the Squire, with great good-nature.

LEONARD.—"Nay, sir, would not that be a great liberty?"

SQUIRE.—"Liberty! To ask a poor sick gentleman how he is? Nonsense. And I say, sir, perhaps as no doubt you have been living in town, and know more of new-fangled notions than I do—perhaps you can tell us whether or not it is all humbug, that new way of doctoring people."

LEONARD.—"What new way, sir. There are so many."

SQUIRE.—"Are there? Folks in London *do* look uncommonly sickly. But my poor cousin (he was never a Solomon) has got hold, he says, of a homely—homely—What's the word, Parson?"

PARSON.—" Homœopathist."

SQUIRE.—" That's it! You see the Captain went to live with one Sharpe Currie, a relation who had a great deal of money, and very little liver;—made the one, and left much of the other in Ingee, you understand. The Captain had *expectations* of the money. Very natural, I dare say; but Lord, sir, what do you think has happened? Sharpe Currie has done him. Would not die, sir; got back his liver, and the Captain has lost his own. Strangest thing you ever heard. And then the ungrateful old Nabob has dismissed the Captain, saying, 'He can't bear to have invalids about him;' and is going to marry, and I have no doubt will have children by the dozen!"

PARSON.—"It was in Germany, at one of the Spas, that Mr. Currie recovered; and as he had the selfish inhumanity to make the Captain go through a course of waters simultaneously with himself, it has so chanced that the same waters that cured Mr. Currie's liver have destroyed Captain Higginbotham's. An English homœopathic physician, then staying at the Spa, has attended the Captain hither, and declares that he will restore him by infinitesimal doses of the same chemical properties that were found in the waters which diseased him. Can there be anything in such a theory?"

LEONARD.—"I once knew a very able, though eccentric homœopathist, and I am inclined to believe there may be something in the system. My friend went to Germany; it may possibly be the same person who attends the Captain. May I ask his name?"

SQUIRE.—"Cousin Barnabas does not mention it. You may ask it of himself, for here we are at his chambers. I say, Parson (whispering slily), if a small dose of what hurt the Captain is to cure him, don't you think the proper thing would be a—legacy? Ha! ha!"

PARSON (trying not to laugh).—"Hush, Squire. Poor human nature! We must be merciful to its infirmities. Come in, Leonard."

Leonard, interested in his doubt whether he might thus chance again upon Dr. Morgan, obeyed the invitation, and with his two companions followed the woman—who " did for the Captain and his rooms "—across the small lobby, into the presence of the sufferer.

## CHAPTER III.

WHATEVER the disposition towards merriment at his cousin's expense entertained by the Squire, it vanished instantly at the sight of the Captain's doleful visage and emaciated figure.

"Very good in you to come to town to see me—very good in you, cousin; and in you too, Mr. Dale. How very well you are both looking. I'm a sad wreck. You might count every bone in my body."

"Hazeldean air and roast beef will soon set you up, my boy," said the Squire, kindly. "You were a great goose to leave them, and these comfortable rooms of yours in the Albany."

"They *are* comfortable, though not showy," said the Captain, with tears in his eyes. "I had done my best to make them so. New carpets—this very chair—(morocco!)—that Japan cat (holds toast and muffins)—just when—just when—(the tears here broke forth, and the Captain fairly whimpered)—just when that ungrateful, bad-hearted man wrote me word 'he was—was dying and lone in the world;' and—and—to think what I've gone through for him;—and to treat me so. Cousin William, he has grown as hale as yourself, and—and—"

"Cheer up, cheer up!" cried the compassionate Squire. "It is a very hard case, I allow. But you see, as the old proverb says, ''tis ill waiting for a dead man's shoes;' and in future—I don't mean offence—but I think if you would calculate less on the livers of your relations, it would be all the better for your own. Excuse me."

"Cousin William," replied the poor Captain, "I am sure I never calculated; but still, if you had seen that deceitful man's good-for-nothing face—as yellow as a guinea—and have gone through all I've gone through, you would have felt cut to the heart, as I do. I can't bear ingratitude. I never could. But let it pass. Will that gentleman take a chair?"

PARSON.—"Mr. Fairfield has kindly called with us, because he knows something of this system of homœopathy which you have adopted, and may, perhaps, know the practitioner. What is the name of your doctor?"

CAPTAIN (looking at his watch).—"That reminds me (swallowing a globule.) A great relief these little pills—

after the physic I've taken to please that malignant man. He always tried his doctor's stuff upon me. But there's another world, and a juster!"

With that pious conclusion, the Captain again began to weep.

"Touched," muttered the Squire, with his forefinger on his forehead, "You seem to have a good tidy sort of a nurse here, Cousin Barnabas. I hope she's pleasant, and lively, and don't let you take on so."

"Hist!—don't talk of her. All mercenary; every bit of her fawning! Would you believe it? I give her ten shillings a week, besides all that goes down of my pats of butter and rolls, and I overheard the jade saying to the laundress that 'I could not last long; and she'd—EXPECTATIONS!' Ah, Mr Dale, when one thinks of the sinfulness there is in this life! But I'll not think of it. No—I'll not. Let us change the subject. You were asking my doctor's name. It is—"

Here the woman with 'expectations' threw open the door, and suddenly announced—"DR. MORGAN."

## CHAPTER IV.

THE Parson started, and so did Leonard.

The Homœopathist did not at first notice either. With an unobservant bow to the visitors, he went straight to the patient, and asked, "How go the symptoms?"

Therewith the Captain commenced, in a tone of voice like a schoolboy reciting the catalogue of the ships in Homer. He had been evidently conning the symptoms, and learning them by heart. Nor was there a single nook or corner in his anatomical organisation, so far as the Captain was acquainted with that structure, but what some symptom or other was dragged therefrom, and exposed to day. The Squire listened with horror to the morbific inventory—muttering at each dread interval, "Bless me! Lord bless me! What, more still! Death would be a very happy release!" Meanwhile the Doctor endured the recital with exemplary patience, noting down in the leaves of his pocket-book what appeared to him the salient points in this fortress of disease to which he had laid siege, and then, drawing forth a minute paper, said—

"Capital—nothing can be better. This powder must be dissolved in eight table-spoonfuls of water; one spoonful every two hours."

"Table-spoonful?"

"Table-spoonful."

"'Nothing can be better,' did you say, sir?" repeated the Squire, who in his astonishment at that assertion applied to the Captain's description of his sufferings, had hitherto hung fire—"nothing can be better?"

"For the diagnosis, sir!" replied Dr. Morgan.

"For the dogs' noses, very possibly," quoth the Squire; "but for the inside of Cousin Higginbotham, I should think nothing could be worse."

"You are mistaken, sir," replied Dr. Morgan. "It is not the Captain who speaks here—it is his liver. Liver, sir, though a noble, is an imaginative organ, and indulges in the most extraordinary fictions. Seat of poetry, and love, and jealousy—the liver. Never believe what it says. You have no idea what a liar it is! But—ahem—ahem. Cott—I think I've seen you before, sir. Surely your name's Hazeldean?"

"William Hazeldean, at your service, Doctor. But where have you seen me?"

"On the hustings at Lansmere. You were speaking on behalf of your distinguished brother, Mr. Egerton."

"Hang it!" cried the Squire: "I think it must have been my liver that spoke there! for I promised the electors that that half-brother of mine would stick by the land; and I never told a bigger lie in my life!"

Here the patient, reminded of his other visitors, and afraid he was going to be bored with the enumeration of the Squire's wrongs, and probably the whole history of his duel with Captain Dashmore, turned with a languid wave of his hand, and said, "Doctor, another friend of mine, the Rev. Mr. Dale,—and a gentleman who is acquainted with homœopathy."

"Dale? What, more old friends!" cried the Doctor, rising; and the Parson came somewhat reluctantly from the window nook, to which he had retired. The Parson and the Homœopathist shook hands.

"We have met before on a very mournful occasion," said the Doctor, with feeling.

"The Parson held his finger to his lips, and glanced towards Leonard. The Doctor stared at the lad, but he did not recognise in the person before him the gaunt, care-worn boy whom he had placed with Mr. Prickett, until Leonard smiled and spoke. And the smile and the voice sufficed.

"Cott—and it *is* the poy!" cried Dr. Morgan; and he actually caught hold of Leonard, and gave him an affectionate Welch hug. Indeed, his agitation at these several surprises became so great that he stopped short, drew forth a globule —"*Aconite*—good against nervous shocks!" and swallowed it incontinently.

"Gad," said the Squire, rather astonished, "'tis the first doctor I ever saw swallow his own medicine! There must be something in it."

The Captain now, highly disgusted that so much attention was withdrawn from his own case, asked, in a querulous voice, "And as to diet? What shall I have for dinner?"

"A friend!" said the Doctor, wiping his eyes.

"Zounds!" cried the Squire, retreating, "do you mean to say, that the British laws (to be sure they are very much changed of late) allow you to diet your patients upon their fellow-men? Why, Parson, this is worse than the donkey sausages."

"Sir," said Dr. Morgan, gravely, "I mean to say, that it matters little what we eat, in comparison with care as to whom we eat with. It is better to exceed a little with a friend, than to observe the strictest regimen, and eat alone. Talk and laughter help the digestion, and are indispensable in affections of the liver. I have no doubt, sir, that it was my patient's agreeable society that tended to restore to health his dyspeptic relative, Mr. Sharpe Currie."

The Captain groaned aloud.

"And, therefore, if one of you gentlemen will stay and dine with Mr. Higginbotham, it will greatly assist the effects of his medicine."

The Captain turned an imploring eye, first towards his cousin, then towards the Parson.

"I'm engaged to dine with my son—very sorry," said the Squire. "But Dale, here—"

"If he will be so kind," put in the Captain, "we might cheer the evening with a game at whist—double dummy."

Now, poor Mr. Dale had set his heart on dining with an old college friend, and having no stupid, prosy double dummy, in which one cannot have the pleasure of scolding one's partner, but a regular orthodox rubber, with the pleasing prospect of scolding all the three other performers. But as his quiet life forbade him to be a hero in great things, the Parson had made up his mind to be a hero in small ones. Therefore, though with rather a rueful face, he accepted the Captain's invitation, and promised to return at six o'clock to dine. Meanwhile he must hurry off to the other end of the town, and excuse himself from the pre-engagement he had already formed. He now gave his card, with the address of a quiet family hotel thereon, to Leonard, and not looking quite so charmed with Dr. Morgan as he was before that unwelcome prescription, he took his leave. The Squire too, having to see a new churn, and execute various commissions for his Harry, went his way (not, however, till Dr. Morgan had assured him that, in a few weeks, the Captain might safely remove to Hazeldean); and Leonard was about to follow, when Morgan hooked his arm in his old *protégé's*, and said, " But I must have some talk with you; and you have to tell me all about the little orphan girl."

Leonard could not resist the pleasure of talking about Helen; and he got into the carriage, which was waiting at the door for the homœopathist.

"I am going in the country a few miles to see a patient," said the Doctor; "so we shall have time for undisturbed consultation. I have so often wondered what had become of you. Not hearing from Prickett, I wrote to him, and received from his heir an answer as dry as a bone. Poor fellow, I found that he had neglected his globules and quitted the globe. Alas, *pulvis et umbra sumus!* I could learn no tidings of you. Prickett's successor declared he knew nothing about you. I hoped the best; for I always fancied you were one who would fall on your legs—bilious-nervous temperament; such are the men who succeed in their undertakings, especially if they take a spoonful of *chamomilla* whenever they are over-excited. So now for your history and the little girl's—pretty little thing —never saw a more susceptible constitution, nor one more suited to *pulsatilla*."

Leonard briefly related his own struggles and success, and informed the good Doctor how they had at last discovered the nobleman in whom poor Captain Digby had confided, and whose care of the orphan had justified the confidence.

Dr. Morgan opened his eyes at hearing the name of Lord L'Estrange. "I remember him very well," said he, "when I practised murder as an allopathist at Lansmere. But to think that wild boy, so full of whim, and life, and spirit, should become staid enough for a guardian to that dear little child, with her timid eyes and *pulsatilla* sensibilities. Well, wonders never cease. And he has befriended you too, you say. Ah, he knew your family."

"So he says. Do you think, sir, that he ever knew—ever saw—my mother?"

"Eh! your mother?—Nora?" exclaimed the Doctor, quickly; and, as if struck by some sudden thought, his brows met, and he remained silent and musing a few moments; then, observing Leonard's eyes fixed on him earnestly, he replied to the question:—

"No doubt he saw her; she was brought up at Lady Lansmere's. Did he not tell you so?"

"No." A vague suspicion here darted through Leonard's mind, but as suddenly vanished. His father! Impossible. His father must have deliberately wronged the dead mother. And was Harley L'Estrange a man capable of such wrong? And had he been Harley's son, would not Harley have guessed it at once, and so guessing, have owned and claimed him? Besides, Lord L'Estrange looked so young;—old enough to be Leonard's father!—he could not entertain the idea. He roused himself and said, falteringly—

"You told me you did not know by what name I should call my father."

"And I told you the truth, to the best of my belief."

"By your honour, sir?"

"By my honour, I do not know it."

There was now a long silence. The carriage had long left London, and was on a high road somewhat lonelier, and more free from houses than most of those which form the entrances to the huge city. Leonard gazed wistfully from the window, and the objects that met his eyes gradually seemed to appeal to his memory. Yes! it was the road by which he had first approached the metropolis, hand in hand with Helen—and hope so busy at his poet's heart. He sighed deeply. He thought he would willingly have resigned all he had won—independence, fame, all—to feel again the clasp of that tender hand—again to be the sole protector of that gentle life.

The Doctor's voice broke on his reverie. "I am going to see a very interesting patient—coats to his stomach quite worn out, sir—man of great learning, with a very inflamed cerebellum. I can't do him much good, and he does me a great deal of harm."

"How harm?" asked Leonard, with an effort at some rejoinder.

"Hits me on the heart, and makes my eyes water;—very pathetic case—grand creature, who has thrown himself away. Found him given over by the allopathists, and in a high state of *delirium tremens*—restored him for a time—took a great liking to him—could not help it—swallowed a great many globules to harden myself against him—would not do—brought him over to England with the other patients, who all pay me well (except Captain Higginbotham). But this poor fellow pays me nothing—costs me a great deal in time and turnpikes, and board and lodging. Thank Heaven I'm a single man, and can afford it! My poy, I would let all the other patients go to the allopathists if I could but save this poor, big, penniless, princely fellow. But what can one do with a stomach that has not a rag of its coats left? Stop—(the Doctor pulled the check-string). This is the stile. I get out here and go across the fields."

That stile—those fields—with what distinctness Leonard remembered them. Ah, where was Helen? Could she ever, ever again be his child-angel?

"I will go with you, if you permit," said he to the good Doctor. "And while you pay your visit, I will saunter by a little brook that I think must run by your way."

"The Brent—you know that brook? Ah, you should hear my poor patient talk of it, and of the hours he has spent angling in it—you would not know whether to laugh or cry. The first day he was brought down to the place, he wanted to go out and try once more, he said, for his old deluding demon —a one-eyed perch."

"Heavens!" exclaimed Leonard, "are you speaking of John Burley?"

"To be sure, that is his name—John Burley."

"Oh, has it come to this? Cure him, save him, if it be in human power. For the last two years I have sought his trace everywhere, and in vain, the moment I had money of my own —a home of my own. Poor, erring, glorious Burley. Take me to him. Did you say there was no hope?"

"I did not say that," replied the Doctor. "But art can only assist nature; and though nature is ever at work to repair the injuries we do to her, yet, when the coats of a stomach are all gone, she gets puzzled, and so do I. You must tell me another time how you came to know Burley, for here we are at the house, and I see him at the window looking out for me."

The Doctor opened the garden gate of the quiet cottage to

which poor Burley had fled from the pure presence of Leonard's child-angel. And with heavy step, and heavy heart, Leonard mournfully followed, to behold the wrecks of him whose wit had glorified orgy, and "set the table in a roar." Alas, poor Yorick!

## CHAPTER V.

AUDLEY EGERTON stands on his hearth alone. During the short interval that has elapsed since we last saw him, events had occurred memorable in English history, wherewith we have nought to do in a narrative studiously avoiding all party politics even when treating of politicians. The new Ministers had stated the general programme of their policy, and introduced one measure in especial that had lifted them at once to the dizzy height of popular power. But it became clear that this measure could not be carried without a fresh appeal to the people. A dissolution of Parliament, as Audley's sagacious experience had foreseen, was inevitable. And Audley Egerton had no chance of return for his own seat—for the great commercial city identified with his name. Oh sad, but not rare, instance of the mutabilities of that same popular favour now enjoyed by his successors! The great commoner, the weighty speaker, the expert man of business, the statesman who had seemed a type of the practical steady sense for which our middle class is renowned—he who, not three years since, might have had his honoured choice of the largest popular constituencies in the kingdom—he, Audley Egerton, knew not one single town (free from the influences of private property or interest) in which the obscurest candidate, who bawled out for the new liberal measure, would not have beaten him hollow. Where one popular hustings, on which that grave sonorous voice that had stilled so often the roar of faction, would not be drowned amidst the hoots of the scornful mob?

True, what were called the close boroughs still existed— true, many a chief of his party would have been too proud of the honour of claiming Audley Egerton for his nominee. But the ex-minister's haughty soul shrunk from this contrast to his past position. And to fight against the popular measure, as member of one of the seats most denounced by the people, —he felt it was a post in the grand army of parties below his dignity to occupy, and foreign to his peculiar mind, which required the sense of consequence and station. And if, in a few months, those seats were swept away—were annihilated from the rolls of Parliament—where was he? Moreover, Egerton, emancipated from the trammels that had bound his will while his party was in office, desired, in the turn of events, to be nominee of no man—desired to stand at least freely and singly on the ground of his own services, be guided by his own penetration; no law for action, but his strong sense and his stout English heart. Therefore he had declined all offers from those who could still bestow seats in Parliament. Seats that he could purchase with hard gold were yet open to him. And the £5000 he had borrowed from Levy were yet untouched.

To this lone public man, public life, as we have seen, was the all in all. But now more than ever it was vital to his very wants. Around him yawned ruin. He knew that it was in Levy's power at any moment to foreclose on his mortgaged lands—to pour in the bonds and the bills which lay within those rosewood receptacles that lined the fatal lair of the sleek usurer—to seize on the very house in which now moved all the pomp of a retinue that vied with the *valetaille* of dukes—to advertise for public auction, under execution, "the costly effects of the Right Hon. Audley Egerton." But, consummate in his knowledge of the world, Egerton felt assured that Levy would not adopt these measures against him while he could still tower in the van of political war—while he could still see before him the full chance of restoration to power, perhaps to power still higher than before—perhaps to power the highest of all beneath the throne. That Levy, whose hate he divined, though he did not conjecture all its causes, had hitherto delayed even a visit, even a menace, seemed to him to show that Levy still thought him one "to be helped," or, at least, one too powerful to crush. To secure his position in Parliament unshackled, unfallen, if but for another year,—new combinations of party might arise, new re-actions take place, in public opinion! And, with his hand pressed to his heart, the stern firm man muttered,—"If not, I ask but to die in my harness, and that men may not know that I am a pauper, until all that I need from my country is a grave."

Scarce had these words died upon his lips ere two quick knocks in succession resounded at the street door. In another moment Harley entered, and, at the same time, the servant in attendance approached Audley, and announced Baron Levy.

"Beg the Baron to wait, unless he would prefer to name his own hour to call again," answered Egerton, with the slightest possible change of colour. "You can say I am now with Lord L'Estrange."

"I had hoped you had done for ever with that deluder of youth," said Harley, as soon as the groom of the chambers had withdrawn. "I remember that you saw too much of him in the gay time, ere wild oats are sown; but now surely you can never need a loan; and if so is not Harley L'Estrange by your side?"

EGERTON.—"My dear Harley!—doubtless he but comes to talk to me of some borough. He has much to do with those delicate negotiations."

HARLEY.—"And I have come on the same business. I claim the priority. I not only hear in the world but I see by the papers, that Josiah Jenkins, Esq., known to fame as an orator who leaves out his h's, and young Lord Willoughby Whiggolin, who is just made a Lord of the Admiralty, because his health is too delicate for the army, are certain to come in for the city which you and your present colleague will as certainly vacate. That is true, is it not?"

EGERTON.—"My old Committee now vote for Jenkins and Whiggolin. And I suppose there will not be even a contest. Go on."

"So my father and I are agreed that you must condescend, for the sake of old friendship, to be once more member for Lansmere?"

"Harley," exclaimed Egerton, changing countenance far more than he had done at the announcement of Levy's portentous visit—"Harley, no, no!"

"No! But why? Wherefore such emotion?" asked L'Estrange, in surprise

Audley was silent.

HARLEY.—"I suggested the idea to two or three of the late Ministers; they all concur in advising you to accede. In the first place, if declining to stand for the place which tempted you from Lansmere, what more natural than that you should fall back on that earlier representation? In the second place, Lansmere is neither a rotten borough, to be bought, nor a close borough, under one man's nomination. It is a tolerably large constituency. My father, it is true, has considerable interest in it, but only what is called the legitimate influence of property. At all events, it is more secure than a contest for a larger town, more dignified than a seat for a smaller. Hesitating still? Even my mother entreats me to say how she desires you to renew that connection."

"Harley," again exclaimed Egerton; and fixing upon his friend's earnest face, eyes which, when softened by emotion, were strangely beautiful in their expression—"Harley, if you could but read my heart at this moment, you would—you would—" His voice faltered, and he fairly bent his proud head upon Harley's shoulder; grasping the hand he had caught! nervously, clingingly—"O Harley, if I ever lose your love, your friendship,—nothing else is left to me in the world."

"Audley, my dear, dear Audley, is it you who speak to me thus? You, my school friend, my life's confidant—you?"

"I am grown very weak and foolish," said Egerton, trying to smile. "I do not know myself. I, too, whom you have so often called 'Stoic,' and likened to the Iron Man in the poem which you used to read by the river-side at Eton."

"But even then, my Audley, I knew that a warm human heart (do what you would to keep it down) beats strong under the iron ribs. And I often marvel now, to think you have gone through life so free from the wilder passions. Happier so!"

Egerton, who had turned his face from his friend's gaze, remained silent for a few moments, and he then sought to divert the conversation, and roused himself to ask Harley how he had succeeded in his views upon Beatrice, and his watch on the Count.

"With regard to Peschiera," answered Harley, "I think we must have overrated the danger we apprehended, and that his wagers were but an idle boast. He has remained quiet enough, and seems devoted to play. His sister has shut her doors both on myself and my young associate during the last few days. I almost fear that in spite of very sage warnings of mine, she must have turned his poet's head, and that either he has met with some scornful rebuff to incautious admiration, or that he himself has grown aware of peril, and declines to face it; for he is very much embarrassed when I speak to him respecting her. But if the Count is not formidable, why, his sister is not needed; and I hope yet to get justice for my Italian friend through the ordinary channels. I have secured an ally in a young Austrian prince, who is now in London, and who has promised to back, with all his influence, a memorial I shall transmit to Vienna. *Apropos*, my dear Audley, now that you have a little breathing time, you must fix an hour for me to present to you my young poet, the son of *her* sister. At moments the expression of his face is so like hers."

"Ay, ay," answered Egerton, quickly, "I will see him as you wish, but later. I have not yet that breathing-time you speak of; but you say he has prospered; and, with your friendship, he is secure from fortune. I rejoice to think so."

"And your own *protégé*, this Randal Leslie, whom you forbid me to dislike—hard task!—what has he decided?"

"To adhere to my fate. Harley, if it please Heaven that I do not live to return to power, and provide adequately for that young man, do not forget that he clung to me in my fall."

"If he still cling to you faithfully, I will never forget it. I will forget only all that now makes me doubt him. But *you* talk of not living, Audley! Pooh!—your frame is that of a predestined octogenarian."

"Nay," answered Audley, "I was but uttering one of those vague generalities which are common upon all mortal lips. And now farewell—I must see this Baron."

"Not yet, until you have promised to consent to my proposal, and be once more member for Lansmere.—Tut! don't shake your head. I cannot be denied. I claim your promise in right of our friendship, and shall be seriously hurt if you even pause to reflect on it."

"Well, well, I know not how to refuse you, Harley; but you have not been to Lansmere yourself since—since that sad event. You must not revive the old wound—*you* must not go; and—and, I own it, Harley; the remembrance of it pains even me. I would rather not go to Lansmere."

"Ah, my friend, this is an excess of sympathy, and I cannot listen to it. I begin even to blame my own weakness, and to feel that we have no right to make ourselves the soft slaves of the past."

"You do appear to me of late to have changed," cried Egerton, suddenly, and with a brightening aspect. "Do tell me that you are happy in the contemplation of your new ties —that I shall live to see you once more restored to your former self."

"All I can answer, Audley," said L'Estrange, with a thoughtful brow, "is, that you are right in one thing—I am changed; and I am struggling to gain strength for duty and for honour. Adieu! I shall tell my father that you accede to our wishes."

## CHAPTER VI.

When Harley was gone, Egerton sunk back on his chair, as if in extreme physical or mental exhaustion, all the lines of his countenance relaxed and jaded.

"To go back to that place—there—there—where—Courage, courage—what is another pang?"

He rose with an effort, and folding his arms tightly across his breast, paced slowly to and fro the large, mournful, solitary room. Gradually his countenance assumed its usual cold and austere composure—the secret eye, the guarded lip, the haughty collected front. The man of the world was himself once more.

"Now to gain time, and to baffle the usurer," murmured Egerton, with that low tone of easy scorn, which bespoke consciousness of superior power and the familiar mastery over hostile natures. He rang the bell: the servant entered.

"Is Baron Levy still waiting?"

"Yes, sir."

"Admit him."

Levy entered.

"I beg your pardon, Levy," said the ex-minister, "for having so long detained you. I am now at your commands."

"My dear fellow," returned the Baron, "no apologies between friends so old as we are; and I fear that my business is not so agreeable as to make you impatient to discuss it.

Egerton (with perfect composure).—"I am to conclude, then, that you wish to bring our accounts to a close. Whenever you will, Levy."

The Baron (disconcerted and surprised).—*Peste! mon cher*, you take things coolly. But if our accounts are closed, I fear you will have but little to live upon."

Egerton.—"I can continue to live on the salary of a Cabinet Minister."

Baron.—"Possibly; but you are no longer a Cabinet Minister."

Egerton.—"You have never found me deceived in a political prediction. Within twelve months (should life be spared to me) I shall be in office again. If the same to you, I would rather wait till then, formally and amicably to resign to you my lands and this house. If you grant that reprieve, our connection can thus close, without the *éclat* and noise, which may be invidious to you, as it would be disagreeable to me. But if that delay be inconvenient, I will appoint a lawyer to examine your accounts, and adjust my liabilities."

The BARON, (soliloquising.)—"I don't like this. A lawyer! That may be awkward."

EGERTON, (observing the Baron, with a curl on his lip.)—" Well, Levy, how shall it be?"

The BARON.—" You know, my dear fellow, it is not my character to be hard on any one, least of all upon an old friend. And if you really think there is a chance of your return to office, which you apprehend that an *esclandre* as to your affairs at present might damage, why, let us see if we can conciliate matters. But, first, *mon cher*, in order to become a Minister, you must at least have a seat in Parliament; and pardon me the question, how the deuce are you to find one?"

EGERTON.—" It is found."

The BARON.—"Ah, I forgot the £5000 you last borrowed."

EGERTON.—"No; I reserve that sum for another purpose."

The BARON, (with a forced laugh.)—" Perhaps to defend yourself against the actions you apprehend from me?"

EGERTON.—" You are mistaken. But to soothe your suspicions I will tell you plainly, that finding any sum I might have insured on my life would be liable to debts preincurred, and (as you will be my sole creditor) might thus at my death pass back to you; and doubting whether, indeed, any office would accept my insurance, I appropriate that sum to the relief of my conscience. I intend to bestow it, while yet in life, upon my late wife's kinsman, Randal Leslie. And it is solely the wish to do what I consider an act of justice, that has prevailed with me to accept a favour from the hands of Harley L'Estrange, and to become again the member for Lansmere."

The BARON.—" Ha!—Lansmere! You will stand for Lansmere?"

EGERTON, (wincing.)—" I propose to do so."

The BARON.—" I believe you will be opposed, subjected to even a sharp contest. Perhaps you may lose your election."

EGERTON.—" If so, I resign myself, and you can foreclose on my estates."

The BARON, (his brow clearing.)—" Look you, Egerton, I shall be too happy to do you a favour."

EGERTON, (with stateliness.)—" Favour! No, Baron Levy,

I ask from you no favour. Dismiss all thought of rendering
me one. It is but a consideration of business on both sides.
If you think it better that we shall at once settle our accounts,
my lawyer shall investigate them. If you agree to the delay
I request, my lawyer shall give you no trouble; and all that
I have, except hope and character, pass to your hands
without a struggle."

The BARON.—"Inflexible and ungracious, favour or not—
put it as you will—I accede, provided, first, that you allow
me to draw up a fresh deed, which will accomplish your part
of the compact; and, secondly, that we saddle the proposed
delay with the condition that you do not lose your election."

EGERTON.—"Agreed. Have you anything further to say?"

The BARON.—"Nothing, except that, if you require more
money, I am still at your service."

EGERTON.—"I thank you. No; I shall take the occasion
of my retirement from office to reduce my establishment. I
have calculated already, and provided for the expenditure I
need, up to the date I have specified, and I shall have no occasion to touch the £5000 that I still retain."

"Your young friend, Mr. Leslie, ought to be very grateful
to you," said the Baron, rising. "I have met him in the
world—a lad of much promise and talent. You should try
and get him also into Parliament."

EGERTON, (thoughtfully.)—"You are a good judge of the
practical abilities and merits of men, as regards worldly success. Do you really think Randal Leslie calculated for public
life—for a Parliamentary career?"

The BARON.—"Indeed I do."

EGERTON, (speaking more to himself than Levy.)—"Parliament without fortune—'tis a sharp trial; still he is prudent,
abstemious, energetic, persevering; and at the onset, under
my auspices and advice, he might establish a position beyond
his years."

The BARON.—"It strikes me that we might possibly get
him into the next Parliament; or, as that is not likely to last
long, at all events, into the Parliament to follow—not for one
of the boroughs which will be swept away, but for a permanent seat, and without expense."

EGERTON.—"Ay—and how?"

The BARON.—"Give me a few days to consider. An idea
has occurred to me. I will call again if I find it practicable.
Good day to you, Egerton, and success to your election for
Lansmere."

## CHAPTER VII.

PESCHIERA had not been so inactive as he had appeared to Harley and the reader. On the contrary, he had prepared the way for his ultimate design, with all the craft and the unscrupulous resolution which belonged to his nature. His object was to compel Riccabocca into assenting to the Count's marriage with Violante, or, failing that, to ruin all chance of his kinsman's restoration. Quietly and secretly he had sought out, amongst the most needy and unprincipled of his own countrymen, those whom he could suborn to depose to Riccabocca's participation in plots and conspiracies against the Austrian dominion. These his former connection with the Carbonari enabled him to track to their refuge in London; and his knowledge of the characters he had to deal with fitted him well for the villanous task he undertook.

He had, therefore, already selected out of these desperadoes a sufficient number, either to serve as witnesses against his kinsman, or to aid him in any more audacious scheme which circumstance might suggest to his adoption. Meanwhile, he had (as Harley had suspected he would) set spies upon Randal's movements; and the day before that young traitor confided to him Violante's retreat, he had, at least, got scent of her father's.

The discovery that Violante was under a roof so honoured, and seemingly so safe as Lord Lansmere's, did not discourage this bold and desperate adventurer. We have seen him set forth to reconnoitre the house at Knightsbridge. He had examined it well, and discovered the quarter which he judged favourable to a *coup-de-main*, should that become necessary.

Lord Lansmere's house and grounds were surrounded by a wall, the entrance being to the high-road, and by a porter's lodge. At the rear there lay fields crossed by a lane or by-road. To these fields a small door in the wall, which was used by the gardeners in passing to and from their work, gave communication. This door was usually kept locked; but the lock was of the rude and simple description common to such entrances, and easily opened by a skeleton key. So far there was no obstacle which Peschiera's experience in conspiracy and gallantry did not disdain as trivial. But the Count was not disposed to abrupt and violent means in the first instance. He had a confidence in his personal gifts, in his address, in his previous triumphs over the sex, which made him naturally desire to hazard the effect of a personal interview; and on this he resolved with his wonted audacity. Randal's description of Violante's personal appearance, and such suggestions as to her character and the motives most likely to influence her actions, as that young lynx-eyed observer could bestow, were all that the Count required of present aid from his accomplice.

Meanwhile we return to Violante herself. We see her now seated in the gardens at Knightsbridge, side by side with Helen. The place was retired, and out of sight from the windows of the house.

VIOLANTE.—" But why will you not tell me more of that early time? You are less communicative even than Leonard."

HELEN, (looking down, and hesitatingly.)—" Indeed there is nothing to tell you that you do not know; and it is so long since, and things are so changed now."

The tone of the last words was mournful, and the words ended with a sigh.

VIOLANTE, (with enthusiasm.)—" How I envy you that past which you treat so lightly! To have been something, even in childhood, to the formation of a noble nature; to have borne on those slight shoulders half the load of a man's grand labour. And now to see Genius moving calm in its clear career; and to say inly, 'Of that genius I am a part!'"

HELEN, (sadly and humbly.)—" A part! Oh, no! A part? I don't understand you."

VIOLANTE.—" Take the child Beatrice from Dante's life, and should we have a Dante? What is a poet's genius but the voice of its emotions? All things in life and in Nature influence genius; but what influences it the most are its own sorrows and affections."

Helen looks softly into Violante's eloquent face, and draws nearer to her in tender silence.

VIOLANTE, (suddenly.)—" Yes, Helen, yes—I know by my own heart how to read yours. Such memories are ineffaceable. Few guess what strange self-weavers of our own destinies we women are in our veriest childhood!" She sunk her voice into a whisper: " How could Leonard fail to be dear to you—dear as you to him—dearer than all others?"

HELEN, (shrinking back, and greatly disturbed.)—" Hush, hush! you must not speak to me thus; it is wicked—I cannot bear it. I would not have it be so—it must not be—it cannot!"

She clasped her hands over her eyes for a moment, and then lifted her face, and the face was very sad, but very calm.

VIOLANTE, (twining her arm round Helen's waist.)—"How have I wounded you?—how offended? Forgive me—but why is this wicked? Why must it not be? Is it because he is below you in birth?"

HELEN.—"No, no—I never thought of that. And what am I? Don't ask me—I cannot answer. You are wrong, quite wrong, as to me. I can only look on Leonard as—as a brother. But—but, you can speak to him more freely than I can. I would not have him waste his heart on me, nor yet think me unkind and distant, as I seem. I know not what I say. But—but—break to him—indirectly—gently—that duty in both forbids us both to—to be more than friends—than—"

"Helen, Helen!" cried Violante, in her warm, generous, passion, "your heart betrays you in every word you say. You weep; lean on me, whisper to me; why—why is this? Do you fear that your guardian would not consent? He not consent? He who—"

HELEN.—"Cease—cease—cease."

VIOLANTE.—"What! You can fear Harley—Lord L'Estrange? Fie; you do not know him."

HELEN, (rising suddenly.)—"Violante, hold; I am engaged to another."

Violante rose also, and stood still, as if turned to stone; pale as death, till the blood came, at first slowly, then with suddenness from her heart, and one deep glow suffused her whole countenance. She caught Helen's hand firmly, and said, in a hollow voice—

"Another! Engaged to another! One word, Helen—not to him—not to—Harley—to—"

"I cannot say—I must not. I have promised," cried poor Helen, and as Violante let fall her hand, she hurried away.

Violante sate down, mechanically; she felt as if stunned by a mortal blow. She closed her eyes and breathed hard. A deadly faintness seized her; and when it passed away, it seemed to her as if she were no longer the same being, nor the world around her the same world—as if she were but one sense of intense, hopeless misery, and as if the universe were but one inanimate void. So strangely immaterial are we really—we human beings, with flesh and blood—that if you suddenly abstract from us but a single, impalpable, airy thought, which our souls have cherished, you seem to curdle the air, to extinguish the sun, to snap every link that connects us to matter, and to benumb everything into death, except woe.

And this warm, young, southern nature, but a moment before was so full of joy and life, and vigorous, lofty hope. It never till now had known its own intensity and depth. The virgin had never lifted the veil from her own soul of woman. What till then, had Harley L'Estrange been to Violante? An ideal—a dream of some imagined excellence—a type of poetry in the midst of the common world. It had not been Harley the man—it had been Harley the Phantom. She had never said to herself, "He is identified with my love, my hopes, my home, my future." How could she? Of such, he himself had never spoken; an internal voice, indeed, had vaguely, yet irresistibly, whispered to her that, despite his light words, his feelings towards her were grave and deep. O false voice! how it had deceived her! Her quick convictions seized the all that Helen had left unsaid. And now suddenly she felt what it is to love, and what it is to despair. So she sate, crushed and solitary, neither murmuring nor weeping, only now and then passing her hand across her brow, as if to clear away some cloud that would not be dispersed; or heaving a deep sigh, as if to throw off some load that no time henceforth could remove. There are certain moments in life in which we say to ourselves, "All is over; no matter what else changes, that which I have made my all is gone evermore —evermore." And our own thought rings back in our ears, "Evermore—evermore!"

## CHAPTER VIII.

As Violante thus sate, a stranger, passing stealthily through the trees, stood between herself and the evening sun. She saw him not. He paused a moment, and then spoke low, in her native tongue, addressing her by the name which she had borne in Italy. He spoke as a relation, and excused his intrusion: "For," said he, "I come to suggest to the daughter the means by which she can restore to her father his country and his honours."

At the word "father" Violante roused herself, and all her love for that father rushed back upon her with double force.

It does so ever—we love most our parents at the moment when some tie less holy is abruptly broken; and when the conscience says, "*there*, at least, is a love that has never deceived thee!"

She saw before her a man of mild aspect and princely form. Peschiera (for it was he) had banished from his dress, as from his countenance, all that betrayed the worldly levity of his character. He was acting a part, and he dressed and looked it.

"My father!" she said, quickly, and in Italian. "What of him? And who are you, signior? I know you not."

Peschiera smiled benignly, and replied in a tone in which great respect was softened by a kind of parental tenderness.

"Suffer me to explain, and listen to me while I speak." Then, quietly seating himself on the bench beside her, he looked into her eyes, and resumed.

"Doubtless, you have heard of the Count di Peschiera?"

VIOLANTE.—"I heard that name, as a child, when in Italy. And when she with whom I then dwelt (my father's aunt) fell ill and died, I was told that my home in Italy was gone, that it had passed to the Count di Peschiera—my father's foe?"

PESCHIERA.—"And your father, since then, has taught you to hate this fancied foe?"

VIOLANTE.—"Nay; my father did but forbid me ever to breathe his name."

PESCHIERA.—"Alas! what years of suffering and exile might have been saved your father, had he but been more just to his early friend and kinsman; nay, had he but less cruelly concealed the secret of his retreat. Fair child, I am that Guilio Franzini, that Count di Peschiera. I am the man you have been told to regard as your father's foe. I am the man on whom the Austrian Emperor bestowed his lands. And now judge if I am, in truth, the foe. I have come hither to seek your father, in order to dispossess myself of my sovereign's gift. I have come but with one desire, to restore Alphonso to his native land, and to surrender the heritage that was forced upon me."

VIOLANTE.—"My father, my dear father! His grand heart will have room once more. Oh! this is noble enmity, true revenge. I understand it, signior, and so will my father, for such would have been his revenge on you. You have seen him?"

PESCHIERA.—"No, not yet. I would not see him till I had

seen yourself; for you, in truth, are the arbiter of his destinies, as of mine."

VIOLANTE.—" I—Count? I—arbiter of my father's destinies? Is it possible?"

PESCHIERA, (with a look of compassionate admiration, and in a tone yet more emphatically parental.)—" How lovely is that innocent joy; but do not indulge it yet. Perhaps it is a sacrifice which is asked from you—a sacrifice too hard to bear. Do not interrupt me. Listen still, and you will see why I could not speak to your father until I had obtained an interview with yourself.—See why a word from you may continue still to banish me from his presence. You know, doubtless, that your father was one of the chiefs of a party that sought to free Northern Italy from the Austrians. I myself was at the onset a warm participator in that scheme. In a sudden moment I discovered that some of its more active projectors had coupled with a patriotic enterprise plots of a dark nature, and that the conspiracy itself was about to be betrayed to the government. I wished to consult with your father; but he was at a distance. I learned that his life was condemned. Not an hour was to be lost. I took a bold resolve, that has exposed me to his suspicions, and to my country's wrath. But my main idea was to save him, my early friend, from death, and my country from fruitless massacre. I withdrew from the intended revolt. I sought at once the head of the Austrian government in Italy, and made terms for the lives of Alphonso and of the other more illustrious chiefs, which otherwise would have been forfeited. I obtained permission to undertake myself the charge of securing my kinsman in order to place him in safety, and to conduct him to a foreign land, in an exile that would cease when the danger was dispelled. But unhappily he deemed that I only sought to destroy him. He fled from my friendly pursuit. The soldiers with me were attacked by an intermeddling Englishman; your father escaped from Italy—concealing his retreat; and the character of his flight counteracted my efforts to obtain his pardon. The government conferred on me half his revenues, holding the other half at its pleasure. I accepted the offer in order to save his whole heritage from confiscation. That I did not convey to him, what I pined to do—viz., the information that I held but in trust what was bestowed by the government, and the full explanation of what seemed blameable in my conduct—was necessarily owing to the secrecy he maintained. I could not discover his refuge; but I never ceased to plead for his recall. This year only I have partially succeeded. He can be restored to his heritage and rank, on one proviso—a guarantee for his loyalty. That guarantee the government has named: it is the alliance of his only child with one whom the government can trust. It was the interest of all the Italian nobility, that the representation of a house so great falling to a female, should not pass away wholly from the direct line;—in a word, that you should ally yourself with a kinsman. But one kinsman, and he the next in blood, presented himself. In short—Alphonso regains all that he lost on the day in which his daughter gives her hand to Guilio Franzini, Count di Peschiera. Ah," continued the Count, mournfully, "you shrink—you recoil. He thus submitted to your choice is indeed unworthy of you. You are scarce in the spring of life. He is in its waning autumn. Youth loves youth. He does not aspire to your love. All that he can say is, love is not the only joy of the heart—it is joy to raise from ruin a beloved father—joy to restore, to a land poor in all but memories, a chief in whom it reverences a line of heroes. These are the joys I offer to you—you, a daughter, and an Italian maid. Still silent! Oh speak to me!"

Certainly this Count Peschiera knew well how woman is to be wooed and won; and never was woman more sensitive to those high appeals which most move all true earnest womanhood, than was the young Violante. Fortune favoured him in the moment chosen. Harley was wrenched away from her hopes, and love a word erased from her language. In the void of the world, her father's image alone stood clear and visible. And she who from infancy had so pined to serve that father, who at first learned to dream of Harley as that father's friend! She could restore to him all for which the exile sighed; and by a sacrifice of self! Self-sacrifice, ever in itself such a temptation to the noble! Still, in the midst of the confusion and disturbance of her mind, the idea of marriage with another seemed so terrible and revolting, that she could not at once conceive it; and still that instinct of openness and honour, which pervaded all her character, warned even her inexperience that there was something wrong in this clandestine appeal to herself.

Again the Count besought her to speak, and with an effort she said, irresolutely—

"If it be as you say, it is not for me to answer you; it is for my father."

"Nay," replied Peschiera. "Pardon, if I contradict you. Do you know so little of your father as to suppose that he will suffer his interest to dictate to his pride? He would refuse, perhaps, even to receive my visit—to hear my explanations; but certainly he would refuse to buy back his inheritance by the sacrifice of his daughter to one whom he has deemed his foe, and whom the mere disparity of years would incline the world to say he had made the barter of his personal ambition. But if I could go to him sanctioned by you—if I could say your daughter overlooks what the father might deem an obstacle—she has consented to accept my hand of her own free choice—she unites her happiness, and blends her prayers with mine—then, indeed, I could not fail of success; and Italy would pardon my errors, and bless your name. Ah! Signorina, do not think of me, save as an instrument towards the fulfilment of duties so high and sacred—think but of your ancestors, your father, your native land, and reject not the proud occasion to prove how you revere them all!"

Violante's heart was touched at the right chord. Her head rose—the colour came back to her pale cheek—she turned the glorious beauty of her countenance towards the wily tempter. She was about to answer and to seal her fate, when at that instant Harley's voice was heard at a little distance, and Nero came bounding towards her, and thrust himself, with rough familiarity, between her and Peschiera. The Count drew back, and Violante, whose eyes were still fixed on his face, started at the change that passed there. One quick gleam of rage sufficed in an instant to light up the sinister secrets of his nature—it was the face of the baffled gladiator. He had time but for few words.

"I must not be seen here," he muttered; "but to-morrow—in these gardens—about this hour. I implore you, for the sake of your father—his hopes, fortunes, his very life, to guard the secret of this interview—to meet me again. Adieu!"

He vanished amidst the trees, and was gone—noiselessly, mysteriously, as he had come.

## CHAPTER IX.

The last words of Peschiera were still ringing in Violante's ears when Harley appeared in sight, and the sound of his voice dispelled the vague and dreamy stupor which had crept over her senses. At that voice there returned the consciousness of a mighty loss, the sting of an intolerable anguish. To meet Harley there, and thus, seemed impossible. She turned abruptly away, and hurried towards the house. Harley called to her by name, but she would not answer, and only quickened her steps. He paused a moment in surprise, and then hastened after her.

"Under what strange taboo am I placed?" said he, gaily, as he laid his hand on her shrinking arm. "I inquire for Helen—she is ill, and cannot see me. I come to sun myself in your presence, and you fly me as if gods and men had set their mark on my brow. Child!—child!—what is this? You are weeping?"

"Do not stay me now—do not speak to me," answered Violante, through her stifling sobs, as she broke from his hand and made towards the house.

"Have you a grief, and under the shelter of my father's roof? A grief that you will not tell to me? Cruel!" cried Harley, with inexpressible tenderness of reproach in his soft tones.

Violante could not trust herself to reply. Ashamed of her self-betrayal—softened yet more by his pleading voice—she could have prayed to the earth to swallow her. At length, checking her tears by a heroic effort, she said, almost calmly, "Noble friend, forgive me. I have no grief, believe me, which—which I can tell to you. I was but thinking of my poor father when you came up; alarming myself about him, it may be, with vain superstitious fears; and so—even a slight surprise—your abrupt appearance, has sufficed to make me thus weak and foolish; but I wish to see my father!—to go home—home!"

"Your father is well, believe me, and pleased that you are here. No danger threatens him; and you, *here*, are safe."

"I safe—and from what?"

Harley mused irresolute. He inclined to confide to her the danger which her father had concealed; but had he the right to do so against her father's will?

" Give me," he said, "time to reflect, and to obtain permission to intrust you with a secret which, in my judgment, you should know. Meanwhile, this much I may say, that rather than you should incur the danger that I believe he exaggerates, your father would have given you a protector—even in Randal Leslie."

Violante started.

" But," resumed Harley, with a calm, in which a certain deep mournfulness was apparent, unconsciously to himself—"but I trust you are reserved for a fairer fate, and a nobler spouse. I have vowed to live henceforth in the common workday world. But for you, bright child, for you, I am a dreamer still!"

Violante turned her eyes for one instant towards the melancholy speaker. The look thrilled to his heart. He bowed his face involuntarily. When he looked up, she had left his side. He did not this time attempt to follow her, but moved away and plunged amidst the leafless trees.

An hour afterwards he re-entered the house, and again sought to see Helen. She had now recovered sufficiently to give him the interview he requested.

He approached her with a grave and serious gentleness.

" My dear Helen," said he, "you have consented to be my wife, my life's mild companion; let it be soon—soon—for I need you. I need all the strength of that holy tie. Helen let me press you to fix the time."

" I owe you too much," answered Helen, looking down, "to have any will but yours. But your mother," she added, perhaps clinging to the idea of some reprieve—" your mother has not yet—"

" My mother—true. I will speak first to her. You shall receive from my family all honour due to your gentle virtues. Helen, by the way, have you mentioned to Violante the bond between us?"

" No—that is, I fear I may have unguardedly betrayed it, against Lady Lansmere's commands too—but—but—"

" So, Lady Lansmere forbade you to name it to Violante. This should not be. I will answer for her permission to revoke that interdict. It is due to Violante and to you. Tell your young friend all. Ah, Helen, if I am at times cold or wayward, bear with me—bear with me; for you love me, do you not?"

## CHAPTER X.

THAT same evening Randal heard from Levy (at whose house he stayed late) of that self-introduction to Violante which (thanks to his skeleton-key) Peschiera had contrived to effect; and the Count seemed more than sanguine—he seemed assured as to the full and speedy success of his matrimonial enterprise. "Therefore," said Levy, "I trust I may very soon congratulate you on the acquisition of your family estates."

"Strange!" answered Randal, "strange that my fortunes seem so bound up with the fate of a foreigner like Beatrice di Negra and her connection with Frank Hazeldean." He looked up at the clock as he spoke, and added—

"Frank by this time has told his father of his engagement."

"And you feel sure that the Squire cannot be coaxed into consent?"

"No; but I feel sure that the Squire will be so choleric at the first intelligence, that Frank will not have the self-control necessary for coaxing; and, perhaps, before the Squire can relent upon this point, he may, by some accident, learn his grievances on another, which would exasperate him still more."

"Ay, I understand—the *post-obit?*"

Randal nodded.

"And what then?" asked Levy.

"The next of kin to the lands of Hazeldean may have his day."

The Baron smiled.

"You have good prospects in that direction, Leslie: look now to another. I spoke to you of the borough of Lansmere. Your patron, Audley Egerton, intends to stand for it."

Randal's heart had of late been so set upon other and more avaricious schemes, that a seat in Parliament had sunk into a secondary object; nevertheless his ambitious and all-grasping nature felt a bitter pang, when he heard that Egerton thus interposed between himself and any chance of advancement."

"So!" he muttered, sullenly—"so. This man, who pretends to be my benefactor, squanders away the wealth of my forefathers—throws me penniless on the world; and, while still encouraging me to exertion and public life, robs me himself of—"

"No!" interrupted Levy—"not robs you; we may prevent that. The Lansmere interest is not so strong in the borough as Dick Avenel's."

"But I cannot stand against Egerton."

"Assuredly not—you may stand with him."

"How?"

"Dick Avenel will never suffer Egerton to come in; and though he cannot, perhaps, carry two of his own politics, he can split his votes upon you."

Randal's eyes flashed. He saw at a glance, that if Avenel did not overrate the relative strength of parties, his seat could be secured.

"But," he said, "Egerton has not spoken to me on such a subject; nor can you expect that he would propose to me to stand with him, if he foresaw the chance of being ousted by the very candidate he himself introduced."

"Neither he nor his party will anticipate that possibility. If he ask you, agree to stand—leave the rest to me."

"You must hate Egerton bitterly," said Randal; "for I am not vain enough to think that you thus scheme but from pure love to me."

"The motives of men are intricate and complicated," answered Levy, with unusual seriousness. "It suffices to the wise to profit by the actions, and leave the motives in shade."

There was silence for some minutes. Then the two drew closer towards each other, and began to discuss details in their joint designs.

Randal walked home slowly. It was a cold moonlit night. Young idlers of his own years and rank passed him by, on their way from the haunts of social pleasure. They were yet in the first fair holiday of life. Life's holiday had gone from him for ever. Graver men, in the various callings of masculine labour—professions, trade, the state—passed him also. Their steps might be sober, and their faces careworn; but no step had the furtive stealth of his—no face the same contracted, sinister, suspicious gloom. Only once, in a lonely thoroughfare, and on the opposite side of the way, fell a footfall, and glanced an eye, that seemed to betray a soul in sympathy with Randal Leslie's.

And Randal, who had heeded none of the other passengers

by the way, as if instinctively, took note of this one. His nerves crisped at the noiseless slide of that form, as it stalked on from lamp to lamp, keeping pace with his own. He felt a sort of awe, as if he had beheld the wraith of himself; and ever as he glanced suspiciously at the stranger, the stranger glanced at him. He was inexpressibly relieved when the figure turned down another street and vanished.

That man was a felon, as yet undetected. Between him and his kind there stood but a thought—a veil air-spun, but impassable, as the veil of the Image at Sais.

And thus moved and thus looked Randal Leslie, a thing of dark and secret mischief—within the pale of the law, but equally removed from man by the vague consciousness that at his heart lay that which the eyes of man would abhor and loathe. Solitary amidst the vast city, and on through the machinery of Civilization, went the still spirit of Intellectual Evil.

## CHAPTER XI.

EARLY the next morning Randal received two notes—one from Frank, written in great agitation, begging Randal to see and propitiate his father, whom he feared he had grievously offended; and then running off, rather incoherently, into protestations that his honour, as well as his affections were engaged irrevocably to Beatrice, and that her, at least, he could never abandon.

And the second note was from the Squire himself—short, and far less cordial than usual—requesting Mr. Leslie to call on him.

Randal dressed in haste, and went first to Limmer's hotel.

He found the Parson with Mr. Hazeldean, and endeavouring in vain to soothe him. The Squire had not slept all night, and his appearance was almost haggard.

"Oho! Mr. young Leslie," said he, throwing himself back in his chair as Randal entered—"I thought you were a friend—I thought you were Frank's adviser. Explain, sir; explain."

"Gently, my dear Mr. Hazeldean," said the Parson. "You do but surprise and alarm Mr. Leslie. Tell him more distinctly what he has to explain."

SQUIRE.—"Did you or did you not tell me or Mrs. Hazeldean, that Frank was in love with Violante Rickeybockey?"

RANDAL, (as in amaze.)—"I! Never, sir. I feared, on the contrary, that he was somewhat enamoured of a very different person. I hinted at that possibility. I could not do more, for I did not know how far Frank's affections were seriously engaged. And indeed, sir, Mrs. Hazeldean, though not encouraging the idea that your son could marry a foreigner and a Roman Catholic, did not appear to consider such objections insuperable, if Frank's happiness were really at stake.

Here the poor Squire gave way to a burst of passion, that involved in one tempest, Frank, Randal, Harry herself, and the whole race of foreigners, Roman Catholics, and women. While the Squire was still incapable of hearing reason, the Parson, taking aside Randal, convinced himself that the whole affair, so far as Randal was concerned, had its origin in a very natural mistake; and that while that young gentleman had been hinting at Beatrice, Mrs. Hazeldean had been thinking of Violante. With considerable difficulty he succeeded in conveying this explanation to the Squire, and somewhat appeasing his wrath against Randal. And the Dissimulator, seizing his occasion, then expressed so much grief and astonishment at learning that matters had gone as far as the Parson informed him—that Frank had actually proposed to Beatrice, been accepted, and engaged himself, before even communicating with his father; he declared so earnestly, that he could never conjecture such evil—that he had had Frank's positive promise to take no step without the sanction of his parents; he professed such sympathy with the Squire's wounded feelings, and such regret at Frank's involvement, that Mr. Hazeldean at last yielded up his honest heart to his consoler—and griping Randal's hand, said, "Well, well, I wronged you—beg your pardon. What now is to be done?"

"Why, you cannot consent to this marriage—impossible," replied Randal; "and we must hope, therefore, to influence Frank by his sense of duty."

"That's it," said the Squire; "for I'll not give way. Pretty pass things have come to, indeed! A widow, too, I hear. Artful jade—thought, no doubt, to catch a Hazeldean of Hazeldean. My estates go to an outlandish Papistical set of mongrel brats! No, no, never!"

"But," said the Parson, mildly, "perhaps we may be unjustly prejudiced against this lady. We should have consented to Violante—why not to her? She is of good family?"

"Certainly," said Randal.

"And good character?"

Randal shook his head, and sighed. The Squire caught him roughly by the arm—"Answer the Parson!" cried he, vehemently.

"Indeed, sir, I cannot speak disrespectfully of the character of a woman,—who may, too, become Frank's wife; and the world is ill-natured, and not to be believed. But you can judge for yourself, my dear Mr. Hazeldean. Ask your brother whether Madame di Negra is one whom he would advise his nephew to marry."

"My brother!" exclaimed the Squire, furiously. "Consult my distant brother on the affairs of my own son?"

"He is a man of the world," put in Randal.

"And of feeling and honour," said the Parson; "and, perhaps, through him, we may be enabled to enlighten Frank, and save him from what appears to be the snare of an artful woman."

"Meanwhile," said Randal, "I will seek Frank, and do my best with him. Let me go now—I will return in an hour or so."

"I will accompany you," said the Parson.

"Nay, pardon me, but I think we two young men can talk more openly without a third person, even so wise and kind as you."

"Let Randal go," growled the Squire. And Randal went.

He spent some time with Frank, and the reader will easily divine how that time was employed. As he left Frank's lodgings, he found himself suddenly seized by the Squire himself.

"I was too impatient to stay at home and listen to the Parson's prosing," said Mr. Hazeldean, nervously. "I have shaken Dale off. Tell me what has passed. Oh! don't fear —I'm a man, and can bear the worst."

Randal drew the Squire's arm within his, and led him into the adjacent park.

"My dear sir," said he, sorrowfully, "this is very confidential what I am about to say. I must repeat it to you, because, without such confidence, I see not how to advise you on the proper course to take. But if I betray Frank, it is for his good, and to his own father;—only do not tell him. He would never forgive me—it would for ever destroy my influence over him."

"Go on, go on," gasped the Squire; "speak out. I'll never tell the ungrateful boy that I learned his secrets from another."

"Then," said Randal, "the secret of his entanglement with Madame di Negra is simply this—he found her in debt—nay, on the point of being arrested—"

"Debt!—arrested! Jezabel!"

"And in paying the debt himself, and saving her from arrest, he conferred on her the obligation which no woman of honour could accept save from an affianced husband. Poor Frank!—if sadly taken in, still we must pity and forgive him!"

Suddenly, to Randal's great surprise, the Squire's whole face brightened up.

"I see, I see!" he exclaimed, slapping his thigh. "I have it —I have it. 'Tis an affair of money! I can buy her off. If she took money from him, the mercenary, painted baggage! why then, she'll take it from me. I don't care what it costs —half my fortune—all! I'd be content never to see Hazeldean Hall again, if I could save my son, my own son, from disgrace and misery; for miserable he will be, when he knows he has broken my heart and his mother's. And for a creature like that! My boy, a thousand hearty thanks to you. Where does the wench live? I'll go to her at once." And as he spoke, the Squire actually pulled out his pocket-book, and began turning over and counting the bank-notes in it.

Randal at first tried to combat this bold resolution on the part of the Squire; but Mr. Hazeldean had seized on it with all the obstinacy of his straightforward English mind. He cut Randal's persuasive eloquence off in the midst.

"Don't waste your breath. I've settled it; and if you don't tell me where she lives, 'tis easily found out, I suppose."

Randal mused a moment. "After all," thought he, "why not? He will be sure so to speak as to enlist her pride against himself, and to irritate Frank to the utmost. Let him go."

Accordingly, he gave the information required; and, insisting with great earnestness on the Squire's promise not to mention to Madame di Negra his knowledge of Frank's pecuniary aid (for that would betray Randal as the informant); and satisfying himself as he best might with the Squire's prompt assurance, "that he knew how to settle matters, without saying why or wherefore, as long as he opened his purse wide enough," he accompanied Mr. Hazeldean back into the street, and there left him—fixing an hour in the evening for an interview at Limmer's, and hinting that it would be best to have that interview without the presence of the Parson. "Excellent good man," said Randal, "but not with sufficient knowledge of the world for affairs of this kind, which *you* understand so well."

"I should think so," quoth the Squire, who had quite recovered his good-humour. "And the Parson is as soft as buttermilk. We must be firm here—firm, sir." And the Squire struck the end of his stick on the pavement, nodded to Randal, and went on to May Fair as sturdily and as confidently as if to purchase a prize cow at a cattle show.

## CHAPTER XII.

"BRING the light nearer," said John Burley—"nearer still."

Leonard obeyed, and placed the candle on a little table by the sick man's bedside.

Burley's mind was partially wandering; but there was method in his madness. Horace Walpole said that "his stomach would survive all the rest of him." That which in Burley survived the last was his quaint wild genius. He looked wistfully at the still flame of the candle: "It lives ever in the air!" said he.

"What lives ever?"

Burley's voice swelled—"Light!" He turned from Leonard, and again contemplated the little flame. "In the fixed star, in the Will-o'-the-wisp, in the great sun that illumes half a world, or the farthing rushlight by which the ragged student strains his eyes—still the same flower of the elements! Light in the universe, thought in the soul—ay—ay—Go on with the simile. My head swims. Extinguish the light! You cannot; fool, it vanishes from your eye, but it is still in the space. Worlds must perish, suns shrivel up, matter and spirit both fall into nothingness, before the combinations whose union makes that little flame, which the breath of a babe can restore to darkness, shall lose the power to form themselves into light once more. Lose the power!—no, the *necessity*:—it is the one *Must* in creation. Ay, ay, very dark riddles grow clear now—now when I could not cast up an addition sum in the baker's bill! What wise man denied that two and two made four? Do they not make four? I can't answer him. But I could answer a question that some wise men have contrived to make much knottier." He smiled softly, and turned his face for some minutes to the wall.

This was the second night on which Leonard had watched by his bedside, and Burley's state had grown rapidly worse. He could not last many days, perhaps many hours. But he had evinced an emotion beyond mere delight at seeing Leonard again. He had since then been calmer, more himself. "I feared I might have ruined you by my bad example," he said, with a touch of humour that became pathos as he added, "That idea preyed on me."

"No, no; you did me great good."

"Say that—say it often," said Burley, earnestly; "it makes my heart feel so light."

He had listened to Leonard's story with deep interest, and was fond of talking to him of little Helen. He detected the secret at the young man's heart, and cheered the hopes that lay there, amidst fears and sorrows. Burley never talked seriously of his repentance; it was not in his nature to talk seriously of the things which he felt solemnly. But his high animal spirits were quenched with the animal power that fed them. Now, we go out of our sensual existence only when we are no longer enthralled by the Present, in which the senses have their realm. The sensual being vanishes when we are in the Past or the Future. The Present was gone from Burley; he could no more be its slave and its king.

It was most touching to see how the inner character of this man unfolded itself, as the leaves of the outer character fell off and withered—a character no one would have guessed in him—an inherent refinement that was almost womanly; and he had all a woman's abnegation of self. He took the cares lavished on him so meekly. As the features of the old man return in the stillness of death to the aspect of youth —the lines effaced, the wrinkles gone—so, in seeing Burley now, you saw what he had been in his spring of promise. But he himself saw only what he had failed to be—powers squandered—life wasted. "I once beheld," he said, "a ship in a storm. It was a cloudy, fitful day, and I could see the ship with all its masts fighting hard for life and for death. Then came night, dark as pitch, and I could only guess that the ship fought on.—Towards the dawn the stars grew visible, and once more I saw the ship—it was a wreck—it went down just as the stars shone forth."

When he had made that allusion to himself, he sate very still for some time, then he spread out his wasted hands, and gazed on them, and on his shrunken limbs. "Good," said he, laughing low; "these hands were too large and rude for handling the delicate webs of my own mechanism, and these strong limbs ran away with me. If I had been a sickly, puny fellow, perhaps my mind would have had fair play. There was too much of brute body here! Look at this hand now! You can see the light through it! Good, good!"

Now, that evening, until he had retired to bed, Burley had been unusually cheerful, and had talked with much of his old eloquence, if with little of his old humour. Amongst other matters, he had spoken with considerable interest of some poems and other papers in manuscript which had been left in the house by a former lodger, and which, the reader may remember, that Mrs. Goodyer had urged him in vain to read, in his last visit to her cottage. But *then* he had her husband Jacob to chat with, and the spirit bottle to finish, and the wild craving for excitement plucked his thoughts back to his London revels. Now poor Jacob was dead, and it was not brandy that the sick man drank from the widow's cruise. And London lay afar amidst its fogs, like a world resolved back into nebulæ. So to please his hostess and distract his own solitary thoughts, he had condescended (just before Leonard found him out) to peruse the memorials of a life obscure to the world, and new to his own experience of coarse joys and woes. "I have been making a romance, to amuse myself, from their contents," said he. "They may be of use to you, brother author. I have told Mrs. Goodyer to place them in your room. Amongst those papers is a sort of journal—a woman's journal; it moved me greatly. A man gets into another world, strange to him as the orb of Sirius, if he can transport himself into the centre of a woman's heart, and see the life there, so wholly unlike our own. Things of moment to us, to it so trivial; things trifling to us, to it so vast. There was this journal—in its dates reminding me of stormy events in my own existence, and grand doings in the world's. And those dates there, chronicling but the mysterious, unrevealed record of some obscure, loving heart! And in that chronicle, O Sir Poet, there was as much genius, vigour of thought, vitality of being, poured and wasted, as ever kind friend will say was lavished on the rude outer world by big John Burley! Genius, genius; are we all alike, then, save when we leash ourselves to some matter-of-fact material, and float over the roaring seas on a wooden plank or a herring tub?" And after he had uttered that cry of a secret anguish, John Burley had begun to show symptoms of growing fever and disturbed brain; and when they had got him into bed, he lay there muttering to himself, until towards midnight, he had asked Leonard to bring the light nearer to him.

So now he again was quiet—with his face turned towards the wall; and Leonard stood by the bedside sorrowfully, and Mrs. Goodyer, who did not heed Burley's talk, and thought only of his physical state, was dipping cloths into iced water to apply to his forehead. But as she approached with these, and addressed him soothingly, Burley raised himself on his arm, and waved aside the bandages. "I do not need them," said he, in a collected voice. "I am better now. I and that pleasant light understand one another, and I believe all it tells me. Pooh, pooh, I do not rave." He looked so smilingly and so kindly into her face, that the poor woman, who loved him as her own son, fairly burst into tears. He drew her towards him, and kissed her forehead.

"Peace, old fool," said he, fondly. "You shall tell anglers hereafter how John Burley came to fish for the one-eyed perch which he never caught; and how, when he gave it up at the last, his baits all gone, and the line broken amongst the weeds, you comforted the baffled man. There are many good fellows yet in the world who will like to know that poor Burley did not die on a dunghill. Kiss me! Come, boy, you too. Now, God bless you, I should like to sleep." His cheeks were wet with the tears of both his listeners, and there was a moisture in his own eyes, which, nevertheless, beamed bright through the moisture.

He laid himself down again, and the old woman would have withdrawn the light. He moved uneasily. "Not that," he murmured—"light to the last!" and putting forth his wan hand, he drew aside the curtain so that the light might fall full on his face. In a few minutes he was asleep, breathing calmly and regularly as an infant.

The old woman wiped her eyes, and drew Leonard softly into the adjoining room, in which a bed had been made up for him. He had not left the house since he had entered it with Dr. Morgan. "You are young, sir," said she with kindness, "and the young want sleep. Lie down a bit: I will call you when he wakes."

"No, I could not sleep," said Leonard. "I will watch for you."

The old woman shook her head. "I must see the last of him, sir; but I know he will be angry when his eyes open on me, for he has grown very thoughtful of others."

"Ah, if he had but been as thoughtful of himself!" murmured Leonard; and he seated himself by the table, on which, as he leaned his elbow, he dislodged some papers placed there. They fell to the ground with a dumb, moaning, sighing sound.

"What is that?" said he, starting.

The old woman picked up the manuscripts and smoothed them carefully.

"Ah, sir, he bade me place these papers here. He thought they might keep you from fretting about him, in case you would sit up and wake. And he had a thought of me, too; for I have so pined to find out the poor young lady, who left them years ago. She was almost as dear to me as he is; dearer perhaps until now—when—when I am about to lose him!"

Leonard turned from the papers, without a glance at their contents: they had no interest for him at such a moment.

The hostess went on—

"Perhaps she is gone to heaven before him; she did not look like one long for this world. She left us so suddenly. Many things of hers besides these papers are still here; but I keep them aired and dusted, and strew lavender over them, in case she ever come for them again. You never heard tell of her, did you, sir?" she added, with great simplicity, and dropping a half curtsey.

"Of her—of whom?"

"Did not Mr. John tell you her name—dear—dear; Mrs. Bertram."

Leonard started; the very name so impressed upon his memory by Harley L'Estrange.

"Bertram!" he repeated. "Are you sure?"

"Oh, yes, sir! And many years after she had left us, and we had heard no more of her, there came a packet addressed to her here, from over sea, sir. We took it in, and kept it, and John would break the seal, to know if it would tell us anything about her; but it was all in a foreign language like —we could not read a word."

"Have you the packet? Pray show it to me. It may be of the greatest value. To-morrow will do—I cannot think of that just now. Poor Burley!"

Leonard's manner indicated that he wished to talk no more, and to be alone. So Mrs. Goodyer left him, and stole back to Burley's room on tiptoe.

The young man remained in deep reverie for some moments. "Light," he murmured. "How often 'Light' is the last word of those round whom the shades are gathering!" * He moved, and straight on his view through the cottage lattice there streamed light, indeed—not the miserable ray lit by a human hand—but the still and holy effulgence of a moonlit heaven. It lay broad upon the humble floors—pierced across the threshold of the death chamber, and halted clear amidst its shadows.

Leonard stood motionless, his eye following the silvery silent splendour.

"And," he said inly—"and does this large erring nature, marred by its genial faults—this soul which should have filled a land, as yon orb the room, with a light that linked earth to heaven—does it pass away into the dark, and leave not a ray behind? Nay, if the elements of light are ever in the space, and when the flames goes out, return to the vital air—so thought once kindled, lives for ever around and about us, a part of our breathing atmosphere. Many a thinker, many a poet, may yet illumine the world, from the thoughts which yon genius, that will have no name, gave forth to wander through air, and recombine again in some new form of light."

Thus he went on in vague speculations, seeking, as youth enamoured of fame seeks too fondly, to prove that mind never works, however erratically, in vain—and to retain yet, as an influence upon earth, the soul about to soar far beyond the atmosphere where the elements that make fame abide. Not thus had the dying man interpreted the endurance of light and thought.

---

* Every one remembers that Goethe's last words are said to have been, "More Light;" and perhaps what has occurred in the text may be supposed a plagiarism from those words. But, in fact, nothing is more common than the craving and demand for light a little before death. Let any consult his own sad experience in the last moments of those whose gradual close he has watched and tended. What more frequent than a prayer to open the shutters and let in the sun? What complaint more repeated, and more touching, than "that it is growing dark?" I once knew a sufferer—who did not then seem in immediate danger—suddenly order the sick room to be lit up as if for a gala. When this was told to the physician, he said, gravely, "No worse sign."

Suddenly, in the midst of his reverie, a loud cry broke on his ear. He shuddered as he heard, and hastened forebodingly into the adjoining room. The old woman was kneeling by the bedside, and chafing Burley's hand—eagerly looking into his face. A glance sufficed to Leonard. All was over. Burley had died in sleep—calmly, and without a groan.

The eyes were half open, with that look of inexpressible softness which death sometimes leaves; and still they were turned towards the light; and the light burned clear. Leonard closed tenderly the heavy lids; and, as he covered the face, the lips smiled a serene farewell.

## CHAPTER XIII.

WE have seen Squire Hazeldean (proud of the contents of his pocket-book, and his knowledge of the mercenary nature of foreign women), set off on his visit to Beatrice di Negra. Randal thus left, musing lone in the crowded streets, revolved with astute complacency the probable results of Mr. Hazeldean's bluff negotiation; and, convincing himself that one of his vistas towards Fortune was becoming more clear and clear, he turned, with the restless activity of some founder of destined cities in a new settlement, to lop the boughs that cumbered and obscured the others. For truly, like a man in a vast Columbian forest, opening entangled space, now with the ready axe, now with the patient train that kindles the slower fire, this child of civilised life went toiling on against surrounding obstacles, resolute to destroy, but ever scheming to construct. And now Randal has reached Levy's dainty business-room, and is buried deep in discussion how to secure to himself, at the expense of his patron, the representation of Lansmere, and how to complete the contract which shall reannex to his forlorn inheritance some fragments of its ancient wealth.

Meanwhile, Chance fought on his side in the boudoir of May Fair. The Squire had found the Marchesa at home—briefly introduced himself and his business—told her she was mistaken if she had fancied she had taken in a rich heir in his son—that, thank Heaven, he could leave his estates to his ploughman, should he so please, but that he was willing to do things liberally; and whatever she thought Frank was worth, he was very ready to pay for.

At another time Beatrice would perhaps have laughed at this strange address; or she might, in some prouder moment, have fired up with all a patrician's resentment and a woman's pride; but now her spirit was crushed, her nerves shattered: the sense of her degraded position, of her dependence on her brother, combined with her supreme unhappiness at the loss of those dreams with which Leonard had for a while charmed her wearied waking life—all came upon her. She listened, pale and speechless; and the poor Squire thought he was quietly advancing towards a favourable result, when she suddenly burst into a passion of hysterical tears; and just at that moment Frank himself entered the room. At the sight of his father, of Beatrice's grief, his sense of filial duty gave way. He was maddened by irritation—by the insult offered to the woman he loved, which a few trembling words from her explained to him; maddened yet more by the fear that the insult had lost her to him—warm words ensued between son and father, to close with the peremptory command and vehement threat of the last.

"Come away this instant, sir! Come with me, or before the day is over I strike you out of my will!"

The son's answer was not to his father; he threw himself at Beatrice's feet.

"Forgive him—forgive us both—"

"What! you prefer that stranger to me—to the inheritance of Hazeldean!" cried the Squire, stamping his foot.

"Leave your estates to whom you will; all that I care for in life is here!"

The Squire stood still a moment or so, gazing on his son, with a strange bewildered marvel at the strength of that mystic passion, which none not labouring under its fearful charm can comprehend, which creates the sudden idol that no reason justifies, and sacrifices to its fatal shrine alike the Past and the Future. Not trusting himself to speak, the father drew his hand across his eyes, and dashed away the bitter tear that sprang from a swelling indignant heart; then he uttered an inarticulate sound, and, finding his voice gone, moved away to the door, and left the house.

He walked through the streets, bearing his head very erect, as a proud man does when deeply wounded, and striving to shake off some affection that he deems a weakness; and his trembling nervous fingers fumbled at the button of his coat, trying to tighten the garment across his chest, as if to confirm a resolution that still sought to struggle out of the revolting heart.

Thus he went on, and the reader, perhaps, will wonder whither, and the wonder may not lessen when he finds the Squire come to a dead pause in Grosvenor Square, and at the portico of his "distant brother's" stately house.

At the Squire's brief inquiry whether Mr. Egerton was at home, the porter summoned the groom of the chambers; and the groom of the chambers, seeing a stranger, doubted whether his master was not engaged, but would take in the stranger's card and see.

"Ay, ay," muttered the Squire, "this is true relationship! —my child prefers a stranger to me. Why should I complain that I am a stranger in a brother's house? Sir," added the Squire aloud, and very meekly—" Sir, please to say to your master that I am William Hazeldean."

The servant bowed low, and without another word conducted the visitor into the statesman's library, and announcing Mr. Hazeldean, closed the door.

Audley was seated at his desk, the grim iron boxes still at his feet, but they were now closed and locked. And the ex-minister was no longer looking over official documents; letters spread open before him, of far different nature; in his hand there lay a long lock of fair silken hair, on which his eyes were fixed sadly and intently. He started at the sound of his visitor's name, and the tread of the Squire's stalwart footstep; and mechanically thrust into his bosom the relic of younger and warmer years, keeping his hand to his heart, which beat loud with disease under the light pressure of that golden hair.

The two brothers stood on the great man's lonely hearth, facing each other in silence, and noting unconsciously the change made in each during the long years in which they had never met.

The Squire, with his portly size, his hardy sun-burnt cheeks, the partial baldness of his unfurrowed open forehead, looked his full age—deep into middle life. Unmistakeably he seemed the *pater familias*—the husband and the father— the man of social domestic ties. But about Audley (really some few years junior to the Squire), despite the lines of care on his handsome face, there still lingered the grace of youth. Men of cities retain youth longer than those of the country— a remark which Buffon has not failed to make and to account for. Neither did Egerton betray the air of the married man·for ineffable solitariness seemed stamped upon one whose private life had long been so stern a solitude. No ray from the focus of Home played round that reserved, unjoyous, melancholy brow. In a word, Audley looked still the man for whom some young female heart might fondly sigh; and not the less because of the cold eye and compressed lip, which challenged interest even while seeming to repel it.

Audley was the first to speak, and to put forth the right hand, which he stole slowly from its place at his breast, on which the lock of hair still stirred to and fro at the heave of the labouring heart. "William," said he, with his rich deep voice, "this is kind. You are come to see me, now that men say I am fallen. The minister you censured is no more; and you see again the brother."

The Squire was softened at once by this address. He shook heartily the hand tendered to him; and then, turning away his head, with an honest conviction that Audley ascribed to him a credit which he did not deserve, he said, "No, no, Audley; I am more selfish than you think me. I have come—I have come to ask your advice—no, not exactly that—your opinion. But you are busy?—"

"Sit down, William. Old days were coming over me when you entered; days earlier still return now—days, too, that leave no shadow when their suns are set."

The proud man seemed to think he had said too much. His practical nature rebuked the poetic sentiment and phrase. He re-collected himself, and added, more coldly, "You would ask my opinion? What on? Some public matter—some Parliamentary bill that may affect your property?"

"Am I such a mean miser as that? Property—property? What does property matter, when a man is struck down at his own hearth? Property, indeed! But you have no child—happy brother!"

"Ay, ay; as you say, I am a happy man; childless! Has your son displeased you? I have heard him well spoken of, too."

"Don't talk of him. Whether his conduct be good or ill is my affair," resumed the poor father with a testy voice—jealous alike of Audley's praise or blame of his rebellious son. Then he rose a moment, and made a strong gulp, as if for air; and laying his broad brown hand on his brother's shoulder, said—"Randal Leslie tells me you are wise—a consummate man of the world. No doubt you are so. And Parson Dale

tells me that he is sure you have warm feelings—which I take
to be a strange thing for one who has lived so long in London,
and has no wife and no child—a widower, and a Member of
Parliament—for a commercial city, too. Never smile; it is
no smiling matter with me. You know a foreign woman,
called Negra or Negro—not a blackymoor, though, by any
means—at least on the outside of her. Is she such a woman
as a plain country gentleman would like his only son to marry
—ay or no?"

"No, indeed," answered Audley, gravely; and I trust
your son will commit no action so rash. Shall I see him,
or her? Speak, my dear William. What would you have
me do?"

"Nothing; you have said enough," replied the Squire,
gloomily; and his head sank on his breast.

Audley took his hand, and pressed it fraternally. "William," said the statesman, "we have been long estranged;
but I do not forget that when we last met, at—at Lord Lansmere's house, and when I took you aside, and said 'William,
if I lose this election, I must resign all chance of public life;
my affairs are embarrassed. I would not accept money from
you—I would seek a profession, and you can help me there,'
you divined my meaning, and said—'Take orders; the Hazeldean living is just vacant. I will get some one to hold it till
you are ordained.' I do not forget that. Would that I had
thought earlier of so serene an escape from all that then
tormented me. My lot might have been far happier."

The Squire eyed Audley with a surprise that broke forth
from his more absorbing emotions. "Happier! Why, all
things have prospered with you; and you are rich enough
now; and—you shake your head. Brother, is it possible! do
you want money? Pooh, not accept money from your
mother's son!—stuff." Out came the Squire's pocket-book.
Audley put it gently aside.

"Nay," said he, "I have enough for myself; but since
you seek and speak with me thus affectionately, I will ask
you one favour. Should I die before I can provide for my
wife's kinsman, Randal Leslie, as I could wish, will you see to
his fortunes, so far as you can, without injury to others—to
your own son?"

"My son! He *is* provided for. He has the Casino estate
—much good may it do him. You have touched on the very
matter that brought me here. This boy, Randal Leslie, seems
a praiseworthy lad, and has Hazeldean blood in his veins.

You have taken him up because he is connected with your late wife. Why should I not take him up, too, when his grandmother was a Hazeldean? My main object in calling was to ask what you mean do to for him; for if you do not mean to provide for him, why, I will, as in duty bound. So your request comes at the right time; I think of altering my will. I can put him into the entail, besides a handsome legacy. You are sure he is a good lad—and it will please you too, Audley!"

"But not at the expense of your son. And stay, William —as to this foolish marriage with Madame di Negra,—who told you Frank meant to take such a step?"

"He told me himself; but it is no matter. Randal and I both did all we could to dissuade him; and Randal advised me to come to you."

"He has acted generously, then, our kinsman Randal—I am glad to hear it"—said Audley, his brow somewhat clearing. "I have no influence with this lady; but, at least, I can counsel her. Do not consider the marriage fixed because a young man desires it. Youth is ever hot and rash."

"Your youth never was," retorted the squire, bluntly. "You married well enough, I'm sure. I will say one thing for you: you have been, to my taste, a bad politician—beg pardon—but you were always a gentleman. You would never have disgraced your family and married a—"

"Hush!" interrupted Egerton, gently. "Do not make matters worse than they are. Madame di Negra is of high birth in her own country; and if scandal—"

"Scandal!" cried the Squire, shrinking and turning pale. "Are you speaking of the wife of a Hazeldean? At least she shall never sit by the hearth at which now sits his mother; and whatever I may do for Frank, her children shall not succeed. No mongrel cross-breed shall kennel in English Hazeldean. Much obliged to you, Audley, for your good feeling—glad to have seen you; and harkye, you startled me by that shake of your head, when I spoke of your wealth; and, from what you say about Randal's prospects, I guess that you London gentlemen are not so thrifty as we are. You *shall* let me speak. I say again, that I have some thousands quite at your service. And though you are not a Hazeldean, still you are my mother's son; and now that I am about to alter my will, I can as well scratch in the name of Egerton as that of Leslie. Cheer up, cheer up: you are younger than I am, and you have no child; so you will live longer than I shall.'

"My dear brother," answered Audley, "believe me I shall never live to want your aid. And as to Leslie, add to the £5000 I mean to give him, an equal sum in your will, and I shall feel that he has received justice."

Observing that the Squire, though he listened attentively, made no ready answer, Audley turned the subject again to Frank; and with the adroitness of a man of the world, backed by cordial sympathy in his brother's distress, he pleaded so well Frank's lame cause, urged so gently the wisdom of patience and delay, and the appeal to filial feeling rather than recourse to paternal threats, that the Squire grew mollified in spite of himself, and left his brother's house a much less angry, and less doleful man.

Mr. Hazeldean was still in the square, when he came upon Randal himself, who was walking with a dark-whiskered, showy gentleman, towards Egerton's house. Randal and the gentleman exchanged a hasty whisper, and the former then exclaimed—

"What, Mr. Hazeldean, have you just left your brother's house? Is it possible?"

"Why, you advised me to go there, and I did. I scarcely knew what I was about. I am very glad I did go. Hang politics! hang the landed interest! what do I care for either now?"

"Foiled with Madame di Negra?" asked Randal, drawing the Squire aside.

"Never speak of her again!" cried the Squire, fiercely. "And as to that ungrateful boy—but I don't mean to behave harshly to him—he shall have money enough to keep her if he likes—keep her from coming to me—keep him, too, from counting on my death, and borrowing post-obits on the Casino—for he'll be doing that next—no, I hope I wrong him there; I have been too good a father for him to count on my death already. After all," continued the Squire, beginning to relax, "as Audley says, the marriage is not yet made; and if the woman has taken him in, he is young, and his heart is warm. Make yourself easy, my boy. I don't forget how kindly you took his part; and before I do anything rash, I'll at least consult with his poor mother."

Randal gnawed his pale lip, and a momentary cloud of disappointment passed over his face.

"True, sir," said he, gently; "true, you must not be rash Indeed, I was thinking of you and poor dear Frank at the very moment I met you. It occurred to me whether we might not make Frank's very embarrassments a reason to induce Madame di Negra to refuse him; and I was on my way to Mr. Egerton, in order to ask his opinion, in company with the gentleman yonder."

"Gentleman yonder. Why should he thrust his long nose into my family affairs? Who the devil is he?"

"Don't ask, sir. Pray let me act."

But the Squire continued to eye askant the dark-whiskered personage thus interposed between himself and his son, and who waited patiently a few yards in the rear, carelessly re-adjusting the camelia in his button-hole.

"He looks very outlandish. Is he a foreigner too?" asked the Squire, at last.

"No, not exactly. However, he knows all about Frank's embarrassments; and—"

"Embarrassments! what, the debt he paid for that woman? How did he raise the money?"

"I don't know," answered Randall, "and that is the reason I asked Baron Levy to accompany me to Egerton's, that he might explain in private what I have no reason—"

"Baron Levy!" interrupted the Squire. "Levy, Levy—I have heard of a Levy who has nearly ruined my neighbour Thornhill—a money-lender. Zounds! is that the man who knows my son's affairs? I'll soon learn, sir."

Randal caught hold of the Squire's arm: "Stop, stop; if you really insist upon learning more about Frank's debts, you must not appeal to Baron Levy directly, and as Frank's father: he will not answer you. But if I present you to him as a mere acquaintance of mine, and turn the conversation, as if carelessly, upon Frank—why, since in the London world, such matters are never kept secret, except from the parents of young men—I have no doubt he will talk out openly."

"Manage it as you will," said the Squire.

Randal took Mr. Hazeldean's arm, and joined Levy—"A friend of mine from the country, Baron." Levy bowed profoundly, and the three walked slowly on.

"By-the-by," said Randal, pressing significantly upon Levy's arm, "my friend has come to town upon the somewhat unpleasant business of settling the debts of another—a young man of fashion—a relation of his own. No one, sir (turning to the Squire), could so ably assist you in such arrangements as could Baron Levy."

BARON (modestly, and with a moralising air).—"I have some experience in such matters, and I hold it a duty to assist the parents and relations of young men who, from want of reflection, often ruin themselves for life. I hope the young gentleman in question is not in the hands of the Jews?"

RANDAL.—"Christians are as fond of good interest for their money as ever the Jews can be."

BARON.—"Granted, but they have not always so much money to lend. The first thing, sir, (addressing the Squire,) —the first thing for you to do is to buy up such of your relation's bills and notes of hand as may be in the market. No doubt we can get them a bargain, unless the young man is heir to some property that may soon be his in the course of nature."

RANDAL.—"Not soon—heaven forbid! His father is still a young man—a fine healthy man," leaning heavily on Levy's arm; " and as to post-obits—"

BARON.—" Post-obits on sound security cost more to buy up, however healthy the obstructing relative may be."

RANDAL.—"I should hope that there are not many sons who can calculate, in cold blood, on the death of their fathers."

BARON.—"Ha, ha—he is young, our friend Randal; eh, sir?"

RANDAL.—"Well, I am not more scrupulous than others, I daresay; and I have often been pinched hard for money, but I would go barefoot rather than give security upon a father's grave! I can imagine nothing more likely to destroy natural feeling, nor to instil ingratitude and treachery into the whole character, than to press the hand of a parent, and calculate when that hand may be dust—than to sit down with strangers and reduce his life to the measure of an insurance table—than to feel difficulties gathering round one, and mutter in fashionable slang, 'But it will be all well if the governor would but die.' And he who has accustomed himself to the relief of post-obits, must gradually harden his mind to all this."

The Squire groaned heavily; and had Randal proceeded another sentence in the same strain, the Squire would have wept outright. "But," continued Randal, altering the tone of his voice, "I think that our young friend, of whom we were talking just now, Levy, before this gentleman joined us, has the same opinions as myself on this head. He may accept bills, but he would never sign post-obits."

BARON, (who with the apt docility of a managed charger to the touch of a rider's hand, had comprehended and complied with each quick sign of Randal's.)—"Pooh! the young fellow we are talking of? Nonsense. He would not be so foolish as to give five times the percentage he otherwise might. Not sign post-obits! Of course he has signed one."

RANDAL.—"Hist—you mistake, you mistake."

SQUIRE, (leaving Randal's arm and seizing Levy's.)—"Were you speaking of Frank Hazeldean?"

BARON.—"My dear sir, excuse me; I never mention names before strangers."

SQUIRE.—"Strangers again! Man, I am the boy's father! Speak out, sir," and his hand closed on Levy's arm with the strength of an iron vice.

BARON.—"Gently; you hurt me, sir: but I excuse your feelings. Randal, you are to blame for leading me into this indiscretion; but I beg to assure Mr. Hazeldean, that though his son has been a little extravagant—"

RANDAL.—"Owing chiefly to the arts of an abandoned woman."

BARON.—"Of an abandoned woman;—still he has shown more prudence than you would suppose; and this very post-obit is a proof of it. A simple act of that kind has enabled him to pay off bills that were running on till they would have ruined even the Hazeldean estate; whereas a charge on the reversion of the Casino—"

SQUIRE.—"He has done it then? He has signed a post-obit?"

RANDAL.—"No, no, Levy must be wrong."

BARON.—"My dear Leslie, a man of Mr. Hazeldean's time of life cannot have your romantic boyish notions. He must allow that Frank has acted in this like a lad of sense—very good head for business has my young friend Frank! And the best thing Mr. Hazeldean can do is quietly to buy up the post-obit, and thus he will place his son henceforth in his power."

SQUIRE.—"Can I see the deed with my own eyes?"

BARON.—"Certainly, or how could you be induced to buy it up? But on one condition; you must not betray me to your son. And, indeed, take my advice, and don't say a word to him on the matter."

SQUIRE.—"Let me see it, let me see it with my own eyes. His mother else will never believe it—nor will I."

BARON.—"I can call on you this evening."

SQUIRE.—"Now—now."

BARON.—"You can spare me, Randal; and you yourself can open to Mr. Egerton the other affair respecting Lansmere. No time should be lost, lest L'Estrange suggest a candidate."

Randal, (whispering.)—Never mind me. This is more important. (Aloud)—Go with Mr. Hazeldean. My dear kind friend, (to the Squire,) do not let this vex you so much. After all, it is what nine young men out of ten would do in the same circumstances. And it is best you should know it; you may save Frank from farther ruin, and prevent, perhaps, this very marriage."

"We will see," exclaimed the Squire, hastily. "Now, Mr. Levy, come."

Levy and the Squire walked on, not arm in arm, but side by side. Randal proceeded to Egerton's house.

"I am glad to see you, Leslie," said the ex-minister. "What is it I have heard? My nephew, Frank Hazeldean, proposes to marry Madame di Negra against his father's consent? How could you suffer him to entertain an idea so wild? And how never confide it to me?"

Randal.—"My dear Mr. Egerton, it is only to-day that I was informed of Frank's engagement. I have already seen him, and expostulated in vain; till then, though I knew your nephew admired Madame di Negra, I could never suppose he harboured a serious intention."

Egerton.—"I must believe you, Randal. I will myself see Madame di Negra, though I have no power, and no right, to dictate to her. I have but little time for all such private business. The dissolution of Parliament is so close at hand."

Randal, (looking down.)—"It is on that subject that I wished to speak to you, sir. You think of standing for Lansmere. Well, Baron Levy has suggested to me an idea that I could not, of course, even countenance, till I had spoken to you. It seems that he has some acquaintance with the state of parties in that borough! He is informed that it is not only as easy to bring in two of our side, as to carry one; but that it would make your election still more safe, not to fight single-handed against two opponents; that if canvassing for yourself alone, you could not carry a sufficient number of plumper votes; that split votes would go from you to one or other of the two adversaries; that, in a word, it is necessary to pair you with a colleague. If it really be so, you of course will learn best from your own Committee; but should they concur in the opinion Baron Levy has formed—do I presume too much on your kindness—to deem it possible that you might allow me to be the second candidate on your side? I should not say this, but that Levy told me you had some wish to see me in Parliament, amongst the supporters of your policy. And what other opportunity can occur? Here the cost of carrying two would be scarcely more than that of carrying one. And Levy says, the party would subscribe for my election; you, of course, would refuse all such aid for your own; and indeed, with your great name, and Lord Lansmere's interest, there can be little beyond the strict legal expenses."

As Randal spoke thus at length, he watched anxiously his patron's reserved, unrevealing countenance.

EGERTON, (drily.)—"I will consider. You may safely leave in my hands any matter connected with your ambition and advancement. I have before told you I hold it a duty to do all in my power for the kinsman of my late wife—for one whose career I undertook to forward—for one whom honour has compelled to share in my own political reverses."

Here Egerton rang the bell for his hat and gloves, and walking into the hall, paused at the street door. There beckoning to Randal, he said, slowly, "You seem intimate with Baron Levy; I caution you against him—a dangerous acquaintance, first to the purse, next to the honour."

RANDAL.—"I know it, sir; and am surprised myself at the acquaintance that has grown up between us. Perhaps its cause is in his respect for yourself."

EGERTON.—"Tut."

RANDAL.—"Whatever it be, he contrives to obtain a singular hold over one's mind, even where, as in my case, he has no evident interest to serve. How is this? It puzzles me!"

EGERTON.—"For his interest, it is most secured where he suffers it to be least evident; for his hold over the mind, it is easily accounted for. He ever appeals to two temptations, strong with all men—Avarice and Ambition. Good day."

RANDAL.—"Are you going to Madame di Negra's? Shall I not accompany you? Perhaps I may be able to back your own remonstrances."

EGERTON.—"No, 1 shall not require you."

RANDAL.—"I trust I shall hear the result of your interview? I feel so much interested in it. Poor Frank!"

Audley nodded. "Of course, of course."

## CHAPTER XIV.

ON entering the drawing-room of Madame di Negra, the peculiar charm which the severe Audley Egerton had been ever reputed to possess with women, would have sensibly struck one who had hitherto seen him chiefly in his relations with men in the business-like affairs of life. It was a charm in strong contrast to the ordinary manners of those who are emphatically called "Ladies' men." No artificial smile, no conventional, hollow blandness, no frivolous gossip, no varnish either of ungenial gaiety or affected grace. The charm was in a simplicity that unbent more into kindness than it did with men. Audley's nature, whatever its faults and defects, was essentially masculine; and it was the sense of masculine power that gave to his voice a music when addressing the gentler sex—and to his manner a sort of indulgent tenderness that appeared equally void of insincerity and presumption.

Frank had been gone about half-an-hour, and Madame di Negra was scarcely recovered from the agitation into which she had been thrown by the affront from the father and the pleading of the son.

Egerton took her passive hand cordially, and seated himself by her side.

"My dear Marchesa," said he, "are we then likely to be near connections? And can you seriously contemplate marriage with my young nephew, Frank Hazeldean? You turn away. Ah, my fair friend, there are but two inducements to a free woman to sign away her liberty at the altar. I say a free woman, for widows are free, and girls are not. These inducements are, first, worldly position; secondly, love. Which of these motives can urge Madame di Negra to marry Mr. Frank Hazeldean?"

"There are other motives than those you speak of—the need of protection—the sense of solitude—the curse of dependence—gratitude for honourable affection. But you men never know women!"

"I grant that you are right there—we never do; neither do women ever know men. And yet each sex contrives to dupe and to fool the other! Listen to me. I have little acquaintance with my nephew, but I allow he is a handsome young gentleman, with whom a handsome young lady in her teens might fall in love in a ball-room. But you who have known the higher order of our species—you who have received the homage of men, whose thoughts and mind leave the small talk of drawing-room triflers so poor and bald—you cannot look me in the face and say that it is any passion resembling love which you feel for my nephew. And as to position, it is right that I should inform you that if he marry you he will have none. He may risk his inheritance. You will receive no countenance from his parents. You will be poor, but not free. You will not gain the independence you seek for. The sight of a vacant discontented face in that opposite chair will be worse than solitude. And as to grateful affection," added the man of the world, "it is a polite synonym for tranquil indifference."

"Mr. Egerton," said Beatrice, "people say you are made of bronze. Did you ever feel the want of a home?"

"I answer you frankly," replied the statesman, "if I had not felt it, do you think I should have been, and that I should be to the last, the joyless drudge of public life? Bronze though you call my nature, it would have melted away long since like wax in the fire, if I had sat idly down and dreamed of a *home!*"

"But we women," answered Beatrice, with pathos, "have no public life, and we do idly sit down and dream. Oh," she continued, after a short pause, and clasping her hands firmly together, "you think me worldly, grasping, ambitious; how different my fate had been had I known a home!—known one whom I could love and venerate—known one whose smiles would have developed the good that was once within me, and the fear of whose rebuking or sorrowful eye would have corrected what is evil."

"Yet," answered Audley, "nearly all women in the great world have had that choice once in their lives, and nearly all have thrown it away. How few of your rank really think of home when they marry—how few ask to venerate as well as to love—and how many, of every rank, when the home has been really gained, have wilfully lost its shelter; some in neglectful weariness—some from a momentary doubt, distrust, caprice—a wild fancy—a passionate fit—a trifle—a straw—a dream! True, you women are ever dreamers. Common sense, common earth, is above or below your comprehension."

Both now are silent. Audley first roused himself with a quick, writhing movement. "We two," said he, smiling half sadly, half cynically—"we two must not longer waste time in talking sentiment. We know both too well what life, as it has been made for us by our faults or our misfortunes, truly is. And once again, I entreat you to pause before you yield to the foolish suit of my foolish nephew. Rely on it, you will either command a higher offer for your prudence to accept; or, if you needs must sacrifice rank and fortune, you, with your beauty and your romantic heart, will see one who, at least for a fair holiday season (if human love allows no more), can repay you for the sacrifice. Frank Hazeldean never can."

Beatrice turned away to conceal the tears that rushed to her eyes.

"Think over this well," said Audley, in the softest tones of his mellow voice. "Do you remember that when you first came to England, I told you that neither wedlock nor love had any lures for me. We grew friends upon that rude avowal, and therefore I now speak to you like some sage of old, wise because standing apart and aloof, from all the affections and ties that mislead our wisdom. Nothing but real love—(how rare it is; has one human heart in a million ever known it?)—nothing but real love can repay us for the loss of freedom—the cares and fears of poverty—the cold pity of the world that we both despise and respect. And all these, and much more, follow the step that you would inconsiderately take—an imprudent marriage."

"Audley Egerton," said Beatrice, lifting her dark, moistened eyes, "you grant that real love does compensate for an imprudent marriage. You speak as if you had known such love—you! Can it be possible?"

"Real love—I thought that I knew it once. Looking back with remorse, I should doubt it now but for one curse that only real love, when lost, has the power to leave evermore behind it."

"What is that?"

"A void here," answered Egerton, striking his heart. "Desolation!—Adieu!"

He rose and left the room.

"Is it," murmured Egerton, as he pursued his way through the streets—"is it that, as we approach death, all the first fair feelings of young life come back to us mysteriously? Thus I have heard, or read, that in some country of old, children scattering flowers, preceded a funeral bier."

## CHAPTER XV.

And so Leonard stood beside his friend's mortal clay, and watched, in the ineffable smile of death, the last gleam which the soul had left there; and so, after a time, he crept back to the adjoining room with a step as noiseless as if he had feared to disturb the dead. Wearied as he was with watching, he had no thought of sleep. He sate himself down by the little table, and leaned his face on his hand, musing sorrowfully. Thus time passed. He heard the clock from below strike the hours. In the house of death the sound of a clock becomes so solemn. The soul that we miss has gone so far beyond the reach of time! A cold, superstitious awe gradually stole over the young man. He shivered, and lifted his eyes with a start, half scornful, half defying. The moon was gone—the grey, comfortless dawn gleamed through the casement, and carried its raw, chilling light through the open doorway into the death-room. And there, near the extinguished fire, Leonard saw the solitary woman, weeping low, and watching still. He returned to say a word of comfort—she pressed his hand, but waved him away. He understood. She did not wish for other comfort than her quiet relief of tears. Again, he returned to his own chamber, and his eye this time fell upon the papers which he had hitherto disregarded. What made his heart stand still, and the blood then rush so quickly through his veins? Why did he seize upon those papers with so tremulous a hand—then lay them down—pause, as if to nerve himself—and look so eagerly again? He recognised the handwriting—those fair, clear characters—so peculiar in their woman-like delicacy and grace—the same as in the wild, pathetic poems, the sight of which had made an era in his boyhood. From these pages the image of the mysterious Nora rose once more before him. He felt that he was with a mother. He went back, and closed the door gently, as if with a jealous piety, to exclude each ruder shadow from the world of spirits, and be alone with that mournful ghost. For a thought written in warm, sunny life, and then suddenly rising up to us, when the hand that traced, and the heart that cherished it, are dust—is verily as a ghost. It is a likeness struck off of the fond human being, and surviving it. Far more truthful than bust or portrait, it bids us see the tear flow, and the pulse beat. What ghost can the churchyard yield to us like the writing of the dead?

The bulk of the papers had been once lightly sewn to each other—they had come undone, perhaps in Burley's rude hands; but their order was easily apparent. Leonard soon saw that they formed a kind of journal—not, indeed, a regular diary, nor always relating to the things of the day. There were gaps in time—no attempt at successive narrative. Some times, instead of prose, a hasty burst of verse, gushing evidently from the heart — sometimes all narrative was left untold, and yet, as it were, epitomised by a single burning line—a single exclamation—of woe or joy! Everywhere you saw records of a nature exquisitely susceptible; and, where genius appeared, it was so artless, that you did not call it genius, but emotion. At the onset the writer did not speak of herself in the first person. The MS. opened with descriptions and short dialogues, carried on by persons to whose names only initial letters were assigned, all written in a style of simple innocent freshness, and breathing of purity and happiness, like a dawn of spring. Two young persons, humbly born—a youth and a girl—the last still in childhood, each chiefly self-taught, are wandering on Sabbath evenings among green dewy fields, near the busy town, in which labour awhile is still. Few words pass between them. You see at once though the writer does not mean to convey it, how far beyond the scope of her male companion flies the heavenward imagination of the girl. It is he who questions—it is she who answers; and soon there steals upon you, as you read, the conviction that the youth loves the girl, and loves in vain. All in this writing, though terse, is so truthful! Leonard, in the youth, already recognises the rude imperfect scholar—the village bard—Mark Fairfield. Then, there is a gap in description—but there are short weighty sentences, which show deepening thought, increasing years, in the writer. And though the innocence remains, the happiness begins to be less vivid on the page.

Now, insensibly, Leonard finds that there is a new phase in the writer's existence. Scenes, no longer of humble, workday rural life, surround her. And a fairer and more dazzling image succeeds to the companion of the Sabbath eves. This image Nora evidently loves to paint—it is akin to her own genius—it captivates her fancy—it is an image that she (inborn artist, and conscious of her art) feels to belong to a brighter and higher school of the Beautiful. And yet the virgin's heart is not awakened—no trace of the heart yet there! The new image thus introduced is one of her own years, perhaps; nay, it may be younger still, for it is a boy that is described, with his profuse fair curls, and eyes new to grief, and confronting the sun as a young eagle's; with veins so full of the wine of life, that they overflow into every joyous whim; with nerves quiveringly alive to the desire of glory; with the frank generous nature, rash in its laughing scorn of the world, which it has not tried. Who was this boy, it perplexed Leonard. He feared to guess. Soon, less told than implied, you saw that this companionship, however it chanced, brings fear and pain on the writer. Again (as before), with Mark Fairfield, there is love on the one side and not on the other;—with her there is affectionate, almost sisterly, interest, admiration, gratitude—but a something of pride or of terror that keeps back love.

Here Leonard's interest grew intense. Were there touches by which conjecture grew certainty; and he recognised, through the lapse of years, the boy-lover in his own generous benefactor?

Fragments of dialogue now began to reveal the suit of an ardent impassioned nature, and the simple wonder and strange alarm of a listener who pitied but could not sympathise. Some great worldly distinction of rank between the two became visible—that distinction seemed to arm the virtue and steel the affections of the lowlier born. Then a few sentences, half blotted out with tears, told of wounded and humbled feelings—some one invested with authority, as if the suitor's parent, had interfered, questioned, reproached, counselled. And it was evident that the suit was not one that dishonoured;—it wooed to flight, but still to marriage.

And now these sentences grew briefer still, as with the decision of a strong resolve. And to these there followed a passage so exquisite, that Leonard wept unconsciously as he read. It was the description of a visit spent at home previous to some sorrowful departure. He caught the glimpse of a proud and vain, but a tender wistful mother—of a father's fonder but less thoughtful love. And then came a quiet soothing scene between the girl and her first village lover, ending thus—" So she put M.'s hand into her sister's, and said: 'You loved me through the fancy, love her with the heart,' and left them comprehending each other, and betrothed."

Leonard sighed. He understood now how Mark Fairfield saw, in the homely features of his unlettered wife, the reflection of the sister's soul and face.

A few words told the final parting—words that were a picture. The long friendless highway, stretching on—on— towards the remorseless city. And the doors of home opening on the desolate thoroughfare—and the old pollard tree beside the threshold, with the ravens wheeling round it and calling to their young. He too had watched that threshold from the same desolate thoroughfare. He too had heard the cry of the ravens. Then came some pages covered with snatches of melancholy verse, or some reflections of dreamy gloom.

The writer was in London, in the house of some highborn patroness—that friendless shadow of a friend which the jargon of society calls "companion." And she was looking on the bright storm of the world as through prison bars. Poor bird, afar from the greenwood, she had need of song—it was her last link with freedom and nature. The patroness seems to share in her apprehensions of the boy suitor, whose wild rash prayers the fugitive had resisted; but to fear least the suitor should be degraded, not the one whom he pursues—fear an alliance ill-suited to a high-born heir. And this kind of fear stings the writer's pride, and she grows harsh in her judgment of him who thus causes but pain where he proffers love. Then there is a reference to some applicant for her hand, who is pressed upon her choice. And she is told that it is her duty so to choose, and thus deliver a noble family from a dread that endures so long as her hand is free. And of this fear, and of this applicant, there breaks out a petulant yet pathetic scorn. After this the narrative, to judge by the dates, pauses for days and weeks, as if the writer had grown weary and listless,—suddenly to re-open in a new strain, eloquent with hopes and with fears never known before. The first person was abruptly assumed—it was the living "I" that now breathed and moved along the lines. How was this? The woman was no more a shadow and a secret unknown to herself. She had assumed the intense and vivid sense of individual being. And love spoke loud in the awakened human heart.

A personage not seen till then appeared on the page. And ever afterwards this personage was only named as "*He*," as if the one and sole representative of all the myriads that walk the earth. The first notice of this prominent character on the scene showed the restless agitated effect produced on the writer's imagination. He was invested with a romance probably not his own. He was described in contrast to the brilliant boy whose suit she had feared, pitied, and now sought to shun—described with a grave and serious, but gentle mien —a voice that imposed respect—an eye and lip that showed collected dignity of will. Alas! the writer betrayed herself. and the charm was in the contrast, not to the character of the earlier lover but her own. And now, leaving Leonard to explore and guess his way through the gaps and chasms of the narrative, it is time to place before the reader what the narrative alone will not reveal to Leonard.

## CHAPTER XVI.

NORA AVENEL had fled from the boyish love of Harley L'Estrange—recommended by Lady Lansmere to a valetudinarian relative of her own, Lady Jane Horton, as companion. But Lady Lansmere could not believe it possible that the low-born girl could long sustain her generous pride, and reject the ardent suit of one who could offer to her the prospective coronet of a countess. She continually urged upon Lady Jane the necessity of marrying Nora to some one of rank less disproportioned to her own, and empowered that lady to assure any such wooer of a dowry far beyond Nora's station. Lady Jane looked around, and saw in the outskirts of her limited social ring, a young solicitor, a peer's natural son, who was on terms of more than business-like intimacy with the fashionable clients whose distresses made the origin of his wealth. The young man was handsome, well-dressed, and bland. Lady Jane invited him to her house; and, seeing him struck with the rare loveliness of Nora, whispered the hint of the dower. The fashionable solicitor, who afterwards ripened into Baron Levy, did not need that hint; for, though then poor, he relied on himself for fortune, and, unlike Randal, he had warm blood in his veins. But Lady Jane's suggestions made him sanguine of success; and when he formally proposed, and was as formally refused, his self-love was bitterly wounded. Vanity in Levy was a powerful passion; and with the vain, hatred is strong, revenge is rankling. Levy retired, concealing his rage; nor did he himself know how vindictive that rage, when it cooled into malignancy, could become, until the arch-fiend OPPORTUNITY prompted its indulgence and suggested its design.

Lady Jane was at first very angry with Nora for the rejection of a suitor whom she had presented as eligible. But the pathetic grace of this wonderful girl had crept into her heart, and softened it even against family prejudice; and she gradually owned to herself that Nora was worthy of some one better than Mr. Levy.

Now, Harley had ever believed that Nora returned his love,

and that nothing but her own sense of gratitude to his parents—her own instincts of delicacy, made her deaf to his prayers. To do him justice, wild and headstrong as he then was, his suit would have ceased at once had he really deemed it persecution. Nor was his error unnatural; for his conversation, till it had revealed his own heart, could not fail to have dazzled and delighted the child of genius; and her frank eyes would have shown the delight. How, at his age, could he see the distinction between the Poetess and the Woman? The poetess was charmed with rare promise in a soul of which the very errors were the extravagances of richness and beauty. But the woman—no! the woman required some nature not yet undeveloped, and all at turbulent, if brilliant strife, with its own noble elements,—but a nature formed and full-grown. Harley was a boy, and Nora was one of those women who must find or fancy an Ideal that commands and almost awes them into love.

Harley discovered, not without difficulty, Nora's new residence. He presented himself at Lady Jane's, and she, with grave rebuke, forbade him the house. He found it impossible to obtain an interview with Nora. He wrote, but he felt sure that his letters never reached her, since they were unanswered. His young heart swelled with rage. He dropped threats, which alarmed all the fears of Lady Lansmere, and even the prudent apprehensions of his friend, Audley Egerton. At the request of the mother, and equally at the wish of the son, Audley consented to visit at Lady Jane's, and make acquaintance with Nora.

"I have such confidence in you," said Lady Lansmere, "that if you once know the girl, your advice will be sure to have weight with her.—You will show her how wicked it would be to let Harley break our hearts and degrade his station."

"I have such confidence in you," said young Harley, "that if you once know my Nora, you will no longer side with my mother. You will recognise the nobility which nature only can create—you will own that Nora is worthy a rank more lofty than mine: and my mother so believes in your wisdom, that, if you plead in my cause, you will convince even her."

Audley listened to both with his intelligent, half-incredulous smile; and wholly of the same opinion as Lady Lansmere, and sincerely anxious to save Harley from an indiscretion that his own notions led him to regard as fatal, he resolved to examine this boasted pearl; and to find out its flaws. Audley Egerton was then in the prime of his earnest, resolute, ambitious youth. The stateliness of his natural manners had then a suavity and polish which, even in later and busier life, it never wholly lost; since, in spite of the briefer words and the colder looks by which care and power mark the official man, the Minister had ever enjoyed that personal popularity which the indefinable, external *something*, that wins and pleases, can alone confer. But he had even then, as ever, that felicitous reserve which Rochefaucault has called the "mystery of the body"—that thin yet guardian veil which reveals but the strong outlines of character, and excites so much of interest by provoking so much of conjecture. To the man who is born with this reserve, which is wholly distinct from shyness, the world gives credit for qualities and talents beyond those that it perceives; and such characters are attractive to others in proportion as these last are gifted with the imagination which loves to divine the unknown.

At the first interview, the impression which this man produced upon Nora Avenel was profound and strange. She had heard of him before as the one whom Harley most loved and looked up to; and she recognised at once in his mien, his aspect, his words, the very tone of his deep tranquil voice, the power to which woman, whatever her intellect, never attains; and to which, therefore, she imputes a nobility not always genuine—viz., the power of deliberate purpose, and self-collected, serene ambition. The effect that Nora produced on Egerton was not less sudden. He was startled by a beauty of face and form that belonged to that rarest order, which we never behold but once or twice in our lives. He was yet more amazed to discover that the aristocracy of mind would bestow a grace that no aristocracy of birth could surpass. He was prepared for a simple, blushing village girl, and involuntarily he bowed low his proud front at the first sight of that delicate bloom, and that exquisite gentleness which is woman's surest passport to the respect of man. Neither in the first, nor the second, nor the third interview, nor, indeed, till after many interviews, could he summon up courage to commence his mission, and allude to Harley. And when he did so at last his words faltered. But Nora's words were clear to him. He saw that Harley was not loved; and a joy, which he felt as guilty, darted through his whole frame. From that interview Audley returned home greatly agitated, and at war with himself. Often, in the course of this story, has it been hinted that, under all

Egerton's external coldness, and measured self-control, lay a nature capable of strong and stubborn passions. Those passions broke forth then. He felt that love had already entered into the heart, which the trust of his friend should have sufficed to guard.

"I will go there no more," said he, abruptly, to Harley.

"But why?"

"The girl does not love you. Cease then to think of her."

Harley disbelieved him, and grew indignant. But Audley had every worldly motive to assist his sense of honour. He was poor, though with the reputation of wealth—deeply involved in debt—resolved to rise in life—tenacious of his position in the world's esteem. Against a host of counteracting influences, love fought single-handed. Audley's was a strong nature; but, alas! in strong natures, if resistance to temptation is of granite, so the passions that they admit are of fire.

Trite is the remark, that the destinies of our lives often date from the impulses of unguarded moments. It was so with this man, to an ordinary eye so cautious and so deliberate. Harley one day came to him in great grief; he had heard that Nora was ill: he implored Audley to go once more and ascertain. Audley went. Lady Jane Horton, who was suffering under a disease which not long afterwards proved fatal, was too ill to receive him. He was shown into the room set apart as Nora's. While waiting for her entrance, he turned mechanically over the leaves of an album which Nora, suddenly summoned away to attend Lady Jane, had left behind her on the table. He saw the sketch of his own features; he read words inscribed below it—words of such artless tenderness, and such unhoping sorrow—words written by one who had been accustomed to regard her genius as her sole confidant, under Heaven; to pour out to it, as the solitary poet-heart is impelled to do, thoughts, feelings, the confession of mystic sighs, which it would never breathe to a living ear, and, save at such moments, scarcely acknowledge to itself. Audley saw that he was beloved, and the revelation, with a sudden light, consumed all the barriers between himself and his own love. And at that moment Nora entered. She saw him bending over the book. She uttered a cry—sprang forward—and then sank down, covering her face with her hands. But Audley was at her feet. He forgot his friend—his trust; he forgot ambition—he forgot the world. It was his own cause that he pleaded—his own love that burst forth from his lips. And when the two that day parted, they were betrothed each to each. Alas for them, and alas for Harley!

And now this man, who had hitherto valued himself as the very type of gentleman—whom all his young contemporaries had so regarded and so revered—had to press the hand of a confiding friend, and bid adieu to truth. He had to amuse, to delay, to mislead his boy-rival—to say that he was already subduing Nora's hesitating doubts—and that with a little time, she could be induced to consent to forget Harley's rank, and his parent's pride, and become his wife. And Harley believed in Egerton, without one suspicion on the mirror of his loyal soul.

Meanwhile, Audley, impatient of his own position—impatient, as strong minds ever are, to hasten what they have once resolved—to terminate a suspense that every interview with Harley tortured alike by jealousy and shame—to pass out of the reach of scruples, and to say to himself, "Right or wrong, there is no looking back; the deed is done;"—Audley, thus hurried on by the impetus of his own power of will, pressed for speedy and secret nuptials—secret, till his fortunes, then wavering, were more assured—his career fairly commenced. This was not his strongest motive, though it was one. He shrank from the discovery of his wrong to his friend—desired to delay the self-humiliation of such announcement, until, as he persuaded himself, Harley's boyish passion was over—had yielded to the new allurements that would naturally beset his way. Stifling his conscience, Audley sought to convince himself that the day would soon come when Harley could hear with indifference that Nora Avenel was another's. "The dream of an hour, at his age," murmured the elder friend; "but at mine the passion of a life!" He did not speak of these latter motives for concealment to Nora. He felt that, to own the extent of his treason to a friend, would lower him in her eyes. He spoke therefore but slightingly of Harley— treated the boy's suit as a thing past and gone. He dwelt only on reasons that compelled self-sacrifice on his side or hers. She did not hesitate which to choose. And so, where Nora loved, so submissively did she believe in the superiority of the lover, that she would not pause to hear a murmur from her own loftier nature, or question the propriety of what he deemed wise and good.

Abandoning prudence in this arch affair of life, Audley still preserved his customary caution in minor details. And this indeed was characteristic of him throughout all his career—

heedless in large things—wary in small. He would not trust Lady Jane Horton with his secret, still less Lady Lansmere. He simply represented to the former, that Nora was no longer safe from Harley's determined pursuit under Lady Jane's roof, and that she had better elude the boy's knowledge of her movements, and go quietly away for a while, to lodge with some connection of her own.

And so, with Lady Jane's acquiescence, Nora went first to the house of a very distant kinswoman of her mother's, and afterwards to one that Egerton took as their bridal home, under the name of Bertram. He arranged all that might render their marriage most free from the chance of premature discovery. But it so happened on the very morning of their bridal, that one of the witnesses he selected (a confidential servant of his own) was seized with apoplexy. Considering, in haste, where to find a substitute, Egerton thought of Levy, his own private solicitor, his own fashionable moneylender, a man with whom he was then as intimate as a fine gentleman is with the lawyer of his own age, who knows all his affairs, and has helped, from pure friendship, to make them as bad as they are! Levy was thus suddenly summoned. Egerton, who was in great haste, did not at first communicate to him the name of the intended bride; but he said enough of the imprudence of the marriage, and his reasons for secresy, to bring on himself the strongest remonstrances; for Levy had always reckoned on Egerton's making a wealthy marriage,—leaving to Egerton the wife, and hoping to appropriate to himself the wealth, all in the natural course of business. Egerton did not listen to him, but hurried him on towards the place at which the ceremony was to be performed; and Levy actually saw the bride before he had learned her name. The usurer masked his raging emotions, and fulfilled his part in the rites. His smile, when he congratulated the bride, might have shot cold into her heart; but her eyes were cast on the earth, seeing there but a shadow from heaven, and her heart was blindly sheltering itself in the bosom to which it was given evermore. She did not perceive the smile of hate that barbed the words of joy. Nora never thought it necessary later to tell Egerton that Levy had been a refused suitor. Indeed, with the exquisite tact of love, she saw that such a confidence, the idea of such a rival, would have wounded the pride of her high-bred, well-born husband.

And now, while Harley L'Estrange, frantic with the news that Nora had left Lady Jane's roof, and purposely misled

into wrong directions, was seeking to trace her refuge in vain
—now Egerton, in an assumed name, in a remote quarter, far
from the clubs, in which his word was oracular—far from
the pursuits, whether of pastime or toil, that had hitherto
engrossed his active mind, gave himself up, with wonder at
his own surrender, to the only vision of fairyland that ever
weighs down the watchful eyelids of hard ambition. The
world for a while shut out, he missed it not. He knew not
of it. He looked into two loving eyes that haunted him ever
after, through a stern and arid existence, and said, murmuringly, "Why, this, then is real happiness!" Often, often, in
the solitude of other years, to repeat to himself the same
words, save that for *is*, he then murmured *was!* And Nora,
with her grand, full heart, all her luxuriant wealth of fancy
and of thought, child of light and of song, did she then never
discover that there was something comparatively narrow and
sterile in the nature to which she had linked her fate? Not
there, could ever be sympathy in feelings, brilliant and shift-
ing as the tints of the rainbow. When Audley pressed her
heart to his own, could he comprehend one finer throb of its
beating? Was all the iron of his mind worth one grain of
the gold she had cast away in Harley's love?

Did Nora already discover this? Surely no. Genius feels
no want, no repining, while the heart is contented. Genius
in her paused and slumbered: it had been as the ministrant
of solitude: it was needed no more. If a woman loves
deeply some one below her own grade in the mental and
spiritual orders, how often we see that she unconsciously
quits her own rank, comes meekly down to the level of the
beloved, is afraid lest he should deem her the superior—she
who would not even be the equal. Nora knew no more that
she had genius; she only knew that she had love.

And so here, the journal which Leonard was reading,
changed its tone, sinking into that quiet happiness which is
but quiet because it is so deep. This interlude in the life of a
man like Audley Egerton could never have been long; many
circumstances conspired to abridge it. His affairs were in
great disorder; they were all under Levy's management.
Demands that had before slumbered, or been mildly urged,
grew menacing and clamorous. Harley, too, returned to
London from his futile researches, and looked out for Audley.
Audley was forced to leave his secret Eden, and re-appear in
the common world; and thenceforward it was only by stealth
that he came to his bridal home—a visitor, no more the

inmate. But more loud and fierce grew the demands of his creditors, now when Egerton had most need of all which respectability, and position, and belief of pecuniary independence can do to raise the man who has encumbered his arms, and crippled his steps towards fortune. He was threatened with writs, with prison. Levy said "that to borrow more would be but larger ruin"—shrugged his shoulders, and even recommended a voluntary retreat to the King's Bench. "No place so good for frightening one's creditors into compounding their claims; but why," added Levy, with covert sneer, "why not go to young L'Estrange—a boy made to be borrowed from!"

Levy, who had known from Lady Jane of Harley's pursuit of Nora, had learned already how to avenge himself on Egerton. Audley could not apply to the friend he had betrayed. And as to other friends, no man in town had a greater number. And no man in town knew better that he should lose them all if he were once known to be in want of their money. Mortified, harassed, tortured—shunning Harley—yet ever sought by him—fearful of each knock at his door, Audley Egerton escaped to the mortgaged remnant of his paternal estate, on which there was a gloomy manor-house, long uninhabited, and there applied a mind, afterwards renowned for its quick comprehension of business, to the investigation of his affairs, with a view to save some wreck from the flood that swelled momently around him.

And now—to condense as much as possible a record that runs darkly on into pain and sorrow—now Levy began to practise his vindictive arts; and the arts gradually prevailed. On pretence of assisting Egerton in the arrangement of his affairs—which he secretly contrived, however, still more to complicate—he came down frequently to Egerton Hall for a few hours, arriving by the mail, and watching the effect which Nora's almost daily letters produced on the bridegroom, irritated by the practical cares of life. He was thus constantly at hand to instil into the mind of the ambitious man a regret for the imprudence of hasty passion, or to embitter the remorse which Audley felt for his treachery to L'Estrange. Thus ever bringing before the mind of the harassed debtor images at war with love, and with the poetry of life, he disattuned it (so to speak) for the reception of Nora's letters, all musical as they were with such thoughts as the most delicate fancy inspires to the most earnest love. Egerton was one of those men who never confide their affairs frankly to women. Nora, when she thus wrote, was wholly in the dark as to the extent of his stern prosaic distress. And so—and so—Levy always near—(type of the prose of life in its most cynic form)—so by degrees, all that redundant affluence of affection, with its gushes of grief for his absence, prayers for his return, sweet reproach if a post failed to bring back an answer to the woman's yearning sighs—all this grew, to the sensible, positive man of real life, like sickly romantic exaggeration. The bright arrows shot too high into heaven to hit the mark set so near to the earth. Ah! common fate of all superior natures! What treasure, and how wildly wasted!

"By-the-by," said Levy one morning, as he was about to take leave of Audley and return to town—"by-the-by, I shall be this evening in the neighbourhood of Mrs. Egerton."

EGERTON.—" Say Mrs. Bertram! "

LEVY.—"Ay; will she not be in want of some pecuniary supplies?"

EGERTON.—" My wife!—Not yet. I must first be wholly ruined before she can want; and if I were so, do you think I should not be by her side?"

LEVY.—" I beg pardon, my dear fellow; your pride of gentleman is so susceptible that it is hard for a lawyer not to wound it unawares. Your wife, then, does not know the exact state of your affairs?"

EGERTON.—" Of course not. Who would confide to a woman things in which she could do nothing, except to tease one the more?"

LEVY.—" True, and a poetess too! I have prevented your finishing your answer to Mrs. Bertram's last letter. Can I take it—it may save a day's delay—that is, if you do not object to my calling on her this evening."

EGERTON, (sitting down to his unfinished letter.)—"Object! no."

LEVY, (looking at his watch.)—" Be quick, or I shall lose the coach."

EGERTON, (sealing the letter.)—" There. And I should be obliged to you if you *would* call; and, without alarming her as to my circumstances, you can just say that you know I am much harassed about important affairs at present, and so soothe the effects of my very short answers—"

LEVY.—" To those doubly-crossed, very long letters—I will."

"Poor Nora," said Egerton, sighing, "she will think this answer brief and churlish enough. Explain my excuses kindly, so that they will serve for the future. I really have no time, and no heart for sentiment. The little I ever had is well-nigh worried out of me. Still I love her fondly and deeply."

LEVY.—"You must have done so. I never thought it in you to sacrifice the world to a woman."

EGERTON.—"Nor I either; but," added the strong man, conscious of that power which rules the world infinitely more than knowledge—conscious of tranquil courage—"but I have not sacrificed the world yet. This right arm shall bear up her and myself too."

LEVY.—"Well said! but in the meanwhile, for heaven's sake, don't attempt to go to London, nor to leave this place; for, in that case, I know you will be arrested, and then adieu to all hopes of Parliament—of a career."

Audley's haughty countenance darkened; as the dog, in his bravest mood, turns dismayed from the stone plucked from the mire, so, when Ambition rears itself to defy mankind, whisper "disgrace and a gaol,"—and, lo, crestfallen, it slinks away! That evening Levy called on Nora, and ingratiating himself into her favour by praise of Egerton, with indirect humble apologetic allusions to his own former presumption, he prepared the way to renewed visits;—she was so lonely, and she so loved to see one who was fresh from seeing Audley—one who would talk to her of *him!* By degrees the friendly respectful visitor thus stole into her confidence; and then, with all his panegyrics on Audley's superior powers and gifts, he began to dwell upon the young husband's worldly aspirations, and care for his career; dwell on them so as vaguely to alarm Nora—to imply that, dear as she was, she was still but second to Ambition. His way thus prepared, he next began to insinuate his respectful pity at her equivocal position, dropped hints of gossip and slander, feared that the marriage might be owned too late to preserve reputation. And then what would be the feelings of the proud Egerton if his wife were excluded from that world, whose opinion he so prized? Insensibly thus he led her on to express (though timidly) her own fear—her own natural desire, in her letters to Audley. When could the marriage be proclaimed? Proclaimed! Audley felt that to proclaim such a marriage, at such a moment, would be to fling away his last cast for fame and fortune. And Harley, too—Harley still so uncured of his frantic love! Levy was sure to be at hand when letters like these arrived.

And now Levy went further still in his determination to alienate these two hearts. He contrived, by means of his various agents, to circulate through Nora's neighbourhood the very slanders at which he had hinted. He contrived that she should be insulted when she went abroad, outraged at home by the sneers of her own servant, and tremble with shame at her own shadow upon her abandoned bridal hearth.

Just in the midst of this intolerable anguish, Levy reappeared. His crowning hour was ripe. He intimated his knowledge of the humiliations Nora had undergone, expressed his deep compassion, offered to intercede with Egerton "to do her justice." He used ambiguous phrases, that shocked her ear and tortured her heart, and thus provoked her on to demand him to explain; and then, throwing her into a wild state of indefinite alarm, in which he obtained her solemn promise not to divulge to Audley what he was about to communicate, he said, with villanous hypocrisy of reluctant shame, "that her marriage was not strictly legal; that the forms required by the law had not been complied with; that Audley, unintentionally or purposely, had left himself free to disown the rite and desert the bride." While Nora stood stunned and speechless at a falsehood which, with lawyer-like show, he contrived to make truth-like to her inexperience, he hurried rapidly on, to re-awake on her mind the impression of Audley's pride, ambition, and respect for worldly position. "These are your obstacles," said he; "but I think I may induce him to repair the wrong, and right you at last." Righted at last—oh infamy!

Then Nora's anger burst forth. She believe such a stain on Audley's honour!

"But where was the honour when he betrayed his friend? Did you not know that he was entrusted by Lord L'Estrange to plead for him. How did he fulfil the trust?"

Plead for L'Estrange; Nora had not been exactly aware of this. In the sudden love preceding those sudden nuptials, so little touching Harley (beyond Audley's first timid allusions to his suit, and her calm and cold reply) had been spoken by either.

Levy resumed. He dwelt fully on the trust and the breach of it, and then said—"In Egerton's world, man holds it far more dishonour to betray a man than to dupe a woman; and if Egerton could do the one, why doubt that he would do the other? But do not look at me with those indignant eyes.

Put himself to the test; write to him to say that the suspicions amidst which you live have become intolerable—that they infect even yourself, despite your reason—that the secrecy of your nuptials, his prolonged absence, his brief refusal, on unsatisfactory grounds, to proclaim your tie, all distract you with a terrible doubt. Ask him, at least, (if he will not yet declare your marriage,) to satisfy you that the rites were legal."

"I will go to him," cried Nora, impetuously.

"Go to him!—in his own house! What a scene, what a scandal! Could he ever forgive you?"

"At least, then, I will implore him to come here. I cannot write such horrible words; I cannot—I cannot—Go, go."

Levy left her, and hastened to two or three of Audley's most pressing creditors—men, in fact, who went entirely by Levy's own advice. He bade them instantly surround Audley's country residence with bailiffs. Before Egerton could reach Nora, he would thus be lodged in a gaol. These preparations made, Levy himself went down to Audley, and arrived, as usual, an hour or two before the delivery of the post.

And Nora's letter came; and never was Audley's grave brow more dark than when he read it. Still, with his usual decision, he resolved to obey her wish—rang the bell, and ordered his servant to put up a change of dress, and send for post-horses.

Levy then took him aside, and led him to the window.

"Look under yon trees. Do you see those men? They are bailiffs. This is the true reason why I come to you to-day. You cannot leave this house."

Egerton recoiled. "And this frantic, foolish letter at such a time," he muttered, striking the open page, full of love in the midst of terror, with his clenched hand.

O Woman, Woman! if thy heart be deep, and its chords tender, beware how thou lovest the man with whom all that plucks him from the hard cares of the work-day world is a frenzy or a folly! He will break thy heart, he will shatter its chords, he will trample out from its delicate framework every sound that now makes musical the common air, and swells into unison with the harps of angels.

"She has before written to me," continued Audley, pacing the room with angry, disordered strides, "asking me when our marriage can be proclaimed, and I thought my replies would have satisfied any reasonable woman. But now, now this is worse, immeasurably worse—she actually doubts my honour! I, who have made such sacrifices—actually doubts whether I, Audley Egerton, an English gentleman, could have been base enough to—"

"What?" interrupted Levy, "to deceive your friend L'Estrange? Did not she know *that* ?"

"Sir," exclaimed Egerton, turning white.

"Don't be angry—all's fair in love as in war; and L'Estrange will live yet to thank you for saving him from such a *mésalliance*. But you are seriously angry: pray, forgive me."

With some difficulty, and much fawning, the usurer appeased the storm he had raised in Audley's conscience. And he then heard, as if with surprise, the true purport of Nora's letter.

"It is beneath me to answer, much less to satisfy, such a doubt," said Audley. "I could have seen her, and a look of reproach would have sufficed; but to put my hand to paper, and condescend to write, 'I am not a villain, and I will give you the proofs that I am not,'—never."

"You are quite right; but let us see if we cannot reconcile matters between your pride and her feelings. Write simply this:—'All that you ask me to say or to explain, I have instructed Levy, as my solicitor, to say and explain for me; and you may believe him as you would myself.'"

"Well, the poor fool, she deserves to be punished; and I suppose that answer will punish her more than a lengthier rebuke. My mind is so distracted, I cannot judge of these trumpery woman-fears and whims; there, I have written as you suggest. Give her all the proof she needs, and tell her that in six months at farthest, come what will, she shall bear the name of Egerton, as henceforth she must share his fate."

"Why say six months?"

"Parliament must be dissolved, and there must be a general election before then. I shall either obtain a seat, be secure from a gaol, have won field for my energies, or—"

"Or what?"

"I shall renounce ambition altogether—ask my brother to assist me towards whatever debts remain when all my property is fairly sold—they cannot be much. He has a living in his gift—the incumbent is old, and, I hear, very ill. I can take orders."

"Sink into a country parson!"

"And learn content. I have tasted it already. She was *then* by my side. Explain all to her. This letter, I fear is too unkind—But to doubt me thus!"

Levy hastily placed the letter in his pocket-book; and, for fear it should be withdrawn, took his leave.

And of that letter he made such use, that the day after he had given it to Nora, she had left the house—the neighbourhood; fled, and not a trace! Of all the agonies in life, that which is most poignant and harrowing—that which for the time most annihilates reason, and leaves our whole organization one lacerated, mangled *heart*—is the conviction that we have been deceived where we placed all the trust of love. The moment the anchor snaps, the storm comes on—the stars vanish behind the cloud.

When Levy returned, filled with the infamous hope which had stimulated his revenge—the hope that if he could succeed in changing into scorn and indignation Nora's love for Audley, he might succeed also in replacing that broken and degraded idol—his amaze and dismay were great on hearing of her departure. For several days he sought her traces in vain. He went to Lady Jane Horton's—Nora had not been there. He trembled to go back to Egerton. Surely Nora would have written to her husband, and, in spite of her promise, revealed his own falsehood; but as days passed and not a clue was found, he had no option but to repair to Egerton Hall, taking care that the bailiffs still surrounded it. Audley had received no line from Nora. The young husband was surprised, perplexed, uneasy—but had no suspicion of the truth.

At length Levy was forced to break to Audley the intelligence of Nora's flight. He gave his own colour to it. Doubtless she had gone to seek her own relations, and, by their advice, take steps to make her marriage publicly known. This idea changed Audley's first shock into deep and stern resentment. His mind so little comprehended Nora's, and was ever so disposed to what is called the common-sense view of things, that he saw no other mode to account for her flight and her silence. Odious to Egerton as such a proceeding would be, he was far too proud to take any steps to guard against it. "Let her do her worst," said he, coldly, masking emotion with his usual self-command; "it will be but a nine days' wonder to the world—a fiercer rush of my creditors on their hunted prey—"

"And a challenge from Lord L'Estrange."

"So be it," answered Egerton, suddenly placing his hand at his heart.

"What is the matter? Are you ill?"

"A strange sensation here. My father died of a complaint of the heart, and I myself was once told to guard, through life, against excess of emotion. I smiled at such a warning then. Let us sit down to business."

But when Levy had gone, and solitude reclosed round that Man of the Iron Mask, there grew upon him more and more the sense of a mighty loss. Nora's sweet loving face started from the shadows of the forlorn walls. Her docile, yielding temper—her generous, self-immolating spirit—came back to his memory, to refute the idea that wronged her. His love, that had been suspended for awhile by busy cares, but which, if without much refining sentiment, was still the master passion of his soul, flowed back into all his thoughts—circumfused the very atmosphere with a fearful, softening charm. He escaped under cover of the night from the watch of the bailiffs. He arrived in London. He himself sought everywhere he could think of for his missing bride. Lady Jane Horton was confined to her bed, dying fast—incapable even to receive and reply to his letter. He secretly sent down to Lansmere to ascertain if Nora had gone to her parents. She was not there. The Avenels believed her still with Lady Jane Horton.

He now grew most seriously alarmed; and in the midst of that alarm, Levy secretly contrived that he should be arrested for debt; but he was not detained in confinement many days. Before the disgrace got wind, the writs were discharged—Levy baffled. He was free. Lord L'Estrange had learned from Audley's servant what Audley would have concealed from him out of all the world. And the generous boy, who, besides the munificent allowance he received from the Earl, was heir to an independent and considerable fortune of his own, when he should attain his majority—hastened to borrow the money and discharge all the obligations of his friend. The benefit was conferred before Audley knew of it, or could prevent. Then a new emotion, and perhaps scarce less stinging than the loss of Nora, tortured the man who had smiled at the warning of science; and the strange sensation at the heart was felt again and again.

And Harley, too, was still in search of Nora—would talk of nothing but her—and looked so haggard and grief-worn. The bloom of the boy's youth was gone. Could Audley then have said, " She you seek is another's; your love is razed out of your life; and, for consolation, learn that your friend has betrayed you?" Could Audley say this? He did not dare. Which of the two suffered the most?

And these two friends, of characters so different, were so singularly attached to each other. Inseparable at school— thrown together in the world, with a wealth of frank confidences between them, accumulated since childhood. And now, in the midst of all his own anxious sorrow, Harley still thought and planned for Egerton. And self-accusing remorse, and all the sense of painful gratitude, deepened Audley's affection for Harley into a devotion as to a superior, while softening it into a reverential pity that yearned to relieve, to atone;—but how—oh, how?

A general election was now at hand, still no news of Nora. Levy kept aloof from Audley, pursuing his own silent search. A seat for the borough of Lansmere was pressed upon Audley, not only by Harley, but his parents especially by the Countess, who tacitly ascribed to Audley's wise counsels Nora's mysterious disappearance.

Egerton at first resisted the thought of a new obligation to his injured friend; but he burned to have it, some day, in his power to repay at least his pecuniary debt: the sense of that debt humbled him more than all else. Parliamentary success might at last obtain for him some lucrative situation abroad, and thus enable him gradually to remove this load from his heart and his honour. No other chance of repayment appeared open to him. He accepted the offer, and went down to Lansmere. His brother, lately married, was asked to meet him; and there, also, was Miss Leslie the heiress, whom Lady Lansmere secretly hoped her son Harley would admire, but who had long since, no less secretly, given her heart to the unconscious Egerton.

Meanwhile, the miserable Nora, deceived by the arts and representations of Levy—acting on the natural impulse of a heart so susceptible to shame—flying from a home which she deemed dishonoured—flying from a lover whose power over her she knew to be so great, that she dreaded lest he might reconcile her to dishonour itself—had no thought save to hide herself for ever from Audley's eye. She would not go to her relations—to Lady Jane; that were to give the clue, and invite the pursuit. An Italian lady of high rank had visited at Lady Jane's—taken a great fancy to Nora—and the lady's husband, having been obliged to precede her return to Italy, had suggested the notion of engaging some companion—the lady had spoken of this to Nora and to Lady Lane Horton, who had urged Nora to accept the offer, elude Harley's pursuit, and go abroad for a time Nora then had refused; for she then had seen Audley Egerton.

To this Italian lady she now went, and the offer was renewed with the most winning kindness, and grasped at in the passion of despair. But the Italian had accepted invitations to English country houses before she finally departed for the Continent. Meanwhile Nora took refuge in a quiet lodging in a sequestered suburb, which an English servant in the employment of the fair foreigner recommended. Thus had she first come to the cottage in which Burley died. Shortly afterwards she left England with her new companion, unknown to all—to Lady Jane as to her parents.

All this time the poor girl was under a moral delirium—a confused fever—haunted by dreams from which she sought to fly. Sound physiologists agree that madness is rarest amongst persons of the finest imagination. But those persons are, of all others, liable to a temporary state of mind in which judgment sleeps—imagination alone prevails with a dire and awful tyranny. A single idea gains ascendancy—expels all others—presents itself everywhere with an intolerable blinding glare. Nora was at that time under the dread one idea—to fly from shame!

But, when the seas rolled, and the dreary leagues interposed, between her and her lover—when new images presented themselves — when the fever slaked, and reason returned—doubt broke upon the previous despair. Had she not been too credulous, too hasty? Fool, fool! Audley have been so poor a traitor! How guilty was she, if she had wronged him! And in the midst of this revulsion of feeling, there stirred within her another life. She was destined to become a mother. At that thought her high nature bowed; the last struggle of pride gave way; she would return to England, see Audley, learn from his lips the truth, and even if the truth were what she had been taught to believe, plead not for herself, but for the false one's child.

Some delay occurred in the then warlike state of affairs on the Continent, before she could put this purpose into execution; and on her journey back, various obstructions lengthened the way. But she returned at last, and resought the suburban cottage in which she had last lodged before quitting England. At night, she went to Audley's London house;

there was only a woman in charge of it. Mr. Egerton was absent — electioneering somewhere — Mr. Levy, his lawyer, called every day for any letters to be forwarded to him. Nora shrank from seeing Levy, shrank from writing even a letter that would pass through his hands. If she had been deceived, it had been by him, and wilfully. But Parliament was already dissolved; the election would soon be over, Mr Egerton was expected to return to town within a week. Nora went back to Mrs. Goodyer's and resolved to wait, devouring her own heart in silence. But the newspapers might inform her where Audley really was; the newspapers were sent for and conned daily.

And one morning this paragraph met her eye:—

"The Earl and Countess of Lansmere are receiving a distinguished party at their country seat. Among the guests is Miss Leslie, whose wealth and beauty have excited such sensation in the fashionable world. To the disappointment of numerous aspirants amongst our aristocracy, we hear that this lady has, however, made her distinguished choice in Mr. Audley Egerton. That gentleman is now a candidate for the borough of Lansmere, as a supporter of the Government; his success is considered certain, and, according to the report of a large circle of friends, few new members will prove so valuable an addition to the Ministerial ranks; a great career may indeed be predicted for a young man so esteemed for talent and character, aided by a fortune so immense as that which he will shortly receive with the hand of the accomplished heiress."

Again the anchor snapt—again the storm descended— again the stars vanished. Nora was now once more under the dominion of a single thought, as she had been when she fled from her bridal home. Then, it was to escape from her lover—now, it was to see him. As the victim stretched on the rack implores to be led at once to death, so there are moments when the annihilation of hope seems more merciful than the torment of suspense.

## CHAPTER XVII.

WHEN the scenes in some long diorama pass solemnly before us, there is sometimes one solitary object, contrasting, perhaps, the view of stately cities or the march of a mighty river, that halts on the eye for a moment, and then glides away, leaving on the mind a strange, comfortless, undefined impression.

Why was the object presented to us? In itself it seemed comparatively insignificant. It may have been but a broken column—a lonely pool with a star-beam on its quiet surface—yet it awes us. We remember it when phantasmal pictures of bright Damascus, or of colossal pyramids—of bazaars in Stamboul, or lengthened caravans that defile slow amidst the sands of Araby—have sated the wondering gaze. Why were we detained in the shadowy procession by a thing that would have been so commonplace had it not been so lone? Some latent interest must attach to it. Was it there that a vision of woe had lifted the wild hair of a Prophet?—there where some Hagar had stilled the wail of her child on her indignant breast? We would fain call back the pageantry procession—fain see again the solitary thing that seemed so little worth the hand of the artist—and ask, "Why art thou here, and wherefore dost thou haunt us?"

Rise up—rise up once more—by the broad great thoroughfare that stretches onward and onward to the remorseless London—Rise up—rise up—O solitary tree with the green leaves on thy bough, and the deep rents in thy heart; and the ravens, dark birds of omen and sorrow, that build their nest amidst the leaves of the bough, and drop with noiseless plumes down through the hollow rents of the heart—or are heard, it may be in the growing shadows of twilight, calling out to their young!

Under the old pollard tree, by the side of John Avenel's house, there cowered, breathless and listening, John Avenel's daughter Nora. Now, when that fatal newspaper paragraph, which lied so like truth, met her eyes, she obeyed the first impulse of her passionate heart—she tore the wedding ring from her finger—she enclosed it, with the paragraph itself, in a letter to Audley—a letter that she designed to convey scorn and pride—alas! it expressed only jealousy and love. She could not rest till she had put this letter into the post with her own hand, addressed to Audley at Lord Lansmere's. Scarce had it left her ere she repented. What had she done?—resigned the birth-right of the child she was so soon to bring into the world—resigned her last hope in her lover's honour—given up her life of life—and from belief in what?—a report in a newspaper! No, no; she would go herself to Lansmere; to her father's home—she could contrive to see Audley before that letter reached his hand. The thought was scarcely conceived before obeyed. She found a vacant place in a coach that started from London some hours before the mail, and went within a few miles of Lansmere; those last miles she travelled on foot. Exhausted—fainting—she gained at last the sight of home, and there halted, for in the little garden in front she saw her parents seated. She heard the murmur of their voices, and suddenly she remembered her altered shape, her terrible secret. How answer the question, "Daughter, where and who is thy husband?" Her heart failed her; she crept under the old pollard tree, to gather up resolve, to watch and to listen. She saw the rigid face of the thrifty prudent mother, with the deep lines that told of the cares of an anxious life, and the chafe of excitable temper and warm affections against the restraint of decorous sanctimony and resolute pride. The dear stern face never seemed to her more dear and more stern. She saw the comely, easy, indolent, good-humoured father; not then the poor, paralytic sufferer, who could yet recognise Nora's eyes under the lids of Leonard, but stalwart and jovial—first bat in the Cricket Club, first voice in the Glee Society, the most popular canvasser of the Lansmere Constitutional True Blue Party, and the pride and idol of the Calvinistical prim wife; never from those pinched lips of hers had come forth even one pious rebuke to the careless social man. As he sate, one hand in his vest, his profile turned to the road, the light smoke curling playfully up from the pipe, over which lips, accustomed to bland smile and hearty laughter, closed as if reluctant to be closed at all, he was the very model of the respectable retired trader in easy circumstances, and released from the toil of making money while life could yet enjoy the delight of spending it.

"Well, old woman," said John Avenel, "I must be off presently to see to those three shaky voters in Fish Lane; they will have done their work soon, and I shall catch 'em at home. They do say as how we may have an opposition; and I know that old Smikes has gone to Lonnon in search of a candidate. We can't have the Lansmere Constitutional Blues beat by a Lonnoner! Ha, ha, ha!"

"But you will be home before Jane and her husband Mark come? How ever she could marry a common carpenter!"

"Yes," said John, "he *is* a carpenter; but he has a vote, and that strengthens the family interest. If Dick was not gone to Amerikay, there would be three on us. But Mark is a real good Blue! A Lonnoner, indeed!—a Yellow from Lonnon beat my Lord and the Blues! Ha, ha!"

"But, John, this Mr. Egerton is a Lonnoner!"

"You don't understand things, talking such nonsense. Mr. Egerton is the Blue candidate, and the Blues are the Country Party; therefore how can he be a Lonnoner? An uncommon clever, well-grown, handsome young man, eh! and my young lord's particular friend."

Mrs. Avenel sighed.

"What are you sighing and shaking your head for?"

"I was thinking of our poor, dear, dear Nora!"

"God bless her!" cried John, heartily.

There was a rustle under the boughs of the old hollow-hearted pollard tree.

"Ha! ha! Hark! I said that so loud that I have startled the ravens!"

"How he did love her!" said Mrs. Avenel, thoughtfully. "I am sure he did; and no wonder, for she looks every inch a lady; and why should not she be my lady, after all?"

"He? Who? Oh, that foolish fancy of yours about my young lord? A prudent woman like you!—stuff! I am glad my little beauty is gone to Lonnon, out of harm's way."

"John—John—John! No harm could ever come to my Nora. She's too pure and too good, and has too proper a pride in her, to—"

"To listen to any young lords, I hope," said John; "though," he added, after a pause, "she might well be a lady too. My lord, the young one, took me by the hand so kindly the other day, and said, 'Have not you heard from her—I mean Miss Avenel—lately?' and those bright eyes of his were as full of tears as—as—as yours are now."

"Well, John, well; go on."

"That is all. My lady came up, and took me away to talk about the election; and, just as I was going, she whispered, 'Don't let my wild boy talk to you about that sweet girl of yours. We must both see that she does not come to disgrace.' 'Disgrace!' that word made me very angry for the moment. But my lady has such a way with her, that she soon put me right again. Yet, I do think Nora must have loved my young lord, only she was too good to show it. What do you say?" And the father's voice was thoughtful.

"I hope she'll never love any man till she's married to him; it is not proper, John," said Mrs. Avenel, somewhat starchly, though very mildly.

"Ha! ha!" laughed John, chucking his prim wife under the chin, "you did not say that to me when I stole your first kiss under that very pollard tree—no house near it then!"

"Hush, John, hush!" and the prim wife blushed like a girl.

"Pooh," continued John, merrily, "I don't see why we plain folks should pretend to be more saintly and prudish like than our betters. There's that handsome Miss Leslie, who is to marry Mr. Egerton—easy enough to see how much she is in love with him—could not keep her eyes off from him even in church, old girl? Ha, ha! What the deuce is the matter with the ravens?"

"They'll be a comely couple, John. And I hear tell she has a power of money. When is the marriage to be?"

"Oh, they say as soon as the election is over. A fine wedding we shall have of it! I daresay my young lord will be bridesman. We'll send for our little Nora to see the gay doings!"

Out from the boughs of the old tree came the shriek of a lost spirit—one of those strange, appalling sounds of human agony, which, once heard, are never forgotten. It is as the wail of Hope, when SHE, too, rushes forth from the Coffer of Woes, and vanishes into viewless space; it is the dread cry of Reason parting from clay—and of Soul, that would wrench itself from life! For a moment all was still—and then a dull, dumb, heavy fall!

The parents gazed on each other, speechless: they stole close to the pales, and looked over. Under the boughs, at the gnarled roots of the oak, they saw—grey and indistinct—a prostrate form. John opened the gate, and went round; the mother crept to the road side, and there stood still.

"Oh, wife, wife!" cried John Avenel, from under the green boughs, "it is our child Nora! Our child—our child!"

And, as he spoke, out from the green boughs started the dark ravens, wheeling round and round, and calling to their young!

\* \* \* \* \*
\* \* \* \* \*

And when they had laid her on the bed, Mrs. Avenel whispered John to withdraw for a moment; and, with set lips but trembling hands, began to unlace the dress, under the pressure of which Nora's heart heaved convulsively. And John went out of the room bewildered, and sate himself down on the landing-place, and wondered whether he was awake or sleeping; and a cold numbness crept over one side of him, and his head felt very heavy, with a loud, booming noise in his ears. Suddenly his wife stood by his side, and said, in a very low voice—

"John, run for Mr. Morgan—make haste. But mind—don't speak to any one on the way. Quick, quick!"

"Is she dying?"

"I don't know. Why not die before?" said Mrs. Avenel, between her teeth. "But Mr. Morgan is a discreet, friendly man."

"A true blue!" muttered poor John, as if his mind wandered; and rising with difficulty, he stared at his wife a moment, shook his head, and was gone.

An hour or two later, a little covered, taxed cart stopped at Mr. Avenel's cottage, out of which stepped a young man with pale face and spare form, dressed in the Sunday suit of a rustic craftsman; then a homely, but pleasant, honest, face, bent down to him, smilingly; and two arms emerging from under covert of a red cloak, extended an infant, which the young man took tenderly. The baby was cross and very sickly; it began to cry. The father hushed, and rocked, and tossed it, with the air of one to whom such a charge was familiar.

"He'll be good when we get in, Mark," said the young woman, as she extracted from the depths of the cart a large basket containing poultry and home-made bread.

"Don't forget the flowers that the Squire's gardener gave us," said Mark the Poet.

Without aid from her husband, the wife took down basket and nosegay, settled her cloak, smoothed her gown, and said, "Very odd!—they don't seem to expect us, Mark. How still the house is! Go and knock; they can't ha' gone to bed yet."

Mark knocked at the door—no answer. A light passed rapidly across the windows on the upper floor, but still no one came to his summons. Mark knocked again. A gentleman dressed in clerical costume, now coming from Lansmere Park, on the opposite side of the road, paused at the sound of Mark's second and more impatient knock, and said, civilly—

"Are you not the young folks my friend John Avenel told me this morning he expected to visit him?"

"Yes, please, Mr. Dale," said Mrs. Fairfield, dropping her curtsey. "You remember me! and this is my dear good man!"

"What! Mark the Poet?" said the curate of Lansmere, with a smile. "Come to write squibs for the election?"

"Squibs, sir!" cried Mark, indignantly.

"Burns wrote squibs," said the curate, mildly.

Mark made no answer, but again knocked at the door. This time, a man, whose face, even seen by the starlight, was much flushed, presented himself at the threshold.

"Mr. Morgan!" exclaimed the curate, in benevolent alarm; "no illness here, I hope?"

"Cott! it is you, Mr. Dale!—Come in, come in; I want a word with you. But who the teuce are these people?"

"Sir," said Mark, pushing through the doorway, "my name is Fairfield, and my wife is Mr. Avenel's daughter!"

"Oh, Jane—and her baby too!—Cood—cood! Come in; but be quiet, can't you? Still, still—still as death!"

The party entered, the door closed; the moon rose, and shone calmly on the pale silent house, on the sleeping flowers of the little garden, on the old pollard with its hollow core. The horse in the taxed-cart dozed, unheeded; the light still at times flitted across the upper windows.—These were the only signs of life, except when a bat, now and then attracted by the light that passed across the windows, brushed against the panes, and then, dipping downwards, struck up against the nose of the slumbering horse, and darted merrily after the moth that fluttered round the raven's nest in the old pollard.

## CHAPTER XVIII.

ALL that day Harley L'Estrange had been more than usually mournful and dejected. Indeed the return to scenes associated with Nora's presence increased the gloom that had settled on his mind since he had lost sight and trace of her. Audley, in the remorseful tenderness he felt for his injured friend, had induced L'Estrange towards evening to leave the Park, and go into a district some miles off, on pretence that he required Harley's aid there to canvass certain important outvoters: the change of scene might rouse him from his reveries. Harley himself was glad to escape from the guests at Lansmere. He readily consented to go. He would not return that night. The outvoters lay remote and scattered—

he might be absent for a day or two. When Harley was gone, Egerton himself sank into deep thought. There was rumour of some unexpected opposition. His partisans were alarmed and anxious. It was clear that the Lansmere interest, if attacked, was weaker than the Earl would believe; Egerton might lose his election. If so, what would become of him? How support his wife, whose return to him he always counted on, and whom it would then become him at all hazards to acknowledge? It was that day that he had spoken to William Hazeldean as to the family living.—"Peace, at least," thought the ambitious man—"I shall have peace!" And the Squire had promised him the rectory if needed; not without a secret pang, for his Harry was already using her conjugal influence in favour of her old schoolfriend's husband, Mr. Dale; and the Squire thought Audley would be but a poor country parson, and Dale—if he would only grow a little plumper than his curacy would permit him to be—would be a parson in ten thousand. But while Audley thus prepared for the worst, he still brought his energies to bear on the more brilliant option; and sate with his Committee, looking into canvass-books, and discussing the characters, politics, and local interests of every elector, until the night was well-nigh gone. When he gained his room, the shutters were unclosed, and he stood a few moments at the window gazing on the moon. At that sight, the thought of Nora, lost and afar, stole over him. The man, as we know, had in his nature little of romance and sentiment. Seldom was it his wont to gaze upon moon or stars. But whenever some whisper of romance did soften his hard, strong mind, or whenever moon or stars did charm his gaze from earth, Nora's bright Muse-like face—Nora's sweet loving eyes, were seen in moon and star-beam—Nora's low tender voice, heard in the whisper of that which we call romance, and which is but the sound of the mysterious poetry that is ever in the air, would we but deign to hear it! He turned with a sigh, undressed, threw himself on his bed, and extinguished his light. But the light of the moon *would* fill the room. It kept him awake for a little time; he turned his face from the calm, heavenly beam, resolutely towards the dull blind wall, and fell asleep. And, in the sleep, he was with Nora;—again in the humble bridal-home. Never in his dreams had she seemed to him so distinct and life-like --her eyes upturned to his—her hands clasped together, and resting on his shoulder, as had been her graceful wont—he voice murmuring meekly, "Has it, then, been my fault that we parted?—forgive, forgive me!"

And the sleeper imagined that he answered, "Never part from me again—never, never!" and that he bent down to kiss the chaste lips that so tenderly sought his own. And suddenly he heard a knocking sound, as of a hammer—regular, but soft, low, subdued. Did you ever, O reader, hear the sound of the hammer on the lid of a coffin in a house of woe,—when the undertaker's decorous hireling fears that the living may hear how he parts them from the dead? Such seemed the sound to Audley—the dream vanished abruptly. He woke, and again heard the knock; it was at his door. He sate up wistfully—the moon was gone—it was morning. "Who is there?" he cried, peevishly.

A low voice from without answered, "Hush, it is I; dress quick; let me see you."

Egerton recognised Lady Lansmere's voice. Alarmed and surprised, he rose, dressed in haste, and went to the door. Lady Lansmere was standing without, extremely pale. She put her finger to her lip, and beckoned him to follow her. He obeyed mechanically. They entered her dressing room, a few doors from his own chamber, and the Countess closed the door.

Then laying her slight firm hand on his shoulder, she said, in suppressed and passionate excitement—

"Oh, Mr. Egerton, you must serve me, and at once—Harley—Harley—save my Harley—go to him—prevent his coming back here—stay with him—give up the election—it is but a year or two lost in your life—you will have other opportunities—make that sacrifice to your friend."

"Speak—what is the matter? I can make no sacrifice too great for Harley!"

"Thanks—I was sure of it. Go then, I say, at once, to Harley; keep him away from Lansmere on any excuse you can invent, until you can break the sad news to him—gently, gently. Oh, how will he bear it—how recover the shock? My boy, my boy!"

"Calm yourself! Explain! Break what news?—recover what shock?"

"True—you do not know—you have not heard. Nora Avenel lies yonder, in her father's house—dead—dead!"

Audley staggered back, clapping his hand to his heart, and then dropping on his knee as if bowed down by the stroke of heaven

"My bride, my wife!" he muttered. "Dead—it cannot be!"

Lady Lansmere was so startled at this exclamation, so stunned by a confession wholly unexpected, that she remained unable to soothe—to explain, and utterly unprepared for the fierce agony that burst from the man she had ever seen so dignified and cold—when he sprang to his feet, and all the sense of his eternal loss rushed upon his heart.

At length he crushed back his emotions, and listened in apparent calm, and in a silence broken but by quick gasps for breath, to Lady Lansmere's account.

One of the guests in the house, a female relation of Lady Lansmere's, had been taken suddenly ill about an hour or two before;—the house had been disturbed, the Countess herself aroused, and Mr. Morgan summoned as the family medical practitioner. From him she had learned that Nora Avenel had returned to her father's house late on the previous evening; had been seized with brain fever, and died in a few hours.

Audley listened, and turned to the door, still in silence.

Lady Lansmere caught him by the arm—"Where are you going? Ah, can I now ask you to save my son from the awful news, you yourself the sufferer? And yet—yet—you know his haste, his vehemence, if he learnt that you were his rival—her husband; you whom he so trusted! What, what would be the result?—I tremble!"

"Tremble not—I do not tremble! Let me go—I will be back soon—and then—(his lips writhed)—*then* we will talk of Harley."

Egerton went forth, stunned and dizzy. Mechanically he took his way across the park to John Avenel's house. He had been forced to enter that house, formally, a day or two before, in the course of his canvass; and his worldly pride had received a shock when the home, the birth, and the manners, of his bride's parents had been brought before him. He had even said to himself, "And is it the child of these persons that I, Audley Egerton, must announce to the world as wife!" Now, if she had been the child of a beggar—nay, of a felon—*now*, if he could but recall her to life, how small and mean would all that dreaded world appear to him! Too late—too late! The dews were glistening in the sun—the birds were singing over head—life waking all around him— and his own heart felt like a charnel-house. Nothing but death and the dead there—nothing! He arrived at the door;

it was open: he called; no one answered: he walked up the narrow stairs, undisturbed, unseen; he came into the chamber of death. At the opposite side of the bed was seated John Avenel; but he seemed in a heavy sleep. In fact, paralysis had smitten him; but he knew it not; neither did any one. Who could heed the strong hearty man in such a moment? Not even the poor anxious wife! He had been left there to guard the house, and watch the dead—an unconscious man; numbed, himself, by the invisible icy hand! Audley stole to the bedside; he lifted the coverlid thrown over the pale still face. What passed within him, during the minute he stayed there, who shall say? But when he left the room, and slowly descended the stairs, he left behind him love and youth, all the sweet hopes and joys of the household human life—for ever and ever!

He returned to Lady Lansmere, who awaited his coming with the most nervous anxiety.

"Now," said he, drily, "I will go to Harley, and I will prevent his returning hither."

"You have seen the parents. Good heavens! do they know of your marriage?"

"No; to Harley I must own it first. Meanwhile, silence?"

"Silence!" echoed Lady Lansmere; and her burning hand rested in Audley's, and Audley's hand was as ice.

In another hour Egerton had left the house, and before noon he was with Harley.

It is necessary now to explain the absence of all the Avenel family, except the poor stricken father.

Nora had died in giving birth to a child—died delirious. In her delirium she had spoken of shame—of disgrace; there was no holy nuptial ring on her finger! Through all her grief, the first thought of Mrs. Avenel was to save the good name of her lost daughter—the unblemished honour of all the living Avenels. No matron, long descended from knights or kings, had keener pride in name and character, than the poor, punctilious Calvinistic trader's wife. "Sorrow later, honour now!" With hard dry eyes she mused and mused, and made out her plan. Jane Fairfield should take away the infant at once, before the day dawned, and nurse it with her own. Mark should go with her, for Mrs. Avenel dreaded the indiscretion of his wild grief. She would go with them herself part of the way, in order to command or reason them into guarded silence. But they could not go back to Hazeldean with another infant; Jane must go where none knew her; the two infants might pass as twins. And Mrs. Avenel, though naturally a humane, kindly woman, and with a mother's heart to infants, looked with almost a glad sternness at Jane's puny babe, and thought to herself, "All difficulty would be over should there be only *one!* Nora's child could thus pass throughout life for Jane's!"

Fortunately for the preservation of the secret, the Avenels kept no servant—only an occasional drudge, who came a few hours in the day, and went home to sleep. Mrs. Avenel could count on Mr. Morgan's silence as to the true cause of Nora's death. And Mr. Dale, why should he reveal the dishonour of a family? That very day, or the next at farthest, she could induce her husband to absent himself, lest he should blab out the tale while his sorrow was greater than his pride. She alone would then stay in the house of death until she could feel assured that all else were hushed into prudence. Ay, she felt, that with due precautions, the *name* was still safe. And so she awed and hurried Mark and his wife away, and went with them in the covered cart—that hid the faces of all three—leaving for an hour or two the house and the dead to her husband's charge, with many an admonition, to which he nodded his head, and which he did not hear! Do you think this woman was unfeeling and inhuman? Had Nora looked from heaven into her mother's heart, Nora would not have thought so. A good name when the burial stone closes over dust, is still a possession upon the earth; on earth it is indeed our only one! Better for our friends to guard for us that treasure than to sit down and weep over perishable clay. And weep!—Oh! stern mother, long years were left to thee for weeping! No tears shed for Nora made such deep furrows on the cheeks as thine did! Yet who ever saw them flow?

Harley was in great surprise to see Egerton; more surprised when Egerton told him that he found he was to be opposed—that he had no chance of success at Lansmere, and had, therefore, resolved to retire from the contest. He wrote to the Earl to that effect; but the Countess knew the true cause, and hinted it to the Earl; so that, as we saw at the commencement of this history, Egerton's cause did not suffer when Captain Dashmore appeared in the borough; and, thanks to Mr. Hazeldean's exertions and oratory, Audley came in by two votes—the votes of John Avenel and Mark Fairfield. For though the former had been removed a little way from the town, and by medical advice—and though, on other matters, the disease that had smitten him left him docile as a child (and he had but vague indistinct ideas of all the circumstances connected with Nora's return, save the sense of her loss)—yet he still would hear how the Blues went on, and would get out of bed to keep his word: and even his wife said, "He is right; better die of it, than break his promise!" The crowd gave way as the broken man they had seen a few days before so jovial and healthful was brought up in a chair to the poll, and said, with his tremulous quavering voice, "I'm a true Blue—Blue for ever!"

Elections are wondrous things! No man who has not seen can guess how the zeal in them triumphs over sickness, sorrow, the ordinary private life of us!

There was forwarded to Audley, from Lansmere Park, Nora's last letter. The postman had left it there an hour or two after he himself had gone. The wedding-ring fell on the ground, and rolled under his feet. And those burning passionate reproaches—all that anger of the wounded dove—explained to him the mystery of her return—her unjust suspicions—the cause of her sudden death, which he still ascribed to brain fever, brought on by excitement and fatigue. For Nora did not speak of the child about to be born; she had not remembered it when she wrote, or she would not have written. On the receipt of this letter, Egerton could not remain in the dull village district—alone, too, with Harley. He said, abruptly, that he must go to London—prevailed on L'Estrange to accompany him; and there, when he heard from Lady Lansmere that the funeral was over, he broke to Harley, with lips as white as the dead, and his hand pressed to his heart, on which his hereditary disease was fastening quick and fierce, the dread truth that Nora was no more. The effect upon the boy's health and spirits was even more crushing than Audley could anticipate. He only woke from grief to feel remorse. "For," said the noble Harley, "had it not been for my passion—my rash pursuit—would she ever have left her safe asylum—ever even have left her native town? And then—and then—the struggle between her sense of duty and her love to me! I see it all—all! But for me she were living still!"

"Oh, no!" cried Egerton—his confession now rushing to his lips. "Believe me, she never loved you as you think. Nay—nay—hear me! Rather suppose that she loved another —fled with him—was perhaps married to him, and—"

"Hold!" exclaimed Harley, with a terrible burst of passion

—"you kill her twice to me if you say that! I can still feel that she lives—lives here, in my heart—while I dream that she loved me—or, at least, that no other lip ever knew the kiss that was denied to mine! But if you tell me to doubt *that;*—you—you—" The boy's anguish was too great for his frame; he fell suddenly back into Audley's arms; he had broken a blood-vessel. For several days he was in great danger; but his eyes were constantly fixed on Audley's, with wistful intense gaze. "Tell me," he muttered, at the risk of re-opening the ruptured veins, and of the instant loss of life—"tell me—you did not mean *that!* Tell me you have no cause to think she loved another —*was* another's!"

"Hush, hush—no cause—none—none. I meant but to comfort you, as I thought—fool that I was—that is all!" cried the miserable friend. And from that hour Audley gave up the idea of righting himself in his own eyes, and submitted still to be the living lie—he, the haughty gentleman!

Now, while Harley was still very weak and suffering, Mr. Dale came to London, and called on Egerton. The curate, in promising secrecy to Mrs. Avenel, had made one condition, that it should not be to the positive injury of Nora's living son. What if Nora were married, after all? And would it not be right, at least, to learn the name of the child's father? Some day he might need a father. Mrs. Avenel was obliged to content herself with these reservations. However, she implored Mr. Dale not to make inquiries. What could they do? If Nora were married, her husband would naturally, of his own accord, declare himself; if seduced and forsaken, it would but disgrace her memory (now saved from stain) to discover the father to a child of whose very existence the world as yet knew nothing. These arguments perplexed the good curate. But Jane Fairfield had a sanguine belief in her sister's innocence; and all her suspicions naturally pointed to Lord L'Estrange. So, indeed, perhaps, did Mrs. Avenel's, though she never owned them. Of the correctness of these suspicions Mr. Dale was fully convinced;—the young lord's admiration, Lady Lansmere's fears, had been too evident to one who had often visited at the Park—Harley's abrupt departure just before Nora's return home—Egerton's sudden resignation of the borough before even opposition was declared, in order to rejoin his friend, the very day of Nora's death—all confirmed his ideas that Harley was the betrayer or the husband. Perhaps there might have been a secret marriage —possibly abroad—since Harley wanted some years of his majority. He would, at least, try to see and to sound Lord L'Estrange. Prevented this interview by Harley's illness, the curate resolved to ascertain how far he could penetrate into the mystery by a conversation with Egerton. There was much in the grave repute which the latter had acquired, and the singular and pre-eminent character for truth and honour with which it was accompanied, that made the curate resolve upon this step. Accordingly, he saw Egerton, meaning only diplomatically to extract from the new member for Lansmere what might benefit the family of the voters who had given him his majority of two.

He began by mentioning, as a touching fact, how poor John Avenel, bowed down by the loss of his child, and the malady which had crippled his limbs and enfeebled his mind, had still risen from his bed to keep his word. And Audley's emotions seemed to him so earnest and genuine, to show so good a heart, that out by little and little came more; first, his suspicions that poor Nora had been betrayed; then his hopes that there might have been private marriage; and as Audley, with his iron self-command, showed just the proper degree of interest, and no more, he went on, till Audley knew that he had a child.

"Inquire no further!" said the man of the world. "Respect Mrs. Avenel's feelings and wishes, I entreat you; they are the right ones. Leave the rest to me. In my position— I mean as a resident of London—I can quietly and easily ascertain more than you could, and provoke no scandal! If I can right this—this—poor—(his voice trembled)—right the lost mother, or the living child—sooner or later you will hear from me; if not, bury this secret where it now rests, in a grave which slander has not reached. But the child—give me the address where it is to be found—in case I succeed in finding the father, and touching his heart."

"Oh, Mr. Egerton, may I not say where you may find that father—who he is?"

"Sir!"

"Do not be angry; and, after all, I cannot ask you to betray any confidence which a friend may have placed in you. I know what you men of high honour are to each other—even in sin. No, no—I beg pardon; I leave all in your hands. I shall hear from you then!"

"Or if not—why, then, believe that all search is hopeless.

My friend! if you mean Lord L'Estrange, he is innocent. I
—I—I—(the voice faltered)—am convinced of it."

The curate sighed, but made no answer, "Oh, ye men of
the world!" thought he. He gave the address which the
member for Lansmere had asked for, and went his way, and
never heard again from Audley Egerton. He was convinced
that the man who had showed such deep feeling had failed in
his appeal to Harley's conscience, or had judged it best to
leave Nora's name in peace, and her child to her own relations
and the care of heaven.

Harley L'Estrange, scarcely yet recovered, hastened to join
our armies on the Continent, and seek the Death which, like
its half-brother, rarely comes when we call it.

As soon as Harley was gone, Egerton went to the village
to which Mr. Dale had directed him, to seek for Nora's child.
But here he was led into a mistake which materially affected
the tenor of his own life, and Leonard's future destinies.
Mrs. Fairfield had been naturally ordered by her mother to
take another name in the village to which she had gone with
the two infants, so that her connection with the Avenel
family might not be traced, to the provocation of inquiry and
gossip. The grief and excitement through which she had
gone, dried the source of nutriment in her breast. She put
Nora's child out to nurse at the house of a small farmer, at a
little distance from the village, and moved from her first
lodging to be nearer to the infant. Her own child was so
sickly and ailing, that she could not bear to intrust it to the
care of another. She tried to bring it up by hand; and the
poor child soon pined away and died. She and Mark could
not endure the sight of their baby's grave; they hastened to
return to Hazeldean, and took Leonard with them. From
that time Leonard passed for the son they had lost.

When Egerton arrived at the village, and inquired for the
person whose address had been given to him, he was referred
to the cottage in which she had last lodged, and was told that
she had been gone some days—the day after her child was
buried. Her child buried! Egerton stayed to inquire no
more; thus he heard nothing of the infant that had been put
out to nurse. He walked slowly into the churchyard, and
stood for some minutes gazing on the small new mound;
then, pressing his hand on the heart to which all emotion had
been forbidden, he re-entered his chaise and returned to
London. The sole reason for acknowledging his marriage
seemed to him now removed. Nora's name had escaped

reproach. Even had his painful position with regard to Harley not constrained him to preserve his secret, there was every motive to the World's wise and haughty son not to acknowledge a derogatory and foolish marriage, now that none lived whom concealment could wrong.

Audley mechanically resumed his former life,—sought to resettle his thoughts on the grand objects of ambitious men. His poverty still pressed on him; his pecuniary debt to Harley stung and galled his peculiar sense of honour. He saw no way to clear his estates, to repay his friend, but by some rich alliance. Dead to love, he faced this prospect first with repugnance, then with apathetic indifference. Levy, of whose treachery towards himself and Nora he was unaware, still held over him the power that the money-lender never loses over the man that has owed, owes, or may owe again. Levy was ever urging him to propose to the rich Miss Leslie; —Lady Lansmere, willing to atone, as she thought, for his domestic loss, urged the same;—Harley, influenced by his mother, wrote from the Continent to the same effect.

"Manage it as you will," at last said Egerton to Levy, "so that I am not a wife's pensioner."

"Propose for me, if you will," he said to Lady Lansmere— "I cannot woo—I cannot talk of love."

Somehow or other the marriage, with all its rich advantages to the ruined gentleman, was thus made up. And Egerton, as we have seen, was the polite and dignified husband before the world—married to a woman who adored him. It is the common fate of men like him to be loved too well!

On her death-bed his heart was touched by his wife's melancholy reproach—"Nothing I could do has ever made you love me!" "It is true," answered Audley, with tears in his voice and eyes—"Nature gave me but a small fund of what women like you call 'love,' and I lavished it all away." And he then told her, though with reserve, some portion of his former history; and that soothed her; for when she saw that he had loved, and *could* grieve, she caught a glimpse of the human heart she *had* not seen before. She died, forgiving him, and blessing.

Audley's spirits were much affected by this new loss. He inly resolved never to marry again. He had a vague thought at first of retrenching his expenditure, and making young Randal Leslie his heir. But when he first saw the clever Eton boy, his feelings did not warm to him, though his intellect appreciated Randal's quick, keen talents. He contented himself with resolving to push the boy;—to do what was merely just to the distant kinsman of his late wife. Always careless and lavish in money matters, generous and princely not from the delight of serving others, but from a *grand Seigneur's* sentiment of what was due to himself and his station, Audley had a mournful excuse for the lordly waste of the large fortune at his control. The morbid functions of the heart had become organic disease. True, he might live many years, and die at last of some other complaint in the course of nature; but the progress of the disease would quicken with all emotional excitement; he might die suddenly—any day— in the very prime, and, seemingly, in the full vigour, of his life. And the only physician in whom he confided what he wished to keep concealed from the world, (for ambitious men would fain be thought immortal,) told him frankly that it was improbable that, with the wear and tear of political strife and action, he could advance far into middle age. Therefore, no son of his succeeding—his nearest relations all wealthy— Egerton resigned himself to his constitutional disdain of money; he could look into no affairs, provided the balance in his banker's hands were such as became the munificent commoner. All else he left to his steward and to Levy. Levy grew rapidly rich—very, very rich—and the steward thrived.

The usurer continued to possess a determined hold over the imperious great man. He knew Audley's secret; he could reveal that secret to Harley. And the one soft and tender side of the statesman's nature—the sole part of him not dipped in the ninefold Styx of practical prosaic life, which renders man so invulnerable to affection—was his remorseful love for the school friend whom he still deceived.

Here then you have the key to the locked chambers of Audley Egerton's character, the fortified castle of his mind. The envied minister—the joyless man;—the oracle on the economies of an empire—the prodigal in a usurer's hands;— the august, high-crested gentleman, to whom princes would refer for the casuistry of honour—the culprit trembling lest the friend he best loved on earth should detect his lie! Wrap thyself in the decent veil that the Arts or the Graces weave for thee, O Human Nature! It is only the statue of marble whose nakedness the eye can behold without shame and offence!

## CHAPTER XIX.

Of the narrative just placed before the reader, it is clear that Leonard could gather only desultory fragments. He could but see that his ill-fated mother had been united to a man she had loved with surpassing tenderness; had been led to suspect that the marriage was fraudulent; had gone abroad in despair, returned repentant and hopeful; had gleaned some intelligence that her lover was about to be married to another, and there the manuscript closed with the blisters left on the page by agonising tears. The mournful end of Nora —her lonely return to die under the roof of her parents—this he had learned before from the narrative of Dr. Morgan.

But even the name of her supposed husband was not revealed. Of him Leonard could form no conjecture, except that he was evidently of higher rank than Nora. Harley L'Estrange seemed clearly indicated in the early boy-lover. If so, Harley must know all that was left dark to Leonard, and to him Leonard resolved to confide the manuscripts. With this resolution he left the cottage, resolving to return and attend the funeral obsequies of his departed friend. Mrs. Goodyer willingly permitted him to take away the papers she had lent to him, and added to them the packet which had been addressed to Mrs. Bertram from the Continent.

Musing in anxious gloom over the record he had read, Leonard entered London on foot, and bent his way towards Harley's hotel; when, just as he had crossed into Bond Street, a gentleman in company with Baron Levy, and who seemed, by the flush on his brow and the sullen tone of his voice, to have had rather an irritating colloquy with the fashionable usurer, suddenly caught sight of Leonard, and, abruptly quitting Levy, seized the young man by the arm.

"Excuse me, sir," said the gentleman, looking hard into Leonard's face; "but unless these sharp eyes of mine are mistaken, which they seldom are, I see a nephew whom, perhaps, I behaved to rather too harshly, but who still has no right to forget Richard Avenel."

"My dear uncle," exclaimed Leonard, "this is indeed a joyful surprise; at a time, too, when I needed joy! No; I have never forgotten your kindness, and always regretted our estrangement."

"That is well said; give us your fist again. Let me look

at you—quite the gentleman, I declare!—still so good-looking too. We Avenels always were a handsome family. Good bye, Baron Levy. Need not wait for me; I am not going to run away. I shall see you again."

"But," whispered Levy, who had followed Avenel across the street, and eyed Leonard with a quick curious searching glance—"but it must be as I say with regard to the borough; or (to be plain) you must cash the bills on the day they are due."

"Very well, sir—very well. So you think to put the screw upon me, as if I were a poor little householder. I understand —my money or my borough?"

"Exactly so," said the Baron, with a soft smile.

"You shall hear from me. (Aside, as Levy strolled away) —D——d tarnation rascal!"

Dick Avenel then linked his arm in his nephew's and strove for some minutes to forget his own troubles, in the indulgence of that curiosity in the affairs of another which was natural to him, and in this instance, increased by the real affection which he had felt for Leonard. But still his curiosity remained unsatisfied; for long before Leonard could overcome his habitual reluctance to speak of his success in literature, Dick's mind wandered back to his rival at Screwstown, and the curse of "over-competition,"—to the bills which Levy had discounted, in order to enable Dick to meet the crushing force of a capitalist larger than himself—and the "tarnation rascal" who now wished to obtain two seats at Lansmere, one for Randal Leslie, one for a rich Nabob whom Levy had just caught as a client; and Dick, though willing to aid Leslie, had a mind to the other seat for himself. Therefore Dick soon broke in upon the hesitating confessions of Leonard, with exclamations far from pertinent to the subject, and rather for the sake of venting his own griefs and resentment, than with any idea that the sympathy or advice of his nephew could serve him.

"Well, well," said Dick, "another time for your history. I see you have thrived, and that is enough for the present. Very odd; but just now I can only think of myself. I'm in a regular fix, sir. Screwstown is not the respectable Screwstown that you remember it—all demoralised and turned topsyturvy by a demoniacal monster capitalist, with steam-engines that might bring the falls of Niagara into your back parlour, sir! And as if that was not enough to destroy and drive into almighty shivers a decent fair-play Britisher like myself, I hear he is just in treaty for some patent infernal invention that will make his engines do twice as much work with half as many hands! That's the way those unfeeling ruffians increase our poor-rates! But I'll get up a riot against him—I will! Don't talk to me of the law! What the devil is the good of the law if it don't protect a man's industry—a *liberal* man, too, like me!" Here Dick burst into a storm of vituperation against the rotten old country in general, and Mr. Dyce, the monster capitalist of Screwstown, in particular.

Leonard started; for Dick now named, in that monster capitalist, the very person who was in treaty for Leonard's own mechanical improvement on the steam-engine.

"Stop, uncle—stop! Why, then, if this man were to buy the contrivance you speak of, it would injure you?"

"Injure me, sir! I should be a bankrupt—that is, if it succeeded; but I dare say it is all a humbug."

"No, it *will* succeed—I'll answer for that!"

"You! You have seen it?"

"Why, I invented it."

Dick hastily withdrew his arm from Leonard's.

"Serpent's tooth!" he said, falteringly, "so it is you, whom I warmed at my hearth, who are to ruin Richard Avenel?"

"No—but to save him! Come into the city and look at my model. If you like it, the patent shall be yours!"

"Cab—cab—cab," cried Dick Avenel, stopping a "Hansom;" "jump in, Leonard—jump in. I'll buy your patent—that is, if it be worth a straw; and as for payment—"

"Payment! Don't talk of that!"

"Well, I won't," said Dick, mildly; "for 'tis not the topic of conversation I should choose myself, just at present. And as for that black-whiskered alligator, the Baron, let me first get out of those rambustious, unchristian, filbert-shaped claws of his, and then— But jump in—jump in—and tell the man where to drive!"

A very brief inspection of Leonard's invention sufficed to show Richard Avenel how invaluable it would be to him. Armed with a patent, of which the certain effects in the increase of power and diminution of labour were obvious to any practical man, Avenel felt that he should have no difficulty in obtaining such advances of money as he required, whether to alter his engines, meet the bills discounted by Levy, or carry on the war with the monster capitalist. It might be necessary to admit into partnership some other monster capitalist—What then? Any partner better than Levy. A bright idea struck him.

"If I can just terrify and whop that infernal intruder on my own ground, for a few months, he may offer, himself, to enter into partnership—make the two concerns a jointstock friendly combination, and then we shall flog the world."

His gratitude to Leonard became so lively, that Dick offered to bring his nephew in for Lansmere instead of himself; and when Leonard declined the offer, exclaimed, "Well, then, any friend of yours; I'm all for reform against those high and mighty right honourable boroughmongers; and what with loans and mortgages on the small householders, and a long course of 'Free and Easies' with the independent freemen, I carry one seat certain, perhaps both seats of the town of Lansmere, in my breeches pocket." Dick then, appointing an interview with Leonard at his lawyer's, to settle the transfer of the invention, upon terms which he declared "should be honourable to both parties," hurried off, to search amongst his friends in the city for some monster capitalist, who might be induced to extricate him from the jaws of Levy, and the engines of his rival at Screwstown, "Mullins is the man, if I can but catch him," said Dick. "You have heard of Mullins?—A wonderful great man; you should see his nails; he never cuts them! Three millions, at least, he has scraped together with those nails of his, sir. And in this rotten old country, a man must have nails a yard long to fight with a devil like Levy!—Good-bye—good-*bye*,— GOOD-bye, my DEAR nephew!"

## CHAPTER XX.

HARLEY L'ESTRANGE was seated alone in his apartments He had just put down a volume of some favourite classic author, and he was resting his hand firmly clenched upon the book. Ever since Harley's return to England, there had been a perceptible change in the expression of his countenance, even in the very bearing and attitudes of his elastic youthful figure. But this change had been more marked since that last interview with Helen which has been recorded. There was a compressed resolute firmness in the lips—a decided character in the brow. To the indolent careless grace of his movements had succeeded a certain indescribable energy, as quiet and self-collected as that which distinguished the determined air of Audley Egerton himself. In fact, if you could have looked into his heart, you would have seen that Harley was, for the first time, making a strong effort over his passions and his humours; that the whole man was nerving himself to a sense of duty. "No," he muttered—"no—I will think only of Helen; I will think only of real life! And what (were I not engaged to another) would that dark-eyed Italian girl be to me?—What a mere fool's fancy is this. I love again—I, who through all the fair spring of my life, have clung with such faith to a memory and a grave! Come, come, come, Harley L'Estrange, act thy part as man amongst men, at last! Accept regard; dream no more of passion. Abandon false ideals. Thou art no poet—why deem that life itself can be a poem?"

The door opened, and the Austrian Prince, whom Harley had interested in the cause of Violante's father, entered with the familiar step of a friend.

"Have you discovered those documents yet?" said the Prince. "I must now return to Vienna within a few days. And unless you can arm me with some tangible proof of Peschiera's ancient treachery, or some more unanswerable excuse for his noble kinsman, I fear that there is no other hope for the exile's recall to his country than what lies in the hateful option of giving his daughter to his perfidious foe."

"Alas!" said Harley, "as yet all researches have been in vain; and I know not what other steps to take, without arousing Peschiera's vigilance, and setting his crafty brains at work to counteract us. My poor friend, then, must rest contented with exile. To give Violante to the Count were dishonour. But I shall soon be married; soon have a home, not quite unworthy of their due rank, to offer both to father and to child."

"Would the future Lady L'Estrange feel no jealousy of a guest so fair as you tell me this young signorina is? And would you be in no danger yourself, my poor friend?"

"Pooh!" said Harley, colouring. "My fair guest would have *two* fathers; that is all. Pray do not jest on a thing so grave as honour."

Again the door opened, and Leonard appeared.

"Welcome," cried Harley, pleased to be no longer alone under the Prince's penetrating eye—"welcome. This is the noble friend who shares our interest for Riccabocca, and who could serve him so well, if we could but discover the document of which I have spoken to you."

"It is here," said Leonard, simply; "may it be all that you require!"

Harley eagerly grasped at the packet, which had been sent from Italy to the supposed Mrs. Bertram, and, leaning his face on his hand, rapidly hurried through the contents.

"Hurrah!" he cried at last, with his face lighted up, and a boyish toss of his right hand. "Look, look, Prince, here are Peschiera's own letters to his kinsman's wife; his avowal of what he calls his 'patriotic designs;' his entreaties to her to induce her husband to share them. Look, look, how he wields his influence over the woman he had once wooed; look how artfully he combats her objections; see how reluctant our friend was to stir, till wife and kinsman both united to urge him."

"It is enough—quite enough," exclaimed the Prince, looking at the passages in Peschiera's letters which Harley pointed out to him.

"No, it is not enough," shouted Harley, as he continued to read the letters with his rapid sparkling eyes. "More still! O villain, doubly damned! Here, after our friend's flight, here is Peschiera's avowal of guilty passion; here, he swears that he had intrigued to ruin his benefactor, in order to pollute the home that had sheltered him. Ah! see how she answers; thank Heaven her own eyes were opened at last, and she scorned him before she died. She was innocent! I said so! Violante's mother was pure. Poor lady, this moves me! Has your Emperor the heart of a man?"

"I know enough of our Emperor," answered the Prince, warmly, "to know that, the moment these papers reach him, Peschiera is ruined, and your friend is restored to his honours. You will live to see the daughter, to whom you would have given a child's place at your hearth, the wealthiest heiress of Italy—the bride of some noble lover, with rank only below the supremacy of kings!"

"Ah!" said Harley, in a sharp accent, and turning very pale—"ah, I shall not see her that! I shall never visit Italy again!—never see her more—never, after she has once quitted this climate of cold iron cares and formal duties—never, never!" He turned his head for a moment, and then came with quick step to Leonard. "But you, O happy poet! No Ideal can ever be lost to you  You are independent of real life. Would that I were a poet!" He smiled sadly.

"You would not say so, perhaps, my dear lord," answered Leonard, with equal sadness, "if you knew how little what you call 'the Ideal' replaces to a poet the loss of one affection in the genial human world. Independent of real life! Alas! no. And I have here the confessions of a true poet-soul, which I will entreat you to read at leisure; and when you have read, say if you would still be a poet!"

He took forth Nora's manuscripts as he spoke.

"Place them yonder, in my *escritoire*, Leonard; I will read them later."

"Do so, and with heed; for to me there is much here that involves my own life—much that is still a mystery, and which I think you can unravel!"

"I!" exclaimed Harley; and he was moving towards the *escritoire*, in a drawer of which Leonard had carefully deposited the papers, when, once more, but this time violently, the door was thrown open, and Giacomo rushed into the room, accompanied by Lady Lansmere.

"Oh, my lord, my lord!" cried Giacomo, in Italian, "the signorina! the signorina!—Violante!"

"What of her? Mother, mother! what of her? Speak, speak!"

"She has gone—left our house!"

"Left! No, no!" cried Giacomo. "She must have been deceived or forced away. The Count! the Count! Oh, my good lord, save her, as you once saved her father!"

"Hold!" cried Harley. "Give me your arm, mother. A *second* such blow in life is beyond the strength of man—at least it is beyond mine. So, so!—I am better now! Thank you, mother. Stand back, all of you—give me air. So the Count has triumphed, and Violante has fled with him! Explain all—I can bear it!"

# BOOK TWELFTH.

### INITIAL CHAPTER.

#### WHEREIN THE CAXTON FAMILY REAPPEAR.

"AGAIN," quoth my father—"again behold us! We who greeted the commencement of your narrative, who absented ourselves in the midcourse when we could but obstruct the current of events, and jostle personages more important—we now gather round the close. Still, as the chorus to the drama, we circle round the altar with the solemn but dubious chant which prepares the audience for the completion of the appointed destinies; though still, ourselves, unaware how the skein is to be unravelled, and where the shears are to descend."

So there they stood, the Family of Caxton—all grouping round me—all eager officiously to question—some overanxious prematurely to criticise.

"Violante can't have voluntarily gone off with that horrid Count," said my mother; "but perhaps she was deceived, like Eugenia by Mr. Bellamy, in the novel of 'CAMILLA.'"

"Ha!" said my father, "and in that case it is time yet to steal a hint from Clarissa Harlowe, and make Violante die less of a broken heart than a sullied honour. She is one of those girls who ought to be killed! All things about her forebode an early tomb!"

"Dear, dear!" cried Mrs. Caxton, "I hope not!"

"Pooh, brother," said the Captain, "we have had enough of the tomb in the history of poor Nora. The whole story grows out of a grave, and if to a grave it must return—if, Pisistratus, you must kill somebody, kill Levy."

"Or the Count," said my mother, with unusual truculence.

"Or Randal Leslie," said Squills. "I should like to have a *post-mortem* cast of his head—it would be an instructive study."

Here there was a general confusion of tongues, all present conspiring to bewilder the unfortunate author with their various and discordant counsels how to wind up his story and dispose of his characters.

"Silence!" cried Pisistratus, clapping his hands to both ears. "I can no more alter the fate allotted to each of the personages whom you honour with your interest than I can change your own; like you, they must go where events lead them, urged on by their own characters and the agencies of others. Providence so pervadingly governs the universe, that you cannot strike it even out of a book. The author may beget a character, but the moment the character comes into action, it escapes from his hands—plays its own part, and fulfils its own inevitable doom."

"Besides," said Mr. Squills, "it is easy to see, from the phrenological development of the organs in those several heads which Pisistratus has allowed us to examine, that we have seen no creations of mere fiction, but living persons, whose true history has set in movement their various bumps of Amativeness, Constructiveness, Acquisitiveness, Ideality, Wonder, Comparison, &c. They must act, and they must end, according to the influences of their crania. Thus we find in Randal Leslie the predominant organs of Constructiveness, Secretiveness, Comparison, and Eventuality—while Benevolence, Conscientiousness, Adhesiveness, are utterly *nil*. Now, to divine how such a man must end, we must first see what is the general composition of the society in which he moves—in short, what other gases are brought into contact with his phlogiston. As to Leonard, and Harley, and Audley Egerton, surveying them phrenologically, I should say that—"

"Hush!" said my father, "Pisistratus has dipped his pen in the ink, and it seems to me easier for the wisest man that ever lived to account for what others have done, than to predict what they should do. Phrenologists discovered that Mr. Thurtell had a very fine organ of Conscientiousness, yet, somehow or other, that erring personage contrived to knock the brains out of his friend's organ of Individuality. Therefore I rise to propose a Resolution—that this meeting be adjourned till Pisistratus has completed his narrative; and we shall then have the satisfaction of knowing that it ought, according to every principle of nature, science, and art, to have been completed differently. Why should we deprive ourselves of that pleasure?"

"I second the motion," said the Captain; "but if Levy

be not hanged, I shall say that there is an end of all poetical justice."

"Take care of poor Helen," said Blanche, tenderly: "not that I would have you forget Violante."

"Pish! and sit down, or they shall both die old maids."

Frightened at that threat, Blanche, with a deprecating look, drew her stool quietly near me, as if to place her two *protégées* in an atmosphere mesmerised to matrimonial attractions; and my mother set hard to work—at a new frock for the baby. Unsoftened by these undue female influences, Pisistratus wrote on at the dictation of the relentless Fates. His pen was of iron, and his heart was of granite. He was as insensible to the existence of wife and baby as if he had never paid a house bill, nor rushed from a nursery at the sound of an infant squall. O blessed privilege of Authorship!

> O testudinis aureæ
> Dulcem quæ strepitum, Pieri temperas!
> O mutis quoque piscibus
> Donatura cycni, si libeat, sonum!" *

## CHAPTER II.

IT is necessary to go somewhat back in the course of this narrative, and account to the reader for the disappearance of Violante.

It may be remembered that Peschiera, scared by the sudden approach of Lord L'Estrange, had little time for farther words to the young Italian, than those which expressed his intention to renew the conference, and press for her decision. But, the next day, when he re-entered the garden, secretly and stealthily, as before, Violante did not appear. And after watching round the precincts till dusk, the Count retreated with an indignant conviction that his arts had failed to enlist on his side either the heart or the imagination of his intended victim. He began now to revolve, and to discuss with Levy, the possibilities of one of those bold and violent measures, which were favoured by his reckless daring, and desperate condition. But Levy treated with such just ridicule any suggestion to abstract Violante by force from Lord Lansmere's house—so scouted the notions of nocturnal assault, with the devices of

---

\* O Muse, who dost temper the sweet sound of the golden shell of the tortoise, and couldst also give, were it needed, to silent fishes the song of the swan!

scaling windows and rope-ladders—that the Count reluctantly abandoned that romance of villany so unsuited to our sober capital, and which would no doubt have terminated in his capture by the police, with the prospect of committal to the House of Correction.

Levy himself found his invention at fault, and Randal Leslie was called into consultation. The usurer had contrived that Randal's schemes of fortune and advancement were so based upon Levy's aid and connivance, that the young man, with all his desire rather to make instruments of other men, than to be himself their instrument, found his superior intellect as completely a slave to Levy's more experienced craft, as ever subtle Genius of air was subject to the vulgar Sorcerer of earth.

His acquisition of the ancestral acres—his anticipated seat in Parliament—his chance of ousting Frank from the heritage of Hazeldean—were all as strings that pulled him to and fro, like a puppet in the sleek, filbert-nailed fingers of the smiling showman, who could exhibit him to the admiration of a crowd, or cast him away into dust and lumber.

Randal gnawed his lip in the sullen wrath of a man who bides his hour of future emancipation, and lent his brain to the hire of the present servitude, in mechanical acquiescence. The inherent superiority of the profound young schemer became instantly apparent over the courage of Peschiera and the practised wit of the Baron.

"Your sister," said Randal, to the former, "must be the active agent in the first and most difficult part of your enterprise. Violante cannot be taken by force from Lord Lansmere's—she must be induced to leave it with her own consent. A female is needed here. Woman can best decoy woman."

"Admirably said," quoth the Count; "but Beatrice has grown restive, and though her dowry, and therefore her very marriage with that excellent young Hazeldean, depend on my own alliance with my fair kinswoman, she has grown so indifferent to my success that I dare not reckon on her aid. Between you and me, though she was once very eager to be married, she now seems to shrink from the notion; and I have no other hold over her."

"Has she not seen some one, and lately, whom she prefers to poor Frank?"

"I suspect that she has; but I know not whom, unless it be that detested L'Estrange."

"Ah—well, well. Interfere with her no farther yourself, but have all in readiness to quit England, as you had before proposed, as soon as Violante be in your power."

"All is in readiness," said the Count. "Levy has agreed to purchase a famous sailing vessel of one of his clients. I have engaged a score or so of determined outcasts, accustomed to the sea—Genoese, Corsicans, Sardinians—ex-Carbonari of the best sort—no silly patriots, but liberal cosmopolitans, who have iron at the disposal of any man's gold. I have a priest to perform the nuptial service, and deaf to any fair lady's 'No.' Once at sea, and wherever I land, Violante will lean on my arm as Countess of Peschiera."

"But Violante," said Randal, doggedly, determined not to yield to the disgust with which the Count's audacious cynicism filled even him—"but Violante cannot be removed in broad daylight at once to such a vessel, nor from a quarter so populous as that in which your sister resides."

"I have thought of that too," said the Count; "my emissaries have found me a house close by the river, and safe for our purpose as the dungeons of Venice."

"I wish not to know all this," answered Randal, quickly; "you will instruct Madame di Negra where to take Violante—my task limits itself to the fair inventions that belong to intellect; what belongs to force is not in my province. I will go at once to your sister, whom I think I can influence more effectually than you can; though later I may give you a hint to guard against the chance of her remorse. Meanwhile as, the moment Violante disappears, suspicion would fall upon you, show yourself constantly in public surrounded by your friends. Be able to account for every hour of your time—"

"An *alibi?*" interrupted the *ci-devant* solicitor.

"Exactly so, Baron. Complete the purchase of the vessel, and let the Count man it as he proposes. I will communicate with you both as soon as I can put you into action. To-day I shall have much to do; it will be done."

As Randal left the room, Levy followed him.

"What you propose to do will be well done, no doubt," quoth the usurer, linking his arm in Randal's; "but take care that you don't get yourself into a scrape, so as to damage your character. I have great hopes of you in public life; and in public life character is necessary—that is, so far as honour is concerned."

"I damage my character!—and for a Count Peschiera!"

said Randal, opening his eyes. "I! What do you take me for?"

The Baron let go his hold.

"This boy ought to rise very high," said he to himself, as he turned back to the Count.

## CHAPTER III.

RANDAL'S acute faculty of comprehension had long since surmised the truth that Beatrice's views and temper of mind had been strangely and suddenly altered by some such revolution as passion only can effect; that pique or disappointment had mingled with the motive which had induced her to accept the hand of his rash young kinsman; and that, instead of the resigned indifference with which she might at one time have contemplated any marriage that could free her from a position that perpetually galled her pride, it was now with a repugnance, visible to Randal's keen eye, that she shrank from the performance of that pledge which Frank had so dearly bought. The temptations which the Count could hold out to her to become his accomplice in designs of which the fraud and perfidy would revolt her better nature, had ceased to be of avail. A dowry had grown valueless, since it would but hasten the nuptials from which she recoiled. Randal felt that he could not secure her aid, except by working on a passion so turbulent as to confound her judgment. Such a passion he recognised in jealousy. He had once doubted if Harley were the object of her love; yet, after all, was it not probable? He knew, at least, of no one else to suspect. If so, he had but to whisper, "Violante is your rival. Violante removed, your beauty may find its natural effect; if not, you are an Italian, and you will be at least avenged." He saw still more reason to suppose that Lord L'Estrange was indeed the one by whom he could rule Beatrice, since, the last time he had seen her, she had questioned him with much eagerness as to the family of Lord Lansmere, especially as to the female part of it. Randal had then judged it prudent to avoid speaking of Violante; and feigned ignorance; but promised to ascertain all particulars by the time he next saw the Marchesa. It was the warmth with which she had thanked him, that had set his busy mind at work to conjecture the cause of her curiosity so earnestly aroused, and to ascribe that cause to jealousy. If Harley loved Violante (as Randal himself had before supposed), the little of passion that the young man admitted to himself was enlisted in aid of Peschiera's schemes. For though Randal did not love Violante, he cordially disliked L'Estrange, and would have gone as far to render that dislike vindictive, as a cold reasoner, intent upon worldly fortunes, will ever suffer mere hate to influence him.

"At the worst," thought Randal, "if it be not Harley, touch the chord of jealousy, and its vibration will direct me right."

Thus soliloquising, he arrived at Madame di Negra's.

Now, in reality, the Marchesa's inquiries as to Lord Lansmere's family had their source in the misguided, restless, despairing interest with which she still clung to the image of the young poet, whom Randal had no reason to suspect. That interest had become yet more keen from the impatient misery she had felt ever since she had plighted herself to another. A wild hope that she might yet escape—a vague regretful thought that she had been too hasty in dismissing Leonard from her presence—that she ought rather to have courted his friendship, and contended against her unknown rival, at times drew her wayward mind wholly from the future to which she had consigned herself. And, to do her justice, though her sense of duty was so defective, and the principles which should have guided her conduct were so lost to her sight, still her feelings towards the generous Hazeldean were not so hard and blunted but what her own ingratitude added to her torment; and it seemed as if the sole atonement she could make to him was to find an excuse to withdraw her promise, and save him from herself. She had caused Leonard's steps to be watched; she had found that he visited at Lord Lansmere's; that he had gone there often, and stayed there long. She had learned in the neighbourhood that Lady Lansmere had one or two young female guests staying with her. Surely this was the attraction—here was the rival!

Randal found Beatrice in a state of mind that favoured his purpose. And first turning his conversation on Harley, and noting that her countenance did not change, by little and little he drew forth her secret.

Then said Randal, gravely, "If one whom you honour with a tender thought visits at Lord Lansmere's house, you have, indeed, cause to fear for yourself, to hope for your brother's success in the object which has brought him to England—for a girl of surpassing beauty is a guest in Lord Lansmere's house; and I will now tell you that that girl is she whom Count Peschiera would make his bride."

As Randal thus spoke, and saw how his listener's brow darkened and her eye flashed, he felt that his accomplice was secured. Violante! Had not Leonard spoken of Violante, and with such praise? Had not his boyhood been passed under her eyes? Who but Violante could be the rival? Beatrice's abrupt exclamations, after a moment's pause, revealed to Randal the advantage he had gained. And partly by rousing her jealousy into revenge—partly by flattering her love with assurances that, if Violante were fairly removed from England, were the wife of Count Peschiera—it would be impossible that Leonard could remain insensible to her own attractions—that he, Randal, would undertake to free her honourably from her engagement to Frank Hazeldean, and obtain from her brother the acquittal of the debt which had first fettered her hand to that confiding suitor—he did not quit the Marchesa until she had not only promised to do all that Randal might suggest, but impetuously urged him to mature his plans, and hasten the hour to accomplish them. Randal then walked some minutes musing and slow along the streets, revolving the next meshes in his elaborate and most subtle web. And here his craft luminously devised its masterpiece.

It was necessary, during any interval that might elapse between Violante's disappearance and her departure from England, in order to divert suspicion from Peschiera (who might otherwise be detained), that some cause for her voluntary absence from Lord Lansmere's should be at least assignable; it was still more necessary that Randal himself should stand wholly clear from any surmise that he could have connived at the Count's designs, even should their actual perpetrator be discovered or conjectured. To effect these objects, Randal hastened to Norwood, and obtained an interview with Riccabocca. In seeming agitation and alarm, he informed the exile that he had reason to know that Peschiera had succeeded in obtaining a secret interview with Violante, and he feared had made a certain favourable impression on her mind; and speaking as if with the jealousy of a lover, he entreated Riccabocca to authorise Randal's direct proposals to Violante, and to require her consent to their immediate nuptials.

The poor Italian was confounded with the intelligence conveyed to him; and his almost superstitious fears of his brilliant enemy, conjoined with his opinion of the susceptibility to outward attractions common to all the female sex, made him not only implicitly credit, but even exaggerate, the dangers that Randal intimated. The idea of his daughter's marriage with Randal, towards which he had lately cooled, he now gratefully welcomed.

But his first natural suggestion was to go, or send, for Violante, and bring her to his own house. This, however, Randal artfully opposed.

"Alas! I know," said he, "that Peschiera has discovered your retreat, and surely she would be far less safe here than where she is now!"

"But, *diavolo!* you say the man has seen her where she is now, in spite of all Lady Lansmere's promises and Harley's precautions."

"True. Of this Peschiera boasted to me. He effected it not, of course, openly, but in some disguise. I am sufficiently, however, in his confidence—(any man may be that with so audacious a braggart)—to deter him from renewing his attempt for some days. Meanwhile, I or yourself will have discovered some surer home than this, to which you can remove, and then will be the proper time to take back your daughter. And for the present, if you will send by me a letter to enjoin her to receive me as her future bridegroom, it will necessarily divert all thought at once from the Count; I shall be able to detect by the manner in which she receives me, how far the Count has overstated the effect he pretends to have produced. You can give me also a letter to Lady Lansmere, to prevent your daughter coming hither. O, sir, do not reason with me. Have indulgence for my lover's fears. Believe that I advise for the best. Have I not the keenest interest to do so?"

Like many a man who is wise enough with pen and paper before him, and plenty of time wherewith to get up his wisdom, Riccabocca was flurried, nervous, and confused, when that wisdom was called upon for any ready exertion. From the tree of knowledge he had taken grafts enough to serve for a forest; but the whole forest could not spare him a handy walking-stick. The great folio of the dead Machiavelli lay useless before him—the living Machiavelli of daily life stood all puissant by his side. The Sage was as supple to the Schemer as the Clairvoyant is to the Mesmerist. And the lean slight fingers of Randal actually dictated almost the very words that Riccabocca wrote to his child and her hostess.

The philosopher would have liked to consult his wife; but he was ashamed to confess that weakness. Suddenly he remembered Harley, and said, as Randal took up the letters which Riccabocca had indited—

"There—that will give us time; and I will send to Lord L'Estrange and talk to him."

"My noble friend," replied Randal, mournfully, "may I entreat you not to see Lord L'Estrange until at least I have pleaded my cause to your daughter—until, indeed, she is no longer under his father's roof."

"And why?"

"Because I presume that you are sincere when you deign to receive me as a son-in-law, and because I am sure that Lord L'Estrange would hear with distaste of your disposition in my favour. Am I not right?"

Riccabocca was silent.

"And though his arguments would fail with a man of your honour and discernment, they might have more effect on the young mind of your child. Think, I beseech you, the more she is set against me, the more accessible she may be to the arts of Peschiera. Speak not, therefore, I implore you, to Lord L'Estrange till Violante has accepted my hand, or at least until she is again under your charge; otherwise take back your letter—it would be of no avail."

"Perhaps you are right. Certainly Lord L'Estrange is prejudiced against you; or rather, he thinks too much of what I have been—too little of what I am."

"Who can see you, and not do so? I pardon him." After kissing the hand which the exile modestly sought to withdraw from that act of homage, Randal pocketed the letters; and, as if struggling with emotion, rushed from the house.

Now, O curious reader, if thou wilt heedfully observe to what uses Randal Leslie put those letters—what speedy and direct results he drew forth from devices which would seem to an honest simple understanding the most round-about, wire-drawn wastes of invention—I almost fear that in thine admiration for his cleverness, thou mayest half forget thy contempt for his knavery.

But when the head is very full, it does not do to have the heart very empty; there is such a thing as being top-heavy!

## CHAPTER IV.

HELEN and Violante had been conversing together, and Helen had obeyed her guardian's injunction, and spoken, though briefly, of her positive engagement to Harley. However much Violante had been prepared for the confidence, however clearly she had divined that engagement, however before persuaded that the dream of her childhood was fled for ever, still the positive truth, coming from Helen's own lips, was attended with that anguish which proves how impossible it is to *prepare* the human heart for the final verdict which slays its future. She did not, however, betray her emotion to Helen's artless eyes; sorrow, deep-seated, is seldom self-betrayed. But, after a little while, she crept away; and, forgetful of Peschiera, of all things that could threaten danger, (what danger could harm her more!) she glided from the house, and went her desolate way under the leafless wintry trees. Ever and anon she paused—ever and anon she murmured the same words: "If she loved him, I could be consoled; but she does not! or how could she have spoken to me so calmly! how could her very looks have been so sad! Heartless!—heartless!"

Then there came on her a vehement resentment against poor Helen, that almost took the character of scorn or hate—its excess startled herself. "Am I grown so mean?" she said; and tears that humbled her, rushed to her eyes. "Can so short a time alter one thus? Impossible!"

Randal Leslie rang at the front gate, inquired for Violante, and, catching sight of her form as he walked towards the house, advanced boldly and openly. His voice startled her as she leant against one of the dreary trees, still muttering to herself—forlorn. "I have a letter to you from your father, Signorina," said Randal. "But, before I give it to your hands, some explanation is necessary. Condescend, then, to hear me." Violante shook her head impatiently, and stretched forth her hand for the letter. Randal observed her countenance with his keen, cold, searching eye; but he still withheld the letter, and continued, after a pause—

"I know that you were born to princely fortunes; and the excuse for my addressing you now is, that your birthright is lost to you, at least unless you can consent to an union with the man who has despoiled you of your heritage—an union which your father would deem dishonour to yourself and him. Signorina, I might have presumed to love you; but I should not have named that love, had your father not encouraged me by his assent to my suit."

Violante turned to the speaker, her face eloquent with haughty surprise. Randal met the gaze unmoved. He continued, without warmth, and in the tone of one who reasons calmly, rather than of one who feels acutely—

"The man of whom I spoke is in pursuit of you. I have cause to believe that this person has already intruded himself upon you. Ah! your countenance owns it; you have seen Peschiera? This house is, then, less safe than your father deemed it. No house is safe for you but a husband's. I offer to you my name—it is a gentleman's; my fortune, which is small; the participation in my hopes of the future, which are large. I place now your father's letter in your hand, and await your answer." Randal bowed slightly, gave the letter to Violante, and retired a few paces.

It was not his object to conciliate Violante's affection, but rather to excite her repugnance, or at least her terror—we must wait to discover why; so he stood apart, seemingly in a kind of self-confident indifference, while the girl read the following letter:—

"My child, receive with favour Mr. Leslie. He has my consent to address you as a suitor. Circumstances, of which it is needless now to inform you, render it essential to my very peace and happiness that your marriage should be immediate. In a word, I have given my promise to Mr. Leslie, and I confidently leave it to the daughter of my house to redeem the pledge of her anxious and tender father."

The letter dropped from Violante's hand. Randal approached, and restored it to her. Their eyes met. Violante recoiled.

"I cannot marry you," said she, passionately.

"Indeed?" answered Randal, drily. "Is it because you cannot love me?"

"Yes."

"I did not expect that you would as yet, and I still persist in my suit. I have promised to your father that I would not recede before your first unconsidered refusal."

"I will go to my father at once."

"Does he request you to do so in his letter? Look again.

Pardon me, but he foresaw your impetuosity; and I have another note for Lady Lansmere, in which he begs her ladyship not to sanction your return to him (should you so wish) until he come or send for you himself. He will do so whenever your word has redeemed his own."

"And do you dare to talk to me thus, and yet pretend to love me?"

Randal smiled ironically.

"I pretend but to wed you. Love is a subject on which I might have spoken formerly, or may speak hereafter. I give you some little time to consider. When I next call, let me hope that we may fix the day for our wedding."

"Never!"

"You will be, then, the first daughter of your house who disobeyed a father; and you will have this additional crime, that you disobeyed him in his sorrow, his exile, and his fall."

Violante wrung her hands.

"Is there no choice—no escape?"

"I see none for either. Listen to me. I love you, it is true; but it is not for my happiness to marry one who dislikes me, nor for my ambition to connect myself with one whose poverty is greater than my own. I marry but to keep my plighted faith with your father, and to save you from a villain you would hate more than myself, and from whom no walls are a barrier, no laws a defence. One person, indeed, might perhaps have preserved you from the misery you seem to anticipate with me; that person might defeat the plans of your father's foe—effect, it might be, terms which could revoke his banishment and restore his honours; that person is—"

"Lord L'Estrange?"

"Lord L'Estrange!" repeated Randal, sharply, and watching her pale parted lips and her changing colour; "Lord L'Estrange! What could he do? Why did you name him?"

Violante turned aside. "He saved my father once," said she, feelingly.

"And has interfered, and trifled, and promised, Heaven knows what, ever since—yet to what end? Pooh! The person I speak of your father would not consent to see—would not believe if he saw her; yet she is generous, noble—could sympathise with you both. She is the sister of your father's enemy—the Marchesa di Negra. I am convinced that she has great influence with her brother—that she has known enough of his secrets to awe him into renouncing all designs on yourself; but it is idle now to speak of her."

"No, no," exclaimed Violante. "Tell me where she lives—I will see her."

"Pardon me, I cannot obey you; and, indeed, her own pride is now aroused by your father's unfortunate prejudices against her. It is too late to count upon her aid. You turn from me—my presence is unwelcome. I rid you of it now. But welcome or unwelcome, later you must endure it—and for life."

Randal again bowed with formal ceremony, walked towards the house, and asked for Lady Lansmere. The Countess was at home. Randal delivered Riccabocca's note, which was very short, implying that he feared Peschiera had discovered his retreat—and requesting Lady Lansmere to retain Violante, whatever her own desire, till her ladyship heard from him again.

The Countess read, and her lip curled in disdain. "Strange!" said she, half to herself.

"Strange!" said Randal, "that a man like your correspondent should fear one like the Count di Peschiera. Is that it?"

"Sir," said the Countess, a little surprised—"strange that any man should fear another in a country like ours!"

"I don't know," said Randal with his low soft laugh; "I fear many men, and I know many who ought to fear me; yet at every turn of the street one meets a policeman!"

"Yes," said Lady Lansmere. "But to suppose that this profligate foreigner could carry away a girl like Violante against her will—a man she has never seen, and whom she must have been taught to hate!"

"Be on your guard, nevertheless, I pray you, madam; 'where there's a will there's a way.'"

Randal took his leave, and returned to Madame di Negra's. He stayed with her an hour, revisited the Count, and then strolled to Limmer's.

"Randal," said the Squire, who looked pale and worn, but who scorned to confess the weakness with which he still grieved and yearned for his rebellious son—"Randal, you have nothing now to do in London; can you come and stay with me, and take to farming? I remember that you showed a good deal of sound knowledge about thin sowing."

"My dear sir, I will come to you as soon as the general election is over."

"What the deuce have you got to do with the general election?"

"Mr. Egerton has some wish that I should enter Parliament; indeed, negotiations for that purpose are now on foot."

The Squire shook his head. "I don't like my half-brother's politics."

"I shall be quite independent of them," cried Randal, loftily; "that independence is the condition for which I stipulate."

"Glad to hear it; and if you do come into Parliament, I hope you'll not turn your back on the land?"

"Turn my back on the land!" cried Randal, with devout horror. "Oh, sir! I am not so unnatural!"

"That's the right way to put it," quoth the credulous Squire; "it is unnatural! It is turning one's back on one's own mother. The land is a mother—"

"To those who live by her, certainly,—a mother," said Randal, gravely. "And though, indeed, my father starves by her rather than lives, and Rood Hall is not like Hazeldean, still—I—"

"Hold your tongue," interrupted the Squire; "I want to talk to you. Your grandmother was a Hazeldean."

"Her picture is in the drawing-room at Rood. People think me very like her."

"Indeed!" said the Squire. "The Hazeldeans are generally inclined to be stout and rosy, which you are certainly not. But no fault of yours. We are all as Heaven made us! However, to the point. I am going to alter my will—(said with a choking gulp). "This is the rough draft for the lawyers to work upon."

"Pray—pray, sir, do not speak to me on such a subject. I cannot bear to contemplate even the possibility of—of—"

"My death? Ha! ha! Nonsense. My own son calculated on the date of it by the insurance tables. Ha, ha, ha! A very fashionable son—eh! Ha, ha!"

"Poor Frank! do not let him suffer for a momentary forgetfulness of right feeling. When he comes to be married to that foreign lady, and be a father himself, he—"

"Father himself!" burst forth the Squire. "Father to a swarm of sallow-faced Popish tadpoles! No foreign frogs shall hop about my grave in Hazeldean churchyard. No, no. But you need not look so reproachful—I'm not going to disinherit Frank."

"Of course not," said Randal, with a bitter curve in the lip that rebelled against the joyous smile which he sought to impose on it.

"No—I shall leave him the life-interest in the greater part of the property; but if he marry a foreigner, her children will not succeed—you will stand after him in that case. But—(now don't interrupt me)—but Frank looks as if he would live longer than you—so small thanks to me for my good intentions, you may say. I mean to do more for you than a mere barren place in the entail. What do you say to marrying?"

"Just as you please," said Randal, meekly.

"Good. There's Miss Sticktorights disengaged — great heiress. Her lands run on to Rood. At one time I thought of her for that graceless puppy of mine. But I can manage more easily to make up the match for you. There's a mortgage on the property; old Sticktorights would be very glad to pay it off. I'll pay it out of the Hazeldean estate, and give up the Right of Way into the bargain. You understand? So come down as soon as you can, and court the young lady yourself."

Randal expressed his thanks with much grateful eloquence; and he then delicately insinuated, that if the Squire ever did mean to bestow upon him any pecuniary favours, (always without injury to Frank,) it would gratify him more to win back some portions of the old estate of Rood, than to have all the acres of the Sticktorights, however free from any other incumbrance than the amiable heiress.

The Squire listened to Randal with benignant attention. This wish the country gentleman could well understand and sympathise with. He promised to inquire into the matter, and to see what could be done with old Thornhill.

Randal here let out that Mr. Thornhill was about to dispose of a large slice of the ancient Leslie estate through Levy, and that he, Randal, could thus get it at a more moderate price than would be natural if Mr. Thornhill knew that his neighbour the Squire would bid for the purchase.

"Better say nothing about it either to Levy or Thornhill."

"Right," said the Squire. "No proprietor likes to sell to another proprietor, in the same shire, as largely acred as himself: it spoils the balance of power. See to the business yourself; and if I can help you with the purchase, (after that boy is married—I can attend to nothing before,) why, I will."

Randal now went to Egerton's. The Statesman was in his library, settling the accounts of his house-steward, and giving brief orders for the the reduction of his establishment to that of an ordinary private gentleman.

"I may go abroad if I lose my election," said Egerton, condescending to assign to his servant a reason for his economy; "and if I do not lose it, still, now I am out of office, I shall live much in private."

"Do I disturb you, sir?" said Randal, entering.

"No—I have just done."

The house-steward withdrew, much surprised and disgusted, and meditating the resignation of his own office—in order, not like Egerton, to save, but to spend. The house-steward had private dealings with Baron Levy, and was in fact the veritable X.Y. of the *Times*, for whom Dick Avenel had been mistaken. He invested his wages and perquisites in the discount of bills; and it was part of his own money that had (though unknown to himself) swelled the last five thousand pounds which Egerton had borrowed from Levy.

"I have settled with our committee; and, with Lord Lansmere's consent," said Egerton, briefly, "you will stand for the borough, as we proposed, in conjunction with myself. And should any accident happen to me—that is, should I vacate this seat from any cause, you may succeed to it—very shortly perhaps. Ingratiate yourself with the electors, and speak at the public-houses for both of us. I shall stand on my dignity, and leave the work of the election to you. No thanks—you know how I hate thanks. Good night."

"I never stood so near to fortune and to power," said Randal, as he slowly undressed. "And I owe it but to knowledge—knowledge of men—life—of all that books can teach us."

So his slight thin fingers dropped the extinguisher on the candle, and the prosperous Schemer laid himself down to rest in the dark. Shutters closed, curtains drawn—never was rest more quiet, never was room more dark!

That evening, Harley had dined at his father's. He spoke much to Helen—scarcely at all to Violante. But it so happened that when later, and a little while before he took his leave, Helen, at his request, was playing a favourite air of his; Lady Lansmere, who had been seated between him and Violante, left the room, and Violante turned quickly towards Harley.

"Do you know the Marchesa di Negra?" she asked, in a hurried voice.

"A little. Why do you ask?"

"That is my secret," answered Violante, trying to smile with her old frank, childlike archness. "But, tell me, do you think better of her than of her brother?"

"Certainly. I believe her heart to be good, and that she is not without generous qualities."

"Can you not induce my father to see her? Would you not counsel him to do so?"

"Any wish of yours is a law to me," answered Harley, gallantly. "You wish your father to see her? I will try and persuade him to do so. Now, in return, confide to me your secret. What is your object?"

"Leave to return to my Italy. I care not for honours—for rank; and even my father has ceased to regret their loss. But the land, the native land—Oh, to see it once more! Oh, to die there!"

"Die! You children have so lately left heaven, that ye talk as if ye could return there, without passing through the gates of sorrow, infirmity, and age! But I thought you were content with England. Why so eager to leave it? Violante, you are unkind to us—to Helen, who already loves you so well."

As Harley spoke, Helen rose from the piano, and approaching Violante, placed her hand caressingly on the Italian's shoulder. Violante shivered, and shrunk away. The eyes both of Harley and Helen followed her. Harley's eyes were very grave and thoughtful.

"Is she not changed—your friend?" said he, looking down.

"Yes, lately—much changed. I fear there is something on her mind—I know not what."

"Ah!" muttered Harley, "it may be so; but at your age and hers, nothing rests on the mind long. Observe, I say the mind—the heart is more tenacious."

Helen sighed softly, but deeply.

"And therefore," continued Harley, half to himself, "we can detect when something is on the mind—some care, some fear, some trouble. But when the heart closes over its own more passionate sorrow, who can discover! who conjecture! Yet you at least, my pure, candid Helen—you might subject mind and heart alike to the fabled window of glass."

"Oh, no!" cried Helen, involuntarily.

"Oh, yes! Do not let me think that you have one secret I may not know, or one sorrow I may not share. For, in our relationship, *that* would be deceit."

He pressed her hand with more than usual tenderness as he spoke, and shortly afterwards left the house.

And all that night Helen felt like a guilty thing—more wretched even than Violante.

## CHAPTER V.

EARLY the next morning, while Violante was still in her room, a letter addressed to her came by the post. The direction was in a strange hand. She opened it, and read, in Italian, what is thus translated :—

"I would gladly see you, but I cannot call openly at the house in which you live. Perhaps I may have it in my power to arrange family dissensions—to repair any wrongs your father may have sustained. Perhaps I may be enabled to render yourself an essential service. But for all this, it is necessary that we should meet and confer frankly. Meanwhile time presses—delay is forbidden. Will you meet me, an hour after noon, in the lane, just outside the private gate of your gardens. I shall be alone, and you cannot fear to meet one of your own sex, and a kinswoman. Ah, I so desire to see you! Come I beseech you.
"BEATRICE."

Violante read, and her decision was taken. She was naturally fearless, and there was little that she would not have braved for the chance of serving her father. And now all peril seemed slight in comparison with that which awaited her in Randal's suit, backed by her father's approval. Randal had said that Madame di Negra alone could aid her in escape from himself. Harley had said that Madame di Negra had generous qualities; and who but Madame di Negra would write herself a kinswoman, and sign herself "Beatrice?"

A little before the appointed hour, she stole unobserved through the trees, opened the little gate, and found herself in the quiet solitary lane. In a few minutes, a female figure came up, with a quick, light step; and, throwing aside her veil, said, with a sort of wild, suppressed energy, "It is you! I was truly told. Beautiful!—beautiful! And, oh! what youth and what bloom!"

The voice dropped mournfully; and Violante, surprised by the tone, and blushing under the praise, remained a moment silent; then she said, with some hesitation—

"You are, I presume, the Marchesa di Negra? And I have heard of you enough to induce me to trust you."

"Of me! From whom?" asked Beatrice, almost fiercely.

"From Mr. Leslie, and—and—"

"Go on—why falter?"

"From Lord L'Estrange."

"From no one else?"

"Not that I remember."

Beatrice sighed heavily, and let fall her veil. Some foot-passengers now came up the lane; and seeing two ladies, of mien so remarkable, turned round, and gazed curiously.

"We cannot talk here," said Beatrice, impatiently; "and I have so much to say—so much to know. Trust me yet more; it is for yourself I speak. My carriage waits yonder. Come home with me—I will not detain you an hour; and I will bring you back."

This proposition startled Violante. She retreated towards the gate with a gesture of dissent. Beatrice laid her hand on the girl's arm, and again lifting her veil, gazed at her with a look, half of scorn, half of admiration.

"I, too, would once have recoiled from one step beyond the formal line by which the world divides liberty from woman. Now see how bold I am. Child, child, do not trifle with your destiny. You may never again have the same occasion offered to you. It is not only to meet you that I am here; I must know something of you—something of your heart. Why shrink?—is not the heart pure?"

Violante made no answer; but her smile, so sweet and so lofty, humbled the questioner it rebuked.

"I may restore to Italy your father," said Beatrice, with an altered voice. "Come!"

Violante approached, but still hesitatingly.

"Not by union with your brother?"

"You dread that so much then?"

"Dread it? No. Why should I dread what is in my power to reject. But if you can really restore my father, and by nobler means, you may save me for—"

Violante stopped abruptly; the Marchesa's eyes sparkled.

"Save you for—ah! I can guess what you leave unsaid. But come, come—more strangers—see; you shall tell me all at my own house. And if you can make one sacrifice, why, I will save you all else. Come, or farewell for ever!"

Violante placed her hand in Beatrice's, with a frank confidence that brought the accusing blood into the Marchesa's cheek.

"We are women both," said Violante, "we descend from the same noble house; we have knelt alike to the same Virgin Mother; why should I not believe and trust you?"

"Why not?" muttered Beatrice, feebly; and she moved

on, with her head bowed on her breast, and all the pride of her step was gone.

They reached a carriage that stood by the angle of the road. Beatrice spoke a word apart to the driver, who was an Italian, in the pay of the Count; the man nodded, and opened the carriage door. The ladies entered. Beatrice pulled down the blinds; the man remounted his box, and drove on rapidly. Beatrice, leaning back, groaned aloud. Violante drew nearer to her side. "Are you in pain?" said she, with her tender, melodious voice; "or can I serve you as you would serve me?"

"Child, give me your hand, and be silent while I look at you. Was I ever so fair as this? Never! And what deeps—what deeps roll between her and me!"

She said this as of some one absent, and again sank into silence; but continued still to gaze on Violante, whose eyes, veiled by their long fringes, drooped beneath the gaze.

Suddenly Beatrice started, exclaiming, "No, it shall not be!" and placed her hand on the check-string.

"What shall not be?" asked Violante, surprised by the cry and the action. Beatrice paused—her breast heaved visibly under her dress.

"Stay," she said, slowly. "As you say, we are both women of the same noble house; you would reject the suit of my brother, yet you have seen him; his the form to please the eye—his the arts that allure the fancy. He offers to you rank, wealth, your father's pardon and recall. If I could remove the objections which your father entertains—prove that the Count has less wronged him than he deems, would you still reject the rank, and the wealth, and the hand of Giulio Franzini?"

"Oh yes, yes, were his hand a king's!"

"Still, then, as woman to woman—both, as you say, akin, and sprung from the same lineage—still, then, answer me—answer me, for you speak to one who has loved—Is it not that you love another?—Speak."

"I do not know. Nay, not love—it was a romance; it is a thing impossible. Do not question—I cannot answer." And the broken words were choked by sudden tears.

Beatrice's face grew hard and pitiless. Again she lowered her veil, and withdrew her hand from the check-string; but the coachman had felt the touch, and halted. "Drive on," said Beatrice, "as you were directed."

Both were now long silent—Violante with great difficulty recovering from her emotion, Beatrice breathing hard, and her arms folded firmly across her breast.

Meanwhile the carriage had entered London—it passed the quarter in which Madame di Negra's house was situated—it rolled fast over a bridge—it whirled through a broad thoroughfare, then through defiles of lanes, with tall blank dreary houses on either side. On it went, and on, till Violante suddenly took alarm. "Do you live so far?" she said, drawing up the blind, and gazing in dismay on the strange ignoble suburb. "I shall be missed already. Oh, let us turn back, I beseech you!"

"We are nearly there now. The driver has taken this road in order to avoid those streets in which we might have been seen together—perhaps by my brother himself. Listen to me, and talk of—of the lover whom you rightly associate with a vain romance. 'Impossible,'—yes, it is impossible!"

Violante clasped her hands before her eyes, and bowed down her head. "Why are you so cruel?" said she. "This is not what you promised. How are you to serve my father—how restore him to his country? This is what you promised!"

"If you consent to one sacrifice, I will fulfil that promise. We are arrived."

The carriage stopped before a tall dull house, divided from other houses by a high wall that appeared to enclose a yard, and standing at the end of a narrow lane, which was bounded on the one side by the Thames. In that quarter the river was crowded with gloomy, dark-looking vessels and craft, all lying lifeless under the wintry sky.

The driver dismounted and rang the bell. Two swarthy Italian faces presented themselves at the threshold.

Beatrice descended lightly, and gave her hand to Violante. "Now, here we shall be secure," said she; "and here a few minutes may suffice to decide your fate."

As the door closed on Violante—who, now waking to suspicion, to alarm, looked fearfully round the dark and dismal hall—Beatrice turned: "Let the carriage wait."

The Italian who received the order bowed and smiled; but when the two ladies had ascended the stairs he re-opened the street-door, and said to the driver, "Back to the Count, and say 'all is safe.'"

The carriage drove off. The man who had given this order barred and locked the door, and, taking with him the huge key, plunged into the mystic recesses of the basement and disappeared. The hall, thus left solitary, had the grim aspect of a prison; the strong door sheeted with iron—the rugged stone stairs, lighted by a high window grimed with the dust of years, and jealously barred—and the walls themselves abutting out rudely here and there, as if against violence even from within.

## CHAPTER VI.

It was, as we have seen, without taking counsel of the faithful Jemima, that the sage recluse of Norwood had yielded to his own fears, and Randal's subtle suggestions, in the concise and arbitrary letter which he had written to Violante; but at night, when churchyards give up the dead, and conjugal hearts the secrets hid by day from each other, the wise man informed his wife of the step he had taken. And Jemima then—who held English notions, very different from those which prevail in Italy, as to the right of fathers to dispose of their daughters without reference to inclination or repugnance —so sensibly yet so mildly, represented to the pupil of Machiavelli that he had not gone exactly the right way to work, if he feared that the handsome Count had made some impression on Violante, and if he wished her to turn with favour to the suitor he recommended—that so abrupt a command could only chill the heart, revolt the will, and even give to the audacious Peschiera some romantic attraction which he had not before possessed—as effectually to destroy Riccabocca's sleep that night. And the next day he sent Giacomo to Lady Lansmere's with a very kind letter to Violante and a note to the hostess, praying the latter to bring his daughter to Norwood for a few hours, as he much wished to converse with both. It was on Giacomo's arrival at Knightsbridge that Violante's absence was discovered. Lady Lansmere, ever proudly careful of the world and its gossip, kept Giacomo from betraying his excitement to her servants, and stated throughout the decorous household that the young lady had informed her she was going to visit some friends that morning, and had no doubt gone through the garden gate, since it was found open; the way was more quiet there than by the highroad, and her friends might have therefore walked to meet her by the lane. Lady Lansmere observed that her only surprise was that Violante had gone earlier than she had expected. Having said this with a composure that compelled belief, Lady Lansmere ordered the carriage, and, taking Giacomo with her, drove at once to consult her son.

Harley's quick intellect had scarcely recovered from the shock upon his emotions, before Randal Leslie was announced.

"Ah," said Lady Lansmere, "Mr. Leslie may know something. He came to her yesterday with a note from her father. Pray let him enter."

The Austrian Prince approached Harley. "I will wait in the next room," he whispered. "You may want me if you have cause to suspect Peschiera in all this."

Lady Lansmere was pleased with the Prince's delicacy, and, glancing at Leonard, said, "Perhaps you, too, sir, may kindly aid us, if you would retire with the Prince. Mr. Leslie may be disinclined to speak of affairs like these, except to Harley and myself."

"True, madam, but beware of Mr. Leslie."

As the door at one end of the room closed on the Prince and Leonard, Randal entered at the other, seemingly much agitated.

"I have just been to your house, Lady Lansmere. I heard you were here; pardon me if I have followed you. I had called at Knightsbridge to see Violante—learned that she had left you. I implore you to tell me how or wherefore. I have the right to ask: her father has promised me her hand."

Harley's falcon eye had brightened up at Randal's entrance. It watched steadily the young man's face. It was clouded for a moment by his knitted brows at Randal's closing words. But he left it to Lady Lansmere to reply and explain. This the Countess did briefly.

Randal clasped his hands. "And she not gone to her father's? Are you sure of that?"

"Her father's servant has just come from Norwood."

"Oh, I am to blame for this! It is my rash suit—her fear of it—her aversion. I see it all!" Randal's voice was hollow with remorse and despair. "To save her from Peschiera, her father insisted on her immediate marriage with myself. His orders were too abrupt, my own wooing too unwelcome. I know her high spirit; she has fled to escape from me. But whither, if not to Norwood?—oh, whither? What other friends has she—what relations?"

"You throw a new light on this mystery," said Lady Lansmere; "perhaps she may have gone to her father's, after all, and the servant may have crossed, but missed her on the way. I will drive to Norwood at once."

"Do so—do; but if she be not there, be careful not to alarm Riccabocca with the news of her disappearance. Caution Giacomo not to do so. He would only suspect Peschiera, and be hurried to some act of violence."

"Do not you, then, suspect Peschiera, Mr. Leslie?" asked Harley, suddenly.

"Ha! is it possible? Yet, no. I called on him this morning with Frank Hazeldean, who is to marry his sister. I was with him till I went on to Knightsbridge, at the very time of Violante's disappearance. He could not then have been a party to it."

"You saw Violante yesterday. Did you speak to her of Madame di Negra?" asked Harley, suddenly recalling the questions respecting the Marchesa which Violante had addressed to him.

In spite of himself, Randal felt that he changed countenance. "Of Madame di Negra? I do not think so. Yet I might. Oh, yes, I remember now. She asked me the Marchesa's address; I would not give it."

"The address is easily found. Can she have gone to the Marchesa's house?"

"I will run there, and see," cried Randal, starting up.

"And I with you. Stay, my dear mother. Proceed, as you propose, to Norwood, and take Mr. Leslie's advice. Spare our friend the news of his daughter's loss—if lost she be—till she is restored to him. He can be of no use meanwhile. Let Giacomo rest here; I may want him."

Harley then passed into the next room, and entreated the Prince and Leonard to await his return, and allow Giacomo to stay in the same room.

He then went quickly back to Randal. Whatever might be his fears or emotions, Harley felt that he had need of all his coolness of judgment and presence of mind. The occasion made abrupt demand upon powers which had slept since boyhood, but which now woke with a vigour that would have made even Randal tremble, could he have detected the wit, the courage, the electric energies, masked under that tranquil self-possession. Lord L'Estrange and Randal soon reached the Marchesa's house, and learned that she had been out since morning in one of Count Peschiera's carriages. Randal stole an alarmed glance at Harley's face. Harley did not seem to notice it.

"Now, Mr. Leslie, what do you advise next?"

"I am at a loss. Ah, perhaps, afraid of her father—knowing how despotic is his belief in paternal rights, and how tenacious he is of his word once passed, as it has been to me, she may have resolved to take refuge in the country—perhaps at the Casino, or at Mrs. Dale's, or Mrs. Hazeldean's.

I will hasten to inquire at the coach-office. Meanwhile, you—"

"Never mind me, Mr. Leslie. Do what you think best. But, if your surmises be just, you must have been a very rude wooer to the high-born lady you aspired to win."

"Not so; but perhaps an unwelcome one. If she has indeed fled from me, need I say that my suit will be withdrawn at once? I am not a selfish lover, Lord L'Estrange."

"Nor I a vindictive man. Yet, could I discover who has conspired against this lady, a guest under my father's roof, I would crush him into the mire as easily as I set my foot upon this glove. Good day to you, Mr. Leslie."

Randal stood still for a few moments as Harley strided on; then his lip sneered as it muttered—"Insolent! But does he love her? If so, I am avenged already."

## CHAPTER VII.

HARLEY went straight to Peschiera's hotel. He was told that the Count had walked out with Mr. Frank Hazeldean and some other gentlemen who had breakfasted with him. He had left word, in case any one called, that he had gone to Tattersall's to look at some horses that were for sale. To Tattersall's went Harley. The Count was in the yard leaning against a pillar, and surrounded by fashionable friends. Lord L'Estrange paused, and, with a heroic effort at self-mastery, repressed his rage. "I may lose all if I show that I suspect him; and yet I must insult and fight him rather than leave his movements free. Ah, is that young Hazeldean? A thought strikes me!" Frank was standing apart from the group round the Count, and looking very absent and very sad. Harley touched him on the shoulder, and drew him aside unobserved by the Count.

"Mr. Hazeldean, your uncle Egerton is my dearest friend. Will you be a friend to me? I want you."

"My lord—"

"Follow me. Do not let Count Peschiera see us talking together."

Harley quitted the yard, and entered St. James's Park by the little gate close by. In a very few words he informed Frank of Violante's disappearance, and of his reasons for suspecting the Count. Frank's first sentiment was that of indignant disbelief that the brother of Beatrice could be so vile; but as he gradually called to mind the cynical and corrupt vein of the Count's familiar conversation—the hints to Peschiera's prejudice that had been dropped by Beatrice herself—and the general character for brilliant and daring profligacy which even the admirers of the Count ascribed to him — Frank was compelled to reluctant acquiescence in Harley's suspicions; and he said, with an earnest gravity very rare to him—"Believe me, Lord L'Estrange, if I can assist you in defeating a base and mercenary design against this poor young lady, you have but to show me how. One thing is clear—Peschiera was not personally engaged in this abduction, since I have been with him all day; and—now I think of it—I begin to hope that you wrong him; for he has invited a large party of us to make an excursion with him to Boulogne next week, in order to try his yacht, which he could scarcely do if—"

"Yacht, at this time of the year! a man who habitually resides at Vienna—a yacht!"

"Spendquick sells it a bargain, on account of the time of year and other reasons; and the Count proposes to spend next summer in cruising about the Ionian Isles. He has some property on those isles, which he has never yet visited."

"How long is it since he bought this yacht?"

"Why I am not sure that it is already bought—that is, paid for.—Levy was to meet Spendquick this very morning to arrange the matter. Spendquick complains that Levy screws him."

"My dear Mr. Hazeldean, you are guiding me through the maze.—Where shall I find Lord Spendquick?"

"At this hour, probably, in bed. Here is his card."

"Thanks. And where lies the vessel?"

"It was off Blackwall the other day. I went to see it—'The Flying Dutchman'—a fine vessel, and carries guns."

"Enough. Now, heed me. There can be no immediate danger to Violante, so long as Peschiera does not meet her—so long as we know his movements. You are about to marry his sister. Avail yourself of that privilege to keep close by his side. Refuse to be shaken off. Make what excuses for the present your invention suggests. I will give you an excuse. Be anxious and uneasy to know where you can find Madame di Negra."

"Madame di Negra!" cried Frank. "What of her? Is she not in Curzon Street?"

"No; she has gone out in one of the Count's carriages. In all probability the driver of that carriage, or some servant in attendance on it, will come to the Count in the course of the day; and, in order to get rid of you, the Count will tell you to see this servant, and ascertain yourself that his sister is safe. Pretend to believe what the man says, but make him come to your lodgings on pretence of writing there a letter for the Marchesa. Once at your lodgings, and he will be safe; for I shall see that the officers of justice secure him. The moment he is there, send an express for me to my hotel."

"But," said Frank, a little bewildered, "if I go to my lodgings, how can I watch the Count?"

"It will not then be necessary. Only get him to accompany you to your lodgings, and part with him at the door."

"Stop, stop — you cannot suspect Madame di Negra of connivance in a scheme so infamous. Pardon me, Lord L'Estrange; I cannot act in this matter—cannot even hear you except as your foe, if you insinuate a word against the honour of the woman I love."

"Brave gentleman, your hand. It is Madame di Negra I would save, as well as my friend's young child. Think but of her, while you act as I entreat, and all will go well. I confide in you. Now, return to the Count."

Frank walked back to join Peschiera, and his brow was thoughtful, and his lips closed firmly. Harley had that gift which belongs to the genius of Action. He inspired others with the light of his own spirit and the force of his own will. Harley next hastened to Lord Spendquick, remained with that young gentleman some minutes, then repaired to his hotel, where Leonard, the Prince, and Giacomo still awaited him.

"Come with me, both of you. You, too, Giacomo. I must now see the police. We may then divide upon separate missions."

"Oh, my dear lord," cried Leonard, "you must have had good news. You seem cheerful and sanguine."

*Seem!* Nay, I *am* so! If I once paused to despond— even to doubt—I should go mad. A foe to baffle, and an angel to save! · Whose spirits would not rise high—whose wits would not move quick to the warm pulse of his heart?"

## CHAPTER VIII.

TWILIGHT was dark in the room to which Beatrice had conducted Violante. A great change had come over Beatrice. Humble and weeping, she knelt beside Violante, hiding her face, and imploring pardon. And Violante, striving to resist the terror for which she now saw such cause as no woman-heart can defy, still sought to soothe, and still sweetly assured forgiveness.

Beatrice had learned—after quick and fierce questions—which at last compelled the answers that cleared away every doubt—that her jealousy had been groundless—that she had no rival in Violante. From that moment the passions that had made her the tool of guilt abruptly vanished, and her conscience startled her with the magnitude of her treachery. Perhaps had Violante's heart been wholly free, or she had been of that mere commonplace, girlish character, which women like Beatrice are apt to despise, the Marchesa's affection for Peschiera, and her dread of him, might have made her try to persuade her young kinswoman at least to receive the Count's visit — at least to suffer him to make his own excuses, and plead his own cause. But there had been a loftiness of spirit in which Violante had first defied the Marchesa's questions, followed by such generous, exquisite sweetness, when the girl perceived how that wild heart was stung and maddened, and such purity of mournful candour when she had overcome her own virgin bashfulness sufficiently to undeceive the error she detected, and confess where her own affections were placed, that Beatrice bowed before her as mariner of old to some fair saint that had allayed the storm.

"I have deceived you!" she cried, through her sobs; "but I will now save you at any cost. Had you been as I deemed—the rival who had despoiled all the hopes of my future life—I could, without remorse, have been the accomplice I am pledged to be. But *now* you!—oh, you—so good and so noble—you can never be the bride of Peschiera. Nay, start not: he shall renounce his designs for ever, or I will go myself to our Emperor, and expose the dark secrets of his life. Return with me quick to the home from which I ensnared you."

Beatrice's hand was on the door while she spoke. Suddenly her face fell—her lips grew white; the door was locked from without. She called—no one answered; the bell-pull in the room gave no sound; the windows were high and barred—they did not look on the river, nor the street, but on a close, gloomy, silent yard—high blank walls all round it— no one to hear the cry of distress, rang it ever so loud and sharp.

Beatrice divined that she herself had been no less ensnared than her companion; that Peschiera, distrustful of her firmness in evil, had precluded her from the power of reparation. She was in a house only tenanted by his hirelings. Not a hope to save Violante, from a fate that now appalled her, seemed to remain. Thus, in incoherent self-reproaches and frenzied tears, Beatrice knelt beside her victim, communicating more and more the terrors that she felt, as the hours rolled on, and the room darkened, till it was only by the dull lamp which gleamed through the grimy windows from the yard without, that each saw the face of the other.

Night came on; they heard a clock from some distant church strike the hours. The dim fire had long since burnt out, and the air became intensely cold. No one broke upon their solitude—not a voice was heard in the house. They felt neither cold nor hunger—they felt but the solitude, and the silence, and the dread of something that was to come.

At length, about midnight, a bell rang at the street door; then there was the quick sound of steps—of sullen bolts withdrawn—of low, murmured voices. Light streamed through the chinks of the door to the apartment—the door itself opened. Two Italians bearing tapers entered, and the Count di Peschiera followed.

Beatrice sprang up, and rushed towards her brother. He laid his hand gently on her lips, and motioned to the Italians to withdraw. They placed the lights on the table, and vanished without a word.

Peschiera then, putting aside his sister, approached Violante.

"Fair kinswoman," said he, with an air of easy but resolute assurance, "there are things which no man can excuse, and no woman can pardon, unless that love, which is beyond all laws, suggests excuse for the one, and obtains pardon for the other. In a word, I have sworn to win you, and I have had no opportunities to woo. Fear not; the worst that can befall you is to be my bride! Stand aside, my sister, stand aside."

"Giulio, no! Giulio Franzini, I stand between you and

her: you shall strike me to the earth before you can touch even the hem of her robe."

"What, my sister!—you turn against me?"

"And unless you instantly retire and leave her free, I will unmask you to the Emperor."

"Too late, *mon infant!* You will sail with us. The effects you may need for the voyage are already on board. You will be witness to our marriage, and by a holy son of the Church. Then tell the Emperor what you will."

With a light and sudden exertion of his strength, the Count put away Beatrice, and fell on his knee before Violante, who, drawn to her full height, death-like pale, but untrembling, regarded him with unutterable disdain.

"You scorn me now," said he, throwing into his features an expression of humility and admiration, "and I cannot wonder at it. But, believe me, that until the scorn yield to a kinder sentiment, I will take no advantage of the power I have gained over your fate."

"Power!" said Violante, haughtily. "You have ensnared me into this house—you have gained the power of a day; but the power over my fate—no!"

"You mean that your friends have discovered your disappearance, and are on your track. Fair one, I provide against your friends, and I defy all the laws and police of England. The vessel that will bear you from these shores waits in the river hard by. Beatrice, I warn you—be still—unhand me. In that vessel will be a priest who shall join our hands, but not before you will recognise the truth, that she who flies with Giulio Peschiera must become his wife, or quit him as the disgrace of her house, and the scorn of her sex."

"Oh, villain! villain!" cried Beatrice.

"*Peste*, my sister, gentler words. You, too, would marry. I tell no tales of you. Signorina, I grieve to threaten force. Give me your hand; we must be gone."

Violante eluded the clasp that would have profaned her, and darting across the room, opened the door, and closed it hastily behind her. Beatrice clung firmly to the Count to detain him from pursuit. But just without the door, close, as if listening to what passed within, stood a man wrapped, from head to foot in a large boat cloak. The ray of the lamp that beamed on the man, glittered on the barrel of a pistol which he held in his right hand.

"Hist!" whispered the man in English; and passing his arm round her—"in this house you are in that ruffian's power; out of it, safe. Ah! I am by your side—I, Violante!"

The voice thrilled to Violante's heart. She started—looked up, but nothing was seen of the man's face, what with the hat and cloak, save a mass of raven curls, and a beard of the same hue.

The Count now threw open the door, dragging after him his sister, who still clung round him.

"Ha—that is well!" he cried to the man, in Italian. "Bear the lady after me, gently; but if she attempt to cry out— why, force enough to silence her, not more. As for you, Beatrice, traitress that you are, I could strike you to the earth—but— No, this suffices." He caught his sister in his arms as he spoke, and regardless of her cries and struggles, sprang down the stairs.

The hall was crowded with fierce, swarthy men. The Count turned to one of them, and whispered; in an instant the Marchesa was seized and gagged. The Count cast a look over his shoulder; Violante was close behind, supported by the man to whom Peschiera had consigned her, and who was pointing to Beatrice, and appeared warning Violante against resistance. Violante was silent, and seemed resigned. Peschiera smiled cynically, and, preceded by some of his hirelings, who held torches, descended a few steps that led to an abrupt landing-place between the hall and the basement story. There, a small door stood open, and the river flowed close by. A boat was moored on the bank, round which grouped four men, who had the air of foreign sailors. At the appearance of Peschiera, three of these men sprang into the boat, and got ready their oars. The fourth carefully re-adjusted a plank thrown from the boat to the wharf, and offered his arm obsequiously to Peschiera. The Count was the first to enter, and, humming a gay opera air, took his place by the helm. The two females were next lifted in, and Violante felt her hand pressed almost convulsively by the man who stood by the plank. The rest followed, and in another minute the boat bounded swiftly over the waves towards a vessel that lay several furlongs adown the river, and apart from all the meaner craft that crowded the stream. The stars struggled pale through the foggy atmosphere; not a word was heard within the boat—no sound save the regular splash of the oars. The Count paused from his lively tune, and gathering round him the ample fold of his fur pelisse, seemed absorbed in thought. Even by the imperfect light of the stars, Peschiera's face wore an air of sovereign triumph. The result had justified that careless and insolent confidence in himself and in fortune, which was the most prominent feature in the character of the man who, both bravo and gamester, had played against the world, with his rapier in one hand and cogged dice in the other. Violante, once in a vessel filled by his own men, was irretrievably in his power. Even her father must feel grateful to learn that the captive of Peschiera had saved name and repute in becoming Peschiera's wife. Even the pride of sex in Violante herself must induce her to confirm what Peschiera, of course, intended to state, viz., that she was a willing partner in a bridegroom's schemes of flight towards the altar, rather than the poor victim of a betrayer, and receiving his hand but from his mercy. He saw his fortune secured, his success envied, his very character rehabilitated by his splendid nuptials. Ambition began to mingle with his dreams of pleasure and pomp. What post in the Court or the State too high for the aspirations of one who had evinced the most incontestable talent for active life—the talent to succeed in all that the will had undertaken? Thus mused the Count, half forgetful of the present, and absorbed in the golden future, till he was aroused by a loud hail from the vessel, and the bustle on board the boat, as the sailors caght at the rope flung forth to them. He then rose and moved towards Violante. But the man who was still in charge of her passed the Count lightly, half-leading, half-carrying his passive prisoner. "Pardon, Excellency," said the man, in Italian, "but the boat is crowded, and rocks so much that your aid would but disturb our footing." Before Peschiera could reply, Violante was already on the steps of the vessel, and the Count paused till, with elated smile, he saw her safely standing on the deck. Beatrice followed, and then Peschiera himself; but when the Italians in his train also thronged towards the sides of the boat, two of the sailors got before them, and let go the rope, while the other two plied their oars vigorously, and pulled back towards shore. The Italians burst into an amazed and indignant volley of execrations. "Silence," said the sailor who had stood by the plank, "we obey orders. If you are not quiet, we shall upset the boat. We can swim; Heaven and Monsignore San Giacomo pity you if you cannot!"

Meanwhile, as Peschiera leapt upon deck, a flood of light poured upon him from lifted torches. That light streamed full on the face and form of a man of commanding stature whose arm was around Violante, and whose dark eyes flashed upon the Count more luminously than the torches. On one side this man stood the Austrian Prince; on the other side (a cloak, and a profusion of false dark locks, at his feet) stood Lord L'Estrange, his arms folded, and his lips curved by a smile in which the ironical humour native to the man was tempered with a calm and supreme disdain. The Count strove to speak, but his voice faltered.

All around him looked ominous and hostile. He saw many Italian faces, but they scowled at him with vindictive hate; in the rear were English mariners, peering curiously over the shoulders of the foreigners, and with a broad grin on their open countenances. Suddenly, as the Count thus stood perplexed, cowering, stupified, there burst from all the Italians present a hoot of unutterable scorn—"*Il traditore! il traditore!*" —(the traitor! the traitor!)

The Count was brave, and at the cry he lifted his head with a certain majesty.

At that moment Harley, raising his hand as if to silence the hoot, came forth from the group by which he had been hitherto standing, and towards him the Count advanced with a bold stride.

"What trick is this?" he said, in French, fiercely. "I divine that it is you whom I can single out for explanation and atonement."

"*Pardieu, Monsieur le Comte,*" answered Harley, in the same language, which lends itself so well to polished sarcasm and high-bred enmity—"let us distinguish. Explanation should come from me, I allow; but atonement I have the honour to resign to yourself. This vessel—"

"Is mine!" cried the Count. "Those men, who insult me, should be in my pay."

"The men in your pay, *Monsieur le Comte*, are on shore, drinking success to your voyage. But, anxious still to procure you the gratification of being amongst your own countrymen, those whom I have taken into my pay are still better Italians than the pirates whose place they supply; perhaps not such good sailors; but then I have taken the liberty to add to the equipment of a vessel, which has cost me too much to risk lightly, some stout English seamen, who are mariners more practised than even your pirates. Your grand mistake, *Monsieur le Comte*, is in thinking that the 'Flying Dutchman' is yours. With many apologies for interfering with your intention to purchase it, I beg to inform you that Lord Spendquick has kindly sold it to me. Nevertheless, *Monsieur le Comte*, for the next few weeks I place it—men and all—at your service."

Peschiera smiled scornfully.

"I thank your lordship; but since I presume that I shall no longer have the travelling companion who alone could make the voyage attractive, I shall return to shore, and will simply request you to inform me at what hour you can receive the friend whom I shall depute to discuss that part of the question yet untouched, and to arrange that the atonement, whether it be due from me or yourself, may be rendered as satisfactory as you have condescended to make the explanation."

"Let not that vex you, *Monsieur le Comte*—the atonement is, in much, made already; so anxious have I been to forestall all that your nice sense of honour would induce so complete a gentleman to desire. You have ensnared a young heiress, it is true; but you see that it was only to restore her to the arms of her father. You have juggled an illustrious kinsman out of his heritage; but you have voluntarily come on board this vessel, first, to enable his highness the Prince Von ———, of whose rank at the Austrian court you are fully aware, to state to your Emperor that he himself has been witness of the manner in which you interpreted his Imperial Majesty's assent to your nuptials with a child of one of the first subjects in his Italian realm; and, next, to commence by an excursion to the seas of the Baltic, the sentence of banishment which I have no doubt will accompany the same act that restores to the chief of your house his lands and his honours."

The Count started.

"That restoration," said the Austrian Prince, who had advanced to Harley's side, "I already guarantee. Disgrace that you are, Giulio Franzini, to the nobles of the Empire, I will not leave my royal master till his hand strike your name from the roll. I have here your own letters, to prove that your kinsman was duped by yourself into the revolt which you would have headed as a Catiline, if it had not better suited your nature to betray it as a Judas. In ten days from this time, these letters will be laid before the Emperor and his Council."

"Are you satisfied, *Monsieur le Comte*," said Harley, "with your atonement so far? if not, I have procured you the occasion to render it yet more complete. Before you stands the kinsman you have wronged. He knows now, that though, for a while, you ruined his fortunes, you failed to sully his hearth. His heart can grant you pardon, and hereafter his hand may give you alms. Kneel then, Giulio Franzini—kneel at the feet of Alphonso, Duke of Serrano."

The above dialogue had been in French, which only a few of the Italians present understood, and that imperfectly; but at the name with which Harley concluded his address to the Count, a simultaneous cry from those Italians broke forth.

"Alphonso the Good!—Alphonso the Good! *Viva—viva*—the good Duke of Serrano!"

And, forgetful even of the Count, they crowded round the tall form of Riccabocco, striving who should first kiss his hand—the very hem of his garments.

Riccabocca's eyes overflowed. The gaunt exile seemed transfigured into another and more kingly man. An inexpressible dignity invested him. He stretched forth his arms, as if to bless his countrymen. Even that rude cry, from humble men, exiles like himself, consoled him for years of banishment and penury.

"Thanks, thanks," he continued; "thanks. Some day or other, you will all perhaps return with me to the beloved land!"

The Austrian Prince bowed his head, as if in assent to the prayer.

"Giulio Franzini," said the Duke of Serrano—for so we may now call the threadbare recluse of the Casino—"had this last villanous design of yours been allowed by Providence, think you that there is one spot on earth on which the ravisher could have been saved from a father's arm? But now, Heaven has been more kind. In this hour let me imitate its mercy;" and with relaxing brow the Duke mildly drew near to his guilty kinsman.

From the moment the Austrian Prince had addressed him, the Count had preserved a profound silence, showing neither repentance nor shame. Gathering himself up, he had stood firm, glaring round him like one at bay. But as the Duke now approached, he waved his hand, and exclaimed, "Back, pedant, back; you have not triumphed yet. And you, prating German, tell your tales to our Emperor. I shall be by his throne to answer—if, indeed, you escape from the meeting to which I will force you by the way." He spoke, and made a rush towards the side of the vessel. But Harley's quick wit had foreseen the Count's intention, and Harley's quick eye had given the signal by which it was frustrated. Seized in the gripe of his own watchful and indignant countrymen, just as he was about to plunge into the stream, Peschiera was dragged back—pinioned down. Then the expression of his whole countenance changed; the desperate violence of the inborn gladiator broke forth. His great strength enabled him to break loose more than once, to dash more than one man to the floor of the deck; but at length, overpowered by numbers, though still struggling—all dignity, all attempt at presence of mind gone, uttering curses the most plebeian, gnashing his teeth, and foaming at the mouth, nothing seemed left of the brilliant Lothario but the coarse fury of the fierce natural man.

Then still preserving that air and tone of exquisite imperturbable irony which the highest comedian might have sought to imitate in vain, Harley bowed low to the storming Count.

"*Adieu, Monsieur le Comte—adieu!* The vessel which you have honoured me by entering is bound to Norway. The Italians who accompany you were sent by yourself into exile, and, in return, they now kindly promise to enliven you with their society, whenever you feel somewhat tired of your own. Conduct the Count to his cabin. Gently there, gently. *Adieu, Monsieur le Comte, adieu! et bon voyage.*"

Harley turned lightly on his heel, as Peschiera, in spite of his struggles, was now fairly carried down to the cabin.

"A trick for the trickster," said L'Estrange to the Austrian Prince. "The revenge of a farce on the would-be tragedian."

"More than that—he is ruined."

"And ridiculous," quoth Harley. "I should like to see his look when they land him in Norway." Harley then passed towards the centre of the vessel, by which, hitherto partially concealed by the sailors, who were now busily occupied, stood Beatrice. Frank Hazeldean, who had first received her on entering the vessel, standing by her side; and Leonard, a little apart from the two, in quiet observation of all that had passed around him. Beatrice appeared but little to heed Frank; her dark eyes were lifted to the dim starry skies, and her lips were moving as if in prayer; yet her young lover was speaking to her in great emotion, low and rapidly.

"No, no—do not think for a moment that we suspect you, Beatrice. I will answer for your honour with my life. Oh, why will you turn from me—why will you not speak?"

"A moment later," said Beatrice, softly. "Give me one moment yet." She passed slowly and falteringly towards Leonard—placed her hand, that trembled, on his arm—and led him aside to the verge of the vessel. Frank, startled by her movement, made a step as if to follow, and then stopped short, and looked on, but with a clouded and doubtful countenance. Harley's smile had gone, and his eye was also watchful.

It was but a few words that Beatrice spoke—it was but a sentence or so that Leonard answered; and then Beatrice extended her hand, which the young poet bent over, and kissed in silence. She lingered an instant; and even by the starlight, Harley noted the blush that overspread her face. The blush faded as Beatrice returned to Frank. Lord L'Estrange would have retired—she signed to him to stay.

"My lord," she said, very firmly, "I cannot accuse you of harshness to my sinful and unhappy brother. His offence might perhaps deserve a heavier punishment than that which you inflict with such playful scorn. But whatever his penance, contempt now or poverty later, I feel that his sister should be by his side to share it. I am not innocent if he be guilty; and, wreck though he be, nothing else on this dark sea of life is now left to me to cling to. Hush, my lord! I shall not leave this vessel. All that I entreat of you is, to order your men to respect my brother, since a woman will be by his side."

"But, Marchesa, this cannot be; and—"

"Beatrice, Beatrice—and me!—our betrothal? Do you forget me?" cried Frank, in reproachful agony.

"No, young and too noble lover; I shall remember you ever in my prayers. But listen. I have been deceived—hurried on, I might say, by others, but also, and far more, by my own mad and blinded heart—deceived, hurried on, to wrong you and to belie myself. My shame burns into me when I think that I could have inflicted on you the just anger of your family—linked you to my own ruined fortunes—my own—"

"Your own generous, loving heart!—that is all I asked!" cried Frank. "Cease, cease—that heart is mine still!"

Tears gushed from the Italian's eyes.

"Englishman, I never loved you; this heart was dead to you, and it will be dead to all else for ever. Farewell. You will forget me sooner than you think for—sooner than I shall forget you—as a friend, as a brother—if brothers had natures as tender and as kind as yours! Now, my lord, will you give me your arm? I would join the Count."

"Stay—one word, madame," said Frank, very pale, and through his set teeth, but calmly, and with a pride on his brow which had never before dignified its habitual careless expression—"one word. I may not be worthy of you in anything else—but an honest love, that never doubted, never suspected—that would have clung to you though all the world were against; such a love makes the meanest man of worth. One word, frank and open. By all that you hold most sacred in your creed, did you speak the truth when you said that you never loved me?"

Beatrice bent down her head; she was abashed before this manly nature that she had so deceived, and perhaps till then undervalued.

"Pardon, pardon," she said, in reluctant accents, half-choked by the rising of a sob.

At her hesitation, Frank's face lighted as if with sudden hope. She raised her eyes, and saw the change in him, then glanced where Leonard stood, mournful and motionless. She shivered, and added firmly—

"Yes—pardon; for I spoke the truth; and I had no heart to give. It might have been as wax to another—it was of granite to you." She paused, and muttered inly—"Granite, and—broken!"

Frank said not a word more. He stood rooted to the spot, not even gazing after Beatrice as she passed on, leaning on the arm of Lord L'Estrange. He then walked resolutely away, and watched the boat that the men were now lowering from the side of the vessel. Beatrice stopped when she came near the place where Violante stood, answering in agitated whispers her father's anxious questions. As she stopped, she leaned more heavily upon Harley. "It is your arm that trembles now, Lord L'Estrange," said she, with a mournful smile, and, quitting him ere he could answer, she bowed down her head meekly before Violante. "You have pardoned me already," she said, in a tone that reached only the girl's ear, "and my last words shall not be of the past. I see your future spread bright before me under those steadfast stars. Love still; hope and trust. These are the last words of her who will soon die to the world. Fair maid, they are prophetic!"

Violante shrunk back to her father's breast, and there hid her glowing face, resigning her hand to Beatrice, who pressed it to her bosom. The Marchesa then came back to Harley, and disappeared with him in the interior of the vessel.

When Harley again came on deck, he seemed much flurried and disturbed. He kept aloof from the Duke and Violante, and was the last to enter the boat, that was now lowered into the water.

As he and his companions reached the land, they saw the vessel in movement, gliding slowly down the river.

"Courage, Leonard, courage!" murmured Harley. "You grieve, and nobly. But you have shunned the worst and most vulgar deceit in civilised life; you have not simulated love. Better that yon poor lady should be, awhile, the sufferer from a harsh truth, than the eternal martyr of a flattering lie! Alas, my Leonard! with the love of the poet's dream are linked only the Graces; with the love of the human heart come the awful Fates!"

"My lord, poets do not dream when they love. You will learn how the feelings are deep in proportion as the fancies are vivid, when you read that confession of genius and woe which I have left in your hands."

Leonard turned away. Harley's gaze followed him with inquiring interest, and suddenly encountered the soft dark grateful eyes of Violante. "The Fates, the Fates!" murmured Harley.

## CHAPTER IX.

WE are at Norwood in the sage's drawing-room. Violante has long since retired to rest. Harley, who had accompanied the father and daughter to their home, is still conversing with the former.

"Indeed, my dear Duke," said Harley—

"Hush, hush! *Diavolo*, don't call me Duke yet; I am at home here once more as Dr. Riccabocca."

"My dear doctor, then, allow me to assure you that you overrate my claim to your thanks. Your old friends, Leonard and Frank Hazeldean, must come in for their share. Nor is the faithful Giacomo to be forgotten."

"Continue your explanation."

"In the first place, I learned, through Frank, that one Baron Levy, a certain fashionable money-lender, and general ministrant to the affairs of fine gentlemen, was just about to purchase a yacht from Lord Spendquick on behalf of the Count. A short interview with Spendquick enabled me to outbid the usurer, and conclude a bargain, by which the yacht became mine;—a promise to assist Spendquick in extricating himself from the claws of the money-lender, (which I trust to do by reconciling him with his father, who is a man of liberality and sense,) made Spendquick readily connive at my scheme for outwitting the enemy. He allowed Levy to suppose that the Count might take possession of the vessel; but affecting an engagement, and standing out for terms, postponed the final settlement of the purchase-money till the next day. I was thus master of the vessel, which I felt sure was destined to serve Peschiera's infamous design. But it was my business not to alarm the Count's suspicions: I therefore permitted the pirate crew he had got together to come on board. I knew I could get rid of them when necessary. Meanwhile, Frank undertook to keep close to the Count until he could see and cage within his lodgings the servant whom Peschiera had commissioned to attend his sister. If I could but apprehend this servant, I had a sanguine hope that I could discover and free your daughter before Peschiera could even profane her with his presence. But Frank, alas! was no pupil of Machiavelli. Perhaps the Count detected his secret thoughts under his open countenance; perhaps merely wished to get rid of a companion very much in his way; but, at all events, he contrived to elude our young friend as cleverly as you or I could have done—told him that Beatrice herself was at Roehampton—had borrowed the Count's carriage to go there—volunteered to take Frank to the house—took him. Frank found himself in a drawing-room; and after waiting a few minutes, while the Count went out on pretence of seeing his sister—in pirouetted a certain distinguished opera-dancer! Meanwhile the Count was fast back on the road to London, and Frank had to return as he could. He then hunted for the Count everywhere, and saw him no more. It was late in the day when Frank found me out with this news. I became seriously alarmed. Peschiera might perhaps learn my counter scheme with the yacht—or he might postpone sailing until he had terrified or entangled Violante into some—in short, everything was to be dreaded from a man of the Count's temper. I had no clue to the place to which your daughter was taken—no excuse to arrest Peschiera—no means even of learning where he was. He had not returned to Mivart's. The Police was at fault, and useless, except in one valuable piece of information. They told me where some of your countrymen, whom Peschiera's perfidy had sent into exile, were to be found. I commissioned Giacomo to seek these men out, and induce them to man the vessel. It might be necessary, should Peschiera or his confidential servants come aboard, after we had expelled or drawn off the pirate crew, that they should find Italians whom they might well mistake for their own hirelings. To these foreigners I added some English sailors who had before served in the same vessel, and on whom Spendquick assured me I could rely. Still these precautions only availed in case Peschiera should resolve to sail, and defer till then all machinations against his captives. While, amidst my fears and uncertainties, I was struggling still to preserve presence of mind, and rapidly discussing with the Austrian Prince if any other steps could be taken, or if our sole resource was to repair to the vessel and take the chance of what might ensue, Leonard suddenly and quietly entered my room. You know his countenance, in which joy or sadness is not betrayed so much by the evidence of the passions as by variations in the intellectual expression. It was but by the clearer brow and the steadier eye that I saw he had good tidings to impart."

"Ah," said Riccabocca—for so, obeying his own request, we will yet call the sage—"ah, I early taught that young man the great lesson inculcated by Helvetius. 'All our errors arise from our ignorance or our passions.' Without ignorance, and without passions, we should be serene, all-penetrating intelligences."

"Mopsticks," quoth Harley, "have neither ignorance nor passions; but as for their intelligence—"

"Pshaw!" interrupted Riccabocca—"Proceed."

"Leonard had parted from us some hours before. I had commissioned him to call at Madame di Negra's, and, as he was familiarly known to her servants, seek to obtain quietly all the information he could collect, and, at all events, procure (what in my haste I had failed to do) the name and description of the man who had driven her out in the morning, and make what use he judged best of every hint he could gather or glean that might aid our researches. Leonard only succeeded in learning the name and description of the coachman, whom he recognised as one Beppo, to whom she had often given orders in his presence. None could say where he then could be found, if not at the Count's hotel. Leonard went next to that hotel. The man had not been there all the day. While revolving what next he should do, his eye caught sight of your intended son-in-law, gliding across the opposite side of the street. One of those luminous, inspiring conjectures, which never occur to you philosophers, had from the first guided Leonard to believe that Randal Leslie was mixed up in this villanous affair."

"Ha! He!" cried Riccabocca. "Impossible! For what interest?—what object!"

"I cannot tell; neither could Leonard; but we had both formed the same conjecture. Brief:—Leonard resolved to follow Randal Leslie, and track all his movements. He did then follow him, unobserved; and at a distance—first to Audley Egerton's house—then to Eaton Square—thence to a house in Bruton Street, which Leonard ascertained to be Baron Levy's. Suspicious that, my dear sage?"

"*Diavolo*—yes!" said Riccabocca, thoughtfully.

"At Levy's, Randal stayed till dusk. He then came out, with his cat-like, stealthy step, and walked quickly into the neighbourhood of Leicester Square. Leonard saw him enter one of those small hotels which are appropriated to foreigners. Wild outlandish fellows were loitering about the door and in the street. Leonard divined that the Count or the Count's confidants were there."

"If that can be proved," cried Riccabocca—"If Randal could have been thus in communication with Peschiera—could have connived at such perfidy—I am released from my promise. Oh, to prove it!"

"Proof will come later, if we are on the right track. Let me go on. While waiting near the door of this hotel, Beppo himself, the very man Leonard was in search of, came forth, and, after speaking a few words to some of the loitering foreigners, walked briskly towards Piccadilly. Leonard here resigned all further heed of Leslie, and gave chase to Beppo, whom he recognised at a glance. Coming up to him, he said, quietly, ' I have a letter for the Marchesa di Negra. She told me I was to send it to her by you. I have been searching for you the whole day.' The man fell into the trap, and the more easily, because—as he since owned in excuse for a simplicity, which, I dare say, weighed on his conscience more than any of the thousand-and-one crimes he may have committed in the course of his illustrious life—he had been employed by the Marchesa as a spy upon Leonard, and, with an Italian's acumen in affairs of the heart, detected her secret."

"What secret?" asked the innocent sage.

"Her love for the handsome young poet. I betray that secret, in order to give her some slight excuse for becoming Peschiera's tool. She believed Leonard to be in love with your daughter, and jealousy urged her to treason. Violante, no doubt, will explain this to you. Well, the man fell into the trap. ' Give me the letter, Signore, and quick.'

## VARIETIES IN ENGLISH LIFE. 401

" ' It is at a hotel close by; come there, and you will have a guinea for your trouble.'

"So Leonard walked our gentleman into my hotel; and having taken him into my dressing-room, turned the key and there left him. On learning this capture, the Prince and myself hastened to see our prisoner. He was at first sullen and silent; but when the Prince disclosed his rank and name, (you know the mysterious terror the meaner Italians feel for an Austrian magnate,) his countenance changed, and his courage fell. What with threats, and what with promises, we soon obtained all that we sought to know; and an offered bribe, which I calculated at ten times the amount the rogue could ever expect to receive from his spendthrift master, finally bound him cheerfully to our service, soul and body. Thus we learned the dismal place to which your noble daughter had been so perfidiously ensnared. We learned also that the Count had not yet visited her, hoping much from the effect that prolonged incarceration might have in weakening her spirit and inducing her submission. Peschiera was to go to the house at midnight, thence to transport her to the vessel. Beppo had received orders to bring the carriage to Leicester Square, where Peschiera would join him. The Count (as Leonard surmised) had taken skulking refuge at the hotel in which Randal Leslie had disappeared. The Prince, Leonard, Frank, (who was then in the hotel,) and myself, held a short council. Should we go at once to the house, and, by the help of the police, force an entrance, and rescue your daughter? This was a very hazardous resource. The abode, which, at various times, had served for the hiding-place of men hunted by the law, abounded, according to our informant, in subterranean vaults and secret passages, and had more than one outlet on the river. At our first summons at the door, therefore, the ruffians within might not only escape themselves, but carry off their prisoner. The door was strong, and before our entrance could be forced, all trace of her we sought might be lost. Again, too, the Prince was desirous of bringing Peschiera's guilty design home to him— anxious to be able to state to the Emperor, and to the great minister, his kinsman, that he himself had witnessed the Count's vile abuse of the Emperor's permission to wed your daughter. In short, while I only thought of Violante, the Prince thought also of her father's recall to his dukedom. Yet still to leave Violante in that terrible house, even for an hour, a few minutes, subjected to the actual presence of

Peschiera, unguarded save by the feeble and false woman who had betrayed, and might still desert her—how contemplate that fearful risk? What might not happen in the interval between Peschiera's visit to the house, and his appearance with his victim on the vessel? An idea flashed on me—Beppo was to conduct the Count to the house; if I could accompany Beppo in disguise—enter the house—myself be present?—I rushed back to our informant, now become our agent; I found the plan still more feasible than I had at first supposed. Beppo had asked the Count's permission to bring with him a brother accustomed to the sea, and who wished to quit England. I might personate that brother. You know that the Italian language, in most of its dialects and varieties of *patois*—Genoese, Piedmontese, Venetian—is as familiar to me as Addison's English! Alas! rather more so. Presto! the thing was settled. I felt my heart, from that moment, as light as a feather, and my sense as keen as the dart which a feather wings. My plans now were formed in a breath, and explained in a sentence. It was right that you should be present on board the vessel, not only to witness your foe's downfall, but to receive your child in a father's arms. Leonard set out to Norwood for you, cautioned not to define too precisely for what object you were wanted, till on board.

"Frank, accompanied by Beppo, (for there was yet time for these preparations before midnight,) repaired to the yacht, taking Giacomo by the way. There our new ally, familiar to most of that piratical crew, and sanctioned by the presence of Frank, as the Count's friend, and prospective brother-in-law, told Peschiera's hirelings that they were to quit the vessel, and wait on shore under Giacomo's auspices till further orders; and as soon as the decks were cleared of these ruffians, (save a few left to avoid suspicion, and who were afterwards safely stowed down in the hold,) and as soon as Giacomo had lodged his convoy in a public house, where he quitted them, drinking his health over unlimited rations of grog, your inestimable servant quietly shipped on board the Italians pressed into the service, and Frank took charge of the English sailors.

"The Prince, promising to be on board in due time, then left me to make arrangements for his journey to Vienna with the dawn. I hastened to a masquerade warehouse, where, with the help of an ingenious stagewright artificer, I disguised myself into a most thorough-paced-looking cut-throat, and then waited the return of my friend Beppo with the most perfect confidence."

"Yet, if that rascal had played false, all these precautions were lost. *Cospetto!* you were not wise," said the prudent philosopher.

"Very likely not. You would have been so wise, that by this time your daughter would have been lost to you for ever."

"But why not employ the police?"

"First—Because I had already employed them to little purpose. Secondly—Because I no longer wanted them. Thirdly—Because to use them for my final catastrophe, would be to drag your name, and your daughter's, perhaps, before a police court; at all events, before the tribunal of public gossip. And lastly—Because, having decided upon the proper punishment, it had too much of equity to be quite consistent with law; and in forcibly seizing a man's person, and shipping him off to Norway, my police would have been sadly in the way. Certainly my plan rather savours of Lope de Vega than of Blackstone. However, you see success atones for all irregularities. I resume:—Beppo came back in time to narrate all the arrangements that had been made, and to inform me that a servant from the Count had come on board just as our new crew were assembled there, to order the boat to be at the place where we found it. The servant, it was deemed prudent to detain and secure. Giacomo undertook to manage the boat. I am nearly at the close of my story. Sure of my disguise, I got on the coach-box with Beppo. The Count arrived at the spot appointed, and did not even honour myself with a question or glance. 'Your brother?' he said to Beppo; 'one might guess that; he has the family likeness. Not a handsome race yours! Drive on.'

"We arrived at the house. I dismounted to open the carriage-door. The Count gave me one look.

"'Beppo says you have known the sea.'

"'Excellency, yes. I am a Genoese.'

"'Ha! how is that! Beppo is a Lombard.'—Admire the readiness with which I redeemed my blunder.

"'Excellency, it pleased Heaven that Beppo should be born in Lombardy, and then to remove my respected parents to Genoa, at which city they were so kindly treated that my mother, in common gratitude, was bound to increase its population. It was all she could do, poor woman. You see she did her best.'

"The Count smiled, and said no more. The door opened—I followed him; your daughter can tell you the rest."

"And you risked your life in that den of miscreants! Noble friend!"

"Risked my life—no; but I risked the Count's. There was one moment when my hand was on my trigger, and my soul very near the sin of justifiable homicide. But my tale is done. The Count is now on the river, and will soon be on the salt seas,—though not bound to Norway as I had first intended. I could not inflict that frigid voyage on his sister. So the men have orders to cruise about for six days, keeping aloof from shore, and they will then land the Count and the Marchesa, by boat, on the French coast. That delay will give time for the Prince to arrive at Vienna before the Count could follow him."

"Would he have that audacity?"

"Do him more justice! Audacity, faith! he does not want for that. But I dreaded not his appearance at Vienna with such evidence against him. I dreaded his encountering the Prince on the road, and forcing a duel, before his character was so blasted that the Prince could refuse it;—and the Count is a dead shot of course;—all such men are!"

"He will return, and you—"

"I!—Oh, never fear; he has had enough of me. And now, my dear friend—now that Violante is safe once more under your own roof—now that my honoured mother must long ere this have been satisfied by Leonard, who left us to go to her, that our success has been achieved without danger, and, what she will value almost as much, without scandal—now that your foe is powerless as a reed floating on the water towards its own rot, and the Prince Von —— is perhaps about to enter his carriage on the road to Dover, charged with the mission of restoring to Italy her worthiest son—let me dismiss you to your own happy slumbers, and allow me to wrap myself in my cloak, and snatch a short sleep on the sofa, till yonder grey dawn has mellowed into riper day. My eyes are heavy, and if you stay here three minutes longer, I shall be out of reach of hearing—in the land of dreams. *Buona notte!*"

"But there is a bed prepared for you."

Harley shook his head in dissent, and composed himself at length on the sofa.

Riccabocca bending, wrapped the cloak round his guest, kissed him on the forehead, and crept out of the room to rejoin Jemima, who still sate up for him, nervously anxious to learn from him those explanations which her considerate affection would not allow her to ask from the agitated and exhausted Violante. "Not in bed!" cried the sage, on seeing her. "Have you no feelings of compassion for my son that is to be? Just, too, when there is a reasonable probability that we can afford a son?"

Riccabocca here laughed merrily, and his wife threw herself on his shoulder, and cried for joy.

But no sleep fell on the lids of Harley L'Estrange. He started up when his host had left him, and paced the apartment, with noiseless but rapid strides. All whim and levity had vanished from his face, which, by the light of the dawn, seemed death-like pale. On that pale face there was all the struggle, and all the anguish of passion.

"These arms have clasped her," he murmured; "these lips have inhaled her breath. I am under the same roof, and she is saved—saved evermore from danger and from penury, and for ever divided from me. Courage, courage! Oh, honour, duty; and thou, dark memory of the past—thou that didst pledge love at least to a grave—support—defend me! Can I be so weak!"

The sun was in the wintry skies, when Harley stole from the house. No one was stirring except Giacomo, who stood by the threshold of the door, which he had just unbarred, feeding the house-dog. "Good day," said the servant, smiling. "The dog has not been of much use, but I don't think the Padrone will henceforth grudge him a breakfast. I shall take him to Italy, and marry him there, in the hope of improving the breed of our native Lombard dogs."

"Ah!" said Harley, "you will soon leave our cold shores. May sunshine settle on you all." He paused, and looked up at the closed windows wistfully.

"The Signorina sleeps there," said Giacomo, in a husky voice, "just over the room in which you slept."

"I knew it," muttered Harley. "An instinct told me of it. Open the gate; I must go home. My excuses to your lord, and to all."

He turned a deaf ear to Giacomo's entreaties to stay till at least the Signorina was up—the Signorina whom he had saved. Without trusting himself to speak further, he quitted the demesne, and walked with swift strides towards London.

## CHAPTER X.

HARLEY had not long reached his hotel, and was still seated before his untasted breakfast, when Mr. Randal Leslie was announced. Randal, who was in the firm belief that Violante was now on the wide seas with Peschiera, entered, looking the very personation of anxiety and fatigue. For, like the great Cardinal Richelieu, Randal had learned the art how to make good use of his own delicate and somewhat sickly aspect. The Cardinal, when intent on some sanguinary scheme requiring unusual vitality and vigour, contrived to make himself look a harmless sufferer at death's door. And Randal, whose nervous energies could at that moment have whirled him from one end of this huge metropolis to the other, with a speed that would have outstripped a prize pedestrian, now sank into a chair with a jaded weariness that no mother could have seen without compassion. He seemed since the last night to have galloped towards the last stage of consumption.

"Have you discovered no trace, my lord? Speak, speak!"

"Speak—certainly. I am too happy to relieve your mind, Mr. Leslie. What fools we were? Ha! ha!"

"Fools—how?" faltered Randal.

"Of course; the young lady was at her father's house all the time."

"Eh? what?"

"And is there now."

"It is not possible!" said Randal, in the hollow dreamy tone of a somnambulist. "At her father's house—at Norwood! Are you sure?"

"Sure."

Randal made a desperate and successful effort at self-control. "Heaven be praised!" he cried. "And just as I had begun to suspect the Count—the Marchesa; for I find that neither of them slept at home last night; and Levy told me that the Count had written to him, requesting the Baron to discharge his bills, as he should be for some time absent from England."

"Indeed! Well that is nothing to us—very much to Baron Levy, if he executes his commission, and discharges the bills. What! are you going already?"

"Do you ask such a question? How can I stay? I must

go to Norwood—must see Violante with my own eyes! Forgive my emotion—I—I—"

Randal snatched at his hat and hurried away. The low scornful laugh of Harley followed him as he went.

"I have no more doubt of his guilt than Leonard has. Violante at least shall not be the prize of that thin-lipped knave. What strange fascination can he possess, that he should thus bind to him the two men I value most—Audley Egerton, and Alphonso di Serrano? Both so wise too!—one in books, one in action. And both suspicious men! While I, so imprudently trustful and frank—Ah! that is the reason; our natures are antipathetic;—cunning, simulation, falsehood, I have no mercy, no pardon for these. Woe to all hypocrites if I were a grand Inquisitor!"

"Mr. Richard Avenel," said the waiter, throwing open the door.

Harley caught at the arm of the chair on which he sate, and grasped it nervously; while his eyes became fixed intently on the form of the gentleman who now advanced into the room. He rose with an effort.

"Mr. Avenel!" he said, falteringly. "Did I hear your name aright? Avenel!"

"Richard Avenel, at your service, my lord," answered Dick. "My family is not unknown to you; and I am not ashamed of my family, though my parents were small Lansmere tradesfolks. And I am—a-hem!—a citizen of the world, and well to do!" added Dick, dropping his kid gloves into his hat, and then placing the hat on the table, with the air of an old acquaintance who wishes to make himself at home.

Lord L'Estrange bowed, and said, as he reseated himself—(Dick being firmly seated already)—"You are most welcome, sir; and if there be anything I can do for one of your name—"

"Thank you, my lord," interrupted Dick. "I want nothing of any man. A bold word to say; but I say it. Nevertheless, I should not have presumed to call on your lordship, unless, indeed, you had done me the honour to call first at my house, Eaton Square, No. * * *.—I should not have presumed to call, if it had not been on business :—public business, I may say—NATIONAL business!"

Harley bowed again. A faint smile flitted for a moment to his lip, but, vanishing, gave way to a mournful, absent expression of countenance, as he scanned the handsome features before him, and, perhaps, masculine and bold though they were, still discovered something of a family likeness to one whose beauty had once been his ideal of female loveliness; for suddenly he stretched forth his hand, and said, with more than his usual cordial sweetness, "Business, or not business, let us speak to each other as friends—for the sake of a name that takes me back to Lansmere—to my youth. I listen to you with interest."

Richard Avenel, much surprised by this unexpected kindliness, and touched, he knew not why, by the soft and melancholy tone of Harley's voice, warmly pressed the hand held out to him: and, seized with a rare fit of shyness, coloured, and coughed, and hemmed, and looked first down, then aside, before he could find the words which were generally ready enough at his command.

"You are very good, Lord L'Estrange; nothing can be handsomer. I feel it here, my lord," striking his buff waistcoat—"I do, 'pon my honour. But not to waste your time, (time's money,) I come to the point. It is about the borough of Lansmere. Your family interest is very strong in that borough. But excuse me if I say that I don't think you are aware that I too have cooked up a pretty considerable interest on the other side. No offence—opinions are free. And the popular tide runs strong with us—I mean with *me*, at the impending crisis—that is at the next election. Now, I have a great respect for the Earl, your father; and so have those who brought me into the world;—my father, John, was always a regular good Blue;—and my respect for yourself since I came into this room has gone up in the market—a very great rise indeed—considerable. So I should just like to see if we could set our heads together, and settle the borough between us two, in a snug private way, as public men ought to do when they get together—nobody else by, and no necessity for that sort of humbug—which is so common in this rotten old country. Eh, my lord?"

"Mr. Avenel," said Harley, slowly, recovering himself from the abstraction with which he had listened to Dick's earlier sentences, "I fear I do not quite understand you; but I have no other interest in the next election for the borough of Lansmere, than as may serve one whom, whatever be your politics, you must acknowledge to be——"

"A humbug!"

"Mr. Avenel, you cannot mean the person I mean. I speak of one of the first statesmen of our time—of Mr. Audley Egerton—of——"

"A stiff-necked, pompous——"

"My earliest and dearest friend."

The rebuke, though gently said, sufficed to silence Dick for a moment; and when he spoke again, it was in an altered tone.

"I beg your pardon, my lord, I am sure. Of course, I can say nothing disrespectful of your friend;—very sorry that he is your friend. In that case, I am almost afraid that nothing is to be done. But Mr. Audley Egerton has not a chance. Let me convince you of this." And Dick pulled out a little book, bound neatly in red.

"Canvass book, my lord. I am no aristocrat. I don't pretend to carry a free and independent constituency in my breeches' pocket. Heaven forbid! But, as a practical man of business—what I do is done properly. Just look at this book. Well kept, eh? Names, promises, inclinations, public opinions, and private interests of every individual Lansmere elector! Now, as one man of honour to another, I show you this book, and I think you will see that we have a clear majority of at least eighty votes as against Mr. Egerton."

"That is your view of the question," said Harley, taking the book and glancing over the names catalogued and ticketed therein. But his countenance became serious as he recognised many names, familiar to his boyhood, as those of important electors on the Lansmere side, and which he now found transferred to the hostile. "But surely there are persons here in whom you deceive yourself—old friends of my family—staunch supporters of our party."

"Exactly so. But this new question has turned all old things topsy-turvy. No relying on any friend of yours. No reliance except in this book!" said Dick, slapping the red cover with calm but ominous emphasis.

"Now, what I want to propose is this: Don't let the Lansmere interest be beaten: it would vex the old Earl—go to his heart, I am sure."

Harley nodded.

"And the Lansmere interest need not be beaten, if you'll put up another man instead of this red-tapist. (Beg pardon.) You see I only want to get in one man—you want to get in another. Why not? Now, there's a smart youth—connection of Mr. Egerton's—Randal Leslie. I have no objection to him, though he is of your colours. Withdraw Mr. Egerton, and I'll withdraw my second man before it comes to the poll; and so we shall halve the borough slick between us. That's the way to do business—eh, my lord?"

"Randal Leslie! Oh, you wish to bring in Mr. Leslie? But he stands with Egerton, not against him."

"Ah!" said Dick, smiling, as if to himself, "so I hear; and we could bring him in over Egerton without saying a word to you. But all our family respect yours, and so I have wished to do the thing handsome and open. Let the Earl and your party be content with young Leslie."

"Young Leslie has spoken to you?"

"Not as to my coming here. Oh no—that's a secret—private and confidential, my lord. And now, to make matters still more smooth, I propose that my man shall be one to your lordship's own heart. I find you have been very kind to my nephew;—does you credit, my lord;—a wonderful young man, though I say it. I never guessed there was so much in him. Yet all the time he was in my house, he had in his desk the very sketch of an invention that is now saving me from ruin—from positive ruin—Baron Levy—the King's Bench—and almighty smash! Now, such a young man ought to be in Parliament. I like to bring forward a relation; that is, when he does one credit; 'tis human nature and sacred ties—one's own flesh and blood; and besides, one hand rubs the other, and one leg helps on the other, and relations get on best in the world when they pull together; that is, supposing that they are the proper sort of relations, and pull one on, not down. I had once thought of standing for Lansmere myself —thought of it very lately. The country wants men like me —I know that; but I have an idea that I had better see to my own business. The country may, or may not, do without me, stupid old thing that she is! But my mill and my new engines, there is no doubt that they cannot do without me. In short, as we are quite alone, and, as I said before, there's no kind of necessity for that sort of humbug which exists when other people are present, provide elsewhere for Mr. Egerton, whom I hate like poison—I have a right to do that, I suppose, without offence to your lordship—and the two younkers, Leonard Fairfield and Randal Leslie, shall be members for the free and independent borough of Lansmere!"

"But does Leonard wish to come into Parliament?"

"No: he says not; but that's nonsense. If your lordship will just signify your wish that he should not lose this noble opportunity to raise himself in life, and get something handsome out of the nation, I'm sure he owes you too much to hesitate—'specially when 'tis to his own advantage. And, besides, one of us Avenels ought to be in Parliament. And if I have not the time and learning, and so forth, and he has, why, it stands to reason that he should be the man. And if he can do something for me one day—not that I want anything—but still a Baronetcy or so would be a compliment to British Industry, and be appreciated as such by myself and the public at large—I say, if he could do something of that sort, it would keep up the whole family; and if he can't, why I'll forgive him."

"Avenel," said Harley, with that familiar and gracious charm of manner which few ever could resist—"Avenel, if as a great personal favour to myself—to me your fellow-townsman—(I was born at Lansmere)—if I asked you to forego your grudge against Audley Egerton, whatever that grudge be, and not oppose his election, while our party would not oppose your nephew's—could you not oblige me? Come, for the sake of dear Lansmere, and all the old kindly feelings between your family and mine, say 'yes—so shall it be.'"

Richard Avenel was almost melted. He turned away his face; but there suddenly rose to his recollection the scornful brow of Audley Egerton, the lofty contempt with which *he*, then the worshipful Mayor of Screwstown, had been shown out of the Minister's office-room; and, the blood rushing over his cheeks, he stamped his foot on the floor, and exclaimed, angrily, "No; I swore that Audley Egerton should smart for his insolence to me, as sure as my name be Richard Avenel; and all the soft soap in the world will not wash out that oath. So there is nothing for it but for you to withdraw that man, or for me to defeat him. And I would do so, ay— and in the way that could most gall him, if it cost me half my fortune. But it will not cost that," said Dick, cooling, "nor anything like it; for when the popular tide runs in one's favour, 'tis astonishing how cheap an election may be. It will cost *him* enough though, and all for nothing—worse than nothing. Think of it, my lord."

"I will, Mr Avenel. And I say, in my turn, that my friendship is as strong as your hate; and that if it costs me, not half, but my whole fortune, Audley Egerton shall come in without a shilling of expense to himself, should we once decide that he stand the contest."

"Very well, my lord—very well," said Dick, stiffly, and drawing on his kid gloves; "we'll see if the aristocracy is always to ride over the free choice of the people in this way. But the people are roused, my lord. The March of Enlightenment is commenced—the Schoolmaster is abroad, and the British Lion—"

"Nobody here but ourselves, my dear Avenel. Is not this rather what you call—*humbug?*"

Dick started, stared, coloured, and then burst out laughing—"Give us your hand again, my lord. You are a good fellow, *that* you are. And for your sake—"

"You'll not oppose Egerton?"

"Tooth and nail—tooth and nail!" cried Dick, clapping his hands to his ears, and fairly running out of the room.

There passed over Harley's countenance that change so frequent to it—more frequent, indeed, to the gay children of the world than those of consistent tempers and uniform habits might suppose. There is many a man whom we call friend, and whose face seems familiar to us as our own; yet, could we but take a glimpse of him when we leave his presence, and he sinks back into his chair alone, we should sigh to see how often the smile on the frankest lip is but a bravery of the drill, only worn when on parade.

What thoughts did the visit of Richard Avenel bequeath to Harley? It were hard to define them.

In his place, an Audley Egerton would have taken some comfort from the visit—would have murmured, "Thank Heaven! I have not to present to the world that terrible man as my brother-in-law." But probably Harley had escaped, in his reverie, from Richard Avenel altogether. Even as the slightest incident in the daytime causes our dreams at night, but is itself clean forgotten—so the name, so the look of the visitor, might have sufficed, but to influence a vision—as remote from its casual suggester, as what we call real life is from that life much more real, that we imagine, or remember, in the haunted chambers of the brain. For what *is* real life? How little the things actually doing around us affect the springs of our sorrow or joy; but the life which our dulness calls romance—the sentiment, the remembrance, the hope, or the fear, that are never seen in the toil of our hands—never heard in the jargon on our lips;—from that life all spin, as the spider from its entrails, the web by which we hang in the sunbeam, or glide out of sight into the shelter of home.

"I must not think," said Harley, rousing himself with a sigh, "either of past or present. Let me hurry on to some fancied future. 'Happiest are the marriages,' said the French philosopher, and still says many a sage, 'in which man asks only the mild companion, and woman but the calm protector.' I will go to Helen."

He rose; and as he was about to lock up his escritoire, he remembered the papers which Leonard had requested him to read. He took them from their deposit, with a careless hand, intending to carry them with him to his father's house. But as his eye fell upon the characters, the hand suddenly trembled, and he recoiled some paces, as if struck by a violent blow. Then, gazing more intently on the writing, a low cry broke from his lips. He reseated himself, and began to read.

## CHAPTER XI.

RANDAL—with many misgivings at Lord L'Estrange's tone, in which he was at no loss to detect a latent irony—proceeded to Norwood. He found Riccabocca exceedingly cold and distant. But he soon brought that sage to communicate the suspicions which Lord L'Estrange had instilled into his mind, and these Randal was as speedily enabled to dispel. He accounted at once for his visits to Levy and Peschiera. Naturally he had sought Levy, an acquaintance of his own—nay, of Audley Egerton's; but whom he knew to be professionally employed by the Count. He had succeeded in extracting from the Baron, Peschiera's suspicious change of lodgment from Mivart's Hotel to the purlieus of Leicester Square;—had called there on the Count—forced an entrance —openly accused him of abstracting Violante; high words had passed between them—even a challenge. Randal produced a note from a military friend of his, whom he had sent to the Count an hour after quitting the hotel. This note stated that arrangements were made for a meeting near Lord's Cricket Ground, at seven o'clock the next morning. Randal then submitted to Riccabocca another formal memorandum from the same warlike friend—to the purport that Randal and himself had repaired to the ground, and no Count been forthcoming. It must be owned that Randal had taken all suitable precautions to clear himself. Such a man is not to blame for want of invention, if he be sometimes doomed to fail.

"I then, much alarmed," continued Randal, "hastened to Baron Levy, who informed me that the Count had written him word that he should be for some time absent from England. Rushing thence, in despair, to your friend Lord L'Estrange, I heard that your daughter was safe with you. And though, as I have just proved, I would have risked my life against so notorious a duellist as the Count, on the mere chance of preserving Violante from his supposed designs, I am rejoiced to think that she had no need of my unskilful arm. But how and why can the Count have left England after accepting a challenge? A man so sure of his weapon, too—reputed to be as fearless of danger as he is blunt in conscience. Explain;—you who know mankind so well—explain. I cannot."

The philosopher could not resist the pleasure of narrating the detection and humiliation of his foe—the wit, ingenuity, and readiness of his friend. So Randal learned, by little and little, the whole drama of the preceding night. He saw, then, that the exile had all reasonable hope of speedy restoration to rank and wealth. Violante, indeed, would be a brilliant prize —too brilliant, perhaps, for Randal—but not to be sacrificed without an effort. Therefore wringing convulsively the hand of his meditated father-in-law, and turning away his head as if to conceal his emotions, the ingenuous young suitor faltered forth,—" That now Dr. Riccabocca was so soon to vanish into the Duke di Serrano, he—Randal Leslie of Rood, born a gentleman, indeed, but of fallen fortunes—had no right to claim the promise which had been given to him while a father had cause to fear for a daughter's future; with the fear ceased the promise. Might Heaven bless father and daughter both!"

This address touched both the heart and honour of the exile. Randal Leslie knew his man. And though, before Randal's visit, Riccabocca was not quite so much a philosopher, but what he would have been well pleased to have found himself released, by proof of the young man's treachery, from an alliance below the rank to which he had all chance of early restoration; yet no Spaniard was ever more tenacious of plighted word than this inconsistent pupil of the profound Florentine. And Randal's probity being now clear to him, he repeated, with stately formalities, his previous offer of Violante's hand.

"But," still falteringly sighed the provident and far-calculating Randal—" but your only child, your sole heiress! Oh, might not your consent to such a marriage (if known before your recall) jeopardize your cause? Your lands, your principalities, to devolve on the child of an humble Englishman! I dare not believe it. Ah, would Violante were not your heiress!"

"A noble wish," said Riccabocca, smiling blandly, "and one that the Fates will realise. Cheer up; Violante will not be my heiress."

"Ah," cried Randal, drawing a long breath—"ah, what do I hear!"

"Hist! I shall soon a second time be a father. And, to judge by the unerring researches of writers upon that most interesting of all subjects, parturitive science, I shall be the father of a son. He will, of course, succeed to the titles of Serrano. And Violante—"

"Will have nothing, I suppose!" exclaimed Randal, trying his best to look overjoyed till he had got his paws out of the trap into which he had so incautiously thrust them.

"Nay, her portion by our laws—to say nothing of my affection—would far exceed the ordinary dower which the daughters of London merchants bring to the sons of British peers. Whoever marries Violante, provided I regain my estates, must submit to the cares which the poets assure us ever attend on wealth."

"Oh!" groaned Randal, as if already bowed beneath the cares, and sympathising with the poets.

"And now, let me present you to your betrothed."

Although poor Randal had been remorselessly hurried along what Schiller calls the "gamut of feeling," during the last three minutes, down to the deep chord of despair at the abrupt intelligence that his betrothed was no heiress after all; thence ascending to vibrations of pleasant doubt as to the unborn usurper of her rights, according to the prophecies of parturitive science; and lastly, swelling into a concord of all sweet thoughts at the assurance that, come what might, she would be a wealthier bride than a peer's son could discover in the matrimonial Potosi of Lombard Street; still the tormented lover was not there allowed to repose his exhausted though ravished soul. For, at the idea of personally confronting the destined bride—whose very existence had almost vanished from his mind's eye, amidst the golden showers that it saw falling divinely round her—Randal was suddenly reminded of the exceeding bluntness with which, at their last interview, it had been his policy to announce his suit, and of the necessity of an impromptu *falsetto* suited to the new variations that tossed him again to and fro on the merciless gamut. However, he could not recoil from her father's proposition, though, in order to prepare Riccabocca for Violante's representation, he confessed pathetically that his impatience to obtain her consent, and baffle Peschiera, had made him appear a rude and presumptuous wooer. The philosopher who was disposed to believe one kind of courtship to be much the same as another, in cases where the result of all courtships was once predetermined—smiled benignly, patted Randal's thin cheek, with a " Pooh, pooh, *pazzie!*" and left the room to summon Violante.

"If knowledge be power," soliloquised Randal, " ability is certainly good luck, as Miss Edgeworth shows in that story of Murad the Unlucky, which I read at Eton ; very clever story it is, too. So nothing comes amiss to *me*. Violante's escape which has cost me the Count's ten thousand pounds, proves to be worth to me, I dare say, ten times as much. No doubt she'll have a hundred thousand pounds at the least. And then, if her father have no other child, after all, or the child he expects die in infancy, why, once reconciled to his government and restored to his estates, the law must take its usual course, and Violante will be the greatest heiress in Europe. As to the young lady herself, I confess she rather awes me ; I know I shall be henpecked. Well, all respectable husbands are. There is something scampish and ruffianly in not being henpecked." Here Randal's smile might have harmonized well with Pluto's " iron tears ; " but, iron as the smile was, the serious young man was ashamed of it. " What am I about," said he, half aloud, " chuckling to myself and wasting time, when I ought to be thinking gravely how to explain away my former cavalier courtship ? Such a masterpiece as I thought it then ! But who could foresee the turn things would take ? Let me think ; let me think. Plague on it, here she comes."

But Randal had not the fine ear of your more romantic lover ; and, to his great relief, the exile entered the room unaccompanied by Violante. Riccabocca looked somewhat embarrassed.

"My dear Leslie, you must excuse my daughter to-day ; she is still suffering from the agitation she has gone through, and cannot see you."

The lover tried not to look too delighted.

"Cruel,' said he ; " yet I would not for worlds force myself on her presence. I hope, Duke, that she will not find it too difficult to obey the commands which dispose of her hand, and intrust her happiness to my grateful charge."

"To be plain with you, Randal, she does at present seem to find it more difficult than I foresaw. She even talks of—"

"Another attachment—Oh, heavens!"

"Attachment, *pazzie!* Whom has she seen? No—a convent! But leave it to me. In a calmer hour she will comprehend that a child must know no lot more enviable and holy than that of redeeming a father's honour. And now, if you are returning to London, may I ask you to convey to young Mr. Hazeldean my assurances of undying gratitude for his share in my daughter's delivery from that poor baffled swindler."

It is noticeable that, now Peschiera was no longer an object of dread to the nervous father, he became but an object of pity to the philosopher, and of contempt to the grandee.

"True," said Randal, "you told me Frank had a share in Lord L'Estrange's very clever and dramatic device. My lord must be by nature a fine actor—comic, with a touch of melodrame! Poor Frank! apparently he has lost the woman he adored—Beatrice di Negra. You say she has accompanied the Count. Is the marriage that was to be between her and Frank broken off?"

"I did not know such a marriage was contemplated. I understood her to be attached to another. Not that that is any reason why she would not have married Mr. Hazeldean. Express to him my congratulations on his escape."

"Nay, he must not know that I have inadvertently betrayed his confidence; but you now guess, what perhaps puzzled you before—viz., how I came to be so well acquainted with the Count and his movements. I was so intimate with my relation Frank, and Frank was affianced to the Marchesa."

"I am glad you give me that explanation; it suffices. After all, the Marchesa is not by nature a bad woman—that is, not worse than women generally are, so Harley says, and Violante forgives and excuses her."

"Generous Violante! But it is true. So much did the Marchesa appear to me possessed of fine, though ill-regulated qualities, that I always considered her disposed to aid in frustrating her brother's criminal designs. So I even said, if I remember right, to Violante."

Dropping this prudent and precautionary sentence, in order to guard against anything Violante might say as to that subtle mention of Beatrice which had predisposed her to confide in the Marchesa, Randal then hurried on,—"But you want repose. I leave you, the happiest, the most grateful of men. I will give your courteous message to Frank."

## CHAPTER XII.

CURIOUS to learn what had passed between Beatrice and Frank, and deeply interested in all that could oust Frank out of the Squire's goodwill, or aught that could injure his own prospects, by tending to unite son and father, Randal was not slow in reaching his young kinsman's lodgings. It might be supposed that having, in all probability, just secured so great a fortune as would accompany Violante's hand, Randal might be indifferent to the success of his scheme on the Hazeldean exchequer. Such a supposition would grievously wrong this profound young man. For, in the first place, Violante was not yet won, nor her father yet restored to the estates which would defray her dower; and, in the next place, Randal, like Iago, loved villany for the genius it called forth in him. The sole luxury the abstemious aspirer allowed to himself was that which is found in intellectual restlessness. Untempted by wine, dead to love, unamused by pleasure, indifferent to the arts, despising literature, save as means to some end of power, Randal Leslie was the incarnation of thought, hatched out of the corruption of will. At twilight we see thin airy spectral insects, all wing and nippers, hovering, as if they could never pause, over some sullen mephitic pool. Just so, methinks, hover over Acheron such gnat-like, noiseless soarers into gloomy air out of Stygian deeps, as are the thoughts of spirits like Randal Leslie's. Wings have they, but only the better to pounce down—draw their nutriment from unguarded material cuticles; and just when, maddened, you strike, and exulting exclaim, "Caught by Jove!" wh—irr flies the diaphanous, ghostly larva, and your blow falls on your own twice-offended cheek.

The young men who were acquainted with Randal said he had not a vice! The fact being that his whole composition was one epic vice, so elaborately constructed that it had not an episode which a critic could call irrelevant. Grand young man!

"But, my dear fellow," said Randal, as soon as he had

learned from Frank all that had passed on board the vessel between him and Beatrice, "I cannot believe this. 'Never loved you?' What was her object, then, in deceiving, not only you, but myself? I suspect her declaration was but some heroical refinement of generosity. After her brother's dejection and probable ruin, she might feel that she was no match for you. Then, too, the Squire's displeasure. I see it all—just like her—noble, unhappy woman!"

Frank shook his head. "There are moments," said he, with a wisdom that comes out of those instincts which awake from the depths of youth's first great sorrow—"moments when a woman cannot feign, and there are tones in the voice of a woman which men cannot misinterpret. She does not love me—she never did love me; I can see that her heart has been elsewhere. No matter—all is over. I don't deny that I am suffering an intense grief; it gnaws like a kind of sullen hunger; and I feel so broken, too, as if I had grown old, and there was nothing left worth living for. I don't deny all that."

"My poor, dear friend, if you would but believe—"

"I don't want to believe anything, except that I have been a great fool. I dont think I can ever commit such follies again. But I'm a man. I shall get the better of this; I should despise myself if I could not. And now let us talk of my dear father. Has he left town?"

"Left last night by the mail. You can write, and tell him you have given up the Marchesa, and all will be well again between you."

"Give her up! Fie, Randal! Do you think I should tell such a lie?—She gave me up; I can claim no merit out of that."

"Oh, yes! I can make the Squire see all to your advantage. Oh, if it were only the Marchesa! but, alas! that cursed *post-obit!* How could Levy betray you? Never trust to usurers again; they cannot resist the temptation of a speedy profit. They first buy the son, and then sell him to the father. And the Squire has such strange notions on matters of this kind."

"He is right to have them. There, just read this letter from my mother. It came to me this morning. I could hang myself if I were a dog; but I'm a man, and so I mus, bear it."

Randal took Mrs. Hazeldean's letter from Frank's trembling hand.—The poor mother had learned, though but imperfectly, Frank's misdeeds from some hurried lines which the Squire had despatched to her; and she wrote, as good, indulgent, but sensible, right-minded mothers alone can write. More lenient to an imprudent love than the Squire, she touched with discreet tenderness on Frank's rash engagements with a foreigner, but severely on his own open defiance of his father's wishes. Her anger was, however, reserved for that unholy *post-obit*. Here the hearty genial wife's love overcame the mother's affection. To count, in cold blood, on that husband's death, and to wound his heart so keenly, just where its jealous, fatherly fondness made it most susceptible!

"O Frank, Frank!" wrote Mrs. Hazeldean, "were it not for this, were it only for your unfortunate attachment to the Italian lady, only for your debts, only for the errors of hasty, extravagant youth, I should be with you now—my arms round your neck, kissing you, chiding you back to your father's heart. But—but the thought that between you and his heart has been the sordid calculation of his death—*that* is a wall between us. I cannot come near you. I should not like to look on your face, and think how my William's tears fell over it, when I placed you new born, in his arms, and bade him welcome his heir. What! you a mere boy still, your father yet in the prime of life, and the heir cannot wait till nature leaves him fatherless. Frank, Frank! this is so unlike you. Can London have ruined already a disposition so honest and affectionate?—No; I cannot believe it. There must be some mistake. Clear it up, I implore you; or, though as a mother I pity you, as a wife I cannot forgive.

"HARRIET HAZELDEAN."

Even Randal was affected by the letter; for, as we know, even Randal felt in his own person the strength of family ties. The poor Squire's choler and bluffness had disguised the parental heart from an eye that, however acute, had not been willing to search for it; and Randal, ever affected through his intellect, had despised the very weakness on which he had preyed. But the mother's letter, so just and sensible, (allowing that the Squire's opinions had naturally influenced the wife to take, what men of the world would call a very exaggerated view of the every-day occurrence of loans raised by a son, payable only at a father's death,)—this letter, I say, if exaggerated according to fashionable notions, so sensible if judged by natural affections, touched the dull heart of the schemer, because approved by the quick tact of his intelligence.

"Frank," said he, with a sincerity that afterwards amazed himself, "go down at once to Hazeldean—see your mother, and explain to her how this transaction really happened. The woman you loved, and wooed as wife, in danger of an arrest —your distraction of mind, Levy's counsels—your hope to pay off the debt, so incurred to the usurer, from the fortune you would shortly receive with the Marchesa. Speak to your mother—she is a woman; women have a common interest in forgiving all faults that arise from the source of their power over us men;—I mean love. Go!"

"No—I cannot go;—you see she would not like to look on my face. And I cannot repeat what you say so glibly. Besides, somehow or other, as I am so dependent upon my father,—and he has said as much—I feel as if it would be mean in me to make any excuses. I did the thing, and must suffer for it. But I'm a m—an—no—I'm not a man here." Frank burst into tears.

At the sight of those tears, Randal gradually recovered from his strange aberration into vulgar and low humanity. His habitual contempt for his kinsman returned; and with contempt came the natural indifference to the sufferings of the thing to be put to use. It is contempt for the worm that makes the angler fix it on the hook, and observe with complacency that the vivacity of its wriggles will attract the bite. If the worm could but make the angler respect, or even fear it, the barb would find some other bait. Few anglers would impale an estimable silkworm, and still fewer the anglers who would finger into service a formidable hornet.

"Pooh, my dear Frank," said Randal; "I have given you my advice; you reject it. Well, what then will you do?"

"I shall ask for leave of absence, and run away somewhere," said Frank, drying his tears. "I can't face London; I can't mix with others. I want to be by myself, and wrestle with all that I feel *here*—in my heart. Then I shall write to my mother, say the plain truth, and leave her to judge as kindly of me as she can."

"You are quite right. Yes, leave town! Why not go abroad? You have never been abroad. New scenes will distract your mind. Run over to Paris."

"Not to Paris—I don't want gaieties; but I did intend to go abroad somewhere—any dull dismal hole of a place. Good-bye! Don't think of me any more for the present."

"But let me know where you go! and meanwhile I will see the Squire."

"Say as little of me as you can to him. I know you mean most kindly—but oh, how I wish there never had been any third person between me and my father! There: you may well snatch away your hand. What an ungrateful wretch to you I am. I do believe I am the wickedest fellow. What! you shake hands with me still. My dear Randal, you have the best heart—God bless you." Frank turned away, and disappeared within his dressing-room.

"They must be reconciled now, sooner or later—Squire and son,"—said Randal to himself, as he left the lodgings. "I don't see how I can prevent that—the Marchesa being withdrawn—unless Frank does it for me. But it is well he should be abroad—something may be made out of that: meanwhile I may yet do all that I could reasonably hope to do—even if Frank had married Beatrice—since he was not to be disinherited. Get the Squire to advance the money for the Thornhill purchase—complete the affair;—this marriage with Violante will help;—Levy must know that; secure the borough;—well thought of. I will go to Avenel's. By-the-by—by-the-by—the Squire might as well keep me still in the entail after Frank—supposing Frank die childless. This love affair may keep him long from marrying. His hand was very hot—a hectic colour;—those strong-looking fellows often go off in a rapid decline, especially if anything preys on their minds—their minds are so very small.

"Ah—the Hazeldean Parson—and with Avenel! That young man, too—who is he? I have seen him before somewhere. My dear Mr. Dale, this is a pleasant surprise. I thought you had returned to Hazeldean with our friend the Squire?"

Mr. Dale.—"The Squire! Has he left town, and without telling me?"

Randal, (taking aside the Parson.)—"He was anxious to get back to Mrs. Hazeldean, who was naturally very uneasy about her son and this foolish marriage; but I am happy to tell you that that marriage is effectually and permanently broken off."

Mr. Dale.—"How, how? My poor friend told me he had wholly failed to make any impression on Frank—forbade me to mention the subject. I was just going to see Frank myself. I always had some influence with him. But, Mr. Leslie, explain this very sudden and happy event—the marriage broken off!"

Randal.—"It is a long story, and I dare not tell you my

humble share in it. Nay, I must keep that secret. Frank might not forgive me. Suffice it that you have my word that the fair Italian has left England, and decidedly refused Frank's addresses. But stay—take my advice—don't go to him;—you see it was not only the marriage that has offended the Squire, but some pecuniary transactions—an unfortunate *post-obit* bond on the Casino property. Frank ought to be left to his own repentant reflections. They will be most salutary—you know his temper—he don't bear reproof; and yet it is better, on the other hand, not to let him treat too lightly what has passed. Let us leave him to himself for a few days. He is in an excellent frame of mind."

MR. DALE, (shaking Randal's hand warmly.)—" You speak admirably—a *post-obit !*—so often as he has heard his father's opinion on such transactions. No—I will not see him—I should be too angry—"

RANDAL, (leading the Parson back, resumes, after an exchange of salutations with Avenel, who, meanwhile, had been conferring with his nephew.)—" You should not be so long away from your rectory, Mr. Dale. What will your parish do without you?"

MR. DALE.—" The old fable of the wheel and the fly. I am afraid the wheel rolls on the same. But if I am absent from my parish, I am still in the company of one who does me honour as an old parishioner. You remember Leonard Fairfield, your antagonist in the Battle of the Stocks?"

MR. AVENEL.—" My nephew, I am proud to say, sir."

Randal bowed with marked civility—Leonard with a reserve no less marked.

MR. AVENEL, (ascribing his nephew's reserve to shyness.)—" You should be friends, you two youngsters. Who knows but you may run together in the same harness? Ah, that reminds me, Leslie—I have a word or two to say to you. Your servant, Mr. Dale. Shall be happy to present you to Mrs. Avenel. My card—Eaton Square—Number ***. You will call on me to-morrow, Leonard. And mind I shall be very angry if you persist in your refusal. Such an opening!" Avenel took Randal's arm, while the Parson and Leonard walked on.

" Any fresh hints as to Lansmere?" asked Randal.

" Yes; I have now decided on the plan of contest. We must fight two and two—you and Egerton against me and (if I can get him to stand, as I hope), my nephew, Leonard."

"What!" said Randal, alarmed; "then, after all, I can hope for no support from you?"

"I don't say that; but I have reason to think Lord L'Estrange will bestir himself actively in favour of Egerton. If so, it will be a very sharp contest; and I must manage the whole election on our side, and unite all our shaky votes, which I can best do by standing myself in the first instance, reserving it to after consideration whether I shall throw up at the last; for I don't particularly want to come in, as I did a little time ago, before I had found out my nephew. Wonderful young man!—with such a head—will do me credit in the rotten old House; and I think I had best leave London, go to Screwstown, and look to my business. No: if Leonard stand, I must first see to get him in; and next, to keep Egerton out. It will probably, therefore, end in the return of one and one on either side, as we thought of before. Leonard on our side; and Egerton shan't be the man on the other. You understand?"

"I do, my dear Avenel. Of course, as I before said, I can't dictate to your party whom they should prefer—Egerton or myself. And it will be obvious to the public that your party would rather defeat so eminent an adversary as Mr. Egerton, than a tyro in politics like me. Of course I cannot scheme for such a result; it would be misconstrued, and damage my character. But I rely equally on your friendly promise."

"Promise! No—I don't promise. I must first see how the cat jumps; and I don't know yet how our friends may like you, nor how they can be managed. All I can say is, that Audley Egerton shan't be M.P. for Lansmere. Meanwhile, you will take care not to commit yourself in speaking, so that our party can't vote for you consistently: they must count on having you—when you get into the House."

"I am not a violent party-man at present," answered Randal, prudently. "And if public opinion prove on your side, it is the duty of a statesman to go with the times."

"Very sensibly said; and I have a private bill or two, and some other little jobs, I want to get through the House, which we can discuss later, should it come to a frank understanding between us. We must arrange how to meet privately at Lansmere, if necessary. I'll see to that. I shall go down this week. I think of taking a hint from the free and glorious land of America, and establishing secret caucuses. Nothing like 'em."

"Caucuses?"

"Small sub-committees that spy on their men night and day, and don't suffer them to be intimidated to vote the other way."

"You have an extraordinary head for public affairs, Avenel. You *should* come into Parliament yourself; your nephew is so very young."

"So are you."

"Yes; but I know the world. Does he?"

"The world knows him, though not by name, and he has been the making of me."

"How? You surprise me."

Avenel first explained about the patent which Leonard had secured to him; and next confided, upon honour, Leonard's identity with the anonymous author whom the Parson had supposed to be Professor Moss.

Randal Leslie felt a jealous pang. What! then—had this village boy—this associate of John Burley—(literary vagabond, whom he supposed had long since gone to the dogs, and been buried at the expense of the parish)—had this boy so triumphed over birth, rearing, circumstance, that, if Randal and Leonard had met together in any public place, and Leonard's identity with the rising author been revealed, every eye would have turned from Randal to gaze on Leonard? The common consent of mankind would have acknowledged the supreme royalty of genius when it once leaves its solitude, and strides into the world. What! was this rude villager the child of Fame, who, without an effort, and unconsciously, had inspired in the wearied heart of Beatrice di Negra a love that Randal knew, by an instinct, no arts, no craft, could ever create for him in the heart of woman? And, now, did this same youth stand on the same level in the ascent to power as he, the well-born Randal Leslie, the accomplished *protégé* of the superb Audley Egerton? Were they to be rivals in the same arena of practical busy life? Randal gnawed his quivering lip.

All the while, however, the young man whom he so envied was a prey to sorrows deeper far than could ever find room or footing in the narrow and stony heart of the unloving schemer. As Leonard walked through the crowded streets with the friend and monitor of his childhood, confiding the simple tale of his earlier trials—when, amidst the wreck of fortune, and in despair of fame, the Child-angel smiled by his side, like Hope—all renown seemed to him so barren, all the future so dark! His voice trembled, and his **countenance**

became so sad, that his benignant listener, divining that
around the image of Helen there clung some passionate grief
that overshadowed all worldly success, drew Leonard gently
and gently on, till the young man, long yearning for some
confidant, told him all;—how, faithful through long years to
one pure and ardent memory, Helen had been seen once more
—the child ripened to woman, and the memory revealing
itself as love.

The Parson listened with a mild and thoughtful brow,
which expanded into a more cheerful expression as Leonard
closed his story.

"I see no reason to despond," said Mr. Dale. "You fear
that Miss Digby does not return your attachment; you dwell
upon her reserve—her distant though kindly manner. Cheer
up!· All young ladies are under the influence of what phrenologists
call the organ of Secretiveness, when they are in the
society of the object of their preference. Just as you
describe Miss Digby's manner to you, was my Carry's manner
to myself."

The Parson here indulged in a very appropriate digression
upon female modesty, which he wound up by asserting, that
that estimable virtue became more and more influenced by
the secretive organ, in proportion as the favoured suitor
approached near and nearer to a definite proposal. It was
the duty of a gallant and honourable lover to make that proposal
in distinct and orthodox form, before it could be
expected that a young lady should commit herself and the
dignity of her sex by the slightest hint as to her own inclinations.

"Next," continued the Parson, "you choose to torment
yourself by contrasting your own origin and fortunes with
the altered circumstances of Miss Digby—the ward of Lord
L'Estrange, the guest of Lady Lansmere. You say that if
Lord L'Estrange could have countenanced such a union, he
would have adopted a different tone with you—sounded your
heart, encouraged your hopes, and so forth. I view things
differently. I have reason to do so; and, from all you have
told me of this nobleman's interest in your fate, I venture to
make you this promise, that if Miss Digby would accept your
hand, Lord L'Estrange shall ratify her choice."

"My dear Mr. Dale," cried Leonard, transported, "you
make me that promise?"

"I do—from what you have said, and from what I myself
know of Lord L'Estrange. Go, then, at once to Knights-

bridge—see Miss Digby—show her your heart—explain to her, if you will, your prospects—ask her permission to apply to Lord L'Estrange, (since he has constituted himself her guardian;) and if Lord L'Estrange hesitate—which, if your happiness be set on this union, I think he will not—let me know, and leave the rest to me."

Leonard yielded himself to the Parson's persuasive eloquence. Indeed, when he recalled to mind those passages in the manuscripts of the ill-fated Nora, which referred to the love that Harley had once borne to her—(for he felt convinced that Harley and the boy suitor of Nora's narrative were one and the same;) and when all the interest that Harley had taken in his own fortunes was explained by his relationship to her (even when Lord L'Estrange had supposed it less close than he would now discover it to be), the young man, reasoning by his own heart, could not but suppose that the noble Harley would rejoice to confer happiness upon the son of her, so beloved by his boyhood.

"And to thee, perhaps, O my mother!" thought Leonard, with swimming eyes—"to thee, perhaps, even in thy grave, I shall owe the partner of my life, as to the mystic breath of thy genius I owe the first pure aspirations of my soul."

It will be seen that Leonard had not confided to the Parson his discovery of Nora's manuscripts, nor even his knowledge of his real birth; for the proud son naturally shrank from any confidence that implicated Nora's fair name, until at least Harley, who, it was clear from those papers, must have intimately known his father, should perhaps decide the question which the papers themselves left so terribly vague—viz., whether he were the offspring of a legal marriage, or Nora had been the victim of some unholy fraud.

While the Parson still talked, and while Leonard still mused and listened, their steps almost mechanically took the direction towards Knightsbridge, and paused at the gates of Lord Lansmere's house.

"Go in, my young friend; I will wait without to know the issue," said the Parson, cheeringly. "Go: and with gratitude to Heaven, learn how to bear the most precious joy that can befall mortal man; or how to submit to youth's sharpest sorrow, with the humble belief that even sorrow is but some mercy concealed."

## CHAPTER XIII.

LEONARD was shown into the drawing-room, and it so chanced that Helen was there alone. The girl's soft face was sadly changed, even since Leonard had seen it last; for the grief of natures, mild, and undemonstrative as hers, gnaws with quick ravages; but at Leonard's unexpected entrance, the colour rushed so vividly to the pale cheeks that its hectic might be taken for the lustre of bloom and health. She rose hurriedly, and in great confusion faltered out, "that she believed Lady Lansmere was in her room—she would go for her," and moved towards the door, without seeming to notice the hand tremulously held forth to her; when Leonard exclaimed in uncontrollable emotions which pierced to her very heart, in the keen accent of reproach—

"Oh, Miss Digby—oh, Helen—is it thus that you greet me —rather thus that you shun me? Could I have foreseen this when we two orphans stood by the mournful bridge;—so friendless—so desolate—and so clinging each to each? Happy time!" He seized her hand suddenly as he spoke the last words, and bowed his face over it.

"I must not hear you. Do not talk so, Leonard—you break my heart. Let me go—let me go."

"Is it that I am grown hateful to you; is it merely that you see my love and would discourage it? Helen, speak to me—speak!"

He drew her with tender force towards him; and, holding her firmly by both hands, sought to gaze upon the face that she turned from him—turned in such despair.

"You do not know," she said at last, struggling for composure—"you do not know the new claims on me—my altered position—how I am bound—or you would be the last to speak thus to me, the first to give me courage—and bid me—bid me—"

"Bid you what?"

"Feel nothing here but duty!" cried Helen, drawing from his clasp both her hands, and placing them firmly on her breast.

"Miss Digby," said Leonard, after a short pause of bitter reflection, in which he wronged, while he thought to divine, her meaning, "you speak of new claims on you, your altered position—I comprehend. You may retain some tender remembrance of the past; but your duty now is to rebuke my presumption. It is as I thought and feared. This vain reputation which I have made is but a hollow sound—it gives me no rank, assures me no fortune. I have no right to look for the Helen of old in the Helen of to-day. Be it so—forget what I have said, and forgive me."

This reproach stung to the quick the heart to which it appealed. A flash brightened the meek, tearful eyes, almost like the flash of resentment—her lips writhed in torture, and she felt as if all other pain were light compared with the anguish that Leonard could impute to her motives which to her simple nature seemed so unworthy of her, and so galling to himself.

A word rushed as by inspiration to her lip, and that word calmed and soothed her.

"Brother!" she said touchingly, "brother!"

The word had a contrary effect on Leonard. Sweet as it was, tender as the voice that spoke it, it imposed a boundary to affection—it came as a knell to hope. He recoiled, shook his head mournfully—"Too late to accept that tie—too late even for friendship. Henceforth—for long years to come—henceforth, till this heart has ceased to beat at your name—to thrill at your presence, we two—are strangers."

"Strangers! Well—yes, it is right—it must be so; we must not meet. O, Leonard Fairfield, who was it that in those days that you recall to me—who was it that found you destitute, and obscure—who, not degrading you by charity, placed you in your right career—opened to you, amidst the labyrinth in which you were well-nigh lost, the broad road to knowledge, independence, fame. Answer me—answer! Was it not the same who reared, sheltered your sister orphan? If I could forget what I have owed to him, should I not remember what he has done for you? Can I hear of your distinction, and not remember it? Can I think how proud she may be who will one day lean on your arm, and bear the name you have already raised beyond all the titles of an hour? Can I think of this, and not remember our common friend, benefactor, guardian? Would you forgive me, if I failed to do so?"

"But," faltered Leonard, fear mingling with the conjectures these words called forth—"but is it that Lord L'Estrange would not consent to our union?—or of what do you speak? You bewilder me."

Helen felt for some moments as if it were impossible to

reply; and the words at length were dragged forth as if from the depth of her very soul.

"He came to me—our noble friend. I never dreamed of it. He did not tell me that he loved me. He told me that he was unhappy, alone; that in me, and only in me, he could find a comforter, a soother—He, he!—And I had just arrived in England—was under his mother's roof—had not then once more seen you; and—and—what could I answer? Strengthen me—strengthen me, you whom I look up to and revere. Yes, yes—you are right. We must see each other no more. I am betrothed to another—to him! Strengthen me!"

All the inherent nobleness of the poet's nature rose at once at this appeal.

"Oh, Helen—sister—Miss Digby, forgive me. You need no strength from me; I borrow it from you. I comprehend you—I respect. Banish all thought of me. Repay our common benefactor. Be what he asks of you—his comforter, his soother; be more—his pride and his joy. Happiness will come to you, as it comes to those who confer happiness and forget self. God comfort you in the passing struggle; God bless you, in the long years to come. Sister—I accept the holy name now, and will claim it hereafter, when I too can think more of others than myself."

Helen had covered her face with her hands, sobbing; but with that soft, womanly constraint which presses woe back into the heart. A strange sense of utter solitude suddenly pervaded her whole being, and by that sense of solitude she knew that he was gone.

## CHAPTER XIV.

In another room in that same house sate, solitary as Helen, a stern, gloomy, brooding man, in whom they who had best known him from his childhood could scarcely have recognised a trace of the humane, benignant, trustful, but wayward and varying Harley, Lord L'Estrange.

He had read that fragment of a memoir, in which, out of all the chasms of his barren and melancholy past, there rose two malignant truths that seemed literally to glare upon him with mocking and demon eyes. The woman whose remembrance had darkened all the sunshine of his life, had loved another. The friend in whom he had confided his whole affectionate loyal soul had been his perfidious rival. He had read from the first word to the last, as if under a spell that held him breathless; and when he closed the manuscript, it was without groan or sigh; but over his pale lips there passed that withering smile, which is as sure an index of a heart overcharged with dire and fearful passions, as the arrowy flash of the lightning is of the tempests that are gathered within the cloud.

He then thrust the papers into his bosom, and, keeping his hand over them, firmly clenched, he left the room, and walked slowly on towards his father's house. With every step by the way, his nature, in the war of its elements, seemed to change and harden into forms of granite. Love, humanity, trust, vanished away. Hate, revenge, misanthropy, suspicion, and scorn of all that could wear the eyes of affection, or speak with the voice of honour, came fast through the gloom of his thoughts, settling down in the wilderness, grim and menacing as the harpies of ancient song—

"——Uncæque manus, et pallida semper Ora."—*

Thus the gloomy man had crossed the threshold of his father's house, and silently entered the apartments still set apart for him. He had arrived about an hour before Leonard; and as he stood by the hearth, with his arms folded on his breast, and his eyes fixed lead-like on the ground, his mother came in to welcome and embrace him. He checked her eager inquiries after Violante—he recoiled from the touch of her hand.

"Hold, madam," said he, startling her ear with the cold austerity of his tone. "I cannot heed your questions—I am filled with the question I must put to yourself. You opposed my boyish love for Leonora Avenel. I do not blame you—all mothers of equal rank would have done the same. Yet, had you not frustrated all frank intercourse with her, I might have taken refusal from her own lips—survived that grief, and now been a happy man. Years since then have rolled away—rolled over her quiet slumbers, and my restless waking life. All this time were you aware that Audley Egerton had been the lover of Leonora Avenel?"

"Harley, Harley! do not speak to me in that cruel voice—do not look at me with those hard eyes!"

"You knew it, then—you, my mother!" continued Harley, unmoved by her rebuke; "and why did you never say, ' Son,

* " Hands armed with fangs, and lips for ever pale."

you are wasting the bloom and uses of your life in sorrowful
fidelity to a lie! You are lavishing trust and friendship on a
perfidious hypocrite?'"

"How could I speak to you thus—how could I dare to do
so—seeing you still so cherished the memory of that unhappy
girl—still believed that she had returned your affection? Had
I said to you what I knew (but not till after her death), as to
her relations with Audley Egerton—"

"Well?—you falter—go on—had you done so?"

"Would you have felt no desire for revenge? Might there
not have been strife between you—danger—bloodshed?
Harley, Harley! Is not such silence pardonable in a mother?
And why deprive you too of the only friend you seemed to
prize—who alone had some influence over you—who concurred with me in the prayer and hope, that some day you
would find a living partner worthy to replace this lost delusion, arouse your faculties—be the ornament your youth promised to your country? For you wrong Audley—indeed
you do!"

"Wrong him! Ah! let me not do that. Proceed."

"I do not excuse him his rivalship, nor his first conceal
ment of it. But believe me, since then, his genuine remorse,
his anxious tenderness for your welfare, his dread of losing
your friendship—"

"Stop—it was doubtless Audley Egerton who induced you
yourself to conceal what you call his 'relations' with her
whom I can now so calmly name—Leonora Avenel?"

"It was so, in truth—and from motives that—"

"Enough—let me hear no more."

"But you will not think too sternly of what is past; you
are about to form new ties. You cannot be wild and wicked
enough to meditate what your brow seems to threaten. You
cannot dream of revenge—risk Audley's life or your own?"

"Tut—tut—tut! What cause here for duels? Single
combats are out of date—civilised men do not slay each other
with sword and pistol. Tut!—revenge! Does it look like
revenge, that one object which brings me hither is to request
my father's permission to charge myself with the care of
Audley Egerton's election? What he values most in the
world is his political position; and here his political existence
is at stake. You know that I have had through life the
character of a weak, easy, somewhat over-generous man.
Such men are not revengeful. Hold! You lay your hand
on my arm—I know the magic of that light touch, mother,

but its power over me is gone. Countess of Lansmere, hear me! Ever from infancy (save in that frantic passion for which I now despise myself), I have obeyed you, I trust, as a duteous son. Now, our relative positions are somewhat altered. I have the right to exact—I will not say to command—the right which wrong and injury bestow upon all men. Madam, the injured man has prerogatives that rival those of kings. I now call upon you to question me no more—not again to breathe the name of Leonora Avenel, unless I invite the subject; and not to inform Audley Egerton by a hint—by a breath—that I have discovered—what shall I call it?—his 'pardonable deceit.' Promise me this, by your affection as mother, and on your faith as gentlewoman—or I declare solemnly, that never in life will you look upon my face again."

Haughty and imperious though the Countess was, her spirit quailed before Harley's brow and voice.

"Is this my son—this my gentle Harley?" she said, falteringly. "Oh! put your arms round my neck—let me feel that I have not lost my child!"

Harley looked softened, but he did not obey the pathetic prayer; nevertheless, he held out his hand, and turning away his face, said, in a milder voice, "Have I your promise?"

"You have—you have; but on condition that there pass no words between you and Audley that can end but in the strife which—"

"Strife!" interrupted Harley. "I repeat that the idea of challenge and duel between me and my friend from our school days, and on a quarrel that we could explain to no seconds, would be a burlesque upon all that is grave in the realities of life and feeling. I accept your promise and seal it thus—"

He pressed his lips to his mother's forehead, and passively received her embrace.

"Hush," he said, withdrawing from her arms, "I hear my father's voice."

Lord Lansmere threw open the door widely, and with a certain consciousness that a door by which an Earl of Lansmere entered ought to be thrown open widely. It could not have been opened with more majesty if a *huissier* or officer of the Household had stood on either side. The Countess passed by her lord with a light step, and escaped.

"I was occupied with my architect in designs for the new infirmary, of which I shall make a present to our county. I have only just heard that you were here, Harley. What is all this about our fair Italian guest? Is she not coming back to us? Your mother refers me to you for explanations."

"You shall have them later, my dear father; at present I can think only of public affairs."

"Public affairs!—they are indeed alarming. I am rejoiced to hear you express yourself so worthily. An awful crisis, Harley! And, gracious heaven! I have heard that a low man, who was born in Lansmere, but made a fortune in America, is about to contest the borough. They tell me he is one of the Avenels—a born Blue—is it possible?"

"I have come here on that business. As a peer you cannot, of course, interfere. But I propose, with your leave, to go down myself to Lansmere, and undertake the superintendence of the election. It would be better, perhaps, if you were not present; it would give us more liberty of action."

"My dear Harley, shake hands; anything you please. You know how I have have wished to see you come forward, and take that part in life which becomes your birth."

"Ah, you think I have sadly wasted my existence hitherto."

"To be frank with you, yes, Harley," said the Earl with a pride that was noble in its nature, and not without dignity in its expression. "The more we take from our country, the more we owe to her. From the moment you came into the world, as the inheritor of lands and honours, you were charged with a trust for the benefit of others, that it degrades one of our order of gentlemen not to discharge."

Harley listened with a sombre brow, and made no direct reply.

"Indeed," resumed the Earl, "I would rather you were about to canvass for yourself than for your friend Egerton. But I grant he is an example that it is never too late to follow. Why, who that had seen you both as youths, notwithstanding Audley had the advantage of being some years your senior—who could have thought that he was the one to become distinguished and eminent—and you to degenerate into the luxurious idler, averse to all trouble and careless of all fame? You, with such advantages, not only of higher fortunes, but, as every one said, of superior talents—you, who had then so much ambition—so keen a desire for glory, sleeping with Plutarch's Lives under your pillow, and only, my wild son, only too much energy. But you are a young man still—it is not too late to redeem the years you have thrown away."

"The years—are nothing—mere dates in an almanack; but the feelings, what can give me back those?—the hope, the enthusiasm, the—no matter! feelings do not help men to rise in the world. Egerton's feelings are not too lively. What I might have been, leave it to me to remember—let us talk of the example you set before me—of Audley Egerton."

"We must get him in," said the Earl, sinking his voice into a whisper. "It is of more importance to him than I even thought for. But you know his secrets. Why did you not confide to me frankly the state of his affairs?"

"His affairs? Do you mean that they are seriously embarrassed? This interests me much. Pray speak; what do you know?"

"He has discharged the greater part of his establishment. That in itself is natural on quitting office; but still it set people talking; and it has got wind that his estates are not only mortgaged for more than they are worth, but that he has been living upon the discount of bills; in short, he has been too intimate with a man whom we all know by sight—a man who drives the finest horses in London, and they tell me (but *that* I cannot believe) lives in the familiar society of the young puppies he snares to perdition. What's the man's name? Levy, is it not?—yes, Levy."

"I have seen Levy with him," said Harley; and a sinister joy lighted up his falcon eyes. "Levy—Levy—it is well."

"I hear but the gossip of the clubs," resumed the Earl. "But they do say that Levy makes little disguise of his power over our very distinguished friend, and rather parades it as a merit with our party, (and, indeed, with all men—for Egerton has personal friends in every party,) that he keeps sundry bills locked up in his desk until Egerton is once more safe in Parliament. Nevertheless if, after all, our friend were to lose his election, and Levy were then to seize on his effects, and proclaim his ruin—it would seriously damage, perhaps altogether destroy, Audley's political career."

"So I conclude," said Harley. "A Charles Fox might be a gamester, and a William Pitt be a pauper. But Audley Egerton is not of their giant stature;—he stands so high because he stands upon heaps of respectable gold. Audley Egerton, needy and impoverished—out of Parliament, and, as the vulgar slang has it, out at elbows, skulking from duns —perhaps in the Bench—"

"No, no—our party would never allow that; we would subscribe—"

"Worse than all, living as the pensioner of the party he aspired to lead! You say truly, his political prospects would be blasted. A man whose reputation lay in his outward respectability! Why, people would say that Audley Egerton has been—a solemn lie; eh, my father?"

"How can you talk with such coolness of your friend? You need say nothing to interest me in his election—if you mean that. Once in Parliament, he must soon again be in office—and learn to live on his salary. You must get him to submit to me the schedule of his liabilities. I have a head for business, as you know. I will arrange his affairs for him. And I will yet bet five to one, though I hate wagers, that he will be prime minister in three years. He is not brilliant, it is true; but just at this crisis we want a safe, moderate, judicious, conciliatory man; and Audley has so much tact, such experience of the House, such knowledge of the world, and," added the Earl, emphatically summing up his eulogies, "he is so thorough a gentleman!"

"A thorough gentleman, as you say—the soul of honour! But, my dear father, it is your hour for riding; let me not detain you. It is settled, then; you do not come yourself to Lansmere. You put the house at my disposal, and allow me to invite Egerton, of course, and what other guests I may please; in short, you leave all to me?"

"Certainly; and if *you* cannot get in your friend, who can? That borough, it is an awkward, ungrateful place, and has been the plague of my life. So much as I have spent there, too—so much as I have done to its trade." And the Earl, with an indignant sigh, left the room.

Harley seated himself deliberately at his writing-table, leaning his face on his hand, and looking abstractedly into space from under knit and lowering brows.

Harley L'Estrange was, as we have seen, a man singularly tenacious of affections and impressions. He was a man, too, whose nature was eminently bold, loyal, and candid; even the apparent whim and levity which misled the world, both as to his dispositions and his powers, might be half ascribed to that open temper which, in its over-contempt for all that seemed to savour of hypocrisy, sported with forms and ceremonials, and extracted humour, sometimes extravagant, sometimes profound—from "the solemn plausibilities of the world." The shock he had now received smote the very foundations of his mind, and, overthrowing all the airier structures which fancy and wit had built upon its surface, left it clear as a new world for the operations of the darker and more fearful passions. When a man of a heart so loving, and a nature so irregularly powerful as Harley's suddenly and abruptly discovers deceit where he had most confided, it is not (as with the calmer pupils of that harsh teacher, Experience) the mere withdrawal of esteem and affection from the one offender—it is, that trust in everything seems gone—it is, that the injured spirit looks back to the Past, and condemns all its kindlier virtues as follies that conduced to its own woe; and looks on to the Future as to a journey beset with smiling traitors, whom it must meet with an equal simulation, or crush with a superior force. The guilt of treason to men like these is incalculable—it robs the world of all the benefits they would otherwise have lavished as they passed—it is responsible for all the ill that springs from the corruption of natures, whose very luxuriance, when the atmosphere is once tainted, does but diffuse disease;—even as the malaria settles not over thin and barren soils, nor over wastes that have been from all time desolate, but over the places in which southern suns had once ripened delightful gardens, or the sites of cities, in which the pomp of palaces has passed away.

It was not enough that the friend of his youth, the confidant of his love, had betrayed his trust—been the secret and successful rival—not enough that the woman his boyhood had madly idolised, and all the while he had sought her traces with pining, remorseful heart—believing she but eluded his suit from the emulation of a kindred generosity—desiring rather to sacrifice her own love than to cost to his the sacrifice of all which youth rashly scorns and the world so highly estimates;—not enough that all this while her refuge had been the bosom of another. This was not enough of injury. His whole life had been wasted on a delusion—his faculties and aims—the wholesome ambition of lofty minds had been arrested at the very onset of fair existence—his heart corroded by a regret for which there was no cause—his conscience charged with the terror that his wild chase had urged a too tender victim to the grave, over which he had mourned. What years that might otherwise have been to himself so serene, to the world so useful, had been consumed in objectless, barren, melancholy dreams! And all this while to whom had his complaints been uttered?—to the man who knew that his remorse was an idle spectre, and his faithful sorrow a mocking self-deceit. Every thought that could gall man's natural pride — every remembrance that could sting into revenge a heart that had loved too deeply not to be accessible to hate—conspired to goad those maddening Furies who come into every temple which is once desecrated by the presence of the evil passions. In that sullen silence of the soul, vengeance took the form of justice. Changed though his feelings towards Leonora Avenel were, the story of her grief and her wrongs embittered still more his wrath against his rival. The fragments of her memoir left naturally on Harley's mind the conviction that she had been the victim of an infamous fraud—the dupe of a false marriage. His idol had not only been stolen from the altar, it had been sullied by the sacrifice—broken with remorseless hand, and thrust into dishonoured clay—mutilated, defamed—its very memory a thing of contempt to him who had ravished it from worship. The living Harley and the dead Nora—both called aloud to their joint despoiler; "Restore what thou hast taken from us, or pay the forfeit!"

Thus, then, during the interview between Helen and Leonard, thus Harley L'Estrange not alone! And as a rude irregular lump of steel, when wheeled round into rapid motion assumes the form of the circle it describes, so his iron purpose, hurried on by his relentless passion, filled the space into which he gazed with optical delusions—scheme after scheme revolving and consummating the circles that clasped a foe.

## CHAPTER XV.

The entrance of a servant, announcing a name which Harley, in the absorption of his gloomy reverie, did not hear, was followed by that of a person on whom he lifted his eyes in the cold and haughty surprise with which a man, much occupied, greets and rebukes the intrusion of an unwelcome stranger.

"It is so long since your lordship has seen me," said the visitor, with mild dignity, "that I cannot wonder you do not recognise my person, and have forgotten my name."

"Sir," answered Harley, with an impatient rudeness, ill in harmony with the urbanity for which he was usually distinguished—"Sir, your person is strange to me, and your name I did not hear; but, at all events, I am not now at leisure to attend to you. Excuse my plainness."

"Yet, pardon me if I still linger. My name is Dale. I was formerly curate at Lansmere; and I would speak to your lordship in the name and the memory of one once dear to you —Leonora Avenel."

HARLEY (after a short pause.)—"Sir, I cannot conjecture your business. But be seated. I remember you now, though years have altered both, and I have since heard much in your favour from Leonard Fairfield. Still let me pray that you will be brief."

MR. DALE.—"May I assume at once that you have divined the parentage of the young man you call Fairfield? When I listened to his grateful praises of your beneficence, and marked with melancholy pleasure the reverence in which he holds you, my heart swelled within me. I acknowledged the mysterious force of nature."

HARLEY.—"Force of nature! You talk in riddles."

MR. DALE, (indignantly.)—"Oh, my lord, how can you so disguise your better self? Surely in Leonard Fairfield you have long since recognised the son of Nora Avenel?"

Harley passed his hand over his face. "Ah!" thought he, "she lived to bear a son, then—a son to Egerton! Leonard is that son. I should have known it by the likeness—by the fond foolish impulse that moved me to him. This is why he confided to me these fearful memoirs. He seeks his father— he shall find him."

MR. DALE, (mistaking the cause of Harley's silence.)—"I honour your compunction, my lord. Oh! let your heart and your conscience continue to speak to your worldly pride."

HARLEY.—"My compunction, heart, conscience! Mr. Dale, you insult me!"

MR. DALE, (sternly.)—"Not so; I am fulfilling my mission, which bids me rebuke the sinner. Leonora Avenel speaks in me, and commands the guilty father to acknowledge the innocent child!"

Harley half rose, and his eyes literally flashed fire; but he calmed his anger into irony. "Ha!" said he, with a sarcastic smile, "so you suppose that I was the perfidious seducer of Nora Avenel—that I am the callous father of the child who came into the world without a name. Very well, sir, taking these assumptions for granted, what is it you demand from me on behalf of this young man?"

"I ask from you his happiness," replied Mr. Dale, imploringly; and yielding to the compassion with which Leonard inspired him, and persuaded that Lord L'Estrange felt a father's love for the boy whom he had saved from the whirlpool of London, and guided to safety and honourable independence, he here, with simple eloquence, narrated all Leonard's feelings for Helen—his silent fidelity to her image, though a child's—his love when he again beheld her as a woman—the modest fears which the Parson himself had combated—the recommendation that Mr. Dale had forced upon him, to confess his affection to Helen, and plead his cause. "Anxious, as you may believe, for his success," continued the Parson, "I waited without your gates till he came from Miss Digby's presence. And oh, my lord, had you but seen his face! —such emotion and such despair! I could not learn from him what had passed. He escaped from me and rushed away. All that I could gather was from a few broken words, and from those words I formed the conjecture (it may be erroneous) that the obstacle to his happiness was not in Helen's heart, my lord, but seemed to me as if it were in yourself. Therefore, when he had vanished from my sight, I took courage, and came at once to you. If he be your son, and Helen Digby be your ward—she herself an orphan, dependent on your bounty—why should they be severed? Equals in years —united by early circumstance—congenial, it seems, in simple habits and refined tastes—what should hinder their union, unless it be the want of fortune?—and all men know your wealth—none ever questioned your generosity. My lord, my lord, your look freezes me. If I have offended, do not visit my offence on him—on Leonard!"

"And so," said Harley, still controlling his rage, "so this boy—whom, as you say, I saved from that pitiless world which has engulfed many a nobler genius—so, in return for all, he has sought to rob me of the last affection, poor and lukewarm though it was, that remained to me in life. He presume to lift his eyes to my affianced bride! He! And for aught I know, steal from me her living heart, and leave to me her icy hand!"

"Oh, my lord, your affianced bride! I never dreamed of this. I implore your pardon. The very thought is so terrible —so unnatural—the son to woo the father's—! Oh, what sin have I fallen into! The sin was mine—I urged and persuaded him to it. He was ignorant as myself. Forgive him, forgive him!"

"Mr. Dale," said Harley, rising, and extending his hand, which the poor Parson felt himself unworthy to take—"Mr. Dale, you are a good man—if, indeed, this universe of liars contains some man who does not cheat our judgment when we deem him honest. Allow me only to ask why you consider Leonard Fairfield to be my son?"

"Was not your youthful admiration for poor Nora evident to me? Remember I was a frequent guest at Lansmere Park; and it was so natural that you, with all your brilliant gifts, should captivate her refined fancy—her affectionate heart."

"Natural—you think so—go on."

"Your mother, as became her, separated you. It was not unknown to me that you still cherished a passion which your rank forbade to be lawful. Poor girl; she left the roof of her protectress, Lady Jane. Nothing was known of her till she came to her father's house to give birth to a child, and die. And the same day that dawned on her corpse, you hurried from the place. Ah! no doubt your conscience smote you—you have never returned to Lansmere since."

Harley's breast heaved—he waved his hand—the Parson resumed—

"Whom could I suspect but you? I made inquiries: they confirmed my suspicions."

"Perhaps you inquired of my friend, Mr. Egerton? He was with me when—when—as you say, I hurried from the place."

"I did, my lord?"

"And he?"

"Denied your guilt; but still, a man of honour so nice, of heart so feeling, could not feign readily. His denial did not deceive me."

"Honest man!" said Harley; and his hand griped at the breast over which still rustled, as if with a ghostly sigh, the records of the dead. "He knew she had left a son, too?"

"He did, my lord; of course, I told him that."

"The son whom I found starving in the streets of London! Mr. Dale, as you see, your words move me very much. I cannot deny that he who wronged, it may be with no common treachery, that young mother—for Nora Avenel was not one to be lightly seduced into error—"

"Indeed, no!"

"And who then thought no more of the offspring of her anguish and his own crime—I cannot deny that that man deserves some chastisement—should render some atonement. Am I not right here? Answer with the plain speech which becomes your sacred calling."

"I cannot say otherwise, my lord," replied the Parson, pitying what appeared to him such remorse. "But if he repent—"

"Enough," interrupted Harley, "I now invite you to visit me at Lansmere; give me your address and I will apprise you of the day on which I will request your presence. Leonard Fairfield shall find a father—I was about to say, worthy of himself. For the rest—stay; reseat yourself. For the rest"—and again the sinister smile broke from Harley's eye and lip—"I will not yet say whether I can, or ought to, resign to a younger and fairer suitor the lady who has accepted my own hand. I have no reason yet to believe that she prefers him. But what think you, meanwhile, of this proposal? Mr. Avenel wishes his nephew to contest the borough of Lansmere—has urged me to obtain the young man's consent. True, that he may thus endanger the seat of Mr. Audley Egerton. What then? Mr. Audley Egerton is a great man, and may find another seat; that should not stand in the way. Let Leonard obey his uncle. If he win the election, why, he'll be a more equal match, in the world's eye, for Miss Digby—that is, should she prefer him to myself; and if she do not, still, in public life, there is a cure for all private sorrow. That is a maxim of Mr. Audley Egerton's; and he, you know, is a man not only of the nicest honour, but the deepest worldly widom. Do you like my proposition?"

"It seems to me most considerate—most generous."

"Then you shall take to Leonard the lines I am about to write."

LORD L'ESTRANGE TO LEONARD FAIRFIELD.

"I have read the memoir you intrusted to me. I will follow up all the clues that it gives me. Meanwhile I request you to suspend all questions—forbear all reference to a subject which, as you may well conjecture, is fraught with painful recollections to myself. At this moment, too, I am compelled to concentre my thoughts upon affairs of a public nature, and yet which may sensibly affect yourself. There are reasons why I urge you to comply with your uncle's wish, and stand for the borough of Lansmere at the approaching election. If the exquisite gratitude of your nature so overrates what I may have done for you, that you think you owe me some obligations, you will richly repay them on the day in which I hear you hailed as member for Lansmere. Relying on that generous principle of self-sacrifice, which actuates all your

conduct, I shall count upon your surrendering your preference to private life, and entering the arena of that noble ambition which has conferred such dignity on the name of my friend Audley Egerton. He, it is true, will be your opponent; but he is too generous not to pardon my zeal for the interests of a youth whose career I am vain enough to think that I have aided. And as Mr. Randal Leslie stands in coalition with Egerton, and Mr. Avenel believes that two candidates of the same party cannot both succeed, the result may be to the satisfaction of all the feelings which I entertain for Audley Egerton, and for you, who, I have reason to think, will emulate his titles to my esteem. "Yours,
"L'Estrange."

"There, Mr. Dale," said Harley, sealing his letter, and giving it into the Parson's hands. "There, you shall deliver this note to your friend. But no—upon second thoughts, since he does not yet know of your visit to me, it is best that he should be still in ignorance of it. For should Miss Digby resolve to abide by her present engagements, it were surely kind to save Leonard the pain of learning that you had communicated to me that rivalry he himself had concealed. Let all that has passed between us be kept in strict confidence."

"I will obey you, my lord," answered the Parson, meekly, startled to find that he who had come to arrogate authority, was now submitting to commands; and all at fault what judgment he could venture to pass upon the man whom he had regarded as a criminal, who had not even denied the crime imputed to him, yet who now impressed the accusing priest with something of that respect which Mr. Dale had never before conceded but to Virtue. Could he have then but looked into the dark and stormy heart, which he *twice* misread!

"It is well—very well," muttered Harley, when the door had closed upon the Parson. "The viper and the viper's brood! So it was this man's son that I led from the dire Slough of Despond; and the son unconsciously imitates the father's gratitude and honour—Ha—ha!" Suddenly the bitter laugh was arrested; a flash of almost celestial joy darted through the warring elements of storm and darkness. If Helen returned Leonard's affection, Harley L'Estrange was free! And through that flash the face of Violante shone upon him as an angel's. But the heavenly light and the angel face vanished abruptly, swallowed up in the black abyss of the rent and tortured soul.

"Fool!" said the unhappy man, aloud, in his anguish—"fool! what then? Were I free, would it be to trust my fate again to falsehood? If, in all the bloom and glory of my youth, I failed to win the heart of a village girl—if, once more deluding myself, it is in vain that I have tended, reared, cherished, some germ of woman's human affection in the orphan I saved from penury—how look for love in the brilliant princess, whom all the sleek Lotharios of our gaudy world will surround with their homage when once she alights on their sphere! If perfidy be my fate—what hell of hells in the thought!—that a wife might lay her head in my bosom—and—oh, horror! horror!—No!—I would not accept her hand were it offered, nor believe in her love were it pledged to me. Stern soul of mine—wise at last, love never more—never more believe in truth!"

## CHAPTER XVI.

As Harley quitted the room, Helen's pale sweet face looked forth from a door in the same corridor. She advanced towards him timidly.

"May I speak with you?" she said, in almost inaudible accents. "I have been listening for your footstep."

Harley looked at her steadfastly. Then, without a word, he followed her into the room she had left, and closed the door.

"I, too," said he, "meant to seek an interview with yourself—but later. You would speak to me Helen—say on.— Ah! child, what mean you? Why this?"—for Helen was kneeling at his feet.

"Let me kneel," she said, resisting the hand that sought to raise her. "Let me kneel till I have explained all, and perhaps won your pardon. You said something the other evening. It has weighed on my heart and my conscience ever since. You said 'that I should have no secret from you; for *that*, in our relation to each other, would be deceit.' I have had a secret; but, oh, believe me! it was long ere it was clearly visible to myself. You honoured me with a suit so far beyond my birth, my merits. You said that I might console and comfort you. At those words, what answer could I give?—I, who owe you so much more than a daughter's duty? And I thought that my affections were free—that they would obey that duty. But—but—but—" continued Helen, bowing her head still lowlier, and in a voice far fainter —" I deceived myself. I again saw *him* who had been all in the world to me, when the world was so terrible—and then— and then—I trembled. I was terrified at my own memories —my own thoughts. Still I struggled to banish the past— resolutely—firmly. Oh, you believe me, do you not? And I hoped to conquer. Yet ever since those words of yours, I felt that I ought to tell you even of the struggle. This is the first time we have met since you spoke them. And now— now—I have seen him again, and—and—though not by a word could she you had deigned to woo as your bride encourage hope in another—though there—there where you now stand—he bade me farewell, and we parted as if for ever;— yet—yet—O Lord L'Estrange! in return for your rank, wealth, your still nobler gifts of nature—what should I bring? —Something more than gratitude, esteem, reverence—at least an undivided heart, filled with your image, and yours alone. And this I cannot give. Pardon me—not for what I say now, but for not saying it before. Pardon me—O my benefactor, pardon me!"

"Rise, Helen," said Harley, with relaxing brow, though still unwilling to yield to one softer and holier emotion. "Rise!" And he lifted her up, and drew her towards the light. "Let me look at your face. There seems no guile here. These tears are surely honest. If I cannot be loved, it is my fate, and not your crime. Now, listen to me. If you grant me nothing else, will you give me the obedience which the ward owes to the guardian—the child to the parent?"

"Yes—oh yes!" murmured Helen.

"Then while I release you from all troth to me, I claim the right to refuse, if I so please it, my assent to the suit of— of the person you prefer. I acquit you of deceit, but I reserve to myself the judgment I shall pass on him. Until I myself sanction that suit, will you promise not to recall in any way the rejection which, if I understand you rightly, you have given to it?"

"I promise."

"And if I say to you, 'Helen, this man is not worthy of you—'"

"No, no! do not say that—I could not believe you."

Harley frowned, but resumed calmly—"If, then, I say, 'Ask me not wherefore, but I forbid you to be the wife of Leonard Fairfield,' what would be your answer?"

"Ah, my lord, if you can but comfort him, do with me as you will! but do not command me to break his heart."

"Oh, silly child," cried Harley, laughing scornfully, "hearts are not found in the race from which that man sprang. But I take your promise, with its credulous condition. Helen, I pity you. I have been as weak as you, bearded man though I be. Some day or other, you and I may live to laugh at the follies at which you weep now. I can give you no other comfort, for I know of none."

He moved to the door, and paused at the threshold. "I shall not see you again for some days, Helen. Perhaps I may request my mother to join me at Lansmere; if so, I shall pray you to accompany her. For the present, let all believe that our position is unchanged. The time will soon come when I may—"

Helen looked up wistfully through her tears.

"I may release you from all duties to me," continued Harley, with grave and severe coldness; "or I may claim your promise in spite of the condition; for your lover's heart will not be broken. Adieu!"

## CHAPTER XVII.

As Harley entered London, he came suddenly upon Randal Leslie, who was hurrying from Eaton Square, having not only accompanied Mr. Avenel in his walk, but gone home with him, and spent half the day in that gentleman's society. He was now on his way to the House of Commons, at which some disclosure as to the day for the dissolution of Parliament was expected.

"Lord L'Estrange," said Randal, "I must stop you. I have been to Norwood, and seen our noble friend. He has confided to me, of course, all that passed. How can I express my gratitude to you! By what rare talent—with what signal courage—you have saved the happiness—perhaps even the honour—of my plighted bride!"

"Your bride! The Duke, then, still holds to the promise you were fortunate enough to obtain from Dr. Riccabocca?"

"He confirms that promise more solemnly than ever. You may well be surprised at his magnanimity."

"No; he is a philosopher—nothing in him can surprise me. But he seemed to think, when I saw him, that there were circumstances you might find it hard to explain."

"Hard! Nothing so easy. Allow me to tender to you the same explanations which satisfied one whom philosophy itself has made as open to truth as he is clear-sighted to imposture."

"Another time, Mr. Leslie. If your bride's father be satisfied, what right have I to doubt? By the way, you stand for Lansmere. Do me the favour to fix your quarters at the Park during the election. You will, of course, accompany Mr. Egerton."

"You are most kind," answered Randal, greatly surprised.

"You accept? That is well. We shall then have ample opportunity for those explanations which you honour me by offering; and, to make your visit still more agreeable, I may, perhaps, induce our friends at Norwood to meet you. Good day."

Harley walked on, leaving Randal motionless in amaze, but tormented with suspicion. What could such courtesies in Lord L'Estrange portend? Surely no good.

"I am about to hold the balance of justice," said Harley to himself.—"I will cast the light-weight of that knave into the scale. Violante never can be mine; but I did not save her from a Peschiera to leave her to a Randal Leslie. Ha, ha! Audley Egerton has some human feeling—tenderness for that youth whom he has selected from the world, in which he left Nora's child to the jaws of Famine. Through that side I can reach at his heart, and prove him a fool like myself, where he esteemed and confided! Good."

Thus soliloquising, Lord L'Estrange gained the corner of Bruton Street, when he was again somewhat abruptly accosted.

"My dear Lord L'Estrange, let me shake you by the hand; for Heaven knows when I may see you again; and you have suffered me to assist in one good action."

"Frank Hazeldean, I am pleased indeed to meet you. Why do you indulge in that melancholy doubt as to the time when I may see you again?"

"I have just got leave of absence I am not well, and am rather hipped, so I shall go abroad for a few weeks."

In spite of himself, the sombre brooding man felt interest and sympathy in the dejection that was evident in Frank's

voice and countenance. "Another dupe to affection," thought
he, as if in apology to himself;—" of course, a dupe; he is
honest and artless—at present." He pressed kindly on the
arm which he had involuntarily twined within his own. "I
conceive how you now grieve, my young friend," said he;
"but you will congratulate yourself hereafter on what this
day seems to you an affliction."

"My dear Lord—"

"I am much older than you, but not old enough for such
formal ceremony. Pray call me L'Estrange."

"Thank you; and I should indeed like to speak to you as
a friend.—There is a thought on my mind which haunts me.
I daresay it is foolish enough, but I am sure *you* will not
laugh at me. You heard what Madame di Negra said to me
last night. I have been trifled with and misled, but I cannot
forget so soon how dear to me that woman was. I am not
going to bore you with such nonsense; but, from what I can
understand, her brother is likely to lose all his fortune; and,
even if not, he is a sad scoundrel. I cannot bear the thought
that she should be so dependent on him—that she may come
to want.—After all, there must be good in her—good in her
to refuse my hand if she did not love me. A mercenary
woman so circumstanced would not have done that."

"You are quite right. But do not torment yourself with
such generous fears. Madame di Negra shall not come to
want—shall not be dependent on her infamous brother. The
first act of the Duke of Serrano, on regaining his estates, will
be a suitable provision for his kinswoman. I will answer for
this."

"You take a load off my mind. I did mean to ask you to
intercede with Riccabocca—that is, the Duke; (it is so hard
to think he can be a Duke!) I, alas! have nothing in my
power to bestow upon Madame di Negra. I may, indeed, sell
my commission; but then I have a debt which I long to pay
off, and the sale of the commission would not suffice even for
that; and perhaps my father might be still more angry if I
do sell it. Well, good-bye. I shall now go away happy—
that is, comparatively. One must bear things like—a
man!"

"I should like, however, to see you again before you go
abroad. I will call on you. Meanwhile, can you tell me the
number of one Baron Levy? He lives in this street, I
know!"

"Levy! Oh, have no dealings with him, I advise—I

entreat you! He is the most plausible, dangerous rascal; and, for Heaven's sake! pray be warned by me, and let nothing entangle you into—a POST-OBIT!"

"Be re-assured, I am more accustomed to lend money than borrow it; and, as to a *post-obit*, I have a foolish prejudice against such transactions."

"Don't call it foolish, L'Estrange; I honour you for it. How I wish I had known you earlier—so few men of the world are like you. Even Randal Leslie, who is so faultless in most things, and never gets into a scrape himself, called my own scruples foolish. However—"

"Stay—Randal Leslie! What! He advised you to borrow on a *post-obit*, and probably shared the loan with you?"

"O no; not a shilling."

"Tell me all about it, Frank. Perhaps, as I see that Levy is mixed up in the affair, your information may be useful to myself, and put me on my guard in dealing with that popular gentleman."

Frank, who somehow or other felt himself quite at home with Harley, and who, with all his respect for Randal Leslie's talents, had a vague notion that Lord L'Estrange was quite as clever, and, from his years and experience, likely to be a safer and more judicious counsellor, was noways loath to impart the confidence thus pressed for.

He told Harley of his debts—his first dealings with Levy; —the unhappy *post-obit* into which he had been hurried by the distress of Madame di Negra;—his father's anger—his mother's letter—his own feelings of mingled shame and pride, which made him fear that repentance would but seem self-interest—his desire to sell his commission, and let its sale redeem in part the *post-obit*; in short, he made what is called a clean breast of it. Randal Leslie was necessarily mixed up with this recital; and the subtle cross-questionings of Harley extracted far more as to that young diplomatist's agency in all these melancholy concerns, than the ingenuous narrator himself was aware of.

"So then," said Harley, "Mr. Leslie assured you of Madame di Negra's affection, when you yourself doubted of it?"

"Yes; she took him in, even more than she did me."

"Simple Mr. Leslie! And the same kind friend—who is related to you—did you say?"

"His grandmother was a Hazeldean."

"Humph. The same kind relation led you to believe that you could pay off this bond with the Marchesa's portion, and that he could obtain the consent of your parents to your marriage with that lady?"

"I ought to have known better; my father's prejudices against foreigners and Papists are so strong."

"And now Mr. Leslie concurs with you, that it is best for you to go abroad, and trust to his intercession with your father. He has evidently, then, gained a great influence over Mr. Hazeldean."

"My father naturally compares me with him—he so clever, so promising, so regular in his habits, and I such a reckless scapegrace."

"And the bulk of your father's property is unentailed—Mr. Hazeldean might disinherit you?"

"I deserve it. I hope he will."

"You have no brothers nor sisters—no relation, perhaps, after your parents, nearer to you than your excellent friend Mr. Randal Leslie?"

"No; that is the reason he is so kind to me, otherwise I am the last person to suit him. You have no idea how well-informed and clever he is," added Frank, in a tone between admiration and awe.

"My dear Hazeldean, you will take my advice—will you not?"

"Certainly. You are too good."

"Let all your family, Mr. Leslie included, suppose you to be gone abroad; but stay quietly in England, and within a day's journey of Lansmere Park. I am obliged to go thither for the approaching election. I may ask you to come over. I think I see a way to serve you; and if so, you will soon hear from me. Now, Baron Levy's number?"

"That is the house with the cabriolet at the door. How such a fellow can have such a horse!—'tis out of all keeping!"

"Not at all; horses are high-spirited, generous, unsuspicious animals. They never know if it is a rogue who drives them. I have your promise, then, and you will send me your address?"

"I will. Strange that I feel more confidence in you than I do even in Randal! Do take care of Levy."

Lord L'Estrange and Frank here shook hands, and Frank, with an anxious groan, saw L'Estrange disappear within the portals of the sleek destroyer.

## CHAPTER XVIII.

Lord L'Estrange followed the spruce servant into Baron Levy's luxurious study.

The Baron looked greatly amazed at his unexpected visitor; but he got up,—handed a chair to my lord with low bow. "This *is* an honour," said he.

"You have a charming abode here," said Lord L'Estrange, looking round, "Very fine bronzes—excellent taste. Your reception-rooms above are, doubtless, a model to all decorators!"

"Would your lordship condescend to see them?" said Levy, wondering, but flattered.

"With the greatest pleasure."

"Lights!" cried Levy, to the servant who answered his bell. "Lights in the drawing-rooms—it is growing dark."

Lord L'Estrange followed the usurer up-stairs; admired everything—pictures, draperies, Sèvres china, to the very shape of the downy *fauteuils*, to the very pattern of the Tournay carpets. Reclining then on one of the voluptuous sofas, Lord L'Estrange said, smilingly, "You are a wise man: there is no advantage in being rich, unless one enjoys one's riches."

"My own maxim, Lord L'Estrange."

"And it is something, too, to have a taste for good society. Small pride would you have, my dear Baron, in these rooms, luxurious though they are, if filled with guests of vulgar exterior and plebeian manners. It is only in the world in which *we* move that we find persons who harmonise, as it were, with the porcelain of Sèvres, and these sofas that might have come from Versailles."

"I own," said Levy, "that I have what some may call a weakness in a *parvenu* like myself. I have a love for the *beau monde*. It is indeed a pleasure to me when I receive men like your lordship."

"But why call yourself a *parvenu?* Though you are contented to honour the name of Levy, we, in society, all know that you are the son of a long-descended English peer. Child of love, it is true; but the Graces smile on those over whose birth Venus presided. Pardon my old-fashioned mythological similes — they go so well with these rooms — *Louis Quinze.*"

"Since you touched on my birth," said Levy, his colour rather heightening, not with shame, but with pride, "I don't deny that it has some effect on my habits and tastes in life. In fact—"

"In fact, own that you would be a miserable man, in spite of all your wealth, if the young dandies, who throng to your banquets, were to cut you dead in the streets;—if, when your high-stepping horse stopped at your club, the porter shut the door in your face;—if, when you lounged into the opera-pit, handsome dog that you are, each spendthrift rake in 'Fop's Alley,' who now waits but the scratch of your pen to endorse *billets-doux* with the charm that can chain to himself for a month some nymph of the *Ballet*, spinning round in a whirlwind of *tulle*,—would shrink from the touch of your condescending forefinger with more dread of its contact than a bailiff's tap in the thick of Pall-Mall could inspire;—if, reduced to the company of city clerks, parasite led-captains—"

"Oh, don't go on, my dear Lord," cried Levy, laughing affectedly. "Impossible though the picture be, it is really appalling. Cut me off from May Fair and St. James's, and I should go into my strong closet and hang myself."

"And yet, my dear Baron, all this may happen if I have the whim just to try;—all this *will* happen, unless, ere I leave your house, you concede the conditions I come here to impose."

"My lord!" exclaimed Levy, starting up, and pulling down his waistcoat with nervous, passionate fingers, "if you were not under my own roof, I would—"

"Truce with mock heroics. Sit down, sir—sit down. I will briefly state my threat—more briefly my conditions. You will be scarcely more prolix in your reply. Your fortune I cannot touch—your enjoyment of it I can destroy. Refuse my conditions—make me your enemy—and war to the knife! I will interrogate all the young dupes you have ruined. I will learn the history of all the transactions by which you have gained the wealth that it pleases you to spend in courting the society and sharing the vices of men who—go with these rooms, *Louis Quinze!* Not a roguery of yours shall escape me, down even to your last notable connivance with an Italian reprobate for the criminal abduction of an heiress. All these particulars I will proclaim in the clubs to which you have gained admittance—in every club in London which you yet hope to creep into. All these I will impart to some such authority in the Press as Mr. Henry Norreys;—all these

I will, upon the voucher of my own name, have so published in some journals of repute, that you must either tacitly submit to the revelations that blast you, or bring before a court of law actions that will convert accusations into evidence. It is but by sufferance that you are now in society—you are excluded when one man like me comes forth to denounce you. You try in vain to sneer at my menace—your white lips show your terror. I have rarely in life drawn any advantage from my rank and position; but I am thankful that they give me the power to make my voice respected and my exposure triumphant. Now, Baron Levy, will you go into your strong closet and hang yourself, or will you grant me my very moderate conditions? You are silent. I will relieve you, and state those conditions. Until the general election, about to take place, is concluded, you will obey me to the letter in all that I enjoin—no demur, and no scruple. And the first proof of obedience I demand is, your candid disclosure of all Mr. Audley Egerton's pecuniary affairs."

"Has my client, Mr. Egerton, authorised you to request of me that disclosure?"

"On the contrary, all that passes between us you will conceal from your client."

"You would save him from ruin? Your trusty *friend*, Mr. Egerton!" said the Baron, with a livid sneer.

"Wrong again, Baron Levy. If I would save him from ruin, you are scarcely the man I should ask to assist me."

"Ah, I guess. You have learned how he—"

"Guess nothing, but obey in all things. Let us descend to your business room."

Levy said not a word until he had reconducted his visitor into his den of destruction—all gleaming with *spoliaria* in rosewood. Then he said this: "If, Lord L'Estrange, you seek but revenge on Audley Egerton, you need not have uttered those threats. I too—hate the man."

Harley looked at him wistfully, and the nobleman felt a pang that he had debased himself into a single feeling which the usurer could share. Nevertheless, the interview appeared to close with satisfactory arrangements, and to produce amicable understanding. For as the Baron ceremoniously followed Lord L'Estrange through the hall his noble visitor said, with marked affability—

"Then I shall see you at Lansmere with Mr. Egerton, to assist in conducting his election. It is a sacrifice of your time worthy of your friendship; not a step farther, I beg. Baron, I have the honour to wish you good evening."

As the street door opened on Lord L'Estrange he again found himself face to face with Randal Leslie, whose hand was already lifted to the knocker.

"Ha, Mr. Leslie!—you too a client of Baron Levy's;—a very useful accommodating man."

Randal stared and stammered. "I come in haste from the House of Commons on Mr. Egerton's business. Don't you hear the newspaper vendors crying out 'Great news—Dissolution of Parliament?'"

"We are prepared. Levy himself consents to give us the aid of his talents. Kindly, obliging—clever person!"

Randal hurried into Levy's study, to which the usurer had shrunk back, and was now wiping his brow with his scented handkerchief, looking heated and haggard, and very indifferent to Randal Leslie.

"How is this?" cried Randal. "I come to tell you first of Peschiera's utter failure, the ridiculous coxcomb, and I meet at your door the last man I thought to find there—the man who foiled us all, Lord L'Estrange. What brought him to you? Ah, perhaps his interest in Egerton's election?"

"Yes," said Levy, sulkily. "I know all about Peschiera. I cannot talk to you now; I must make arrangements for going to Lansmere."

"But don't forget my purchase from Thornhill. I shall have the money shortly from a surer source than Peschiera."

"The Squire?"

"Or a rich father-in-law."

In the meanwhile, as Lord L'Estrange entered Bond Street, his ears were stunned by vociferous cries from the Stentors employed by *Standard, Sun,* and *Globe,*—"Great news. Dissolution of Parliament—great news!" The gas-lamps were lighted—a brown fog was gathering over the streets, blending itself with the falling shades of night. The forms of men loomed large through the mist. The lights from the shops looked red and lurid. Loungers usually careless as to politics, were talking eagerly and anxiously of King, Lords, Commons, "Constitution at stake"—"Triumph of liberal opinions,"—according to their several biases. Hearing, and scorning—unsocial, isolated—walked on Harley L'Estrange. With his direr passions had been roused up all the native powers, that made them doubly dangerous. He became proudly conscious of his own great faculties, but exulted in them only so far as they could minister to the purpose which had invoked them.

"I have constituted myself a Fate," he said inly; "let the gods be but neutral—while I weave the meshes. Then, as Fate itself when it has fulfilled its mission, let me pass away into shadow, with the still and lonely stride that none may follow.

'Oh for a lodge in some vast wilderness.'

How weary I am of this world of men!" And again the cry "Great news—National crisis—Dissolution of Parliament— Great news!" rang through the jostling throng. Three men, arm-in-arm, brushed by Harley, and were stopped at the crossing by a file of carriages. The man in the centre was Audley Egerton. His companions were an ex-minister like himself, and one of those great proprietors who are proud of being above office, and vain of the power to make and unmake Governments.

"You are the only man to lead us, Egerton," said this last personage. "Do but secure your seat, and as soon as this popular fever has passed away, you must be something more than the leader of Opposition—you must be the first man in England."

"Not a doubt of that," chimed in the fellow ex-minister— a worthy man—perfect red-tapist, but inaudible in the reporters' gallery. "And your election is quite safe, eh? All depends on that. You must not be thrown out at such a time, even for a month or two. I hear that you will have a contest—some townsmen of the borough, I think. But the Lansmere interest must be all-powerful; and, I suppose L'Estrange will come out and canvass for you. You are not the man to have lukewarm friends!"

"Don't be alarmed about my election. I am as sure of that as of L'Estrange's friendship."

Harley heard, with a grim smile, and passing his hand within his vest, laid it upon Nora's memoir.

"What could we do in Parliament without you!" said the great pro-pretor, almost piteously.

"Rather what could I do without Parliament? Public life is the only existence I own. Parliament is all in all to me. But we may cross now."

Harley's eye glittered cold as it followed the tall form of the statesman towering high above all other passers-by.

"Ay," he muttered—"ay, rest as sure of my friendship as

I was of thine! And be Lansmere our field of Philippi! There, where thy first step was made in the only life that thou own'st as existence, shall the ladder itself rot from under thy footing. There, where thy softer victim slunk to death from the deceit of thy love, shall deceit like thine own dig a grave for thy frigid ambition. I borrow thy quiver of fraud; its still arrows shall strike thee; and thou too shalt say, when the barb pierces home, 'This comes from the hand of a friend.' Ay, at Lansmere, at Lansmere, shall the end crown the whole! Go, and dot on the canvas the lines for a lengthened perspective, where my eyes note already the vanishing point of the picture."

Then through the dull fog, and under the pale gas-lights Harley L'Estrange pursued his noiseless way, soon distinguished no more amongst the various, motley, quick-succeeding groups, with their infinite sub-divisions of thought, care, and passion; while, loud over all their low murmurs, or silent hearts, were heard the tramp of horses and din of wheels, and the vociferous discordant cry that had ceased to attract an interest in the ears it vexed—" Great News, Great News— Dissolution of Parliament—Great News!"

## CHAPTER XIX.

THE scene is at Lansmere Park—a spacious pile, commenced in the reign of Charles II.; enlarged and altered in the reign of Anne. Brilliant interval in the History of our National Manners, when even the courtier dreaded to be dull, and Sir Fopling raised himself on tiptoe to catch the ear of a wit—when the names of Devonshire and Dorset, Halifax and Carteret, Oxford and Bolingbroke, unite themselves, brother-like, with those of Hobbes and of Dryden, of Prior and Bentley, or Arbuthnot, Gay, Pope, and Swift; and still, wherever we turn, to recognise some ideal of great Lord or fine Gentleman—the Immortals of Literature stand by his side.

The walls of the rooms at Lansmere were covered with the portraits of those who illustrate that time which Europe calls the Age of Louis XIV. A L'Estrange, who had lived through the reigns of four English princes, (and with no mean importance through all,) had collected those likenesses of noble contemporaries. As you passed through the chambers—

opening one on the other in that pomp of parade introduced with Charles II. from the palaces of France, and retaining its mode till Versailles and the Trianon passed, themselves, out of date—you felt you were in excellent company. What saloons of our day, demeaned to tailed coats and white waistcoats, have that charm of high breeding which speaks out from the canvas of Kneller and Jervis, Vivien and Rigaud? And withal, notwithstanding lace and brocade—the fripperies of artificial costume—still those who give interest or charm to that day, look from their portraits like men—raking or *debonnair*, if you will—never mincing nor feminine. Can we say as much of the portraits of Lawrence? Gaze there on fair Marlborough—what delicate perfection of features, yet how easy in boldness, how serene in the conviction of power! So fair and so tranquil he might have looked through the cannon-reek at Ramillies and Blenheim, suggesting to Addison the image of an angel of war. Ah, there, Sir Charles Sedley, the Lovelace of wits! Note that strong jaw and marked brow;—do you not recognise the courtier who scorned to ask one favour of the king with whom he lived as an equal, and who stretched forth the right hand of man to hurl from a throne the king who had made his daughter—a Countess?\*

Perhaps, from his childhood thus surrounded by the haunting faces—that spoke of their age as they looked from the walls—that age and those portraits were not without influence on the character of Harley L'Estrange. The whim and the daring—the passion for letters and reverence for genius—the mixture of levity and strength—the polished sauntering indolence, or the elastic readiness of energies once called into action—all might have found their prototypes in the lives which those portraits rekindled. The deeper sentiment, the more earnest nature, which in Harley L'Estrange were commingled with the attributes common to a former age—these, indeed, were of his own. *Our* age so little comprehended, while it colours us from its atmosphere!—so full of mysterious and profound emotions, which our ancestors never knew!—will those emotions be understood by our descendants?

In this stately house were now assembled, as Harley's

---

\* Sedley was so tenacious of his independence, that when his affairs were most embarrassed, he refused all pecuniary aid from Charles II. His bitter sarcasm, in vindication of the part he took in the deposition of James II., who had corrupted his daughter, and made her Countess of Dorchester, is well known. "As the King has made my daughter a Countess, the least I can do, in common gratitude, is to assist in making his majesty's daughter—a Queen!"

guests, many of the more important personages whom the slow length of this story has made familiar to the reader. The two candidates for the borough in the True Blue interest —Audley Egerton and Randal Leslie;—and Levy — chief among the barons to whom modern society grants a seignorie of pillage, which, had a baron of old ever ventured to arrogate, burgess and citizen, socman and bocman, villein and churl, would have burned him alive in his castle; — the Duke di Serrano, still fondly clinging to his title of Doctor and pet name of Riccabocca;—Jemima, not yet with the airs of a duchess, but robed in very thick silks, as the chrysalis state of a duchess;—Violante, too, was there, sadly against her will, and shrinking as much as possible into the retirement of her own chamber. The Countess of Lansmere had deserted her lord, in order to receive the guests of her son ; my lord himself, ever bent on being of use in some part of his country, and striving hard to distract his interest from his plague of a borough, had gone down into Cornwall to inquire into the social condition of certain troglodytes who worked in some mines which the Earl had lately had the misfortune to wring from the Court of Chancery, after a lawsuit commenced by his grandfather; and a Blue Book, issued in the past session by order of Parliament, had especially quoted the troglodytes thus devolved on the Earl as bipeds who were in considerable ignorance of the sun, and had never been known to wash their feet since the day that they came into the world—their world underground, chipped off from the Bottomless Pit!

With the Countess came Helen Digby, of course; and Lady Lansmere, who had hitherto been so civilly cold to the wife elect of her son, had, ever since her interview with Harley at Knightsbridge, clung to Helen with almost a caressing fondness  The stern Countess was tamed by fear; she felt that her own influence over Harley was gone; she trusted to the influence of Helen—in case of what ?—ay, what? It was because the danger was not clear to her, that her bold spirit trembled : superstitions, like suspicions, are "as bats among birds, and fly by twilight." Harley had ridiculed the idea of challenge and strife between Audley and himself; but still Lady Lansmere dreaded the fiery emotions of the last, and the high spirit and austere self-respect which were proverbial to the first. Involuntarily she strengthened her intimacy with Helen. In case her alarm should appear justified, what mediator could be so persuasive in appeasing the angrier passions, as one whom courtship and betrothal sanctified to the gentlest?

On arriving at Lansmere, the Countess, however, felt somewhat relieved. Harley had received her, if with a manner less cordial and tender than had hitherto distinguished it, still with easy kindness and calm self-possession. His bearing towards Audley Egerton still more reassured her: it was not marked by an exaggeration of familiarity or friendship—which would at once have excited her apprehensions of some sinister design—nor, on the other hand, did it betray, by covert sarcasms, an ill-suppressed resentment. It was exactly what, under the circumstances, would have been natural to a man who had received an injury from an intimate friend, which, in generosity or discretion, he resolved to overlook, but which those aware of it could just perceive had cooled or alienated the former affection. Indefatigably occupying himself with all the details of the election, Harley had fair pretext for absenting himself from Audley, who, really looking very ill, and almost worn out, pleaded indisposition as an excuse for dispensing with the fatigues of a personal canvass, and, passing much of his time in his own apartments, left all the preparations for contest to his more active friends. It was not till he had actually arrived at Lansmere that Audley became acquainted with the name of his principal opponent. Richard Avenel! the brother of Nora! rising up from obscurity, thus to stand front to front against him in a contest on which all his fates were cast. Egerton quailed as before an appointed avenger. He would fain have retired from the field;—he spoke to Harley.

"How can *you* support all the painful remembrances which the very name of my antagonist must conjure up?"

"Did you not tell me," answered Harley, "to strive against such remembrances—to look on them as sickly dreams? I am prepared to brave them. Can you be more sensitive than I?"

Egerton durst not say more. He avoided all further reference to the subject. The strife raged around him, and he shut himself out from it—shut himself up in solitude with his own heart. Strife enough there! Once, late at night, he stole forth and repaired to Nora's grave. He stood there, amidst the rank grass, and under the frosty starlight, long, and in profound silence. His whole past life seemed to rise before him; and, when he regained his lonely room, and strove to survey the future, still he could behold only that past and that grave.

In thus declining all active care for an election, to his prospects so important, Audley Egerton was considered to have excuse, not only in the state of his health, but in his sense of dignity. A statesman so eminent, of opinions so well known, of public services so incontestable, might well be spared the personal trouble that falls upon obscurer candidates. And besides, according to current report, and the judgment of the Blue committee, the return of Mr. Egerton was secure. But, though Audley himself was thus indulgently treated, Harley and the Blue Committee took care to inflict double work upon Randal. That active young spirit found ample materials for all its restless energies. Randal Leslie was kept on his legs from sunrise to starlight. There does not exist in the Three Kingdoms a constituency more fatiguing to a candidate than that borough of Lansmere. As soon as you leave the High Street, wherein, according to immemorial usage, the Blue canvasser is first led, in order to put him into spirits for the toils that await him—(delectable, propitious, constitutional High Street, in which at least two-thirds of the electors—opulent tradesmen employed at the Park—always vote for "my lord's man," and hospitably prepare wine and cakes in their tidy back-parlours!)—as soon as you quit this stronghold of the party, labyrinths of lanes and defiles stretch away into the farthest horizon; level ground is found nowhere; it is all up hill and down hill—now rough, craggy pavements that blister the feet, and at the very first tread upon which all latent corns shook prophetically—now deep, muddy ruts, into which you sink ankle-deep—oozing slush creeping into the pores, and moistening the way for catarrh, rheum, cough, sore throat, bronchitis, and phthisis. Black sewers, and drains Acherontian, running before the thresholds, and so filling the homes behind with effluvia, that, while one hand clasps the grimy paw of the voter, the other instinctively guards from typhus and cholera your abhorrent nose. Not in those days had mankind ever heard of a sanitary reform! and, to judge of the slow progress which that reform seems to make, sewer and drain would have been much the same if they had. Scot-and-lot voters were the independent electors of Lansmere, with the additional franchise of Freemen. Universal suffrage could scarcely more efficiently swamp the franchises of men who care a straw what becomes of Great Britain! With all Randal Leslie's profound diplomacy, all his art in talking over, deceiving, and (to borrow Dick Avenel's vernacular phrase) "humbugging" educated men,

his eloquence fell flat upon minds invulnerable to appeals
whether to State or to Church, to Reform or to Freedom.
To catch a Scot-and-lot voter by such frivolous arguments,—
Randal Leslie might as well have tried to bring down a
rhinoceros by a pop-gun charged with split peas! The young
man who so firmly believed that "knowledge was power,"
was greatly disgusted. It was here the ignorance that foiled
him. When he got hold of a man with some knowledge,
Randal was pretty sure to trick him out of a vote.

Nevertheless, Randal Leslie walked and talked on, with
most creditable perseverance. The Blue Committee allowed
that he was an excellent canvasser. They conceived a liking
for him, mingled with pity. For, though sure of Egerton's
return, they regarded Randal's as out of the question. He
was merely there to keep split votes from going to the
opposite side; to serve his patron, the ex-minister; shake
the paws, and smell the smells which the ex-minister was too
great a man to shake and to smell. But, in point of fact,
none of that Blue Committee knew anything of the prospects
of the election. Harley received all the reports of each
canvass-day. Harley kept the canvass-book, locked up from
all eyes but his own, or it might be Baron Levy's, as Audley
Egerton's confidential, if not strictly professional adviser;—
Baron Levy, the millionaire, had long since retired from all
acknowledged professions. Randal, however—close, observant, shrewd—perceived that he himself was much stronger
than the Blue Committee believed. And, to his infinite
surprise, he owed that strength to Lord L'Estrange's exertions
on his behalf. For though Harley, after the first day on
which he ostentatiously showed himself in the High Street,
did not openly canvass with Randal, yet when the reports
were brought in to him, and he saw the names of the voters
who gave one vote to Audley, and withheld the other from
Randal, he would say to Randal, dead beat as that young
gentleman was, "Slip out with me, the moment dinner is
over, and before you go the round of the public-houses; there
are some voters we must get for you to-night." And sure
enough a few kindly words from the popular heir of the
Lansmere baronies usually gained over the electors, from
whom, though Randal had proved that all England depended
on their votes in his favour, Randal would never have extracted more than a "Wu'll, I shall waute gin the Dauy
coomes!" Nor was this all that Harley did for the younger
candidate. If it was quite clear that only one vote could be

won for the Blues, and the other was pledged to the Yellows, Harley would say, "Then put it down to Mr. Leslie;"—a request the more readily conceded, since Audley Egerton was considered so safe by the Blues, and alone worth a fear by the Yellows.

Thus Randal, who kept a snug little canvass-book of his own, became more and more convinced that he had a better chance than Egerton, even without the furtive aid he expected from Avenel; and he could only account for Harley's peculiar exertions in his favour, by supposing that Harley, unpractised in elections, and deceived by the Blue Committee, believed Egerton to be perfectly safe, and sought, for the honour of the family interest, to secure *both* the seats.

Randal's public cares thus deprived him of all opportunity of pressing his courtship on Violante; and, indeed, if ever he did find a moment in which he could steal to her reluctant side, Harley was sure to seize that very moment to send him off to canvass an hesitating freeman, or harangue in some public-house.

Leslie was too acute not to detect some motive hostile to his wooing, however plausibly veiled in the guise of zeal for his election, in this officiousness of Harley's. But Lord L'Estrange's manner to Violante was so little like that of a jealous lover, and he was so well aware of her engagement to Randal, that the latter abandoned the suspicion he had before conceived, that Harley was his rival. And he was soon led to believe that Lord L'Estrange had another, more disinterested, and less formidable motive for thus stinting his opportunities to woo the heiress.

"Mr. Leslie," said Lord L'Estrange, one day, "the Duke has confided to me his regret at his daughter's reluctance to ratify his own promise; and, knowing the warm interest I take in her welfare—for his sake and her own; believing, also, that some services to herself, as well as to the father she so loves, gives me a certain influence over her inexperienced judgment, he has even requested me to speak a word to her in your behalf."

"Ah! if you would!" said Randal, surprised.

"You must give me the power to do so. You were obliging enough to volunteer to me the same explanations which you gave to the Duke, his satisfaction with which induced him to renew, or confirm the promise of his daughter's hand. Should those explanations content me, as they did him, I hold the Duke bound to fulfil his engagement, and I am convinced that his daughter would, in that case, not be inflexible to your suit. But, till such explanations be given, my friendship for the father, and my interest in the child, do not allow me to assist a cause which, however, at present, suffers little by delay."

"Pray, listen at once to those explanations."

"Nay, Mr. Leslie, I can now only think of the election. As soon as that is over, rely on it you shall have the amplest opportunity to dispel any doubts which your intimacy with Count di Peschiera and Madame di Negra may have suggested. Apropos of the election — here is a list of voters you must see at once in Fish Lane.—Don't lose a moment."

In the meanwhile, Richard Avenel and Leonard had taken up their quarters in the hotel appropriated to the candidates for the Yellows; and the canvass on that side was prosecuted with all the vigour which might be expected from operations conducted by Richard Avenel, and backed by the popular feeling.

The rival parties met from time to time, in the streets and lanes, in all the pomp of war—banners streaming, fifes resounding, (for bands and colours were essential proofs of public spirit, and indispensable items in a candidate's bills, in those good old days.) When they thus encountered, very distant bows were exchanged between the respective chiefs. But Randal, contriving ever to pass close to Avenel, had ever the satisfaction of perceiving that gentleman's countenance contracted into a knowing wink, as much as to say, "All right, in spite of this tarnation humbug."

But now that both parties were fairly in the field, to the private arts of canvassing were added the public arts of oratory. The candidates had to speak—at the close of each day's canvass—out from wooden boxes, suspended from the windows of their respective hotels, and which looked like dens for the exhibition of wild beasts. They had to speak at meetings of Committees—meetings of electors—go the nightly round of enthusiastic public-houses, and appeal to the sense of an enlightened people through wreaths of smoke and odours of beer.

The alleged indisposition of Audley Egerton had spared him the excitement of oratory, as well as the fatigue of canvassing. The practised debater had limited the display of his talents to a concise, but clear and masterly exposition of his own views on the leading public questions of the day, and the state of parties, which, on the day after his arrival at Lansmere, was delivered at a meeting of his general Committee.—

in the great room of their hotel—and which was then printed and circulated amongst the voters.

Randal, though he expressed himself with more fluency and self-possession than are usually found in the first attempts of a public speaker, was not effective in addressing an unlettered crowd;—for a crowd of this kind is all heart—and we know that Randal Leslie's heart was as small as heart could be. If he attempted to speak at his own intellectual level, he was so subtle and refining as to be incomprehensible; if he fell into the fatal error—not uncommon to inexperienced orators—of trying to lower himself to the intellectual level of his audience, he was only elaborately stupid. No man can speak too well for a crowd—as no man can write too well for the stage; but in neither case should he be rhetorical, or case in periods the dry bones of reasoning. It is to the emotions, or to the humours, that the speaker of a crowd must address himself; his eye must brighten with generous sentiment, or his lip must expand in the play of animated fancy or genial wit. Randal's voice, too, though pliant and persuasive in private conversation, was thin and poor when strained to catch the ear of a numerous assembly. The falsehood of his nature seemed to come out, when he raised the tones which had been drilled into deceit. Men like Randal Leslie may become sharp debaters—admirable special pleaders; they can no more become orators than they can become poets. Educated audiences are essential to them, and the smaller the audience (that is, the more the brain supersedes the action of the heart) the better they can speak.

Dick Avenel was generally very short and very pithy in his addresses. He had two or three favourite topics, which always told. He was a fellow-townsman—a man who had made his own way in life—he wanted to free his native place from aristocratic usurpation—it was the battle of the electors, not his private cause, &c. He said little against Randal—"Pity a clever young man should pin his future to two yards of worn-out red tape"—"He had better lay hold of the strong rope, which the People, in compassion to his youth, were willing yet to throw out to save him from sinking," &c. But as for Audley Egerton, "the gentleman who would not show, who was afraid to meet the electors, who could only find his voice in a hole-and-corner meeting, accustomed all his venal life to dark and nefarious jobs"—Dick, upon that subject, delivered philippics truly Demosthenian. Leonard, on the contrary, never attacked Harley's friend, Mr. Egerton; but he was merciless against the youth who had filched reputation from John Burley, and whom he knew that Harley despised as heartily as himself. And Randal did not dare to retaliate, (though boiling over with indignant rage,) for fear of offending Leonard's uncle. Leonard was unquestionably the popular speaker of the three. Though his temperament was a writer's, not an orator's—though he abhorred what he considered the theatrical exhibition of self, which makes what is called "delivery" more effective than ideas—though he had little interest at any time in party politics—though at this time his heart was far away from the Blues and Yellows of Lansmere, sad and forlorn—yet, forced into action, the eloquence that was natural to his conversation poured itself forth. He had warm blood in his veins; and his dislike to Randal gave poignancy to his wit, and barbed his arguments with impassioned invective. In fact, Leonard could conceive no other motive for Lord L'Estrange's request to take part in the election than that nobleman's desire to defeat the man whom they both regarded as an impostor. And this notion was confirmed by some inadvertent expressions which Avenel let fall, and which made Leonard suspect that, if he were not in the field, Avenel would have exerted all his interest to return Randal instead of Egerton. With Dick's dislike to that statesman, Leonard found it impossible to reason; nor, on the other hand, could all Dick's scoldings or coaxings induce Leonard to divert his siege on Randal to an assault upon the man who, Harley had often said, was dear to him as a brother.

In the meanwhile, Dick kept the canvass-book of the Yellows as closely as Harley kept that of the Blues; and, in despite of many pouting fits and gusts of displeasure, took precisely the same pains for Leonard as Harley took for Randal. There remained, however, apparently unshaken by the efforts on either side, a compact body of about a Hundred and Fifty voters, chiefly freemen. Would they vote Yellow? Would they vote Blue? No one could venture to decide; but they declared that they would all vote the same way. Dick kept his secret "caucuses," as he called them, constantly nibbling at this phalanx. A hundred and fifty voters!—they had the election in their hands! Never were hands so cordially shaken—so caressingly clung to—so fondly lingered upon! But the votes still stuck as firm to the hands as if a part of the skin, or of the dirt—which was much the same thing!

## CHAPTER XX.

WHENEVER Audley joined the other guests of an evening—while Harley was perhaps closeted with Levy and committeemen, and Randal was going the round of the public-houses—the one with whom he chiefly conversed was Violante. He had been struck at first, despite his gloom, less perhaps by her extraordinary beauty, than by something in the expression of her countenance which, despite differences in feature and complexion, reminded him of Nora; and when, by his praises of Harley, he drew her attention, and won into her liking, he discovered, perhaps, that the likeness which had thus impressed him, came from some similarities in character between the living and the lost one—the same charming combination of lofty thought and childlike innocence—the same enthusiasm—the same rich exuberance of imagination and feeling. Two souls that resemble each other will give their likeness to the looks from which they beam. On the other hand, the person with whom Harley most familiarly associated, in his rare intervals of leisure, was Helen Digby. One day, Audley Egerton, standing mournfully by the window of the sitting-room appropriated to his private use, saw the two, whom he believed still betrothed, take their way across the park, side by side, "Pray Heaven, that she may atone to him for all!" murmured Audley. "But ah, that it had been Violante! Then I might have felt assured that the Future would efface the Past—and found the courage to tell him all. And when last night I spoke of what Harley ought to be to England, how like were Violante's eyes and smile to Nora's, when Nora listened in delighted sympathy to the hopes of my own young ambition." With a sigh he turned away, and resolutely sat down to read and reply to the voluminous correspondence which covered the table of the busy public man. For, Audley's return to Parliament being considered by his political party as secure, to him were transmitted all the hopes and fears of the large and influential section of it whose members looked up to him as their future chief, and who in that general election, (unprecedented for the number of eminent men it was fated to expel from Parliament, and the number of new politicians it was fated to send into it,) drew their only hopes of regaining their lost power from Audley's sanguine confidence in the reaction of that Public Opinion which he had hitherto so profoundly comprehended; and it was too clearly seen, that the seasonable adoption of his counsels would have saved the existence and popularity of the late Administration, whose most distinguished members could now scarcely show themselves on the hustings.

Meanwhile Lord L'Estrange led his young companion towards a green hill in the centre of the Park, on which stood a circular temple, that commanded a view of the country round for miles. They had walked in silence till they gained the summit of the sloped and gradual ascent; and then, as they stood still, side by side, Harley thus spoke—

"Helen, you know that Leonard is in the town, though I cannot receive him at the Park, since he is standing in opposition to my guests, Egerton and Leslie."

HELEN.—"But that seems to me so strange. How—how could Leonard do anything that seems hostile to you?"

HARLEY.—"Would his hostility to me lower him in your opinion? If he knew that I am his rival, does not rivalry include hate?"

HELEN.—"Oh, Lord L'Estrange, how can you speak thus? —how so wrong yourself? Hate—hate to you! and from Leonard Fairfield!"

HARLEY.—"You evade my question. Would his hate or hostility to me affect your sentiments towards him?"

HELEN, (looking down.)—"I could not force myself to believe in it."

HARLEY.—"Why?"

HELEN.—"Because it would be so unworthy of him."

HARLEY.—"Poor child! You have the delusion of your years. You deck a cloud in the hues of the rainbow, and will not believe that its glory is borrowed from the sun of your own fancy. But here, at least, you are not deceived. Leonard obeys but my wishes, and, I believe, against his own will. He has none of man's noblest attribute, Ambition."

HELEN.—"No ambition!"

HARLEY.—"It is vanity that stirs the poet to toil—if toil the wayward chase of his own chimeras can be called. Ambition is a more masculine passion."

Helen shook her head gently, but made no answer.

HARLEY.—"If I utter a word that profanes one of your delusions, you shake your head and are incredulous. Pause, listen one moment to my counsels—perhaps the last I may ever obtrude upon you. Lift your eyes; look around. Far as your eye can reach, nay, far beyond the line which the horizon forms in the landscape, stretch the lands of my inheritance. Yonder you see the home in which my forefathers for many generations lived with honour and died lamented. All these, in the course of nature, might one day have been your own, had you not rejected my proposals. I offered you, it is true, not what is commonly called Love; I offered you sincere esteem, and affections the more durable for their calm. You have not been reared by the world in the low idolatry of rank and wealth. But even romance cannot despise the power of serving others, which rank and wealth bestow. For myself, hitherto indolence, and lately disdain, rob fortune of these nobler attributes. But she who will share my fortune may dispense it so as to atone for my sins of omission. On the other side, grant that there is no bar to your preference for Leonard Fairfield, what does your choice present to you?—Those of his kindred with whom you will associate are unrefined and mean. His sole income is derived from precarious labours; the most vulgar of all anxieties—the fear of bread itself for the morrow—must mingle with all your romance, and soon steal from love all its poetry. You think his affection will console you for every sacrifice. Folly! —the love of poets is for a mist—a moonbeam—a denizen of air—a phantom that they call an Ideal. They suppose for a moment that they have found that Ideal in Chloe or Phyllis —Helen or a milkmaid. Bah!—the first time you come to the poet with the baker's bill, where flies the Ideal? I knew one more brilliant than Leonard—more exquisitely gifted by nature—that one was a woman: she saw a man hard and cold as that stone at your feet—a false, hollow, sordid worldling; she made him her idol—beheld in him all that history would not recognise in a Cæsar—that mythology would scarcely grant to an Apollo: to him she was the plaything of an hour —she died, and before the year was out he had married for money! I knew another instance—I speak of myself. I loved before I was your age. Had an angel warned me then, I would have been incredulous as you. How that ended, no matter: but had it not been for that dream of maudlin delirium, I had lived and acted as others of my kind and my sphere—married from reason and judgment—been now a useful and happy man. Pause, then. Will you still reject me for Leonard Fairfield? For the last time you have the option—me and all the substance of waking life—Leonard Fairfield and the shadows of a fleeting dream. Speak! You hesitate. Nay, take time to decide."

HELEN.—"Ah! Lord L'Estrange, you who have felt what it is to love, how can you doubt my answer?—how think that I could be so base, so ungrateful as take from yourself what you call the substance of waking life, while my heart was far away—faithful to what you call a dream?"

HARLEY.—"But, can you not dispel the dream?"

HELEN, (her whole face one flush.)—"It was wrong to call it dream! It is the reality of life to me. All things else are as dreams."

HARLEY, (taking her hand and kissing it with respect.)—"Helen, you have a noble heart, and I have tempted you in vain. I regret your choice, though I will no more oppose it. I regret it, though I shall never witness your disappointment. As the wife of that man, I shall see and know you no more."

HELEN.—"Oh, no!—do not say that. Why?—wherefore?"

HARLEY, (his brows meeting.)—"He is the child of fraud and of shame. His father is my foe, and my hate descends to the son. He, too, the son, filches from me——but complaints are idle. When the next few days are over, think of me but as one who abandons all right over your actions, and is a stranger to your future fate. Pooh!—dry your tears: so long as you love Leonard or esteem me, rejoice that our paths do not cross."

He walked on impatiently; but Helen, alarmed and wondering, followed close, took his arm timidly, and sought to soothe him. She felt that he wronged Leonard—that he knew not how Leonard had yielded all hope when he learned to whom she was affianced. For Leonard's sake she conquered her bashfulness, and sought to explain. But at her first hesitating, faltered words, Harley, who with great effort suppressed the emotions which swelled within him, abruptly left her side, and plunged into the recesses of thick, far-spreading groves, that soon wrapt him from her eye.

While this conversation occurred between Lord L'Estrange and his ward, the *soi-disant* Riccabocca and Violante were walking slowly through the gardens. The philosopher, unchanged by his brightening prospects—so far as the outer man was concerned—still characterised by the red umbrella, and the accustomed pipe—took the way mechanically towards the sunniest quarter of the grounds, now and then glancing tenderly at Violante's downcast, melancholy face, but not speaking; only, at each glance, there came a brisker cloud from the pipe, as if obedient to a fuller heave of the heart.

At length, in a spot which lay open towards the south, and seemed to collect all the gentlest beams of the November sun, screened from the piercing east by dense evergreens, and flanked from the bleak north by lofty walls, Riccabocca paused and seated himself. Flowers still bloomed on the sward in front, over which still fluttered the wings of those later and more brilliant butterflies that, unseen in the genial days of our English summer, come with autumnal skies, and sport round the mournful steps of the coming winter—types of those thoughts which visit and delight the contemplation of age, while the current yet glides free from the iron ice, and the leaves yet linger on the boughs; thoughts that associate the memories of the departed summer with messages from suns that shall succeed the winter, and expand colours the most steeped in light and glory, just as the skies through which they gleam are darkening, and the flowers on which they hover fade from the surface of the earth—dropping still seeds, that sink deep out of sight below.

"Daughter," said Riccabocca, drawing Violante to his side with caressing arm—"Daughter! Mark, how they who turn towards the south can still find the sunny side of the landscape! In all the seasons of life, how much of chill or of warmth depends on our choice of the aspect! Sit down—let us reason."

Violante sate down passively, clasping her father's hand in both her own. Reason!—harsh word to the ears of Feeling!

"You shrink," resumed Riccabocca, "from even the courtship, even the presence of the suitor in whom my honour binds me to recognise your future bridegroom."

Violante drew away her hands, and placed them before her eyes, shudderingly.

"But," continued Riccabocca, rather peevishly, "this is not listening to reason. I may object to Mr. Leslie, because he has not an adequate rank or fortune to pretend to a daughter of my house; that would be what every one would allow to be reasonable in a father; except, indeed," added the poor sage, trying hard to be sprightly, and catching hold of a proverb to help him—"except, indeed, those wise enough to recollect that admonitory saying, 'Casa il figlio quando vuoi, e la figlia quando puoi,'—(Marry your son when you will, your daughter when you can.) Seriously, if I overlook those objections to Mr. Leslie, it is not natural for a young girl to enforce them. What is reason in you is quite another thing from reason in me. Mr. Leslie is young, not ill-looking, has the air of a gentleman, is passionately enamoured of you, and has proved his affection by risking his life against that villanous Peschiera—that is, he would have risked it had Peschiera not been shipped out of the way. If, then, you will listen to reason, pray what can reason say against Mr. Leslie?"

"Father, I detest him!"

"*Cospetto!*" persisted Riccabocca, testily, "you have no reason to detest him. If you had any reason, child, I am sure that I should be the last person to dispute it. How can you know your own mind in such a matter? It is not as if you had seen any one else you could prefer. Not another man of your own years do you even know—except, indeed, Leonard Fairfield, whom, though I grant he is handsomer, and with more imagination and genius than Mr. Leslie, you still must remember as the boy who worked in my garden. Ah! to be sure, there is Frank Hazeldean—fine lad—but his affections are pre-engaged. In short," continued the sage, dogmatically, "there is no one else you *can*, by any possible caprice, prefer to Mr. Leslie; and for a girl, who has no one else in her head, to talk of detesting a well-looking, well-dressed, clever young man, is—a nonsense—'chi lascia il poco per haver l'assai nè l'uno, nè l'altro avera mai;'—which may be thus paraphrased—The young lady who refuses a mortal in the hope of obtaining an angel, loses the one, and will never fall in with the other. So now, having thus shown that the darker side of the question is contrary to reason—let us look to the brighter. In the first place—"

"Oh, father, father!" cried Violante, passionately, "you to whom I once came for comfort in every childish sorrow! Do not talk to me with this cutting levity. See, I lay my head upon your breast—I put my arms around you—and now, can you reason me into misery?"

"Child, child, do not be so wayward. Strive, at least, against a prejudice that you cannot defend. My Violante, my darling, this is no trifle. Here I must cease to be the fond, foolish father, whom you can do what you will with. Here I am Alphonso, Duke di Serrano; for here my honour as noble, and my word as man, are involved. I, then, but a helpless exile—no hope of fairer prospects before me—trembling like a coward at the wiles of my unscrupulous kinsman —grasping at all chances to save you from his snares—I myself offered your hand to Randal Leslie—offered, promised, pledged it;—and now that my fortunes seem assured, my rank in all likelihood restored, my foe crushed, my fears at rest—now, does it become me to retract what I myself had urged? It is not the noble, it is the parvenu, who has only to grow rich, in order to forget those whom in poverty he hailed as his friends.* Is it for me to make the poor excuse, never heard on the lips of an Italian prince, 'that I cannot command the obedience of my child,'—subject myself to the galling answer—'Duke of Serrano, you could once command that obedience, when, in exile, penury, and terror, you offered me a bride without a dower.' Child—Violante—daughter of ancestors on whose honour never slander set a stain, I call on you to redeem your father's plighted word."

"Father, must it be so? Is not even the convent open to me? Nay, look not so coldly on me. If you could but read my heart! And, oh! I feel so assured of your own repentance hereafter—so assured that this man is not what you believe him. I so suspect that he has been playing throughout some secret and perfidious part."

"Ha!" interrupted Riccabocca, "Harley has perhaps infected you with that notion."

"No—no. But is not Harley—is not Lord L'Estrange one whose opinion you have cause to esteem? And if he distrust Mr. Leslie—",

"Let him make good his distrust by such proof as will absolve my word, and I shall share your own joy. I have told him this. I have invited him to make good his suspicions —he puts me off. He cannot do so," added Riccabocca, in a dejected tone; "Randal has already so well explained all that Harley deemed equivocal. Violante, my name and my honour rest in your hands. Cast them away if you will; I cannot constrain you, and I cannot stoop to implore. *Noblesse oblige* —With your birth you took its duties. Let them decide between your vain caprice and your father's solemn remonstrance."

Assuming a sternness that he was far from feeling, and putting aside his daughter's arms, the exile walked away.

Violante paused a moment, shivered, looked round as if taking a last farewell of joy, and peace, and hope on earth, and then approaching her father with a firm step, she said,—"I never rebelled, father; I did but entreat. What you say is my law

---

\* " Quando 'l villano è divenuto ricco
Non ha (*i. e.*, riconosce) parent nè amico."
*Italian Proverb.*

now, as it has ever been; and come what may, never shall you hear complaint or murmur from me. Poor father, you will suffer more than I shall. Kiss me!"

About an hour afterwards, as the short day closed in, Harley, returning from his solitary wanderings, after he had parted from Helen, encountered on the terrace, before the house, Lady Lansmere and Audley Egerton arm in arm.

Harley had drawn his hat over his brows, and his eyes were fixed on the ground, so that he did not see the group upon which he came unawares, until Audley's voice started him from his reverie.

"My dear Harley," said the ex-minister, with a faint smile, "you must not pass us by, now that you have a moment of leisure from the cares of the election. And, Harley, though we are under the same roof, I see you so little." Lord L'Estrange darted a quick glance towards his mother—a glance that seemed to say, "You leaning on Audley's arm! Have you kept your promise?" And the eye that met his own reassured him.

"It is true," said Harley: "but you, who know that, once engaged in public affairs, one has no heart left for the ties of private life, will excuse me. And this election is so important!"

"And you, Mr. Egerton," said Lady Lansmere, "whom the election most concerns, seem privileged to be the only one who appears indifferent to success."

"Ay—but you are not indifferent?" said Lord L'Estrange, abruptly.

"No. How can I be so, when my whole future career may depend on it?"

Harley drew Egerton aside. "There is one voter you ought at least to call upon and thank. He cannot be made to comprehend that, for the sake of any relation, even for the sake of his own son, he is to vote against the Blues—against you; I mean, of course, Nora's father, John Avenel. His vote and his son-in-law's gained your majority at your first election."

EGERTON.—"Call on John Avenel! Have *you* called?"

HARLEY, (calmly.)—"Yes. Poor old man, his mind has been affected ever since Nora's death. But your name as the candidate for the borough at that time—the successful candidate for whose triumph the joy-bells chimed with her funeral knell—your name brings up her memory; and he talks in a breath of her and of you. Come, let us walk together to his house; it is close by the Park Lodge."

The drops stood on Audley's brow! He fixed his dark handsome eyes, in mournful amaze, upon Harley's tranquil face.

"Harley, at last, then, you have forgotten the Past."

"No; but the Present is more imperious. All my efforts are needed to requite your friendship. You stand against her brother—yet her father votes for you. And her mother says to her son, 'Let the old man alone. Conscience is all that is well alive in him; and he thinks if he were to vote against the Blues, he would sin against honour.' 'An electioneering prejudice,' some sceptics would say. But you must be touched by this trait of human nature—in her father, too—you, Audley Egerton, who are the soul of honour. What ails you?"

EGERTON.—"Nothing—a spasm at the heart—my old complaint. Well, I will call on the poor man later, but not now —not with you. Nay, nay, I will not—I cannot. Harley, just as you joined us, I was talking to your mother."

HARLEY.—"Ay, and what of?"

EGERTON.—"Yourself. I saw you from my windows walking with your betrothed. Afterwards I observed her coming home alone; and by the glimpse I caught of her gentle countenance, it seemed sad. Harley, do you deceive us?"

HARLEY.—"Deceive—l!—How!"

EGERTON.—"Do you really feel that your intended marriage will bestow on you the happiness, which is my prayer, as it must be your mother's?"

HARLEY.—"Happiness—I hoped so. But perhaps—"

EGERTON.—"Perhaps what?"

HARLEY.—"Perhaps the marriage may not take place. Perhaps I have a rival—not an open one—a secret, stealthy wooer—in one, too, whom I have loved, served, trusted. Question me not now. Such instances of treachery make one learn more how to prize a friendship honest, devoted, faithful as your own, Audley Egerton. But here comes your *protégé*, released awhile from his canvass, and your confidential adviser, Baron Levy. He accompanied Randal through the town to-day. So anxious is he to see that that young man does not play false, and regard his own interest before yours. Would that surprise you?"

EGERTON.—"You are too severe upon Randal Leslie. He is ambitious, worldly—has no surplus of affection at the command of his heart—"

HARLEY.—"Is it Randal Leslie you describe?"

EGERTON, (with a languid smile.)—"Yes, you see I do not

flatter. But he is born and reared a gentleman; as such he would scarcely do anything mean. And, after all, it is with me that he must rise or fall. His very intellect must tell him that. But again I ask, do not strive to prepossess me against him. I am a man who could have loved a son. I have none. Randal, such as he is, is a sort of son. He carries on my projects and my interest in the world of men beyond the goal of the tomb."

Audley turned kindly to Randal.

"Well, Leslie, what report of the canvass?"

"Levy has the book, sir. I think we have gained ten fresh votes for you, and perhaps seven for me."

"Let me rid you of your book, Baron Levy," said Harley.

Just at this time Riccabocca and Violante approached the house, both silent. The Italian caught sight of Randal, and made him a sign to join them. The young lover glanced fearfully towards Harley, and then with alacrity bounded forward, and was soon at Violante's side. But scarce had Harley, surprised by Leslie's sudden disappearance, remarked the cause, than with equal abruptness he abandoned the whispered conference he had commenced with Levy, and hastening to Randal, laid hand on the young man's shoulder, exclaiming, "Ten thousand pardons to all three! But I cannot allow this waste of time, Mr. Leslie. You have yet an hour before it grows dark. There are three outvoters six miles off, influential farmers, whom you must canvass in person with my father's steward. Hasten to the stables; choose your own horse. To saddle—to saddle! Baron Levy, go and order my lord's steward, Mr. Smart, to join Mr. Leslie at the stables; then come back to me—quick. What! —loitering still, Mr. Leslie! You will make me throw up your whole cause in disgust at your indolence and apathy."

Alarmed at this threat, Randal lifted his accusing eyes to heaven, and withdrew.

Meanwhile Audley had drawn close to Lady Lansmere, who was leaning, in thought, over the balustrade of the terrace.

"Do you note," said Audley, whispering, "how Harley sprang forward when the fair Italian came in sight? Trust me, I was right. I know little of the young lady, but I have conversed with her. I have gazed on the changes in her face. If Harley ever love again, and if ever love influence and exalt his mind, wish with me that his choice may yet fall where I believe that his heart inclines it."

LADY LANSMERE.—"Ah! that it were so. Helen, I own, is charming; but—but—Violante is equal in birth! Are you not aware that she is engaged to your young friend, Mr. Leslie?"

AUDLEY.—"Randal told me so; but I cannot believe it. In fact, I have taken occasion to sound that fair creature's inclinations, and if I know aught of women, her heart is not with Randal. I cannot believe her to be one whose affections are so weak as to be easily constrained; nor can I suppose that her father could desire to enforce a marriage that is almost a *mésalliance*. Randal must deceive himself; and from something Harley just let fall, in our painful but brief conversation, I suspect that his engagement with Miss Digby is broken off. He promises to tell me more, later. Yes," continued Audley, mournfully, "observe Violante's countenance, with its ever-varying play; listen to her voice, to which feeling seems to give the expressive music, and tell me whether you are not sometimes reminded of—of—In one word, there is one who, even without rank or fortune, would be worthy to replace the image of Leonora, and be to Harley—what Leonora could not; for sure I am that Violante loves him."

Harley, meanwhile, had lingered with Riccabocca and Violante, speaking but on indifferent subjects, obtaining short answers from the first, and none from the last—when the sage drew him a little aside, and whispered, "She has consented to sacrifice herself to my sense of honour. But, O Harley! if she be unhappy, it will break my heart. Either you must give me sufficient proof of Randal's unworthiness, to absolve me from my promise—or I must again entreat you to try and conciliate the poor child in his favour. All you say has weight with her; she respects you as — a second father."

Harley did not seem peculiarly flattered by that last assurance, but he was relieved from an immediate answer, by the appearance of a man who came from the direction of the stables, and whose dress, covered with dust, and travel-stained, seemed like that of a foreign courier. No sooner did Harley catch sight of this person, than he sprang forward, and accosted him briefly and rapidly.

"You have been quick; I did not expect you so soon. You discovered the trace? You gave my letter—"

"And have brought back the answer, my lord," replied the man, taking the letter from a leathern pouch at his side. Harley hastily broke open the seal, and glanced over the contents, which were comprised in a few lines.

"Good. Say not whence you came. Do not wait here;—return at once to London."

Harley's face seemed so unusually cheerful as he rejoined the Italians, that the Duke exclaimed—

"A despatch from Vienna! My recall!"

"From Vienna, my dear friend? Not possible yet. I cannot calculate on hearing from the Prince till a day or two before the close of this election. But you wish me to speak to Violante. Join my mother yonder. What can she be saying to Mr. Egerton? I will address a few words apart to your fair daughter, that may at least prove the interest in her fate taken by—her second father."

"Kindest of friends," said the unsuspecting pupil of Machiavelli; and he walked towards the terrace. Violante was about to follow. Harley detained her.

"Do not go till you have thanked me; for you are not the noble Violante for whom I take you, unless you acknowledge gratitude to any one who delivers you from the presence of an admirer in Mr. Randal Leslie."

VIOLANTE.—"Ought I to hear this of one whom—whom—"

HARLEY.—"One whom your father obstinately persists in obtruding on your repugnance. Yet, O dear child, you who, when almost an infant, ere yet you knew what snares and pitfalls, for all who trust to another, lie under the sward at our feet, even when decked the fairest with the flowers of spring—you who put your small hands around my neck, and murmured in your musical voice, 'Save us—save my father;' you at least I will not forsake, in a peril worse than that which menaced you then—a peril which affrights you more than that which threatened you in the snares of Peschiera. Randal Leslie may thrive in his meaner objects of ambition;—those I fling to him in scorn;—but *you!* the presuming varlet!" Harley paused a moment, half stifled with indignation. He then resumed, calmly—"Trust to me, and fear not. I will rescue this hand from the profanation of Randal Leslie's touch; and then farewell, for life, to every soft emotion. Before me expands the welcome solitude. The innocent saved, the honest righted, the perfidious stricken by a just retribution—and then—what then? Why, at least I shall have studied Machiavelli with more effect than your wise father; and I shall lay him aside, needing no philosophy to teach me never again to be deceived." His brow darkened; he turned abruptly away, leaving Violante lost in amaze, fear—and a delight, vague, yet more vividly felt than all.

## CHAPTER XXI.

THAT night, after the labours of the day, Randal had gained the sanctuary of his own room, and seated himself at his table, to prepare the heads of the critical speech he would have now very soon to deliver on the day of nomination—critical speech when, in the presence of foes and friends, reporters from London, and amidst all the jarring interests that he sought to weave into the sole self-interest of Randal Leslie, he would be called upon to make the formal exposition of his political opinions. Randal Leslie, indeed, was not one of those speakers whom either modesty, fastidiousness, or conscientious desire of truth predisposes towards the labour of written composition. He had too much cleverness to be in want of fluent period or ready commonplace—the ordinary materials of oratorical impromptu—too little taste for the Beautiful to study what graces of diction will best adorn a noble sentiment —too obtuse a conscience to care if the popular argument were purified from the dross which the careless flow of a speech wholly extemporaneous rarely fails to leave around it. But this was no ordinary occasion. Elaborate study here was requisite, not for the orator, but the hypocrite. Hard task, to please the Blues, and not offend the Yellows;— appear to side with Audley Egerton, yet insinuate sympathy with Dick Avenel;—confront, with polite smile, the younger opponent whose words had lodged arrows in his vanity, which rankled the more gallingly because they had raised the skin of his conscience.

He had dipped his pen into the ink and smoothed the paper before him, when a knock was heard at the door.

"Come in," said he, impatiently. Levy entered, saunteringly.

"I am come to talk over matters with you, *mon cher*," said the Baron, throwing himself on the sofa. "And, first, I wish you joy of your prospects of success."

Randal postponed his meditated composition with a quick sigh, drew his chair towards the sofa, and lowered his voice into a whisper. "You think with me, that the chance of my success—is good?"

"Chance!—Why, it is a rubber of whist, in which your partner gives you all the winnings, and in which the adversary is almost sure to revoke. Either Avenel or his nephew, it is true, must come in; but not both. Two parvenus aspiring to make a family seat of an Earl's borough! Bah! too absurd."

"I hear from Riccabocca (or rather the Duke di Serrano) that this same young Fairfield is greatly indebted to the kindness of Lord L'Estrange. Very odd that he should stand against the Lansmere interest."

"Ambition, *mon cher*. You yourself are under some obligations to Mr. Egerton. Yet, in reality, he has more to apprehend from you than from Mr. Fairfield."

"I disown obligations to Mr. Egerton. And if the electors prefer me to him (whom, by-the-by, they once burned in effigy,) it is no fault of mine: the fault, if any, will rest with his own dearest friend, L'Estrange. I do not understand how a man of such clear sense, as L'Estrange undoubtedly possesses, should be risking Egerton's election in his zeal for mine. Nor do his formal courtesies to myself deceive me. He has even implied that he suspects me of connivance with Peschiera's schemes on Violante. But those suspicions he cannot support. For of course, Levy, you would not betray me?"

"I! What possible interest could I serve in that?"

"None that I can discover, certainly," said Randal, relaxing into a smile. "And when I get into Parliament, aided by the social position which my marriage will give me, I shall have so many ways to serve you. No, it is certainly your interest not to betray me. And I shall count on you as a witness, if a witness can be required."

"Count on me, certainly, my dear fellow," said the Baron. "And I suppose there will be no witness the other way. Done for eternally is my poor dear friend Peschiera, whose cigars, by-the-by, were matchless;—I wonder if there will be any for sale. And if he were not so done for, it is not you, it is L'Estrange, that he would be tempted to do for."

"We may blot Peschiera out of the map of the future," rejoined Randal. "Men from whom henceforth we have nothing to hope or to fear, are to us as the races before the deluge."

"Fine remark," quoth the Baron, admiringly. "Peschiera, though not without brains, was a complete failure. And when the failure of one I have tried to serve is complete, the rule I have adopted through life is to give him up altogether."

"Of course," said Randal.

"Of course," echoed the Baron. "On the other hand, you know that I like pushing forward young men of mark and promise. You really are amazingly clever; but how comes it you don't speak better? Do you know, I doubt whether you will do in the House of Commons all that I expected from your address and readiness in private life."

"Because I cannot talk trash vulgar enough for a mob? Pooh! I shall succeed wherever knowledge is really power. Besides, you must allow for my infernal position. You know, after all, that Avenel, if he can only return himself or his nephew, still holds in his hands the choice of the candidate upon our side. I cannot attack him—I cannot attack his insolent nephew—"

"Insolent!—not that, but bitterly eloquent. He hits you hard. You are no match for him, Randal, before a popular audience; though *en petit comité*, the devil himself were hardly a match for *you*. But now to a somewhat more serious point. Your election you will win—your bride is promised to you; but the old Leslie lands, in the present possession of Squire Thornhill, you have not gained—and your chance of gaining them is in great jeopardy. I did not like to tell you this morning—it would have spoiled your temper for canvassing; but I have received a letter from Thornhill himself. He has had an offer for the property, which is only £1000 short of what he asks. A city alderman, called Jobson, is the bidder; a man it seems, of large means and few words. The alderman has fixed the date on which he must have a definite answer; and that date falls on the —th, two days after that fixed for the poll at Lansmere. The brute declares he will close with another investment, if Thornhill does not then come into his terms. Now, as Thornhill will accept these terms unless I can positively promise him better, and as those funds on which you calculated (had the marriage of Peschiera with Violante, and Frank Hazeldean with Madame di Negra, taken place) fail you, I see no hope for your being in time with the money—and the old lands of the Leslies must yield their rents to a Jobson."

"I care for nothing on earth like those old lands of my forefathers," said Randal, with unusual vehemence—"I reverence so little amongst the living—and I do reverence the dead. And my marriage will take place so soon; and the dower would so amply cover the paltry advance required."

"Yes; but the mere prospect of a marriage to the daughter of a man whose lands are still sequestered, would be no security to a money-lender."

"Surely," said Randal, "you who once offered to assist me

when my fortunes were more precarious, might now accommodate me with this loan, as a friend, and keep the title-deeds of the estate as—"

"As a money-lender," added the Baron, laughing pleasantly. "No, *mon cher*, I will still lend you half the sum required in advance, but the other half is more than I can afford as friend, or hazard as money-lender; and it would damage my character—be out of all rule—if, the estates falling, by your default of payment, into my own hands, I should appear to be the real purchaser of the property of my own distressed client. But, now I think of it, did not Squire Hazeldean promise you his assistance in this matter?"

"He did so," answered Randal, "as soon as the marriage between Frank and Madame di Negra was off his mind. I meant to cross over to Hazeldean immediately after the election. How can I leave the place till then?"

"If you do, your election is lost. But why not write to the Squire?"

"It is against my maxim to write where I can speak. However, there is no option; I will write at once. Meanwhile, communicate with Thornhill; keep up his hopes; and be sure, at least, that he does not close with this greedy alderman before the day fixed for decision."

"I have done all that already, and my letter is gone. Now, do your part: and if you write as cleverly as you talk, you would coax the money out from a stonier heart than poor Mr. Hazeldean's. I leave you now—Good night."

Levy took up his candlestick, nodded, yawned, and went.

Randal still suspended the completion of his speech, and indited the following epistle :—

"My dear Mr. Hazeldean,—I wrote to you a few hasty lines on leaving town, to inform you that the match you so dreaded was broken off, and proposing to defer particulars till I could visit your kind and hospitable roof, which I trusted to do for a few hours during my stay at Lansmere, since it is not a day's journey hence to Hazeldean. But I did not calculate on finding so sharp a contest. In no election throughout the kingdom do I believe that a more notable triumph, or a more stunning defeat, for the great landed interest can occur. For in this town—so dependent on agriculture—we are opposed by a low and sordid manufacturer, of the most revolutionary notions, who has, moreover, the audacity to force his own nephew—that very boy whom I chastised for impertinence on your village green—son of a common carpenter—actually the audacity, I say, to attempt to force this peasant of a nephew, as well as himself, into the representation of Lansmere, against the Earl's interest, against your distinguished brother—of myself I say nothing. You should hear the language in which these two men indulge against all your family! If we are beaten by such persons in a borough supposed to be so loyal as Lansmere, every one with a stake in the country may tremble at such a prognostic of the ruin that must await not only our old English Constitution, but the existence of property itself. I need not say that on such an occasion I cannot spare myself. Mr. Egerton is ill too. All the fatigue of the canvass devolves on me. I feel, my dear and revered friend, that I am a genuine Hazeldean, fighting your battle; and that thought carries me through all. I cannot, therefore, come to you till the election is over; and meanwhile you, and my dear Mrs. Hazeldean, must be anxious to know more about the affair that so preyed on both your hearts, than I have yet informed you, or can well trust to a letter. Be assured, however, that the worst is over; the lady has gone abroad. I earnestly entreated Frank (who showed me Mrs. Hazeldean's most pathetic letter to him) to hasten at once to the Hall and relieve your minds. Unfortunately he would not be ruled by me, but talked of going abroad too—not, I trust, (nay, I feel assured,) in pursuit of Madame di Negra; but still—In short, I should be so glad to see you, and talk over the whole. Could you not come hither?—pray do. And now, at the risk of your thinking that in this I am only consulting my own interest, (but no—your noble English heart will never so misjudge me!) I will add with homely frankness, that if you could accommodate me immediately with the loan you not long since so generously offered, you would save those lands once in my family from passing away from us for ever. A city alderman—one Jobson—is meanly taking advantage of Thornhill's necessities, and driving a hard bargain for those lands. He has fixed the —th inst. for Thornhill's answer, and Levy (who is here assisting Mr. Egerton's election) informs me that Thornhill will accept his offer, unless I am provided with £10,000 beforehand; the other £10,000, to complete the advance required, Levy will lend me. Do not be surprised at the usurer's liberality; he knows that I am about shortly to marry a very great heiress, (you will be pleased when you learn whom, and will then be able to account for my indifference to

Miss Sticktorights,) and her dower will amply serve to repay his loan and your own, if I may trust to your generous affection for the grandson of a Hazeldean! I have the less scruple in this appeal to you, for I know how it would grieve you that a Jobson, who perhaps never knew a grandmother, should foist your own kinsman from the lands of his fathers. Of one thing I am convinced—we squires, and sons of squires, must make common cause against those great monied capitalists, or they will buy us all out in a few generations. The old race of country gentlemen is already much diminished by the grasping cupidity of such leviathans; and if the race be once extinct, what will become of the boast and strength of England!

"Yours, my dear Mr. Hazeldean, with most affectionate and grateful respect,

"RANDAL LESLIE."

## CHAPTER XXII.

NOTHING to Leonard could as yet be more distasteful or oppressive than his share in this memorable election. In the first place, it chafed the secret sores of his heart to be compelled to resume the name of Fairfield, which was a tacit disavowal of his birth. It had been such delight to him that the same letters which formed the name of Nora, should weave also that name of Oran, to which he had given distinction, which he had associated with all his nobler toils, and all his hopes of enduring fame—a mystic link between his own career and his mother's obscurer genius. It seemed to him as if it were rendering to her the honours accorded to himself—subtle and delicate fancy of the affections, of which only poets would be capable, but which others than poets may perhaps comprehend! That earlier name of Fairfield was connected in his memory with all the ruder employments, the meaner trials of his boyhood;—the name of Oran, with poetry and fame. It was his title in the ideal world, amongst all fair shapes and spirits. In receiving the old appellation, the practical world, with its bitterness and strife, returned to him as at the utterance of a spell. But in coming to Lansmere he had no choice. To say nothing of Dick, and Dick's parents, with whom his secret would not be safe, Randal Leslie knew that he had gone by the name of Fairfield—knew his supposed parentage, and would be sure to proclaim them. How account for the later name without setting curiosity to decipher the anagram it involved, and perhaps guiding suspicion to his birth from Nora, to the injury of her memory, yet preserved from stain?

His feelings as connected with Nora—sharpened and deepened as they all had been by his discovery of her painful narrative—were embittered still more by coming in contact with her parents. Old John was in the same helpless state of mind and body as before—neither worse nor better; but waking up at intervals with vivid gleams of interest in the election at the wave of a blue banner—at the cry of "Blue for ever!" It was the old broken-down charger, who, dozing in the meadows, starts at the roll of the drum. No persuasions Dick could employ would induce his father to promise to vote even one Yellow. You might as well have expected the old Roman, with his monomaniac cry against Carthage, to have voted for choosing Carthaginians for consuls. But poor John, nevertheless, was not only very civil, but very humble to Dick—"very happy to oblige the gentleman."

"Your own son!" bawled Dick; "and here is your own grandson."

"Very happy to serve you both; but you see you are the wrong colour."

Then as he gazed at Leonard, the old man approached him with trembling knees, stroked his hair, looked into his face piteously. "Be thee my grandson?" he faltered. "Wife, wife, Nora had no son, had she? My memory begins to fail me, sir; pray excuse it; but you have a look about the eyes that—" Old John began to weep, and his wife led him away.

"Don't come again," she said to Leonard, harshly, when she returned. "He'll not sleep all night now." And then, observing that the tears stood in Leonard's eyes, she added, in softened tones—"I am glad to see you well and thriving, and to hear that you have been of great service to my son Richard, who is a credit and an honour to the family, though poor John cannot vote for him or for you against his conscience; and he should not be asked," she added, firing up; "and it is a sin to ask it, and he so old, and no one to defend him but me. But defend him I will while I have life!"

The poet recognised woman's brave, loving, wife-like heart here, and would have embraced the stern grandmother, if she had not drawn back from him; and, as she turned towards the room to which she had led her husband, she said over her shoulder—

"I'm not so unkind as I seem, boy; but it is better for you, and for all, that you should not come to this house again —better that you had not come into the town."

"Fie, mother!" said Dick, seeing that Leonard, bending his head, silently walked from the room. "You should be prouder of your grandson than you are of me."

"Prouder of him who may shame us all yet?"

"What do you mean?"

But Mrs. Avenel shook her head and vanished.

"Never mind her, poor old soul," said Dick, as he joined Leonard at the threshold; "she always had her tempers. And since there is no vote to be got in this house, and one can't set a caucus on one's own father—at least in this extraordinarily rotten and prejudiced old country, which is quite in its dotage—we'll not come here to be snubbed any more. Bless their old hearts, nevertheless!"

Leonard's acute sensibility in all that concerned his birth, deeply wounded by Mrs. Avenel's allusions which he comprehended better than his uncle did, was also kept on the edge by the suspense to which he was condemned by Harley's continued silence as to the papers confided to that nobleman. It seemed to Leonard almost unaccountable that Harley should have read those papers—be in the same town with himself—and yet volunteer no communication. At length he wrote a few lines to Lord L'Estrange, bringing the matter that concerned him so deeply before Harley's recollection, and suggesting his own earnest interest in any information that could supply the gaps and omissions of the desultory fragments. Harley, in replying to this note, said, with apparent reason, "that it would require a long personal interview to discuss the subject referred to, and that such an interview, in the thick of the contest between himself and a candidate opposed to the Lansmere party would be sure to get wind, be ascribed to political intrigues, be impossible otherwise to explain—and embarrass all the interests confided to their respective charge. That for the rest, he had not been unmindful of Leonard's anxiety, which must now mainly be to see justice done to the dead parent, and learn the name, station, and character of the parent yet surviving. And in this Harley trusted to assist him as soon as the close of the poll would present a suitable occasion." The letter was unlike Harley's former cordial tone: it was hard and dry.

Leonard respected L'Estrange too much to own to himself that it was unfeeling. With all his rich generosity of nature, he sought excuses for what he declined to blame. Perhaps something in Helen's manner or words had led Harley to suspect that she still cherished too tender an interest in the companion of her childhood; perhaps under this coldness of expression there lurked the burning anguish of jealousy. And, oh Leonard so well understood, and could so nobly compassionate even in his prosperous rival, that torture of the most agonising of human passions, in which all our reasonings follow the distorted writhings of our pain.

And Leonard himself, amidst his other causes of disquiet, was at once so gnawed and so humbled by his own jealousy Helen, he knew, was still under the same roof as Harley. They, the betrothed, could see each other daily, hourly. He would soon hear of their marriage. She would be borne afar from the very sphere of his existence—carried into a loftier region—accessible only to his dreams. And yet to be jealous of one to whom both Helen and himself were under such obligations, debased him in his own esteem—jealousy here was so like ingratitude. But for Harley, what could have become of Helen, left to his boyish charge?—he who had himself been compelled, in despair, to think of sending her from his side, to be reared into smileless youth in his mother's humble cottage, while he faced famine alone, gazing on the terrible river, from the bridge by which he had once begged for very alms—begged of that Audley Egerton, to whom he was now opposed as an equal;—or flying from the fiend that glared at him under the lids of the haunting Chatterton. No, jealousy here was more than agony—it was degradation—it was crime! But, ah! if Helen were happy in these splendid nuptials! Was he sure even of that consolation? Bitter was the thought either way—that she should wholly forget him, in happiness from which he stood excluded as a thing of sin—or sinfully herself remember, and be wretched!

With that healthful strength of will which is more often proportioned to the susceptibility of feeling than the world suppose, the young man at last wrenched himself for awhile from the iron that had entered into his soul, and forced his thoughts to seek relief in the very objects from which they otherwise would have the most loathingly recoiled. He aroused his imagination to befriend his reason; he strove to divine some motive not explained by Harley, not to be referred to

the mere defeat, by counter-scheme, of the scheming Randal
—nor even to be solved, by any service to Audley Egerton,
which Harley might evolve from the complicated meshes of
the election;—some motive that could more interest his own
heart in the contest, and connect itself with Harley's promised aid in clearing up the mystery of his parentage. Nora's
memoir had clearly hinted that his father was of rank and
station far beyond her own. She had thrown the glow of
her glorious fancies over the ambition and the destined career
of the lover in whom she had merged her ambition as poetess,
and her career as woman. Possibly the father might be more
disposed to own and to welcome the son, if the son could
achieve an opening, and give promise of worth, in that grand
world of public life in which alone reputation takes prece-
dence of rank. Possibly, too, if the son thus succeeded, and
became one whom a proud father could with pride acknowledge, possibly he might not only secure a father's welcome,
but vindicate a mother's name. This marriage, which Nora
darkly hinted she had been led to believe was fraudulent,
might, after all, have been legal—the ceremony concealed,
even till now, by worldly shame at disparity of rank. But if
the son could make good his own footing—there were rank
itself owned its chiefs in talent—that shame might vanish.
These suppositions were not improbable ; nor were they
uncongenial to Leonard's experience of Harley's delicate
benignity of purpose. Here, too, the image of Helen allied
itself with those of his parents, to support his courage and
influence his new ambition. True, that she was lost to him
for ever. No worldly success, no political honours, could now
restore her to his side. But she might hear him named with
respect in those circles in which alone she would hereafter
move, and in which parliamentary reputation ranks higher
than literary fame. And perhaps in future years, when love,
retaining its tenderness, was purified from its passion, they
might thus meet as friends. He might without a pang, take
her children on his knees, and say, perhaps in their old age,
when he had climbed to a social equality even with her high-
born lord, " It was the hope to regain the privilege bestowed
on our childhood, that strengthened me to seek distinction
when you and happiness forsook my youth." Thus regarded,
the election, which had before seemed to him so poor and
vulgar an exhibition of vehement passions for petty objects,
with its trumpery of banners and its discord of trumpets,
suddenly grew into vivid interest, and assumed dignity and

importance. It is ever thus with all mortal strife. In proportion as it possesses, or is void of, the diviner something that quickens the pulse of the heart, and elevates the wing of the imagination, it presents a mockery to the philosopher, or an inspiration to the bard. Feel *that something*, and no contest is mean! Feel it not, and, like Byron, you may class with the slaughter of Cannæ that field which, at Waterloo, restored the landmarks of nations; or may jeer with Juvenal at the dust of Hannibal, because he sought to deliver Carthage from ruin, and free a world from Rome.

## CHAPTER XXIII.

ONCE then, grappling manfully with the task he had undertaken, and constraining himself to look on what Riccabocca would have called " the southern side of things," whatever there was really great in principle or honourable to human nature, deep below the sordid details and pitiful interests apparent on the face of the agitated current, came clear to his vision. The ardour of those around him began to be contagious; the generous devotion to some cause, apart from self, which pervades an election, and to which the poorest voter will often render sacrifices that may be called sublime—the warm personal affection which community of zeal creates for the defender of beloved opinions—all concurred to dispel that indifference to party politics, and counteract that disgust of their baser leaven, which the young poet had first conceived. He even began to look with complacency, for itself, on a career of toil and honours strange to his habitual labours and intellectual ambition. He threw the poetry of idea within him (as poets ever do) into the prose of action to which he was hurried forward. He no longer opposed Dick Avenel when that gentleman represented how detrimental it would be to his business at Screwstown if he devoted to his country the time and the acumen required by his mill and its steam-engine; and how desirable it would be, on all accounts, that Leonard Fairfield should become the parliamentary representative of the Avenels. " If, therefore," said Dick, " two of us cannot come in, and one must retire, leave it to me to arrange with the committee that you shall be the one to persist. Oh, never fear but what all scruples of honour shall be satisfied. I would not for the sake of the Avenels, have a word said against their representative."

"But," answered Leonard, "if I grant this, I fear that you have some intention of suffering the votes that your resignation would release, to favour Leslie at the expense of Egerton."

"What the deuce is Egerton to you?"

"Nothing, except through my gratitude to his friend Lord L'Estrange."

"Pooh! I will tell you a secret. Levy informs me privately that L'Estrange will be well satisfied if the choice of Lansmere fall upon Leslie instead of Egerton; and I think I convinced my Lord—for I saw him in London—that Egerton would have no chance, though Leslie might."

"I must think that Lord L'Estrange would resist to the utmost any attempt to prefer Leslie—whom he despises—to Egerton, whom he honours. And, so thinking, I too would resist it, as you may judge by the speeches which have so provoked your displeasure."

"Let us cut short a yarn of talk which, when it comes to likings and dislikings, might last to almighty crack: I'll ask you to do nothing that Lord L'Estrange does not sanction. Will that satisfy you?"

"Certainly, provided I am assured of the sanction."

And now, the important day preceding the poll, the day in which the candidates were to be formally nominated, and meet each other in all the ceremony of declared rivalship, dawned at last. The town-hall was the place selected for the occasion; and before sunrise, all the streets were resonant with music, and gay with banners.

Audley Egerton felt that he could not—without incurring some just sarcasm on his dread to face the constituency he had formerly represented, and by the malcontents of which he had been burned in effigy—absent himself from the town-hall, as he had done from balcony and hostel. Painful as it was to confront Nora's brother, and wrestle in public against all the secret memories that knit the strife of the present contest with the anguish that recalled the first—still the thing must be done; and it was the English habit of his life to face with courage whatever he had to do.

## CHAPTER XXIV.

The chiefs of the Blue party went in state from Lansmere Park; the two candidates in open carriages, each attended with his proposer and seconder. Other carriages were devoted to Harley and Levy, and the principal members of the committee. Riccabocca was seized with a fit of melancholy or cynicism, and declined to join the procession. But just before they started, as all were assembling without the front door, the postman arrived with his welcome bag. There were letters for Harley, some for Levy, many for Egerton, one for Randal Leslie.

Levy, soon hurrying over his own correspondence, looked, in the familiar freedom wherewith he usually treated his particular friends, over Randal's shoulder.

"From the Squire?" said he. "Ah, he has written at last! What made him delay so long? Hope he relieves your mind?"

"Yes," cried Randal, giving way to a joy that rarely lighted up his close and secret countenance—"yes, he does not write from Hazeldean—not there when my letter arrived—in London—could not rest at the Hall—the place reminded him too much of Frank—went again to town, on the receipt of my first letter concerning the rupture of the marriage, to see after his son, and take up some money to pay off his *post-obit*. Read what he says :—' So, while I was about a mortgage—(never did I guess that I should be the man to encumber the Hazeldean estate)—I thought I might as well add £20,000 as £10,000 to the total. Why should you be indebted at all to that Baron Levy? Don't have dealings with money-lenders. Your grandmother was a Hazeldean; and from a Hazeldean you shall have the whole sum required in advance for those Rood lands—good light soil some of them. As to repayment, we'll talk of that later.' If Frank and I come together again, as we did of old, why, my estates will be his some day; and he'll not grudge the mortgage, so fond as he always was of you; and if we don't come together, what do I care for hundreds or thousands, either more or less? So I shall be down at Lansmere the day after to-morrow, just in the thick of your polling. Beat the manufacturer, my boy, and stick up for the land. Tell Levy to have all ready. I shall bring the money down in good bank-notes, and a brace of pistols in my coat pocket to take care of them in case robbers get scent of the notes and attack me on the road, as they did my grandfather sixty years ago, come next Michaelmas. A Lansmere election puts one in mind of pistols. I once fought a duel with an officer in his Majesty's service, R.N., and had a ball lodged in my right shoulder, on account of an election at Lansmere; but I have forgiven Audley his share in that transaction. Remember me to him kindly. Don't get into a duel yourself; but I suppose manufacturers don't fight;—not that I blame them for that—far from it."

The letter then ran on to express surprise, and hazard conjecture, as to the wealthy marriage which Randal had announced as a pleasing surprise to the Squire.

"Well," said Levy, returning the letter, "you *must* have written as cleverly as you talk, or the Squire is a booby indeed."

Randal smiled, pocketed his letter, and responding to the impatient call of his proposer, sprang lightly into the carriage.

Harley, too, seemed pleased with the letters delivered to himself, and now joined Levy, as the candidates drove slowly off.

"Has not Mr. Leslie received from the Squire an answer to that letter of which you informed me?"

"Yes, my lord, the Squire will be here to-morrow."

"To-morrow? Thank you for apprising me; his rooms shall be prepared."

"I suppose he will only stay to see Leslie and myself, and pay the money."

"Aha! Pay the money. Is it so, then?"

"Twice the sum, and, it seems, as a gift, which Leslie only asked as a loan. Really, my lord, Mr. Leslie is a very clever man; and though I am at your commands, I should not like to injure him. With such matrimonial prospects, he could be a very powerful enemy; and if he succeed in Parliament, still more so."

"Baron, these gentlemen are waiting for you. I will follow by myself."

## CHAPTER XXV.

In the centre of the raised platform in the town-hall sat the Mayor. On either hand of that dignitary now appeared the candidates of the respective parties. To his right, Audley Egerton and Leslie; to his left, Dick Avenel and Leonard. The place was as full as it could hold. Rows of grimy faces peeped in, even from the upper windows outside the building. The contest was one that created intense interest, not only from public principles, but local passions. Dick Avenel, the son of a small tradesman, standing against the Right Honourable Audley Egerton, the choice of the powerful Lansmere aristocratic party—standing too, with his nephew by his side —taking, as he himself was wont to say, "the tarnation Blue Bull by both its oligarchical horns!" There was a pluck and gallantry in the very impudence of the attempt to convert the important borough—for one member of which a great Earl had hitherto striven, "with labour dire and weary woe,"— into two family seats for the house of Avenel and the triumph of the Capelocracy.

This alone would have excited all the spare passions of a country borough; but, besides this, there was the curiosity that attached to the long-deferred public appearance of a candidate so renowned as the ex-minister—a man whose career had commenced with his success at Lansmere, and who now, amidst the popular tempest that scattered his colleagues, sought to refit his vessel in the same harbour from which it had first put forth. New generations had grown up since the name of Audley Egerton had first fluttered the dovecotes in that Corioli. The questions that had then seemed so important, were, for the most part, settled and at rest. But those present who remembered Egerton in the former day, were struck to see how the same characteristics of bearing and aspect which had distinguished his early youth revived their interest in the mature and celebrated man. As he stood up for a few moments, before he took his seat beside the Mayor, glancing over the assembly, with its uproar of cheers and hisses, there was the same stately erectness of form and steadfastness of look—the same indefinable and mysterious dignity of externals, that imposed respect, confirmed esteem, or stilled dislike. The hisses involuntarily ceased.

The preliminary proceedings over, the proposers and seconders commenced their office.

Audley was proposed, of course, by the crack man of the party—a gentleman who lived on his means in a white house in the High Street—had received a University education, and was a cadet of a "County Family." This gentleman spoke much about the Constitution, something about Greece and Rome—compared Egerton with William Pitt, also with Aristides; and sat down, after an oration esteemed classical by the few, and pronounced prosy by the many. Audley's seconder, a burly and important maltster, struck a bolder key. He dwelt largely upon the necessity of being represented by gentlemen of wealth and rank, and not by "upstarts and adventurers." (Cheers and groans.) Looking at the candidates on the other side, it was an insult to the respectability of Lansmere to suppose its constituents could elect a man who had no pretensions whatever to their notice, except that he had once been a little boy in the town, in which his father kept a shop—and a very noisy, turbulent, dirty little boy he was!" Dick smoothed his spotless shirt-front, and looked daggers, while the Blues laughed heartily, and the Yellows cried "Shame!" "As for the other candidate on the same side, he (the maltster) had nothing to say against him. He was, no doubt, seduced into presumption by his uncle and his own inexperience. It was said that that candidate, Mr. Fairfield, was an author and a poet; if so, he was unknown to fame, for no bookseller in the town had ever even heard of Mr. Fairfield's works. Then it was replied Mr. Fairfield had written under another name. What would that prove? Either that he was ashamed of his name, or that the works did him no credit. For his part, he (the maltster) was an Englishman; he did not like anonymous scribblers; there was something not right in whatever was concealed. A man should never be afraid to put his name to what he wrote. But, grant that Mr. Fairfield was a great author and a great poet, what the borough of Lansmere wanted was, not a member who would pass his time in writing sonnets to Peggy or Moggy, but a practical man of business—a statesman—such a man as Mr. Audley Egerton—a gentleman of ancient birth, high standing, and princely fortune. The member for such a place as Lansmere should have a proper degree of wealth." ("Hear, hear!" from the Hundred and Fifty Hesitators, who all stood in a row at the bottom of the hall; and "Gammon!" "Stuff!" from some revolutionary, but incorruptible Yellows.) Still the allusion to Egerton's private fortune had considerable effect with the bulk of the audience, and the maltster was much cheered on concluding. Mr. Avenel's proposer and seconder—the one a large grocer, the other the proprietor of a new shop for ticketed prints, shawls, blankets, and counterpanes, (a man who, as he boasted, dealt with the People for ready money, and no mistake—at least none that *he* ever rectified,) next followed. Both said much the same thing. Mr. Avenel had made his fortune by honest industry—was a fellow townsman—must know the interests of the town better than strangers—upright public principles—never fawn on governments—would see that the people had their rights, and cut down army, navy, and all other jobs of a corrupt aristocracy, &c. &c. &c. Randal Leslie's proposer, a captain on half-pay, undertook a long defence of army and navy, from the unpatriotic aspersions of the preceding speakers; which defence diverted him from the due praise of Randal, until cries of "Cut it short," recalled him to that subject; and then the topics he selected for eulogium were "amiability of character, so conspicuous in the urbane manners of his young friend;"— "coincidence in the opinions of that illustrious statesman with whom he was conjoined;"—"early tuition in the best principles—only fault, youth—and that was a fault which would diminish every day." Randal's seconder was a bluff yeoman, an out-voter of weight with the agricultural electors. He was too straightforward by half—adverted to Audley Egerton's early desertion of questions espoused by the landed interest—"hoped he had had enough of the large towns; and he (the yeoman) was ready to forgive and forget, but trusted that there would be no chance of burning their member again in effigy. As to the young gentleman, whose nomination he had the pleasure to second—did not know much about him; but the Leslies were an old family in the neighbouring county, and Mr. Leslie said he was nearly related to Squire Hazeldean—as good a man as ever stood upon shoe leather. He (the yeoman) liked a good breed in sheep and bullocks; and a good breed in men he supposed was the same thing. He (the yeoman) was not for abuses—he was for King and Constitution. He should have no objection, for instance, to have tithes lowered, and the malt-tax repealed— not the least objection. Mr. Leslie seemed to him a likely young chap, and uncommon well-spoken; and, on the whole, for aught he (the yeoman) could see, would do quite as well in Parliament as nine-tenths of the gentlemen sent there." The yeoman sat down, little cheered by the Blues—much by the Yellows—and with a dim consciousness that somehow or other he had rather damaged than not the cause of the party he had been chosen to advocate. Leonard was not particularly fortunate in his proposer—a youngish gentleman—who, having tried various callings, with signal unsuccess, had come into a small independence, and set up for a literary character. This gentleman undertook the defence of poets, as the half-pay captain had undertaken that of the army and navy; and after a dozen sentences spoken through the nose, about the "moonlight of existence," and "the oasis in the desert," suddenly broke down, to the satisfaction of his impatient listeners. This failure was, however, redeemed by Leonard's seconder—a master tailor—a practised speaker and an earnest, thinking man—sincerely liking, and warmly admiring, Leonard Fairfield. His opinions were delivered with brief simplicity, and accompanied by expressions of trust in Leonard's talents and honesty, that were effective, because expressed with feeling.

These preparatory orations over, a dead silence succeeded, and Audley Egerton arose.

At the first few sentences, all felt they were in the presence of one accustomed to command attention, and to give to opinions the weight of recognised authority. The slowness of the measured accents, the composure of the manly aspect, the decorum of the simple gestures—all bespoke and all became the Minister of a great empire, who had less agitated assemblies by impassioned eloquence, than compelled their silent respect to the views of sagacity and experience. But what might have been formal and didactic in another, was relieved in Egerton by that air, tone, bearing of *gentleman*, which have a charm for the most plebeian audience. He had eminently these attributes in private life; but they became far more conspicuous whenever he had to appear in public. The "*senatorius decor*" seemed a phrase coined for him.

Audley commenced with notice of his adversaries in that language of high courtesy which is so becoming to superior station, and which augurs better for victory than the most pointed diatribes of hostile declamation. Inclining his head towards Avenel, he expressed regret that he should be opposed by a gentleman whose birth naturally endeared him to the town, of which he was a distinguished native, and whose honourable ambition was in itself a proof of the admirable nature of that Constitution, which admitted the lowliest to rise to its distinctions, while it compelled the loftiest to labour and compete for those honours which were the most coveted because they were derived from the trust of their countrymen, and dignified by the duties which the sense of responsibility entailed. He paid a passing but generous compliment to the reputed abilities of Leonard Fairfield; and, alluding with appropriate grace to the interest he had ever taken in the success of youth striving for place in the van of the new generation that marched on to replace the old, he implied that he did not consider Leonard as opposed to himself, but rather as an emulous competitor for a worthy prize with his "own young and valued friend, Mr. Randal Leslie." "They are happy at their years!" said the statesman, with a certain pathos. "In the future they see nothing to fear, in the past they have nothing to defend. It is not so with me." And then, passing on to the vague insinuations or bolder charges against himself and his policy proffered by the preceding speakers, Audley gathered himself up, and paused; for his eye here rested on the Reporters seated round the table just below him; and he recognised faces not unfamiliar to his recollection when metropolitan assemblies had hung on the words which fell from lips then privileged to advise a King. And involuntarily it occurred to the ex-minister to escape altogether from this contracted audience—this election, with all its associations of pain—and address himself wholly to that vast and invisible Public, to which those Reporters would transmit his ideas. At this thought his whole manner gradually changed. His eye became fixed on the farthest verge of the crowd; his tones grew more solemn in their deep and sonorous swell. He began to review and to vindicate his whole political life. He spoke of the measures he had aided to pass—of his part in the laws which now ruled the land. He touched lightly, but with pride, on the services he had rendered to the opinions he had represented. He alluded to his neglect of his own private fortunes; but in what detail, however minute, in the public business committed to his charge, could even an enemy accuse him of neglect? The allusion was no doubt intended to prepare the public for the news, that the wealth of Audley Egerton was gone. Finally, he came to the questions that then agitated the day; and made a general but masterly exposition of the policy which, under the changes he foresaw, he should recommend his party to adopt.

Spoken to the motley assembly in that town-hall, Audley's speech extended to a circle of interest too wide for their sympathy. But that assembly he heeded not—he forgot it. The reporters understood him, as their flying pens followed words which they presumed neither to correct nor to abridge. Audley's speech was addressed to the nation;—the speech of a man in whom the nation yet recognised a chief—desiring to clear all misrepresentation from his past career—calculating, if life were spared to him, on destinies higher than he had yet fulfilled—issuing a manifesto of principles to be carried later into power, and planting a banner round which the divided sections of a broken host might yet rally for battle and for conquest. Or, perhaps, in the deeps of his heart (not even comprehended by reporters, nor to be divined by the public), the uncertainty of life was more felt than the hope of ambition; and the statesman desired to leave behind him one full vindication of that *public* integrity and honour, on which, at least, his conscience acknowledged not a stain. "For more than twenty years," said Audley, in conclusion, "I have known no day in which I have not lived for my country. I may at times have opposed the wish of the People—I may oppose it now—but, so far as I can form a judgment, only because I prefer their welfare to their wish. And if —as I believe—there have been occasions on which as one amongst men more renowned, I have amended the laws of England—confirmed her safety, extended her commerce, upheld her honour—I leave the rest to the censure of my enemies, and (his voice trembled) to the charity of my friends."

Before the cheers that greeted the close of this speech were over, Richard Avenel arose. What is called "the more respectable part" of an audience—viz., the better educated and better clad, even on the Yellow side of the question— winced a little for the credit of their native borough, when they contemplated the candidate pitted against the Great Commoner, whose lofty presence still filled the eye, and whose majestic tones yet sounded in the ear. But the vast majority on both sides, Blue and Yellow, hailed the rise of Dick Avenel as a relief to what, while it had awed their attention, had rather strained their faculties. The Yellows cheered and the Blues groaned; there was a tumultuous din of voices, and a reel to and fro of the whole excited mass of unwashed faces and brawny shoulders. But Dick had as much pluck as Audley himself; and, by degrees, his pluck and his handsome features, and the curiosity to hear what he had to say, obtained him a hearing; and that hearing, Dick having once got, he contrived to keep. His self-confidence was backed by a grudge against Egerton, that attained to the elevation of malignity. He had armed himself for this occasion with an arsenal of quotations from Audley's speeches, taken out of Hansard's debates; and, garbling these texts in the unfairest and most ingenious manner, he contrived to split consistency into such fragments of inconsistency—to cut so many harmless sentences into such unpopular, arbitrary, tyrannical segments of doctrine—that he made a very pretty case against the enlightened and incorruptible Egerton, as shuffler and trimmer, defender of jobs, and eulogist of Manchester massacres, &c., &c. And all told the more because it seemed courted and provoked by the ex-minister's elaborate vindication of himself. Having thus, as he declared, "triumphantly convicted the Right Honourable Gentleman out of his own mouth," Dick considered himself at liberty to diverge into what he termed "the just indignation of a free-born Briton;" in other words, into every variety of abuse which bad taste could supply to acrimonious feeling. But he did it so roundly and dauntlessly, in such true hustings style, that for the moment, at least, he carried the bulk of the crowd along with him sufficiently to bear down all the resentful murmurs of the Blue Committee men, and the abashed shakes of the head with which the more aristocratic and well-bred among the Yellows signified to each other that they were heartily ashamed of their candidate. Dick concluded with an emphatic declaration that the Right Honourable Gentleman's day was gone by; that the people had been pillaged and plundered enough by pompous red-tapists, who only thought of their salaries, and never went to their offices except to waste the pen, ink, and paper which they did not pay for; that the Right Honourable Gentleman had boasted he had served his country for twenty years. Served his country!—he should have said served her *out!* (Much laughter.) Pretty mess his country was in now. In short, for twenty years the Right Honourable Gentleman had put his hands into his country's pockets.—"And I ask you," bawled Dick, "whether any of you are a bit the better for all that he has taken out of them!" The Hundred and Fifty Hesitators shook their heads. "Noa, that we ben't!" cried the Hundred and Fifty, dolorously. "*You* hear THE PEOPLE!" said Dick, turning majestically to Egerton, who, with his arms folded on his breast, and his upper lip slightly curved, sat like "Atlas unremoved"—"You hear THE PEOPLE! They condemn you and the whole set of you. I repeat here what I once vowed on a less public occasion—'As sure as my name is Richard Avenel, you shall smart for'—(Dick hesitated)—'smart for your contempt of the just rights, honest claims, and enlightened aspirations of your indignant countrymen. The schoolmaster is abroad, and the British Lion is aroused!'"

Dick sat down. The curve of contempt had passed from Egerton's lip;—at the name of Avenel, thus harshly spoken, he had suddenly shaded his face with his hand.

But Randal Leslie next arose, and Audley slowly raised his eyes, and looked towards his *protégé* with an expression of kindly interest. What better *debût* could there be for a young man warmly attached to an eminent patron, who had been coarsely assailed—for a political aspirant vindicating the principles which that patron represented? The Blues, palpitating with indignant excitement, all prepared to cheer every sentence that could embody their sense of outrage;—even the meanest amongst the Yellows, now that Dick had concluded, dimly aware that their orator had laid himself terribly open, and richly deserved (more especially from the friend of Audley Egerton) whatever punishing retort could vibrate from the heart of a man to the tongue of an orator. A better opportunity for an honest young *debutant* could not exist;— a more disagreeable, annoying, perplexing, unmanageable opportunity for Randal Leslie, the malice of the Fates could not have contrived. How could *he* attack Dick Avenel!—he who counted upon Dick Avenel to win his election? How could he exasperate the Yellows, when Dick's solemn injunction had been—"Say nothing to make the Yellows not vote for you!" How could he identify himself with Egerton's policy, when it was his own policy to make his opponents believe him an unprejudiced, sensible youth, who would come all right and all Yellow one of these days! Demosthenes himself would have had a sore throat, worse than when he swallowed the golden cup of Harpalus, had Demosthenes been placed in so cursed a fix. Therefore Randal Leslie may well be excused if he stammered and boggled—if he was appalled by a cheer when he said a word in vindication of Egerton— and looked cringing and pitiful when he sneaked out a counter civility to Dick. The Blues were sadly disappointed— damped; the Yellows smirked and took heart. Audley Egerton's brows darkened. Harley, who was on the platform, half seen behind the front row, a quiet listener, bent over and whispered drily to Audley—"You should have given a lesson beforehand to your clever young friend. His affection for you overpowers him!"

Audley made no rejoinder, but tore a leaf out of his pocket-book, and wrote, in pencil, these words—"Say that you may well feel embarrassed how to reply to Mr. Avenel, because I had especially requested you not to be provoked to one angry expression against a gentleman whose father and brother-in-law gave the majority of two by which I gained my first seat in Parliament;—then plunge at once into general politics." He placed this paper in Randal's hand, just as that unhappy young man was on the point of a thorough break-down. Randal paused, took breath, read the words attentively, and amidst a general titter; his presence of mind returned to him —he saw a way out of the scrape—collected himself—suddenly raised his head—and in tones unexpectedly firm and fluent, enlarged on the text afforded to him—enlarged so well that he took the audience by surprise—pleased the Blues by an evidence of Audley's generosity—and touched the Yellows by so affectionate a deference to the family of their two candidates. Then the speaker was enabled to come at once to the topics on which he had elaborately prepared himself, and delivered a set harangue—very artfully put together—temporising it is true, and trimming, but full of what would have been called admirable tact and discretion in an old stager who did not want to commit himself to anybody or to anything. On the whole, the display became creditable, at least as an evidence of thoughtful reserve, rare in a man so young—too refining and scholastic for oratory, but a very good essay—upon both sides of the question. Randal wiped his pale forehead and sat down, cheered, especially by the lawyers present, and self-contented. It was now Leonard's turn to speak. Keenly nervous, as men of the literary temperament are—constitutionally shy, his voice trembled as he began. But he trusted, unconsciously, less to his intellect than his warm heart and noble temper—and the warm heart prompted his words, and the noble temper gradually dignified his manner. He took advantage of the sentences which Audley had put into Randal's mouth, in order to efface the impression made by his uncle's rude assault. "Would that the Right Honourable Gentleman had himself made that generous and affecting allusion to the services which he had deigned to remember, for, in that case, he (Leonard) was confident that Mr. Avenel would have lost all the bitterness which political contest was apt to engender in proportion to the earnestness with which political opinions were entertained. Happy it was when some such milder sentiment as that which Mr. Egerton had instructed Mr. Leslie to convey, preceded the sharp encounter, and reminded antagonists, as Mr. Leslie had so emphatically done, that every shield had two sides, and that it was possible to maintain the one side to be golden, without denying the truth of the champion who asserted the other side to be silver." Then, without appearing to throw over his uncle, the young speaker contrived to insinuate an apology on his uncle's behalf, with such exquisite grace and good feeling, that he was loudly cheered by both parties; and even Dick did not venture to utter the dissent which struggled to his lips.

But if Leonard dealt thus respectfully with Egerton, he had no such inducements to spare Randal Leslie. With the intuitive penetration of minds accustomed to analyse character and investigate human nature, he detected the varnished insincerity of Randal's artful address. His colour rose—his voice swelled—his fancy began to play, and his wit to sparkle —when he came to take to pieces his younger antagonist's rhetorical mosaic. He exposed the falsehood of its affected moderation—he tore into shreds the veil of words, with their motley woof of yellow and blue—and showed that not a single conviction could be discovered behind it. "Mr. Leslie's speech," said he, "puts me in mind of a ferry-boat; it seems made for no purpose but to go from one side to the other." The simile hit the truth so exactly, that it was received with a roar of laughter: even Egerton smiled. "For myself," concluded Leonard, as he summed up his unsparing analysis, "I am new to party warfare; yet if I were not opposing Mr. Leslie as a candidate for your suffrages, if I were but an elector—belonging, as I do, to the people by my condition and my labours—I should feel that he is one of those politicians in whom the welfare, the honour, the moral elevation of the people, find no fitting representative."

Leonard sate down amidst great applause, and after a speech that raised the Yellows in their own estimation, and materially damaged Randal Leslie in the eyes of the Blues. Randal felt this, with a writhing of the heart, though a sneer on the lips. He glanced furtively towards Dick Avenel, on whom, after all, his election, in spite of the Blues, might depend. Dick answered the furtive glance by an encouraging wink. Randal turned to Egerton, and whispered to him— "How I wish I had had more practice in speaking, so that I could have done you more justice!"

"Thank you, Leslie; Mr. Fairfield has supplied any omission of yours, so far as I am concerned. And you should excuse him for his attack on yourself, because it may serve to convince you where your fault as a speaker lies."

"Where?" asked Leslie, with jealous sullenness.

"In not believing a single word that you say," answered Egerton, very drily; and then turning away, he said aloud to his proposer, and with a slight sigh, "Mr. Avenel may be proud of his nephew! I wish that young man were on our side; I could train him into a great debater."

And now the proceedings were about to terminate with a show of hands, when a tall brawny elector in the middle of the hall suddenly arose, and said he had some questions to put. A thrill ran through the assembly, for this elector was the demagogue of the Yellows—a fellow whom it was impossible to put down—a capital speaker, with lungs of brass. "I shall be very short," said the demagogue. And therewith, under the shape of questions to the two Blue candidates, he commenced a most furious onslaught on the Earl of Lansmere, and the Earl's son, Lord L'Estrange, accusing the last of the grossest intimidation and corruption, and citing instances thereof as exhibited towards various electors in Fish Lane and the Back Slums, who had been turned from Yellow promises by the base arts of Blue aristocracy, represented in the person of the noble lord, whom he now dared to reply. The orator paused, and Harley suddenly passed into the front of the platform, in token that he accepted the ungracious invitation. Great as had been the curiosity to hear Audley Egerton, yet greater, if possible, was the curiosity to hear Lord L'Estrange. Absent from the place for so many years—heir to such immense possessions—with a vague reputation for talent that he had never proved—strange, indeed, if Blue and Yellow had not strained their ears and hushed their breaths to listen.

It is said that the poet is born, and the orator made—a saying only partially true. Some men have been made poets, and some men have been born orators. Most probably Harley L'Estrange had hitherto never spoken in public, and he had not now spoken five minutes before all the passions and humours of the assembly were as much under his command as the keys of the instrument are under the hands of the musician. He had taken from nature a voice capable of infinite variety of modulation, a countenance of the most flexible play of expression; and he was keenly alive (as profound humourists are) equally to the ludicrous and the graver side of everything presented to his vigorous understanding. Leonard had the eloquence of a poet—Audley Egerton that of a parliamentary debater. But Harley had the rarer gift of eloquence in itself, apart from the matter it conveys or adorns —that gift which Demosthenes meant by his triple requisite of an orator, which has been improperly translated "action," but means in reality "the *acting*,"—" the stage-play." Both Leonard and Audley spoke well, from the good sense which their speeches contained; but Harley could have talked nonsense, and made it more effective than sense—even as a Kemble or Macready could produce effects from the trash talked by "The Stranger," which your merely accomplished performer would fail to extract from the beauties of Hamlet. The art of oratory, indeed, is allied more closely to that of the drama than to any other; and throughout Harley's whole nature there ran, as the reader may have noted, (though quite unconsciously to Harley himself,) a tendency towards that concentration of thought, action, and circumstance, on a single purpose, which makes the world form itself into a stage, and gathers various and scattered agencies into the symmetry and compactness of a drama. This tendency, though it often produces effects that appear artificially theatrical, is not uncommon with persons the most genuine and single-minded. It is, indeed, the natural inclination of quick energies springing from warm emotions. Hence the very history of nations in their fresh, vigorous, half-civilised youth, always shapes itself into dramatic forms; while, as the exercise of sober reason expands with civilisation, to the injury of the livelier faculties and more intuitive impulses, people look to the dramatic form of expression, whether in thought or in action, as if it were the antidote to truth, instead of being its abstract and essence.

But to return from this long and somewhat metaphysical digression, whatever might be the cause why Harley L'Estrange spoke so wonderfully well, there could be no doubt that wonderfully well he did speak. He turned the demagogue and his attack into the most felicitous ridicule, and yet with the most genial good-humour; described that virtuous gentleman's adventures in search of corruption through the pure regions of Fish Lane and the Back Slums; and then summed up the evidence on which the demagogue had founded his charge, with a humour so caustic and original that the audience were convulsed with laughter. From laughter Harley hurried his audience almost to the pathos of tears—for he spoke of the insinuations against his father, so that every son and every father in the assembly felt moved as at the voice of Nature.

A turn in a sentence, and a new emotion seized the assembly. Harley was identifying himself with the Lansmere electors. He spoke of his pride in being a Lansmere man, and all the Lansmere electors suddenly felt proud of him. He talked with familiar kindness of old friends remembered in his schoolboy holidays, rejoicing to find so many alive and prospering. He had a felicitous word to each.

"Dear old Lansmere!" said he, and the simple exclamation won him the hearts of all. In fine, when he paused, as if to retire, it was amidst a storm of acclamation. Audley grasped his hand, and whispered—"I am the only one here not surprised, Harley. Now you have discovered your powers, never again let them slumber. What a life may be yours if you no longer waste it!" Harley extricated his hand, and his eye glittered. He made a sign that he had more to say, and the applause was hushed. "My Right Honourable friend chides me for the years that I have wasted. True; my years have been wasted—no matter how nor wherefore! But *his!* —how have *they* been spent: in such devotion to the public that those who know him not as I do, have said that he had not one feeling left to spare to the obscurer duties and more limited affections, by which men of ordinary talents and humble minds rivet the links of that social order which it is the august destiny of statesmen—like him who now sits beside me—to cherish and defend. But, for my part, I think that there is no being so dangerous as the solemn hypocrite, who, because he drills his cold nature into serving mechanically some conventional abstraction—whether he calls it 'the Constitution' or 'the Public'—holds himself dispensed from whatever, in the warm blood of private life, wins attachment to goodness, and confidence to truth. Let others, then, praise my Right Honourable friend as the incorruptible politician. Pardon me if I draw his likeness as the loyal sincere man, who might say with the honest priest, 'that he could not tell a lie to gain Heaven by it!'—and with so fine a sense of honour, that he would hold it a lie merely to conceal the truth." Harley then drew a brilliant picture of the type of chivalrous honesty—of the ideal which the English attach to the phrase of "a perfect gentleman," applying each sentence to his Right Honourable friend with an emphasis that seemed to burst from his heart. To all of the audience, save two, it was an eulogium which the fervent sincerity of the eulogist alone saved from hyperbole. But Levy rubbed his hands, and chuckled inly; and Egerton hung his head, and moved restlessly on his seat. Every word that Harley uttered lodged an arrow in Audley's breast. Amidst the cheers that followed this admirable sketch of the "loyal man," Harley recognised Leonard's enthusiastic voice. He turned sharply towards the young man: "Mr. Fairfield cheers this description of integrity, and its application; let him imitate the model set before him, and he may live to hear praise as genuine as mine from some friend who has tested his worth as I have tested Mr. Egerton's. Mr. Fairfield is a poet: his claim to that title was disputed by one of the speakers who preceded me! —unjustly disputed! Mr. Fairfield is every inch a poet. But, it has been asked, 'Are poets fit for the business of senates? Will they not be writing sonnets to Peggy and Moggy, when you want them to concentrate their divine imagination on the details of a beer bill!' Do not let Mr. Fairfield's friends be alarmed. At the risk of injury to the two candidates whose cause I espouse, truth compels me to say, that poets, when they stoop to action, are not less prosaic than the dullest amongst us: they are swayed by the same selfish interests—they are moved by the same petty passions. It is a mistake to suppose that any detail in common life, whether in public or private, can be too mean to seduce the exquisite pliances of their fancy. Nay, in public life, we may trust them better than other men; for vanity is a kind of second conscience, and, as a poet has himself said—

> 'Who fears not to do ill, yet fears the name,
> And free from conscience, is a slave to shame.'

In private life alone we do well to be on our guard against these children of fancy, for they so devote to the Muse all their treasury of sentiment, that we can no more expect them to waste a thought on the plain duties of men, than we can expect the spendthrift, who dazzles the town, 'to fritter away his money in paying his debts.' But all the world are agreed to be indulgent to the infirmities of those who are their own deceivers and their own chastisers. Poets have more enthusiasm, more affection, more heart than others; but only for fictions of their own creating. It is in vain for us to attach them to ourselves by vulgar merit, by commonplace obligations—strive and sacrifice as we may. They are ungrateful to us, only because gratitude is so very unpoetical a subject. We lose them the moment we attempt to bind. Their love,

> 'Light as air, at sight of human ties,
> Spreads its light wings, and in a moment flies.'

They follow their own caprices—adore their own delusions—and, deeming the forms of humanity too material for their fantastic affections, conjure up a ghost, and are chilled to death by its embrace!"

Then, suddenly aware that he was passing beyond the comprehension of his audience, and touching upon the bounds of his bitter secret, (for here he was thinking, not of Leonard, but of Nora,) Harley gave a new and more homely direction to his terrible irony—turned into telling ridicule the most elevated sentiments Leonard's speech had conveyed—hastened on to a rapid view of political questions in general—defended Leslie with the same apparent earnestness and latent satire with which he had eulogised Audley—and concluded a speech which, for popular effect, had never been equalled in that hall, amidst a diapason of cheers that threatened to bring down the rafters.

In a few minutes more the proceedings were closed—a show of hands taken. The show was declared by the Mayor, who was a thorough Blue, in favour of the Right Hon. Audley Egerton and Randal Leslie, Esquire.

Cries of "No," "Shame," "Partial," &c.—a poll demanded on behalf of the other two candidates—and the crowd began to pour out of the hall.

Harley was the first who vanished, retreating by the private entrance. Egerton followed; Randal, lingering, Avenel came up and shook hands with him openly, but whispered, privately, "Meet me to-night in Lansmere Park, in the oak copse, about three hundred yards from the turnstile, at the town end of the park. We must see how to make all right. What a confounded humbug this has been!"

## CHAPTER XXVI.

If the vigour of Harley's address had taken by surprise both friend and foe, not one in that assembly—not even the conscience-stricken Egerton—felt its effect so deeply as the assailed and startled Leonard. He was at first perfectly stunned by sarcasms which he so ill deserved; nor was it till after the assembly had broken up, that Leonard could even conjecture the cause which had provoked the taunt and barbed its dart. Evidently Harley had learned (but learned only in order to misconceive and to wrong) Leonard's confession of love to Helen Digby. And now those implied accusations of disregard to the duties of common life not only galled the young man's heart, but outraged his honour. He felt the generous indignation of manhood. He must see Lord L'Estrange at once, and vindicate himself—vindicate Helen; for thus to accuse one, was tacitly to asperse the other.

Extricating himself from his own enthusiastic partisans, Leonard went straight on foot towards Lansmere House. The Park palings touched close upon the town, with a small turnstile for foot passengers. And as Leonard, availing himself of this entrance, had advanced some hundred yards or so through the park, suddenly, in the midst of that very copse in which Avenel had appointed to meet Leslie, he found himself face to face with Helen Digby herself.

Helen started, with a faint cry. But Leonard, absorbed in his own desire to justify both, hailed the sight, and did not pause to account for his appearance, nor to soothe her agitation.

"Miss Digby!" he exclaimed, throwing into his voice and manner that respect which often so cruelly divides the past familiarity from the present alienation—"Miss Digby, I rejoice to see you—rejoice to ask your permission to relieve myself from a charge, that in truth wounds even you, while levelled but at me. Lord L'Estrange has just implied, in public, that I—I—who owe him so much—who have honoured him so truly, that even the just resentment I now feel, half seems to me the ingratitude with which he charges me—has implied that—ah! Miss Digby, I can scarcely command words to say what it so humiliates me to have heard. But you know how false is all accusation that either of us could deceive our common benefactor. Suffer me to repeat to your guardian, what I presumed to say to you when we last met—what you answered—and state how I left your presence."

"Oh, Leonard! yes: clear yourself in his eyes. Go! Unjust that he is—ungenerous Lord L'Estrange!"

"Helen Digby!" cried a voice, close at hand. "Of whom do you speak thus?"

At the sound of that voice Helen and Leonard both turned, and beheld Violante standing before them, her young beauty rendered almost sublime by the noble anger that lit her eyes, glowed in her cheeks, animated her stately form.

"Is it you who thus speak of Lord L'Estrange? You—Helen Digby—*you!*"

From behind Violante now emerged Mr. Dale. "Softly, children," he said; and placing one hand on Violante's shoulder, he extended the other to Leonard. "What is this? Come hither to me, Leonard, and explain."

Leonard walked aside with the Parson, and in a few sentences gave vent to his swelling heart.

The Parson shared in Leonard's resentment; and having soon drawn from him all that had passed in his memorable interview with Helen, exclaimed—

"Enough! Do not yet seek Lord L'Estrange yourself; I am going to see him—I am here at his request. His summons, indeed, was for to-morrow; but the Squire having written me a hurried line, requesting me to meet him at Lansmere to-morrow and proceed with him afterwards in search of poor Frank, I thought I might have little time for communications with Lord L'Estrange, unless I forestalled his invitation and came to-day. Well that I did so. I only arrived an hour since—found he was gone to the Town Hall—and joined the young ladies in the Park. Miss Digby, thinking it natural that I might wish to say something in private to my old young friend Violante, walked a few paces in advance. Thus, fortunately, I chanced to be here, to receive your account, and I trust to remove misunderstanding. Lord L'Estrange must now be returned. I will go back to the house. You, meanwhile, return to the town, I beseech you. I will come to you afterwards at your inn. Your very appearance in these grounds—even the brief words that have passed between Helen and you—might only widen the breach between yourself and your benefactor. I cannot bear to anticipate this. Go back, I entreat you. I will explain all, and Lord L'Estrange shall right you! That *is*—that must be his intention!"

"*Is*—*must* be his intention—when he has just so wronged me!"

"Yes, yes," faltered the poor Parson, mindful of his promise to L'Estrange not to reveal his own interview with that nobleman, and yet not knowing otherwise how to explain or to soothe. But, still believing Leonard to be Harley's son and remembering all that Harley had so pointedly said of atonement, in apparent remorse for crime. Mr. Dale was wholly at a loss himself to understand why Harley should have thus prefaced atonement by an insult. Anxious, however, to prevent a meeting between Harley and Leonard while both were under the influence of such feelings towards each other, he made an effort over himself, and so well argued in favour of his own diplomacy, that Leonard reluctantly consented to wait for Mr. Dale's report.

"As to reparation or excuse," said he, proudly, "it must rest with Lord L'Estrange. I ask it not. Tell him only this—that if, the instant I heard that she whom I loved and held sacred for so many years was affianced to him, I resigned even the very wish to call her mine—if that were desertion of man's duties, I am guilty. If to have prayed night and day that she who would have blessed my lonely and toilsome life, may give some charm to his, not bestowed by his wealth and his greatness—if that were ingratitude, I am ungrateful; let him still condemn me. I pass out of his sphere—a thing that has crossed it a moment, and is gone. But Helen he must not blame—suspect—even by a thought. One word more. In this election—this strife for objects wholly foreign to all my habits, unsuited to my poverty, at war with aspirations so long devoted to fairer goals, though by obscurer paths—I obeyed but his will or whim; at a moment too when my whole soul sickened for repose and solitude. I had forced myself at last to take interest in what I had before loathed. But in every hope for the future—every stimulant to ambition—Lord L'Estrange's esteem still stood before me. Now, what do I here longer? All of his conduct, save his contempt for myself, is an enigma. And unless he repeat a wish, which I would fain still regard as a law, I retire from the contest he has embittered—I renounce the ambition he has poisoned; and, mindful of those humble duties which he implies that I disdain, I return to my own home."

The Parson nodded assent to each of these sentences, and Leonard, passing by Violante and Helen, with a salutation equally distant to both, retraced his steps towards the town.

Meanwhile Violante and Helen had also been in close conference, and that conference had suddenly endeared each to the other; for Helen, taken by surprise, agitated, overpowered, had revealed to Violante that confession of another attachment, which she had made to Lord L'Estrange—the rupture of her engagement with the latter. Violante saw that Harley was free. Harley, too, had promised to free herself. By a sudden flash of conviction, recalling his words, looks, she felt that she was beloved—deemed that honour alone (while either was yet shackled) had forbidden him to own that love. Violante stood a being transformed, "blushing celestial rosy red"—Heaven at her heart, joy in her eyes;—she loved so well, and she trusted so implicitly! Then from out the overflow of her own hope and bliss she poured forth such sweet comfort to Helen, that Helen's arm stole around her—cheek touched cheek—they were as sisters.

At another moment, Mr. Dale might have felt some amazement at the sudden affection which had sprung up between these young persons; for in his previous conversation with Violante, he had, as he thought, very artfully, and in a pleasant vein, sounded the young Italian as to her opinion of her fair friend's various good qualities—and Violante had rather shrunk from the title of "friend;" and though she had the magnanimity to speak with great praise of Helen, the praise did not sound cordial. But the good man was at this moment occupied in preparing his thoughts for his interview with Harley,—he joined the two girls in silence, and, linking an arm of each within his own, walked slowly towards the house. As he approached the terrace he observed Riccabocca and Randal pacing the gravel walk side by side.

Violante, pressing his arm, whispered, "Let us go round the other way; I would speak with you a few minutes undisturbed."

Mr. Dale, supposing that Violante wished to dispense with the presence of Helen, said to the latter, "My dear young lady, perhaps you will excuse me to Dr. Riccabocca—who is beckoning to me, and no doubt very much surprised to see me here—while I finish what I was saying to Violante when we were interrupted."

Helen left them, and Violante led the Parson round through the shrubbery, towards a side door in another wing of the house.

"What have you to say to me?" asked Mr. Dale, surprised that she remained silent.

"You will see Lord L'Estrange. Be sure that you convince him of Leonard's honour. A doubt of treachery so grieves his noble heart, that perhaps it may disturb his judgment."

"You seem to think very highly of the heart of this Lord L'Estrange, child!" said the Parson, in some surprise.

Violante blushed, but went on firmly, and with serious earnestness. "Some words which he—that is, Lord L'Estrange—said to me very lately, make me so glad that you are here—

that you will see him; for I know how good you are, and how wise—dear, dear Mr. Dale. He spoke as one who had received some grievous wrong, which had abruptly soured all his views of life. He spoke of retirement—solitude; he on whom his country has so many claims. I know not what he can mean—unless it be that his—his marriage with Helen Digby is broken off."

"Broken off! Is that so?"

"I have it from herself. You may well be astonished that she could even think of another after having known him!"

The Parson fixed his eyes very gravely on the young enthusiast. But though her cheek glowed, there was in her expression of face so much artless, open innocence, that Mr. Dale contented himself with a slight shake of the head, and a dry remark:

"I think it quite natural that Helen Digby should prefer Leonard Fairfield. A good girl, not misled by vanity and ambition; temptations of which it behoves us all to beware— nor least, perhaps, young ladies suddenly brought in contact with wealth and rank. As to this nobleman's merits, I know not yet whether to allow or to deny them; I reserve my judgment till after our interview. This is all you have to say to me?"

Violante paused a moment. "I cannot think," she said, half smiling—"I cannot think that the change that has occurred in him—for changed he is—that his obscure hints as to injury received, and justice to be done, are caused merely by his disappointment with regard to Helen. But you can learn that; learn if he be so very much disappointed. Nay, I think not!"

She slipped her slight hand from the Parson's arm, and darted away through the evergreens. Half concealed amidst the laurels, she turned back, and Mr. Dale caught her eye— half arch—half melancholy; its light came soft through a tear.

"I don't half like this," muttered the Parson; "I shall give Dr. Riccabocca a caution." So muttering he pushed open the side door, and finding a servant, begged admittance to Lord L'Estrange.

Harley at that moment was closeted with Levy, and his countenance was composed and fearfully stern. "So, so, by this time to-morrow," said he, "Mr. Egerton will be tricked out of his election by Mr. Randal Leslie—good! By this time to-morrow his ambition will be blasted by the treachery of his friends—good! By this time to-morrow the bailiffs will seize his person—ruined, beggared, pauper, and captive—all because he has trusted and been deceived—good! And if he blame you, prudent Baron Levy—if he accuse smooth Mr. Randal Leslie—forget not to say, 'We were both but the blind agents of your friend Harley L'Estrange. Ask *him* why you are so miserable a dupe.'"

"And might I now ask your lordship for one word of explanation?"

"No, sir!—it is enough that I have spared *you*. But you were never my friend; I have no revenge against a man whose hand I never even touched."

The Baron scowled, but there was a power about his tyrant that cowed him into actual terror. He resumed, after a pause—

"And though Mr. Leslie is to be member for Lansmere—thanks to you—you still desire that I should—"

"Do exactly as I have said. My plans now never vary a hair's breadth."

The groom of the chambers entered.

"My lord, the Reverend Mr. Dale wishes to know if you can receive him."

"Mr. Dale! he should have come to-morrow. Say that I did not expect him to-day: that I am unfortunately engaged till dinner, which will be earlier than usual. Show him into his room; he will have but little time to change his dress. By the way, Mr. Egerton dines in his own apartment."

## CHAPTER XXVII.

THE leading members of the Blue Committee were invited to dine at the Park, and the hour for the entertainment was indeed early, as there might be much need yet of active exertion on the eve of a poll in a contest expected to be so close, and in which the inflexible Hundred and Fifty "Waiters upon Providence" still reserved their very valuable votes.

The party was gay and animated, despite the absence of Audley Egerton, who, on the plea of increased indisposition, had shut himself up in his rooms the instant that he had returned from the Town Hall, and sent word to Harley that he was too unwell to join the party at dinner.

Randal was really in high spirits, despite the very equivocal success of his speech. What did it signify if a speech failed, provided the election was secure? He was longing for the appointment with Dick Avenel, which was to make "all right!" The Squire was to bring the money for the purchase of the coveted lands the next morning. Riccabocca had assured him, again and again, of Violante's hand. If ever Randal Leslie could be called a happy man, it was as he sate at that dinner taking wine with Mr. Mayor and Mr. Alderman, and looking, across the gleaming silver *plateau*, down the long vista into wealth and power.

The dinner was scarcely over, when Lord L'Estrange, in a brief speech, reminded his guests of the work still before them; and after a toast to the health of the future members for Lansmere, dismissed the Committee to their labours.

Levy made a sign to Randal, who followed the Baron to his own room.

"Leslie, your election is in some jeopardy. I find, from the conversation of those near me at dinner, that Egerton has made such way amongst the Blues by his speech, and they are so afraid of losing a man who does them so much credit, that the Committee men not only talk of withholding from you their second votes and of plumping Egerton, but of subscribing privately amongst themselves to win over that coy body of a Hundred and Fifty, upon whom, I know that Avenel counts in whatever votes he may be able to transfer to you."

"It would be very unhandsome in the Committee, which pretends to act for both of us, to plump Egerton," said Randal, with consistent anger. "But I don't think they can get those Hundred and Fifty without the most open and exorbitant bribery—an expense which Egerton will not pay, and which it would be very discreditable to Lord L'Estrange or his father to countenance."

"I told them flatly," returned Levy, "that, as Mr. Egerton's agent, I would allow no proceedings that might vitiate the election; but that I would undertake the management of these men myself; and I am going into the town in order to do so. I have also persuaded the leading Committee men to reconsider their determination to plump Egerton: they have decided to do as L'Estrange directs; and I know what he will say. You may rely on me," continued the Baron, who spoke with a dogged seriousness, unusual to his cynical temper, "to obtain for you the preference over Audley, if it be in my power to do so. Meanwhile, you should really see Avenel this very night."

"I have an appointment with him at ten o'clock; and, judging by his speech against Egerton, I cannot doubt on his aid to me, if convinced by his poll-books that he is not able to return both himself and his impertinent nephew. My speech, however sarcastically treated by Mr. Fairfield, must at least have disposed the Yellow party to vote rather for me than for a determined opponent like Egerton."

"I hope so; for your speech and Fairfield's answer have damaged you terribly with the Blues. However, your main hope rests on my power to keep those Hundred and Fifty rascals from splitting their votes on Egerton, and to induce them, by all means short of bringing myself before a Committee of the House of Commons for positive bribery—which would hurt most seriously my present social position—to give one vote to you. I shall tell them, as I have told the Committee, that Egerton is safe, and will pay nothing; but that you want the votes, and that I—in short, if they can be bought *upon tick*, I will buy them. Avenel, however, can serve you best here; for, as they are all Yellows at heart, they make no scruple of hinting that they want twice as much for voting Blue as they will take for voting Yellow. And Avenel being a townsman, and knowing their ways, could contrive to gain them, and yet not bribe."

RANDAL (shaking his head incredulously).—"Not bribe!"

LEVY.—"Pooh! Not bribe so as to be found out."

There was a knock at the door. A servant entered and presented Mr. Egerton's compliments to Baron Levy, with a request that the Baron would immediately come to his rooms for a few minutes.

"Well," said Levy, when the servant had withdrawn, "I must go to Egerton, and the instant I leave him I shall repair to the town. Perhaps I may pass the night there." So saying, he left Randal, and took his way to Audley's apartment.

"Levy," said the statesman, abruptly, upon the entrance of the Baron, "have you betrayed my secret—my first marriage —to Lord L'Estrange?"

"No, Egerton; on my honour, I have not betrayed it."

"You heard his speech! Did you not detect a fearful irony under his praises?—or is it but—but—my conscience?" added the proud man, through his set teeth.

"Really," said Levy, "Lord L'Estrange seemed to me to

select for his praise precisely those points in your character which any other of your friends would select for panegyric."

"Ay, any other of my friends!—What friends?" muttered Egerton, gloomily. Then, rousing himself, he added, in a voice that had none of its accustomed clear firmness of tone—"Your presence here in this house, Levy, surprised me, as I told you at the first; I could not conceive its necessity Harley urged you to come?—he with whom you are no favourite! You and he both said that your acquaintance with Richard Avenel would enable you to conciliate his opposition. I cannot congratulate you on your success."

"My success remains to be proved. The vehemence of his attack to-day may be but a feint to cover his alliance to-morrow."

Audley went on without notice of the interruption. "There is a change in Harley—to me and to all; a change, perhaps, not perceptible to others—but I have known him from a boy."

"He is occupied for the first time with the practical business of life.—That would account for a much greater change than you remark."

"Do you see him familiarly?— converse with him often?"

"No, and only on matters connected with the election. Occasionally, indeed, he consults me as to Randal Leslie, in whom, as your special *protégée*, he takes considerable interest."

"That, too, surprises me. Well, I am weary of perplexing myself.—This place is hateful; after to-morrow I shall leave it, and breathe in peace. You have seen the reports of the canvass; I have had no heart to inspect them. Is the election as safe as they say?"

"If Avenel withdraws his nephew, and the votes thus released split off to you, you are secure."

"And you think his nephew will be withdrawn? Poor young man!—defeat at his age, and with such talents, is hard to bear." Audley sighed.

"I *must* leave you now, if you have nothing important to say," said the Baron, rising. "I have much to do, as the election is yet to be won, and—to you the loss of it would be—"

"Ruin, I know. Well, Levy, it is, on the whole, to your advantage that I should not lose. There may be more to get from me yet. And, judging by the letters I received this morning, my position is rendered so safe by the absolute necessity of my party to keep me up, that the news of my pecuniary difficulties will not affect me so much as I once feared. Never was my career so free from obstacle—so clear towards the highest summit of ambition—never, in my day of ostentatious magnificence, as it is now, when I am prepared to shrink into a lodging, with a single servant."

"I am glad to hear it, and I am the more anxious to secure your election, upon which this career must depend, because—nay, I hardly like to tell you—"

"Speak on."

"I have been obliged, by a sudden rush on all my resources, to consign some of your bills and promissory notes to another, who, if your person should not be protected from arrest by parliamentary privilege, might be harsh and—"

"Traitor!" interrupted Egerton, fiercely, all the composed contempt with which he usually treated the usurer giving way, "say no more.—How could I ever expect otherwise! you have foreseen my defeat, and have planned my destruction. Presume no reply. Sir, begone from my presence!"

"You will find that you have worse friends than myself," said the Baron, moving to the door; "and if you are defeated —if your prospects for life are destroyed—I am the last man you will think of blaming. But I forgive your anger, and trust that to-morrow you will receive those explanations of my conduct which you are now in no temper to bear. I go to take care of the election."

Left alone, Audley's sudden passion seemed to forsake him.

He gathered together, in that prompt and logical precision which the habit of transacting public business bestows, all his thoughts, and sounded all his fears; and most vivid of every thought, and most intolerable of every fear, was the belief that the Baron had betrayed him to L'Estrange.

"I cannot bear this suspense," he cried aloud and abruptly. "I will see Harley myself. Open as he is, the very sound of his voice will tell me at once if I am a bankrupt even of human friendship. If *that* friendship be secure—if Harley yet clasp my hand with the same cordial warmth—all other oss shall not wring from my fortitude one complaint."

He rang the bell; his valet, who was waiting in the anteroom, appeared.

"Go and see if Lord L'Estrange is engaged. I would speak with him."

The servant came back in less than two minutes.

"I find that my lord is now particularly engaged, since he has given strict orders that he is not to be disturbed."

"Engaged!—on what?—whom with?"

"He is in his own room, sir, with a clergyman, who arrived, and dined here, to-day. I am told that he was formerly curate of Lansmere."

"Lansmere—curate! His name—his name! Not Dale?"

"Yes, sir, that is the name—the Reverend Mr. Dale."

"Leave me," said Audley in a faint voice. "Dale! the man who suspected Harley, who called on me in London, spoke of a child—my child—and sent me to find but another grave! He closeted with Harley—he!"

Audley sank back on his chair, and literally gasped for breath. Few men in the world had a more established reputation for the courage that dignifies manhood, whether the physical courage or the moral. But at that moment it was not grief, not remorse, that paralysed Audley—it was fear. The brave man saw before him, as a thing visible and menacing, the aspect of his own treachery—that crime of a coward; and into cowardice he was stricken. What had he to dread? Nothing save the accusing face of an injured friend—nothing but that. And what more terrible? The only being, amidst all his pomp of partisans, who survived to love him—the only being for whom the cold statesman felt the happy, living, human tenderness of private affection, lost to him for ever. He covered his face with both hands, and sate in suspense of something awful, as a child sits in the dark—the drops on his brow, and his frame trembling.

## CHAPTER XXVIII.

MEANWHILE Harley had listened to Mr. Dale's vindication of Leonard with cold attention.

"Enough," said he, at the close. "Mr. Fairfield (for so we will yet call him) shall see me to-night; and if apology be due to him, I will make it. At the same time, it shall be decided whether he continue this contest or retire. And now, Mr. Dale, it was not to hear how this young man wooed, or shrunk from wooing, my affianced bride, that I availed myself of your promise to visit me at this house. We agreed that the seducer of Nora Avenel deserved chastisement, and I promised that Nora Avenel's son should find a father. Both these assurances shall be fulfilled to-morrow. And you, sir," continued Harley, rising, his whole form gradually enlarged by the dignity of passion, "who wear the garb appropriated to the holiest office of Christian charity—you who have presumed to think that, before the beard had darkened my cheek, I could first betray the girl who had been reared under this roof, then abandon her—sneak like a dastard from the place in which my victim came to die—leave my own son, by the woman thus wronged, without thought, or care, through the perilous years of tempted youth, till I found him, by chance, an outcast in a desert more dread than Hagar's—you, sir, who have for long years thus judged of me, shall have the occasion to direct your holy anger towards the rightful head; and in me, you who have condemned the culprit, shall respect the judge."

Mr. Dale was at first startled, and almost awed, by this unexpected burst. But, accustomed to deal with the sternest and the darkest passions, his calm sense and his habit of authority over those whose souls were bared to him, nobly recovered from their surprise. "My lord," said he, "first, with humility I bow to your rebuke, and entreat your pardon for my erring, and, as you say, my uncharitable opinions. We, dwellers in a village, and obscure pastors of a humble flock—we, mercifully removed from temptation, are too apt, perhaps, to exaggerate its power over those whose lots are cast in that great world which has so many gates ever open to evil. This is my sole excuse if I was misled by what appeared to me strong circumstantial evidence. But forgive me again if I warn you not to fall into an error perhaps little lighter than my own. Your passion, when you cleared yourself from reproach, became you. But ah! my lord, when with that stern brow and those flashing eyes, you launched your menace upon another over whom you would constitute yourself the judge, forgetful of the divine precept, 'Judge not,' I felt that I was listening no longer to honest self-vindication—I felt that I was listening to fierce revenge."

"Call it revenge, or what you will," said Harley, with sullen firmness. "But I have been stung too deeply not to sting. Frank with all, till the last few days, I have ever been. Frank to you, at least, even now, this much I tell you: I pretend to no virtue in what I still hold to be justice; but no declamations nor homilies tending to prove that justice is sinful, will move my resolves. As man I have been outraged, and as man I will retaliate. The way and the mode—the true criminal and his fitting sentence—you will soon learn, sir. I have much to do to-night: forgive me if I adjourn for the present all further conference."

"No, no; do not dismiss me. There is something, in spite of your present language, which so commands my interest, I see that there has been so much suffering where there is now so much wrath, that I would save you from the suffering worse than all—remorse. O pause, my dear lord, pause and answer me but two questions; then I will leave your after course to yourself."

"Say on, sir," said Lord L'Estrange, touched, and with respect.

"First, then, analyse you own feelings. Is this anger merely to punish an offender and to right the living?—for who can pretend to right the dead? Or is there not some private hate that stirs, and animates, and confuses all?"

Harley remained silent. Mr. Dale renewed.

"You loved this poor girl. Your language even now reveals it. You speak of treachery: perhaps you had a rival who deceived you; I know not—guess not, whom. But if you would strike the rival, must you not wound the innocent son? And, in presenting Nora's child to his father, as you pledge yourself to do, can you mean some cruel mockery that, under seeming kindness, implies some unnatural vengeance?"

"You read well the heart of man," said Harley; "and I have owned to you that I am but man. Pass on; you have another question."

"And one more solemn and important. In my world of a village, revenge is a common passion; it is the sin of the uninstructed. The savage deems it noble! but Christ's religion, which is the sublime Civiliser, emphatically condemns it. Why? Because religion ever seeks to ennoble man; and nothing so debases him as revenge. Look into your own heart, and tell me whether, since you have cherished this passion, you have not felt all sense of right and wrong confused—have not felt that whatever would before have seemed to you mean and base, appears now but just means to your heated end. Revenge is ever a hypocrite—rage, at least, strikes with the naked sword; but revenge, stealthy and patient, conceals the weapon of the assassin. My lord, your colour changes. What is your answer to my question?"

"Oh," exclaimed Harley, with a voice thrilling in its mournful anguish, "it is not since I have cherished the revenge that I am changed—that right and wrong grow dark to me—that hypocrisy seems the atmosphere fit for earth. No; it is since the discovery that demands the vengeance. It is useless, sir," he continued, impetuously—"useless to argue with me. Were I to sit down patient and impotent, under the sense of the wrong which I have received, I should feel, indeed, that debasement which you ascribe to the gratification of what you term revenge. I should never regain the self-esteem which the sentiment of power now restores to me—I should feel as if the whole world could perceive and jeer at my meek humiliation. I know not why I have said so much—why I have betrayed to you so much of my secret mind, and stooped to vindicate my purpose. I never meant it. Again I say, we must close this conference." Harley here walked to the door, and opened it significantly.

"One word more, Lord L'Estrange—but one. You will not hear me. I am a comparative stranger, but you have a friend, a friend dear and intimate, now under the same roof. Will you consent, at least, to take counsel of Mr. Audley Egerton? None can doubt his friendship for you; none can doubt, that whatever he advise will be that which best becomes your honour. What, my lord, you hesitate?—you feel ashamed to confide to your dearest friend a purpose which his mind would condemn? Then I will seek him—I will implore him to save you from what can but entail repentance."

"Mr. Dale, I must forbid you to see Mr. Egerton. What has passed between us ought to be as sacred to you as a priest of Rome holds confession. This much, however, I will say to content you: I promise that I will do nothing that shall render me unworthy of Mr. Audley Egerton's friendship, or which his fine sense of honour shall justify him in blaming. Let that satisfy you."

"Ah, my lord," cried Mr. Dale, pausing irresolute at the doorway, and seizing Harley's hand, "I should indeed be satisfied if you would submit yourself to higher counsel than mine—than Mr. Egerton's—than man's. Have you never felt the efficacy of prayer?"

"My life has been wasted," replied Harley, "and I dare not, therefore, boast that I have found prayer efficacious. But, so far back as I can remember, it has at least been my habit to pray to Heaven, night and morning, until, at least—until—" The natural and obstinate candour of the man forced out the last words, which implied reservation. He stopped short.

"Until you have cherished revenge? You have not dared

to pray since? Oh! reflect what evil there is within us, when we dare not come before Heaven—dare not pray for what we wish. You are moved—I leave you to your own thoughts."

Harley inclined his head, and the Parson passed him by, and left him alone—startled indeed; but was he softened?

As Mr. Dale hurried along the corridor, much agitated, Violante stole from a recess formed by a large bay window, and, linking her arm in his, said anxiously, but timidly: "I have been waiting for you, dear Mr. Dale; and so long! You have been with Lord L'Estrange?"

"Well!"

"Why do you not speak? You have left him comforted—happier?"

"Happier! No."

"What!" said Violante, with a look of surprise, and a sadness not unmixed with petulance in her quick tone. "What! does he then so grieve that Helen prefers another?"

Despite the grave emotions that disturbed his mind, Mr. Dale was struck by Violante's question, and the voice in which it was said. He loved her tenderly. "Child, child," said he, "I am glad that Helen has escaped Lord L'Estrange. Beware, oh beware! how he excite any gentler interest in yourself. He is a dangerous man—more dangerous for glimpses of a fine original nature. He may well move the heart of the innocent and inexperienced, for he has strangely crept into mine. But *his* heart is swollen with pride, and ire, and malice."

"You mistake: it is false!" cried Violante, impetuously. "I cannot believe one word that would asperse him who has saved my father from a prison, or from death. You have not treated him gently. He fancies he has been wronged by Leonard—received ingratitude from Helen. He has felt the sting in proportion to his own susceptible and generous heart, and you have chided where you should have soothed. Poor Lord L'Estrange! And you have left him still indignant and unhappy!"

"Foolish girl! I have left him meditating sin; I have left him afraid to pray; I have left him on the brink of some design—I know not what—but which involves more than Leonard in projects of revenge; I have left him so, that if his heart be really susceptible and generous, he will wake from wrath to be the victim of long and unavailing remorse. If your father has influence over him, tell Dr. Riccabocca what I say, and bid him seek, and in his turn save, the man who saved himself. He has not listened to religion—he may be more docile to philosophy. I cannot stay here longer—I must go to Leonard."

Mr. Dale broke from Violante and hurried down the corridor; Violante stood on the same spot, stunned and breathless. Harley on the brink of some strange sin—Harley to wake the victim of remorse—Harley to be saved, as he had saved her father! Her breast heaved—her colour went and came—her eyes were raised—her lips murmured. She advanced with soft footsteps up the corridor—she saw the lights gleaming from Harley's room, and suddenly they were darkened, as the inmate of the room shut to the door, with angry and impatient hand.

An outward act often betrays the inward mind. As Harley had thus closed the door, so had he sought to shut his heart from the intrusion of softer and holier thoughts. He had turned to his hearthstone, and stood on it, resolved and hardened. The man who had loved with such pertinacious fidelity for so many years, could not at once part with hate. A passion once admitted to his breast, clung to it with such rooted force! But woe, woe to thee, Harley L'Estrange if to-morrow at this hour thou stand at the hearthstone, thy designs accomplished, knowing that, in the fulfilment of thy blind will, thou hast met falsehood with falsehood, and deception with deceit! What though those designs now seem to consummate so just, so appropriate, so exquisite a revenge—seem to thee the sole revenge wit can plan and civilised life allow—wilt thou ever wash from thy memory the stain that will sully thine honour? Thou, too, professing friendship still, and masking perfidy under smiles! Grant that the wrong be great as thou deem it—be ten times greater—the sense of thy meanness, O gentleman and soldier, will bring the blush to thy cheek in the depth of thy solitude. Thou, who now thinkest others unworthy a trustful love, wilt feel thyself for ever unworthy theirs. Thy seclusion will know not repose. The dignity of man will forsake thee. Thy proud eye will quail from the gaze. Thy step will no longer spurn the earth that it treads on. He who has once done a base thing is never again wholly reconciled to honour. And woe—thrice woe, if thou learn too late that thou hast exaggerated thy fancied wrong: that there is excuse, where thou seest none; that thy friend may have erred, but that his error is venial compared to thy fancied retribution!

Thus, however, in the superb elation of conscious power, though lavished on a miserable object—a terrible example of what changes one evil and hateful thought, cherished to the exclusion of all others, can make in the noblest nature—stood, on the hearth of his fathers, and on the abyss of a sorrow and a shame from which there could be no recall, the determined and scornful man.

A hand is on the door, he does not hear it; a form passes the threshold—he does not see it; a light step pause—a soft eye gazes. Deaf and blind still to both.

Violante came on, gathering courage, and stood at the hearth, by his side.

## CHAPTER XXIX.

"Lord L'Estrange—noble friend!"

"You!—and here—Violante? Is it I whom you seek? For what? Good heavens! what has happened? Why are you so pale?—why tremble?"

"Have you forgiven Helen?" asked Violante, beginning with evasive question, and her cheek was pale no more.

"Helen—the poor child! I have nothing in her to forgive, much to thank her for. She has been frank and honest."

"And Leonard—whom I remember in my childhood—you have forgiven him?"

"Fair mediator," said Harley, smiling, though coldly, "happy is the man who deceives another; all plead for him. And if the man deceived cannot forgive, no one will sympathise or excuse."

"But Leonard did not deceive you?"

"Yes, from the first. It is a long tale, and not to be told to you. But I cannot forgive him."

"Adieu! my lord. Helen must, then, still be very dear to you!" Violante turned away. Her emotion was so artless, her very anger so charming, that the love, against which, in the prevalence of his later and darker passions, he had so sternly struggled, rushed back upon Harley's breast; but it came only in storm.

"Stay, but talk not of Helen!" he exclaimed. "Ah! if Leonard's sole offence had been what you appear to deem it, do you think I could feel resentment? No; I should have

gratefully hailed the hand that severed a rash and ungenial
tie. I would have given my ward to her lover with such a
dower as it suits my wealth to bestow. But his offence dates
from his very birth. To bless and to enrich the son of a man
who—Violante, listen to me. We may soon part, and for
ever. Others may misconstrue my actions; you, at least,
shall know from what just principle they spring. There was
a man whom I singled out of the world as more than a
brother. In the romance of my boyhood I saw one who
dazzled my fancy, captivated my heart. It was a dream of
Beauty breathed into waking life. I loved—I believed myself beloved. I confided all my heart to this friend—this
more than brother; he undertook to befriend and to aid my
suit. On that very pretext he first saw this ill-fated girl;—
saw—betrayed—destroyed her;—left me ignorant that her
love, which I had thought mine, had been lavished so wildly
on another;—left me to believe that my own suit she had fled,
but in generous self-sacrifice—for she was poor and humbly
born; that—oh, vain idiot that I was!—the self-sacrifice had
been too strong for a young human heart, which had broken
in the struggle;—left me to corrode my spring of life in
remorse;—clasped my hand in mocking comfort:—smiled at
my tears of agony—not one tear himself for his own poor
victim! And suddenly, not long since, I learned all this.
And, in the father of Leonard Fairfield, you behold the man
who has poisoned all the well-spring of joy to me. You
weep! O, Violante!—the Past he has blighted and embittered
—*that* I could forgive; but the Future is blasted too. For,
just ere this treason was revealed to me, I had begun to awake
from the torpor of my dreary penance, to look with fortitude
towards the duties I had slighted—to own that the pilgrimage
before me was not barren. And then, oh then, I felt that all
love was not buried in a grave. I felt that you, had fate so
granted, might have been all to my manhood which youth
only saw through the delusion of its golden mists. True, I
was then bound to Helen; true, that honour to her might forbid me all hope. But still, even to know that my heart was
not all ashes—that I could love again—that that glorious
power and privilege of our being was still mine, seemed to
me so heavenly sweet. But then this revelation of falsehood burst on me, and all truth seemed blotted from the universe. I am freed from Helen; ah, freed, forsooth—because
not even rank and wealth, and benefits and confiding tenderness, could bind to me one human heart! Free from her; but

between me and your fresh nature stands Suspicion as an Upas tree. Not a hope that would pass through the tainted air, and fly to you, but falls dead under the dismal boughs. *I* love! Ha, ha! I—*I*, whom the past has taught the impossibility to be loved again. No: if those soft lips murmured 'Yes' to the burning prayer that, had I been free but two short weeks ago, would have rushed from the frank deeps of my heart, I should but imagine that you deceived yourself—a girl's first fleeting delusive fancy—nothing more! Were you my bride, Violante, I should but debase your bright nature by my own curse of distrust. At each word of tenderness, my heart would say, 'How long will this last?—when will the deception come?' Your beauty, your gifts, would bring me but jealous terror; eternally I should fly from the Present to the Future, and say, 'These hairs will be grey, while flattering youth will surround her in the zenith of her charms.' Why then do I hate and curse my foe? Why do I resolve upon revenge? I comprehend it now. I knew that there was something more imperious than the ghost of the Past that urged me on. Gazing on you, I feel that it was the dim sense of a mighty and priceless loss; it is not the dead Nora—it is the living Violante. Look not at me with those reproachful eyes; they cannot reverse my purpose; they cannot banish suspicion from my sickened soul; they cannot create a sunshine in the midst of this ghastly twilight. Go, go; leave me to the sole joy that bequeathes no disappointment—the sole feeling that unites me to social man; leave me to my revenge."

"Revenge! Oh, cruel!" exclaimed Violante, laying her hand on his arm. "And in revenge, it is your own life that you will risk!"

"My life, simple child! This is no contest of life against life. Could I bear to all the world my wrongs for their ribald laughter, I should only give to my foe the triumph to pity my frenzy—to shun the contest; or grant it, if I could find a second—and then fire in the air. And all the world would say, 'Generous Egerton—soul of honour!'"

"Egerton, Mr. Egerton! He cannot be this foe? It is not on him you can design revenge?—you who spend all your hours in serving his cause—you to whom he trusts so fondly—you who leant yesterday on his shoulder, and smiled so cheeringly in his face?"

"Did I? Hypocrisy against hypocrisy—snare against snare: *that* is my revenge!"

"Harley, Harley! Cease, cease!"

The storm of passion rushed on unheeding.

"I seem to promote his ambition, but to crush it into the mire. I have delivered him from the gentler gripe of an usurer, so that he shall hold at my option alms or a prison—"

"Friend, friend! Hush, hush!"

"I have made the youth he has reared and fostered into treachery like his own (your father's precious choice—Randal Leslie), mine instrument in the galling lesson how ingratitude can sting. His very son shall avenge the mother, and be led to his father's breast as victor, with Randal Leslie, in the contest that deprives sire and benefactor of all that makes life dear to ambitious egotism. And if, in the breast of Audley Egerton, there can yet lurk one memory of what I was to him and to truth, not his least punishment will be the sense that his own perfidy has so changed the man whose very scorn of falsehood has taught him to find in itself fraud the power of retribution."

"If this be not a terrible dream!" murmured Violante, recoiling, it is not your foe alone that you will deprive of all that makes life dear. Act thus—and what, in the future, is left to me?"

"To you! Oh, never fear. I may give Randal Leslie a triumph over his patron, but in the same hour I will unmask his villany, and sweep him for ever from your path. What in the future is left to you?—your birthright and your native land; hope, joy, love, felicity. Could it be possible that in the soft but sunny fancy which plays round the heart of maiden youth, but still sends no warmth into its deeps—could it be possible that you had honoured me with a gentler thought, it will pass away, and you will be the pride and delight of one of your own years, to whom the vista of Time is haunted by no chilling spectres—one who can look upon that lovely face, and not turn away to mutter—'Too fair, too fair for me!'"

"Oh agony!" exclaimed Violante, with sudden passion. "In my turn hear me. If, as you promise, I am released from the dreadful thought that he, at whose touch I shudder, can claim this hand, my choice is irrevocably made. The altars which await me will not be those of a human love. But oh, I implore you—by all the memories of your own life, hitherto, if sorrowful, unsullied—by the generous interest you yet profess for me, whom you will have twice saved from a danger to which death were mercy—leave, oh leave to me the right to regard your image as I have done from the first dawn of childhood. Leave me the right to honour and revere it. Let not an act accompanied with a meanness—oh that I should say the word!—a meanness and a cruelty that give the lie to your whole life—make even a grateful remembrance of you an unworthy sin. When I kneel within the walls that divide me from the world, oh let me think that I can pray for you as the noblest being that the world contains! Hear me! hear me!"

"Violante!" murmured Harley, his whole frame heaving with emotion, "bear with me. Do not ask of me the sacrifice of what seems to me the cause of manhood itself—to sit down, meek and patient, under a wrong that debases me, with the consciousness that all my life I have been the miserable dupe to affections I deemed so honest—to regrets that I believed so holy. Ah! I should feel more mean in my pardon than you can think me in revenge! Were it an acknowledged enemy, I could open my arms to him at your bidding; but the perfidious friend!—ask it not. My check burns at the thought, as at the stain of a blow. Give me but to-morrow— one day—I demand no more—wholly to myself and to the past, and mould me for the future as you will. Pardon, pardon the ungenerous thoughts that extended distrust to *you*. I retract them; they are gone—dispelled before those touching words, those ingenuous eyes. At your feet, Violante, I repent and I implore! Your father himself shall banish your sordid suitor. Before this hour to-morrow you will be free. Oh then, then! will you not give me this hand to guide me again into the paradise of my youth? Violante, it is in vain to wrestle with myself—to doubt—to reason—to be wisely fearful—I love, I love you. I trust again in virtue and faith. I place my fate in your keeping."

If at times Violante may appear to have ventured beyond the limit of strict maiden bashfulness, much may be ascribed to her habitual candour, her solitary rearing, and remoteness from the world—the very innocence of her soul, and the warmth of heart which Italy gives its daughters. But now that sublimity of thought and purpose which pervaded her nature, and required only circumstances to develop, made her superior to all the promptings of love itself. Dreams realised which she had scarcely dared to own—Harley free— Harley at her feet;—all the woman struggling at her heart, mantling in her blushes,—still stronger than love—stronger than the joy of being loved again—was the heroic will—will to save him—who in all else ruled her existence—from the eternal degradation to which passion had blinded his own confused and warring spirit.

Leaving one hand in his impassioned clasp, as he still knelt before her, she raised on high the other, "Ah!" she said, scarce audibly—"ah! if Heaven vouchsafe me the proud and blissful privilege to be allied to your fate, to minister to your happiness, never should I know one fear of your distrust. No time, no change, no sorrow—not even the loss of your affection—could make me forfeit the right to remember that you had once confided to me a heart so noble. But"—Here her voice rose in its tone, and the glow fled from her cheek— "But, O Thou the Ever Present, hear and receive the solemn vow. If to me he refuse to sacrifice the sin that would debase him, that sin be the barrier between us evermore. And may my life, devoted to Thy service, atone for the hour in which he belied the nature he received from Thee. Harley, release me! I have spoken: firm as yourself, I leave the choice to you."

"You judge me harshly," said Harley, rising, with sullen anger. "But at least I have not the meanness to sell what I hold as justice, though the bribe may include my last hope of happiness."

"Meanness! Oh unhappy, beloved Harley!" exclaimed Violante, with such a gush of exquisite reproachful tenderness, that it thrilled him as the voice of the parting guardian angel. "Meanness! But it is that from which I implore you to save yourself. You cannot judge, you cannot see. You are dark, dark. Lost Christian that you are, what worse than heathen darkness to feign the friendship the better to betray—to punish falsehood by becoming yourself so false— to accept the confidence even of your bitterest foe, and then to sink below his own level in deceit? And oh—worse, worse than all—to threaten that a son—son of the woman you professed to love—should swell your vengeance against a father. No! it was not you that said this—it was the Fiend!"

"Enough!" exclaimed Harley, startled, conscience-stricken, and rushing into resentment, in order to escape the sense of shame. "Enough! you insult the man you professed to honour."

"I honoured the prototype of gentleness and valour. I honoured one who seemed to me to clothe with life every grand and generous image that is born from the souls of poets. Destroy that ideal, and you destroy the Harley whom I honoured. He is dead to me for ever. I will mourn for him as his widow—faithful to his memory—weeping over the thought of what he was." Sobs choked her voice; but as Harley, once more melted, sprang forward to regain her side, she escaped with a yet quicker movement, gained the door, and darting down the corridor, vanished from his sight.

Harley stood still one moment, thoroughly irresolute—nay, almost subdued. Then sternness, though less rigid than before, gradually came to his brow. The demon had still its hold in the stubborn and marvellous pertinacity with which the man clung to all that once struck root at his heart. With a sudden impulse, that still withheld decision, yet spoke of sore-shaken purpose, he strode to his desk, drew from it Nora's manuscript, and passed from his room.

Harley had meant never to have revealed to Audley the secret he had gained, until the moment when revenge was consummated. He had contemplated no vain reproach. His wrath would have spoken forth in deeds, and then a word would have sufficed as the key to all. Willing, perhaps, to hail some extenuation of perfidy, though the possibility of such extenuation he had never before admitted, he determined on the interview which he had hitherto so obstinately shunned, and went straight to the room in which Audley Egerton still sate solitary and fearful.

## CHAPTER XXX.

EGERTON heard the well-known step advancing near and nearer up the corridor—heard the door open and reclose—and he felt, by one of those strange and unaccountable instincts which we call forebodings, that the hour he had dreaded for so many secret years had come at last. He nerved his courage, withdrew his hands from his face, and rose in silence. No less silent, Harley stood before him. The two men gazed on each other; you might have heard their breathing.

"You have seen Mr. Dale?" said Egerton, at length. "You know—"

"All!" said Harley, completing the arrested sentence.

Audley drew a long sigh. "Be it so; but no, Harley; you

deceive yourself; you cannot know all, from any one living, save myself."

"My knowledge comes from the dead," answered Harley, and the fatal memoir dropped from his hand upon the table. The leaves fell with a dull, low sound, mournful and faint as might be the tread of a ghost, if the tread gave sound. They fell, those still confessions of an obscure, uncomprehended life, amidst letters and documents eloquent of the strife that was then agitating millions, the fleeting, turbulent fears and hopes that torture parties and perplex a nation; the stormy business of practical public life, so remote from individual love and individual sorrow.

Egerton's eye saw them fall. The room was but partially lighted. At the distance where he stood, he did not recognise the characters, but involuntarily he shivered, and involuntarily drew near.

"Hold yet awhile," said Harley. "I produce my charge, and then I leave you to dispute the only witness that I bring. Audley Egerton, you took from me the gravest trust one man can confide to another. You knew how I loved Leonora Avenel. I was forbidden to see and urge my suit; you had the access to her presence which was denied to myself. I prayed you to remove scruples that I deemed too generous, and to woo her not to dishonour, but to be my wife. Was it so? Answer."

"It is true," said Audley, his hand clenched at his heart.

"You saw her whom I thus loved—her thus confided to your honour. You wooed her for yourself. Is it so?"

"Harley, I deny it not. Cease here. I accept the penalty; —I resign your friendship;—I quit your roof;—I submit to your contempt;—I dare not implore your pardon. Cease; let me go hence, and soon!"—The strong man gasped for breath.

Harley looked at him steadfastly, then turned away his eyes, and went on. "Nay," said he, is that ALL? You wooed her for yourself—you won her. Account to me for that life which you wrenched from mine. You are silent. I will take on myself your task; you took that life and destroyed it."

"Spare me, spare me!"

"What was the fate of her who seemed so fresh from heaven when these eyes beheld her last? A broken heart—a dishonoured name—an early doom—a forgotten gravestone."

"No, no—forgotten—no!"

"Not forgotten! Scarce a year passed, and you were

married to another. I aided you to form those nuptials which secured your fortunes. You have had rank, and power, and fame. Peers call you the type of English gentlemen. Priests hold you as a model of Christian honour. Strip the mask, Audley Egerton; let the world know you for what you are!"

Egerton raised his head, and folded his arms calmly; but he said, with a melancholy humility—"I bear all from you; it is just. Say on."

"You took from me the heart of Nora Avenel. You abandoned her—you destroyed. And her memory cast no shadow over your daily sunshine; while over my thoughts—over my life—oh, Egerton—Audley, Audley—how could you have deceived me thus!" Here the inherent tenderness under all this hate—the fount imbedded under the hardening stone —broke out. Harley was ashamed of his weakness, and hurried on.

"Deceived—not for an hour, a day, but through blighted youth, through listless manhood—you suffered me to nurse the remorse that should have been your own;—her life slain, mine wasted; and shall neither of us have revenge?"

"Revenge! Ah, Harley, you have had it!"

"No, but I await it! Not in vain from the charnel have come to me the records I produce. And whom did fate select to discover the wrongs of the mother?—whom appoint as her avenger? Your son—your own son; your abandoned, nameless son!"

"Son—son!"

"Whom I delivered from famine, or from worse; and who, in return, has given into my hands the evidence which proclaims in you the perjured friend of Harley L'Estrange, and the fraudulent seducer, under mock marriage forms—worse than all franker sin—of Leonora Avenel."

"It is false—false!" exclaimed Egerton, all his stateliness and all his energy restored to him. "I forbid you to speak thus to me. I forbid you by one word to sully the memory of my lawful wife."

"Ah!" said Harley, startled. "Ah! false! prove *that*, and revenge is over! Thank Heaven!"

"Prove it! What so easy? And wherefore have I delayed the proof—wherefore concealed, but from tenderness to you —dread, too—a selfish but human dread—to lose in you the sole esteem that I covet;—the only mourner who would have shed one tear over the stone inscribed with some lying epitaph, in which it will suit a party purpose to proclaim the gratitude of a nation. Vain hope. I resign it! But you spoke of a son. Alas, alas! you are again deceived. I heard that I had a son—years, long years ago. I sought him, and found a grave. But bless you, Harley, if you succoured one whom you even erringly suspect to be Leonora's child!" He stretched forth his hands as he spoke.

"Of your son we will speak later," said Harley, strangely softened. "But before I say more of him, let me ask you to explain—let me hope that you can extenuate what—"

"You are right," interrupted Egerton with eager quickness. "You would know from my own lips at last the plain tale of my own offence against you. It is due to both. Patiently hear me out."

Then Egerton told all; his own love for Nora—his struggles against what he felt as treason to his friend—his sudden discovery of Nora's love for him;—on that discovery, the overthrow of all his resolutions; their secret marriage—their separation; Nora's flight, to which Audley still assigned but her groundless vague suspicion that their nuptials had not been legal, and her impatience of his own delay in acknowledging the rite.

His listener interrupted him here with a few questions; the clear and prompt replies to which enabled Harley to detect Levy's plausible perversion of the facts; and he vaguely guessed the cause of the usurer's falsehood, in the criminal passion which the ill-fated bride had inspired.

"Egerton," said Harley, stifling with an effort his own wrath against the vile deceiver both of wife and husband, "if, on reading those papers, you find that Leonora had more excuse for her suspicions and flight than you now deem, and discover perfidy in one to whom you trusted your secret, leave his punishment to Heaven. All that you say convinces me more and more that we cannot even see through the cloud, much less guide the thunderbolt. But proceed."

Audley looked suprised and startled, and his eye turned wistfully towards the papers; but after a short pause he continued his recital. He came to Nora's unexpected return to her father's house—her death—his conquest of his own grief, that he might spare Harley the abrupt shock of learning her decease. He had torn himself from the dead, in remorseful sympathy with the living. He spoke of Harley's illness, so nearly fatal—repeated Harley's jealous words, "that he would rather mourn Nora's death, than take comfort from the thought that she had loved another." He spoke of his journey to the village where Mr. Dale had told him Nora's child was placed—"and, hearing that child and mother were alike gone, whom now could I right by acknowledging a bond that I feared would so wring your heart?" Audley again paused a moment, and resumed in short, nervous, impressive sentences. This cold, austere man of the world for the first time bared his heart—unconscious, perhaps, that he did so—unconscious that he revealed how deeply, amidst state cares and public distinctions, he had felt the absence of affections — how mechanical was that outer circle in the folds of life which is called "a career"—how valueless wealth had grown— none to inherit it. Of his gnawing and progressive disease alone he did not speak; he was too proud and too masculine to appeal to pity for physical ills. He reminded Harley how often, how eagerly, year after year, month after month, he had urged his friend to rouse himself from mournful dreams, devote his native powers to his country, or seek the surer felicity of domestic ties. "Selfish in these attempts I might be," said Egerton; "it was only if I saw you restored to happiness that I could believe you could calmly hear my explanation of the past, and on the floor of some happy home grant me your forgiveness. I longed to confess, and I dared not. Often have the words rushed to my lips—as often some chance sentence from you repelled me. In a word, with you were so entwined all the thoughts and affections of my youth —even those that haunted the grave of Nora—that I could not bear to resign your friendship, and, surrounded by the esteem and honour of a world I cared not for, to meet the contempt of your reproachful eye."

Amidst all that Audley said—amidst all that admitted of no excuse—two predominant sentiments stood clear, in unmistakable and touching pathos. Remorseful regret for the lost Nora—and self-accusing, earnest, almost feminine tenderness for the friend he had deceived. Thus, as he continued to speak, Harley more and more forgot even the remembrance of his own guilty and terrible interval of hate; the gulf that had so darkly yawned between the two closed up, leaving them still standing, side by side, as in their schoolboy days. But he remained silent, listening—shading his face from Audley, and as if under some soft but enthralling spell, till Egerton thus closed—

"And now, Harley, all is told. You spoke of revenge?"

"Revenge!" muttered Harley, starting.

"And believe me," continued Egerton, "were revenge in

your power, I should rejoice at it as an atonement. To receive an injury in return for that which, first from youthful passion, and afterwards from the infirmity of purpose that concealed the wrong, I have inflicted upon you—why, that would soothe my conscience, and raise my lost self-esteem. The sole revenge you can bestow takes the form which most humiliates me;—to revenge, is to pardon."

Harley groaned; and still hiding his face with one hand, stretched forth the other, but rather with the air of one who entreats than who accords forgiveness. Audley took and pressed the hand thus extended.

"And now, Harley, farewell. With the dawn I leave this house. I cannot now accept your aid in this election. Levy shall announce my resignation. Randal Leslie, if you so please it, may be returned in my stead. He has abilities which, under safe guidance, may serve his country; and I have no right to reject, from vain pride, whatever will promote the career of one whom I undertook, and have failed, to serve."

"Ay, ay," muttered Harley; "think not of Randal Leslie; think but of your son."

"My son! But are you sure that he still lives? You smile; you—you—oh, Harley—I took from you the mother—give to me the son; break my heart with gratitude. Your revenge is found!"

Lord L'Estrange rose with a sudden start—gazed on Audley for a moment—irresolute, not from resentment, but from shame. At that moment he was the man humbled; he was the man who feared reproach, and who needed pardon. Audley, not divining what was thus passing in Harley's breast, turned away.

"You think that I ask too much; and yet all that I can give to the child of my love and the heir of my name, is the worthless blessing of a ruined man. Harley, I say no more. I dare not add, 'You too loved his mother! and with a deeper and a nobler love than mine.'" He stopped short, and Harley flung himself on his breast.

"Me—me—pardon me, Audley! Your offence has been slight to mine. You have told me your offence; never can I name to you my own. Rejoice that we have both to exchange forgiveness, and in that exchange we are equal still, Audley—brother still. Look up—look up; think that we are boys now as we were once;—boys who have had their wild quarrel—and who, the moment it is over, feel dearer to each other than before."

"Oh, Harley, this *is* revenge! It strikes home," murmured Egerton, and tears gushed fast from eyes that could have gazed unwinking on the rack. The clock struck; Harley sprang forward.

"I have time yet," he cried. "Much to do and to undo. You are saved from the grasp of Levy—your election will be won—your fortunes in much may be restored—you have before you honours not yet achieved—your career as yet is scarce begun—your son will embrace you to-morrow. Let me go—your hand again! Ah, Audley, we shall be so happy yet!"

## CHAPTER XXXI.

"THERE is a hitch," said Dick, pithily, when Randal joined him in the oak copse at ten o'clock. "Life is full of hitches."

RANDAL.—"The art of life is to smoothe them away. What hitch is this, my dear Avenel?"

DICK.—"Leonard has taken huff at certain expressions of Lord L'Estrange's at the nomination to-day, and talks of retiring from the contest."

RANDAL, (with secret glee.)—"But his resignation would smoothe a hitch—not create one. The votes promised to him would thus be freed, and go to—"

DICK.—"The Right Honourable Red-Tapist!"

RANDAL.—"Are you serious?"

DICK.—"As an undertaker! The fact is, there are two parties among the Yellows as there are in the Church—High Yellow and Low Yellow. Leonard has made great way with the High Yellows, and has more influence with them than I; and the High Yellows infinitely preferred Egerton to yourself. They say 'Politics apart, he would be an honour to the borough.' Leonard is of the same opinion; and if he retires, I don't think I could coax either him or the Highflyers to make you any the better by his resignation."

RANDAL.—"But surely your nephew's sense of gratitude to you would induce him not to go against your wishes?"

DICK.—"Unluckily, the gratitude is all the other way. It is I who am under obligations to him—not he to me. As for Lord L'Estrange, I can't make head or tail of his real intentions; and why he should have attacked Leonard in that way, puzzles me more than all, for he wished Leonard to stand. And Levy has privately informed me that, in spite of my lord's friendship for the Right Honourable, you are the man he desires to secure."

RANDAL.—"He has certainly shown that desire throughout the whole canvass."

DICK.—"I suspect that the borough-mongers have got a seat for Egerton elsewhere; or, perhaps, should his party come in again, he is to be pitchforked into the Upper House."

RANDAL, (smiling.)—"Ah, Avenel, you are so shrewd; you see through everything. I will also add, that Egerton wants some short respite from public life in order to nurse his health and attend to his affairs, otherwise I could not even contemplate the chance of the electors preferring me to him, without a pang."

DICK.—"Pang!—stuff—considerable. The oak trees don't hear us! You want to come into Parliament, and no mistake. If I am the man to retire—as I always proposed, and had got Leonard to agree to, before this confounded speech of L'Estrange's—come into Parliament you will, for the Low Yellows I can twist round my finger, provided the High Yellows will not interfere; in short, I could transfer to you votes promised to me, but I can't answer for those promised to Leonard. Levy tells me you are to marry a rich girl, and will have lots of money; so, of course, you will pay my expenses if you come in through my votes."

RANDAL.—"My dear Avenel, certainly I will."

DICK.—"And I have two private bills I want to smuggle through Parliament."

RANDAL.—"They shall be smuggled, rely on it. Mr. Fairfield being on one side of the House, and I on the other, we two could prevent all unpleasant opposition. Private bills are easily managed—with that tact which I flatter myself I possess."

DICK.—"And when the bills are through the House, and you have had time to look about you, I daresay you will see that no man can go against Public Opinion, unless he wants to knock his own head against a stone wall; and that Public Opinion is decidedly Yellow."

RANDAL, (with candour.)—"I cannot deny that Public Opinion is Yellow; and, at my age, it is natural that I should not commit myself to the policy of a former generation. Blue is fast wearing out. But, to return to Mr. Fairfield—you do not speak as if you had no hope of keeping him straight to what I understand to be his agreement with yourself. Surely his honour is engaged to it?"

Dick.—" I don't know as to honour; but he has now taken a fancy to public life; at least so he said no later than this morning before we went into the hall; and I trust that matters will come right. Indeed, I left him with Parson Dale, who promised me that he would use all his best exertions to reconcile Leonard and my lord, and that Leonard should do nothing hastily."

Randal.—" But why should Mr. Fairfield retire because Lord L'Estrange wounds his feelings? I am sure Mr. Fairfield has wounded mine, but that does not make me think of retiring."

Dick.—" Oh, Leonard is a poet, and poets are quite as crotchety as L'Estrange said they were. And Leonard is under obligations to Lord L'Estrange, and thought that Lord L'Estrange was pleased by his standing: whereas, now—in short, it is all Greek to me, except that Leonard has mounted his high horse, and if that throws him, I am afraid it will throw you. But still I have great confidence in Parson Dale—a good fellow, who has much influence with Leonard. And though I thought it right to be above-board, and let you know where the danger lies, yet one thing I can promise—if I resign, you shall come in; so shake hands on it."

Randal.—" My dear Avenel! And your wish is to resign?"

Dick.—" Certainly. I should do so a little time after noon, contriving to be below Leonard on the poll. You know Emanuel Trout, the captain of the Hundred and Fifty 'Waiters on Providence,' as they are called?"

Randal.—" To be sure I do."

Dick.—" When Emanuel Trout comes into the booth, you will know how the election turns. As he votes, all the Hundred and Fifty will vote. Now I must go back. Good night. You'll not forget that my expenses are to be paid. Point of honour. Still, if they are *not* paid, the election can be upset —petition for bribery and corruption; and if they *are* paid, why Lansmere may be your seat for life."

Randal.—" Your expenses shall be paid the moment my marriage gives me the means to pay them—and that must be very soon."

Dick.—" So Levy says. And my little jobs—the private bills?"

Randal.—" Consider the bills passed and the jobs done."

Dick.—" And one must not forget one's country. One

must do the best one can for one's principles. Egerton is infernally Blue. You allow Public Opinion—is—"

RANDAL.—" Yellow. Not a doubt of it."

DICK.—" Good night. Ha—ha—humbug, eh?"

RANDAL.—" Humbug! Between men like us—oh no. Good night, my dear friend—I rely on you."

DICK.—"Yes; but mind, I promise nothing if Leonard Fairfield does not stand."

RANDAL.—" He must stand; keep him to it. Your affairs —your business—your mill—"

DICK.—"Very true. He *must* stand. I have great faith in Parson Dale."

Randal glided back through the park. When he came on the terrace, he suddenly encountered Lord L'Estrange. "I have just been privately into the town, my dear lord, and heard a strange rumour, that Mr. Fairfield was so annoyed by some remarks in your lordship's admirable speech, that he talks of retiring from the contest. That would give a new feature to the election, and perplex all our calculations. And I fear, in that case, there might be some secret coalition between Avenel's friends and our Committee, whom, I am told, I displeased by the moderate speech which your lordship so eloquently defended—a coalition by which Avenel would come in with Mr. Egerton, whereas, if we all four stand, Mr. Egerton, I presume, will be quite safe; and I certainly think I have an excellent chance."

LORD L'ESTRANGE.—" So Mr. Fairfield would retire in consequence of my remarks! I am going into the town, and I intend to apologise for those remarks, and retract them."

RANDAL, (joyously.)—" Noble!"

Lord L'Estrange looked at Leslie's face, upon which the stars gleamed palely. "Mr. Egerton has thought more of your success than of his own," said he, gravely, and hurried on.

Randal continued on the terrace. Perhaps Harley's last words gave him a twinge of compunction. His head sunk musingly on his breast, and he paced to and fro the long gravel walk, summoning up all his intellect to resist every temptation to what could injure his self-interest.

"Skulking knave!" muttered Harley. "At least there will be nothing to repent, if I can do justice on him. That is not revenge. Come, that must be fair retribution. Besides, how else can I deliver Violante?"—He laughed gaily, his heart was so light; and his foot bounded on as fleet as the deer that he startled amongst the fern.

A few yards from the turnstile he overtook Richard Avenel, disguised in a rough greatcoat and spectacles. Nevertheless, Harley's eye detected the Yellow candidate at the first glance. He caught Dick familiarly by the arm. "Well met—I was going to you. We have the election to settle."

"On the terms I mentioned to your lordship?" said Dick, startled. "I will agree to return one of your candidates; but it must not be Audley Egerton." Harley whispered close in Avenel's ear.

Avenel uttered an exclamation of amazement. The two gentlemen walked on rapidly, and conversing with great eagerness.

"Certainly," said Avenel, at length stopping short, "one would do a great deal to serve a family connection—and a connection that does a man so much credit; and how can one go against one's own brother-in-law?—a gentleman of such high standing—pull up the whole family! How pleased Mrs. Richard Avenel will be! Why the devil did not I know it before? And poor—dear—dear Nora. Ah that she were living!" Dick's voice trembled.

"Her name will be righted; and I will explain why it was my fault that Egerton did not before acknowledge his marriage, and claim you as a brother. Come, then, it is all fixed and settled."

"No, my lord; I am pledged the other way. I don't see how I can get off my word—to Randal Leslie. I'm not over nice, nor what is called Quixotic, but still my word is given, that if I retire from the election, I will do my best to return Leslie instead of Egerton."

"I know that through Baron Levy. But if your nephew retires?"

"Oh, that would solve all difficulties. But the poor boy has now a wish to come into Parliament; and he has done me a service in the hour of need.

"Leave it to me. And as to Randal Leslie, he shall have an occasion himself to acquit you and redeem himself; and happy, indeed, will it be for him if he has yet one spark of gratitude, or one particle of honour."

The two continued to converse for a few moments—Dick seeming to forget the election itself, and ask questions of more interest to his heart, which Harley answered so, that Dick wrung L'Estrange's hand with great emotion—and muttered, "My poor mother! I understand now why she would never talk to me of Nora. When may I tell her the truth?"

"To-morrow evening, after the election, Egerton shall embrace you all."

Dick started, and saying—"See Leonard as soon as you can—there is no time to lose," plunged into a lane that led towards the obscurer recesses of the town. Harley continued his way with the same light elastic tread which (lost during his abnegation of his own nature) was now restored to the foot, that seemed loath to leave a print upon the mire.

At the commencement of the High Street he encountered Mr. Dale and Fairfield, walking slowly, arm in arm.

HARLEY.—"Leonard, I was coming to you. Give me your hand. Forget for the present the words that justly stung and offended you. I will do more than apologise—I will repair the wrong. Excuse me, Mr. Dale—I have one word to say in private to Leonard." He drew Fairfield aside.

"Avenel tells me that if you were to retire from this contest, it would be a sacrifice of inclination. Is it so?"

"My Lord, I have sorrows that I would fain forget; and, though I at first shrunk from the strife in which I have been since engaged, yet now a literary career seems to me to have lost its old charm; and I find that, in public life, there is a distraction to the thoughts which embitter solitude, that books fail to bestow. Therefore, if you still wish me to continue this contest, though I know not your motive, it will not be as it was to begin it—a reluctant and a painful obedience to your request."

"I understand. It was a sacrifice of inclination to begin the contest—it would be now a sacrifice of inclination to withdraw!"

"Honestly—yes, my lord."

"I rejoice to hear it, for I ask that sacrifice; a sacrifice which you will recall hereafter with delight and pride; a sacrifice sweeter, if I read your nature aright—oh, sweeter far, than all which commonplace ambition could bestow! And when you learn why I make this demand, you will say, 'This, indeed, is reparation for the words that wounded my affections, and wronged my heart.'"

"My lord, my lord!" exclaimed Leonard, "the injury is repaired already. You give me back your esteem, when you so well anticipate my answer. Your esteem!—life smiles again. I can return to my more legitimate career without a sigh. I have no need of distraction from thought now. You will believe that, whatever my past presumption, I can pray sincerely for your happiness."

"Poet! you adorn your career; you fulfil your mission, even at this moment; you beautify the world; you give to the harsh form of Duty the cestus of the Graces," said Harley, trying to force a smile to his quivering lips. "But we must hasten back to the prose of existence. I accept your sacrifice. As for the time and mode I must select, in order to insure its result, I will ask you to abide by such instructions as I shall have occasion to convey through your uncle. Till then, no word of your intentions—not even to Mr. Dale. Forgive me if I would rather secure Mr. Egerton's election than yours. Let that explanation suffice for the present. What think you, by the way, of Audley Egerton?"

"I thought when I heard him speak, and when he closed with those touching words—implying that he left all of his life not devoted to his country, 'to the charity of his friends'— how proudly, even as his opponent, I could have clasped his hand; and if he had wronged me in private life, I should have thought it ingratitude to the country he had so served, to remember the offence."

Harley turned away abruptly, and joined Mr. Dale.

"Leave Leonard to go home by himself; you see that I have healed whatever wounds I inflicted on him."

PARSON.—"And, your better nature thus awakened, I trust, my dear lord, that you have altogether abandoned the idea of—"

HARLEY.—"Revenge?—no. And if you do not approve that revenge to-morrow, I will never rest till I have seen you —a bishop!"

MR. DALE, (much shocked.)—"My lord, for shame!"

HARLEY, (seriously.)—"My levity is but lip-deep, my dear Mr. Dale. But sometimes the froth on the wave shows the change in the tide."

The Parson looked at him earnestly, and then seized him by both hands with holy gladness and affection.

"Return to the Park now," said Harley, smiling; "and tell Violante, if it be not too late to see her, that she was even more eloquent than you."

Lord L'Estrange bounded forward.

Mr. Dale walked back through the park to Lansmere house. On the terrace he found Randal, who was still pacing to and fro, sometimes in the starlight, sometimes in the shadow

Leslie looked up, and seeing Mr. Dale, the close astuteness of his aspect returned; and stepping out of the starlight deep into the shadow, he said—

"I was sorry to learn that Mr. Fairfield had been so hurt by Lord L'Estrange's severe allusions. Pity that political differences should interfere with private friendships; but I hear that you have been to Mr. Fairfield—and, doubtless, as the peacemaker. Perhaps you met Lord L'Estrange by the way? He promised me that he would apologise and retract."

"Good young man," said the unsuspecting Parson, "he has done so."

"And Mr. Leonard Fairfield will, therefore, I presume, continue the contest?"

"Contest—ah, this election! I suppose so, of course. But I grieve that he should stand against you, who seem to be disposed towards him so kindly."

"Oh," said Randal, with a benevolent smile, "we have fought before, you know, and I beat him then. I may do so again!"

And he walked into the house, arm-in-arm with the Parson. Mr. Dale sought Violante—Leslie retired to his own room, and felt his election was secured.

Lord L'Estrange had gained the thick of the streets—passing groups of roaring enthusiasts—Blue and Yellow—now met with a cheer—now followed by a groan. Just by a public-house that formed the angle of a lane with the High-street, and which was all ablaze with light, and all alive with clamour, he beheld the graceful Baron leaning against the threshold, smoking his cigar, too refined to associate its divine vapour with the wreaths of shag within, and chatting agreeably with a knot of females, who were either attracted by the general excitement, or waiting to see husband, brother, father, or son, who were now joining in the chorus of "Blue for ever!" that rang from tap-room to attic of the illumined hostelry. Levy, seeing Lord L'Estrange, withdrew his cigar from his lips, and hastened to join him. "All the Hundred and Fifty are in there," said the Baron, with a backward significant jerk of his thumb towards the inn. "I have seen them all privately, in tens at a time; and I have been telling the ladies without that it will be best for the interest of their families to go home, and let us lock up the Hundred and Fifty safe from the Yellows, till we bring them to the poll. But I am afraid," continued Levy, "that the rascals are not to be relied upon unless I actually pay them beforehand; and that would be disreputable, immoral—and, what is more, it would upset the election. Besides, if they are paid beforehand, query, is it quite sure how they will vote afterwards?"

"Mr. Avenel, I daresay, can manage them," said Harley. "Pray do nothing immoral, and nothing that will upset the election. I think you might as well go home."

"Home! No, pardon me, my lord; there must be some head to direct the Committee, and keep our captains at their posts upon the doubtful electors. A great deal of mischief may be done between this and the morrow; and I would sit up all night—ay, six nights a-week for the next three months —to prevent any awkward mistake by which Audley Egerton can be returned."

"His return would really grieve you so much?" said Harley.

"You may judge of that by the zeal with which I enter into all your designs."

Here there was a sudden and wondrously loud shout from another inn—a Yellow inn, far down the lane, not so luminous as the Blue hostelry; on the contrary, looking rather dark and sinister, more like a place for conspirators or felons than honest, independent electors.—"Avenel for ever!—Avenel and the Yellows!"

"Excuse me, my lord, I must go back and watch over my black sheep, if I would have them blue!" said Levy; and he retreated towards the threshold. But at that shout of "Avenel for ever!" as if at a signal, various electors of the redoubted Hundred and Fifty rushed from the Blue hostelry, sweeping past Levy, and hurrying down the lane to the dark little Yellow inn, followed by the female stragglers, as small birds follow an owl. It was not, however, very easy to get into that Yellow inn, Yellow Reformers, eminent for their zeal on behalf of purity of election, were stationed outside the door, and only strained in one candidate for admittance at a time. "After all," thought the Baron, as he passed into the principal room of the Blue tavern, and proposed the national song of "Rule Britannia"—"after all, Avenel hates Egerton as much as I do, and both sides work to the same end." And thrumming on the table, he joined with a fine bass, in the famous line,

"For Britons never will be slaves!"

In the interim, Harley had disappeared within the "Lansmere Arms," which was the head quarters of the Blue Committee.

Not, however, mounting to the room in which a few of the more indefatigable were continuing their labours, receiving reports from scouts, giving orders, laying wagers, and very muzzy with British principles and spirits, Harley called aside the landlord, and inquired if the stranger, for whom rooms had been prepared, was yet arrived. An affirmative answer was given, and Harley followed the host up a private stair, to a part of the house remote from the rooms devoted to the purposes of the election. He remained with this stranger about half an hour, and then walked into the Committee-room, got rid of the more excited, conferred with the more sober, issued a few brief directions to such of the leaders as he felt he could most rely upon, and returned home as rapidly as he had quitted it.

Dawn was grey in the skies when Harley sought his own chamber. To gain it, he passed by the door of Violante's. His heart suffused with grateful ineffable tenderness, he paused and kissed the threshold. When he stood within his room, (the same that he had occupied in his early youth,) he felt as if the load of years were lifted from his bosom. The joyous divine elasticity of spirit, that in the morning of life springs towards the Future as a bird soars into heaven, pervaded his whole sense of being. A Greek poet implies, that the height of bliss is the sudden relief of pain: there is a nobler bliss still—the rapture of the conscience at the sudden release from a guilty thought. By the bedside at which he had knelt in boyhood, Harley paused to kneel once more. The luxury of prayer, interrupted since he had nourished schemes of which his passions had blinded him to the sin, but which, nevertheless, he dared not confess to the All-Merciful, was restored to him. And yet, as he bowed his knee, the elation of spirits he had before felt forsook him. The sense of the danger his soul had escaped—the full knowledge of the guilt to which the fiend had tempted—came dread before his clearing vision; he shuddered in horror of himself. And he who but a few hours before had deemed it so impossible to pardon his fellow-man, now felt as if years of useful and beneficent deeds could alone purify his own repentant soul from the memory of one hateful passion.

## CHAPTER XXXII.

But while Harley had thus occupied the hours of night with cares for the living, Audley Egerton had been in commune with the dead. He had taken from the pile of papers amidst which it had fallen, the record of Nora's silenced heart. With a sad wonder he saw how he had once been loved. What had all which successful ambition had bestowed on the lonely statesman to compensate for the glorious empire he had lost—such realms of lovely fancy; such worlds of exquisite emotion; that infinite which lies within the divine sphere that unites spiritual genius with human love? His own positive and earthly nature attained, for the first time, and as if for its own punishment, the comprehension of that loftier and more ethereal visitant from the heavens, who had once looked with a seraph's smile through the prison bars of his iron life;—that celestial refinement of affection, that exuberance of feeling which warms into such varieties of beautiful idea, under the breath of the earth-beautifier, Imagination;—all from which, when it was all his own, he had turned half weary and impatient, and termed the exaggerations of a visionary romance—now that the world had lost them evermore, he interpreted aright as truths. Truths they were, although illusions. Even as the philosopher tells us that the splendour of colours which deck the universe is not on the surface whereon we think to behold it, but in our own vision; yet, take the colours from the universe, and what philosophy can assure us that the universe has sustained no loss?

But when Audley came to that passage in the fragment which, though but imperfectly, explained the true cause of Nora's flight;—when he saw how Levy, for what purpose he was unable to conjecture, had suggested to his bride the doubts that had offended him—asserted the marriage to be a fraud—drawn from Audley's own brief resentful letters to Nora, proof of the assertion—misled so naturally the young wife's scanty experience of actual life, and maddened one so sensitively pure into the conviction of dishonour—his brow darkened, and his hand clenched. He rose and went at once to Levy's room. He found it deserted—inquired—learned that Levy was gone forth, and had left word he might not be at home for the night. Fortunate, perhaps, for Audley—for tunate for the Baron—that they did not then meet. Revenge, in spite of his friend's admonition, might at that hour have been as potent an influence on Egerton as it had been on Harley, and not, as with the latter, to be turned aside.

Audley came back to his room and finished the tragic record. He traced the tremor of that beloved hand through the last tortures of doubt and despair;—he saw where the hot tears had fallen,—he saw where the hand had paused, the very sentence not concluded;—mentally he accompanied his fated bride in the dismal journey to her maiden home, and beheld her before him as he had last seen, more beautiful even in death than the face of living woman had ever since appeared to him;—and as he bent over the last words, the blank that they left on the leaf, stretching pale beyond the quiver of the characters and the blister of the tears—pale and blank as the void which departed love leaves behind it—he felt his heart suddenly stand still, its course arrested as the record closed. It beat again, but feebly—so feebly! His breath became labour and pain, his sight grew dizzy. But the constitutional firmness and fortitude of the man clung to him in the stubborn mechanism of habit—his will yet fought against his disease—life rallied as the light flickers up in the waning taper.

The next morning, when Harley came into his friend's room, Egerton was asleep. But the sleep seemed much disturbed; the breathing was hard and difficult; the bed-clothes were partially thrown off, as if in the tossing of disturbed dreams; the sinewy strong arm, the broad athletic breast, were partly bare. Strange that so deadly a disease within should leave the frame such apparent power that, to the ordinary eye, the sleeping sufferer seemed a model of healthful vigour. One hand was thrust with uneasy straining over the pillows—it had its hold on the fatal papers; a portion of the leaves was visible; and where the characters had been blurred by Nora's tears, were the traces, yet moist, of tears perhaps more bitter.

Harley felt deeply affected; and while he still stood by the bed, Egerton sighed heavily and woke. He stared round him, as if perplexed and confused—till his eyes resting on Harley, he smiled and said—

"So early! Ah—I remember, it is the day for our great boat-race. We shall have the current against us; but you and I together—when did we ever lose?"

Audley's mind was wandering; it had gone back to the old

Eton days. But Harley thought that he spoke in metaphorical allusion to the present more important contest.

"True, my Audley—you and I together—when did we ever lose? But will you rise? I wish you would be at the polling-place to shake hands with your voters as they come up. By four o'clock you will be released, and the election won."

"The election! How!—what!"—said Egerton, recovering himself. "I recollect now. Yes—I accept this last kindness from you. I always said I would die in harness. Public life —I have no other. Ah, I dream again! Oh, Harley!—my son—my son!"

"You shall see him after four o'clock. You will be proud of each other. But make haste and dress. Shall I ring the bell for your servant?"

"Do," said Egerton, briefly, and sinking back. Harley quitted the room, and joined Randal and some of the more important members of the Blue Committee, who were already hurrying over their breakfast.

All were anxious and nervous except Harley, who dipped his dry toast into his coffee, according to his ordinary abstemious Italian habit, with serene composure. Randal in vain tried for an equal tranquillity. But though sure of his election, there would necessarily follow a scene trying to the nerve of his hypocrisy. He would have to affect profound chagrin in the midst of vile joy; have to act the part of decorous high-minded sorrow, that by some untoward chance—some unaccountable cross-splitting, Randal Leslie's gain should be Audley Egerton's loss. Besides, he was flurried in the expectation of seeing the Squire, and of appropriating the money which was to secure the dearest object of his ambition. Breakfast was soon despatched. The Committee men, bustling for their hats, and looking at their watches, gave the signal for departure; yet no Squire Hazeldean had made his appearance. Harley, stepping from the window upon the terrace, beckoned to Randal, who took his hat and followed.

"Mr. Leslie," said Harley, leaning against the balustrade, and carelessly patting Nero's rough, honest head, "you remember that you were good enough to volunteer to me the explanation of certain circumstances in connexion with the Count di Peschiera, which you gave to the Duke di Serrano; and I replied that my thoughts were at present engaged on the election, but as soon as that was over, I should be very willing to listen to any communications affecting yourself and my old friend the Duke, with which you might be pleased to favour me."

This address took Randal by surprise, and did not tend to calm his nerves. However, he replied readily.

"Upon that, as upon any other matter that may influence the judgment you form of me, I shall be but too eager to remove a single doubt that, in your eyes, can rest upon my honour."

"You speak exceedingly well, Mr. Leslie; no man can express himself more handsomely; and I will claim your promise with the less scruple because the Duke is powerfully affected by the reluctance of his daughter to ratify the engagement that binds his honour, in case your own is indisputably cleared. I may boast of some influence over the young lady, since I assisted to save her from the infamous plot of Peschiera; and the Duke urges me to receive your explanation, in the belief that, if it satisfy me, as it has satisfied him, I may conciliate his child in favour of the addresses of a suitor who would have hazarded his very life against so redoubted a duellist as Peschiera."

"Lord L'Estrange," replied Randal, bowing, "I shall indeed owe you much if you can remove that reluctance on the part of my betrothed bride, which alone clouds my happiness, and which would at once put an end to my suit, did I not ascribe it to an imperfect knowledge of myself, which I shall devote my life to improve into confidence and affection."

"No man *can* speak more handsomely," reiterated Harley, as if with profound admiration; and indeed he did eye Randal as we eye some rare curiosity. "I am happy to inform you, too," continued L'Estrange, "that if your marriage with the Duke of Serrano's daughter take place—"

"*If !*" echoed Randal.

"I beg pardon for making an hypothesis of what you claim the right to esteem a certainty—I correct my expression: *when* your marriage with that young lady takes place, you will at least escape the rock on which many young men of ardent affections have split at the onset of the grand voyage. You will form no imprudent connection. In a word, I received yesterday a despatch from Vienna, which contains the full pardon and formal restoration of Alphonso Duke di Serrano. And I may add, that the Austrian government (sometimes misunderstood in this country) is bound by the laws it administers, and can in no way dictate to the Duke, once restored, as to the choice of his son-in-law, or as to the heritage that may devolve on his child."

"And does the Duke yet know of his recall?" exclaimed Randal, his cheeks flushed and his eyes sparkling.

"No. I reserve that good news, with other matters, till after the election is over. But Egerton keeps us waiting sadly. Ah, here comes his valet."

Audley's servant approached. "Mr. Egerton feels himself rather more poorly than usual, my lord; he begs you will excuse his going with you into the town at present. He will come later if his presence is absolutely necessary."

"No. Pray tell him to rest and nurse himself. I should have liked him to witness his own triumph—that is all. Say I will represent him at the polling place. Gentlemen, are you ready? We will go on."

The polling booth was erected in the centre of the market-place. The voting had already commenced; and Mr. Avenel and Leonard were already at their posts, in order to salute and thank the voters in their cause who passed before them. Randal and L'Estrange entered the booth amidst loud hurrahs, and to the national air of "See the Conquering Hero comes." The voters defiled in quick succession. Those who voted entirely according to principle or colour—which came to much the same thing—and were therefore above what is termed "management," flocked in first, voting straight-forwardly for both Blues or both Yellows. At the end of the first half-hour the Yellows were about ten ahead of the Blues. Then sundry split votes began to perplex conjecture as to the result; and Randal, at the end of the first hour, had fifteen majority over Audley Egerton, two over Dick Avenel—Leonard Fairfield heading the poll by five. Randal owed his place in the lists to the voters that Harley's personal efforts had procured for him; and he was well pleased to see that Lord L'Estrange had not withdrawn from him a single promise so obtained. This augured well for Harley's ready belief in his appointed "explanations." In short, the whole election seemed going just as he had calculated. But by twelve o'clock there were some changes in the relative position of the candidates. Dick Avenel had gradually gained ground—passing Randal, passing even Leonard. He stood at the head of the poll by a majority of ten. Randal came next. Audley was twenty behind Randal, and Leonard four behind Audley.

More than half the constituency had polled, but none of the Committee on either side, nor one of the redoubted corps of a Hundred and Fifty.

The poll now slackened sensibly. Randal, looking round,

and longing for an opportunity to ask Dick whether he really meant to return himself instead of his nephew, saw that Harley had disappeared; and presently a note was brought to him requesting his presence in the Committee-Room. Thither he hastened.

As he forced his way through the bystanders in the lobby, towards the threshold of the room, Levy caught hold of him and whispered—"They begin to fear for Egerton. They want a compromise in order to secure him. They will propose to you to resign, if Avenel will withdraw Leonard. Don't be entrapped. L'Estrange may put the question to you; but—a word in your ear—he would be glad enough to throw over Egerton. Rely upon this, and stand firm."

Randal made no answer, but, the crowd giving way for him, entered the room. Levy followed. The doors were instantly closed. All the Blue Committee were assembled. They looked heated, anxious, eager. Lord L'Estrange, alone calm and cool, stood at the head of the long table. Despite his composure, Harley's brow was thoughtful. "Yes," said he to himself, "I will give this young man the fair occasion to prove gratitude to his benefactor; and if he here acquit himself, I will spare him at least, public exposure of his deceit to others. So young, he must have some good in him—at least towards the man to whom he owes all."

"Mr. Leslie," said L'Estrange, aloud, "you see the state of the poll. Our Committee believe that, if you continue to stand, Egerton must be beaten. They fear that, Leonard Fairfield having little chance, the Yellows will not waste their second votes on him, but will transfer them to you, in order to keep out Egerton. If you retire, Egerton will be safe. There is reason to suppose that Leonard would, in that case, also be withdrawn."

"You can hope and fear nothing more from Egerton," whispered Levy. "He is utterly ruined; and, if he lose, will sleep in a prison. The bailiffs are waiting for him."

Randal was still silent, and at that silence an indignant murmur ran through the more influential members of the Committee. For, though Audley was not personally very popular, still a candidate so eminent was necessarily their first object, and they would seem very small to the Yellows if their great man was defeated by the very candidate introduced to aid him—a youth unknown. Vanity and patriotism both swelled that murmur. "You see, young sir," cried a rich blunt master-butcher, "that it was an honourable understanding that Mr. Egerton was to be safe. You had no claim on us, except as fighting second to him. And we are all astonished that you don't say at once, 'Save Egerton, of course.' Excuse my freedom, sir. No time for palaver."

"Lord L'Estrange," said Randal, turning mildly from the butcher, "do you, as the first here in rank and influence, and as Mr. Egerton's especial friend, call upon me to sacrifice my election, and what appear to be the inclinations of the majority of the constituents, in order to obtain what is, after all, a doubtful chance of returning Mr. Egerton in my room?"

"I do not call upon you, Mr. Leslie. It is a matter of feeling or of honour, which a gentleman can very well decide for himself?"

"Was any such compact made between your lordship and myself, when you first gave me your interest and canvassed for me in person?"

"Certainly not. Gentlemen, be silent. No such compact was mentioned by me."

"Neither was it by Mr. Egerton. Whatever might be the understanding spoken of by the respected elector who addressed me, I was no party to it. I am persuaded that Mr. Egerton is the last person who would wish to owe his election to a trick upon the electors in the midst of the polling, and to what the world would consider a very unhandsome treatment of myself, upon whom all the toil of the canvass has devolved."

Again the murmur rose; but Randal had an air so determined, that it quelled resentment, and obtained a continued, though most chilling and half-contemptuous hearing.

"Nevertheless," resumed Randal, "I would at once retire were I not under the firm persuasion that I shall convince all present, who now seem to condemn me, that I act precisely according to Mr. Egerton's own private inclinations. That gentleman, in fact, has never been amongst you—has not canvassed in person—has taken no trouble, beyond a speech, that was evidently meant to be but a general defence of his past political career. What does this mean? Simply that his standing has been merely a form, to comply with the wish of his party, against his own desire."

The Committee men looked at each other amazed and doubtful. Randal saw he had gained an advantage; he pursued it with a tact and ability which showed that, in spite of his mere oratorical deficiencies, he had in him the elements of a dexterous debater. "I will be plain with you, gentlemen. My character, my desire to stand well with you all, oblige me to be so. Mr. Egerton does not wish to come into Parliament at present. His health is much broken; his private affairs need all his time and attention. I am, I may say, as a son to him. He is most anxious for my success; Lord L'Estrange told me but last night, very truly, 'more anxious for my success than his own.' Nothing could please him more than to think I were serving in Parliament, however humbly, those great interests which neither health nor leisure will, in this momentous crisis, allow himself to defend with his wonted energy. Later, indeed, no doubt, he will seek to return to an arena in which he is so distinguished; and when the popular excitement, which produces the popular injustice of the day, is over, what constituency will not be proud to return such a man? In support and proof of what I have thus said, I now appeal to Mr. Egerton's own agent—a gentleman who, in spite of his vast fortune and the rank he holds in society, has consented to act gratuitously on behalf of that great statesman. I ask you, then, respectfully, Baron Levy—Is not Mr. Egerton's health much broken, and in need of rest?"

"It is," said Levy.

"And do not his affairs necessitate his serious and undivided attention?"

"They do indeed," quoth the Baron. "Gentlemen, I have nothing to urge in behalf of my distinguished friend as against the statement of his adopted son, Mr. Leslie."

"Then all I can say," cried the butcher, striking his huge fist on the table, "is, that Mr. Egerton has behaved d——d unhandsome to us, and we shall be the laughing-stock of the borough."

"Softly, softly," said Harley. "There is a knock at the door behind. Excuse me."

Harley quitted the room, but only for a minute or two. On his return he addressed himself to Randal.

"Are we then to understand, Mr. Leslie, that your intention is not to resign?"

"Unless your lordship actually urge me to the contrary, I should say, 'Let the election go on, and all take our chance.' That seems to me the fair, manly, ENGLISH (great emphasis on the last adjective), honourable course."

"Be it so," replied Harley; "'let all take their chance.' Mr. Leslie, we will no longer detain you. Go back to the polling place—one of the candidates should be present; and you, Baron Levy, be good enough to go also, and return thanks to those who may yet vote for Mr. Egerton."

Levy bowed, and went out arm-in-arm with Randal.

"Capital, capital," said the Baron. "You have a wonderful head."

"I did not like L'Estrange's look, nevertheless. But he can't hurt me now; the votes he got for me instead of for Egerton have already polled. The Committee, indeed, may refuse to vote for me; but then there is Avenel's body of reserve. Yes, the election is virtually over. When we get back, Hazeldean will have arrived with the money for the purchase of my ancestral property;—Dr. Riccabocca is already restored to the estates and titles of Serrano;—what do I care farther for Lord L'Estrange? Still, I do not like his look."

"Pooh, you have done just what he wished. I am forbidden to say more. Here we are at the booth. A new placard since we left. How are the numbers? Avenel forty ahead of you; you thirty above Egerton; and Leonard Fairfield still last on the poll. But where are Avenel and Fairfield?"

Both those candidates had disappeared, perhaps gone to their own Committee-Room.

Meanwhile, as soon as the doors had closed on Randal and the Baron, in the midst of the angry hubbub succeeding to their departure, Lord L'Estrange sprang upon the table. The action and his look stilled every sound.

"Gentlemen, it is in our hands to return one of our candidates, and to make our own choice between the two. You have heard Mr. Leslie and Baron Levy. To their statement I make but this reply—Mr. Egerton is needed by the country; and whatever his health or his affairs, he is ready to respond to that call. If he has not canvassed—if he does not appear before you at this moment, the services of more than twenty years plead for him in his stead. Which, then, of the two candidates do you choose as your member—a renowned statesmen, or a beardless boy? Both have ambition and ability;— the one has identified those qualities with the history of a country, and (as it is now alleged to his prejudice) with a devotion that has broken a vigorous frame and injured a princely fortune. The other evinces his ambition by inviting you to prefer him to his benefactor; and proves his ability by the excuses he makes for ingratitude. Choose between the two—an Egerton or a Leslie.

"Egerton for ever!" cried all the assembly, as with a single voice, followed by a hiss for Leslie.

"But," said a grave and prudent Committee-man, "have we really the choice?—does not that rest with the Yellows? Is not your lordship too sanguine?"

"Open that door behind; a deputation from our opponents waits in the room on the other side the passage. Admit them."

The Committee were hushed in breathless silence while Harley's order was obeyed. And soon, to their great surprise, Leonard Fairfield himself, attended by six of the principal members of the Yellow party, entered the room.

LORD L'ESTRANGE.—"You have a proposition to make to us, Mr. Fairfield, on behalf of yourself and Mr. Avenel, and with the approval of your committee?"

LEONARD, (advancing to the table.)—"I have. We are convinced that neither party can carry both its candidates. Mr. Avenel is safe. The only question is, which of the two candidates on your side it best becomes the honour of this constituency to select. My resignation, which I am about to tender, will free sufficient votes to give the triumph either to Mr. Egerton or to Mr. Leslie."

"Egerton for ever!" cried once more the excited Blues.

"Yes—Egerton for ever!" said Leonard, with a glow upon his cheek. "We may differ from his politics, but who can tell us those of Mr. Leslie? We may differ from the politician, but who would not feel proud of the senator? A great and incalculable advantage is bestowed on that constituency which returns to Parliament a distinguished man. His distinction ennobles the place he represents—it sustains public spirit—it augments the manly interest in all that effects the nation. Every time his voice hushes the assembled Parliament, it reminds us of our common country; and even the discussion amongst his constituents which his voice provokes—clears their perceptions of the public interest, and enlightens themselves, from the intellect which commands their interest, and compels their attention. Egerton, then, for ever! If our party must subscribe to the return of one opponent, let all unite to select the worthiest. My Lord L'Estrange, when I quit this room, it will be to announce my resignation, and to solicit those who have promised me their votes to transfer them to Mr. Audley Egerton."

Amidst the uproarious huzzas which followed this speech, Leonard drew near to Harley! "My Lord, I have obeyed your wishes, as conveyed to me by my uncle, who is engaged at this moment elsewhere in carrying them into effect."

"Leonard," said Harley, in the same undertone, "you have insured to Audley Egerton what you alone could do—the triumph over a perfidious dependent—the continuance of the sole career in which he has hitherto found the solace or the zest of life. He must thank you with his own lips. Come to the Park after the close of the poll. There and then shall the explanations yet needful to both be given and received."

Here Harley bowed to the assembly and raised his voice: "Gentlemen, yesterday, at the nomination of the candidates, I uttered remarks that have justly pained Mr. Fairfield. In your presence I wholly retract and frankly apologise for them. In your presence I entreat his forgiveness, and say, that if he will accord me his friendship, I will place him in my esteem and affection side by side with the statesman whom he has given to his country."

Leonard grasped the hand extended to him with both his own, and then, overcome by his emotions, hurried from the room; while Blues and Yellows exchanged greetings, rejoiced in the compromise that would dispel all party irritation, secure the peace of the borough, and allow quiet men, who had detested each other the day before, and vowed reciprocal injuries to trade and custom, the indulgence of all amiable and fraternal feelings—until the next general election.

In the meanwhile the polling had gone on slowly as before, but still to the advantage of Randal. "Not two-thirds of the constituency will poll," murmured Levy, looking at his watch. "The thing is decided. Aha, Audley Egerton! you who once tortured me with the unspeakable jealousy that bequeaths such implacable hate—you who scorned my society, and called me 'scoundrel'—disdainful of the very power your folly placed within my hands—aha, your time is up!—and the spirit that administered to your own destruction strides within the circle to seize its prey."

"You shall have my first frank, Levy," said Randal, "to enclose your letter to Mr. Thornhill's solicitor. This affair of the election is over; we must now look to what else rests on our hands."

"What the devil is that placard?" cried Levy, turning pale.

Randal looked, and right up the market-place, followed by

an immense throng, moved, high over the heads of all, a Yellow Board that seemed marching through the air, comet-like:—

*Two o'clock p.m.*

## RESIGNATION OF FAIRFIELD.

## YELLOWS!
### VOTE FOR
## AVENEL AND EGERTON!
(Signed) TIMOTHY ALLJACK.

*Yellow Committee Room.*

"What infernal treachery is this?" cried Randal, livid with honest indignation.

"Wait a moment; there is Avenel!" exclaimed Levy; and at the head of another procession that emerged from the obscurer lanes of the town, walked, with grave majesty, the surviving Yellow candidate. Dick disappeared for a moment within a grocer's shop in the broadest part of the place, and then culminated, at the height of a balcony on the first story, just above an enormous yellow canister, significant of the profession and the politics of the householder. No sooner did Dick, hat in hand, appear on this rostrum, than the two processions halted below, bands ceased, flags drooped round their staves, crowds rushed within hearing, and even the poll-clerks sprang from the booth. Randal and Levy themselves pressed into the throng. Dick on the balcony was the *Deus ex Machinâ*.

"Freemen and electors!" said Dick, with his most sonorous accents—"finding that the public opinion of this independent and enlightened constituency is so evenly divided, that only one Yellow candidate can be returned, and only one Blue has a chance, it was my intention last night to retire from the contest, and thus put an end to all bickerings and ill-blood—(Hold your tongues there, can't you!)—I say honestly, I should have preferred the return of my distinguished and talented young nephew—honourable relation—to my own; but he would not hear of it; and talked all our Committee into the erroneous but high-minded notion, that the town would cry shame if the nephew rode into Parliament by breaking the back of the uncle." (Loud cheers from the mob, and partial cries of "We'll have you both!")

"You'll do no such thing, and you know it; hold your jaw,"

resumed Dick, with imperious good humour. "Let me go on, can't you?—time presses. In a word, my nephew resolved to retire, if, at two o'clock this day, there was no chance of returning both of us; and there is none. Now, then, the next thing for the Yellows, who have not yet voted, is to consider how they will give their second votes. If I had been the man to retire, why, for certain reasons, I should have recommended them to split with Leslie—a clever chap, and pretty considerable sharp."

"Hear, hear, hear!" cried the Baron, lustily.

"But I'm bound to say that my nephew has an opinion of his own—as an independent Britisher, let him be twice your nephew, ought to have; and his opinion goes the other way, and so does that of our Committee."

"Sold!" cried the Baron, and some of the crowd shook their heads, and looked grave—especially those suspected of a wish to be bought.

"Sold!—Pretty fellow you with the nosegay in your buttonhole to talk of selling! You who wanted to sell your own client—and you know it. (Levy recoiled.) Why, gentlemen, that's Levy the Jew, who talks of selling! And if he asperses the character of this constituency, I stand here to defend it:— And there stands the parish pump, with a handle for the arm of Honesty, and a spout for the lips of Falsehood!"

At the close of this magniloquent period, borrowed, no doubt, from some great American orator, Baron Levy involuntarily retreated towards the shelter of the polling-booth, followed by some frowning Yellows with very menacing gestures.

"But the calumniator sneaks away; leave him to the reproach of his conscience," resumed Dick, with a generous magnanimity.

"SOLD!—(the word rang through the place like the blast of a trumpet)—Sold! No, believe me, not a man who votes for Egerton instead of Fairfield will, so far as I am concerned, be a penny the better—(chilling silence)—or (with a scarce perceivable wink towards the anxious faces of the Hundred and Fifty who filled the background)—or a penny the worse. (Loud cheers from the Hundred and Fifty, and cries of 'Noble!') I don't like the politics of Mr. Egerton. But I am not only a politician—I am a MAN! The arguments of our respected Committee—persons in business, tender husbands, and devoted fathers—have weight with me. I myself am a husband and a father. If a needless contest be prolonged to the last, with all the irritations it engenders, who suffer?—why, the tradesmen and the operative. Partiality, loss of custom, tyrannical demands for house rent, notices to quit—in a word, the screw!"

"Hear, hear!" and "Give us the Ballot!"

"The Ballot—with all my heart, if I had it about me! And if we had the Ballot, I should like to see a man dare to vote Blue. (Loud cheers from the Yellows.) But, as we have not got it, we must think of our families. And I may add, that though Mr. Egerton may come again into office, yet (added Dick, solemnly) I will do my best, as his colleague, to keep him straight; and your own enlightenment (for the schoolmaster is abroad) will show him that no minister can brave public opinion, nor quarrel with his own bread and butter. (Much cheering.) In these times the aristocracy must endear themselves to the middle and working class; and a member in office has much to give away in the Stamps and Excise, in the Customs, the Post Office, and other State departments in this rotten old—I mean this magnificent empire—by which he can benefit his constituents, and reconcile the prerogatives of aristocracy with the claims of the people—more especially in this case, the people of the borough of Lansmere. (Hear, hear.)

"And therefore, sacrificing party inclinations (since it seems that I can in no way promote them) on the Altar of General Good Feeling, I cannot oppose the resignation of my nephew —honourable relation—nor blind my eyes to the advantages that may result to a borough so important to the nation at large, if the electors think fit to choose my Right Honourable broth—I mean the Right Honourable Blue candidate—as my brother colleague. Not that I presume to dictate, or express a wish one way or the other—only, as a Family Man, I say to you, Electors and Freemen, having served your country in returning me, you have nobly won the right to think of the little ones at home."

Dick put his hand to his heart, bowed gracefully, and retired from the balcony amidst unanimous applause.

In three minutes more Dick had resumed his place in the booth in his quality of candidate. A rush of Yellow electors poured in, hot and fast. Up came Emanuel Trout, and, in a firm voice, recorded his vote—"Avenel and Egerton." Every man of the Hundred and Fifty so polled. To each question, "Whom do you vote for?" "Avenel and Egerton" knelled on the ears of Randal Leslie with "damnable iteration." The young man folded his arms across his breast in dogged despair. Levy had to shake hands for Mr. Egerton, with a rapidity that took away his breath. He longed to slink away—longed to get at L'Estrange, whom he supposed would be as wroth at this turn in the wheel of fortune as himself. But how, as Egerton's representative, escape from the continuous gripes of those horny hands? Besides, there stood the parish pump, right in face of the booth, and some huge truculent-looking Yellows loitered round it, as if ready to pounce on him the instant he quitted his present sanctuary. Suddenly the crowd round the booth receded—Lord L'Estrange's carriage drove up to the spot, and Harley, stepping from it, assisted out of the vehicle an old grey-haired, paralytic man. The old man stared round him, and nodded smilingly to the mob. "I'm here—I'm come; I'm but a poor creature, but I'm a good Blue to the last!"

"Old John Avenel—fine old John!" cried many a voice.

And John Avenel, still leaning on Harley's arm, tottered into the booth, and plumped for "Egerton."

"Shake hands, father," said Dick, bending forward, "though you'll not vote for me."

"I was a Blue before you were born," answered the old man, tremulously. "But I wish you success all the same, and God bless you, my boy!"

Even the poll-clerks were touched; and when Dick, leaving his place, was seen by the crowd assisting Lord L'Estrange to place poor John again in the carriage—that picture of family love in the midst of political difference—of the prosperous, wealthy, energetic son, who, as a boy, had played at marbles in the very kennel, and who had risen in life by his own exertions, and was now virtually M.P. for his native town—tending on the broken-down, aged father, whom even the interests of a son he was so proud of could not win from the colours which he associated with truth and rectitude—had such an effect upon the rudest of the mob there present, that you might have heard a pin fall—till the carriage drove away back to John's humble home, and then there rose such a tempest of huzzas! John Avenel's vote for Egerton gave another turn to the vicissitudes of that memorable election. As yet Avenel had been ahead of Audley; but a plumper in favour of Egerton, from Avenel's own father, set an example and gave an excuse to many a Blue who had not yet voted, and could not prevail on himself to split his vote between Dick and Audley: and, therefore, several leading tradesmen, who, seeing that Egerton was safe, had previously resolved not to vote at all, came up in the

last hour, plumped for Egerton, and carried him to the head
of the poll; so that poor John, whose vote, involving that of
Mark Fairfield, had secured the first opening in public life to
the young ambition of the unknown son-in-law, still contributed to connect with success and triumph, but also with
sorrow, and, it may be, with death, the names of the high-born
Egerton and the humble Avenel.

The great town-clock strikes the hour of four; the returning
officer declares the poll closed; the formal announcement of
the result will be made later. But all the town knows that
Audley Egerton and Richard Avenel are the members for
Lansmere. And flags stream, and drums beat, and men shake
each other by the hand heartily; and there is talk of the chair-
ing to-morrow; and the public-houses are crowded; and there
is an indistinct hubbub in street and alley, with sudden bursts
of uproarious shouting; and the clouds to the west look red
and lurid round the sun, which has gone down behind the
church tower—behind the yew trees that overshadow the
quiet grave of Nora Avenel.

## CHAPTER XXXIII.

AMIDST the darkening shadows of twilight, Randal Leslie
walked through Lansmere Park towards the house. He had
slunk away before the poll was closed—crept through by-
lanes, and plunged into the leafless copses of the Earl's stately
pasture grounds. Amidst the bewilderment of his thoughts—
at a loss to conjecture how this strange mischance had befallen
him—inclined to ascribe it to Leonard's influence over Avenel
—but suspecting Harley, and half doubtful of Baron Levy, he
sought to ascertain what fault of judgment he himself had
committed—what wile he had forgotten—what thread in his
web he had left ragged and incomplete. He could discover
none. His ability seemed to him unimpeachable—*totus, teres,
atque rotundus*. And then there came across his breast a sharp
pang—sharper than that of baffled ambition—the feeling that
he had been deceived and bubbled, and betrayed. For so vital
a necessity to all living men is TRUTH, that the vilest traitor
feels amazed and wronged—feels the pillars of the world
shaken, when treason recoils on himself. " That Richard
Avenel, whom I trusted, could so deceive me!" murmured
Randal, and his lip quivered.

He was still in the midst of the Park, when a man with a
yellow cockade in his hat, and running fast from the direction

of the town, overtook him with a letter, on delivering which
the messenger, waiting for no answer, hastened back the way
he had come. Randal recognised Avenel's hand on the address
—broke the seal, and read as follows:—

(" *Private and Confidential.*)

"DEAR LESLIE,—Don't be down-hearted—you will know
to-night or to-morrow why I have had cause to alter my
opinion as to the Right Honourable; and you will see that I
could not, as a Family Man, act otherwise than I have done.
Though I have not broken my word to you—for you remember
that all the help I promised was dependent on my own resignation, and would go for nothing if Leonard resigned instead
—yet I feel you must think yourself rather bamboozled. But
I have been obliged to sacrifice you, from a sense of Family
Duty, as you will soon acknowledge. My own nephew is
sacrificed also; and I have sacrificed my own concerns, which
require the whole man of me for the next year or two at
Screwstown. So we are all in the same boat, though you
may think you are set adrift by yourself. But I don't mean
to stay in Parliament. I shall take the Chiltern Hundreds,
pretty considerable soon. And if you keep well with the
Blues, I'll do my best with the Yellows to let you walk over
the course in my stead. For I don't think Leonard will want
to stand again. And so a word to the wise—and you may yet
be member for Lansmere.—R. A."

In this letter, Randal, despite all his acuteness, could not
detect the honest compunction of the writer.—He could at
first only look at the worst side of human nature, and fancy
that it was a paltry attempt to stifle his just anger and ensure
his discretion. But, on second thoughts, it struck him that
Dick might very naturally be glad to be released to his
mill, and get a *quid pro quo* out of Randal, under the comprehensive title—" repayment of expenses."—Perhaps Dick
was not sorry to wait until Randal's marriage gave him the
means to make the repayment. Nay, perhaps Randal had been
thrown over for the present, in order to wring from him
better terms in a single election. Thus reasoning, he took
comfort from his belief in the mercenary motives of another.
True, it might be but a short disappointment. Before the
next Parliament was a month old, he might yet take his seat
in it as member for Lansmere. But all would depend on his
marriage with the heiress; he must hasten that.

Meanwhile, it was necessary to knit and gather up all his

thought, courage, and presence of mind. How he shrunk from return to Lansmere House — from facing Egerton, Harley—all. But there was no choice. He would have to make it up with the Blues—to defend the course he had adopted in the Committee-Room. — There, no doubt, was Squire Hazeldean awaiting him with the purchase-money for the lands of Rood—there was the Duke di Serrano restored to wealth and honour—there was his promised bride, the great heiress, on whom depended all that could raise the needy gentleman into wealth and position. Gradually, with the elastic temper that is essential to a systematic schemer, Randal Leslie plucked himself from the pain of brooding over a plot that was defeated, to prepare himself for consummating those that yet seemed so near success.—After all, should he fail in regaining Egerton's favour, Egerton was of use no more. He might rear his head, and face out what some might call "ingratitude," provided he could but satisfy the Blue Committee. Dull dogs, how could he fail to do that! He could easily talk over the Machiavellian sage. He should have small difficulty in explaining all to the content of Audley's distant brother, the Squire. Harley alone—but Levy had so positively assured him that Harley was not sincerely anxious for Egerton; and as to the more important explanation relative to Peschiera, surely what had satisfied Violante's father ought to satisfy a man who had no peculiar right to demand explanations at all; and if these explanations did not satisfy, the onus to disprove them must rest with Harley; and who or what could contradict Randal's plausible assertions—assertions in support of which he himself could summon a witness, in Baron Levy? Thus nerving himself to all that could task his powers, Randal Leslie crossed the threshold of Lansmere House, and in the hall he found the Baron awaiting him.

"I can't account," said Levy, "for what has gone so cross in this confounded election. It is L'Estrange that puzzles me but I know that he hates Egerton. I know that he will prove that hate by one mode of revenge, if he has lost it in another. —But it is well, Randal, that you are secure of Hazeldean's money and the rich heiress's hand; otherwise—"

"Otherwise, what?"

"I should wash my hands of you, *mon cher;* for, in spite of all your cleverness, and all I have tried to do for you, somehow or other I begin to suspect that your talents will never secure your fortune. A carpenter's son beats you in public speaking, and a vulgar mill-owner tricks you in private negotiation. Decidedly, as yet, Randal Leslie, you are—a failure. And, as you so admirably said, 'a man from whom we have nothing to hope or fear, we must blot out of the map of the future.'"

Randal's answer was cut short by the appearance of the groom of the chambers.

"My lord is in the saloon, and requests you and Mr. Leslie will do him the honour to join him there." The two gentlemen followed the servant up the broad stairs.

The saloon formed the centre room of the suite of apartments. From its size, it was rarely used save on state occasions. It had the chilly and formal aspect of rooms reserved for ceremony.

Riccabocca, Violante, Helen, Mr. Dale, Squire Hazeldean, and Lord L'Estrange, were grouped together by the cold Florentine marble table, not littered with books and female work, and the endearing signs of habitation, that give a living smile to the face of home; nothing thereon save a great silver candelabrum, that scarcely lighted the spacious room, and brought out the portraits on the walls as a part of the assembly, looking, as portraits do look, with searching curious eyes upon every eye that turns to them.

But as soon as Randal entered, the Squire detached himself from the group, and, coming to the defeated candidate, shook hands with him heartily.

"Cheer up, my boy; 'tis no shame to be beaten. Lord L'Estrange says you did your best to win, and man can do no more. And I'm glad, Leslie, that we don't meet for our little business till the election is over; for, after annoyance, something pleasant is twice as acceptable. I've the money in my pocket. Hush—and I say, my dear, dear boy, I cannot find out where Frank is, but it is really all off with that foreign woman—eh?"

"Yes, indeed, sir, I hope so. I'll talk to you about it when we can be alone. We may slip away presently, I trust."

"I'll tell you a secret scheme of mine and Harry's," said the Squire, in a still low whisper. "We must drive that marchioness, or whatever she is, out of the boy's head, and put a pretty English girl into it instead. That will settle him in life too. And I must try and swallow that bitter pill of the *post-obit*. Harry makes worse of it than I do, and is so hard on the poor fellow that I've been obliged to take his part. I've no idea of being under petticoat government—it is not the way with the Hazeldeans. Well, but to come back to the point—whom do you think I mean by the pretty girl?"

"Miss Sticktorights!"

"Zounds, no!—your own little sister, Randal. Sweet pretty face! Harry liked her from the first, and then you'll be Frank's brother, and your sound head and good heart will keep him right. And as you are going to be married too, (you must tell me all about that later,) why, we shall have two marriages, perhaps, in the family the same day."

Randal's hand grasped the Squire's, and with an emotion of human gratitude—for we know that, hard to all else, he had natural feelings for his fallen family; and his neglected sister was the one being on earth whom he might almost be said to love. With all his intellectual disdain for honest simple Frank, he knew no one in the world with whom his young sister could be more secure and happy. Transferred to the roof, and improved by the active kindness, of Mrs. Hazeldean—blest in the manly affection of one not too refined to censure her own deficiencies of education—what more could he ask for his sister, as he pictured her to himself, with her hair hanging over her ears, and her mind running into seed over some trashy novel. But before he could reply, Violante's father came to add his own philosophical consolations to the Squire's downright comfortings.

"Who could ever count on popular caprice? The wise of all ages had despised it. In that respect, Horace and Machiavelli were of the same mind," &c. &c. "But," said the Duke, with emphatic kindness, "perhaps your very misfortune here may serve you elsewhere. The female heart is prone to pity, and ever eager to comfort. Besides, if I am recalled to Italy, you will have leisure to come with us, and see the land where, of all others, ambition can be most readily forgotten, even (added the Italian, with a sigh)—even by her own sons!"

Thus addressed by both Hazeldean and the Duke, Randal recovered his spirits. It was clear that Lord L'Estrange had not conveyed to them any unfavourable impression of his conduct in the Committee-Room. While Randal had been thus engaged, Levy had made his way to Harley, who retreated with the Baron into the bay of the great window.

"Well, my lord, do you comprehend this conduct on the part of Richard Avenel? He secure Egerton's return!—he!"

"What so natural, Baron Levy—his own brother-in-law?"

The Baron started, and turned very pale.

"But how did he know that? I never told him. I meant indeed—"

"Meant, perhaps, to shame Egerton's pride at the last, by publicly declaring his marriage with a shopkeeper's daughter. A very good revenge still left to you; but revenge for what? A word with you, now, Baron, that our acquaintance is about to close for ever. You know why I have cause for resentment against Egerton. I do but suspect yours; will you make it clear to me?"

"My lord, my lord," faltered Baron Levy, "I, too, wooed Nora Avenel as my wife; I, too, had a happier rival in the haughty worldling who did not appreciate his own felicity; I too—in a word, some women inspire an affection that mingles with the entire being of a man, and is fused with all the currents of his life-blood. Nora Avenel was one of those women."

Harley was startled. This burst of emotion from a man so corrupt and cynical arrested even the scorn he felt for the usurer. Levy soon recovered himself. "But our revenge is not baffled yet. Egerton, if not already in my power, is still in yours. His election may save him from arrest, but the law has other modes of public exposure and effectual ruin."

"For the knave, yes—as I intimated to you in your own house—you who boast of your love to Nora Avenel, and know in your heart that you were her destroyer—you who witnessed her marriage, and yet dared to tell her that she was dishonoured!"

"My lord—I—how could you know—I mean, how think that—that—" faltered Levy, aghast.

"Nora Avenel has spoken from her grave," replied Harley, solemnly. "Learn that, wherever man commits a crime, Heaven finds a witness!"

"It is on me, then," said Levy, wrestling against a superstitious thrill at his heart—"on me that you now concentre your vengeance; and I must meet it as I may. But I have fulfilled my part of our compact. I have obeyed you implicitly —and—"

"I will fulfil my part of our bond, and leave you undisturbed in your wealth."

"I knew I might trust to your lordship's honour," exclaimed the usurer, in servile glee.

"And this vile creature nursed the same passions as myself; and but yesterday we were partners in the same purpose, and influenced by the same thought," muttered Harley to himself. "Yes," he said aloud, "I dare not, Baron Levy, constitute myself your judge. Pursue your own path—all roads meet at last before the common tribunal. But you are not yet released from our compact; you must do some good in spite of yourself. Look yonder, where Randal Leslie stands, smiling secure, between the two dangers he has raised up for himself. And as Randal Leslie himself has invited me to be his judge, and you are aware that he cited yourself this very day as his witness, here I must expose the guilty—for here the innocent still live, and need defence."

Harley turned away, and took his place by the table. "I have wished," said he, raising his voice, "to connect with the the triumph of my earliest and dearest friend the happiness of others in whose welfare I feel an interest. To you, Alphonso, Duke of Serrano, I now give this despatch, received last evening by a special messenger from the Prince Von ——, announcing your restoration to your lands and honours."

The Squire stared with open mouth. "Rickeybockey a duke? Why, Jemima's a duchess! Bless me, she is actually crying!" And his good heart prompted him to run to his cousin and cheer her up a bit.

Violante glanced at Harley, and flung herself on her father's breast. Randal involuntarily rose, and moved to the Duke's chair.

"And you, Mr. Randal Leslie," continued Harley, "though you have lost your election, see before you at this moment such prospects of wealth and happiness, that I shall only have to offer you congratulations to which those that greet Mr. Audley Egerton may well appear lukewarm and insipid, provided you prove that you have not forfeited the right to claim that promise which the Duke di Serrano has accorded to the suitor of his daughter's hand. Some doubts resting on my mind, you have volunteered to dispel them. I have the duke's permission to address to you a few questions, and I now avail myself of your offer to reply to them."

"Now—and here, my lord?" said Randal, glancing round the room, as if deprecating the presence of so many witnesses.

"Now—and here. Nor are those present so strange to your explanations as your question would imply. Mr. Hazeldean, it so happens that much of what I shall say to Mr. Leslie concerns your son."

Randal's countenance fell. An uneasy tremor now seized him.

"My son!—Frank? Oh then, of course, Randal will speak out. Speak, my boy!"

Randal remained silent. The Duke looked at his working face, and drew away his chair.

"Young man, can you hesitate?" said he. "A doubt is expressed which involves your honour."

"'Sdeath!" cried the Squire, also gazing on Randal's cowering eye and quivering lip—"What are you afraid of?"

"Afraid!" said Randal, forced into speech, and with a hollow laugh—"afraid?—I? What of? I was only wondering what Lord L'Estrange could mean."

"I will dispel that wonder at once. Mr. Hazeldean, your son displeased you first by his proposals of marriage to the Marchesa di Negra against your consent; secondly by a *post-obit* bond granted to Baron Levy. Did you understand from Mr. Randal Leslie that he had opposed or favoured the said marriage—that he had countenanced or blamed the said *post-obit?*"

"Why, of course," cried the Squire, "that he had opposed both the one and the other."

"Is it so, Mr. Leslie?"

"My lord—I—I—my affection for Frank, and my esteem for his respected father—I—I—" (He nerved himself, and went on with firm voice.)—"Of course, I did all I could to dissuade Frank from the marriage; and as to the *post-obit*, I know nothing about it."

"So much at present for this matter. I pass on to the graver one, that affects your engagement with the Duke di Serrano's daughter. I understand from you, Duke, that to save your daughter from the snares of Count di Peschiera, and in the belief that Mr. Leslie shared in your dread of the Count's designs, you, while in exile and in poverty, promised to that gentleman your daughter's hand? When the probabilities of restoration to your principalities seemed well-nigh certain, you confirmed that promise on learning from Mr. Leslie that he had, however ineffectively, struggled to preserve your heiress from a perfidious snare. Is it not so?"

"Certainly. Had I succeeded to a throne, I could not recall the promise that I had given in penury and banishment—I could not refuse to him who would have sacrificed worldly ambition in wedding a penniless bride, the reward of his own generosity. My daughter subscribes to my views."

Violante trembled, and her hands were locked together; but her gaze was fixed on Harley.

Mr. Dale wiped his eyes, and thought of the poor refugee feeding on minnows, and preserving himself from debt amongst the shades of the Casino.

"Your answer becomes you, Duke," resumed Harley. "But should it be proved that Mr. Leslie, instead of wooing the Princess for herself, actually calculated on the receipt of money for transferring her to Count Peschiera—instead of saving her from the dangers you dreaded, actually suggested the snare from which she was delivered—would you still deem your honour engaged to—"

"Such a villain! No, surely not!" exclaimed the Duke. "But this is a groundless hypothesis! Speak, Randal."

"Lord L'Estrange cannot insult me by deeming it otherwise than a groundless hypothesis!" said Randal, striving to rear his head.

"I understand, then, Mr. Leslie, that you scornfully reject such a supposition?"

"Scornfully—yes. And," continued Randal, advancing a step, "since the supposition has been made, I demand from Lord L'Estrange, as his equal, (for all gentlemen are equals where honour is to be defended at the cost of life,) either instant retractation or instant proof."

"That's the first word you have spoken like a man," cried the Squire. "I have stood my ground myself for a less cause. I have had a ball through my right shoulder."

"Your demand is just," said Harley, unmoved. "I cannot give the retractation—I will produce the proof."

He rose and rang the bell;—the servant entered, received his whispered order, and retired. There was a pause painful to all. Randal, however, ran over in his fearful mind what evidence could be brought against him—and foresaw none. The folding doors of the saloon were thrown open and the servant announced—

THE COUNT DI PESCHIERA.

A bombshell descending through the roof could not have produced a more startling sensation. Erect, bold, with all the imposing effect of his form and bearing, the Count strode into the centre of the ring; and, after a slight bend of haughty courtesy, which comprehended all present, reared up his lofty head, and looked round, with calm in his eye and a curve on his lip—the self-assured, magnificent, high-bred Daredevil.

"Duke di Serrano," said the Count, in English, turning towards his astounded kinsman, and in a voice that, slow, clear, and firm, seemed to fill the room, "I returned to England on the receipt of a letter from my Lord L'Estrange, and with a view, it is true, of claiming at his hands the satisfaction which men of our birth accord to each other, where affront, from what cause soever, has been given or received. Nay, fair kinswoman"—and the Count, with a slight but grave smile, bowed to Violante, who had uttered a faint cry—" that intention is abandoned. If I have adopted too lightly the old courtly maxim, that 'all stratagems are fair in love,' I am bound also to yield to my Lord L'Estrange's arguments, that the counter stratagems must be fair also. And, after all, it becomes me better to laugh at my own sorry figure in defeat, than to confess myself gravely mortified by an ingenuity more successful than my own." The Count paused, and his eye lightened with sinister fire, which ill suited the raillery of his tone, and the polished ease of his bearing. "*Ma foi!*" he continued, "it is permitted me to speak thus, since at least I have given proofs of my indifference to danger, and my good fortune when exposed to it. Within the last six years I have had the honour to fight nine duels, and the regret to wound five, and dismiss from the world four, as gallant and worthy gentlemen as ever the sun shone upon."

"Monster!" faltered the Parson.

The Squire stared aghast, and mechanically rubbed the shoulder which had been lacerated by Captain Dashmore's bullet. Randal's pale face grew yet more pale, and the eye he had fixed upon the Count's hardy visage quailed and fell.

"But," resumed the Count, with a graceful wave of the hand, "I have to thank my Lord L'Estrange for reminding me that a man whose courage is above suspicion is privileged not only to apologise if he has injured another, but to accompany apology with atonement. Duke of Serrano, it is for that purpose that I am here. My lord, you have signified your wish to ask me some questions of serious import as regards the Duke and his daughter—I will answer them without reserve."

"*Monsieur le Comte*," said Harley, "availing myself of your courtesy, I presume to inquire who informed you that this young lady was a guest under my father's roof?"

"My informant stands yonder—Mr. Randal Leslie. And I call upon Baron Levy to confirm my statement."

"It is true," said the Baron, slowly, and as if overmastered by the tone and mien of an imperious chieftain.

There came a low sound like a hiss from Randal's livid lips.

"And was Mr. Leslie acquainted with your project for securing the person and hand of your young kinswoman?"

"Certainly—and Baron Levy knows it." The Baron bowed assent. "Permit me to add—for it is due to a lady nearly related to myself—that it was, as I have since learned, certain erroneous representations made to her by Mr. Leslie, which alone induced that lady, after my own arguments had failed, to lend her aid to a project which otherwise she would have condemned as strongly as, Duke di Serrano, I now with unfeigned sincerity do myself condemn it."

There was about the Count, as he thus spoke, so much of that personal dignity which, whether natural or artificial, imposes for the moment upon human judgment—a dignity so supported by the singular advantages of his superb stature, his handsome countenance, his patrician air, that the Duke, moved by his good heart, extended his hand to the perfidious kinsman, and forgot all the Machiavellian wisdom which should have told him how little a man of the Count's hardened profligacy was likely to be influenced by any purer motives, whether to frank confession or to manly repentance. The Count took the hand thus extended to him, and bowed his face, perhaps to conceal the smile which would have betrayed his secret soul. Randal still remained mute, and pale as death. His tongue clove to his mouth. He felt that all present were shrinking from his side. At last, with a violent effort, he faltered out, in broken sentences—

"A charge so sudden may well—may well confound me. But—but—who can credit it? Both the law and common sense pre-suppose some motive for a criminal action; what could be my motive here? I—myself the suitor for the hand of the Duke's daughter—*I* betray her! Absurd—absurd. Duke—Duke, I put it to your own knowledge of mankind—whoever goes thus against his own interest—and—and his wn heart?"

This appeal, however feebly made, was not without effect on the philosopher. "That is true," said the Duke, dropping his kinsman's hand; "I see no motive."

"Perhaps," said Harley, "Baron Levy may here enlighten us. Do you know of any motive of self-interest that could have actuated Mr. Leslie in assisting the Count's schemes?"

Levy hesitated. The Count took up the word. "*Pardieu!*" said he, in his clear tone of determination and will—"*Pardieu!* I can have no doubt thrown on my assertion, least of all by those who know of its truth; and I call upon you, Baron Levy, to state whether, in case of my marriage with the Duke's daughter, I had not agreed to present my sister with a sum, to which she alleged some ancient claim, and which would have passed through your hands?"

"Certainly, that is true," said the Baron.

"And would Mr. Leslie have benefited by any portion of that sum?"

Levy paused again.

"Speak, sir," said the Count, frowning.

"The fact is," said the Baron, "that Mr. Leslie was anxious to complete a purchase of certain estates that had once belonged to his family, and that the Count's marriage with the Signora, and his sister's marriage with Mr. Hazeldean, would have enabled me to accommodate Mr. Leslie with a loan to effect that purchase."

"What! what!" exclaimed the Squire, hastily buttoning his breast pocket with one hand, while he seized Randal's arm with the other—"my son's marriage! You lent yourself to that, too? Don't look so like a lashed hound! Speak out like a man, if man you be!"

"Lent himself to that, my good sir!" said the Count. "Do you suppose that the Marchesa di Negra could have condescended to an alliance with a Mr. Hazeldean—"

"Condescended!—a Hazeldean of Hazeldean!" exclaimed the Squire, turning fiercely, and half choked with indignation.

"Unless," continued the Count, imperturbably, "she had been compelled by circumstances to do that said Mr. Hazeldean the honour to accept a pecuniary accommodation, which she had no other mode to discharge. And here, sir, the family of Hazeldean, I am bound to say, owe a great debt of gratitude to Mr. Leslie; for it was he who most forcibly represented to her the necessity for this *mésalliance;* and it was he, I believe, who suggested to my friend, the Baron, the mode by which Mr. Hazeldean was best enabled to afford the accommodation my sister deigned to accept."

"Mode!—the *post-obit!*" ejaculated the Squire, relinquishing his hold of Randal, to lay his gripe upon Levy.

The Baron shrugged his shoulders. "Any friend of Mr. Frank Hazeldean's would have recommended the same, as the most economical mode of raising money."

Parson Dale, who had at first been more shocked than any one present at these gradual revelations of Randal's treachery, now turning his eyes towards the young man, was so seized with commiseration at the sight of Randal's face, that he laid his hand on Harley's arm, and whispered him—"Look, look at that countenance!—and one so young! Spare him, spare him!"

"Mr. Leslie," said Harley, in softened tones, "believe me that nothing short of justice to the Duke di Serrano—justice even to my young friend, Mr. Hazeldean, has compelled me to this painful duty. Here let all inquiry terminate."

"And," said the Count, with exquisite blandness, "since I have been informed by my Lord L'Estrange, that Mr. Leslie has represented as a serious act on his part, that personal challenge to myself, which I understood was but a pleasant and amicable arrangement in our baffled scheme—let me assure Mr. Leslie, that if he be not satisfied with the regret that I now express for the leading share I have taken in these disclosures, I am wholly at Mr. Leslie's service."

"Peace, homicide," cried the Parson, shuddering; and he glided to the side of the detected sinner, from whom all else had recoiled in loathing.

Craft against craft, talent against talent, treason against treason—in all this Randal Leslie would have risen superior to Giulio di Peschiera. But what now crushed him, was not the superior intellect—it was the sheer brute power of audacity and nerve. Here stood the careless, unblushing villain, making light of his guilt, carrying it away from disgust itself, with resolute look and front erect. There stood the abler, subtler, profounder criminal—cowering, abject, pitiful; the power of mere intellectual knowledge shivered into pieces against the brazen metal with which the accident of constitution often arms some ignobler nature.

The contrast was striking, and implied that truth so universally felt, yet so little acknowledged in actual life, that men with audacity and force of character can subdue and paralyse those far superior to themselves in ability and intelligence. It was these qualities which made Peschiera Randal's master; nay, the very physical attributes of the Count, his very voice and form; his bold front and unshrinking eye, overpowered the acuter mind of the refining schemer, as in a popular assembly some burly Cleon cows into timorous silence every dissentient sage. But Randal turned in sullen impatience from the Parson's whisper, that breathed comfort or urged repentance; and at length said, with clearer tones than he had yet mustered—

"It is not a personal conflict with the Count di Peschiera that can vindicate my honour; and I disdain to defend myself against the accusations of a usurer, and of a man who—"

"*Monsieur!*" said the Count, drawing himself up.

"A man who," persisted Randal, though he trembled visibly, "by his own confession, was himself guilty of all the schemes in which he would represent me as his accomplice, and who now, not clearing himself, would yet convict another—"

"*Cher petit Monsieur!*" said the Count, with his grand air of disdain, "when men like me make use of men like you, we reward them for a service if rendered, or discard them if the service be not done; and, if I condescend to confess and apologise for any act I have committed, surely Mr. Randal Leslie might do the same without disparagement to his dignity. But I should never, sir, have taken the trouble to appear against you, had you not, as I learn, pretended to the hand of the lady whom I had hoped, with less presumption, to call my bride; and in this, how can I tell that you have not tricked and betrayed me? Is there anything in our past acquaintance that warrants me to believe that, instead of serving me, you sought but to serve yourself? Be that as it may, I had but one mode of repairing to the head of my house the wrongs I have done him—and that was by saving his daughter from a derogatory alliance with an impostor who had abetted my schemes for hire, and who now would filch for himself their fruit."

"Duke!" exclaimed Randal.

The Duke turned his back. Randal extended his hands to the Squire. "Mr. Hazeldean—what? you, too, condemn me, and unheard?"

"Unheard!—zounds, no! If you have anything to say, speak truth, and shame the devil."

"I abet Frank's marriage!—I sanction the *post-obit!*—Oh!" cried Randal, clinging to a straw, "If Frank himself were but here!"

Harley's compassion vanished before this sustained hypocrisy.

"You wish for the presence of Frank Hazeldean. It is just." Harley opened the door of the inner room, and Frank appeared at the entrance.

"My son—my son!" cried the Squire, rushing forward, and clasping Frank to his broad, fatherly breast.

This affecting incident gave a sudden change to the feelings of the audience, and for a moment Randal himself was forgotten. The young man seized that moment. Reprieved, as it were, from the glare of contemptuous, accusing eyes—

slowly he crept to the door, slowly and noiselessly, as the
viper, when it is wounded, drops its crest and glides writhing
through the grass. Levy followed him to the threshold, and
whispered in his ear—

"I could not help it—you would have done the same by
me. You see you have failed in everything; and when a man
fails completely, we both agreed that we must give him up
altogether."

Randal said not a word, and the Baron marked his shadow
fall on the broad stairs, stealing down, down, step after step,
till it faded from the stones.

"But he was of some use," muttered Levy. "His treachery
and his exposure will gall the childless Egerton. Some little
revenge still!"

The Count touched the arm of the musing usurer—

"*J'ai bien joué mon rôle, n'est ce pas?*"—(I have well
played my part, have I not?)

"Your part! Ah! but my dear Count, I do not quite
understand it."

"*Ma foi*—you are passably dull. I had just been landed
in France, when a letter from L'Estrange reached me. It
was couched as an invitation, which I interpreted to—the
*duello*. Such invitations I never refuse. I replied. I came
hither—took my lodgings at an inn. My lord seeks me last
night. I begin in the tone you may suppose. *Pardieu!* he is
clever, *milord!* He shows me a letter from the Prince
Von ——, Alphonso's recall, my own banishment. He
places before me, but with admirable suavity, the option of
beggary and ruin, or an honourable claim on Alphonso's
gratitude. And as for that *petit Monsieur*, do you think I
could quietly contemplate my own tool's enjoyment of all I
had lost myself? Nay, more, if that young Harpagon were
Alphonso's son-in-law, could the Duke have a whisperer at
his ear more fatal to my own interests? To be brief, I saw
at a glance my best course. I have adopted it. The difficulty was to extricate myself as became a man '*de sang et de
feu*.' If I have done so, congratulate me. Alphonso has
taken my hand, and I now leave it to him—to attend to my
fortunes, and clear up my repute."

"If you are going to London," said Levy, "my carriage,
ere this, must be at the door, and I shall be proud to offer
you a seat, and converse with you on your prospects. But,
*peste, mon cher*, your fall has been from a great height, and
any other man would have broken his bones."

"Strength is ever light," said the Count, smiling; "and it does not fall; it leaps down and rebounds."

Levy looked at the Count, and blamed himself for having disparaged Peschiera and overrated Randal.

While this conference went on, Harley was by Violante's side.

"I have kept my promise to you," said he, with a kind of tender humility. Are you still so severe on me?"

"Ah!" answered Violante, gazing on his noble brow, with all a woman's pride in her eloquent, admiring eyes—"I have heard from Mr. Dale that you have achieved a conquest over yourself, which makes me ashamed to think that I presumed to doubt how your heart would speak when a moment of wrath (though of wrath so just) had passed away."

"No, Violante—do not acquit me yet; witness my revenge, (for I have not foregone it,) and then let my heart speak, and breathe its prayer that the angel voice, which it now beats to hear, may still be its guardian monitor."

"What is this?" cried an amazed voice; and Harley, turning round, saw that the Duke was by his side; and, glancing with ludicrous surprise, now to Harley, now to Violante, "Am I to understand that you—"

"Have freed you from one suitor for this dear hand, to become, myself, your petitioner!"

"*Corpo di Bacco!*" cried the sage, almost embracing Harley, "this, indeed, is joyful news. But I must not again make a rash pledge—not again force my child's inclinations. And Violante, you see, is running away."

The Duke stretched out his arm, and detained his child. He drew her to his breast, and whispered in her ear. Violante blushed crimson, and rested her head on his shoulder. Harley eagerly pressed forward.

"There," said the Duke, joining Harley's hand with his daughter's—"I don't think I shall hear much more of the convent; but anything of this sort I never suspected. If there be a language in the world for which there is no lexicon nor grammar, it is that which a woman thinks in, but never speaks."

"It is all that is left of the language spoken in paradise," said Harley.

"In the dialogue between Eve and the serpent—yes," quoth the incorrigible sage. "But who comes here?—our friend Leonard."

Leonard now entered the room; but Harley could scarcely greet him, before he was interrupted by the Count.

"*Milord*," said Peschiera, beckoning him aside, "I have fulfilled my promise, and I will now leave your roof. Baron Levy returns to London, and offers me a seat in his carriage, which is already, I believe, at your door. The Duke and his daughter will readily forgive me, if I do not ceremoniously bid them farewell. In our altered positions, it does not become me too intrusively to claim kindred; it became me only to remove, as I trust I have done, a barrier against the claim. If you approve my conduct, you will state your own opinion to the Duke." With a profound salutation the Count turned to depart; nor did Harley attempt to stay him, but attended him down the stairs with polite formality.

"Remember only, my lord, that I solicit nothing. I may allow myself to accept. *Voila tout.*" He bowed again, with the inimitable grace of the old *régime*, and stepped into the Baron's travelling carriage.

Levy, who had lingered behind, paused to accost L'Estrange.

"Your lordship will explain to Mr. Egerton how his adopted son deserved his esteem, and repaid his kindness. For the rest, though you have bought up the more pressing and immediate demands on Mr. Egerton, I fear that even your fortune will not enable you to clear those liabilities, which will leave him, perhaps, a pauper!"

"Baron Levy," said Harley abruptly, "if I have forgiven Mr. Egerton, cannot you too forgive? Me he has wronged—you have wronged him, and more foully."

"No, my lord, I cannot forgive him. You he has never humiliated—you he has never employed for his wants, and scorned as his companion. You have never known what it is to start in life with one whose fortunes were equal to your own, whose talents were not superior. Look you, Lord L'Estrange — in spite of this difference between me and Egerton, that he has squandered the wealth that he gained without effort, while I have converted the follies of others into my own ample revenues—the spendthrift in his penury has the respect and position which millions cannot bestow upon me. You would say that I am an usurer, and he is a statesman. But do you know what I should have been, had I not been born the natural son of a peer? Can you guess what I should have been, if Nora Avenel had been my wife? The blot on my birth, and the blight on my youth—and the knowledge that he who was rising every year into the rank which entitled him to reject me as a guest at his table—he whom the world called the model of a gentleman—was a coward and a liar to the friend of his youth: all this made me look on the world with contempt; and, despising Audley Egerton, I yet hated him and envied. You, whom he wronged, stretch your hand as before to the great statesman; from my touch you would shrink as pollution. My lord, you may forgive him whom you love and pity; I cannot forgive him whom I scorn and envy. Pardon my prolixity. I now quit your house."

The Baron moved a step—then, turning back, said with a withering sneer—

"But you will tell Mr. Egerton how I helped to expose the son he adopted! I thought of the childless man when your lordship imagined I was but in fear of your threats. Ha! ha!—that will sting."

The Baron gnashed his teeth as hastily entering the carriage, he threw down the blinds. The post-boys cracked their whips, and the wheels rolled away.

"Who can judge," thought Harley, "through what modes retribution comes home to the breast? That man is chastised in his wealth—ever gnawed by desire for what his wealth cannot buy!" He roused himself, cleared his brow, as from a thought that darkened and troubled; and, entering the saloon, laid his hand upon Leonard's shoulder, and looked, rejoicing, into the poet's mild, honest, lustrous eyes. "Leonard," said he, gently, "your hour is come at last."

## CHAPTER XXXIV.

AUDLEY EGERTON was alone in his apartment. A heavy sleep had come over him, shortly after Harley and Randal had left the house in the early morning; and that sleep continued till late in the day. All the while the town of Lansmere had been distracted in his cause—all the while so many tumultuous passions had run riot in the contest that was to close or re-open, for the statesman's ambition, the Janus gates of political war—the object of so many fears and hopes, schemes and counter schemes, had slumbered quietly as an infant in the cradle. He woke but in time to receive Harley's despatch, announcing the success of his election; and adding, "Before the night you shall embrace your son. Do not join us below when I return. Keep calm—*we* will come to you."

In fact, though not aware of the dread nature of Audley's

complaint, with its warning symptoms, Lord L'Estrange wished to spare to his friend the scene of Randal's exposure.

On the receipt of that letter Egerton rose. At the prospect of seeing his son—Nora's son—the very memory of his disease vanished. The poor, weary, over-laboured heart indeed beat loud, and with many a jerk and spasm. He heeded it not. The victory, that restored him to the sole life for which he had hitherto cared to live, was clean forgotten. Nature claimed her own—claimed it in scorn of death, and in oblivion of renown.

There sate the man, dressed with his habitual precision! the black coat, buttoned across the broad breast; his countenance, so mechanically habituated to self-control, still revealing little of emotion, though the sickly flush came and went on the bronzed cheek, and the eye watched the hand of the clock, and the ear hungered for a foot-tread along the corridor. At length the sound was heard—steps—many steps. He sprung to his feet—he stood on the hearth. Was the hearth to be solitary no more? Harley entered first. Egerton's eyes rested on him eagerly for a moment, and strained onward across the threshold. Leonard came next—Leonard Fairfield, whom he had seen as his opponent! He began to suspect—to conjecture—to see the mother's tender eyes in the son's manly face. Involuntarily he opened his arms; but, Leonard remaining still, let them fall with a deep sigh, and fancied himself deceived.

"Friend," said Harley, "I give to you a son proved in adversity, and who has fought his own way to fame. Leonard, in the man to whom I prayed you to sacrifice your own ambition—of whom you have spoken with such worthy praise —whose career of honour you have promoted—and whose life, unsatisfied by those honours, you will soothe with your filial love—behold the husband of Nora Avenel! Kneel to your father! O Audley, embrace your son!"

"Here—here," exclaimed Egerton, as Leonard bent his knee—"here to my heart! Look at me with those eyes!— kindly, forgivingly: they are your mother's!" His proud head sunk on his son's shoulder.

"But this is not enough," said Harley, leading Helen, and placing her by Leonard's side. "You must open your heart for more. Take into its folds my sweet ward and daughter. What is a home without the smile of woman? They have loved each other from children. Audley, yours be the hand to join—yours be the lips to bless."

Leonard started anxiously. "Oh, sir!—oh, my father!—this generous sacrifice may not be; for he—he who has saved me for this surpassing joy—he too loves her!"

"Nay, Leonard," said Harley, smiling, "I am not so neglectful of myself. Another home woos you, Audley. He whom you long so vainly sought to reconcile to life, exchanging mournful dreams for happy duties—he, too, presents you to his bride. Love her for my sake—for your own. She it is, not I, who presides over this hallowed re-union. But for her, I should have been a blinded, vindictive, guilty, repentant man; and—" Violante's soft hand was on his lips.

"Thus," said the Parson, with mild solemnity, "Man finds that the Saviour's precepts, 'Let not the sun go down upon thy wrath,' and 'Love one another,' are clues that conduct us through the labyrinth of human life, when the schemes of fraud and hate snap asunder, and leave us lost amidst the maze."

Egerton reared his head, as if to answer; and all present were struck and appalled by the sudden change that had come over his countenance. There was a film upon the eye—a shadow on the aspect; the words failed his lips—he sunk on the seat beside him. The left hand rested droopingly upon the piles of public papers and official documents, and the fingers played with them, as the bed-ridden dying sufferer plays with the coverlid he will soon exchange for the winding-sheet. But his right hand seemed to feel, as through the dark, for the recovered son; and having touched what it sought, feebly drew Leonard near and nearer. Alas! that blissful PRIVATE LIFE—that close centre round the core of being in the individual man—so long missed and pined for—slipped from him, as it were, the moment it reappeared; hurried away, as the circle on the ocean, which is scarce seen ere it vanishes amidst infinity. Suddenly both hands were still; the head fell back. Joy had burst asunder the last ligaments, so fretted away in unrevealing sorrow. Afar, their sound borne into that room, the joy-bells were pealing triumph; mobs roaring out huzzas; the weak cry of John Avenel might be blent in those shouts, as the drunken zealots reeled by his cottage door, and startled the screaming ravens that wheeled round the hollow oak. The boom which is sent from the waves on the surface of life, while the deeps are so noiseless in their march, was wafted on the wintry air into the chamber of the statesman it honoured, and over the grass sighing low upon Nora's grave. But there was one in the chamber, as in the grave, for whom the boom on the wave had no sound, and the march of the deep had no tide. Amidst promises of home, and union, and peace, and fame, Death strode into the household ring, and, seating itself, calm and still, looked life-like; warm hearts throbbing round it; lofty hopes fluttering upward; Love kneeling at its feet; Religion, with lifted finger, standing by its side.

## FINAL CHAPTER.

SCENE—*The Hall in the Old Tower of* CAPTAIN ROLAND DE CAXTON.

"BUT you have not done?" said Augustine Caxton
PISISTRATUS.—"What remains to do?"
MR. CAXTON.—"What!—why the *Final Chapter*,!—the last news you can give us of those whom you have introduced to our liking or dislike."
PISISTRATUS.—"Surely it is more dramatic to close the work with a scene that completes the main design of the plot, and leave it to the prophetic imagination of all whose flattering curiosity is still not wholly satisfied, to trace the streams of each several existence, when they branch off again from the lake in which their waters converge, and by which the sybil has confirmed and made clear the decree, that 'Conduct is Fate.'"
MR. CAXTON.—" More dramatic, I grant; but you have not written a drama. A novelist should be a comfortable, garrulous, communicative, gossiping fortune-teller; not a grim, laconical, oracular sibyl. I like a novel that adopts all the old-fashioned customs prescribed to its art by the rules of the Masters, more especially a novel which you style 'My Novel,' *par* emphasis."
CAPTAIN ROLAND.—"A most vague and impracticable title 'My Novel.' It must really be changed before the work goes in due form to the public."
MR. SQUILLS.—"Certainly the present title cannot be even pronounced by many without inflicting a shock upon their nervous system. Do you think, for instance, that my friend, Lady Priscilla Graves—who is a great novel-reader indeed, but holds all female writers unfeminine deserters to the standard of Man—could ever come out with, ' Pray, sir, have you had time to look at—MY NOVEL?'—She would rather die first. And yet to be silent altogether on the latest acquisition to the circulating libraries, would bring on a functional de-

rangement of her ladyship's organs of speech. Or how could pretty Miss Dulcet—all sentiment, it is true, but all bashful timidity—appal Captain Smirke from proposing, with, 'Did not you think the Parson's sermon a little too dry in MY NOVEL?' It will require a face of brass, or at least a long course of citrate of iron, before a respectable lady or unassuming young gentleman, with a proper dread of being taken for scribblers, could electrify a social circle with, 'The reviewers don't do justice to the excellent things in—MY NOVEL.'"

CAPTAIN ROLAND.—"Awful consequences, indeed, may arise from the mistakes such a title gives rise to.—Counsellor Digwell, for instance—a lawyer of literary tastes, but whose career at the bar was long delayed by an unjust suspicion amongst the attorneys that he had written a 'Philosophical Essay'—imagine such a man excusing himself for being late at a dinner of big-wigs, with 'I could not get away from— MY NOVEL.' It would be his professional ruin! I am not fond of lawyers in general, but still I would not be a party to taking the bread out of the mouth of those with a family; and Digwell has children—the tenth an innocent baby in arms."

MR. CAXTON.—"As to Digwell in particular, and lawyers in general, they are too accustomed to circumlocution, to expose themselves to the danger your kind heart apprehends; but I allow that a shy scholar like myself, or a grave college tutor, might be a little put to the blush, if he were to blurt forth inadvertently with, 'Don't waste your time over trash like— MY NOVEL.' And that thought presents to us another and more pleasing view of this critical question. The title you condemn places the work under universal protection. Lives there a man or a woman, so dead to self-love as to say, 'What contemptible stuff is—MY NOVEL?' Would he or she not rather be impelled by that strong impulse of an honourable and virtuous heart, which moves us to stand as well as we can with our friends, to say—'Allow that there is really a good thing now and then in—MY NOVEL.' Moreover, as a novel aspires to embrace most of the interests or the passions that agitate mankind—to generalise, as it were, the details of life that come home to us all—so, in reality, the title denotes that, if it be such as the author may not unworthily call his Novel, it must also be such as the reader, whoever he be, may appropriate in part to himself, representing his own ideas— expressing his own experience—reflecting, if not in full, at least in profile, his own personal identity. Thus, when we glance at the looking-glass in another man's room, our likeness for the moment appropriates the mirror; and according to the humour in which we are, or the state of our spirits and health, we say to ourselves, 'Bilious and yellow!—I might as well take care of my diet!' Or, 'Well, I've half a mind to propose to dear Jane; I'm not such an ill-looking dog as I thought for!' Still, whatever result from that glance at the mirror, we never doubt that 'tis our likeness we see; and each says to the phantom reflection, 'Thou art myself,' though the mere article of furniture that gives the reflection belongs to another. It is my likeness if it be his glass. And a narrative that is true to the Varieties of Life is every Man's Novel, no matter from what shores, by what rivers, by what bays, in what pits were extracted the sands, and the silex, the pearlash, the nitre and quicksilver which form its materials: no matter who the craftsman who fashioned its form; no matter who the vendor that sold, or the customer who bought: still, if I but recognise some trait of myself, 'tis my likeness that makes it 'MY Novel.'"

MR. SQUILLS, (puzzled, and therefore admiring.)—" Subtle, sir—very subtle. Fine organ of Comparison in Mr. Caxton's head, and much called into play this evening."

MR. CAXTON, (benignly.) — " Finally, the author, by this most admirable and much signifying title dispenses with all necessity of preface. He need insinuate no merits—he need extenuate no faults; for, by calling his work thus curtly 'MY Novel,' he doth delicately imply that it is no use wasting talk about faults or merits."

PISISTRATUS, (amazed.)—" How is that, sir ? "

MR. CAXTON.—" What so clear ? You imply that, though a better novel may be written by others, you do not expect to write a novel to which, taken as a novel, you would more decisively and unblushingly prefix that voucher of personal authorship and identity conveyed in the monosyllable 'My.' And if you have written your best, let it be ever so bad, what can any man of candour and integrity require more from you ? Perhaps you will say that, if you had lived two thousand years ago, you might have called it *The Novel*, or the *Golden* Novel, as Lucius called his story 'The Ass;' and Apuleius, to distinguish his own more elaborate Ass from all Asses preceding it, called his tale 'The Golden Ass.' But living in the present day, such a designation—implying a merit in general, not the partial and limited merit corresponding only with your individual abilities—would be presumptuous and offensive. True—I here anticipate the observation I see Squills is about to make—"

SQUILLS.—" I, sir?—"

MR. CAXTON.—"You would say that, as Scarron called his work of fiction 'The Comic Novel,' so Pisistratus might have called his 'The Serious Novel,' or 'The Tragic Novel.' But, Squills, that title would not have been inviting nor appropriate, and would have been exposed to comparison with Scarron, who being dead is inimitable. Wherefore—to put the question on the irrefragable basis of mathematics—wherefore as A B 'My Novel,' is not equal to B C 'The Golden Novel,' nor to D E 'The Serious or Tragic Novel,' it follows, that A B 'My Novel' is equal to P C 'Pisistratus Caxton,' and P C 'Pisistratus Caxton' must therefore be just equal, neither more nor less, to A B 'My Novel'—Which was to be demonstrated." My father looked round triumphantly, and observing that Squills was dumb-founded, and the rest of his audience posed, he added mildly—

"And so now, *non quieta movere*, proceed with the Final Chapter, and tell us first what became of that youthful Giles Overreach, who was himself his own Marrall?"

"Ay!" said the Captain, "what became of Randal Leslie? Did he repent and reform?"

"Nay," quoth my father with a mournful shake of the head, "you can regulate the warm tide of wild passion—you can light into virtue the dark errors of ignorance; but where the force of the brain does but clog the free action of the heart—where you have to deal, not with ignorance misled, but intelligence corrupted—small hope of reform; for reform here will need re-organisation. I have somewhere read (perhaps in Hebrew tradition) that of the two orders of fallen spirits—the Angels of Love, and the Angels of Knowledge—the first missed the stars they had lost, and wandered back through the darkness, one by one into heaven; but the last, lighted on by their own lurid splendours, said, 'Wherever *we* go, there is heaven!' And deeper and lower descending, lost their shape and their nature, till, deformed and obscene, the bottomless pit closed around them."

MR. SQUILLS.—"I should not have thought Mr. Caxton, that a book-man like you would be thus severe upon Knowledge."

MR. CAXTON, (in wrath.)—"Severe upon knowledge! O Squills—Squills—Squills! Knowledge perverted, is knowledge no longer. Vinegar, which, exposed to the sun, breeds small serpents, or at best slimy eels, not comestible, once was wine. If I say to my grandchildren, 'Don't drink that sour stuff, which the sun itself fills with reptiles;' does that prove me a foe to sound sherry? Squills, if you had but received a scholastic education, you would know the wise maxim that saith, 'All things the worst are corruptions from things originally designed as the best.' Has not freedom bred anarchy, and religion fanaticism? And if I blame Marat calling for blood, or Dominic racking a heretic, am I severe on the religion that canonised Francis de Sales, or the freedom that immortalised Thrasybulus?"

Mr. Squills, dreading a catalogue of all the saints in the calendar, and an epitome of Ancient History, exclaimed eagerly —"Enough, sir—I am convinced!"

Mr. Caxton.—"Moreover, I have thought it a natural stroke of art in Pisistratus, to keep Randal Leslie, in his progress towards the rot of the intellect unwholesomely refined, free from all the salutary influences that deter ambition from settling into egotism. Neither in his slovenly home, nor from his classic tutor at his preparatory school, does he seem to have learned any truths, religious or moral, that might give sap to fresh shoots, when the first rank growth was cut down by the knife; and I especially noted, as illustrative of Egerton, no less than of Randal, that though the statesman's occasional hints of advice to his *protégé* are worldly wise in their way, and suggestive of honour as befitting the creed of a gentleman, they are not such as much influence a shrewd reasoner like Randal, whom the example of the playground at Eton had not served to correct of the arid self-seeking, which looked to knowledge for no object but power. A man tempted by passions like Audley, or seduced into fraud by a cold subtle spirit like Leslie, will find poor defence in the elegant precepts, 'Remember to act as a gentleman.' Such moral embroidery adds a beautiful scarf to one's armour; but it is not the armour itself! Ten o'clock——as I live——Push on, Pisistratus! and finish the chapter."

Mrs. Caxton, (benevolently.)—"Don't hurry. Begin with that odious Randal Leslie, to oblige your father; but there are others whom Blanche and I care much more to hear about."

Pisistratus, since there is no help for it, produces a supplementary manuscript, which proves that, whatever his doubt as to the artistic effect of a Final Chapter, he had foreseen that his audience would not be contented without one.

---

Randal Leslie, late at noon the day after he quitted Lansmere Park, arrived on foot at his father's house. He had walked all the way, and through the solitudes of the winter night; but he was not sensible of fatigue till the dismal home closed round him, with its air of hopeless ignoble poverty; and then he sunk upon the floor, feeling himself a ruin amidst the ruins. He made no disclosure of what had passed to his relations. Miserable man, there was not one to whom he could confide, or from whom he might hear the truths that connect repentance with consolation! After some weeks passed in sullen and almost unbroken silence, he left as abruptly as he had appeared, and returned to London. The sudden death of a man like Egerton had even in those excited times created intense, though brief sensation. The particulars of the election, that had been given in detail in the provincial papers, were copied into the London journals;—among those details, Randal Leslie's conduct in the Committee Room, with many an indignant comment on selfishness and ingratitude. The political world of all parties formed one of those judgments on the great man's poor dependant, which fix a stain upon the character, and place a barrier in the career, of ambitious youth. The important personages who had once noticed Randal for Audley's sake, and who, on their subsequent and not long-deferred restoration to power, could have made his fortune, passed him in the streets without a nod. He did not venture to remind Avenel of the promise to aid him in another election for Lansmere, nor dream of filling up the vacancy which Egerton's death had created. He was too shrewd not to see that all hope of that borough was over;—he would have been hooted in the streets and pelted from the hustings. Forlorn in the vast metropolis as Leonard had once been, in his turn he loitered on the bridge, and gazed on the remorseless river. He had neither money nor connections—nothing save talents and knowledge to force his way back into the lofty world in which all had smiled on him before; and talents and knowledge, that had been exerted to injure a benefactor, made him but the more despised. But even now, Fortune, that had bestowed on the pauper heir of Rood advantages so numerous and so dazzling, out of which he had cheated himself, gave him a chance, at least, of present independence, by which, with patient toil, he might have won, if not to the highest places, at least to a position in which he could have forced the world to listen to his explanations, and perhaps receive his excuses. The £5000 that Audley designed for him, and which, in a private memorandum, the statesman had entreated Harley to see safely rescued from the fangs of the law, were made over to Randal by Lord L'Estrange's solicitor; but this sum seemed to him so small after the loss of such gorgeous hopes, and the up-hill path seemed so slow after such short cuts to power, that Randal looked upon the unexpected bequest simply as an apology for adopting no profession. Stung to the quick by the contrast between his past and his present place in the English world, he hastened abroad. There, whether in distraction from thought, or from the curiosity of a restless intellect to explore the worth of things yet untried, Randal Leslie, who had hitherto been so dead to the ordinary amusements of youth, plunged into the society of damaged gamesters and third-rate *roués*. In this companionship his very talents gradually degenerated, and their exercise upon low intrigues and miserable projects but abased his social character, till, sinking step after step as his funds decayed, he finally vanished out of the sphere in which even profligates still retain the habits, and cling to the *caste*, of gentlemen. His father died; the neglected property of Rood devolved on Randal, but out of its scanty proceeds he had to pay the portions of his brother and sister, and his mother's jointure; the surplus left was scarcely visible in the executor's account. The hope of restoring the home and fortunes of his forefathers had long ceased. What were the ruined hall and its bleak wastes, without that hope which had once dignified the wreck and the desert? He wrote from St. Petersburg ordering the sale of the property. No one great proprietor was a candidate for the unpromising investment; it was sold in lots among small freeholders and retired traders. A builder bought the Hall for its materials. Hall, lands and name were blotted out of the map and the history of the county.

The widow, Oliver, and Juliet removed to a provincial town in another shire. Juliet married an ensign in a marching regiment, and died of neglect after childbirth. Mrs. Leslie did not long survive her. Oliver added to his little fortune by marriage with the daughter of a retail tradesman, who had amassed a few thousand pounds. He set up a brewery, and contrived to live without debt, though a large family, and his own constitutional inertness, extracted from his business small profits and no savings. Nothing of Randal had been heard of for years after the sale of Rood, except that he had taken up his residence either in Australia or the United States; it was not known which, but presumed to be the latter. Still Oliver had been brought up with so high a veneration of his brother's talents, that he cherished the sanguine belief that Randal would some day appear, wealthy and potent, like the uncle in a comedy; lift up the sunken family, and rear into graceful ladies and accomplished gentlemen the clumsy little boys and the vulgar little girls who now crowded round Oliver's dinner-table, with appetites altogether disproportioned to the size of the joints.

One winter day, when from the said dinner-table wife and children had retired, and Oliver sate sipping his half-pint of bad port, and looking over unsatisfactory accounts, a thin terrier, lying on the thread-bare rug by the niggard fire, sprang up and barked fiercely. Oliver lifted his dull blue eyes, and saw opposite to him, at the window, a human face. The face was pressed close to the panes, and was obscured by the haze which the breath of its lips drew forth from the frosty rime that had gathered on the glass.

Oliver, alarmed and indignant, supposing this intrusive spectator of his privacy to be some bold and lawless tramper, stepped out of the room, opened the front door, and bade the stranger go about his business; while the terrier still more inhospitably yelped and snapped at the stranger's heels. Then a hoarse voice said, "Don't you know me, Oliver? I am your brother Randal! Call away your dog and let me in." Oliver stared aghast—he could not believe his slow senses—he could not recognise his brother in the gaunt grim apparition before him. But at length he came forward, gazed into Randal's face, and, grasping his hand in amazed silence, led him into the little parlour. Not a trace of the well-bred refinement which had once characterized Randal's air and person was visible. His dress bespoke the last stage of that terrible decay which is significantly called the "shabby genteel." His mien was that of the skulking, timorous, famished, vagabond. As he took off his greasy tattered hat, he exhibited, though still young in years, the signs of premature old age. His hair, once so fine and silken, was of a harsh iron grey, bald in ragged patches; his forehead and visage were ploughed into furrows; intelligence were still in the aspect, but an intelligence that instinctively set you on your guard—sinister—gloomy—menacing.

Randal stopped short all questioning. He seized the small modicum of wine on the table, and drained it at a draught. "Pooh," said he, "have you nothing that warms a man better than this?" Oliver, who felt as if under the influence of a frightful dream, went a cupboard and took out a bottle of brandy three parts-full. Randal snatched at it eagerly, and put his lips to the mouth of the bottle. "Ah," said he, after a short pause, "this comforts; now give me food." Oliver hastened himself to serve his brother; in fact, he felt ashamed that even the slip-shod maid-servant should see his visitor. When he returned with such provisions as he could extract from the larder, Randal was seated by the fire, spreading over the embers emaciated bony hands, like the talons of a vulture.

He devoured the cold meat set before him with terrible voracity, and nearly finished the spirits left in the bottle; but the last had no effect in dispersing his gloom. Oliver stared at him in fear—the terrier continued to utter a low suspicious growl.

"You would know my history?" at length said Randal, bluntly. "It is short. I have tried for fortune and failed—I am without a penny and without a hope. You seem poor—I suppose you cannot much help me. Let me at least stay with you for a time—I know not where else to look for bread and for shelter."

Oliver burst into tears, and cordially bade his brother welcome. Randal remained some weeks at Oliver's house, never stirring out of the doors, and not seeming to notice, though he did not scruple to use, the new habiliments, which Oliver procured ready-made, and placed, without remark, in his room. But his presence soon became intolerable to the mistress of the house, and oppressive even to its master. Randal, who had once been so abstemious that he had even regarded the most moderate use of wine as incompatible with clear judgment and vigilant observation, had contracted the habit of drinking spirits at all hours of the day; but though they sometimes intoxicated him into stupor, they never unlocked his heart nor enlivened his sullen mood. If he observed less acutely than of old, he could still conceal just as closely. Mrs. Oliver Leslie, at first rather awed and taciturn, grew cold and repelling, then pert and sarcastic, at last undisguisedly and vulgarly rude. Randal made no retort; but his sneer was so galling that the wife flew at once to her husband, and declared that either she or his brother must leave the house. Oliver tried to pacify and compromise, with partial success; and, a few days afterwards, he came to Randal and said timidly, "You see, my wife brought me nearly all I possess, and you don't condescend to make friends with her.

Your residence here must be as painful to you as to me. But
I wish to see you provided for; and I could offer you something—only it seems, at first glance, so beneath—"

"Beneath what?" interrupted Randal, witheringly. "What
I was—or what I am? Speak out!"

"To be sure you are a scholar; and I have heard you say
fine things about knowledge and so forth; and you'll have
plenty of books at your disposal, no doubt; and you are still
young, and may rise—and—"

"Hell and torments! Be quick—say the worst or the best!"
cried Randal, fiercely.

"Well then," said poor Oliver, still trying to soften the
intended proposal, "you must know that our poor sister's
husband was nephew to Dr. Felpem, who keeps a very respectable school. He is not learned himself, and attends chiefly to
arithmetic and book-keeping, and such matters—but he wants
an usher to teach the classics; for some of the boys go to
college. And I have written to him, just to sound—I did not
mention your name till I knew if you would like it; but he
will take my recommendation. Board—lodging—fifty pounds
a-year; in short, the place is yours if you like it."

Randal shivered from head to foot, and was long before he
answered. "Well, be it so; I have come to that. Ha, ha!
yes, knowledge is power!" He paused a few moments. "So,
the old Hall is razed to the ground, and you are a tradesman
in a small country town, and my sister is dead, and I henceforth am—John Smith! You say that you did not mention
my name to the schoolmaster—still keep it concealed; forget
that I once was a Leslie. Our tie of brotherhood ceases when
I go from your hearth. Write, then, to your head master,
who attends to arithmetic, and secure the rank of his usher
in Latin and Greek for—John Smith!"

Not many days afterwards, the *protégé* of Audley Egerton
entered on his duties as usher in one of those large, cheap
schools, which comprise a sprinkling of the sons of gentry
and clergymen designed for the learned professions, with a
far larger proportion of the sons of traders, intended, some
for the counting-house, some for the shop and the till.
There, to this day, under the name of John Smith, lives
Randal Leslie.

It is probably not pride alone that induces him to persist in
that change of name, and makes him regard as perpetual the
abandonment of the one that he took from his forefathers,
and with which he had once identified his vaulting ambition;

for shortly after he had quited his brother's house, Oliver read in the weekly newspaper, to which he bounded his lore of the times in which he lived, an extract from an American journal, wherein certain mention was made of an English adventurer who, among other aliases, had assumed the name of Leslie— that extract caused Oliver to start, turn pale, look round, and thrust the paper into the fire. From that time he never attempted to violate the condition Randal had imposed on him—never sought to renew their intercourse, nor to claim a brother. Doubtless, if the adventurer thus signalised was the man Oliver suspected, whatever might be imputed to Randal's charge that could have paled a brother's cheek, it was none of the more violent crimes to which law is inexorable, but rather, (in that progress made by ingratitude and duplicity, with Need and Necessity urging them on,) some act of dishonesty which may just escape from the law, to sink, without redemption, the name. However this be, there is nothing in Randal's present course of life which forbodes any deeper fall. He has known what it is to want bread, and his former restlessness subsides into cynic apathy.

He lodges in the town near the school, and thus the debasing habit of unsocial besotment is not brought under the eyes of his superior. The dram is his sole luxury—if it be suspected, it is thought to be his sole vice. He goes through the ordinary routine of tuition with average credit; his spirit of intrigue occasionally shows itself in attempts to conciliate the favour of the boys whose fathers are wealthy—who are born to higher rank than the rest; and he lays complicated schemes to be asked home for the holidays. But when the schemes succeed, and the invitation comes, he recoils and shrinks back —he does not dare to show himself on the borders of the brighter world he once hoped to sway; he fears that he may be discovered to be—a Leslie! On such days, when his taskwork is over, he shuts himself up in his room, locks the door, and drugs himself into insensibility.

Once he found a well-worn volume running the round of delighted schoolboys—took it up, and recognised Leonard's earliest popular work, which had, many years before, seduced himself into pleasant thoughts and gentle emotions. He carried the book to his own lodgings—read it again; and when he returned it to its young owner, some of the leaves were stained with tears. Alas! perhaps but the maudlin tears of broken nerves, not of the awakened soul—for the leaves smelt strongly of whisky. Yet, after that re-perusal,

Randal Leslie turned suddenly to deeper studies than his habitual drudgeries required. He revived and increased his early scholarship; he chalked the outline of a work of great erudition, in which the subtlety of his intellect found field in learned and acute criticism. But he has never proceeded far in this work. After each irregular and spasmodic effort, the pen drops from his hand, and he mutters, " But to what end? I can never *now* raise a name. Why give reputation to—John Smith!"

Thus he drags on his life; and perhaps, when he dies, the fragments of his learned work may be discovered in the desk of the usher, and serve as hints to some crafty student, who may filch ideas and repute from the dead Leslie, as Leslie had filched them from the living Burley.

While what may be called poetical justice has thus evolved itself from the schemes in which Randal Leslie had wasted rare intellect in baffling his own fortunes, no outward signs of adversity evince the punishment of Providence on the head of the more powerful offender, Baron Levy. No fall in the Funds has shaken the sumptuous fabric, built from the ruined houses of other men. Baron Levy is still Baron Levy the *millionaire;* but I doubt if at heart he be not more acutely miserable than Randal Leslie, the usher. For Levy is a man who has admitted the fiercer passions into his philosophy of life; he has not the pale blood and torpid heart which allow the scotched adder to doze away its sense of pain. Just as old age began to creep upon the fashionable usurer, he fell in love with a young opera-dancer, whose light heels had turned the lighter heads of half the *élégans* of Paris and London. The craft of the dancer was proof against all lesser bribes than that of marriage; and Levy married her. From that moment his house, *Louis Quinze*, was more crowded than ever by the high-born dandies whose society he had long so eagerly courted. That society became his curse. The Baroness was an accomplished *coquette;* and Levy (with whom, as we have seen, jealousy was the predominant passion) was stretched on an eternal rack. His low estimate of human nature—his disbelief in the possibility of virtue—added strength to the agony of his suspicions, and provoked the very dangers he dreaded. His sole self-torturing task was that of the spy upon his own hearth. His banquets were haunted by a spectre; the attributes of his wealth were as the goad and the scourge of Nemesis. His gay cynic smile changed into a sullen scowl—his hair blanched into white—

his eyes were hollow with one consuming care. Suddenly he left his costly house; left London; abjured all the society which it had been the joy of his wealth to purchase; buried himself and his wife in a remote corner of the provinces; and there he still lives. He seeks in vain to occupy his days with rural pursuits; he to whom the excitements of a metropolis, with all its corruption and its vices, were the sole sources of the turbid stream that he called "pleasure." There, too, the fiend of jealousy still pursues him: he prowls round his demesnes with the haggard eye and furtive step of a thief; he guards his wife as a prisoner, for she threatens every day to escape. The life of the man who had opened the prison to so many is the life of a jailer. His wife abhors him, and does not conceal it; and still slavishly he dotes on her. Accustomed to the freest liberty—demanding applause and admiration as her rights—wholly uneducated, vulgar in mind, coarse in language, violent in temper—the beautiful Fury he has brought to his home, makes that home a hell. Thus, what might seem to the superficial most enviable, is to their possessor most hateful. He dares not ask a soul to see how he spends his gold—he has shrunk into a mean and niggardly expenditure, and complains of reverse and poverty, in order to excuse himself to his wife for debarring her the enjoyments which she anticipated from the Money Bags she had married. A vague consciousness of retribution has awakened remorse, to add to his other stings. And the remorse coming from superstition, not religion, (sent from below, not descending from above,) brings with it none of the consolations of a genuine repentance. He never seeks to atone—never dreams of some redeeming good action. His riches flow around him, spreading wider and wider—out of his own reach.

The Count di Peschiera was not deceived in the calculations which had induced him to affect repentance, and establish a claim upon his kinsman. He received from the generosity of the Duke di Serrano an annuity not disproportioned to his rank, and no order from his court forbade his return to Vienna. But, in the very summer that followed his visit to Lansmere, his career came to an abrupt close. At Baden-Baden he paid court to a wealthy and accomplished Polish widow; and his fine person and terrible repute awed away all rivals, save a young Frenchman, as daring as himself, and much more in love. A challenge was given and accepted. Peschiera appeared on the fatal ground, with his customary *sang-froid*, humming an opera air, and looking so diabolically gay that his opponent's nerves were affected in spite of his courage, and, the Frenchman's trigger going off before he had even taken aim, to his own ineffable astonishment, he shot the Count through the heart, dead.

Beatrice di Negra lived for some years after her brother's death in strict seclusion, lodging within a convent, though she did not take the veil, as she at first proposed. In fact, the more she saw of the sisterhood, the more she found that human regrets and human passions (save in some rarely gifted natures) find their way through the barred gates and over the lofty walls. Finally, she took up her abode in Rome, where she is esteemed for a life not only marked by strict propriety, but active benevolence. She cannot be prevailed on to accept from the Duke more than a fourth of the annuity that had been bestowed on her brother; but she has few wants, save those of charity; and when charity is really active, it can do so much with so little gold! She is not known in the gayer circles of the city; but she gathers around her a small society composed chiefly of artists and scholars, and is never so happy as when she can aid some child of genius—more especially if his country be England.

The Squire and his wife still flourish at Hazeldean, where Captain Barnabas Higginbotham has taken up his permanent abode. The Captain is a confirmed hypochondriac, but he brightens up now and then when he hears of any illness in the family of Mr. Sharpe Currie, and, at such times, is heard to murmur, "If those seven sickly children should go off, I might still have very great—EXPECTATIONS." For the which he has been roundly scolded by the Squire, and gravely preached at by the Parson. Upon both, however, he takes his revenge in a fair and gentlemanlike way, three times a-week, at the whist-table, the Parson no longer having the Captain as his constant partner, since a fifth now generally cuts in at the table—in the person of that old enemy and neighbour, Mr. Sticktorights. The Parson, thus fighting his own battles unallied to the Captain, observes with melancholy surprise that there is a long run of luck against him, and that he does not win so much as he used to do. Fortunately that is the sole trouble—except Mrs. Dale's "little tempers," to which he is accustomed—that ever disturbs the serene tenor of the Parson's life. We must now explain how Mr. Sticktorights came to cut in at the Hazeldean whist-table. Frank has settled at the Casino with a wife who suits him exactly, and that wife was Miss Sticktorights. It was two years before Frank recovered the disappointment with which the loss of Beatrice saddened his spirits, but sobered his habits and awoke his reflection. An affection, however misplaced and ill-requited, if honestly conceived and deeply felt, rarely fails to advance the self-education of man. Frank became steady and serious; and, on a visit to Hazeldean, met at a county ball Miss Sticktorights, and the two young persons were instantly attracted towards each other, perhaps by the very feud that had so long existed between their houses. The marriage settlements were nearly abandoned, at the last moment, by a discussion between the parents as to the Right of Way. But the dispute was happily appeased by Mr. Dale's suggestion, that as both properties would be united in the children of the proposed marriage, all cause for litigation would naturally cease, since no man would go to law with himself. Mr. Sticktorights and Mr. Hazeldean, however, agreed in the precaution of inserting a clause in the settlements, (though all the lawyers declared that it could not be of any legal avail,) by which it was declared, that if, in default of heritable issue by the said marriage, the Sticktorights' estate devolved on some distant scion of the Sticktorights family, the right of way from the wood across the waste land would still remain in the same state of delectable dispute in which it then stood. There seems, however, little chance of a lawsuit thus providently bequeathed to the misery of distant generations—since two sons and two daughters are already playing at hide-and-seek on the terrace where Jackeymo once watered the orange trees, and in the Belvidere where Riccabocca had studied his Machiavelli.

Jackeymo, though his master has assessed the long arrears of his wages at a sum which would enable him to have orange-groves and servants of his own, still clings to his former duties, and practises his constitutional parsimony. His only apparent deviation into profusion consists in the erection of a chapel to his sainted namesake, to whom he burns many a votive taper;—the tapers are especially tall, and their sconces are wreathed with garlands whenever a letter with the foreign post-mark brings good news of the absent Violante and her English lord.

Riccabocca was long before he reconciled himself to the pomp of his principalities and his title of Duke. Jemima accommodated herself much more readily to greatness, but she retained all her native Hazeldean simplicity at heart, and is adored by the villagers around her, especially by the young of both sexes, whom she is always ready to marry and to portion;—convinced, long ere this, of the redeemable qualities of the male sex by her reverence for the Duke, who continues to satirise women and wedlock, and deem himself—thanks to his profound experience of the one, and his philosophical endurance of the other—the only happy husband in the world. Longer still was it before the sage, who had been so wisely anxious to rid himself of the charge of a daughter, could wean his thoughts from the remembrance of her tender voice and loving eyes. Not, indeed, till he seriously betook himself to the task of educating the son with whom, according to his scientific prognostics, Jemima presented him shortly after his return to his native land. The sage began betimes with his Italian proverbs, full of hard-hearted worldly wisdom, and the boy was scarce out of the hornbook before he was introduced to Machiavelli. But somehow or other the simple goodness of the philosopher's actual life, with his high-wrought patrician sentiments of integrity and honour, so counteract the theoretical lessons, that the Heir of Serrano is little likely to be made more wise by the proverbs, or more wicked by the Machiavelli, than those studies have practically made the progenitor, whose opinions his countrymen still shame with the title of "Alphonso the Good."

The Duke long cherished a strong curiosity to know what had become of Randal. He never traced the adventurer to his closing scene. But once (years before Randal had crept into his present shelter) in a visit of inspection to the hospital at Genoa, the Duke, with his peculiar shrewdness of observation in all matters except those which concerned himself, was remarking to the officer in attendance, "that for one dull, honest man, whom fortune drove to the hospital or the jail, he had found, on investigation of their antecedents, three sharp-witted knaves who had thereto reduced themselves"—when his eye fell upon a man asleep in one of the sick wards, and recognising the face, not then so changed as Oliver had seen it, he walked straight up, and gazed upon Randal Leslie.

"An Englishman," said the official. "He was brought hither insensible, from a severe wound on the head, inflicted, as we discovered, by a wellknown *chevalier d'industrie*, who declared that the Englishman had outwitted and cheated him. That was not very likely, for a few crowns were all we could find on the Englishman's person, and he had been obliged to leave his lodgings for debt. He is recovering—but there is fever still."

The Duke gazed silently on the sleeper, who was tossing restlessly on his pallet, and muttering to himself; then he placed his purse in the official's hand. "Give this to the Englishman," said he; "but conceal my name. It is true—it is true—the proverb is very true"—resumed the Duke, descending the stairs—"*Più pelli di volpi che di asini vanno in Pellicciaria.*" (More hides of foxes than of asses find their way to the tanner's.)

Dr. Morgan continues to prescribe globules for grief, and to administer infinitesimally to a mind diseased. Practising what he prescribes, he swallows a globule of "*caustic*" whenever the sight of a distressed fellow-creature moves him to compassion—a constitutional tendency which, he is at last convinced, admits of no radical cure. For the rest, his range of patients has notably expanded; and under his sage care his patients unquestionably live as long — as Providence pleases. No allopathist can say more.

The death of poor John Burley found due place in the obituary of "literary men." Admirers, unknown before, came forward and subscribed for a handsome monument to his memory in Kensall Green. They would have subscribed for the relief of his widow and children, if he had left any. Writers in magazines thrived for some months on collections of his humorous sayings, anecdotes of his eccentricities, and specimens of the eloquence that had lightened through the tobacco-reek of tavern and club-room. Leonard ultimately made a selection from his scattered writings which found place in standard libraries, though their subjects were either of too fugitive an interest, or treated in too capricious a manner to do more than indicate the value of the ore had it been purified from its dross and subjected to the art of the mint. These specimens could not maintain their circulation as the coined money of Thought, but they were hoarded by collectors as rare curiosities. Alas, poor Burley!

The Pompleys sustained a pecuniary loss by the crash of a railway company, in which the Colonel had been induced to take several shares by one of his wife's most boasted "connections," whose estate the said railway proposed to traverse, on paying £400 an acre, in that golden age when railway companies respected the rights of property. The Colonel was no longer able, in his own country, to make both ends meet at Christmas. He is now straining hard to achieve that feat in Boulogne, and has in the process grown so red in the face, that those who meet him in his morning walk on the pier, bargaining for fish, shake their heads and say, " Old Pompley will go off in a fit of apoplexy ; a great loss to society; genteel people the Pompleys! and very highly 'connected.'"

The vacancy created in the borough of Lansmere by Audley Egerton's death, was filled up by our old acquaintance, Haveril Dashmore, who had unsuccessfully contested that seat on Egerton's first election. The naval officer was now an admiral, and perfectly reconciled to the Constitution, with all its alloy of aristocracy.

Dick Avenel did not retire from Parliament so soon as he had anticipated. He was not able to persuade Leonard, whose brief fever of political ambition was now quenched in the calm fountain of the Muse, to supply his place in the senate, and he felt that the house of Avenel needed one representative. He contrived, however, to devote, for the first year or two, much more of his time to his interests at Screwstown than to the affairs of his country, and succeeded in baffling the over competition to which he had been subjected, by taking the competitor into partnership. Having thus secured a monopoly at Screwstown, Dick, of course, returned with great ardour to his former enlightened opinions in favour of free trade. He remained some years in Parliament; and though far too shrewd to venture out of his depth as an orator, distinguished himself so much by his exposure of "humbug" on an important Committee, that he acquired a very high reputation as a man of business, and gradually became so in request amongst all members who moved for "Select Committees," that he rose into consequence; and Mrs. Avenel, courted for his sake, more than her own, obtained the wish of her heart, and was received as an acknowledged *habituée* into the circles of fashion.—Amidst these circles, however, Dick found that his home entirely vanished; and when he came home from the House of Commons, tired to death, at two in the morning, disgusted at always hearing that Mrs. Avenel was not yet returned from some fine lady's ball, he formed a sudden resolution of cutting Parliament, Fashion, and London altogether; withdrew his capital, now very large, from his business; bought the remaining estates of Squire Thornhill; and his chief object of ambition is in endeavouring to coax or bully out of their holdings all the small freeholders round, who had subdivided amongst them, into poles and furlongs, the fated inheritance of Randal Leslie.

An excellent justice of the peace, though more severe than your old family proprietors generally are;—a spirited landlord, as to encouraging and making, at a proper percentage, all permanent improvements on the soil, but formidable to meet if the rent be not paid to the day, or the least breach of covenant be heedlessly incurred on a farm that he could let for more money;—employing a great many hands in productive labour, but exacting rigorously from all the utmost degree of work at the smallest rate of wages which competition and the poor-rate permit;—the young and robust in his neighbourhood never stinted in work, and the aged and infirm, as lumber worn out, stowed away in the workhouse;—Richard Avenel holds himself an example to the old race of landlords; and, taken altogether, is no very bad specimen of the rural civilisers whom the application of spirit and capital raise up in the new.

From the wrecks of Egerton's fortune, Harley, with the aid of his father's experience in business, could not succeed in saving, for the statesman's sole child and heir, more than a few thousand pounds; and but for the bonds and bills which, when meditating revenge, he had bought from Levy, and afterwards thrown into the fire—paying dear for that detestable whistle—even this surplus would not have been forthcoming.

Harley privately paid out of his own fortune the £5000 Egerton had bequeathed to Leslie; perhaps not sorry, now that the stern duty of exposing the false wiles of the schemer was fulfilled, to afford some compensation even to the victim who had so richly deserved his fate; and pleased, though mournfully, to comply with the solemn request of the friend whose offence was forgotten in the remorseful memory of his own projects of revenge.

Leonard's birth and identity were easily proved, and no one appeared to dispute them. The balance due to him as his father's heir, together with the sum Avenel ultimately paid to him for the patent of his invention, and the dowry which Harley insisted upon bestowing on Helen, amounted to that happy competence which escapes alike the anxieties of poverty and (what to one of contemplative tastes and retired habits are often more irksome to bear) the show and responsibilities of wealth. His father's death made a deep impression upon Leonard's mind; but the discovery that he owed his birth to a statesman of so great a repute, and occupying a position in society so conspicuous, contributed not to confirm, but to still the ambition which had for a short time diverted him from his more serene aspirations. He had no longer to win a rank which might equal Helen's. He had no longer a parent, whose affections might be best won through pride. The memories of his earlier peasant life, and his love for retirement—in which habit confirmed the constitutional tendency—made him shrink from what a more worldly nature would have considered the enviable advantages of a name that secured the entrance into the loftiest sphere of our social world.—He wanted not that name to assist his own path to a rank far more durable than that which kings can confer. And still he retained in the works he had published, and still he proposed to bestow on the works more ambitious that he had, in leisure and competence, the facilities to design with care, and complete with patience, the name he had himself invented, and linked with the memory of the low-born mother. Therefore, though there was some wonder, in drawing-rooms and clubs, at the news of Egerton's first unacknowledged marriage, and some curiosity expressed as to what the son of that marriage might do—and great men were prepared to welcome, and fine ladies to invite and bring out, the heir to the statesman's grave repute—yet wonder and curiosity soon died away; the repute soon passed out of date, and its heir was soon forgotten. Politicians who fall short of the highest renown are like actors; no applause is so vivid while they are on the stage—no oblivion so complete when the curtain falls on the last farewell.

Leonard saw a fair tomb rise above Nora's grave, and on the tomb was engraved the word of WIFE, which vindicated her beloved memory. He felt the warm embrace of Nora's mother, no longer ashamed to own her grandchild; and even old John was made sensible that a secret weight of sorrow was taken from his wife's stern silent heart. Leaning on Leonard's arm, the old man gazed wistfully on Nora's tomb, and muttering—"Egerton! Egerton! 'Leonora, the first wife of the Right Honourable Audley Egerton!' Ha! I voted for him. She married the right colour. Is that the date? Is it so long since she died? Well, well! I miss her sadly. But wife says we shall both now see her soon; and wife once thought we should never see her again—never; but I always knew better. Thank you, sir. I'm a poor creature, but these tears don't pain me—quite otherwise. I don't know why, but I'm very happy. Where's my old woman? She does not mind how much I talk about Nora now. Oh, there she is! Thank you, sir, humbly; but I'd rather lean on my old woman—I'm more used to it; and—wife, when shall we go to Nora?"

Leonard had brought Mrs. Fairfield to see her parents, and Mrs. Avenel welcomed her with unlooked-for kindness. The name inscribed upon Nora's tomb softened the mother's heart to her surviving daughter. As poor John had said—"She could *now* talk about Nora;" and in that talk, she and the child she had so long neglected discovered how much they had in common. So when, shortly after his marriage with Helen, Leonard went abroad, Jane Fairfield remained with the old couple. After their death, which was within a day of each other, she refused, perhaps from pride, to take up her residence with Leonard, but she settled near the home which he subsequently found in England. Leonard remained abroad for some years. A quiet observer of the various manners and intellectual development of living races—a rapt and musing student of the monuments that revive the dead—his experience of mankind grew large in silence, and his perceptions of the Sublime and Beautiful brightened into tranquil art under their native skies.

On his return to England he purchased a small house amidst the most beautiful scenes of Devonshire, and there patiently commenced a work in which he designed to bequeath to his country his noblest thoughts in their fairest forms. Some men best develop their ideas by constant exercise; their thoughts spring from their brain ready-armed, and seek, like the fabled goddess, to take constant part in the wars of men. And such are, perhaps, on the whole, the most vigorous and lofty writers; but Leonard did not belong to this class. Sweetness and serenity were the main characteristics of his genius; and these were deepened by his profound sense of his domestic happiness. To wander alone with Helen by the banks of the murmurous river—to gaze with her on the deep still sea—to feel that his thoughts, even when most silent, were comprehended by the intuition of love, and reflected on that translucent sympathy so yearned for and so rarely found by poets—these were the Sabbaths of his soul, necessary to fit him for its labours: for the Writer has this advantage over other men, that his repose is not indolence. His duties, rightly fulfilled, are discharged to earth and men in other capacities than those of action. If he is not seen among those who act, he is all the while maturing some noiseless influence, which will guide or illumine, civilize or elevate, the restless men whose noblest actions are but the obedient agencies of the thoughts of writers. Call not, then, the Poet whom we place amidst the Varieties of Life, the sybarite of literary ease, if, returning on Summer eves, Helen's light footstep by his musing side, he greets his sequestered home, with its trellised flowers smiling out from amidst the lonely cliffs in which it is embedded;—while lovers still, though wedded long, they turn to each other, with such deep joy in their speaking eyes, grateful that the world, with its various distractions and noisy conflicts, lies so far from their actual existence—only united to them by the happy link that the writer weaves invisibly with the hearts that he moves and the souls that he inspires. No! Character and circumstance alike unfitted Leonard for the strife of the thronged literary democracy; they led towards the development of the gentler and purer portions of his nature—to the gradual suppression of the more combative and turbulent. The influence of the happy light under which his genius so silently and calmly grew, was seen in the exquisite harmony of its colours, rather than the gorgeous diversities of their glow. His contemplation, intent upon objects of peaceful beauty, and undisturbed by rude anxieties and vehement passions, suggested only kindred reproductions to the creative faculty by which it was vivified; so that the whole man was not only a poet, but, as it were, a poem—a living idyl, calling into pastoral music every reed that sighed and trembled along the stream of life. And Helen was so suited to a nature of this kind, she so guarded the ideal existence in which it breathes! All the little cares and troubles of the common practical life she appropriated so quietly to herself—the stronger of the two, as should be a poet's wife, in the necessary household virtues of prudence and forethought. Thus, if the man's genius made the home a temple, the woman's wisdom gave to the temple the security of the fortress. They have only one child—a girl; they call her Nora. She has the father's soul-lit eyes, and the mother's warm human smile. She assists Helen in the morning's noiseless domestic duties; she sits in the evening at Leonard's feet, while he reads or writes. In each light grief of childhood she steals to the mother's knee; but in each young impulse of delight, or each brighter flash of progressive reason, she springs to the father's breast. Sweet Helen, thou has taught her this, taking to thyself the shadows even of thine infant's life, and leaving to thy partner's eyes only its rosy light!

But not here shall this picture of Helen close. Even the Ideal can only complete its purpose by connection with the Real. Even in solitude the writer must depend upon Mankind.

Leonard at last has completed the work, which has been the joy and the labour of so many years—the work which he regards as the flower of all his spiritual being, and to which he has committed all the hopes that unite the creature of to-day with the generations of the future. The work has gone through the press, each line lingered over with the elaborate patience of the artist, loath to part with the thought he has sculptured into form, while an improving touch can be imparted by the chisel. He has accepted an invitation from Norreys. In the restless excitement, (strange to him since his first happy maiden effort,) he has gone to London. Unrecognised in the huge metropolis, he has watched to see if the world acknowledge the new tie he has woven between its busy life and his secluded toil. And the work came out in an unpropitious hour; other things were occupying the public; the world was not at leisure to heed him, and the book did not penetrate into the great circle of readers. But a savage critic has seized on it, and mangled, distorted, deformed it, confounding together defect and beauty in one mocking ridicule; and the beauties have not yet found an exponent, nor the defects a defender; and the publisher shakes his head, points to groaning shelves, and delicately hints that the work which was to be the epitome of the sacred life within life, does not hit the taste of the day. Leonard thinks over the years that his still labour has cost him, and knows that he has exhausted the richest mines of his intellect, and that long years will elapse before he can recruit that capital of ideas which is necessary to sink new shafts and bring to light fresh ore; and the deep despondency of intellect, frustrated in its highest aims, has seized him, and all he has before done is involved in failure by the defeat of the crowning effort. Failure, and irrecoverable, seems his whole ambition as writer; his whole existence in the fair Ideal seems to have been a profitless dream, and the face of the Ideal itself is obscured. And even Norreys frankly, though kindly, intimates that the life of a metropolis is essential to the healthful intuition of a writer in the intellectual wants of his age; since every great writer supplies a want in his own generation, for some feeling to be announced, some truth to be revealed; and as this maxim is generally sound, as most great writers have lived in cities,

Leonard dares not dwell on the exception; it is only success that justifies the attempt to be an exception to the common rule; and with the blunt manhood of his nature, which is not a poet's, Norreys sums up with, "What then? One experiment has failed; fit your life to your genius, and try again." Try again! Easy counsel enough to the man of ready resource and quick combative mind; but to Leonard, how hard and how harsh! "Fit his life to his genius!"—renounce contemplation and Nature for the jostle of Oxford Street!—would that life not scare away the genius for ever? Perplexed and despondent, though still struggling for fortitude, he returns to his home, and there at his hearth awaits the Soother, and there is the voice that repeats the passages most beloved, and prophesies so confidently of future fame; and gradually all around smiles from the smile of Helen. And the profound conviction that Heaven places human happiness beyond the reach of the world's contempt or praise, circulates through his system and restores its serene calm. And he feels that the duty of the intellect is to accomplish and perfect itself —to harmonise its sounds into music that may be heard in heaven, though it wake not an echo on the earth. If this be done, as with some men, best amidst the din and the discord, be it so; if, as with him, best in silence, be it so too. And the next day he reclines with Helen by the sea-shore, gazing calmly as before on the measureless sunlit ocean; and Helen, looking into his face, sees that it is sunlit as the deep. His hand steals within her own, in the gratitude that endears beyond the power of passion, and he murmurs gently, "Blessed be the woman who consoles."

The work found its way at length into fame, and the fame sent its voices loud to the poet's home. But the applause of the world had not a sound so sweet to his ear, as, when, in doubt, humiliation, and sadness, the lips of his Helen had whispered "Hope! and believe."

Side by side with this picture of Woman the Consoler, let me place the companion sketch. Harley L'Estrange, shortly after his marriage with Violante, had been induced, whether at his bride's persuasions, or to dissipate the shadow with which Egerton's death still clouded his wedded felicity, to accept a temporary mission, half military, half civil, to one of our colonies. On this mission he had evinced so much ability, and achieved so signal a success, that on his return to England he was raised to the peerage, while his father yet lived to rejoice that the son who would succeed to his honours had achieved the nobler dignity of honours not inherited, but won. High expectations were formed of Harley's parliamentary success; but he saw that such success, to be durable, must found itself on the knowledge of wearisome details, and the study of that practical business, which jarred on his tastes, though it suited his talents. Harley had been indolent for so many years—and there is so much to make indolence captivating to a man whose rank is secured, who has nothing to ask from fortune, and who finds at his home no cares from which he seeks a distraction;—so he laughed at ambition in the whim of his delightful humours, and the expectations formed from his diplomatic triumph died away. But then came one of those political crises, in which men ordinarily indifferent to politics rouse themselves to the recollection, that the experiment of legislation is not made upon dead matter, but on the living form of a noble country. And in both Houses of Parliament the strength of party is put forth.

It is a lovely day in spring, and Harley is seated by the window of his old room at Knightsbridge—now glancing to the lively green of the budding trees—now idling with Nero, who, though in canine old age, enjoys the sun like his master —now repeating to himself, as he turns over the leaves of his favourite Horace, some of those lines that make the shortness of life the excuse for seizing its pleasures and eluding its fatigues, which formed the staple morality of the polished epicurean—and Violante (into what glorious beauty her maiden bloom has matured!) comes softly into the room, seats herself on a low stool beside him, leaning her face on her hands, and looking up at him through her dark, clear, spiritual eyes; and as she continues to speak, gradually a change comes over Harley's aspect — gradually the brow grows thoughtful, and the lips lose their playful smile. There is no hateful assumption of the would-be "superior woman"—no formal remonstrance, no lecture, no homily which grates upon masculine pride, but the high theme and the eloquent words elevate unconsciously of themselves, and the Horace is laid aside—a Parliamentary Blue Book has been, by some marvel or other been conjured there in its stead—and Violante now moves away as softly as she entered. Harley's hand detains her.

"Not so. Share the task, or I quit it. Here is an extract I condemn you to copy. Do you think I would go through this labour if you were not to halve the success?—halve the labour as well!"

And Violante, overjoyed, kisses away the implied rebuke, and sits down to work, so demure and so proud by his side. I do not know if Harley made much way in the Blue Book that morning; but a little time after, he spoke in the Lords, and surpassed all that the most sanguine had hoped from his talents. The sweetness of fame, and the consciousness of utility once fully tasted, Harley's consummation of his proper destinies was secure. A year later, and his voice was one of the influences of England. His boyish love of glory revived; no longer vague and dreamy, but ennobled into patriotism, and strengthened into purpose. One night, after a signal triumph, he returned home, with his father, who had witnessed it, and Violante—who all lovely, all brilliant, though she was, never went forth in her lord's absence, to lower among fops and flatterer's, the dignity of the name she so aspired to raise —sprang to meet him. Harley's eldest son—a boy yet in the nursery—had been kept up later than usual; perhaps Violante had anticipated her husband's triumph, and wished the son to share it. The old Earl beckoned the child to him, and laying his hand on the infant's curly locks, said with unusual seriousness—

"My boy, you may see troubled times in England before these hairs are as grey as mine; and your stake in England's honour and peace will be great. Heed this hint from an old man who had no talents to make a noise in the world, but who yet has been of some use in his generation. Neither sounding titles, nor wide lands, nor fine abilities will give you real joy, unless you hold yourself responsible for all to your God and to your country; and when you are tempted to believe that the gifts you may inherit from both entail no duties, or that duties are at war with true pleasure, remember how I placed you in your father's arms, and said, 'Let him be as proud of you some day, as I at this hour am of him.'"

The boy clung to his father's breast, and said manfully, "I will try!" Harley bent his fair smooth brow over the young earnest face, and said softly, "Your mother speaks in you!"

Then the old Countess, who had remained silent and listening on her elbow-chair, rose and kissed the Earl's hand reverently. Perhaps in that kiss there was the repentant consciousness how far the active goodness she had often secretly undervalued had exceeded, in its fruits, her own cold unproductive powers of will and mind. Then passing on to Harley, her brow grew elate, and the pride returned to her eye.

"At last," she said, laying on his shoulder that light firm hand, from which he no longer shrunk—"at last, O my noble son, you have fulfilled all the promise of your youth!"

"If so," answered Harley, "it is because I have found what I then sought in vain." He drew his arm around Violante, and added, with half tender, half solemn smile—"Blessed is the woman who exalts!"

---

So, symbolled forth in these twin and fair flowers which Eve saved for Earth out of Paradise, each with the virtue to heal or to strengthen, stored under the leaves that give sweets to the air;—here, soothing the heart when the world brings the trouble—here recruiting the soul which our sloth or our senses enervate, leave we Woman, at least in the place Heaven assigns to her amidst the multiform "Varieties of Life."

Farewell to thee, gentle Reader; and go forth to the world, O MY NOVEL!

THE END.

www.ingramcontent.com/pod-product-compliance
Lightning Source LLC
Chambersburg PA
CBHW021228300426
44111CB00007B/464